Leonie Wittershagen
The Transfer of Personal Data from the European Union to the United Kingdom post-Brexit

Global and Comparative Data Law

Edited by
Moritz Hennemann
Lea Katharina Kumkar
Linda Kuschel
Björn Steinrötter

Volume 1

Leonie Wittershagen

The Transfer of Personal Data from the European Union to the United Kingdom post-Brexit

—

DE GRUYTER

ISBN 978-3-11-099933-4
e-ISBN (PDF) 978-3-11-098825-3
e-ISBN (EPUB) 978-3-11-098866-6
ISSN 2751-0174

Library of Congress Control Number: 2022944286

Bibliographic information published by the Deutsche Nationalbibliothek
The Deutsche Nationalbibliothek lists this publication in the Deutsche Nationalbibliografie;
detailed bibliographic data are available on the internet at http://dnb.dnb.de.

© 2023 Walter de Gruyter GmbH, Berlin/Boston
Cover image: peshkov / iStock / Getty Images
Printing and binding: CPI books GmbH, Leck

www.degruyter.com

Dedicated to my parents

Foreword and Acknowledgements

This study was accepted as a dissertation by the Faculty of Law of the University of Passau in the summer semester 2022. It was completed in March 2022; new developments were taken into account until May 2022.

First and foremost, I would like to thank my doctoral supervisor Professor Dr. Moritz Hennemann, M.Jur. (Oxford) for the excellent supervision of my doctoral thesis in every respect, especially for his invaluable guidance and feedback. I would also like to thank Professor Dr. Kai von Lewinski for his intensive examination of my thesis and the immediate second review.

My special thanks go to my friends who supported me in many ways. In a very special way, I would like to thank Aron Heidtke for providing me with unfailing and invaluable support and continuous encouragement during the entire doctoral period. Finally, I must express my deepest gratitude to my family, especially my parents Christina and Tilman Wittershagen. This accomplishment would not have been possible without them. Their belief in me has kept my spirits and motivation high throughout this process.

Berlin, June 2022   Leonie Wittershagen

https://doi.org/10.1515/9783110988253-001

Contents

List of Abbreviations

£	Pounds
AC	Appeal Cases
Art. 29 Working Party	Article 29 Data Protection Working Party
art/artt	Article/Articles
B.U. L. Rev.	Boston University Law Review
BCRs	Binding Corporate Rules
BGH	German Federal Court of Justice
BVerfG	German Federal Constitutional Court
CCZ	Corporate Compliance Zeitschrift ("Corporate Compliance Journal")
cf	confer (compare)
CFR or Charter	Charter of Fundamental Rights of the EU
CJEU or the Court	Court of Justice of the European Union
CLJ	Cambridge Law Journal
CLSR	Computer Law & Security Review
CML Rev	Common Market Law Review
CNIL	Commission Nationale de l'Informatique et des Libertés
CoC	Codes of Conduct
Convention 108	Council of Europe's Convention for the Protection of Individuals with regard to Automatic Processing of Personal Data of 28 January 1981
Convention 108+	Modernised Convention for the Protection of Individuals with Regard to the Processing of Personal Data
CR	Computer und Recht ("Computer and Law")
Cri	Computer Law Review International
Data Retention Directive	Directive 2006/24/EC of the European Parliament and of the Council on the retention of data generated or processed in connection with the provision of publicly available electronic communications services or of public communications networks and amending Directive 2002/58/EC [2006] OJ L 105/54
DCMS	Department for Digital, Culture Media and Sport
Directive 95/46	Directive 95/46/EC of the European Parliament and of the Council [2016] OJ L 344/83
DPA 1984	Data Protection Act 1984
DPA 1998	Data Protection Act 1998
DPA 2018	Data Protection Act 2018
DRAR	Data Retention and Acquisition Regulations 2018/1123
DRIPA	Data Retention and Investigatory Powers Act 2014
DuD	Datenschutz und Datensicherheit ("Data Protection and Data Security")
DVBl	Deutsches Verwaltungsblatt ("German Administrative Journal")
e.g.	for example
ECA	European Communities Act from 1972
ECHR	European Convention of Human Rights

https://doi.org/10.1515/9783110988253-002

ECHR (in case citings)	Reports of Judgments and Decisions
ECtHR or Strasbourg Court	European Court of Human Rights
EDPB	European Data Protection Board
EDPL	European Data Protection Law Review
EDPS	European Data Protection Supervisor
EEA	European Economic Area
EHRLR	European Human Rights Law Review
ELJ	European Law Journal
ERE	Edinburgh Research Explorer
et seq.	et sequens
et seqq.	et sequentia
EU	European Union
EU Commission	European Commission
EUConst	European Constitutional Law Review
EUR	Euro
EuR	Zeitschrift Europarecht ("Journal of European Law")
Euratom	European Atomic Energy Community
Eur. Law Rev	European Law Review
EUWA 2018	European Union (Withdrawal) Act from 2018
EuZW	Europäische Zeitschrift für Wirtschaftsrecht ("European Journal of Business Law")
GCHQ	Government Communications Headquarter
GDPR	General Data Protection Regulation
Geo. L.J.	Georgetown Law Journal
Geo. Wash. Int'l L. Rev.	George Washington International Law Review
Georget. J. Int. Aff.	Georgetown Journal of International Affairs
GLPR	Global Privacy Law Review
GRUR-Prax	Gewerblicher Rechtsschutz und Urheberrecht, Praxis im Immaterial-güter- und Wettbewerbsrecht ("Intellectual Property and Copyright Law, Practice in Intellectual Property and Competition Law")
HBR	Harvard Business Review
HRA 1998	Human Rights Act 1998
ibid	ibidem ("in the very same place")
IC	Information Commissioner
ICO	Information Commissioner's Office
IDPL	International Data Privacy Law
Int. Rev.Law Comput.	International Review of Law, Computers & Technology
IP completion day	The end of the implementation period put in place to enable the UK to transition away from the EU's laws and institutions
IPA 2016	Investigatory Powers Act 2016
IPC	Investigatory Powers Commissioner
IPCO	Investigatory Powers Commissioner's Office
IPT	Investigatory Powers Tribunal
ISC	Parliament's Intelligence and Security Committee
JCHR	UK Parliament's Joint Committee of Human Rights
LED	Law Enforcement Directive

LQR	Law Quarterly Review
LRZ	Legal Revolutionary
MMR	Multimedia und Recht ("Multimedia and Law")
Mod. L. Rev.	The Modern Law Review
NI Legal Quarterly	Northern Ireland Legal Quarterly
NJW	Neue Juristische Wochenschrift ("New Legal Weekly")
no	number
nos	numbers
NVwZ	Neue Zeitschrift für Verwaltungsrecht ("New Journal of Administrative Law")
Nw. U. L. Rev.	Northwestern University Law Review
N.Y.U. L. Rev.	New York University Law Review
NZA	Neue Zeitschrift für Arbeitsrecht ("New Journal of Labour Law")
OECD	Organisation for Economic Co-operation and Development
para/paras	paragraph/paragraphs
pt/pts	part/parts
PinG	Privacy in Germany
PL&B Reports	Privacy Laws & Business International Report
Privacy Shield	Commission Implementing Decision (EU) 2016/1250 pursuant to Directive 95/46/EC of the European Parliament and of the Council on the adequacy of the protection provided by the EU-U.S. Privacy Shield [2016] OJ L 207/1
PL	Public Law
QB	Queen's Bench
RabelsZ	Rabels Zeitschrift für ausländisches und internationales Privatrecht ("The Rabel Journal of Comparative and International Private Law")
Safe Harbor	Commission Decision 2000/520/EC pursuant to Directive 95/46/EC of the European Parliament and of the Council on the adequacy of the protection provided by the safe harbor privacy principles and related frequently asked questions issued by the US Department of Commerce [2000] OJ L 215/7
sch/schs	schedule/schedules
s/ss	section/sections
sub-s/sub-ss	subsection/subsections
TCA	Trade and Cooperation Agreement between the European Union and the European Atomic Energy Community, of the one part, and the United Kingdom of Great Britain and Northern Ireland, of the other part, OJ L 444/14 ("Brexit-Deal")
TEU	Treaty on European Union
TFEU	Treaty on the Functioning of the European Union
UDHR	UN's Universal Declaration of Human Rights of 1948
UK	United Kingdom of Great Britain and Northern Ireland
UK Adequacy Decision	Commission Implementing Decision (EU) 2021/1772 pursuant to Regulation (EU) 2016/679 of the European Parliament and of the Council on the Adequate Protection of Personal Data by the United Kingdom [2021] OJ L 360/1
UK GDPR	UK General Data Protection Regulation

UK-US Agreement	Agreement on Access to Electronic Data for the Purpose of Countering Serious Crime
US	United States of America
v	versus
Withdrawal Agreement	Agreement on the Withdrawal of the United Kingdom of Great Britain and Northern Ireland from the European Union and the European Atomic Energy Community, 12 November 2019, OJ C 384 I
WPg	Die Wirtschaftsprüfung ("The audit Journal")
Yale J. Int'l L.	Yale Journal of International Law
YEL	Yearbook of European Law
ZD	Zeitschrift für Datenschutzrecht ("Journal of Data Protection Law")
ZfDR	Zeitschrift für Digitalisierung und Recht ("Journal of Digialisation and Law")
ZWeR	Zeitschrift für Wettbewerbsrecht ("Journal of Competition Law")

Chapter 1 Introduction

In a globally connected world, personal data is constantly transferred cross-border, inside and outside the EU. These data flows are necessary for the expansion of international trade and international cooperation.[1] However, such international data flows have raised new challenges and concerns about the protection of personal data.[2] Cross-border data transfer may impose a risk to the right to privacy if the recipient country ensures only a lower level of protection of personal data than the sender country.[3] In such cases, the transferred personal data loses a certain standard of protection. In the EU, the GDPR establishes the free flow of personal data as an element of the European Single Market since all member states are bound to the same level of data protection. The export of personal data to countries outside the EU – so-called third countries – and to international organisations is regulated by Chapter V of the GDPR. The EU data transfer provisions follow a location-centric approach.[4] Only within the statutory permissions set out by Article 45 et seqq. GDPR transfer to third countries is allowed. The protection of the personal data even after their export must be ensured, the level of protection of natural persons guaranteed by the GDPR shall not be undermined.[5] Generally, the recipient country must ensure an "adequate level of protection"[6]. If this is not the case, data transfer is only permitted if other appropriate safeguards[7] are established or if the transfer takes place under exceptional and specific circumstances[8].

In the past years, the topic of data transfer has been discussed almost exclusively in the context of transatlantic data transfer. Since the exit of the UK from the EU (so-called "Brexit") and the UK's subsequent status of a third country in terms of the GDPR, a focus in the discussion has shifted to the data transfer from the EU to the UK *post*-Brexit. The UK formally left the EU on 31 January 2020. In

---

1 GDPR, recital 101.
2 GDPR, recital 101.
3 For a detailed overview on international regulation of transborder data flows see Christopher Kuner, *Transborder Data Flow and Data Privacy Law* (Oxford University Press 2013) 25 et seqq.
4 Julian Wagner, 'The Transfer of Personal Data to Third Countries under the GDPR: When Does a Recipient Country Provide an Adequate Level of Protection?' (2018) 8 IDPL 318, 320.
5 GDPR, art 44.
6 GDPR, art 45.
7 GDPR, art 46.
8 GDPR, art 49.

https://doi.org/10.1515/9783110988253-003

2019, the EU and the UK signed the Withdrawal Agreement,[9] in which both parties had agreed on a transitional period until 31 December 2020[10], during which EU law continued to apply in and to the UK[11]. Since 1 January 2021, the EU-UK Trade and Cooperation Agreement (after this: TCA)[12], commonly referred to as "Brexit-Deal", applies. Article FINPROV 10 A TCA stipulated a "bridging mechanism" to enable free data to flow from the EU to the UK until 30 June 2021.[13] Only, on 28 June 2021, the EU Commission adopted two adequacy decisions on the UK, one under the GDPR[14] and another under the Law Enforcement Directive[15] (after this: LED). Such adequacy decisions granted by the EU Commission are the only mechanisms that allow completely free and unhindered data flow from the EU to third countries to continue to take place. The adoption of an adequacy decision was crucial for the UK since there is a strong dependence on uncontrolled data flow between the EU and UK *post*-Brexit on the part of the UK: From 2015 to 2016, 75 % of the UK's cross border data flows were with EU countries.[16] Furthermore, the UK's economy is primarily based on service industries that generate vast volumes of personal data in behavioural, profile, and transactional data. They ac-

---

9 Agreement on the Withdrawal of the United Kingdom of Great Britain and Northern Ireland from the EU and the Euratom, 12 November 2019, OJ C 384I, approved on 25 November 2018 (Withdrawal Agreement). The Withdrawal Agreement was later incorporated into domestic law by the European Union (Withdrawal Agreement) Act 2020, which was given Royal Assent on 23 January 2021.

10 Withdrawal Agreement, art 126; the deadline of 1 July 2020 set out by Art. 132 of the Withdrawal Agreement for the extension of the transition period has elapsed without an extension being agreed by the Joint Committee.

11 Withdrawal Agreement, art 127.

12 Trade and Cooperation Agreement between the EU and the Euratom, of the one part, and the UK, of the other part, 31 December 2020, OJ L 444/14 (TCA).

13 The bridging mechanism only applied as long as the UK did not amend the data protection legislation, which was saved and incorporated by the European Union (Withdrawal) Act 2018 and did not exercise the designated powers listed in Art. FINPROV 10 A (3) without the agreement of the Union within the Partnership Council.

14 EU Commission, 'Commission Implementing Decision Pursuant to Regulation (EU) 2016/679 of the European Parliament and of the Council on the Adequate Protection of Personal Data by the United Kingdom' C/2021/4800

(UK Adequacy Decision).

15 EU Commission, 'Commission Implementing Decision Pursuant to Regulation (EU) 2016/679 of the European Parliament and of the Council on the Adequate Protection of Personal Data by the United Kingdom' C/2021/4801

(UK Adequacy Decision LED).

16 Department for Exiting the European Union, 'The Exchange and Protection of Personal Data. A Future Partnership Paper' (2017) 3 referring to The UK Digital Sectors after Brexit' by Frontier Economics (2017) 10 and 37.

counted for 79.6 % of the UK's GDP in 2019[17], thus making the UK's economy essentially dependant on the processing of personal data. In light of this, the UK Government under former Prime Minister *Theresa May* declared in August 2017: "Unhindered flow of data [...] is essential to the UK forging its path as an ambitious trading partner. This is why the UK Government will be seeking to ensure that data flows between the UK and the EU, and also appropriately between the UK and third countries and international organisations, remain uninterrupted after the UK's exit from the EU."[18] Additionally, the aggregate cost to UK firms of no adequacy decision, which would stem from additional compliance obligations – such as setting up standard contractual clauses (SCCs) or other appropriate safeguards, would likely be up to £1.6 billion.[19] With no adequacy decision in place, other economic implications, such as the increased risk of GDPR fines, reduction in EU-UK trade, especially digital trade, reduced investment, as well as the relocation of business functions, infrastructure, and personnel outside the UK, would occur.[20] Consequently, the adequacy decision was broadly welcomed, especially by the UK Government[21] and businesses[22]. The UK Information Commissioner *Elizabeth Denham* has commented: "Approved adequacy means that businesses can continue to receive data from the EU without having to make any changes to their data protection practice. Adequacy is

---

17 Office of National Statistics, 'Index of Services, UK: January 2020' (2020) <https://www.ons. gov.uk/economy/economicoutputandproductivity/output/bulletins/indexofservices/jan uary2020>.
18 Department for Digital, Culture, Media & Sport, 'A New Data Protection Bill: Our Planned Reforms' (2017) Statement of Intent 24 <https://assets.publishing.service.gov.uk/government/ uploads/system/uploads/attachment_data/file/635900/2017-08-07_DP_Bill_-_Statement_of_In tent.pdf>.
19 Duncan McCann, Oliver Patel and Javier Ruiz, 'The Cost of Data Inadequacy' *New Economics Foundation* (23 November 2020) <https://neweconomics.org/2020/11/the-cost-of-data-in adequacy>. SCCs and other appropriate safeguards pursuant to Article 46 GDPR will be discussed in detail in Chapter 4, A and B.
20 ibid.
21 Department for Digital, Culture, Media & Sport, 'EU Adopts "Adequacy" Decisions Allowing Data to Continue Flowing Freely to the UK. UK Businesses and Other Organisations Will Benefit from Unrestricted Personal Data Transfers' (2021) Press Release of 28 June 2021 <https://www. gov.uk/government/news/eu-adopts-adequacy-decisions-allowing-data-to-continue-flowing-free ly-to-the-uk>.
22 For example, the global software alliance *BSA* welcome the EU member states' endorsement, commenting that adequacy frameworks were pivotal for personal data transfers of thousands of businesses operating in Europe, cf *BSA*, 'BSA Welcomes EU Decision For UK Adequacy, Encourages Global Convergence on Data Flows' (2018) <https://www.bsa.org/news-events/news/bsa-welcomes-eu-decision-for-uk-adequacy-encourages-global-convergence-on-data-flows>.

the best outcome as it means organisations can carry on with data protection as usual. Moreover, people will continue to enjoy the protections that their data will be used fairly, lawfully, and transparently."[23]

A Research Subject

With the adoption of the EU Commission's adequacy decision on the UK on 28 June 2021 pursuant to Article 45(3) GDPR, the UK obtained the status of an adequate third country. Personal data can thus be transferred from the EU to the UK without further obstacles. The main subject of this study is the assessment of the level of protection of personal data transferred under such an adequacy decision from the EU to the UK and whether the UK's adequacy status was granted by the EU Commission in compliance with EU law. Subject of this study is also the data transfer regime of EU data protection law, which includes Article 7 and Article 8 CFR, and the relevant provisions of the GDPR. A focus here lies on the data transfer regime under the GDPR, established in Chapter V. In this context, the "adequacy" requirements and their interpretation by the CJEU play an essential role. All relevant rulings of the CJEU concerning data transfers to a third country or relevant in the context of transferring personal data to the UK are also covered in the course of this study. A detailed assessment of the relevant law in the UK *post*-Brexit and the implementation of such legislation will be provided. Also, any foreseeable developments and changes in the UK data protection regime *post*-Brexit are considered.

B Thematic Exclusion

In light of the comprehensive interest in knowledge outlined above it is necessary to make thematic limitations and exclusions. Therefore, the study will not go into details about Brexit concerning other legal areas other than data protection. The study will only focus on the data flow from the EU to the UK and not *vice versa*. The UK already deemed the EEA adequate, allowing a free data flow to continue from the UK to the EEA.[24] Furthermore, at this point, the UK has largely

---

23 Elizabeth Dunham, 'ICO Statement in Response to the EU Commission's Announcement on the Approval of the UK's Adequacy' (28 June 2021) <https://ico.org.uk/about-the-ico/news-and-events/news-and-blogs/2021/06/ico-statement-in-response-to-the-eu-commission-s-announcement-on-the-approval-of-the-uk-s-adequacy>.
24 DPA 2018, sch 21 paras 4 and 5(1)(a).

implemented Chapter V of the GDPR in the UK GDPR. Since the UK GDPR largely mirrors the GDPR, only provisions that might be problematic in the context of data transfer from the EU to the UK will be discussed. Also, this study will not include the assessment of any other adequacy decision, such as the former US adequacy decisions *Safe Harbor*[25] and *Privacy Shield*[26] or the recent adequacy decisions on Japan[27] and South Korea[28]. This study does not further deal with the question of whether the UK should be held to provide adequate protection to personal data transferred to it from the EU for law enforcement purposes (including concerning access by the UK law enforcement agencies to the relevant EU databases and bodies) under Article 36 of the LED. Although the LED is based on the same principles as the GDPR and also must be read in the light CFR, the assessment is distinct. This study also largely excludes the assessment of Article 48 GDPR, since at this point it does not appear to be of wider relevance for the data transfer between the EU and the UK under the GDPR.[29]

---

25 Commission Decision 2000/520/EC pursuant to Directive 95/46/EC of the European Parliament and of the Council on the adequacy of the protection provided by the safe harbor privacy principles and related frequently asked questions issued by the US Department of Commerce [2000] OJ L 215/7 (*Safe Harbor* Decision).

26 Commission Implementing Decision (EU) 2016/1250 pursuant to Directive 95/46/EC of the European Parliament and of the Council on the adequacy of the protection provided by the EU-U.S. Privacy Shield [2016] OJ L 207/1 (*Privacy Shield* Decision).

27 Commission Implementing Decision (EU) 2019/419 pursuant to Regulation (EU) 2016/679 of the EU Parliament and of the Council on the adequate protection of personal data by Japan under the Act on the Protection of Personal Information [2019] OJ L 76/1 (Japan Adequacy Decision).

28 Commission Implementing Decision pursuant to Regulation (EU) 2016/679 of the European Parliament and of the Council on the adequate protection of personal data by the Republic of Korea under the Personal Information Protection Act, C(2021) 4800 final (South Korea Adequacy Decision).

29 Overall, Article 48 GDPR is ascribed a clarification function and symbolic approach, which would be used to interpret Article 49(1) GDPR. It clarifies a public interest of a third country and the obligation to comply with decisions of the third country cannot alone legitimise a transfer to the third country; the GDPR protects personal data from sovereign acts of third countries (cf instead of many Peter Schantz, 'Art. 48' in Spiros Simitis, Gerrit Hornung and Indra Spiecker (eds), *Kommentar: Datenschutz: DSGVO mit BDSG* (1st edn, Nomos 2019) para 1, with further references).

C Course of the Study

To understand under which circumstances the European level of protection of personal data is undermined, one must first take a look at and define the level of data protection guaranteed within the EU. The right to the protection of personal data in the EU is guaranteed and protected through different instruments and their synergy: The EU's primary law (Article 16 TFEU, Articles 7 and 8 CFR), the ECHR (Article 8 ECHR) and the EU's secondary law, the GDPR. The GDPR aims to "protect fundamental rights and freedoms of natural persons and in particular their right to the protection of personal data" (Article 1(2) GDPR). The level of protection provided under those provisions will be examined in Chapter 2. Generally, the EU views that its high data protection standards are compromised if personal data are made available to recipients in third countries. Hence, in a second step, the provisions and mandatory requirements under which the GDPR permits the transfer of personal data outside the EU are examined. Here, the CJEU's interpretation of adequacy must also be analysed. Eventually, the findings of Chapter 2 should provide the essential basis for the assessment of whether the transfers of personal data from the EU to the UK *post*-Brexit would undermine the European data protection level (Chapter 3). Chapter 3 – the main part of this study – contains the assessment of whether the EU Commission's adequacy decision on the UK is coherent and compliant with EU law and the relevant CJEU's case law. This assessment constitutes the main part of this study. For this, the criteria set out in Article 45(2) GDPR must be taken into account. A particular focus will be laid on exemptions established in the Data Protection Act 2018, the Investigatory Powers Act 2016 and the UK's onward transfer practices, especially within the transatlantic cooperation framework with the USA. Also, the fundamental privacy and data protection rights in the *post*-Brexit UK will be evaluated. Suppose the assessment would show a lack of adequacy within the UK data protection regime, it is reasonable to assume that the CJEU will declare the adequacy decision towards the UK invalid. In that case, businesses must switch to alternative transfer tools provided by the GDPR. Consequently, the extent to which such alternative tools are suitable for transferring data from the EU to the UK are evaluated (Chapter 4). In the last step, any indications on possible future developments in (global) data protection in the UK and the EU are outlined as far as it might allow conclusions to be drawn about the future of the UK's adequacy decision (Chapter 5).

D Research Aim

This study pursues to provide an examination of the level of protection of personal data within the EU and the data protection level provided in the UK. The primary objective of this study is to assess and clarify whether the EU Commission's adequacy decision on the UK is compliant with EU law. The study seeks to determine whether and to what extent the UK provides an adequate level of protection for personal data transferred. The chances of an invalidation of the adequacy decision by the CJEU will also be evaluated. Given the aforementioned possibility of an invalidation of the adequacy decision, another aim is to examine the extent to which alternative safeguards would be suitable as a basis for data transfer to the UK for businesses.

Chapter 2 Transfer of Personal Data to Third Countries under the European Data Protection Law

The GDPR allows free data flow within the EEA "as an element of the European Single Market, with all member states bound to the same data protection level set by the GDPR."[30] The following Chapter focuses on transfers of personal data outside the EU. These cross-border flows are necessary for the expansion of international trade and international cooperation.[31] However, such international data flows have raised new challenges and concerns about the protection of personal data.[32] The transfer of personal data outside the EU bears the risk that the respective third country ensures a lower level of data protection than within the EU. A transfer outside the EU might lead to personal data losing their high European level of protection.[33] The GDPR aims to prevent the risk of undermining the EU's high protection standard.[34] Such transfers are regulated by Chapter V of the GDPR and may only be carried out fully compliant to those provisions.

To understand under which circumstances the European level of protection of personal data is undermined, one must first take a look at and define the level of data protection guaranteed within the EU as the relevant comparator. At first, the following focuses on providing a general overview of the protection of personal data in the EU (under A.). In a second step, the provisions and mandatory requirement under which the GDPR permits the transfer of personal data outside the EU are examined (under B.). Eventually, the findings of this Chapter provide the essential basis for the assessment of whether the transfers of personal data from the EU to the UK *post*-Brexit would undermine the European data protection level (Chapter 3).

A Data Protection Law in the EU

The data protection regime established in the EU can be classified as "omnibus regime" ("one-size-fits-all"), contrary to the concept of a "sectorial regime" or

---

30 Wagner (n 4) 320.
31 GDPR, recital 101.
32 GDPR, recital 101.
33 Wagner (n 4) 320.
34 GDPR, art 44.

https://doi.org/10.1515/9783110988253-004

"limited regime".[35] In an omnibus regime, the data protection rules apply to public and private actors and are sector-neutral; independent supervisory authorities are responsible for enforcing such rules. [36] In contrary, the USA takes a sectoral approach to data protection: there is no overarching data protection law, but (only) sectoral protection provisions for certain constellations in which the individual is considered particularly in need of protection.[37] The European data protection system is based on a human rights perspective.[38] The EU engages in a "right-focused legal discourse" that concentrates on the individual whose data are processed.[39] The right to the protection of personal data is a "fundamental right anchored in interests of dignity, personality, and self-determination".[40] The EU data protection system does not grant individuals "proprietary rights" over their personal data or allow contractual agreements according to their individual data protection preferences.[41] Instead, the EU's regime cannot be circumvented due to its "fundamental rights character".[42]

The protection of personal data within the EU derives from different provisions and instruments.[43] In 2007, the Treaty of Lisbon introduced data protection as a fundamental right guaranteed by EU institutions in Article 16(1) of the TFEU.[44] Article 16(2) TFEU provides a specific legal basis for adopting rules on personal data protection. Further, Article 8 CFR enshrines personal data protection as a fundamental right (under I.). Also, Article 7 CFR, protecting the right to respect private and family life, includes the protection of personal data (under

---

35 Orla Lynskey, *The Foundations of EU Data Protection Law* (Oxford University Press 2015) 15.
36 ibid.
37 For more information on the different approaches taken by the EU and the US see for example, Franz-Stefan Gady, 'EU/U.S. Approaches to Data Privacy and the "Brussels Effect": A Comparative Analysis' (2014) Georget. J. Int. Aff. 12.
38 Paul M Schwartz and Karl-Nikolaus Peifer, 'Transatlantic Data Privacy Law' (2017) 119 Geo. L.J. 115, 122; Lynskey (n 35) 35, 36 and 38 et seqq.
39 Schwartz and Peifer (n 38) 122.
40 ibid 123 et seqq.
41 ibid.
42 ibid.
43 See in detail Nikolaus Marsch, *Das Europäische Datenschutzrecht* (Mohr Siebeck 2018).
44 With the entry into force of the Treaty of Lisbon in 2009, Article 16 TFEU replaced Article 286 of the former Treaty establishing the European Community. Article 16(1) TFEU has the exact wording as Article 8(1) CFR and guarantees everyone the right to the protection of personal data. Next to Article 8 CFR, Article 16(1) TFEU has a more symbolic meaning, cf Stephanie Schiedermair, 'Einleitung' in Spiros Simitis, Gerrit Hornung and Indra Spiecker (eds) (n 29) para 177. Consequently, it will not be further discussed in the following.

II.).[45] Individuals should be granted enhanced control over their data in order to embrace self-determination.[46] The fundamental right to privacy can be traced back to Article 8 ECHR, a treaty documented drafted by the Council of Europe in 1950. The ECtHR has extended the right to privacy to data protection (under III.).[47] Since all EU member states are among the forty-seven signatories of the ECHR, all EU citizens also benefit from the ECHR's privacy rules. Although the EU has not yet acceded to the ECHR, the fundamental rights and freedoms established in the Charter must comply with those established in the ECHR.[48]

On the secondary-law level, the personal data is protected by the GDPR, which replaced the Directive 95/46[49] (under IV.). According to Article 1(2) GDPR, the GDPR mainly protects a natural person's right to the protection of personal data. This wording is a reference (to Article 16(1) TEU and) to Article 8(1) CFR.[50] Consequently, although the GDPR is the essential and primary instrument in the European data protection law context, all its provisions must necessarily be interpreted in light of the aforementioned fundamental rights.[51] The key judicial institutions within and outside the EU that protect the data protection rights are CJEU and the ECtHR. Also, national supervisory authorities in each EU member state play an essential role in securing and protecting data protection rights (under I.5. and V.4.). The EDPS and the EDPB also fulfil important institutional roles in data protection.

The following focuses on the fundamental rights to data protection and the provisions of the GDPR. It gives an overview of the data protection level guaranteed in the EU. As aforementioned, this is crucial to understand the requirements for the data transfer outside the EU in Chapter V of the GDPR, which main purpose is to prevent undermining the level of protection guaranteed in the EU when transferring data (under B.).

---

45 Gerrit Hornung and Indra Spiecker, 'Art. 1 DSGVO' in Spiros Simitis, Gerrit Hornung and Indra Spiecker (n 29) para 37.
46 Lynskey (n 35) 11.
47 cf *Copland v the United Kingdom*, no 62617/00, para 252, ECHR 2007-I.
48 CFR, art 52(3).
49 GDPR, art 94(1).
50 GDPR, recital 1.
51 Judgement of 20 May 2003, *Österreichischer Rundfunk and Others*, C-465/00, C-138/01 and C-139/01, EU:C:2003:294, para 68.

I Article 8 CFR

Article 8 CFR guarantees everyone the right to protect personal data concerning them. Article 8 CFR addresses institutions, bodies, offices and agencies of the EU as well as member states implementing EU law[52]. Article 8 CFR was "designed to meet the challenges of current and future development of information technologies".[53] It is of outstanding importance in the modern age for a wide range of matters, which is also shown by the fact that Article 8 CFR is the subject of numerous proceedings before the CJEU. Article 8 CFR was based on Article 286 Treaty establishing the European Community (which was later replaced by Article 16 TFEU), on the Directive 95/46, on Article 8 of the ECHR and the Convention 108[54].[55] These various legal sources shall be used for Article 8 CFR's interpretation. In the following, the scope of application, the requirements and principles of legitimate processing, the specific rights guaranteed by Article 8 CFR, and the role of supervisory authorities will be further reviewed.

1 Scope of Application

According to Article 8(1) CFR, everyone has the right to the protection of their personal data. The term "everyone" includes only natural persons as data subjects but no legal persons.[56] The material scope of application of Article 8 CFR is defined by the concept of "personal data" and the concept of "processing" personal data.[57] The term "personal data" is interpreted broadly and includes all information relating to an identified or identifiable person – not just sensitive

---

52 CFR, art 51(1).

53 EU Commission, 'Communication from the Commission on the Legal Nature of the Charter of Fundamental Rights of the European Union' COM(2014) 644 final 2 <https://eur-lex.europa.eu/LexUriServ/LexUriServ.do?uri=COM:2000:0644:FIN:EN:PDF>.

54 Council of Europe, 'Convention for the Protection of Individuals with Regard to Automatic Processing of Personal Data 28 January 1981.' (1981) European Treaty Series – No 108 (Convention 108). The Convention was modernised in May 2018.

55 Explanatory Note on Article 8 CFR.

56 Judgement of 9 November 2010, *Volker and Markus Schecke and Eifert*, C-92/09 and C-93/09, EU:C:2010:662, para 53. For a different view see Heinrich Amadeus Wolff, 'Art. 8 GRC' in Matthias Pechstein, Carsten Nowak and Ulrich Häde (eds), *Frankfurter Kommentar EUV/GRC/AEUV*, vol 1 (1st edn, C.H. Beck 2017) para 11.

57 The material scope of application of the GDPR is also defined by "processing personal data". The concept of "personal data" as well as the concept of "processing" will be explained and clarified in more detail under A.IV.1.a.aa. and bb.

data.[58] The concept of "processing" is also to be interpreted widely to ensure that all possible ways of data use are taken into account.[59] Unlike the material scope of the GDPR, Article 8 CFR is neither exclusive to partly or fully automated personal data processing nor data processing leading to a structured set or file.[60]

2 General Limitations

Article 52 CFR specifies the scope and the interpretation of the fundamental rights and principles.[61] According to its first paragraph, "[a]ny limitation on the exercise of the rights and freedoms recognised by this Charter must be provided for by law and respect the essence of those rights and freedoms. Subject to the principle of proportionality, limitations may only be made if they are necessary and genuinely meet objectives of general interest recognised by the European Union or the need to protect the rights and freedoms of others."[62] These requirements also apply for Article 8 CFR.[63] Most recently, the CJEU emphasised that Article 8 CFR is no absolute right and must be considered in relation to its function in society.[64] In the view of the CJEU, the requirement "provided by law" "implies that the legal basis which permits the interference with those rights must itself define the scope of the limitation on the exercise of the right concerned."[65]

Article 52(1) refers to three different elements as regards the substantive justification for limiting rights: (a) the need to "respect the essence" of the Charter rights and freedoms; (b) the "principle of proportionality"; and (c) the requirement that any limitations must be "necessary" and "genuinely meet" the objectives or other rights being protected. "Objectives of general interest recognised by the EU" covers both the objectives mentioned in Article 3 TEU and other interests protected by specific provisions of the Treaties such as Article 4(1) of the TEU

---

58 Norbert Bernsdorff, 'Art. 8 GRCh' in Jürgen Meyer and Sven Höscheidt (eds), *Nomos Kommentar: Charta der Grundrechte der Europäischen Union* (5th edn, Nomos 2019) para 20.
59 ibid para 22.
60 Frank Hendrick, 'Art. 8 – Protection of Personal Data' in Filip Dorssemont and others (eds) (1st edn, 2019) 260.
61 For more details on the case law about Article 52 CFR see Steve Peers and Sacha Prechal, 'Art. 52 CFR' in Steve Peers and others (eds), *The EU Charter of Fundamental Rights: A Commentary* (2nd edn, Nomos 2021).
62 ibid para 52.14 et seqq.
63 *Volker and Markus Schecke and Eifert* (n 56) para 50.
64 Judgement of 16 July 2020, *Facebook Ireland and Schrems*, C-311/18, EU:C:2020:559, para 172 et seqq.
65 ibid para 175 (and case law cited).

and Article 35(3), 36 and 346 of the TFEU. "[T]he need to protect the rights and freedoms of others" encompasses the rights protected in the Charter itself ("conflict of rights" scenario).

a Respect to the Essence

The "respect to essence"[66], shows that all fundamental rights, also those subject to permissible limitations, should be understood as including the inviolable essence that allows neither limitations nor balancing.[67] The essence "represents the untouchable core or inner circle of a fundamental right that cannot be diminished, restricted or interfered with. Interference with the essence of a fundamental right makes the right lose its value for society and, consequently, for the right holders".[68] The CJEU has not yet explicitly identified the essence of the rights to private life and data protection. In its prominent judgement in *Maximilian Schrems v Data Protection Commissioner and Facebook Ireland* (after this: *Schrems*), which will be discussed in detail below[69], the CJEU found an interference with the essence of a fundamental right for the first time in its history.[70] The Court stated that "a rule that allows the authorities to access the content of electronic communications generally violates the essence of the fundamental right to respect for private life guaranteed by Article 7 of the Charter."[71] Furthermore, legislation not providing legal remedies for an individual to have access to their data or to obtain the rectification or erasure of it violated the essence of the right to effective judicial protection in Article 47 CFR.[72] In other rulings, the CJEU found that mass data retention did not affect the essence of the right to privacy under Article 7 CFR since it did not lead to knowledge of the content of elec-

---

66 The notion of essence also appears in several constitutions of EU member states: Estonia (art 17(2)), Germany (art 19(2)), Hungary (art 1(3)), Poland (art 31(3)), Portugal (art 18), Romania (art 53(2)), Slovakia (art 13(4)), Spain (art 53(1)).

67 Tuomas Ojanen, 'Making the Essence of Fundamental Rights Real: The Court of Justice of the European Union Clarifies the Structure of Fundamental Rights under the Charter. ECJ 6 October 2015, Case C-362/14, Maximilian Schrems v Data Protection Commissioner.' (2016) 12 EuConst 318, 328.

68 Maja Brkan, 'The Concept of Essence of Fundamental Rights in the EU Legal Order: Peeling the Onion to Its Core' (2018) 14 EuConst 332, 333 with further references. This article provides an in-depth analysis of the notion of the essence of fundamental rights.

69 B.I.3.a.aa.

70 cf Ojanen (n 67).

71 Judgement of 6 October 2015, *Schrems*, C-362/14, EU:C:2015:665, para 94.

72 ibid para 187.

tronic communications.[73] However, the view that only content data would trigger the essence of the right to privacy appears to be overruled by the *Schrems* ruling, where mere access by the public authorities on a generalised basis would compromise the essence of privacy.[74] *Thomas Ojanen* also criticised that the CJEU did not find that metadata (such as traffic and location data) could trigger the essence of privacy, calling the differentiation "orthodox, even obsolete".[75] *Johannes Eichenhofer* elaborated from the CJEU judgements that in order to interfere with the essence of fundamental rights access to the electronic communication must be general: The essence of Article 7 CFR would not be affected if a single communication (e.g. a telephone conversation or a single e-mail) is intercepted or read. However, this would be the case if, for example, all communications stored on the server of a communication intermediary can be accessed.[76] *Jens Ambrock* and *Moritz Karg* agreed, arguing that the disclosure of a data subject's situation, even if it is susceptible, can be a severe intrusion of privacy for the person concerned but does not automatically undermine the data subject's fundamental right to data protection because each data can only describe a small part of what constitutes the individual.[77]

In *Schrems*, the CJEU only found a violation of the essence of Article 7 CFR but not of Article 8 CFR. The violation of the essence of Article 8 CFR could depend on whether the recipient third country's regulation contains a minimum level of restrictions and limitation of data processing.[78] This view appears to be consistent with the findings in the *Digital Rights Ireland* ruling. Here, the Court denied the affection of essence since providers of electronic communication services or public communications networks were required to respect "principles of data protection and security"[79]. Also, the CJEU found that transfer of PNR data to Canada did not violate the essence of Articles 7 and 8 CFR. This was due to the nature of the information at issue being limited to certain aspects

---

73 Judgement of 8 April 2014, *Digital Rights Ireland and Seitlinger and Others*, C-293/12, EU: C:2014:238, para 39.
74 Ojanen (n 67) 327.
75 ibid 328.
76 Johannes Eichenhofer, '"e-Privacy" im Europäischen Grundrechtsschutz: Das "Schrems"-Urteil des EuGH' [2016] EuR 76, 84.
77 Jens Ambrock and Moritz Karg, 'Ausnahmetatbestände der DS-GVO als Rettungsanker des internationalen Datenverkehrs? Analyse der Neuerungen zur Angemessenheit des Datenschutzniveaus' [2017] ZD 154, 158.
78 In *Schrems* (n 71), the Court did not address specific content, limitations and specifications of the relevant US-provisions and did not determine whether those violate the essence of Article 8 CFR due to a lack of sufficient limitation of processing powers.
79 *Digital Rights Ireland and Seitlinger and Others* (n 73) para 39.

of private life (about Article 7 CFR), and the fact that the purposes for which PNR may be processed contained rules protecting the security, confidentiality and integrity of the data (about Article 8 CFR).[80]

b Principle of Necessity and Proportionality

The CJEU found the following about the principle of proportionality: "The legislation in question must lay down clear and precise rules governing the scope of application of the measure in question and imposing minimum safeguards so that the persons whose data has been transferred have sufficient guarantees to protect their personal data against the risk of abuse effectively. It must indicate in what circumstances, and under which conditions a measure providing for the processing of such data may be adopted, thereby ensuring that the interference is limited to what is strictly necessary. The need for such safeguards is all the greater where personal data is subject to automated processing. Those considerations particularly apply where the protection of the particular category of personal data that is sensitive data is at stake."[81] The principle of necessity is implicit in the proportionality rule.[82]

3 Legitimate Processing

The first sentence of Article 8(2) CFR gives various requirements for legitimate processing of personal data: Personal data "must be processed fairly for specified purposes and based on the consent of the person concerned or some other legitimate basis laid down by law".[83] These requirements for legitimate

---

80 Opinion of 26 July 2017, Avis 1/15 – *Accord PNR EU-Canada*, EU:C:2017:592, paras 151 et seq.

81 *Digital Rights Ireland and Seitlinger and Others* (n 73) paras 54 et seq.; Judgement of 21 December 2016, *Tele2 Sverige*, C-203/15 and C-698/15, EU:C:2016:970, paras 109 and 117; *Accord PNR EU-Canada* (n 80) para 141; *Facebook Ireland and Schrems* (n 64) para 176.

82 Peers and Prechal (n 61) para 52.82.

83 Despite Article 16(1) TFEU and Article 52(2) CFR, Article 8(2) CFR is applicable. Unlike Article 16 TFEU, Article 8(2) CFR adds that personal data shall only be processed fairly for specified purposes as well as with the consent of the person concerned or based on some other legitimate legal ground. According to Article 52(2) CFR, rights that are recognised by the Charter, for which provisions are made in the TEU or TFEU shall be exercised under the condition and within limits defined by the Treaties. As Article 16 TFEU does not provide any limitations to the right to data protection, Article 52(2) CFR would consequently lead to the inapplicability of Article 8(2) CFR. However, it is somewhat aberrant to assume a right to protect personal data without any limitations or restrictions. It would be considered impractical due to the increasing digitalisation. The purpose of Article 52(2) CFR was to ensure that rights already included in the TFEU were not modified or relativised by the Charter. Article 52(2) CFR thus does not include

processing are also established in the GDPR. Since the GDPR's predecessor, Directive 95/46, was one of the sources of Article 8 CFR, the GDPR definitions can be used as a reference to define the requirements of legitimate processing under Article 8(2) CFR.[84]

4 Right to Access and Right to Rectification

The second sentence of Article 8(2) CFR guarantees the data subject a right to access[85] and rectify[86] the collected data. Since these rights are also established in Article 15 and 16 GDPR, they are discussed below.[87]

5 Independent Supervisory Authorities

Article 8(3) CFR states that compliance with data protection rules shall be subject to control by an independent authority. The existence of independent supervisory authorities constitutes an "essential component" of protecting individuals concerning the processing of personal data.[88] In the case *Commission v Germany* the CJEU interpreted the notion of "complete independence" of the supervisory authorities widely: "[it] precludes not only any influence exercised by the supervised bodies, but also any directions or any other external influence, whether direct or indirect, which could call into question the performance by those authorities of their task."[89] The authorities "should remain above any suspicion of partiality".[90] The tasks and powers of a supervisory authority under the GDPR will be outlined below.[91]

---

articles in the TEU and TFEU, which only came into force with the Lisbon Treaty. This would also include Article 16(1) TFEU. Against this background, in the case of Article 8(2) CFR, Article 52(2) CFR should find no application, cf Thorsten Kingreen, 'Art. 8 EU-GRCharta' in Christian Callies and Matthias Ruffert (eds), *EUV/AEUV – Das Verfassungsrecht der Europäischen Union mit Europäischer Grundrechtecharta* (6th edn, C.H. Beck 2022) para 4.

84 For the principle of fairness see below under IV.2.a., for purpose limitation see below under IV.2.b., for consent and other legitimate basis see below under IV.3.

85 The right to access collected personal data is also guaranteed in Article 15(1) GDPR.

86 The right to rectify collected personal data is also guaranteed in Article 16 GDPR.

87 IV.4.b. and c.

88 Directive 95/46, recital 62. Also, in Judgement of 9 March 2010, *Commission v Germany*, C-518/07, EU:C:2010:125, para 23 and in Judgement of 16 October 2012, *Commission v Austria*, C-614/10, EU:C:2012:631, paras 36 et seq.

89 Judgement of 9 March 2010, *Commission v Germany*, C-518/07, EU:C:2010:125, para 30.

90 ibid para 36.

91 IV.6.

II Article 7 CFR

According to Article 7 CFR, everyone has the right to respect for his or her private and family life, home and communications. As the explanatory note to Article 8 CFR shows, the roots of the right to data protection lie in the right to privacy.[92] Both rights are "closely connected" with each other.[93] The CJEU even refers to them as "fused species"[94] ("the right to respect for private life with regard to the processing of personal data, recognised by Articles 7 and 8").[95] According to the CJEU, "[t]he protection of personal data resulting from the explicit obligation laid down in Article 8(1) of the Charter is especially important for the right to respect for private life enshrined in Article 7 of the Charter."[96] Both rights constitute an essential prerequisite for a free society.[97] However, the right to privacy and data protection are not the same.[98] The CJEU stated that as far as personal data relating to private life is concerned, both Article 7 and Article 8 CFR apply next to each other.[99] Some argue that Article 8 CFR is *lex specialis* to Article 7.[100] Others argue that the protection scope of Article 8 CFR is narrower than the one of Article 7 CFR. This is because it only refers to data processing and is also broader since it includes all personal data of a data subject and not just the data that protect privacy.[101] According to this view, the right to privacy protects social and communicative spaces of retreat, while the right to data protection concerns the lawfulness of data processing.[102] More precisely, Article 7 CFR would protect privacy spaces by adopting the perspective of the private sphere and protecting the individual in developing their personality from exploration

---

92 Helge Kranenborg, 'Art. 8 CFR' in Steve Peers and others (eds) (n 61) para 08.21.

93 *Volker and Markus Schecke and Eifert* (n 56) para 47; *Digital Rights Ireland and Seitlinger and Others* (n 73) para 29.

94 Lynskey (n 35) 173.

95 *Volker and Markus Schecke and Eifert* (n 56) para 52; Judgement of 13 May 2014, *Google Spain and Google*, C-131/12, EU:C:2014:317, para 74.

96 *Digital Rights Ireland and Seitlinger and Others* (n 73) para 53.

97 Kirsten Bock and Malte Engeler, 'Die verfassungsrechtliche Wesensgehaltsgarantie als absolute Schranke im Datenschutzrecht' (2016) 131 DVBl 593, 569.

98 See Walther Michl, 'Das Verhältnis zwischen Art. 7 und Art. 8 GRCh – Zur Bestimmung der Grundlage des Datenschutzgrundrechts im EU-Recht' (2017) 41 DuD 349 for more details on the relationship between Articles 7 and 8 CFR.

99 *Volker and Markus Schecke and Eifert* (n 56) para 52; *Digital Rights Ireland and Seitlinger and Others* (n 73) para 29.

100 Instead of many: Bernsdorff (n 58) para 13; Wolff (n 56) para 3.

101 Bock and Engeler (n 97) 595.

102 ibid; Johannes Eichenhofer, 'Privatheit im Internet als Vertrauensschutz. Eine Neukonstruktion der Europäischen Grundrechte auf Privatleben und Datenschutz' (2016) 55 Der Staat 41, 62.

and influence, while Article 8 CFR would address the power asymmetries that become entrenched in favour of organisations due to modern data processing between organisations and individuals in an unregulated manner.[103] Others state that, by applying the two norms in combination, the CJEU underlines a particular ideal division of tasks between them: Article 7 CFR would represent human rights tradition and the more profound meaning that data protection serves; Article 8 CFR would represent the Charter's modernity by showing that it explicitly addresses the issue of digitalisation.[104] Article 8 CFR also provides detailed rules that would be more difficult to derive from the broader Article 7 CFR.[105]

III ECHR

The right to respect for private and family life, home and communication is also protected in Article 8 ECHR. The ECHR is an international treaty signed on 4 November 1950 by twelve member states of the Council of Europe. Although the EU has not (yet) accessed the ECHR,[106] all of the EU's member states are members of the Council of Europe and have therefore signed the ECHR. The ECHR obliges its parties to comply, but how they choose to comply is up to them; it has no direct effects on domestic law. The supra-national character of the Charter makes it is much more deeply entrenched in domestic law. The ECHR lacks a serious enforcement mechanism as there is no public enforcement by way of infringement proceedings (unlike in Article 258 TFEU), nor does it provide for the possibility of private enforcement by having a direct effect. Yet, at least in practice, the ECHR is almost consistently followed by member states.[107] The ECtHR is a court of individual petition, meaning citizens of contracting States can seek a ruling from the ECtHR for violation of an ECHR right by their government (or its executive agencies). However, before applying to the ECtHR, the individuals must exhaust all

---

103 Bock and Engeler (n 97) 596; Eichenhofer (n 102) 62; critical examination and different approach in Michl (n 98) 352 and 353.
104 This view was also held in the Opinion of Advocate General *Sharpston* of 17 June 2010 in *Volker and Markus Schecke and Eifert*, EU:C:2010:353, C-92/09 and C-93/09, para 71, suggesting that privacy is "a classic right" while data protection is a "more modern right".
105 Michl (n 98) 353.
106 The accession of the EU to the ECHR is intended (TEU, art 6(2) and ECHR, art 59(2)). However, the CJEU declared the accession of the EU to the ECHR under the Accession Convention, which had been drafted since 2010, to be contrary to EU law in light of the autonomy of the Union legal order, cf Avis 2/13, EU:C:2014:2454 (Opinion) (18 December 2014).
107 BVerfG, 14 October 2014 – 2 BvR 1481/104 = BVerfGE 111, 307 (*Görgülü*).

national remedies.[108] The ECtHR's judgements are legally binding to the contracting states[109] but apply only to the member states concerned in the dispute.

According to Article 52(3) CFR, the rights guaranteed by the Charter must be consistent with the corresponding rights – rights with the same meaning and scope – laid down in the ECHR. However, Article 52(3) CFR makes clear that the Charter rights may provide more extensive protection. Therefore, Article 8 ECHR and the relevant case law of the ECtHR is relevant when applying the right to data protection; however, not necessarily conclusive when assessing whether a situation is compliant with Article 8 CFR.[110]

1 Article 8 ECHR

Like Article 7 CFR, Article 8 ECHR protects the right to respect private and family life, home, and communication.[111] Although Article 8 ECHR protects the right to respect private and family life, home and communication and mainly corresponds to Article 7 CFR, the CJEU decided it should also be considered when interpreting Article 8 CFR.[112] Article 8 ECHR still plays a vital role in data protection as the ECtHR developed a broad notion of privacy, which also includes the right to the protection of personal data.[113] The protection of personal data is of fundamental importance to a person's enjoyment of their right to respect for privacy and family life.[114] As stated by the ECtHR, Article 8 of the Convention provides "the right to a form of informational self-determination[115], allowing individuals to rely on their right to privacy as regards data which, albeit neutral, are collected, processed and disseminated collectively and in such a form or manner that their Article 8 rights may be engaged."[116]

---

108 ECHR, art 35(1).

109 ECHR, art 46(1).

110 Kranenborg (n 92) para 08.50.

111 See for more information: ECHR, 'Guide on Article 8 of the European Convention on Human Rights' (2020) <https://www.echr.coe.int/documents/guide_art_8_eng.pdf>.

112 *Volker and Markus Schecke and Eifert* (n 56) para 52.

113 *Rotaru v Romania* [GC], no 28341/95, paras 42 et seq. and 172, ECHR 2000-V; critically is Kranenborg (n 92) para 08.156.

114 *Satakunnan Markkinapörssi Oy and Satamedia Oy v Finland* [GC], no 931/13, para 137, 27 June 2017.

115 Kai von Lewinski, *Die Matrix des Datenschutzes – Besichtigung und Ordnung eines Begriffsfeldes*, vol 1 (Mohr Siebeck 2014) 46 et seq. classifies data protection in its current form as a right to "informational heteronomy".

116 *Satakunnan Markkinapörssi Oy and Satamedia Oy v Finland* (n 114) para 133.

Article 8(2) ECHR requires that an interference with the right to respect for private life is in "accordance with the law", serves a legitimate purpose and is "necessary in a democratic society". As for an interference to be "in accordance with the law", it is necessary that the law is adequately accessible and foreseeable. The legal basis must be formulated with sufficient precision to enable the individual to regulate his conduct.[117] For example, in the *Rotaru v Romania* case, the Romanian law did not provide an apparent limit on the exercise of power by the state to collect and store data, and there was no procedure under which the subject of the information could consult it, find out its nature or seek to correct it. The Strasbourg Court decided that, where the national law fails to indicate with clarity a scope and manner of the exercise of the State's powers, the interference with the private life of the natural person is not "in accordance with the law".[118] As to the second and third condition of the second paragraph, interference will be considered "necessary in democratic society" for a legitimate aim if it answers a "pressing social need", if it is not out of proportion compared to the legitimate aim pursued and, if the reasons adduce by the national authorities are "relevant and sufficient".[119] This is not the case, where the natural person concerned has no effective access to court to challenge an interference by state authorities.[120] Domestic law must afford appropriate safeguards to prevent any such use of personal data that may be inconsistent with the guarantees of Article 8 ECHR.[121] When personal data undergo automatic processing or is used for police purposes, the ECtHR defines the need for such safeguards as "all the greater".[122] Domestic law must ensure that such data are relevant and guarantee against the risk of abuse, misuse and arbitrariness.[123] Therefore national law should ensure that personal data "are relevant and not excessive in relation to the purpose for which they are stored" and also "preserved in a form which permits identification of the data subjects for no longer than is required for the purpose for which those data are stored".[124] When assessing whether the collection, retention, the use or the disclosure of the information complies with the abovementioned requirements, the ECtHR takes several factors into account, including

---

117 See for instance: *S and Marper v United Kingdom* [GC], nos 30562/04 and 30566/04, para 95, ECHR 2008.

118 Instead of many *Rotaru v Romania* (n 113).

119 *S and Marper v United Kingdom* (n 117) para 101.

120 *M.N. and others v San Marino*, no 28005/12, 17 July 2015.

121 *S and Marper v United Kingdom* (n 117) para 103.

122 ibid.

123 *Gardel v France*, no 16428/05, para 62, ECHR 2009.

124 *S and Marper v United Kingdom* (n 117) para 103.

the privacy expectation of the person concerned,[125] the nature of the data,[126] control mechanisms given to the data subject,[127] the existence of independent oversight mechanisms,[128] and installed security measures[129].[130] Regarding disclosure of personal data, the public interest must outweigh the individual's right to privacy regarding the aim pursued and the safeguards surrounding its use.[131]

2 Convention 108

The Convention 108 is an international agreement established by the Council of Europe in 1981.[132] The Council of Europe "has been enormously influential in shaping regulatory discourse in the field, primarily within Europe but also beyond" ("Strasbourg Effect").[133] It played a decisive role in developing European data protection law.[134] The Convention 108 summarised the most important fundamental principles present, which were present in national data protection statutes, and burst the framework of isolated, national reactions regarding the necessary creation of legally binding regulation for the processing of personal data.[135] Each of the Convention 108's principles are to be regarded as part of internationally accepted rules of conduct. [136] Convention 108 is open to non-European states and consists now of 53 parties – the latest being Mexico.[137] The Convention does not provide rights for individuals and is not directly applicable between private parties but obliges the member countries to implement its pro-

---

125 *Von Hannover v Germany*, no 59320/00, paras 51 and 69, ECHR 2004-VI.

126 *Z v Finland*, 25 February 1997, paras 96 et seqq., *Reports of Judgements and Decisions* 1997-I.

127 *Gaskin v United Kingdom*, 7 July 1989, para 49, Series A no 160.

128 *Klass and Others v Germany*, 6 September 1978, para 50, Series A no 28.

129 *I v Finland*, no 20511/03, paras 38 et seqq., 17 July 2008.

130 Listing of the relevant factors found in Kranenborg (n 92) para 08.56.

131 Instead of many: *Z v Finland* (n 126) para 95.

132 Convention 108. See for more background information in Kuner, *Transborder Data Flow and Data Privacy Law* (n 3) 36 et seqq.

133 Lee A Bygrave, 'The "Strasbourg Effect" on Data Protection in Light of the "Brussels Effect": Logic, Mechanics and Prospects' (2020) 40 CLSR 2 <https://doi.org/10.1016/j.clsr.2020.105460>.

134 Schiedermair (n 44) para 137.

135 ibid.

136 ibid.

137 Council of Europe, 'Welcome to Mexico, 53rd Party to Convention 108' (2018) Press Release of 28 June 2018 <https://www.coe.int/en/web/data-protection/-/welcome-to-mexico-53rd-party-to-convention-108>; a comprehensive overview map of all parties to the Convention 108 and Convention 108+ is provided by Research Centre for Law and Digitalisation, 'Parties to the CoE Convention 108 / 108+' (last revised on 23 August 2021) <https://www.jura.uni-passau.de/fileadmin/dokumente/fakultaeten/jura/lehrstuehle/hennemann/Mapping_Global_Data_Law/I02_-_Convention_108_and_108__.pdf>.

visions in their law.[138] According to recital 11 of the former Directive 95/46, the Directive gives substance to and amplifies the principles contained in Convention 108.[139] The Directive 95/46 and the GDPR can be seen as the successors of Convention 108 and implementing its principle and thus must be interpreted in the light of the Convention. An Amending Protocol to the Convention 108 was recently adopted by the Council of Europe's Committee of Ministers in 2018 (after this: Convention 108+).[140] The purpose of this modernisation was to "better address emerging privacy challenges resulting from the increasing use of new information and communication technologies (IT), the globalisation of processing operations and the ever greater flows of personal data, and, at the same time, to strengthen the Convention 108's evaluation and follow up mechanism."[141] Article 9 of Convention 108 provides that derogations from the general data protection principles (Article 5 "Quality of data"), the rules governing special categories of data (Article 6 "Special categories of data") and data subject rights (Article 8 "Additional safeguards to the data subject") are only permissible when such derogation is provided for by the law of the party. This constitutes a necessary measure in a democratic society in the interests of protecting state security, public safety, the monetary interests of the state or the suppression of criminal offences, or for protecting the data subject or the rights and freedoms of others. The EU Commission is currently promoting the EU to become a party to the Convention 108.[142]

IV GDPR

The GDPR entered into force on 25 May 2018 in the EU and on 20 July 2018 in the non-EU member states of the EEA, Iceland, Liechtenstein, and Norway.[143] The

---

138 Council of Europe, 'Explanatory Report to Protocol Amending the Convention for the Protection of Individuals with Regard to Automatic Processing of Personal Data' CM(2018)2-addfinal (Explanatory Report to Convention 108+) para 38.
139 Directive 95/46, recital 11.
140 Council of Europe, Protocol amending the Convention for the Protection of Individuals with regard to Automatic Processing of Personal Data, No 233, 18 May 2018.
141 Explanatory Report to Convention 108+, para 1.
142 EU Commission, 'Communication from the Commission to the European Parliament and Council. Exchanging and Protecting Personal Data in a Globalised World' (2017) COM(2017) 7 final 9.
143 In this study, references to the EU in the context of the GDPR are to be understood as references to the entire EEA area.

GDPR, as secondary legislation, fully harmonises[144] the data protection law and data protection standard within the EEA. As "[r]apid technological developments and globalisation have brought new challenges for the protection for personal data" and "[t]he scale of the collection and sharing of personal data has increased significantly", [145] the Directive 95/46 could no longer prevent "fragmentation in the way personal data protection is implemented across the Union, legal uncertainty and a widespread public perception that there are significant risks associated notably with online activity"[146]. Absent EU harmonisation allowed companies to locate their data processing in member states without adequate data protection rules.[147] Therefore, the introduction of the GDPR aimed to provide "a stronger and more coherent data protection framework in the EU, backed by strong enforcement that allowed the digital economy to develop across the internal market, put individuals in control of their data and reinforce legal and practical certainty for economic operators and public authorities".[148] According to Article 1(3) GDPR, the exchange of personal data must remain free throughout the EU. Member states are precluded from taking national measures to protect personal data and justifying a restriction of fundamental freedoms as an important general interest,[149] from changing the scope of the GDPR provisions,[150] and from exceeding or falling below the GDPR's data protection level.[151] Exemptions are only permissible as far as the GDPR explicitly al-

---

144 Consequently, neither a softer nor a stricter interpretation of the provisions of the GDPR in member states is possible.

145 GDPR, recital 5; EU Commission, 'Proposal for a Regulation of the European Parliament and of the Council on the Protection of Individuals with Regard to the Processing of Personal Data and on the Free Movement of Such Data (General Data Protection Regulation)' (2012) COM(2012) 11 final 2.

146 ibid.

147 Anu Bradford, *The Brussels Effect: How the European Union Rules the World* (Oxford University Press 2020) 138. The author also reviews the process of the adoption of the GDPR and the involvement of different parties (e.g. companies, NGO's, foreign states) in more detail.

148 GDPR, recital 7; EU Commission, 'Proposal for a Regulation of the European Parliament and of the Council on the Protection of Individuals with Regard to the Processing of Personal Data and on the Free Movement of Such Data (General Data Protection Regulation)' (n 145) 2.

149 Peter Schantz, 'Art. 1 DS-GVO' in Heinrich Amadeus Wolff and Stefan Brink (eds), *Beck'-scher Onlinekommentar: Datenschutzrecht* (38th edn, C.H. Beck 2022) para 9.

150 Judgement of 24 November 2011, *ASNEF*, C-468/10 and C-469/10, EU:C:2011:777, paras 32 and 34.

151 Schantz (n 149) para 10.

lows it in its "opening clauses" (for instance, in Article 8(1), Article 9(2)(a) and Article 9(4) GDPR).[152]

The provisions of the GDPR, insofar as they govern the processing of personal data liable to infringe fundamental freedoms, must necessarily be interpreted in the light of the fundamental rights which, in line with the settled case law of the CJEU, "form an integral part of the general principles of law" whose observance the CJEU ensures.[153]

1 Scope of Application

In the following, the scope of the GDPR, in both material and territorial dimensions, will be further clarified. The ultimate purpose of the GDPR, protecting the fundamental rights and freedoms of natural persons and their right to privacy, should be kept in mind when assessing the scope of the GDPR.[154]

a Material Scope

The GDPR's material scope of application covers "the processing of personal data wholly or partly by automated means and to the processing other than by automated means of personal data which form part of a filing system or are intended to form part of a filing system."[155] Just like Article 8 CFR, the material scope of application depends on the two key concepts "processing" and "personal data". The GDPR conceptually pursues a technologically neutral[156] "one-size-fits-all" approach, regardless of whether private or state data processing is at issue.[157]

---

152 Other opening clauses can be found in Article 88(1) GDPR, Article 37(4) GDPR, Article 17(3) (b) GDPR, allowing the national legislator to specify, supplement and modify certain GDPR provisions.

153 See by analogy: Judgement of 6 March 2001, *Conolly/Commission*, C-274/99, EU:C:2001:127, para 37; *Österreichischer Rundfunk and Others* (n 51) para 68.

154 Daniel Rücker, 'B. Scope of Application of the GDPR' in Sebastian Dienst and Daniel Rücker (eds), *New European General Data Protection Regulation: A Practitioner's Guide* (1st edn, Nomos 2018) para 49.

155 GDPR, art 2(1).

156 cf GDPR, recital 15.

157 Stefan Ernst, 'Art. 2 DS-GVO' in Boris P Paal and Daniel A Pauly (eds), *Datenschutz-Grundverordnung. Bundesdatenschutzgesetz: DS-GVO BDSG* (3rd edn, C.H. Beck 2021) paras 2 and 5.

aa Personal Data

"Personal data" is the central concept of data protection law:[158] Not only does it define the scope of the primary law protection under Article 8 CFR, but also the scope of the GDPR. The concept of personal data is to be interpreted as "extremely broad".[159] Article 4(1) GDPR defines "personal data" as "any information relating to an identified or identifiable natural person ("data subject")".[160] "[T]he use of the expression "any information" in the definition of the concept of "personal data" reflects the aim of the EU legislature to assign a wide scope to that concept, which is not restricted to information that is sensitive or private, but potentially encompasses all kinds of information, not only objective, but also subjective , in the form of opinions and assessments."[161] The scope of personal data is limited to information with a sufficiently close link to a natural person. Consistent with the Article 29 Working Party, this is the case where data "refers to the identity, characteristics or behaviour of an individual or if such information is used to determine or influence the way in which that person is treated or evaluated".[162] Legal persons are excluded from the scope of protection.[163] The GDPR does not apply to "information which does not relate to an identified or identifiable natural person or to personal data rendered anonymous in such a manner that the data subject is not or no longer identifiable" (anonymous information).[164] An "identifiable natural person is one who can be identified, directly or indirectly, in particular by reference to an identifier such as a name, an identification number, location data, an online identifier or to one or more factors specific to the physical, physiological, genetic, mental, economic, cultural or social identity of that natural person" (Article 4(1) GDPR). In the digital world, individuals are associated with online identifiers, including internet protocol addresses or cookie identifiers, leaving traces that may be used, combined with other information received by the servers, to create profiles of the persons concerned and identify them.[165] For the assessment of the identifiability of a natural

---

158 Brendan van Alsenoy, *Data Protection Law in the EU: Roles, Responsibilities and Liability* (Cambridge University Press 2019) para 36.
159 ibid para 37.
160 Recitals 26 – 30 GDPR must be taken into account for the interpretation and application of Article 4(1) GDPR.
161 Judgement of 20 December 2017, *Nowak*, C-434/16, EU:C:2017:994, para 34.
162 Art. 29 Data Protection Working Party, 'Working Document on Data Protection Issues Related to RFID Technology' (2005) WP 105 8.
163 Wolfganz Ziebarth, 'Art. 4 DSGVO' in Gernot Sydow (ed), *Nomos Kommentar: Europäische Datenschutzgrundverordnung* (2nd edn, Nomos 2018) para 13.
164 GDPR, recital 26.
165 GDPR, recital 30.

person, "account should be taken of all the means reasonably likely to be used [...] either by the controller or by another person to identify the natural person directly or indirectly."[166] All objective factors[167], such as cost and required time for identification, must be considered depending on the available technology at the time of the processing.[168] The CJEU found that the abstract possibility of access to information held by a third party is sufficient to assume a "likely reasonable use" to identify the data subject.[169] Hence, all information enabling the identification do not necessarily must be held by one person. [170]

bb Processing of Personal Data

"Processing of personal data" is understood as "any operation or set of operations which is performed on personal data or sets of personal data, whether or not by automated means, such as collection, recording, organisation, structuring, storage, adaptation or alteration, retrieval, consultation, use, disclosure by transmission, dissemination or otherwise making available, alignment or combination, restriction, erasure or destruction".[171] The concept of processing is also broad.[172] The definition of the term "automated means" is left open in the GDPR as it also intends to comprehensively cover further future technological developments. Recital 15 GDPR demands a "technologically neutral protection of natural persons [...] in order to prevent creating a serious risk of circumvention". "Non-automated processing" of personal data means processing by manual means.[173] Regarding manual processing, the GDPR only applies to the extent that the personal data is included in a filing system or intended to be part of a filing system, which is defined as any structured set of personal data

---

166 GDPR, recital 26.

167 In the relevant literature, it is discussed to what extent knowledge and means of a third party, which it may use to identify a person, must be taken into account to confirm identifiability: Matthias Berg, 'Die Bestimmbarkeit als Grundproblem des Datenschutzrechts. Überblick über den Theorienstreit und Lösungsvorschlag' [2015] ZD 365 et seq.; Stefan Brink and Jens Eckhardt, 'Wann ist ein Datum ein personenbezogenes Datum? Anwendungsbereich des Datenschutzrechts' [2015] ZD 205 et seq.

168 GDPR, recital 26. The CJEU found that legally prohibited means would not fall under the term "likely to be used", cf Judgment of 19 October 2016, *Breyer*, C-582/14, EU:C:2016:779, para 46.

169 *Breyer* (n 168) paras 47 et seq.

170 ibid para 43.

171 GDPR, art 4(2).

172 van Alsenoy (n 158) para 40; Rücker (n 154) para 52.

173 GDPR, recital 15.

which is accessible according to specific criteria.[174] As a consequence, member states may legislate in this area of data processing.[175] However, in a modern world, there would be only very few practical irrelevant scenarios in which a collection of paper would be filed away randomly and according to no criteria or system.[176] Also, the term "intended to be part of a filing system" is to be understood broadly so that the mere prospect of a system is sufficient.[177]

cc Exemptions

The GDPR does not apply in the course of an activity which falls outside the scope of EU law.[178] It does not regulate activities concerning national security, according to Article 4(2) TEU they remain the "sole responsibility of each Member State".[179] However, it could be questioned whether certain activities in the context of national security can be assessed against the requirements in the GDPR, particularly activities involving personal data that were initially collected by private entities (e.g. telecommunication providers). Second, the GDPR does not apply where member states carry out activities that fall within the scope of Chapter 2 of Title V of the TEU[180].[181] Third, the GDPR is inapplicable in the course of a natural person's purely personal or household activity[182].[183] Finally, the GDPR does not apply to actions by competent authorities "for the prevention, investigation, detection or prosecution of criminal offences or the execution of criminal penalties, including the safeguarding against and the prevention of

---

174 GDPR, art 4(6). This definition is partly criticised since it could lead to a protection gap regarding the fundamental right of data protection in Article 8 CFR, which covers all manual processing of personal data without any differentiation. Jürgen Kühling and Johannes Raab, 'Art. 2 DS-GVO' in Jürgen Kühling and Benedikt Buchner (eds), *Datenschutz-Grundverordnung, Bundesdatenschutzgesetz: DS-GVO/BDSG* (3rd edn, C.H. Beck 2020) para 19 state that this lack of protection might be avoided by extending national law to include non-automated processing without a file system (the harmonising effect of the GDPR would not oppose, as it is limited by its scope).
175 Examples for the extension of national law in this context would be Section 26(7) BDSG (German Federal Data Protection Act) and Article 2(1) BayDSG (Bavarian Data Protection Act).
176 Alexander Roßnagel, 'Art. 2 DSGVO' in Spiros Simitis, Gerrit Hornung and Indra (eds) (n 29) para 16; Kai von Lewinski, 'Art. 2 DSGVO' in Martin Eßer, Philipp Kramer and Kai von Lewinski (eds), *Auernhammer, DSGVO/BDSG – Kommentar* (7th edn, Carl Heymanns Verlag 2020) para 5.
177 Ernst (n 157) para 10.
178 GDPR, art 2(2)(a).
179 GDPR, recital 16.
180 'Specific Provisions of the Common Foreign and Security Policy'.
181 GPDR, art 2(2)(b).
182 See in detail von Lewinski, 'Art. 2 DSGVO' (n 176) paras 25 et seqq.
183 GDPR, art 2(2)(c).

threats to public security" ("law enforcement processing").[184] This field is governed by the LED[185] and by Regulation No 45/2001 for EU bodies and institutions.[186]

b Personal Scope

"Controllers" and "processors" are the two bodies bound by the GDPR. However, they have different roles and are responsible to a different extent and so, the differentiation between controllers and processors is essential.[187] A controller is the body with the primary responsibility and liability for data protection compliance.[188] The term "controller" is defined as "the natural or legal person, public authority, agency or other body which, alone or jointly with others, determines the purposes and means of the processing of personal data".[189] This may either be determined by law or may depend on who has the greater substantial influence on the determination. However, it is possible to be a controller without a specific competence or formal power to control data conferred by law. All relevant circumstances that may create the relevant factual influence need to be considered, including the terms of a contract, which assign specific rights and control to a particular person or entity.[190] Two or more controllers collectively determine the purposes and means of processing are "joint controllers".[191]

A "processor" is "a natural or legal person, public authority, agency or other body, which processes personal data on behalf of the controller".[192] Unlike the controller, the processor does not process personal data in its interest to fulfil its purposes, but only in the interest of the controller in the context of fulfilling the purposes of the controller and consistent with strict instructions of the con-

---

184 GDPR, art 2(2)(d).

185 Directive (EU) 2016/680 of the EU Parliament and of the Council of 27 April 2016 on the protection of natural persons with regard to the processing of personal data by competent authorities for the purposes of the prevention, investigation, detection or prosecution of criminal offences or the execution of criminal penalties, and on the free movement of such data, and repealing Council Framework Decision 2008/977/JHA, *OJ L 119/89*.

186 Such data processing, including data transfers by the competent authorities for law enforcement purposes, will not be further covered in the course of this study.

187 Rücker (n 154) para 115.

188 ibid para 120.

189 GDPR, art 4(7).

190 In analogy cf Art. 29 Data Protection Working Party, 'Opinion 1/2010 on the Concepts of "Controller" and "Processor"' (2010) WP 169 8 (referring to the former Directive 95/46).

191 GDPR, art 26(1). However, there is no privilege for the exchange of personal data between joint controllers.

192 GDPR, art 4(8).

troller.[193] The GDPR privileges the processor compared to the controller due to the processor's acting as an extended arm of the controller with very little room for own decision-making.[194]

c Territorial Scope

Due to the wide range of technical options regarding data processing and storage, the territorial scope of application of the European data protection law does not depend on the "physical location" of data processing or even storage.[195] Therefore, the GDPR's territorial scope of the application contains different points of reference.[196]

aa Establishment Principle

The GDPR has an extraterritorial reach as it applies to processing outside the EU as long as it is being carried out "in the context of the activities of an establishment of the controller or processor" located within the EU.[197] The notion of establishment is not defined in the GDPR. The term entails "the effective and real exercise of activity through stable arrangements" regardless the legal form of such arrangements is irrelevant.[198] The main establishment does not necessarily have to be located in the EU.[199] According to the CJEU, "both the degree of stability of the arrangements and the effective exercise of activities [...] should be assessed in the light of the specific nature of the economic activities and the provision of services concerned."[200] Therefore, in some circumstances, the presence of one single representative acts with a sufficient degree of stability "through the presence of the necessary equipment for provision of the specific services concerned in the member states in question."[201] On the other side, the mere accessibility of a website would not suffice to constitute an establish-

---

193 Rücker (n 154) para 154.
194 ibid para 155.
195 Stefan Ernst, 'Art. 3 DS-GVO' in Boris P Paal and Daniel A Pauly (eds) (n 157) para 1.
196 For a detailed assessment on Article 3 GDPR in the context of private and public international law see Marian Thon, 'Transnationaler Datenschutz: Das Internationale Datenprivatrecht Der DS-GVO' (2020) 84 RabelsZ 25.
197 GDPR, art 3(1).
198 GDPR, recital 22.
199 Pascal Schumacher, 'B. Scope of Application of the GDPR' in Tobias Kugler and Daniel Rücker (eds), *New European General Data Protection Regulation: A Practitioner's Guide* (1st edn, Nomos 2018) para 190.
200 Judgement of 1 October 2015, *Weltimmo*, C-230/14, EU:C:2015:639, para 29.
201 ibid para 30.

ment.[202] The notion "context of activities" does not imply that the law of the member state is applicable where the controller or processor is established, but rather where an establishment of the controller or processor is involved in activities relating to data processing, considering its degree of involvement in the processing activities, the nature of the activities and the need to guarantee effective data protection.[203] A clear link must exist between the processing at issue and the activities of the establishment.[204] However, the establishment itself must not be actively engaged in the processing.[205] The term "the context of activities" should not be interpreted as too restrictive to ensure the purpose of the GDPR in Article 1(2) GDPR, guaranteeing effective and complete protection of natural persons' fundamental rights and freedoms.[206]

bb Marketplace Principle

The GDPR also "applies to the processing of personal data of data subjects who are in the Union by a controller or processor not established in the Union, where the processing activities are related to (a) the offering of goods or services, irrespective of whether a payment of the data subject is required, to such data subjects in the Union; or (b) the monitoring of their behaviour as far as their behaviour takes place within the Union" (marketplace principle).[207] The marketplace principle is a much-discussed innovation of the GDPR.[208] It assumes that players doing business in the Union should also comply with the rules of the European Single Market and should not have any advantages over those established in the Union.[209] Natural persons are should not be deprived of the protection of the

---

202 Judgement of 28 July 2016, *Verein für Konsumenteninformation*, C-191/15, EU:C:2016:388, para 76.
203 By analogy: Art. 29 Data Protection Working Party, 'Opinion 8/2010 on Applicable Law' (2010) WP 179 14 (referring to the former Directive 95/46).
204 Brendan van Alsenoy 'Reconciling the (extra)territorial reach of the GDPR with public international law' in Gert Vermeulen and Eva Lievens, *Data Protection and Privacy under Pressure – Transatlantic Tensions, EU Surveillance, and Big Data* (2017) 84.
205 *Google Spain and Google* (n 95) para 52.
206 ibid para 53.
207 GDPR, art 3(2).
208 For a detailed and critical evaluation of the marketplace principle see Manuel Klar, 'Die extraterritoriale Wirkung des neuen europäischen Datenschutzrechts' (2017) 41 DuD 533; Manuel Klar, 'Art. 3 DS-GVO' in Jürgen Kühling and Benedikt Buchner (eds) (n 174); Jens Brauneck, 'Marktortprinzip der DSGVO: Weltgeltung für EU-Datenschutz?' [2019] EuZW 494.
209 Gerrit Hornung, 'Art. 3 DSGVO' in Spiros Simitis, Gerrit Hornung and Indra Spiecker (eds) (n 29) para 4; for a critical assessment of the market principle in the larger context of "competition" between different data protection laws see Moritz Hennemann, 'Wettbewerb der Daten-

GDPR.[210] Thus, the market principle provides the clear advantage of preventing the establishment of data protection "havens".[211] The processing activities must either be related to (a) "the offering of goods or services" or (b) "the monitoring of [the data subject's] behaviour". To determine whether a controller or processor is offering goods or services to individuals in the EU, the decisive factor is whether the controller or processor apparently "envisages offering services to data subjects in one or more Member States".[212] In this context, conduct on the part of the controller or processor which demonstrates its intention to offer goods or services to data subjects located in the EU is required.[213] The mere accessibility of a website is considered insufficient to ascertain such an intention; however, "the use of a language or a currency generally used in one or more member states with the possibility of ordering goods and services in that other language, or the mentioning of customers or users who are in the Union, may make it apparent that the controller envisages offering goods or services to data subjects in the Union."[214]

Whether a processing activity relates to monitoring the behaviour of data subjects[215] (lit. b) depends on "whether natural persons are tracked on the internet including potential subsequent use of personal data processing techniques which consist of profiling a natural person, particularly in order to take decisions concerning her or him for analysing or predicting her or his personal preferences, behaviours and attitudes".[216] This shows that this provision mainly concerns online tracking and profiling activities.[217] However, the wording is sufficiently broad and might also cover other behavioural monitoring techniques.[218] In

---

schutzrechtsordnungen? – Zur Rezeption der Datenschutz-Grundverordnung –' (2020) 84 RabelsZ 864, 279 et seqq.

210 GDPR, recital 23.

211 Hennemann, 'Wettbewerb Der Datenschutzrechtsordnungen? – Zur Rezeption Der Datenschutz-Grundverordnung –' (n 209) 19.

212 GDPR, recital 23.

213 EDPB, 'Guidelines 3/2018 on the Territorial Scope of the GDPR (Article 3)' (2019) 17.

214 GDPR, recital 23. It shows consistency with the CJEU's decision in Judgement of 7 December 2010, *Pammer v Alpenhof*, EU:C:2010:740, C-585/08 and C-144/09) regarding Article 17 of the Regulation EU/1215/2012 (jurisdiction over consumer contracts).

215 Recital 24 GDPR does not refer to any intention of the controller or processor to monitor behaviour of data subjects in the EU; the only requirement is that monitoring behaviour concerns the performance taking place in the EU.

216 GDPR, recital 24.

217 van Alsenoy (n 158) para 45.

218 van Alsenoy 'Reconciling the (extra)territorial reach of the GDPR with public international law' (n 204) 88; Merlin Gömann, 'The New Territorial Scope of EU Data Protection Law: Deconstruction a Revolutionary Achievement' (2017) 54 CML Rev 567, 588.

this context, the approach in Article 3(2)(b) GDPR is partly criticised, on the one side, for the consequence of creating a *de facto* worldwide application of the GDPR and a "data imperialism"[219], and on the other side for its lack of clearness and predictability[220].

2 Key Principles

To protect individuals regarding the processing of their personal data, the GDPR requires controllers' and processors' compliance with several key principles. These principles are provided in Article 5 GDPR. Article 5 GDPR partly takes up the guarantees established in Article 8(2) CFR.[221] Article 83(5)(a) GDPR enforces the possibilities of severe administrative fines in case of any violations of the principles in Article 5 GDPR. In the following, these key principles will be further explained.

a Lawfulness, Fairness and Transparency

Personal data must be processed "lawfully, fairly and in a transparent manner".[222] The European Data Protection Supervisor (after this: EDPS)[223] called these the "core principles".[224] The principle of lawfulness and fairness also appears in Article 8(2) CFR. The principle of lawfulness stipulates that data processing is generally prohibited unless a legal ground legitimises the processing as an exception.[225] Personal data have to be processed "fairly". The guarantee of fair processing implies predictability and transparency:[226] The Council of Europe de-

---

219 Kai von Lewinski, 'Art. 3 DSGVO' in Martin Eßer, Philipp Kramer and Kai von Lewinski (eds) (n 176) para 24 who recognises an imperial tendency also for lit.a; Klar, 'Art. 3 DS-GVO' (n 208) para 24. Such an "imperial tendency" of the GDPR is also reviewed in Chapter 5, B.I.3.
220 See for instance Gömann (n 218) 587 et seq.
221 Alexander Roßnagel, 'Art. 5 DSGVO' in Spiros Simitis, Gerrit Hornung and Indra Spiecker (eds) (n 29) para 2; Eike Michael Frenzel, 'Art. 5 DS-GVO' in Boris P Paal and Daniel A Pauly (eds) (n 157) para 3.
222 GDPR, art 5(1)(a).
223 The EDPS is the EU's independent data protection authority. More information is available at the following link <https://edps.europa.eu/about-edps_en> accessed 9 June 2022
224 EDPS, 'Opinion 8/2016 on Coherent Enforcement of Fundamental Rights in the Age of Big Data' (2016) 8; see further Lee A Bygrave, *Data Privacy Law: An International Perspective* (2014) 145 et seqq. discussing "core principles" of data privacy law in an international context.
225 Sebastian Dienst, 'C. Lawful Processing of Personal Data in Companies under the General Data Protection Regulation' in Tobias Kugler and Daniel Rücker (eds) (n 199) para 249.
226 Wolff (n 56) para 34.

fined fair processing (under the Directive 95/46) as transparent processing.[227] It remains unclear if, next to the principle of transparency under the GDPR, the principle of fairness has an independent meaning.[228] It should be transparent to natural persons that personal data concerning them are processed and to what extent the personal data are or will be processed.[229] Any information and communication relating to the processing of those personal data must be easily understandable and, also, clear and plain language must be used.[230] The data subjects must be provided with all the relevant information on the controller and the processing.[231] The data controller or processor is obliged to educate the data subjects of "risks, rules, safeguards and their rights in relation to the processing of personal data as well as how to exercise their rights".[232]

b Purpose Limitations

Personal data must be "collected for specified, explicit and legitimate purposes and not further processed in a manner that is incompatible with those purposes."[233] The principle of purpose limitation is also found in Article 8(2) CFR. The purpose limitation principle comprises two rules: the specification of the purpose and the limitation of the use of data.[234] It can be seen as the most crucial data protection principle as the evaluation of whether other principles are infringed chiefly depends on the specified purpose.[235] First, the purpose must be specified, explicit and legitimate. The controller must consider the purpose(s) for which the personal data will be used.[236] As stated by the Article 29 Working Party, "specified" means that any purpose has to be sufficiently defined before collecting data to enable the implementation of any necessary data protection safeguards and to delimit the scope of the processing operation.[237] However,

---

227 European Union Agency for Fundamental Rights and others (eds), *Handbook on European Data Protection Law* (2014) 73.

228 Dienst (n 225) para 253; See for more information on the principle of fairness: Damian Clifford and Jef Ausloos, 'Data Protection and the Role of Fairness' (2018) 37 YEL 130.

229 GDPR, recital 39.

230 GDPR, recital 39.

231 GDPR, recital 39.

232 GDPR, recital 39.

233 GDPR, art 5(1)(b).

234 van Alsenoy (n 158) para 49.

235 Dienst (n 225) para 262; Art. 29 Data Protection Working Party, 'Opinion 03/2013 on Purpose Limitation' (2013) WP 203 4 (referring to Article 7 Directive 95/46).

236 Art. 29 Data Protection Working Party, 'Opinion 03/2013 on Purpose Limitation' (2013) WP 203 15.

237 ibid.

the degree of specification and detail depends on the context of personal data and its nature.[238] An explicit purpose is "sufficiently unambiguous and revealed, explained or expressed in some intelligible form".[239] When specifying the purpose(s), the controller must do so without any vagueness or ambiguity regarding the purpose's meaning or intent; no doubt or difficulty in understanding should arise.[240] Hence, the risk that the data subject's expectations differ from the controller's or processor's expectations is reduced.[241] For the purposes to be "legitimate", the data processing must begin at all different stages and at all times be based on at least one of the legal grounds provided for in Article 6 GDPR.[242] Moreover, the purpose must be in accordance with all provisions of applicable protection law as well as other applicable law, including written and common law, primary and secondary legislation, municipal degrees, judicial precedents, constitutional principles, fundamental rights and other legal principles as well as jurisprudence, as such law would be interpreted and taken into account by courts, as the requirement of the legitimacy of the purpose is more comprehensive than Article 6 GDPR's scope.[243]

Secondly, the controller must assess whether further processing is compatible with the original purposes. Any further processing is still authorised as long as it is compatible and simultaneously fulfils lawfulness requirements.[244] However, processing data for a different purpose does not automatically lead to incompatibility; compatibly, instead, needs to be assessed in each case.[245] Different factors that should be taken into account for the assessment, such as a link between the purpose(s) for the initial collection and the purposes for the intended further processing, the context of the processing – especially the relationship between the data subject and the controller –, the nature of the personal data, possible consequences of the intended further processing for the data subject and the existence of appropriate safeguards.[246] The principle of purpose limitation is strongly linked to the principle of transparency as it helps all (natural

---

238 Art. 29 Data Protection Working Party, 'Opinion 03/2013 on Purpose Limitation' (2013) WP 203 16.
239 ibid 17.
240 ibid.
241 ibid.
242 ibid.
243 ibid.
244 Dienst (n 225) para 280.
245 Art. 29 Data Protection Working Party, 'Opinion 03/2013 on Purpose Limitation' (n 235) 3.
246 GDPR, art 6(4).

or legal) persons involved to have a common understanding of how data in question can or will be used.[247]

c Data Minimisation

The processing of personal data should be limited to data that is "adequate, relevant and limited to what is necessary for relation to the purposes for which they are processed (data minimisation)".[248] With its reference to the purpose of processing, data minimisation complements the abovementioned principle of purpose limitation.[249] A sufficiently narrow connection in terms of adequacy and relevancy needs to exist between the legitimate purpose pursued by the controller and the data being collected.[250] According to recital 39 GDPR, the concept of necessity requires that personal data be processed only where the purpose of processing cannot be "reasonably fulfilled by other means".[251] The controller shall implement appropriate technical and organisation measures designed to implement data minimisation effectively and integrate the necessary safeguards into the processing ("privacy by design")[252], and, which ensure that by default, only necessary data for each specified purpose is processed ("privacy by default")[253]. Privacy by default applies to the amount of personal data collected, to the extent of their processing, to the period of their storage, as well as to their accessibility.[254]

d Accuracy

Every controller is obligated to ensure the accuracy of the personal data processed.[255] "Accurate means as to a matter of fact."[256] The principle of accuracy ena-

---

247 Art. 29 Data Protection Working Party, 'Opinion 03/2013 on Purpose Limitation' (n 235) 13 et seq. and 17.
248 GDPR, art 5 (1)(c).
249 Tobias Herbst, 'Art. 5 DS-GVO' in Jürgen Kühling and Benedikt Buchner (eds) (n 174) para 56.
250 van Alsenoy (n 158) para 51.
251 GDPR, recital 39.
252 GDPR, art 25(1).
253 GDPR, art 25(2).
254 GDPR, art 25(2).
255 GDPR, art 5(1)(d); see in detail Moritz Hennemann, 'Datenrichtigkeit. Beitragsreihe "Input Control – Datenqualität und Datenvalidität als Grundlage rechtlicher Automatisierungsprozesse" [2020] LRZ 77.

bles the reconstruction of facts, a situation or characteristics of a person and is essential to create a representation of reality.[257] Whether personal data are accurate or inaccurate has to be evaluated on a case-by-case basis in the context of the relevant purpose for which they are processed.[258] Personal data may be inaccurate if they are not complete or embedded in a wrong context.[259] The controller needs to ensure that inaccurate personal data are erased or rectified without delay.[260] The controller is obligated to take "every reasonable step". Furthermore, the controller must keep the data up to date where necessary. However, it is not clear if such updating is only required by demand of the data subject or even requires a periodic review.[261] Periodically review of data might be difficult and expensive, especially for extensive databases.[262] However, in several situations where data remained inaccurate, the potential damage caused to the data subject can overweigh these expenses.[263]

e Storage limitation

The principle of storage limitation complements the principle of purpose limitation.[264] Personal data may not be kept in a form that permits identification of data subjects for longer than necessary to realise the purpose for which the data were collected or for which they are further processed ("storage limitation"), e. g. by establishing time limits for erasure or a periodic review[265].[266]

f Integrity and Confidentiality

Personal data may only be processed in a manner that ensures appropriate security of the personal data, including protection against unauthorised or unlawful processing and accidental loss, destruction or damage, using appropriate technical and organisational measures to ensure the confidentiality and security

---

256 Art. 29 Data Protection Working Party, 'Guidelines on the Implementation of the Court of Justice of the European Union Judgement on "Google Spain and Inc v Agencia Espanola de Protección de Datos (AEPD) and Mario Costeja González"' (2014) WP 225 15.
257 Frenzel (n 221) para 39; Gernot Sydow, 'Einleitung' in Gernot Sydow (ed) (n 163) para 68.
258 European Union Agency for Fundamental Rights and others (n 227) 71.
259 Dienst (n 225) para 328.
260 The right to erasure and the right to rectification are outlined under 4.c.
261 Dienst (n 225) para 330.
262 ibid.
263 ibid.
264 Frenzel (n 221) para 43; Herbst (n 249) para 65.
265 GDPR, recital 39.
266 GDPR, art 5(1)(e).

of processing.[267] Confidentiality is understood as keeping the content of information secret from all parties except those authorised to access it.[268] This principle of confidentiality is further specified in Article 25(1) GDPR ("privacy by design") as well as in Article 32(1) GDPR, which enumerates some concrete examples of technical and organisational measures. The controller must prevent unauthorised disclosure, access and processing of personal data. Integrity means ensuring that data has not been altered by unauthorised or unknown means.[269]

g Accountability

The controller shall be responsible for and demonstrates compliance with the principles relating to the processing of personal data (Article 5(2) GDPR). Furthermore the controller must implement appropriate technical and organisational measures to ensure and to be able to demonstrate that processing is compliant with the GDPR.[270] These measures shall include implementing appropriate data protection policies by the controller.[271] The measures adopted by controllers must be tailored to the nature, scope, context and purposes of the processing and the risks presented by the processing.[272] The GDPR provides several specific obligations that aim to give further substance to the accountability principle, such as data protection by design and by default,[273] the legal binding of processors,[274] keeping appropriate records of the processing,[275] co-operation with the supervisory authorities,[276] personal data breach notification,[277] data protection impact assessments and prior consultation,[278] designation of data protection officer[279] and, last but not least, codes of conduct and certification[280].[281]

---

267 GDPR, art 5(1)(f).
268 van Alsenoy (n 158) para 60.
269 GDPR, artt 32(2), 32(4), 28(3)(b) and 29.
270 GDPR, art 24(1).
271 GDPR, art 24(2).
272 GDPR, recital 74.
273 GDPR, art 25.
274 GDPR, art 28(3).
275 GPDR, art 30.
276 GDPR, art 30.
277 GDPR, artt 33 and 34.
278 GDPR, artt 35 and 36.
279 GDPR, artt 37 et seqq.
280 GDPR, artt 40 et seqq.
281 van Alsenoy (n 158).

3 Legal Basis for Data Processing

According to Article 6(1) GDPR, processing of personal data "shall be lawful only if and to the extent that (a) the data subject has given consent to the processing, that the processing is (b) necessary for the performance of a contract to which the data subject is party, (c) necessary for compliance with a legal obligation to which the controller is subject, (d) necessary in order to protect the vital interest of the data subject, (e) necessary for the performance of a task carried out in the public interest or (f) necessary for the purposes of the legitimate interest pursued by the controller or by a third party".[282] No legal distinction between these grounds is made, and thus, no hierarchy exists among them.[283] However, the different legal grounds provide different rights under the GDPR: The right to erasure, portability, and object must always be provided to the data subject. The right to object and data portability must only be provided where data are processed based on consent.[284] Most legal bases, except for data processing based on the data subject's consent, require the data processing to be "necessary". The processing of personal data is necessary if the controller cannot reasonably achieve the same purpose without such processing or by less intrusive means by ensuring proportionality between the processing and the purpose.[285] In the following, the different legal grounds will be further reviewed.

a Consent

Consent[286] as a legal basis for data processing is explicitly mentioned in Article 8(2) CFR.[287] Under Article 4(11) GDPR "consent of the data subject means any freely given, specific, informed and unambiguous indication of the data subject's wishes by which he or she, by a statement or by a clear affirmative

---

282 Article 6(1) GDPR implements the legal basis-requirement of Article 8(2) CFR ("on the basis of the consent of the person concerned or some other legitimate basis laid down by law").
283 In analogy Art. 29 Data Protection Working Party, 'Opinion 15/2011 on the Definition of Consent' (2011) WP 187 7; Art. 29 Data Protection Working Party, 'Opinion 06/2014 on the Notion of Legitimate Interests of the Data Controller under Article 7 of Directive 95/46/EC' (2014) WP 217 10 (both referring to the similar Article 7 Directive 95/46).
284 Elena Gil González and Paul de Hert, 'Understanding the Legal Provisions That Allow Processing and Profiling of Personal Data—an Analysis of GDPR Provisions and Principles' (2019) 19 ERA Forum 597, 599.
285 ibid 600.
286 See in detail Kai von Lewinski in Kai von Lewinski, Giselher Rüpke, Jens Eckhardt, *Datenschutzrecht* (1st edn, C.H.Beck 2018) 180 et seqq.; Marlene Voigt, *Die Datenschutzrechtliche Einwilligung. Zum Spannungsfeld von informationeller Selbstbestimmung und ökonomischer Verwertung personenbezogener Daten* (Nomos 2020).
287 A.I.3.

action, signifies agreement to the processing of personal data relating to him or her." Most importantly, the data subject has the unconditional right to withdraw his or her consent at any time.[288]

First, consent requires an indication of the data subject's wishes signifying agreement. The requirement for establishing consent under the GDPR have been tightened beyond those in the Directive 45/96[289], as the GPDR added the requirements of an "unambiguous" indication "by a statement or by a clear affirmative action".[290] This wording implies that the lack of any action, for instance, the absence of any behaviour or passive behaviour, cannot be interpreted as an indication of agreement.[291] Silence, pre-ticked boxes or inactivity do not constitute consent.[292] The consent does not necessarily have to be given in writing but can also be given in an oral statement or electronic means.[293] In the latter case, the request must be "clear, concise and not unnecessarily disruptive to the use of the service for which it is provided."[294] Special categories of sensitive data require explicit consent that needs to be expressed in writing.[295] It is unclear whether implied consent may constitute a valid legal basis for non-sensitive data processing.[296] The wording in recital 32 GDPR ("another statement or conduct which clearly indicates in this context the data subject's acceptance") does indicate that implied consent may be sufficient as long as the data subject's conduct signifies agreement to the processing.[297]

Second, consent needs to be given freely. Consent is not be given freely "if the data subject has no genuine or free choice or is unable to refuse or withdraw consent without detriment".[298] The data subject needs to be given a proper choice, without the risk of deception, intimidation, coercion, or significant negative consequences if the data subject does not consent.[299] Consent does not provide a valid legal ground for processing personal data in scenarios with a "clear

---

288 GDPR, art 7(3).
289 Directive 45/96, art 2(h).
290 Dienst (n 225) para 432; González and de Hert (n 284) 600.
291 Dienst (n 225) para 435.
292 GDPR, recital 32; Judgement of 1 October 2019, *Planet49*, C-673/17, EU:C:2019:801.
293 GDPR, recital 32.
294 GDPR, recital 32.
295 GDPR, art 9.
296 Dienst (n 225) para 441. Article 9(2)(a) GDPR requires an "explicit" consent for data processing for special categories of personal data.
297 ibid para 441.
298 GDPR, recital 42.
299 Art. 29 Data Protection Working Party, 'Opinion 15/2011 on the Definition of Consent' (n 283) 12.

imbalance between the data subject and the controller" (e.g. the controller is public authority).[300] Another scenario could be where the data exporter has a certain level of market power so that the consumer has no equivalent alternatives.[301] Relevant for the assessment on whether consent is given freely is also whether "the performance of a contract, including the provision of a service, is conditional on consent to the processing of personal data that is not necessary for the performance of that contract".[302] Also, consent is presumed not to be freely given if it does not allow separate consent to be given to different personal data processing operations despite it being appropriate in the individual case, or if the performance of a contract, including the provision of a service, is dependent on the consent despite such consent not being necessary for such performance.[303]

Third, the consent must be specific. It means that the consent must be "intelligible", defining "clearly and precisely the scope and consequences of the data processing" and thus, does not cover an "open ended set" of processing.[304] It covers all the processing activities carried out for the same purpose; in case of different purposes, consent must necessarily be given on each processing.[305]

Fourth, the consent also must be informed. "For consent to be informed, the data subject should be aware at least of the identity of the controller and the purposes of the processing for which the personal data are intended".[306] The data subject must be informed of their right to withdraw the consent.[307] In the relevant literature, there is disagreement about whether the controller must additionally fulfil Article 13 and 14 GDPR for the consent to be informed.[308]

---

300 Recital 43 GDPR; Boris P Paal, 'Marktmacht im Daten(schutz)recht' (2020) 18 ZWeR 215, 230 et seq. who differentiates according to whether the public authority and the data subject interfere in a relationship of superiority and inferiority or meet on an equal level.

301 cf Paal 'Marktmacht im Daten(schutz)recht' (n 300).

302 GDPR, art 7(4).

303 GDPR, recital 43.

304 Art. 29 Data Protection Working Party, 'Opinion 15/2011 on the Definition of Consent' (n 283) 17.

305 GDPR, recital 32.

306 GDPR, recital 42.

307 GDPR, art 7(3).

308 Philipp Kramer, 'Art. 6 DSGVO' in Martin Eßer, Philipp Kramer and Kai von Lewinski (eds) (n 176) para 21 argues that Articles 13 and 14 GDPR must only be fulfilled at the time of the personal data collection, while the valid consent must be given before the collection; Bastian Stemmer, 'Art. 6 DS-GVO' in Heinrich Amadeus Wolff and Stefan Brink (eds) (n 149) paras 55 and 69 argues that the data subject's knowledge of the significance and scope of the consent must be present when the consent is given, so that the information must therefore precede the consent in terms of time.

Finally, the consent also needs an unambiguous indication of agreement. In the Article 29 Working Party's view, the consent must leave no doubt regarding the data subject's intention to deliver consent. "In other words, the indication by which the data subject signifies [their] agreement must leave no room for ambiguity regarding his/her content. If there is a reasonable doubt about the individual's intention, there is ambiguity."[309]

b Contract or Pre-Contractual Relations

Article 6(1)(b) GDPR provides a legal ground in situations where the processing of personal data is "necessary for the performance of a contract to which the data subject is a party or in order to take steps at the request of the data subject before entering into a contract." The first scenario requires the data subject to be a party to the relevant contract. The controller does not necessarily have to be a party to the contracts. It also applies to the processing of personal data to perform contracts between the data subject and a third party.[310] As understood by the Article 29 Working Party, the provision requires a strict interpretation and does not include a situation where the processing is unilaterally imposed on the data subject but is not necessary for the performance of a contract.[311] An evaluation on a case-by-case basis is necessary about the "exact rationale of the relevant contract, i.e. its substance and fundamental objective, as it is against this that it will be tested whether data processing is necessary for its performance."[312] The limitation of what is necessary for the actual performance of a contract implies that the provision does not legitimise all data processing due to any contractual non-compliance or all other incidents in the execution of a contract.[313] For example, fraud prevention or customer profiling would be typically beyond what is strictly necessary for the actual performance of a sales contract.[314] The second scenario under Article 6(1)(b) GDPR covers pre-contractual relations.[315] It requires the data to be processed at the data subject's request and not initiated by the controller or a third party. This scenario appears to be the case with requests for product and service information or price quotes, but

---

309 Art. 29 Data Protection Working Party, 'Opinion 15/2011 on the Definition of Consent' (n 283) 21.
310 Dienst (n 225) para 369.
311 Art. 29 Data Protection Working Party, 'Opinion 06/2014 on the Notion of Legitimate Interests of the Data Controller under Article 7 of Directive 95/46/EC' (n 283) 16.
312 ibid 17.
313 ibid.
314 ibid 18.
315 Dienst (n 225) para 374.

not with solvency or credit reference checks and any direct marketing activities at the initiative by the controller.[316]

c Legal Obligation

Article 6(1)(c) GDPR provides a legal ground where the processing of personal data is "necessary for compliance with a legal obligation to which the controller is subject". In these situations, the controller does not have a choice whether or not to fulfil the obligation.[317] As evident in this provision, legal obligations under the laws of any third country will not be deemed a suitable basis for this legal ground unless they are officially recognised and integrated in the member state's legal order, e. g. in an international agreement.[318] The legal obligation does not inevitably require a legislative act adopted by a parliament.[319] Nonetheless, the obligation needs to be "clear and precise and its application should be foreseeable to the persons subject to it, in accordance with the case law of the Court of Justice of the European Union [...] and European Court of Human Rights."[320] This does, however, not mean that a specific law for each processing is required; a law may provide a sufficient basis for several processing operations.[321]

d Vital Interests

Article 6(1)(d) GDPR covers situations where the processing of personal data is "necessary in order to protect the vital interests of the data subject". "Vital interest" is an interest that is "essential for the life of the data subject or that of another natural person".[322] However, the application of this legal ground is limited, as Article 6(1)(d) GDPR is only subsidiary in relation to other legal bases.[323]

---

316 Art. 29 Data Protection Working Party, 'Opinion 06/2014 on the Notion of Legitimate Interests of the Data Controller under Article 7 of Directive 95/46/EC' (n 283) 18. Credit reference checks prior to the grant of a loan are usually not made upon request of the data subject, but rather under lit. f or lit. c. in compliance with a legal obligation of banks to consult an official list of registered debtors.

317 Dienst (n 225) para 376.

318 Art. 29 Data Protection Working Party, 'Opinion 06/2014 on the Notion of Legitimate Interests of the Data Controller under Article 7 of Directive 95/46/EC' (n 283) 19; however, compliance with laws of any third countries may represent a legitimate interest of the controller pursuant to Article 6(1)(f) GDPR.

319 GDPR, recital 41.

320 GDPR, recital 41.

321 GDPR, recital 45.

322 GDPR, recital 46.

323 GDPR, recital 46.

e Public Interest

Article 6(1)(e) GDPR provides a legal ground in a situation where the processing of personal data is "necessary for the performance of a task carried out in the public interest or the exercise of official authority vested in the controller." "Official authority" refers to an authority granted by the EU or a member state.[324] The provision excludes any tasks carried out in the public interest(s) of a third country or by an official authority vested by the laws of any third country unless officially recognised or integrated in the legal order of the member state concerned. It does not cover situations where the controller does not have official authority but is requested by a third party as having such authority to disclose data.[325]

f Legitimate Interests

Of more practical importance is Article 6(1)(f) GDPR, which provides a legal ground in situations where the processing of personal data "is necessary for the purposes of the legitimate interest pursued by the controller or by a third party, except where such interests are overridden by the interests or fundamental rights and freedoms of the data subject which require protection personal data, in particular where the data subject is a child." The legal ground in question requires a legitimate interest of the controller or a third party. The term "interest" means the overall value or intention the controller wants to fulfil by processing data.[326] The interest should be "real and present", respectively "something that corresponds with current activities or benefits that are expected in the very near future."[327] Vague or speculative interests are insufficient.[328] For the interest to be considered "legitimate", the purpose must be consistent with the data protection and other applicable EU and member state laws.[329] The existence of a legitimate interest must be assessed carefully, considering whether the processing of personal data for the specific purpose from the data subject's perspective could "reasonably [be] expected at the time and in the context of the collection of the personal data".[330] According to the Article 29 Working Party, the term "legitimate interest" covers a wide range of interests, "trivial or very compelling,

---

324 GDPR, art 6(3).
325 Unlike Article 7(e) of Directive 95/46.
326 González and de Hert (n 284) 606.
327 Art. 29 Data Protection Working Party, 'Opinion 06/2014 on the Notion of Legitimate Interests of the Data Controller under Article 7 of Directive 95/46/EC' (n 283) 24.
328 ibid.
329 Dienst (n 225) para 399.
330 GDPR, recital 47.

straightforward or more controversial".[331] However, in a second step, these interests must be balanced against the data subject's interests and rights. It must be assessed whether the controller's legitimate interests are outweighed by the data subject's interests, fundamental rights, and freedoms. Here, "a more restricted approach and more substantive analysis should be taken".[332]

Situations in which legitimate interest may exist could be where the "data subject is a client or in the service of the controller" and where the data are processed to prevent fraud or for direct marketing purposes[333]. Furthermore, in cases of transmission within the group of undertakings for internal administrative purposes, including the processing of the personal data of clients or employees [334] as well as in cases of processing to ensure network and information security, including preventing unauthorised access to electronic communications networks, malicious code distribution and stopping "denial of service" attacks and damage to computer and electronic communication systems[335].[336] The Article 29 Working Party specifies other situations where the controller's legitimate interest may be given the enforcement of legal claims, the prevention of money laundering, the processing for historical, scientific or statistical purposes or research purposes.[337] The data processing further must be necessary for realising the legitimate interest. There must be no better suited and no less invasive alternative.

---

331 Art. 29 Data Protection Working Party, 'Opinion 06/2014 on the Notion of Legitimate Interests of the Data Controller under Article 7 of Directive 95/46/EC' (n 283) 24.

332 ibid.

333 GDPR, recital 47.

334 GDPR, recital 48.

335 GDPR, recital 49.

336 See also BGH, 12 July 2018 – III ZR 183/17 = BGHZ 219, 243: The heirs' right of access to the "digital inheritance" of a testator represents a legitimate interest, since the heirs could enter into the contractual position of the deceased and, if necessary, use the "digital inheritance" to obtain information about inherited claims and liabilities. See also BGH, 12 October 2021 – VI ZR 488/19 and VI ZR 489/19: The operator of a rating portal for medical services pursued legitimate interests protected by Article 11 CFR and Article 16 CFR. The BGH found that the associated processing of the personal data does not go beyond what is necessary for this purpose; the balancing of the conflicting rights and interests to be carried out according to the specific circumstances of the individual case does not turn out in favour of the data subject with regard to the design elements of the portal operation.

337 Art. 29 Data Protection Working Party, 'Opinion 06/2014 on the Notion of Legitimate Interests of the Data Controller under Article 7 of Directive 95/46/EC' (n 283) 25.

4 Data Subject's Rights

Article 12 GDPR[338] and the following articles contain rights data subjects can exercise towards controllers and processors if their personal data is processed.[339] The following rights aim to improve the control by and the position of the data subject in the context of data processing.[340] Article 83(5)(b) GDPR enforces the possibilities of severe administrative fines in case of any violations of the data subject's rights.

a Duty to Inform

Article 13 and Article 14 of the GDPR specify which types of information controllers must provide to data subjects regarding the processing of their personal data.[341] It especially obliges the controller to inform about the purpose of processing and automated decision-making's lawful basis or existence. Article 13 GDPR addresses the scenario in which the information is obtained directly from the data subject, and Article 14 GDPR addresses the scenario in which the information is collected indirectly, for instance, from an entity other than the data subject.

b Right to Access

Article 15(1) GDPR provides the data subject with the right to obtain confirmation whether or not personal data concerning him or her are (being) processed, and

---

338 Article 12 GDPR unifies technical and procedural aspects of the exercise of various information and access rights. The controller is required to communicate about the exercise of the rights of the data subject "in a concise, transparent, intelligible and easily accessible form, using clear a plain language" (GDPR, art 12(1)) requires the controller. Furthermore, the controller is obligated to "facilitate the exercise of the rights of the data subject" (GDPR, art 12(2)) and thus, must provide mechanisms that allow data subjects to exercise their rights more efficiently, e.g. facilitate electronic requests (GDPR, recital 59). The controller must respond to a request concerning the data subject's rights with unnecessary delay, at least within one month of receiving the request (GDPR, art 12(4)). If the controller does not act on the data subject's request, they must inform the subject without delay, at the latest within one month (GDPR, art 12(4)). Furthermore, the data subject can exercise their rights free of charge (GDPR, art 12(5)).

339 As relevant case law for instance: Judgement of 7 May 2009, *Rijkeboer*, C-553/07, EU:C:2009:293; Judgement of 12 December 2013, *X*, C-486/12, EU:C:2013:836; *Google Spain and Google* (n 95); Judgement of 17 July 2014, *YS and Others*, C-141/12 and C-372/12, EU:C:2014:2081.

340 PTJ Wolters, 'The Control by and Rights of the Data Subject under the GDPR' (2018) 22 Journal of Internet Law 7, 7.

341 See for instance: Judgement of 7 November 2013, *IPI*, C-473/12, EU:C:2013:715; Judgement of 1 October 2015, *Bara and Others*, C-201/14, EU:C:2015:638.

where this is the case, access to the personal data[342] and information about the processing, including (a) the purposes, (b) the categories of personal data concerned, (c) the recipients of the personal data, (d) the envisaged period of storage, (e) the existence of the right to rectification, erasure, restriction and to object to such processing, (f) the right to lodge a complaint with a supervisory authority (f).[343] Article 15(3) GDPR grants the data subject the right to copy the processed data, free of charge. In order to exercise most of the data subject's rights, the right to access is indispensable, as, for example, a data subject cannot effectively request a correction if he or she is not aware of incorrect personal data.[344]

c Right to Rectification, Erasure and Restriction

Article 16 GDPR provides the data subject with the right to obtain from the controller without any unnecessary delay, rectify inaccurate personal data concerning him or her,[345] and the right to have incomplete data completed.[346] The right to rectification goes hand in hand with the principle of accuracy.[347] Article 17 GDPR stipulates data subjects with the right to obtain the erasure of personal data in several circumstances (right to be forgotten)[348].[349] Article 18 GDPR provides the right to obtain the restriction of processing from the controller under certain circumstances[350].[351] Article 19 GDPR provides that the data subject has the right to

---

342 The right to access to personal data collected is also guaranteed by Article 8(2) CFR (under A.I.4).

343 See for instance: *Rijkeboer* (n 339); *X* (n 339); *YS and Others* (n 339); *Nowak* (n 161).

344 Wolters (n 340) 7 et seq.

345 The right to rectification of personal data collected is also guaranteed by Article 8(2) CFR (under A.I.4).

346 See for instance: *Rijkeboer* (n 339); *X* (n 339); *YS and Others* (n 339); *Schrems* (n 71); *Nowak* (n 161); Judgement of 24 September 2019, *Google (Territorial scope of de-referencing)*, C-507/17, EU: C:2019:772.

347 GDPR, art 5(1)(d) (under 2.d).

348 The most relevant judgement in this context is the CJEU's Judgement of 13 May 2014, *Google Spain and Google* (n 95). It is one of the CJEU landmark privacy rulings involving Google searches in Spain. The "right to be forgotten" refers to the internet user's right to demand all data on them to be permanently deleted upon request. Also relevant in this context is the Judgement of 9 March 2017, *Manni*, EU:C:2017:197, C- 398/15. See for further information on the right for erasure Jef Ausloos, *The Right to Erasure: Safeguard for Informational Self-Determination in a Digital Society?* (Oxford University Press 2018).

349 This is in line with the principle of accuracy (under 2.d) and the principle of storage limitation (under 2.e).

350 Article 18 GDPR applies where "(a) the accuracy of the personal data is contested by the data subject, for a period enabling the controller to verify the accuracy of the personal data,

demand from the controller to "communicate any rectification or erasure of personal data or restriction of processing carried out in accordance with Article 16, Article 17(1) and Article 18 GDPR to each recipient to whom the data have been disclosed, unless it proves impossible or involves disproportionate effort." Also, the data subject can request information about those recipients from the controller.

d Data Portability

The right to data portability is one of the novelties of the GDPR.[352] It expands the right to access in several ways and grants the data subject better control over personal data concerning them. Article 20(1) GDPR provides that the data subject has a right to transmit a set of data to another controller. Article 20(2) GDPR grants him the right to transmit the data directly from one controller to another. The right to data portability primarily pursues competition law interests as it intends to prevent data-induced lock-in effects.[353] It is of no relevance for an assessment of a third country's adequacy level. Consequently, it should be disregarded in the assessment of adequacy.

e Right to Object

Article 21(1) GDPR gives the data subject the right to object to processing their personal data based on Article 6(1) (e) or (f) GDPR[354].[355] However, the controller can continue with the processing if he or she demonstrates compelling legitimate grounds for the processing which override the interests, rights, and free-

---

(b) the processing is unlawful and the data subject opposes the erasure of the personal data and requests the restriction of their use instead, (c) the controller no longer needs the data for the purposes of the processing, but they are required by the data subject for the establishment, exercise or defence of legal claims, (d) the data subject has objected to processing pursuant to Article 21(1) GDPR pending the verification whether the legitimate grounds of the controller override those of the data subject".

351 See for instance: *Rijkeboer* (n 339); *Google Spain and Google* (n 95).

352 See in detail Moritz Hennemann, 'Datenportabilität' [2017] PinG 5; a comprehensive overview map of countries recognising a right to data portability is provided by the Research Centre for Law and Digitalisation in Passau, 'Right to the Personal Data Portability' (last revised 20 October 2021) <https://www.jura.uni-passau.de/fileadmin/dokumente/fakultaeten/jura/lehrstuehle/hennemann/Mapping_Global_Data_Law/R01_-_Right_to_Personal_Data_Portability_.pdf>.

353 See in detail ibid 6; Boris P Paal, 'Art. 20 DS-GVO' in Boris P Paal and Daniel A Pauly (eds) (n 157) para 6.

354 3.e. and f.

355 See for instance: *Google Spain and Google* (n 95); *Manni* (n 348); *Nowak* (n 161).

doms of the data subject or for the establishment, exercise or defence of legal claims. Article 21(2) GDPR provides the right to object to data processing for "direct marketing purposes". If the data subject exercises this right, the controller is no longer allowed to process the data for the purposes (Article 21(3) GDPR). However, the controller can continue with the processing if necessary for the performance of a task carried out for reasons of the public interest.

f Right to Obtain Human Intervention

Article 22(1) GDPR gives the data subject the right not to be subject to decisions based exclusively on automated processing or profiling, producing legal effects on the data subject: "This shall apply if the decision (a) is necessary for entering into, or the performance of, a controller between the data subject and the controller, (b) is authorised by Union or Member State law to which the controller is subject and which also lays down suitable measures to safeguard the data subject's rights and freedoms and legitimate interests, or (c) is based on the data subject's explicit consent." In these cases, the controller is obligated to "implement suitable measures to safeguard the data subject's rights, freedom and legitimate interests"; the data subject should "at least have the right to obtain human intervention, to express his or her point of view and to contest the decisions".[356] Human intervention must be based on an assessment of all the relevant data, including any additional information provided by the data subject, and it should be carried out by someone with appropriate authority and capability to change the decisions.[357] Two other suitable safeguards would be receiving specific information, explaining the decision reached after such assessment, and challenging the decisions.[358]

5 Restrictions

Article 23 GDPR recognises that the abovementioned data subject's rights and the corresponding key principles established in the GDPR may be restricted under specific conditions set out in this provision and inspired by the Charter, especially Article 52 CFR. Article 23 GDPR reflects the nature of the fundamental right to protect personal data as a non-absolute right that must be considered in

---

356 GDPR, art 22(3).
357 Art. 29 Data Protection Working Party, 'Guidelines on Automated Individual Decision-Making and Profiling for the Purposes of Regulation 2016/679' (2017) WP 251 rev.01 27.
358 GDPR, recital 71.

relation to its function in society[359].[360] The EDPB has provided guidelines to member states and EU legislators for the use of Article 23 GDPR.[361] According to Article 23(1) GDPR, a restriction of data subject's rights and principles must respect the essence of the fundamental rights and freedoms[362] and be necessary and proportionate measure in a democratic society to safeguard: (a) national security, (b) defence, (c) public security, (d) the prevention, investigation, detection or prosecution of criminal offences or the execution of criminal penalties, including the safeguarding against and the prevention of threats to public security, (e) other important objectives of general public interest of the Union or of a member state (e.g. important economic or financial interest) (f) the protection of judicial independence and proceedings, (g) the prevention, investigation, detection and prosecution of breaches of ethics for regulated professions, (h) monitoring, inspection or regulatory function connected, even occasionally, to the exercise of official authority in the cases referred to in points (a) to (e) and (g), (i) the protection of the data subject or the rights and freedoms of others, (j) the enforcement of civil law claims. Article 23(2) GDPR imposes an obligation for a "legislative measure", adopted by the Union or member state, to contain, where relevant, specific provisions on the matters listed in points (a) to (h) that include the purposes of the processing or categories of processing, the categories of personal data, the scope of the restrictions introduced, the safeguards to prevent abuse or unlawful access or transfer, the specification of the controller or categories of controllers, the storage periods and the applicable safeguards taking into account the nature, scope and purposes of the processing or categories of processing, the risks to the rights and freedoms of data subjects; and the right of data subjects to be informed about the restriction, unless that may be prejudicial to the purpose of the restriction.

6 Supervisory Authorities and Procedural and Enforcement Mechanisms

Member states must have an independent supervisory authority dedicated to monitoring compliance in place.[363] On the European level, the EDPB[364] is com-

---

359 This is shown by Article 8(2) and Article 52(1) CFR. See also *Volker and Markus Schecke and Eifert* (n 55) para 48.

360 Dominique Moore, 'Art. 23 GDPR' in Christopher Kuner, Lee A Bygrave and Christopher Docksey (eds), *The EU General Data Protection Regulation (GDPR). A Commentary* (Oxford University Press 2020) 545.

361 EDPB, 'Guidelines 10/2020 on Restrictions under Article 23 GDPR. Version 1.0.' (2020).

362 A.I.2.a.

363 GDPR, art 51.

364 The EDPB replaced the Art. 29 Working Party under the Directive 95/46.

posed of a representative of the supervisory authority of each member state (Article 68(3) GDPR). The establishment of independent supervisory authorities is also required by Article 8(3) CFR.[365] The supervisory authority must act completely independently while carrying out its task and exercising its powers.[366] The members of each supervisory authority shall remain free from direct or indirect external influence and shall not seek or take instructions from anybody while performing their tasks and exercising their powers.[367] In order to guarantee this, all members of the supervisory authority are to be appointed in a transparent procedure.[368] They should act with integrity, "refrain from any action that is incompatible with their duties and should [...] engage in any incompatible occupation, whether gainful or not".[369] However, the independence of supervisory authorities does not prevent the supervisory authorities from becoming subject to judicial review.[370] The establishment of supervisory authorities immediately protects the data subject's rights and freedoms as they perform the tasks specified in Article 57(1) GDPR.[371] Each supervisory authority shall have investigative powers to carry out investigations and to obtain all the information necessary to perform its task, corrective powers such as the power to order a controller or processor to comply with the data protection regime as well as authorisation and advisory powers, in particular in cases of complaints from natural persons, and without prejudice to the powers of prosecutorial authorities under member state law, to bring infringements of the GDPR to the attention of the judicial authorities and engage in legal proceedings.[372] Individuals who feel their rights and freedoms are being harmed by the processing of personal data have the right to lodge a complaint with the relevant supervisory authority and the right to be informed about the complaint's progress and outcome.[373] A data subject has the right to seek "effective judicial remedy" when data processing is non-compliant.[374] The GDPR also introduced a framework for imposing administrative fines.[375] Each supervi-

---

365 A.I.5.
366 GDPR, art 52(1).
367 GDPR, art 52(2).
368 GDPR, recital 121.
369 GDPR, art 52(3).
370 GDPR, recital 118.
371 GDPR, recital 117.
372 GDPR, art 58.
373 GDPR, art 77.
374 GDPR, art 78.
375 This is also reviewed in Chapter 4, E.

sory authority needs to ensure that the imposition of the fines is "effective, proportionate and dissuasive".[376]

V Conclusion to A

The data protection law in the EU guarantees a very high standard of protection of personal data – if not, in fact, the highest standard worldwide. The above shows that the EU data protection regime has a "fundamental rights character". The right to the protection of personal data in the EU is guaranteed and protected through different instruments and their synergy: The EU's primary law (Articles 7 and 8 CFR), the ECHR (Article 8 ECHR) and the EU's secondary law, the GDPR. The GDPR aims to "protect fundamental rights and freedoms of natural persons and in particular their right to the protection of personal data".[377] Consequently, the Regulation must always be read in the light of the CFR.[378] The fundamental rights character of the EU system is reflected in the design and interpretation of the GDPR's provisions.[379]. The regime provides a "high level of default protection" and must not be circumvented.[380] EU data protection law has a vast scope of (material and territorial) application and, therefore, an extensive range of protection of individuals.

The EU regime legitimises the processing of personal data. The system can be defined as "prohibitive" insofar as the processing of personal data is prohibited unless there is a legal basis, and the processing complies with a specified data protection safeguard.[381] The scope of application is very wide.[382] In regard to the territorial scope, the presence of a relevant establishment of a controller or processor on EU territory (Article 3(1) GDPR), as well as the monitoring or targeting of EU data subjects (Article 3(2) GDPR), trigger the application of the GDPR.[383]

---

376 GDPR, art 83(1).
377 GDPR, art 1(2).
378 *Schrems* (n 71) para 78.
379 Lynskey (n 35) 38 et seq.
380 ibid.
381 Lynskey (n 35) 30, taking into account that the EU data protection system could at the same time be classified as 'permissive' insofar as it sets out a system which facilitates personal data processing by legitimising it once certain provisions are respected.
382 IV.1.a.
383 The third trigger is the processing of personal data by a controller not established in the Union, but in a place where member state law applies by virtue of public international law (GDPR, art 3(3)).

With the introduction of the market principle in Article 3(2) GDPR, the Regulation has attained an even more excellent standing worldwide.[384]

The Charter and the GDPR provide various key principles, such as lawfulness, purpose limitation, data minimisation and accuracy,[385] which form a fundamental basis for data protection law in the EU. These key principles go hand in hand with the various rights guaranteed to the data subjects concerned. [386]

The data protection system and compliance with the key principles and the individual's rights are supervised by the competent supervisory authority, equipped with the powers necessary to enforce data controllers' compliance with the principles and the data subjects' rights.[387] Furthermore, the data subjects are provided legal remedies, which are essential to comply with the fundamental right guaranteed by Article 47 CFR.

B Transfer of Personal Data to a Third Country under the GDPR

The level of protection of fundamental rights and freedoms guaranteed within the EU is also crucial when assessing the lawfulness of data transfers outside the EU. The European protection system and its provisions should be kept in mind for the further course of this study when assessing the requirements for such transfers.

Where personal data leave the EU, the risk of unrestricted use of data in the recipient country arises.[388] The third country may ensure a lower level of data protection than the one established in the EU. Therefore, the transfer of personal data outside the EU is only permitted when compliant with specific requirements set out in the GDPR. To determine whether a particular transfer of personal data to recipients in third countries is legitimate under the GDPR, companies must carry out a two-step admissibility check:[389] In a first step it must be ensured that the planned transfer complies with the general principles and requirements of the GDPR. The transmission of personal data to any third party under the

---

384 See for a critical assessment Hennemann, 'Wettbewerb der Datenschutzrechtsordnungen? – Zur Rezeption der Datenschutz-Grundverordnung –' (n 209) 879 et seqq.
385 IV.2.
386 IV.4.
387 IV.6.
388 Daniel A Pauly, 'Art. 44 DS-GVO' in Boris P Paal and Daniel A Pauly (eds) (n 157) para 1.
389 cf Tim Wybitul, Lukas Ströbel and Marian Ruess, 'Übermittlung personenbezogener Daten in Drittländer. Überblick und Checkliste für die Prüfung nach der DS-GVO' [2017] ZD 503, 504.

GDPR irrespective of its location falls under the term data processing[390] and must be compliant with the GDPR's key principles.[391] Most importantly, the processing of personal data must be lawful and be based on one of the legal grounds established in Article 6 GDPR.[392] A second step is to verify whether the specific transfer requirements outlined in Chapter V are met. Article 44 GDPR intends "to ensure that the level of protection of natural persons guaranteed by the Regulation is not undermined" where personal data is transferred to a recipient outside the EU.[393] Article 44 GDPR restricts the transfer of personal data to third countries and only allows the transfers if one of the – three-tiered structured[394]– legal bases for data transfer outside the EU is given. A transfer to a recipient in a third country is permitted if the recipient is located in a country in respect of which the Commission adopted an adequacy decision (Article 45 GDPR) (under I.), in the absence of such adequacy decision if the transfer is subject to appropriate safeguards (Article 46 GDPR) (under II.) or in the absence of an adequacy decision and appropriate safeguards a derogation set out in the GDPR applies (Article 49 GDPR) (under III.). Notably, Article 44 GDPR further clarifies that the specific requirements for data transfer outside the EU apply to onward transfers of personal data from the third country to another third country.

I Data Transfer to Third Countries on the Ground of an Adequacy Decision (Article 45 GDPR)

According to Article 45(1) GDPR, a transfer of personal data to a recipient located in a third country, may take place if the EU Commission has decided that the third country, a territory or one or more specified sectors within that third country in question ensures an adequate level of protection.[395] Such adequacy deci-

---

390 cf GDPR, art 4(2) (A.IV.1.a.bb.).

391 A.IV.2.

392 A.IV.3.

393 GDPR, art 44, second sentence and recital 101.

394 Christopher Kuner, 'Art. 45 GDPR' in Christopher Kuner, Lee A Bygrave and Christopher Docksey (eds) (n 360) 774.

395 The term adequacy is further used in Article 2(1) of the Additional Protocol to the Convention for the Protection of Individuals with regard to Automatic Processing of Personal Data, regarding supervisory authorities and transborder data flows No 181 (available at the following link <https://rm.coe.int/1680080626>) and in the OECD Privacy Framework (2013) <https://www.oecd.org/sti/ieconomy/oecd_privacy_framework.pdf>; see in detail Wagner (n 4) 327 et seqq.

sions, adopted by the EU Commission under Article 45(3) GDPR guarantee the highest standard of protection for transfers outside the EU. With an adequacy decision in place, there is no need for any further (specific) authorisation when transferring personal data to a third country. It allows completely free and unhindered data flow from the EUU to the respective country.

1 Adequacy Decisions

The following provides general information on adequacy decisions and the (adoption) process of adequacy.

a Nature and Enforcement

Adequacy decisions are implementing acts by the EU Commission within the meaning of Article 291 TFEU[396] and thus binding for all member states and their supervisory authorities[397]. Member states and their supervisory authorities cannot adopt measures contrary to that adequacy decisions, e. g. suspend or prohibit a transfer of personal data to that particular country.[398] Adequacy decisions as a measure of an EU institution are presumed to be lawful and produce a legal effect.[399] This presumption is crucial to guarantee legal certainty by ensuring that EU law is applied uniformly.[400] However, when a person lodges a complaint under Article 77(1) GDPR with the competent supervisory authority, that authority must examine whether the transfer of personal data at issue complies with the requirements laid down by the GDPR. Suppose in the supervisory authority's view the arguments put forward by that person to challenge the validity of an adequacy decision are well-founded. In that case, it must bring an action before the national courts in order for them to make a reference to the CJEU for a preliminary ruling to examine the validity of that decision.[401] When the national supervisory authority rejects the claim as unfounded, the individual concerned must have access to judicial remedies to contest this decision before national courts; the national courts must make a reference to the CJEU for a preliminary ruling on validity in cases they consider the grounds for invalidity put forward by

---

396 GDPR, art 45(3).
397 TFEU, art 288(4).
398 *Schrems* (n 71) para 52.
399 Judgement of 21 May 1987, *Albako Margarinefabrik*, C-249/85, EU:C:1987:245, para 17; Judgement of 13 February 2014, *Mediaset*, C-69/13, EU:C:2014:71, para 23.
400 *Schrems* (n 71) paras 61 et seq.
401 ibid paras 63 and 65.

the parties.[402] The lodge of the complaint must be interpreted as concerning the issue of whether that decision is compatible with the criteria of Chapter V of the GDPR.[403]

b Process of Adoption

The EU Commission must conduct an assessment of the level of protection that a third country, a territory or one or more specified sectors within a country ensures the adequacy level of data protection. After such an assessment and the EU Commission concludes that such adequate level of protection is provided, the EU Commission may adopt an adequacy decision pursuant to Article 45(3) GDPR. This adoption process should be following the examination procedure referred to in Article 93(2) GDPR.

Before reaching an adequacy decision, the EU Commission consults with the EDPB, which issues its own – non-binding – opinion on the EU Commission's findings.[404] Adequacy decisions must include a detailed explanation of how a country ensures an adequate level of protection.[405] The implementing act shall also provide a periodic review mechanism, considering all relevant developments in the third country at least every four years.[406] Also, the act must specify the territorial and sectoral scope of application. Where applicable, it shall also specify the supervisory authority.[407]

c Repeal, Amendment or Suspension

Once the adequacy decision is adopted the EU Commission is obliged to monitor developments in third countries ongoing, affecting the adequacy decisions adopted according to Article 45(3) GDPR or Directive 95/46.[408] If the EU Commission becomes aware that a third country, territory, or specifies sector within a third country that was subject to an adequacy decision no longer ensures an adequate level of protection, the EU Commission shall repeal, amend or suspend the adequacy decision to the extent necessary without retroactive effective (*ex nunc*).[409] Furthermore, in this situation, the EU Commission shall consult with

---

402 *Schrems* (n 71) paras 53 and 64.
403 ibid paras 59 (referring to Article 25(6) and Article 28(4) of Directive 95/46) and 158.
404 Art. 29 Data Protection Working Party, 'Adequacy Referential' (2018) WP 254 rev.01 4.
405 *Schrems* (n 71) para 83.
406 GDPR, art 45(3).
407 GDPR, art 45(2)(b).
408 GDPR, art 45(4).
409 GDPR, art 45(5).

the third county to remedy the situation giving rise to said decisions.[410] To this date, the EU Commission has not yet repealed, amended or suspended an adequacy decision.[411] The CJEU may also declare such an adequacy decision invalid following a reference for a preliminary ruling or a plea of illegality.[412]

d Current Adequacy Decisions

So far, Andorra, Argentina, Canada, Faroe Islands, Guernsey, Israel, Isle of Man, Japan, Jersey, New Zealand, Switzerland, UK, Uruguay and, most recently, South Korea[413], officially provide adequate data protection.[414] The EU Commission only adopted three adequacy decisions under the GDPR, on Japan, the UK and South Korea. Article 45(9) GDPR specifies that adequacy decisions previously issued under Directive 95/46 remain in force until amended, replaced or repealed by a Commission Decision or invalidated by the CJEU. The adequacy decision regarding Canada differs from the other adequacy decisions that are currently in place since it does not cover all data transfers to Canada and applies only to private entities that fall under the scope of the Canadian Personal Information Protection and Electronic Documents Act.[415] Three former adequacy decisions are no longer in force after the CJEU invalidated the data transfer mechanisms upon which they were based: The 2004 decision on the transfer of passenger name record data to the United States' Bureau of Customs and Border Protec-

---

410 GDPR, art 45(6).

411 This was considered with regard to the Swiss adequacy decision, but became obsolete when in 2020 a new Swiss data protection law was introduced, cf Moritz Hennemann, 'Das Schweizer Datenschutzrecht im Wettbewerb der Rechtsordnungen' in Boris P. Paal, Dörte Poelzig, Oliver Fehrenbacher (eds), *Deutsches, Europäisches und vergleichendes Wirtschaftsrecht: Festschrift für Werner F. Ebke zum 70. Geburtstag* (C.H.Beck 2021) 377. The new Swiss data protection law clearly approximates the GDPR in various areas, cf Lukas Bühlmann and Michael Reinle 'DSG Revision: Vergleich zum geltendem Recht und zur EU-DSGVO' <https://www.mll-news.com/wp-content/uploads/2020/10/DSG-Revision_Gegenüberstellung.pdf>.

412 The CJEU did so in *Schrems* (n 71) and in *Facebook Ireland and Schrems* (n 64).

413 Adequacy Decision South Korea (n 28).

414 A comprehensive overview map of all adequacy decisions by the EU Commission is provided by Research Centre for Law and Digitalisation, 'Adequacy Decisions by the European Commission' (last revised on 23 August 2021) <https://www.jura.uni-passau.de/fileadmin/dokumente/fakultaeten/jura/lehrstuehle/hennemann/Mapping_Global_Data_Law/I01_-_Adequacy_Decisions.pdf>.

415 Commission Decision 2002/2/EC pursuant to Directive 95/46/EC of the EU Parliament and of the Council on the adequate protection of personal data provided by the Canadian Personal Information Protection and Electronic Documents Act [2001] OJ L 2/13.

tion[416]; the 2000 decision on the EU-US *Safe Harbor* agreement[417] and, in July 2020, the 2016 decision on the EU-US *Privacy Shield* agreement was declared invalid by the CJEU[418]. On 25 March 2022, the EU Commission and the US announced that they have agreed in principle on a new Trans-Atlantic Data Privacy Framework.[419] The adequacy decision regarding the transfer of PNR data of air passengers to the Canada Border Service Agency expired in 2009.[420] After the CJEU rendered the Safe Harbor agreement invalid in Schrems[421], the EU Commission amended the previous adequacy decisions, changing each Article 3 and adding a new Article 3a. This new provision establishes the following: (1) member states are required to inform the EU Commission when they suspend or ban data flows to third countries, (2) the EU Commission is required to monitor developments in the legal order of the third country that could affect the functioning of the adequacy decision, (3) member states and the EU Commission must keep each other informed of indications that interferences by public authorities responsible for national security, law enforcement or other public interest go beyond what is strictly necessary or that there is no effective legal protection against such interferences. The EU Commission is required to inform the third country's competent authority and propose draft measures to repeal or suspend the decision or limit its scope where evidence shows that an adequate level of protection is no longer guaranteed.[422]

---

416 Council Decision of 17 May 2004 on the conclusion of an Agreement between the European Community and the USA on the processing and transfer of PNR data by Air Carriers to the United States Department of Homeland Security, Bureau of Customs and Border Protection, OJ L 183/83. PNR means Passenger Name Record. It was declared invalid by the CJEU in its Judgement of 30 May 2006, *Parliament v Council*, C- 317/04 and C-318/04, EU:C:2006:346.
417 *Safe Harbor* Decision (n 25), which was invalidated by the CJEU in *Schrems* (n 71). The *Schrems* judgement is further reviewed under I.3.a.aa.
418 *Privacy Shield* Decision (n 26). Due to the absent of general data protection legislation in the United States, the *Privacy Shield* was based on a system of self-certification by which U.S. organisations commit to a set of privacy principles; the decision was invalidated by the CJEU in *Facebook Ireland and Schrems* (n 64), which is further reviewed under I.3.a.bb.
419 EU Commission, 'European Commission and United States Joint Statement on Trans-Atlantic Data Privacy Framework' (2022) Press release of 19 February 2021 <https://ec.europa.eu/commission/presscorner/detail/en/ip_22_2087>.
420 Commission Decision 2006/253/EC on the adequate protection of personal data contained in the Passenger Name Record of air passengers transferred to the Canada Border Services Agency [2005] OJ L 91/49.
421 3.a.aa.
422 cf Commission Implementing Decision (EU) 2016/2295 amending Decisions 2000/518/EC, 2002/2/EC, 2003/490 EC, 2003/821/EC, 2004/411/EC, 2008/393/EC, 2010/146/EU, 2010/625/EU, 2011/61/EU and Implementing Decisions 2012/848/EU, 2013/65/EU on the adequate protection

e International Instruments

In addition to adequacy decisions, the transfer of personal data may be legalised by an international agreement.[423] These agreements must also ensure an adequate level of protection for personal data transferred under such instrument. However, the investigation of data protection standards when negotiating an international agreement may not be as thorough as the one for adequacy findings.[424] However, to keep trade deals politically uncontroversial, the EU Commission prefers to legalise data transfer outside the EU by adequacy decisions.[425] As EU Commission spokesperson *Mina Andreeva* stated: "For the EU, privacy is not a commodity to be traded", "[d]ialogues on data protection and trade negotiations with third countries follow separate tracks".[426]

The CJEU once gave an opinion on a draft agreement for processing and transferring passenger name records (so-called "PNR") data between the EU and Canada, signed on 25 June 2014[427].[428] The Court assessed whether the envisaged agreement was compatible with Article 8 CFR. It found that an international agreement may meet the requirements of a "law" as defined in Article 8(2) and 52(1) CFR.[429] The CJEU clarified that the case law on adequacy decisions, discussed below, also applies to international agreements.[430] In the case of the proposed EU-Canada PNR transfer agreement, the CJEU criticised the lack of sufficient preciseness and sufficient protection for sensitive data[431], the lack of individual re-examination by non-automated means in cases of automated anal-

---

of personal data by certain countries, pursuant to Article 25(6) of Directive 95/46/EC of the European Parliament and of the Council [2016] OJ L 344/83.

423 cf recital 102 GDPR stating that the GDPR is "without prejudice to international agreements concluded between the Union and third countries regulating the transfer of personal data including appropriate safeguards for data subjects"; see also CJEU's Opinion *Accord PNR EU-Canada* (n 80) para 214.

424 Christopher Kuner, 'Art. 45 GDPR' (n 394) 777.

425 Jakob Hanke Vela, Joanna Plucinska and Hans von der Burchard, 'EU Trade, the Martin Selmayr Way' *Politico* (18 October 2017) <https://www.politico.eu/article/eu-trade-the-martin-selmayr-way/>.

426 cf Hanke Vela, Plucinska and von der Burchard (n 428). The EU Commission's approach to the adequacy process will be discussed in Chapter 5, B.

427 EU Commission, 'Proposal for a Council Decision on the Conclusion of the Agreement between Canada and the European Union on the Transfer and Processing of Passenger Name Record Data' COM/2013/0528 final.

428 *Accord PNR EU-Canada* (n 80).

429 ibid paras 145 et seqq.

430 ibid paras 134 and 214.

431 Ibid (n 80) para 165.

ysis of PNR data, [432] and the lack of sufficient oversight mechanisms pursuant to Article 8(3) GDPR[433]. Thus, the draft agreement could not be concluded in its form at the point in time.

2 Criteria for the Adequacy

The assessment and the adequacy decision are mainly based on the level of data protection abroad and whether it can be considered adequate compared to the level of protection under the European data protection law.[434] The criteria that must be taken into account in the assessment of adequacy set out in Article 45(2) GDPR:

> "(a) the rule of law, respect for human rights and fundamental freedoms, relevant legislation, both general and sectoral, including concerning public security, defence, national security and criminal law and the access of public authorities to personal data, as well as the implementation of such legislation, data protection rules, professional rules and security measures, including rules for the onward transfer of personal data to another third country or international organisation which are complied within that country or international organisation, case law, as well as effective and enforceable data subject rights and effective administrative and judicial redress for the data subjects whose personal data are being transferred;

> (b) the existence and effective functioning of one or more independent supervisory authorities in the third country or to which an international organisation is subject, with responsibility for ensuring and enforcing compliance with the data protection rules, including adequate enforcement powers, for assisting and advising the data subjects in exercising their rights and for cooperation with the supervisory authorities of the Member States; and

> (c) the international commitments the third country or international organisation concerned has entered into, or other obligations arising from legally binding conventions or instruments as well as from its participation in multilateral or regional systems, in particular in relation to the protection of personal data."

The wording ("in particular") shows that this list is non-exhaustive and only gives a few indications of how to determine whether the third country guarantees an adequate level of data protection.[435] In the following, the different criteria are examined in more detail.

---

432 *Accord PNR EU-Canada* (n 80) para 173.
433 ibid para 231.
434 EU Commission, 'Communication from the Commission to the European Parliament and Council. Exchanging and Protecting Personal Data in a Globalised World' (n 142) 6.
435 Daniel A Pauly, 'Art. 45 DS-GVO' in Boris P Paal and Daniel A Pauly (eds) (n 157) para 4.

a Article 45(2)(a) GDPR

The third country's legislation and case law must essentially be considered. As a minimum requirement, the third country must respect the rule of law and international human rights norms and standards.[436] The term "the rule of law"[437] can be found in other EU provisions, such as in Article 2, 6 and 21 TEU, defining the fundament of the EU, but also in Article 49 TEU, requiring accessing states to the EU to respect the values of the rule of law. In 2014, the EU Commission started a new EU Framework to strengthen the rule of law, citing and interpreting the relevant CJEU case law.[438] It states that according to the relevant case law, "the rule of law" is the source of fully justiciable principles applicable within the EU legal system, including the principle of legality, legal certainty, prohibition of arbitrariness of executive powers, and independent and effective judicial review, including the respect for fundamental rights and equality before the law.[439] This interpretation is also the premise for the "rule of law" in the context of Article 45(2)(a) GDPR. The term "human rights" refers to the rights, freedoms, and principles guaranteed in the ECHR, which the EU acknowledges in Article 6 TEU and have the same legal value as the Treaties and fundamental rights guaranteed in the Charter. Although the term "legislation" is to be understood broadly in this context, as it also explicitly includes the legislation concerning public security, defence, national security, and criminal law, it becomes clear from Article 45(2)(a) GDPR, particularly the third country's data protection law, is highly important for the EU Commission's assessment.

b Article 45(2)(b) GDPR

Article 45(2)(b) GDPR requires the existence of an effective, functioning, and independent data protection supervisory authority in the respective third country. The supervisory authority should assist the data subject in exercising their right and cooperating with EU member states' supervisory authorities. The requirements demanded by Article 8(3) CFR, as well as the requirements demanded

---

436 GDPR, recital 104.

437 See for further information: Thomas von Danwitz, 'The Rule of Law in the Recent Jurisprudence of the ECJ' (2014) 37 Fordham International Law Journal 1311; Nicolas Hachez and Jan Wouters, 'Promoting the Rule of Law: A Benchmarks Approach' (Leuven Centre for Global Governance Studies 2013) Working Paper No 105 1 and 6 et seqq. <https://www.fp7-frame.eu/wp-content/materiale/w-papers/WP105-Hachez-Wouters.pdf>.

438 EU Commission, 'Communication from the Commission to the European Parliament and the Council. A New EU Framework to Strengthen the Rule of Law' (2014) COM(2014) 158 final.

439 ibid Annex 1 and 2.

by the GDPR for an independent and effective data protection supervisory authority, were already laid out above.[440]

c Article 45(2)(c) GDPR

Article 45(2)(c) expands the scope of the relevant law in Article 45(2)(a) GDPR to international commitments. This shows an openness to public international law and explicitly allows reference to international treaties in the interpretation of the European data export regime.[441] In particular, the third country's accession to Convention 108, an international treaty entered into force in 1981, is relevant to the adequacy assessment.[442] This Convention 108 and its updated version Convention 108+ were already discussed above.[443] Other international commitments could be the OECD Privacy Guidelines[444].[445]. However, the OECD Guidelines are not legally binding on the member states but rather provide a supplementary framework.[446]

3 Further Interpretation of and Criteria for Adequacy

Article 45 GDPR does not define the term "adequacy" in any way or define which standard the abovementioned criteria must fulfil to guarantee an adequate level of protection. Therefore, in the following, the relevant case law of the CJEU as well as the relevant Working Papers of the Art. 29 Working Party and the EDPB will be further evaluated to understand better the requirements which

---

440 For an overview of the requirements in Article 8(3) of the Charter and the GDPR see under A.I.5 and A.IV.6.

441 Wagner (n 4) 327.

442 GDPR, recital 105.

443 A.III.2.

444 OECD, 'Recommendation of the Council concerning Guidelines governing the Protection of Privacy and Transborder Flows of Personal Data' (2013), C(80)58/Final (as amended on 11 July 2013 by C(2013)79) <https://www.oecd.org/sti/ieconomy/2013-oecd-privacy-guidelines.pdf>.

445 For African Union countries a relevant factor under Article 45(2)(a) GDPR could be the 'African Union Convention on Cyber Security and Personal Data African Union Convention on Cyber Security and Personal Data', adopted on 27 June 2014 <https://au.int/sites/default/files/treaties/29560-treaty-0048_-_african_union_convention_on_cyber_security_and_personal_data_protection.pdf>. However, the Convention has not yet entered into force since it has not been signed by all African Union member states (art. 35). See for more information on data protection regimes in Africa in Moritz Hennemann, Patricia Boshe and Ricarda von Meding, 'Current Regulatory Approaches, Policy Initiatives, and the Way Forward' (2022) 3 Global Privacy Law Review 56.

446 Wagner (n 4) 328; Kuner, *Transborder Data Flow and Data Privacy Law* (n 3) 35.

the third country's legislation concerning data protection has to provide in order to guarantee an adequate level of data protection.

a CJEU's interpretation of Adequacy

The CJEU has dealt with the adequacy level in its ruling *Schrems*.[447] In *Schrems*, the CJEU invalidated the decision of the EU Commission, finding the EU-US *Safe Harbor* agreement[448] to provide only inadequate protection for data transfers under Article 25 of Directive 95/46[449]. More recently, in July 2020, the CJEU decided on the adequacy level under the GDPR in its ruling *Schrems and Facebook Ireland* and invalidated the EU Commission's decision on the adequacy of the EU-US *Privacy Shield* agreement.[450] The *Safe Harbor* and the *Privacy Shield* were self-certifying agreements, with companies agreeing to comply with data protection principles and requirements set out in the agreement. In both decisions, the CJEU did not provide a detailed set of requirements or framework for assessing the third country's data protection but emphasised single aspects and factors that the third country's legislation must provide to ensure an adequate level of protection. Although both judgements concerned adequacy decisions under Article 25(1) of the former Directive 95/46, the case law also applies to adequacy decisions under the GDPR.

aa Schrems

First, the CJEU declared that the EU Commission's discretion regarding the adequacy assessment is reduced to a minimum, with a strict review of the requirements deriving from Article 25 of Directive 95/46 read in the light CFR.[451] Consequently, the EU Commission must periodically check whether the adequacy

---

447 *Schrems* (n 71).
448 *Safe Harbor* Decision (n 25).
449 Article 25(2) of the Directive 95/46 stated that the adequacy level afforded by a third county "shall be assessed in the light of all the circumstances surrounding a data transfer operation or set of data transfer operations", including "the nature of the data, the purpose and duration of the proposed processing operation [...], the country of origin and country of final destination, the rules of law, both general and sectoral, in force in the third country in question and the professional rules and security measures which are complied with in that country".
450 *Facebook Ireland and Schrems* (n 64). Prior to the judgement, the EU Commission found in its third annual review in October 2019 that the *"Privacy Shield"* still ensures an adequate level of protection (Report from the Commission to the EU Parliament and the Council on the third annual review of the functioning of the EU-U.S. Privacy Shield (2019) COM(2019) 495 final).
451 *Schrems* (n 71) para 78, referring to *Digital Rights Ireland and Seitlinger and Others* (n 73) paras 47 et seq.

assessment is still justified and consider all circumstances after adopting the decision.[452] Second, the CJEU highlights that the European provisions on data transfer to third countries essentially implement the right to the protection of personal data as laid down in Article 8 CFR by ensuring that the high level of protection continues after the data has been exported.[453] The word "adequate" clarifies that a third country does not necessarily need to guarantee an identical level of protection as the EU.[454] "Adequate" requires the third country "to ensure, because of its domestic law or its international commitments, a level of protection of fundamental rights and freedoms that is essentially equivalent to that guaranteed within the European Union".[455] Briefly, "adequate" is defined as "essentially equivalent".[456] Consistent with the interpretation of the term "adequacy", as in not "identical", "the means used by the third country for the purpose of ensuring such a level of protection may differ from those implemented within the EU. However, the provisions must prove effective in practice.[457] The CJEU's requirement of "essential equivalency" is now implemented in recital 104 GDPR.

The CJEU has defined the Charter as the comparative "benchmark" for the regulation of data transfer to third countries:[458] The third country must establish "effective detection" and "supervision mechanisms".[459] The Court underlined that the provisions of the adequacy decision must essentially meet EU legal standards in terms of purpose limitation, necessity and proportionality, and clearness and precision. [460] In the specific case, *Safe Harbor* did not contain any finding concerning limitations on the powers of public authorities in the USA to interfere with fundamental rights.[461] The relevant legislation was "not limited to what is strictly necessary where it authorises, on a generalised

---

452 *Schrems* (n 71) paras 76 et seq. This obligation to the EU Commission is now implemented in Article 45(4) GDPR.

453 ibid para 72.

454 ibid para 73.

455 ibid. The equation of the terms adequacy and equivalence has been critisised in the relevant literature, see Christian Schröder, 'Art. 45 DS-GVO' in Jürgen Kühling and Benedikt Buchner (eds) (n 174) para 11 and footnote 19 with further references.

456 Critically ibid para 11.

457 *Schrems* (n 71) para 74.

458 This shows the CJEU's dynamic approach as the Charter had not been elevated to the level of EU primary law at the time *Safe Harbor* was enacted in 2000, but the CJEU still used it as a standard of reference. The CJEU evaluates whether the adequacy decision meets the legal standard in force at time that it makes its judgement.

459 *Schrems* (n 71) para 81.

460 cf ibid paras 90 et seq.

461 ibid para 88.

basis, storage of all the personal data of all the persons whose data has been transferred from the European Union to the United States without any differentiation, limitation or exception being made in the light of the objective pursued and without an objective criterion being laid down by which to determine the limits of the access of the public authorities to the data, and of its subsequent use, for purposes which are specific, strictly restricted and capable of justifying the interference which both access to that data and its use entail".[462] The CJEU evaluates that "[l]egislation permitting the public authorities to have access on a generalised basis to the content of electronic communications must be regarded as compromising the essence of the fundamental right to respect for private life, as guaranteed by Article 7 CFR".[463] Also, the CJEU emphasised the importance that the third country's legislation provides the individual with a possibility to pursue legal remedies to get access to personal data relating to them or to obtain the right to rectify, erase such data, in order to respect the essence of the right to effective judicial protection enshrined in Article 47 CFR[464].[465]

bb Facebook Ireland and Schrems

Although the main subject in *Facebook Ireland and Schrems* was the validity of the EU Commission's Decision 2010/87/EU concerning a set of standard contractual clauses[466], the CJEU also decided on the adequacy level of protection provided by the EU-US *Privacy Shield*. Essentially, the CJEU's line of the jurisdiction in the *Schrems* decision was continued.[467]

---

462 *Schrems* (n 71) para 93.

463 ibid para 94. See also under A.I.2.a.

464 Article 47 CFR states: "(1) Everyone whose rights and freedoms guaranteed by the law of the Union are violated has the right to an effective remedy before a tribunal in compliance with the conditions laid down in this Article. (2) Everyone is entitled to a fair and public hearing within a reasonable time by an independent and impartial tribunal previously established by law. (3) Everyone shall have the possibility of being advised, defended and represented. Legal aid shall be made available to those who lack sufficient resources in so far as such aid is necessary to ensure effective access to justice".

465 *Schrems* (n 71) para 95.

466 The *Facebook Ireland and Schrems* judgement (n 64) concerning the standard contractual clauses is evaluated in more detail in Chapter 4 under A.

467 See for a critical assessment of the CJEU's *Facebook Ireland and Schrems* judgement Jens Brauneck, 'Privacy Shield – zu Recht für ungültig erklärt? Zugleich Besprechung von EuGH, Urt. v. 16.7.2020 in der Rs. C-311/18 – Schrems II' [2020] EuZW 933.

The Court assessed whether interferences arising from US surveillance programs[468] are covered by requirements ensuring, subject to the principle of proportionality, a level of protection "essentially equivalent" to that guaranteed by Article 52(1) CFR[469].[470] Legal grounds for surveillance measures that do not themselves define the scope of limitation on the exercise of the right concerned by laying down "clear and precise rules governing the scope and application of the measure in question and imposing minimum safeguards" are not compatible with the principle of proportionality.[471] Furthermore, to ensure that the third country's level of data protection is adequate, the Court assessed whether there are "effective and enforceable data subject rights" for data subjects whose personal data are transferred – as now required by Article 45(2)(a) GDPR.[472] The third country's legislation must provide the data subjects with actionable rights against authorities before the courts.[473] The Court further evaluated the compliance of the *Privacy Shield* with Article 47 CFR – which, as it already became clear from the CJEU's judgement in *Schrems*, also "contributes" to the level of protection in the EU.[474] The Court states that "the very existence of effective judicial review designed to ensure compliance with provisions of EU law is inherent in the existence of the rule of law."[475] In this context, the CJEU also refers to Article 45(2)(a) GDPR requiring the EU Commission to take into account "effective administrative and judicial redress for the data subject whose personal data are being transferred", and to recital 104 GDPR, which states that the third country "should ensure effective independent data protection supervision and should provide for cooperation mechanism with the Member States' data protection authorities".[476] The ombudsperson mechanism, established in the *Privacy Shield* agreement, did not provide data subjects with any cause of action before a body that offers guarantees substantially equivalent to those required by Arti-

---

468 These surveillance programs are based on section 702 of the Foreign Intelligence Surveillance Act (FISA) and Executive Order (E.O.) 12333.
469 A.I.2.b.
470 ibid paras 178 et seqq.
471 ibid para 176.
472 ibid para 177.
473 cf ibid para 181. In the specific case, the Presidential Policy Directive 28 (PPD-28) did provide requirements that had to be complied with by the US authorities when carrying out the surveillance programmes in question. However, these requirements did not guarantee any rights that could have can be enforced against the US authorities in court by EU data subjects. The *Privacy Shield* also did not include sufficient judicial remedies.
474 ibid para 186.
475 ibid para 187.
476 ibid paras 188 et seq.

cle 47 CFR. It was also found that both the independence of the ombudsperson and the ombudsperson's power to adopt decisions that are binding on US intelligence services were not sufficiently ensured.[477]

b Art 29 Working Party's and EDPB's Interpretation of Adequacy

The Art. 29 Working Party released some guidelines in Working Paper 12 (after this: WP 12) on assessing the adequacy of a third country's level of protection. The EDPB, Art. 29 Working Party's predecessor, has adopted the guidelines defined in an updated working paper (WP 254).[478] These guidelines are also used as guidance to assess third countries' data protection levels when the EDPB (or under the Directive 95/46, the Art. 29 Working Party) is asked to adopt an opinion for the EU Commission's decision.[479] The EDPB's working papers are non-binding and only serve as guidance on the interpretation of Article 45 GPDR.

In line with the Art. 29 Working Party and the EDPB, the system of the third country must contain the following content of rules: The third country's legislation should reflect and be consistent with the key concepts enshrined in the GDPR.[480] However, the GDPR terminology does not have to be mirrored.[481] The processing must be "lawfully, fairly and legitimate".[482] The legitimate bases for processing "should be set out in a sufficiently clear manner".[483] Data should be processed for a specific purpose and afterwards used only in a, with this purpose, compatible way ("purpose limitation principle").[484] Data should be accurate and kept up to date (where necessary) as well as adequate, relevant and proportionate to the processing purpose ("data quality and proportionality principle").[485] Data should not be kept longer than necessary for the purposes of data processing ("data retention principle").[486] The controller or processor

---

477 *Facebook Ireland and Schrems* (n 64) paras 194 et seqq. Prior to the CJEU judgement, the EU Commission found that the "ombudsperson mechanism" ensured a level of data protection adequate to Article 47 CFR, EU Commission, 'Report from to the European Parliament and the Council on the Third Annual Review of the Functioning of the EU-U.S. Privacy Shield' (2019) COM(2019) 495 final recitals 115 et seq.
478 The EDPB endorsed all WP29 Guidelines related to the GDPR (<https://edpb.europa.eu/node/89>).
479 Wagner (n 4) 324.
480 Art. 29 Data Protection Working Party, 'Adequacy Referential' (n 404) 4.
481 ibid.
482 ibid.
483 ibid.
484 ibid.
485 ibid.
486 ibid.

shall ensure a secure way of processing personal data, including protection against unauthorised or unlawful processing and accidental loss, destruction or damage, by using technical and organisational measures ("security and confidentiality principle").[487] The controller should provide the data subject with all the necessary information "in a clear, easily accessible, concise, transparent and intelligible form", including the purpose of processing and the identity of the data controller ("transparency principle").[488] The data subject should have the right to access all data concerning them, the right to obtain rectification of their data as appropriate, when they are inaccurate or incomplete, the right to erasure, when their processing is no longer necessary or lawful and the right to object on compelling legitimate grounds relating to their particular situation at any time to the processing of their personal data.[489] However, these rights may be restricted for important objectives of general public interests.[490] Finally, restrictions on onward transfers should exist as they should only be allowed if the designated recipient is also bound by rules that establish an adequate protection level.[491] WP 254 also provides examples of "additional content principles to be applied in specific situations of processing", including situations where special categories of data are involved, where data is processed for direct marketing or where a decision is based solely on automated decision making.[492]

Regarding procedural and enforcement mechanisms, the Art. 29 Working Party and the EDPB requested that the system in question contain the following: The third country needs a competent, independent supervisory authority, which is monitoring, ensuring and enforcing compliance with data protection provisions.[493] The data protection system should ensure a good level of compliance by the existence of effective and dissuasive sanctions or systems of direct verification.[494] The third country data protection framework should obligate controllers to comply with it and be able to demonstrate such compliance to the competent supervisory authority.[495] The data subject should be able to pursue legal remedies to enforce his or her rights rapidly, effectively and without prohibitive

---

487 Art. 29 Data Protection Working Party, 'Adequacy Referential' (n 404) 4.
488 ibid 5.
489 ibid.
490 ibid.
491 ibid.
492 ibid 5 et seq.
493 ibid 6.
494 ibid.
495 ibid.

costs.[496] To do so, the data protection system must ensure supervision mechanisms allowing for the investigation of complaints and enabling any infringements of the right of data protection and privacy to be identified and punished.[497] Also, where rules are not complied with, the data subject should be provided with effective administrative and judicial redress, such as compensation for damages.[498]

The above shows that the Art. 29 Working Party and the EDPB have established narrow and strict requirements for an adequate level of data protection, *de facto* demanding an identical level of data protection through almost identical means as the one provided by the GDPR.[499] It appears that the Art. 29 Working Party and the EDPB do not grant flexibility in the adequacy assessment since they basically request that the data protection regime of a third country contains all of the GDPR's data protection principles. This is contrary to the term "adequate", which cannot be understood as "identical"[500] as well as the CJEU's approach stressing that there is no need for a point-to-point-replication of EU rules.[501] In the case of a required identity, no consideration of the values and legal ideas of the recipient country would be possible.[502] The CJEU emphasised the importance of the third country's data protection system as a whole being effective in practice, providing a standard of data protection "essential equivalent" to the one within the EU. However, the Court did not define a detailed set of requirements or framework for the assessment, but instead highlighted essential aspects deriving from the Charter, which a third country's legislation must necessarily provide in order to be deemed adequate.

4 Conclusion to I

Assessing the adequate level of data protection ensured in a third country is a highly demanding process, which entails a detailed study and a comparison of the rules and practices prevailing in the third country with the protection stand-

---

496 Art. 29 Data Protection Working Party, 'Adequacy Referential' (n 404) 7.
497 ibid.
498 ibid.
499 See Hennemann, 'Wettbewerb der Datenschutzrechtsordnungen? – Zur Rezeption der Datenschutz-Grundverordnung –' (n 209) 888.
500 Schrems (n 71) para 73.
501 ibid para 74.
502 See Hennemann, Wettbewerb der Datenschutzrechtsordnungen? – Zur Rezeption der Datenschutz-Grundverordnung –' (n 209) 888 et seqq. who analyses why the path of the Art. 29 Working Group and the EDPB is problematic in the context of functional and contextual comparative law. See also below in Chapter V, B.

ards within the EU.[503] Adequacy decisions are not just a formality, and the adequacy process is not a trivial matter.[504] A high standard of fundamental rights protection must be provided, which needs to be evaluated in a strict manner. It must be determined that the law, in theory, corresponds to the data subject's reality. The adequacy assessment must include analysing whether the third country has a functioning and effective legal system that allows recourse if the law is breached.[505] The CJEU's interpretation of adequacy as "essentially equivalent"[506] to the level of data protection guaranteed within the EU is now constituted in recital 104 GDPR and defines every EU Commission's adequacy decision.[507] The means ensuring the level of data protection may differ from the means in the European data protection law as long as they prove as effective in practice.[508] The essential criteria for an adequate level of data protection established from above can be summarised as follows:

The third country's legislation shall not violate the fundamental right guaranteed in Articles 7, 8 and 47 CFR.[509] Interferences may be permitted only within the scope of EU legal standards as required by Articles 52(1) and 8(2) CFR.[510] Third country public authorities shall not have access to personal data without any limitations regarding the access and its subsequent use; access shall only be granted where it is strictly necessary to protect value such as national security.[511]

Regarding the procedural and enforcement mechanism, in order to enforce compliance, the third country must establish "effective detection and supervision mechanisms enabling any infringements of the rules ensuring the protection of fundamental right".[512] The CJEU stresses that any supervisory mechanism requires guaranteeing independence from the executive and providing the power

---

503 Also, Opinion of Advocate General *Saugmandsgaard Øe* of 19 December 2019, *Facebook Ireland and Schrems*, C-311/18, EU:C:2019:1145, para 202.

504 cf Hans Graux and others, 'Study Requested by the European Parliament's LIBE Committee: The Future EU-UK Relationship: Options in the Field of the Protection of Personal Data for General Processing Activities and for Processing for Law Enforcement Purposes' (Policy Department for Citizens' Rights and Constitutional Affairs 2018) 28 <https://www.europarl.europa.eu/RegData/etudes/STUD/2018/604976/IPOL_STU(2018)604976_EN.pdf>.

505 cf Graux and others (n 504) 25 et seq.

506 *Schrems* (n 71) para 72.

507 Also, EU Commission, 'Communication from the Commission to the European Parliament and Council. Exchanging and Protecting Personal Data in a Globalised World' (n 142) 4.

508 *Schrems* (n 71) para 74.

509 *Facebook Ireland and Schrems* (n 64) paras 168 et seqq.

510 cf ibid para 91; *Facebook Ireland and Schrems* (n 64) paras 72 et seqq. (A.I.2. and 3.).

511 cf *Schrems* (n 71) para 93.

512 ibid para 81.

to adopt decisions binding on national authorities.[513] Also, where rules are not complied with, the data subject should be provided with effective and appropriate administrative and judicial redress.[514] It is essential for the third country's legislation to comply with the right of effective remedy and to a fair trial guaranteed Article 47 CFR: According to the CJEU, the third country's legislation must provide the data subject with legal remedies to enforce their right to access, erasure and rectification.[515]

II Data Transfer to Third Countries with Appropriate Safeguards (Article 46 GDPR)

> "In the absence of a decision pursuant to Article 45(3) GDPR, a controller or processor may transfer personal data to a third country or an international organisation only if the controller or processor has provided appropriate safeguards, and on condition that enforceable data subject rights and effective legal remedies for data subjects available."

The appropriate safeguards established in Article 46(1) GDPR are more limited in scope than adequacy decisions, do only concern the data transfer of personal data in *inter partes* relations and are tailored to specific transfers or types of transfers. Controllers and processors can implement appropriate safeguards to facilitate a data transfer to a third country under the GDPR. According to Article 46(2) GDPR appropriate safeguards without the requirement of an authorisation by the supervisory authority may be provided by

> "(a) a legally binding and enforceable instrument between public authorities or bodies; (b) binding corporate rules in accordance with Article 47 GDPR; (c) standard data protection clauses adopted by the Commission in accordance with the examination procedure referred to in Article 93(2) GDPR; (d) standard data protection clauses adopted by a supervisory authority and approved by the Commission pursuant to the examination procedure referred to in Article 93(2) GDPR; (e) an approved code of conduct pursuant to Article 40 GDPR together with binding and enforceable commitments of the controller or processor in the third country to apply the appropriate safeguards, including as regards data subjects' rights; or (f) an approved certification mechanism pursuant to Article 42 GDPR together with binding and enforceable commitments of the controller or processor in the third country to apply the appropriate safeguards, including as regards data subjects' rights."

---

513 cf *Facebook Ireland and Schrems* (n 64) paras 195 et seq.
514 Art. 29 Data Protection Working Party, 'Adequacy Referential' (n 404) 7.
515 *Schrems* (n 71) para 95; *Facebook Ireland and Schrems* (n 64) paras 187 et seqq.

By abolishing the requirement of prior notification to and specific authorisation by the data protection authorities of each transfer to a third country based on appropriate safeguards, which was perceived as a significant obstacle for data flow – especially for smaller businesses – the GDPR's system of appropriate safeguards was simplified.[516] Further appropriate safeguards may be provided by "(a) contractual clauses between the controller or processor and the controller, processor or the recipient of the personal data in the third country; or (b) provision to be inserted into administrative arrangements between public authorities or bodies which include enforceable and effective data subject rights" – both requiring an additional authorisation from the competent supervisory authority.[517] In the following, the different appropriate safeguards will be further examined. The focus will be on binding corporate rules (after this: BCRs) and standard contractual clauses (after this: SCCs), the latter being the most popular appropriate safeguard.[518] The appropriate safeguards as effective alternative tools for data transfer from the EU to the UK are further evaluated in Chapter 4.

1 Legally Binding and Enforceable Instrument

Legally binding and enforceable instruments between public authorities or bodies may provide an appropriate safeguard without additional authorisation from a supervisory authority. A legal definition for the term "instruments" is not provided.[519] Such instruments can be administrative arrangements, for example, a "memorandum of understanding". When administrative arrangements lack a legally binding nature, an additional authorisation by the competent supervisory authority is required.[520]

2 Binding Corporate Rules

BCRs are defined as "personal data protection policies which are adhered to by a controller or processor established on the territory of a Member State for trans-

---

516 EU Commission, 'Communication from the Commission to the European Parliament and Council. Exchanging and Protecting Personal Data in a Globalised World' (n 142) 5.

517 GDPR, art 46(3).

518 According to IAPP, 'IAPP-EY Annual Governance Report 2019' <https://iapp.org/store/books/a191P000003Qv5xQAC/> the most popular method for data transfers to outside the EU is use of SCCs (88% of respondents). 91% of the respondents reported that they intend to use SCCs for data-transfer compliance after Brexit.

519 Daniel A Pauly, 'Art. 46 DS-GVO' in Boris P Paal and Daniel A Pauly (eds) (n 157) para 15; Christian Schröder, 'Art. 46 DS-GVO' in Jürgen Kühling and Benedikt Buchner (eds) (n 174) para 23.

520 GDPR, art 46(3)(b) and recital 108.

fers or a set of transfers of personal data to a controller or processor in one or more third countries within a group of undertakings, or group of enterprises engaged in a joint economic activity".[521] BCRs apply to transfers to recipients inside a group of undertakings or enterprises. The notion "group of undertaking" is defined as "a controlling undertaking and its controlled undertakings".[522] A definition of the term "group of enterprises engaged in a joint economic activity" cannot be found in the GDPR. However, the term "enterprise" is defined as "a natural or legal person engaged in an economic activity, irrespective of its legal form, including partnerships or associations regularly engaged in an economic activity".[523] Thus, the notion "group of enterprises engaged in a joint economic activity" could be interpreted as a group of at least two natural or legal persons, whether affiliated or not, which collaborate for economic activity but not necessarily forming part of the same corporate group.[524] In the negotiations of the GDPR, it was agreed that a joint economic activity should be stable.[525] For example, the unrestricted subcontracting to sub-processors through their inclusion in a cooperation of enterprises, in which not every relationship with the sub-processor would prove to be sufficiently stable, would not fall under the scope of Article 47(1)(a) GDPR.[526] Enterprises with only a loose connection to each other usually do not fulfil the mandatory requirements cited in Article 47(2) GDPR[527].[528] Data transfer between different groups that have enacted BCRs separately would probably have to comply with the conditions for onwards transfers set out in the BCRs.[529]

The BCRs must be approved by the competent supervisory authority by the consistency mechanisms set out in Article 63 et seqq. GDPR.[530] The consistency mechanism is a concept newly introduced by the GDPR that enhances and formalises the cooperation of supervisory authorities through their participation in the EDPB. The supervisory authority of the (primary) establishment of the con-

---

521 GDPR, art 4(20).
522 GDPR, art 4(19).
523 GDPR, art 4(18).
524 Tobias Kugler, 'E. Practical Examples' in Tobias Kugler and Daniel Rücker (eds) (n 199) 872.
525 As an example an airline alliance was mentioned, cf Christopher Kuner, 'Art. 47 GDPR' in Christopher Kuner, Lee A Bygrave and Christopher Docksey (eds) (n 360) 820.
526 Daniel A. Pauly, 'Art. 47 DS-GVO' in Boris P Paal and Daniel A Pauly (eds) (n 157) para 4.
527 The mandatory requirements will be looked at in in Chapter 4, B.I.
528 Christian Schröder, 'Art. 47 DS-GVO' in Jürgen Kühling and Benedikt Buchner (eds) (n 174) para 13. In the case of loose cooperation between companies of the same sector, one will rather have to resort to codes of conduct requiring approval according to Art. 46 (2) lit.e, Art. 40 GDPR.
529 Kuner, 'Art. 47 GDPR' (n 525) 820.
530 GDPR, art 47(1).

troller or processor is the lead supervisory authority and only interlocutor for cross-border processing[531] but must cooperate and exchange information with other supervisory authorities.[532] Under the consistency mechanism, the EDPB is the established EU body, issuing opinions where a competent supervisory authority intends to approve BCRs.[533] Once approval from the EDPB is obtained, no further supervisory authorisation is necessary.[534] This process is an important innovation compared to the situation under the former Directive 95/46, which was characterised by inconsistencies in the individual EU member states.[535] The GDPR brings EU-wide standardisation and simplifies the application of BCRs for a large part of the member states.[536] The EU Commission is allowed to specify the format and procedures for exchanging information between all players for BCRs by implementing acts consistent with the examination procedure set out in Article 93(2) GDPR.[537]

3 Standard Contractual Clauses

SCCs are model contracts, (only) binding to the parties, the controller established in the EU and the recipient (either controller or processor) established in the third country. SCCs do not provide any protection where their content is changed and modified.[538] However, the use of SCCs should not prevent controllers or processors from including the SCCs in a wider contract, e. g. a contract between the processor and another processor, or from adding other clauses or additional safeguards as long as they do not contradict the SCCs or prejudice the fundamental rights or freedoms of the data subject.[539] Instead, the controllers and processors should be encouraged to provide additional safeguards via contractual commitments supplementing SCCs.[540] There are two different types of SCCs: SCCs adopted by the EU Commission (in accordance with the examination procedure

---

531 GDPR, art 56(6).

532 GDPR, art 60.

533 GDPR, art 64(1)(f).

534 GDPR, artt 64(1)(f) and 46(2)(b).

535 Lisa-Marie Lange and Alexander Filip, 'Art. 47 DS-GVO' in Heinrich Amadeus Wolff and Stefan Brink (eds) (n 149) para 17.

536 ibid para 19.

537 GDPR, art 7(3). To the author's knowledge, this has not yet been done.

538 Thomas Zerdick, 'Art. 46 DS-GVO' in Eugen Ehmann and Martin Selmayr (eds), *Beck'scher Kurz-Kommentare: DSGVO* (2nd edn, C.H. Beck 2018) para 10.

539 GDPR, recital 109.

540 GDPR, recital 109. Such contractual commitments are discussed in detail below under III.2.b.

referred to in Article 93(2) GDPR) and SCCs adopted by a member state supervisory authority and approved by the EU Commission (pursuant to the examination procedure referred to in Article 93(2) GDPR)[541].[542] To this date, the latter has not yet been adopted. The EU Commission has adopted two different sets of SCCs based on Article 26(4) of the Directive 95/46: The EU Commission adopted SCCs concerning the transfer of personal data from a controller within the EU to a controller established in a third country (Decision 2001/497/EC)[543] and Decision 2004/915/EC.[544] Furthermore, the EU Commission adopted a set of SCCs for data transfer from controllers within the EU to processors located in third countries (Decision 2010/87/EU).[545] These different sets of SCCs all show structural similarities: The EU Commission's decision, describing the purpose and scope of the SCCs, is followed by the Annex, providing the specific contract to be filled in and signed by the parties.[546] Each set of SCCs includes clauses defining the mutual rights and obligations, including the parties' liability, the obligation to cooperate with supervisory authorities, options for termination and amendment, and defining the rights to be granted to third parties through third-party beneficiaries clauses.[547] The validity of the SCCs for transferring personal data to processors established in third countries (adopted by Decision 2010/87/EU) was challenged in front of the CJEU in *Facebook Ireland and Schrems*. It was eventually declared valid, although SCCs do not bind third-country authorities and thus, do not constitute a sufficient means to ensure effective protection of data transferred to third countries in all situations.[548] Following the *Facebook Ireland and Schrems* judgement, the EU Commission adopted a new set of

---

541 Article 93(2) GDPR refers to Article 5 of the 'Regulation (EU) No 182/2011 (Regulation (EU) No 182/2011 of the EU Parliament and of the Council of 16 February 2011 laying down the rules and general principles concerning mechanisms for control by member states of the EU Commission's exercise of implementing powers', OJ L 55/13.

542 GDPR, art 46(2)(c) and (d).

543 Commission Decision 2001/497/EC on standard contractual clauses for the transfer of personal data to third countries, under Directive 95/46 [2001] OJ L 181/19.

544 Commission Decision 2004/915/EC amending Decision 2001/497/EC as regards the introduction of an alternative set of standard contractual clauses for the transfer of personal data to third countries [2004] OJ L 385/74.

545 Commission Decision (EU) 2010/87 on standard contractual clauses for the transfer of personal data to processors established in third countries under Directive 95/46 of the EU Parliament and of the Council [2010] OJ L 39/5.

546 Pauly, 'Art. 46 DS-GVO' (n 519) para 22.

547 ibid.

548 This will be further discussed in Chapter 4, A.I.

SCCs under the GDPR (Decision 2021/914)[549], discussed in Chapter 4.[550] This new set of SCCs replaced the "old" sets of SCCs three months after entering into force on 21 June 2021. Chapter 4 provides practical guidance for businesses on using SCCs as an alternative transfer tool.

4 Codes of Conduct

An alternative appropriate safeguard may be provided through an approved code of conducts (after this: CoC) pursuant to Article 40 GDPR in combination with binding and enforceable commitment of the controller or processor in the third country to apply those safeguards. CoC are voluntary accountability tools that set out specific data protection rules for categories of controllers and processors.[551] Controllers and processors in third countries shall make binding and enforceable commitments, by contractual or other legally binding instruments, to apply the codes of conduct approved by a supervisory authority[552] and those approved by the EU Commission and with general validity[553].

CoC may be prepared by associations or other bodies representing categories of controllers or processors (so-called code owners), such as trade and representative associations, sectoral organisations, academic organisations, and interest groups.[554] The competent supervisory authority must approve the CoC intended for the transfer. The EDPB must provide an opinion to the draft decision of a supervisory authority to approve a code intended for transfer.[555] The GDPR even provides the option that the EU Commission may adopt an implementing act deciding that a code, intended for transfers and approved by a supervisory authority, has general validity within the EU ("transnational codes").[556] Most importantly, only those codes granted general validity within the EU may be relied upon for framing transfers.[557] To this date, no CoC have been granted general validity

---

549 Commission Implementing Decision (EU) 2021/914 on standard contractual clauses for the transfer of personal data to third countries pursuant to Regulation (EU) 2016/679 of the European Parliament and of the Council [2021] OJ L 199/13 (SCCs Decision 2021).
550 Chapter 4, A.II.
551 EDPB, 'Guidelines 1/2019 on Codes of Conduct and Monitoring Bodies under Regulation 2016/679 – Version 2.0' (2019) 7.
552 GDPR, art 40(5).
553 GDPR, art 40(9).
554 EDPB, 'Guidelines 04/2021 on Codes of Conduct as Tools for Transfers' (2021) para 16.
555 GDPR, artt 40(7) and 64(1)(b).
556 GDPR, art 40(9).
557 GDPR, art 40(3). Also, EDPB, 'Guidelines 04/2021 on Codes of Conduct as Tools for Transfers' (n 554) para 20; Lisa-Marie Lange and Alexander Filip, 'Art. 49 DS-GVO' in Heinrich Amadeus Wolff and Stefan Brink (eds) (n 149) para 53.

by the EU Commission. The EDPB provides a flowchart that details the procedural steps for adopting a code of conduct intended for transfers in different scenarios.[558] The guarantees to be provided under CoC intended for data transfer will be examined in Chapter 4.[559] A monitoring body accredited by the competent supervisory authority in line with Article 41 GDPR must effectively monitor that third country controllers and processors adhere to the CoC and comply with the rules set out in the code.[560] Those monitoring bodies acting could be located either only inside or also outside of the EU provided that the concerned monitoring body has a "main" and "controlling" establishment, which has the "final decision-making power" and can be held accountable in the EU.[561]

5 Certification

Another appropriate safeguard is the approved certification mechanism under Article 42 GDPR, together with binding and enforceable commitments of the controller or processor in the third country, made via contractual or other legally binding instruments to apply safeguards. Certification can be issued by a certification body[562] or the competent supervisory authority based on criteria approved by the competent supervisory authority[563] or by the EDPB[564]. Certification bodies must be accredited by the competent supervisory authority, or the national accreditation body named in accordance with Regulation (EC) No 765/2008 of the EU Parliament and the Council in accordance with EN-ISO/IEC 17065/2012[565].[566] Where the EDPB approves certification criteria, they are classified as "common certification". The approved certification mechanisms are not limited in their scope of application to specific data transfers. Hence, they could be suitable for controllers and processors in third countries receiving personal data regularly from the EU.[567] Also, recital 108 GDPR must be respected. To this date, no

---

558 Annex to EDPB, 'Guidelines 04/2021 on Codes of Conduct as Tools for Transfers' (n 554).
559 Chapter 4, B.II.
560 EDPB, 'Guidelines 1/2019 on Codes of Conduct and Monitoring Bodies under Regulation 2016/679 – Version 2.0' (n 551) 19 et seqq.
561 EDPB, 'Guidelines 04/2021 on Codes of Conduct as Tools for Transfers' (n 554) para 18.
562 GDPR, art 43.
563 GDPR, art 58(3).
564 GDPR, art 63.
565 For example, in Germany the national accreditation body is Deutsche Akkreditierungsstelle (DAkks).
566 GDPR, art 43. The EDPB has published guidelines on accreditation of certification bodies EDPB, 'Guidelines 4/2018 on the Accreditation of Certification Bodies under Article 43 of the General Data Protection Regulation (2016/679) – Version 3.0' (2019).
567 Kugler (n 524) para 905.

certification mechanism to transfer personal data to third countries has been approved.

6 Individual Authorisation of Contractual Clauses

Alternative appropriate safeguards and subjects to the authorisation from the competent supervisory authority may also be (a) contractual clauses between the controller or processor and the controller, processor, or the recipient of the personal data in the third country or (b) provisions included into administrative arrangements between public authorities or bodies which contain enforceable and effective data subject rights.[568] The supervisory authority must apply the consistency mechanism referred to in Article 63 GDPR (Article 46(3) GDPR). Authorisations by a member state or supervisory authority based on Article 26(2) of Directive 95/46 shall remain valid until amended, replaced, or repealed, Article 46(5) GDPR. Due to the authorisation requirements and the consistency mechanism, it is to assume that the appropriate safeguards in Article 46(3) GDPR are of relevance in only a few individual cases.[569]

III Derogation for Specific Situations (Article 49 GDPR)

Article 49(1) GDPR provides derogations where a transfer or a set of transfers of personal data to a third country still can occur in specific scenarios. The Art. 29 Working Party and (later) the EDPB have advocated as best practice a layered approach: data exporters should first endeavour possibilities to frame the transfer with one of the mechanisms established in Article 45 and 46 GDPR and only in their absence use the derogations provided in Article 49(1) GDPR.[570] According to the Art. 29 Working Party and the EDPB, the derogations in Article 49 should be interpreted restrictively.[571] Recital 114 GDPR could be interpreted so that implementing appropriate safeguards should be favoured over using the derogation. It states that in the absence of an adequacy decision, "the controller or processor should make use of solutions that provide data subjects with enforceable and effective rights as regards the processing of their data in the Union once those

---

568 GDPR, art 46(3).
569 Kugler (n 524) para 907.
570 Art. 29 Data Protection Working Party, 'Working Document on a Common Interpretation of Article 26(1) of Directive 95/46/EC of 24 October 1995' (2005) WP 114 9; EDPB, 'Guidelines 2/2018 on Derogations of Article 49 under Regulation 2016/679' (2018) 3 et seq.
571 EDPB, 'Guidelines 2/2018 on Derogations of Article 49 under Regulation 2016/679' (n 570) 5.

data have been transferred so that that they will continue to benefit from fundamental rights and safeguards". Whether this approach is convincing and practicable, especially for transfer based on the data subject's consent, is to be discussed in Chapter 4.[572]

1 Consent

According to Article 49(1)(a) GDPR, transfer of personal data to a third country is permitted if the data subject explicitly gives consent to the proposed transfer to a third country after he or she has been informed of the possible risks of such transfer which might arise due to the absence of an adequacy decision and appropriate safeguards. The GDPR's definition of consent as the personal expression of will and outflow of the core idea of informational self-determination has already been reviewed.[573] In general, the data subject's will must be respected if they consciously decide to send their data to a third country without adequate data protection law and leave it there to the free play of forces.[574] Article 49(1)(a) GDPR goes even further than Article 6(1)(a) GDPR and requires, like Article 9(1)(a) GDPR (consent concerning special categories of personal data), explicit consent, excluding any implied consent form. Blanket consent is not sufficient.[575] The general requirements in Article 7 GDPR apply.

Under Article 49(1)(a) GDPR, before giving an explicit consent, the data subject must initially be informed of the absence of an adequacy decision and appropriate safeguards and further of the possible risks of such transfer for the data subject resulting from the lack of an adequacy decision and appropriate safeguards.[576] The level of detail of the information about the risks given to the data subject is unclear. Some authors state that the intended use of the data and the collection and processing practices in the third country must be described in such detail that the data subject is aware of the possible consequences of transferring his or her data to a country with a different level of protection.[577]

---

572 Chapter 4, C.I. and II.
573 Above under A.IV.3.a.
574 Ambrock and Karg (n 77) 157.
575 Boris P Paal and Lea Katharina Kumkar, 'Datenübermittlungen nach dem Unwirksamwerden des EU-US-Privacy Shield. Bestandsaufnahme und Handlungsempfehlungen nach der EuGH- Entscheidung "Schrems II"' [2020] MMR 733, 737.
576 The general transparency requirements of Articles 13 and 14 GDPR also apply (to all derogations established in Article 49 GDPR).
577 Jens Ambrock, 'Nach Safe Harbor: Schiffbruch des Transatlantischen Datenverkehrs?' [2015] NZA 1493, 1496; Jürgen Kühling and Johanna Heberlein, 'EuGH "reloaded": "unsafe Harbor" USA vs. "Datenfestung" EU' [2016] NVwZ 7, 10; Paal and Kumkar (n 575) 737 et seq.

It is convincing because under Article 49(1)(a) GDPR, the level of protection guaranteed by the European law should in general not be undermined when transferring personal data. [578] A higher level of detail, including information about specific risks from specific use of personal data permitted by national legislation in the specific third country in question, as well as the lack of protection offered by the GDPR, would be required.[579]

2 Other Derogations

According to Article 49(1)(b) GDPR data may also be transferred to a third country "if the transfer is necessary for the performance of a contract between the data subject and the controller or the implementation of pre-contractual measures taken at the data subject's request".[580] Article 49(1)(c) GDPR allows the transfer of personal data to a third country if "the transfer is necessary for the conclusion or performance of a contract concluded in the interest of the data subject between the controller and another natural or legal person". In this constellation, the data subject is not a party to the agreement; however, the contract must be concluded in his interest between the controller and a third party. Article 49(1)(d) GDPR permits a transfer of personal data to a third country where the transfer is "necessary for important reasons of public interest". The public interest must be recognised by the law of the EU or the member state to which the controller is subject.[581] Personal data may further be transferred to a third country if "the transfer is necessary for the establishment, exercise or defence of legal claims" (Article 49(1)(e) GDPR). According to Article 49(1) (f) GDPR, personal data may also be transferred to a third country "if the transfer is necessary in order to protect the vital interest of the data subject or of other persons, where the data subject is physically or legally incapable of giving consent". Article 49(1)(g) GDPR permits the transfer of personal data to a third country "from a register which according to Union or member state law is intended to provide information to the public and which is open to consultation either by the public in general or by any person who can demonstrate a legitimate interest, but only to the extent that the conditions laid down by Union or member

---

578 Kugler (n 524) para 918; Ambrock and Karg (n 77) 157 stating that in cases of data transfer to the US this would mean that key findings on the collection and processing practices of the US intelligence services shall be included.
579 ibid.
580 See also above in A.IV.3.b. regarding Article 6(1)(b) GDPR.
581 GDPR, art 49(4).

state law for consultation are fulfilled in the particular case." It would not be logical to exclude a person established in a third country from consulting a register that can be accessed by anyone in the country or any person with a legitimate interest in doing so.[582] However, a transfer based on this derogation, "shall not involve the entirety of the personal data or entire categories of the personal data contained in the register. Where the register is intended for consultation by persons having a legitimate interest, the transfer shall be made only at the request of those persons or if they are to be the recipients".[583]

The second sentence of Article 49(1) GDPR contains another derogation, which is subsidiary to data transfers based on Article 45 and 46 GDPR and the other derogations in the first sentence of Article 49(1) GDPR.[584] This derogation allows data transfer to take place only "if the transfer is not repetitive, concerns only a limited number of data subjects, is necessary for the purposes of compelling legitimate interest pursued by the controller which are not overridden by interest or rights and freedoms of the data subject, and the controller has assessed all the circumstances surrounding the data transfer and has on the basis of that assessment provided suitable safeguards with regard to the protection of personal data." These derogations will be further reviewed in Chapter 4.[585]

IV Conclusion to B

The lawfulness of data transfer to a third country must be assessed in two steps: In the first step, it must be ensured that the planned transfer complies with the general principles and requirements of the GDPR applicable to the respective processing of personal data. In a second step, it is to be verified whether the specific transfer requirements outlined in Article 44 GDPR and the following articles are met. The GDPR provides various legal bases for the transfer of personal data outside the EU: Adequacy decisions (Article 45 GDPR), appropriate safeguards (Article 46 GDPR) or derogations (Article 49 GPDR).

The transfer based on an adequacy decision provides the most legal certain and comfortable way of exporting data outside the EU. No additional safety measures have to be established by the data exporter. However, there are very high

---

582 Art. 29 Data Protection Working Party, 'Working Document on a Common Interpretation of Article 26(1) of Directive 95/46/EC of 24 October 1995' (n 570) 16.
583 GDPR, art 49(2).
584 See in detail Ambrock and Karg (n 77) 159 et seqq.
585 Chapter 4, C.III.

standards to be fulfilled by a third country desiring an adequacy decision by the Commission. The CJEU requires the third country's legislation to protect personal data "essentially equivalent" to the one guaranteed within the EU by the Charter and the GDPR. The declaration of the *Privacy Shield* agreement as invalid by the Court questions the ability to maintain EU levels of protection where the third country's legislation have "extensive surveillance focus".[586] The judgement demonstrates that the CJEU is unwilling to accept any protection for personal data transferred lower than the one guaranteed in the EU. This finding must be kept in mind for Chapter 3, in which the level of protection of personal data provided in the UK *post*-Brexit will be discussed. Also, as the EU Commission can repeal, amend or suspend the adequacy decision to the extent necessary without retroactive effect, and the CJEU may render an adequacy decision invalid, the data exporter needs to anticipate changes and act accordingly. Especially when the adequacy decision is rendered invalid by the CJEU, there is no transitional period for businesses to change data export provisions.[587]

Compared to data transfers based on an adequacy decision, alternative transfer tools, established in Article 46 and 49 GDPR, require far more supervisory and control measures. These alternative transfer tools will be the focus in Chapter 4. Since the CJEU's ruling in *Data Protection Commissioner v Facebook Ireland and Maximilian Schrems* (after this: *Facebook Ireland and Schrems*), data exporters as well as (subsidiary) the competent supervisory authorities are obliged to fulfil strict oversight – mainly to supervise the legal situation in the recipient country regarding the fundamental rights of the data subject concerned, and where necessary to suspend the data transfer.[588]

C Conclusion to Chapter 2

This chapter gave a comprehensive overview of the European data protection law, provided by the primary law (Articles 7 and 8 CFR), Article 8 ECHR, and the secondary law, the GDPR. It showed that these provisions and their interplay with

---

586 Genna Chuches and Monika Zalnieriute, 'A Groundhog Day in Brussels. Schrems II and International Data Transfer' (*Verfassungsblog*, 16 July 2020) <https://verfassungsblog.de/a-groundhog-day-in-bruessels/>.

587 EDPB, 'Frequently Asked Questions on the Judgement of the Court of Justice of the European Union in Case C-311/18 – Data Protection Commissioner v Facebook Ireland Ltd and Maximillian Schrems' (2020) No 3 <https://edpb.europa.eu/sites/default/files/files/file1/20200724_edpb_faqoncjeuc31118_en.pdf>.

588 In detail in Chapter 4, A.I.3 and 4.

each other guarantee a very high standard of protecting a natural person's data within the EU. The GDPR calls for lawful, fair, and transparent data processing[589], limits the quantity and purpose of data collection, and requires all data controllers or processors to ensure data integrity, security, and accuracy[590] and data can only be stored for a limited period.[591] The GDPR further provides an extensive catalogue of data subject's rights (directly applicable across all member states), including the right to access obtained personal data[592], rectify[593], ask for the erasure[594], and restrict[595] specific data. Member states are obliged to establish an independent data protection authority to guarantee the enforcement of the GDPR.[596] The GDPR is also enforced utilising heavy sanctions in cases of non-compliance.[597]

Generally, the EU fears that its high privacy standards are compromised if personal data are made available to recipients in third countries. Notably, the GDPR has an extraterritorial reach due to the introduction of the marketplace principle.[598] Undermining the protection standard guaranteed within the EU when transferring personal data is not permitted.[599] Where a third country fails to ensure "an adequate level of protection of personal data", transfers are generally not allowed without further requirements.[600] The CJEU defines "adequate" as "essentially equivalent".[601] Only under strict conditions, data exporters can use other transfer tools[602] or exceptionally transfer data in specific situations laid down by the GDPR[603].The European data protection law standard must be kept in mind when assessing the UK's legislation and data protection system in the following. It is the relevant comparator when evaluating whether the UK system provides a data protection standard "essential equivalent" to the one guaranteed within the EU. Also important to consider are the CJEU findings in *Schrems* and *Facebook Ireland and Schrems* concerning previous adequacy decisions.

---

589 GDPR, art 5(1)(a).

590 GDPR, artt 5(1)(b) and (c).

591 GDPR, artt 5(1)(d) and (f).

592 GDPR, art 15.

593 GDPR, art 16.

594 GDPR, art 17.

595 GDPR, art 18.

596 CFR, art 8(3).

597 GDPR, art 83 (Chapter 4, E.).

598 GDPR, art 3(2).

599 GDPR, art 44.

600 GDPR, art 45.

601 *Schrems* (n 71); *Facebook Ireland and Schrems* (n 64).

602 GDPR, art 46.

603 GDPR, art 49.

Chapter 3 The Adequacy of the Level of Data Protection in the UK

On 28 June 2021 the EU Commission adopted two adequacy decisions on the UK, one under the GDPR[604] and another under the LED[605].[606] In order for the EU Commission to adopt an adequacy decision under Article 45(3) GDPR, the UK's legislation must provide an adequate level of protection for personal data transferred from the EU that in the view of the CJEU is defined as "essentially equivalent" [607] to the level within the EU. As it became clear from Chapter 2, the adoption of the adequacy decision by the EU Commission on the UK was not merely a formality but a very complex process. The EU Commission had to examine the relevant UK legislation in detail and assess whether the legal system of the UK would also be effective in its implementation. Although the UK has a unique position as a former member state and the UK's data protection law has evolved hand in hand with the EU's, an adequacy decision could not have been adopted automatically.[608] The EU Commission has undertaken this review and concluded that the UK ensures an adequate level of protection for personal data transferred within the scope of the GDPR from the EU to the UK.[609] It found that the UK data protection framework, consisting of the UK GDPR and the DPA 2018, ensures a level of protection for personal data "essentially equivalent" to the one guaranteed within the EU.[610] Furthermore, the EU Commission concluded that violations could be identified and punished in practice because of sufficient oversight mechanisms and redress avenues in UK law. [611] Legal remedies would be provided to the data subject to obtain access to personal data relating to them and, eventually, the rectification or erasure of such data.[612] Any interference with the fundamental

---

604 UK Adequacy Decision (n 14).

605 UK Adequacy Decision LED (n 15).

606 This study does not deal with the questionof whether the UK should be held to provide adequate protection to personal data transferred to it from the EU for law enforcement purposes (including in relation to access by the UK law enforcement agencies to the relevant EU databases and bodies) under Article 36 LED. Although the LED is based on the same principles as the GDPR and also must be read in the light of the Charter, the adequacy assessment under the LED differs from the one under the GDPR.

607 *Schrems* (n 71) para 73. In detail in Chapter 2, B.I.3.

608 Graux and others (n 504) 29.

609 UK Adequacy Decision (n 14) recital 276.

610 ibid recital 273.

611 ibid recital 274.

612 ibid.

https://doi.org/10.1515/9783110988253-005

rights of the individuals whose personal data are transferred from the EU to the UK by UK public authorities for law enforcement and national security purposes would be limited to what is strictly necessary to achieve the legitimate objective in question, and that effective legal protection against such interference exists.[613]

Since, such an adequacy decision is the only mechanism that allows completely free and unhindered data flow from the EU to the UK, the adoption of the adequacy decision was broadly welcomed, especially by the UK Government and businesses.[614] Yet, the adoption of the adequacy decision has received much criticism. The EDPB called on the EU Commission to study and assess its decision further.[615] Also, Members of the EU Parliament adopted a resolution, requesting the EU Commission to revise its decision.[616]

This Chapter evaluates whether the EU Commission's adequacy decision is coherent and compliant with EU law and the relevant CJEU's case law. Suppose this was not the case, the CJEU would likely declare the adequacy decision towards the UK invalid.[617] A particular focus would be laid on exemptions established in the Data Protection Act 2018 (after this: DPA 2018) (under B.), the Investigatory Powers Act 2016 (after this: IPA 2016) (under C.) and the UK's onward transfer within the transatlantic cooperation framework with the USA (under D.). In the first part (under A.), the fundamental privacy and data protection rights in *post*-Brexit UK is further evaluated.

A Fundamental Rights in the post-Brexit UK

When deciding on adequacy, "the respect for human rights and fundamental freedoms" in the third country must be considered.[618] One of the main reasons

---

613 UK Adequacy Decision (n 14) recital 275.

614 The UK's economy is heavenly dependent on the data flow from the EU. This was already briefly outlined in Chapter 1 and is discussed in more detail in Chapter 5, A.IV.

615 EDPB, 'Opinion 14/2021 Regarding the European Commission Draft Implementing Decision Pursuant to Regulation (EU) 2016/679 on the Adequate Protection of Personal Data in the United Kingdom' (2021).

616 EU Parliament, 'Resolution on the Adequate Protection of Personal Data by the United Kingdom' (2021) (2021/2594(RSP)).

617 Notably, due to the GDPR's extra-territorial scope (Chapter 2, A.IV.1.c.) the GDPR will continue to apply to UK established data controllers and processors when processing personal data relating to the offering of goods or services to individuals in the EU or were monitoring the behaviour of individuals in the Member States ("marketplace principle" pursuant to Article 3(2) GDPR).

618 GDPR, art 45(2).

why the EU Commission found that the UK provides an adequate level of data protection compared to the one within the EU is that the UK has remained a member of the EU privacy "family" by committing to remain a party to the ECHR and the Convention 108.[619] The UK does not have "a codified constitution in an entrenched constitutive document" that governs fundamental rights.[620] Fundamental rights of individuals have been developed through common law, statutes, such as the Magna Carta, the Bill of Rights of 1689 and Human Rights Act 1998 (HRA 1998), and international treaties, in particular the ECHR, which the UK ratified in 1951.[621] Also, the Charter played a significant role in shaping and evolving fundamental rights in the last years. In the following, the data subject's fundamental rights in *post*-Brexit UK are looked at closely. In the course of this, the role of the Charter (under I.), the ECHR and the HRA 1998 (under II,), the common law (under III.) and other international commitments (under IV.) in *post*-Brexit UK are examined. Finally, the proposed British Bill of Rights is reviewed (under V.).

I Role of the Charter in post-Brexit UK

The following focuses on the Charter's role, in particular the role of Articles 7, 8 and 47 CFR, in *post*-Brexit UK (under 3.). Crucial in this context is the EUWA 2018, which legislated the preservation of EU law in UK law after Brexit (under 2.). First, the former role of the Charter in the UK prior to Brexit is looked at (under 1.).

1 Role of the Charter in the UK prior to Brexit
The UK always had a somewhat strained relationship with the Charter in the past.[622] The UK Government constantly opposed the Charter's originally planned binding character (under the Constitutional Treaty) and was concerned about the

---

619 EU Commission, 'Data Protection: European Commission Launches Process on Personal Data Flows to UK' (2021) Press release of 19 February 2021 <https://ec.europa.eu/commission/presscorner/detail/en/ip_21_661>.
620 cf UK Adequacy Decision (n 14) recital 9.
621 ibid.
622 Catherine Barnard, 'So Long, Farewell, Auf Wiedersehen, Adieu: Brexit and the Charter of Fundamental Rights' (2019) 82 Mod. L. Rev. 350.

effect of solidarity provisions, including social and economic rights on its labour market policies.[623]

a Protocol (No 30)

The UK's relationship with the Charter was sharpened by the content of the Protocol (No 30).[624] Its adoption was supposed to protect the UK and Poland from consequences of the changes of status caused by the Lisbon Treaty, which gave the Charter the "same legal value" as the leading EU Treaties[625].[626] The UK Government not only "feared" the CJEU's extensive interpretation of the "scope of Community law"[627] but also the role of general principles, a source of EU law, which would be even superior to positive primary domestic law.[628] The fear was that any principle of social rights valid in one member state could become a general principle.[629]

While the former UK Government under *Tony Blair* presented the Protocol (No 30) as an "opt-out" from the Charter, [630] this point of view was not shared

---

623 Rosalind English, 'The EU Charter: Are we in or out?' (*UK Human Rights Blog*, 1 March 2011) <https://ukhumanrightsblog.com/2011/03/01/the-eu-charter-are-we-in-or-out/>.
624 Article 1(1) of Protocol (No 30) states: "The Charter does not extend the ability of the Court of Justice of the European Union, or any court or tribunal of Poland or of the United Kingdom, to find that the laws, regulations or administrative provisions, practices or action of Poland or of the United Kingdom are inconsistent with the fundamental rights, freedoms and principles that it reaffirms." According to Article 2(2) of Protocol (No 30) "[t]o the extent that a provision of the Charter refers to national laws and practices, it shall only apply to Poland or the United Kingdom to the extent that the rights or principles that it contains are recognized in the law or practices of Poland or of the United Kingdom."
625 cf Treaty of Lisbon, art 6(1).
626 cf former Prime Minister *Tony Blair* stating to the Liaison Committee "we will not accept a treaty that allows the charter of fundamental rights to change UK law in any way", House of Commons, European Scrutiny Committee, Thirty-Fifth Report of Session 2019–21, 'Documents Considered by the Committee on 3 February 2021', HC Paper 229 para 52 <https://committees.parliament.uk/publications/4604/documents/46687/default/>.
627 Judgement of 18 June 1991, *ERT v DEP*, C-260/89, EU:C:1991:254.
628 Vojtech Belling, 'Supranational Fundamental Rights or Primacy of Sovereignty? Legal Effects of the So-Called Opt-Out from the EU Charter of Fundamental Rights' (2012) 18 ELJ 251, 254.
629 Judgement of 22 November 2005, *Mangold*, C-144/04, EU:C:2005:709.
630 See Barnard (n 622) 355 et seqq. who gives an overview of the UK government's display of the Protocol (No 30) and its perception in the press. However, later, the House of Lords' European Scrutiny Committee confirmed that the Protocol (No 30) does not provide an 'opt-out' (cf House of Lords, European Union Committee, Tenth Report of Session 2007–08, 'The Treaty of Lisbon: An Impact Assessment', HL Paper 62-I para 5.87 <https://publications.parliament.uk/pa/ld200708/ldselect/ldeucom/62/62.pdf>).

by the prevailing view in literature.[631] The CJEU too disagreed with the Government's interpretation and clarified that "Protocol (No 30) does not call into question the applicability of the Charter in the United Kingdom or in Poland".[632] Article 1(1) of Protocol (No 30) solely clarified the normative content of Article 51 CFR.[633] It did not shift powers at the expense of the UK or Poland or extended the scope of application of EU law beyond the control of the EU established in the Treaties, nor did it question the validity of the Charter for the UK and Poland[634].[635] Article 2 of Protocol (No 30) reinforced Article 52(4) and (6) CFR, which stipulate that the Charter rights must be "interpreted in harmony" with the constitutional tradition of the member states, and national laws and practices must be taken into complete account.[636] The Protocol (No 30) does not provide the UK and Poland with a "general opt-out" from the Charter. Article 2 of Protocol (No 30) exclusively applies to provisions of the Charter that reference national laws and practices.[637] In the end, Article 1(2) and Article 2 of Protocol (No 30) are commonly understood to have clarified existing provisions of the Charter.

b UK Courts and the Charter

Furthermore, it appears that the Charter did not have a significant impact on the UK court's interpretation of national law implementing EU law.[638] *Catherine Barnard* bases this theory on the fact that from 1 December 2009 to 1 December 2018, only 25 preliminary references by a referring UK court expressively asked questions concerning an issue with the Charter.[639] In particular, the Supreme Court made only little reference to the Charter.[640] Consequently, one could say that

---

631 Steve Peers, 'The "Opt-out" That Fell to Earth: The British and Polish Protocol Concerning the EU Charter of Fundamental Rights' (2012) 12 Human rights Law Review 375, 378 et seqq. who gives an overview of the academic comments on the Protocol and provides respective references.
632 Judgement of 21 December 2011, *N.S and Others*, C-411/10 and C-493/10, EU:C:2011:865, para 119.
633 ibid para 120.
634 Judgement of 30 April 2014, *Pfleger*, C-390/12, EU:C:2014:281.
635 Opinion of Advocate General *Trstenjak* of 22 September 2011, *N.S and Others*, C-411/10 and C-493/10 EU:C:2011:611, para 169.
636 ibid.
637 ibid para 176.
638 Barnard (n 622) 358.
639 ibid Annex 1.
640 ibid 358 et seq. referring to *Pham v Secretary of State for the Home Department* [2015] UKSC 19 [42] and to *R (HS2 Action Alliance Limited) v The Secretary of State for Transport* [2014] UKSC 3, [2014] 1 WLR 324 [106].

the loss of the Charter would only have little impact on the UK courts.[641] Nevertheless, many of the cases in which UK courts referred to the Charter or issued preliminary references to the CJEU were related to the right to the protection of personal data.[642] In protecting personal data, the Charter plays a more significant role before the British higher courts.[643] Thus, the loss of the Charter could have a noticeable impact on data protection.

2 European Union (Withdrawal) Act 2018

The EUWA 2018 repealed the European Communities Act from 1972[644] (after this: the ECA). The ECA made the legal provisions of the UK's accession to the three European Communities (EEA, Euratom, ECSC).[645] The EUWA 2018 then terminated the ability of EU institutions to legislate for the UK after Brexit. It came wholly into effect on 31 January 2020. The EUWA 2018 preserved (most of) the existing EU law when leaving the EU, converting it into domestic law to guarantee legal certainty and avoid chaos resulting from sudden excising the vast part of EU-derived law from the statute book (so-called "retained EU law"). Below, the most relevant provisions of the EUWA 2018 are reviewed.

a Acquis of EU Law

Sections 2–4 EUWA 2018 establish the mechanism whereby the *acquis* of EU law is converted into domestic UK law. These provisions provide "the architectural heart" of the EUWA 2018. According to Section 3(1) EUWA 2018, direct EU legislation is implemented in domestic law. Direct EU legislation includes any EU regulation, decision, or tertiary legislation[646] as it has effect in EU law immediately before IP completion day[647], so far as operative immediately before IP comple-

---

641 Barnard (n 622) 360.

642 Cian C Murphy, 'Bulletin on the EU Charter of Fundamental Rights: An Introduction: Part 2' [2016] EHRLR 273, 278.

643 *Secretary of State for the Home Department v Davis* [2015] EWCA Civ 1185, [2016] HRLR 1; *Google Inc v Vidal-Hall* [2015] EWCA Civ 311; *The Christian Institute and Others v The Scottish Ministers* [2015] CSIH 64.

644 The EUWA 2018 is available at the following link <https://www.legislation.gov.uk/ukpga/1972/68/contents> accessed 9 June 2022.

645 EUWA 2018, s 6.

646 As far as the legislation is not an exempt EU instrument, nor an EU decision addressed only toa member state other than the UK, where effect is not reproduced in an enactment to which Section 2(1) applies (Section 3(2)(a) EUWA 2018).

647 IP completion day was on 31 December 2020. The EUWA 2018 was amended by the European Union (Withdrawal Agreement) Act 2020. The latter incorporates the Withdrawal Agree-

tion day. Accordingly, the GDPR, including its recitals,[648] has been incorporated into UK national law. Hence, under the EUWA 2018 the GDPR continues to have effect in the UK upon Brexit.[649] Section 4 EUWA 2018 states that other directly effective EU law continues to apply. Furthermore, "EU-derived domestic legislation" is saved by Section 2 EUWA 2018. Retained EU law may be amended by secondary legislation, "as the Minister considers appropriate to prevent, remedy or mitigate (a) any failure of retained EU law to operate effectively, or (b) any other deficiency in retained EU law arising from withdrawal" (so-called Henry VIII[650]-clause).[651]

b Principle of Supremacy

Under the principle of supremacy, a provision of national law that falls within the scope of EU law and infringes a fundamental right of the Charter or a general principle of EU law must be disapplied by national courts.[652] Under the EUWA 2018, the principle of supremacy continues to apply "so far as relevant to the interpretation, disapplication or quashing of any enactment or the rule of law passed or made before IP completion day".[653] It will however, "not apply to any enactment or rule of law passed or made on or after IP completion day"[654]. The principle of supremacy applies to modifications made on or after the IP completion day of any enactment or the rule of law passed or made before

---

ment between the UK and the EU into domestic law once the UK has formally left the EU on 29 March 2019. The European Union (Withdrawal Agreement) Act 2020 provided for an "implementation period" until 31 December 2020 ("IP completion day"), during which the UK remained bound by the ECA.

648 Explanatory Notes to the EUWA 2018, para 83.

649 For more information on the GDPR in a *post*-Brexit UK see below in the introduction to B.

650 The expression is a reference to King Henry VIII's supposed preference for legislating directly by proclamation rather than through Parliament, cf UK Parliament, Glossary, "Henry VIII clauses" <https://www.parliament.uk/site-information/glossary/henry-viii-clauses/> accessed on 13 March 2022.

651 EUWA 2018, s 8(1); limitations to these delegated powers are established in Section 8(7) EUWA 2018.

652 Judgement of 5 February 1963, *Van Gend en Loos v Administratie der Belastingen*, C-26/62, EU:C:1963:1; Judgement of 15 July 1964, *Costa/E.N.E.L.*, C-6–64, EU:C:1964:66; Judgement of 17 December 1970, *Internationale Handelsgesellschaft mbH v Einfuhr- und Vorratsstelle fur Getreide und Futtermittel*, C-11/70, EU:C:1970:114; Judgement of 9 March 1978, *Amministrazione delle finanze dello Stato v Simmenthal*, C-106–77, EU:C:1978:49; Judgement of 13 November 1990, *Marleasing v Comercial Internacional de Alimentación*, C-106–89, EU:C:1990:395.

653 EUWA 2018, s 5(2).

654 EUWA 2018, s 5(1).

IP completion day if the application of the supremacy principle is consistent with the intention of the modification.[655]

However, Section 5(4) EUWA 2018 explicitly excludes the Charter rights from being incorporated into domestic law. Consequently, this also applies to Articles 7, 8 and 47 CFR. According to Section 5(5) EUWA 2018, this exclusion, however, should not affect "the retention in domestic law [...] of any fundamental rights or principles which exist irrespective of the Charter (and references to the Charter in any case law are, so far as necessary for this purpose, to be read as if they were references to any corresponding retained fundamental rights or principles)." The corresponding Explanatory Note inclines a broad interpretation of the provision, stating that "the Charter did not create any new rights but rather reaffirmed rights and principles which already existed in EU law."[656] Taking this interpretation into regard, removing the Charter does not hinder converted EU law to be interpreted in light of those "underlying rights and principles".[657] Underlying rights and principles are "substantive rights" which otherwise have existed and exist elsewhere in EU law and are converted into UK law. The Explanatory Note mirrors the view of the UK Government referring to the Preamble to Protocol (No 30)[658], which states that the Charter was intended to make fundamental rights that already existed in EU law more visible by bringing them together in a single document.[659] This interpretation was strongly criticised. If the Charter only "reaffirmed" rights that were already binding on actions, the UK "would [only] benefit from such codification as an easy, and accessible source of rights, listed and clarified, for the interpretation and application of retained law."[660]

General principles of EU law can be part of domestic law, provided that the CJEU thus recognised them before IP completion day.[661] However, there is no right of action in domestic law, on or after IP completion day, based on a failure

---

655 EUWA 2018, s 5(3).

656 Explanatory Note to the EUWA 2018, para 106.

657 Explanatory Note to the EUWA 2018, para 107; also Barnard (n 622) 363.

658 Consolidated version of the Treaty on the Functioning of the European Union – Protocol (No 30) on the application of the Charter of Fundamental Rights of the European Union to Poland and to the United Kingdom, OJ C 115/313 and 115/314.

659 Department for Exiting the European Union, 'Legislating for the United Kingdom's Withdrawal from the European Union' (2017) CM 9446 2.21–2.25 <https://assets.publishing.service.gov.uk/gover nment/uploads/system/uploads/attachment_data/file/604514/Great_repeal_bill_-white_paper_ print.pdf>.

660 Joelle Grogan, 'Rights and Remedies at Risk: Implications of the Brexit Process on the Future of Rights in the UK' [2019] PL 683, 692.

661 EUWA 2018, sch 1 para 2.

to comply with general principles of EU law.[662] On or after IP completion day, no court or tribunal or other public authority may disapply or quash any enactment or the other rule of law, quash any conduct or otherwise decide that it is unlawful because it is incompatible with any general principle of EU law[663]. This provision intensifies the division established by Section 5(4) EUWA 2018.[664]

Ultimately, according to Schedule 1 Paragraph 4 EUWA 2018, the rule regarding damages in the *Francovich* decision[665] will not further apply.

These provisions impact the level and scope of protection of the rights guaranteed in Articles 7, 8 and 47 CFR. The extent of this impact is discussed below.[666]

c Interpretation by UK courts

Section 6 EUWA 2018 addresses how the retained EU law, including the GDPR, must be interpreted by UK courts.[667] A UK court or tribunal is still bound by any principles laid down or any decisions made before IP completion day by the CJEU, and it can refer any matter to it on or after IP completion day.[668] The courts and the tribunals may regard any decision by the CJEU or any other EU body, "so far as it is relevant to any matter before the court or the tribunal."[669] While the

---

662 EUWA 2018, sch 1 para 3(1).

663 EUWA 2018, sch 1 para 3(2).

664 Mark Elliot and Stephen Tierney, 'Political Pragmatism and Constitutional Principle: The European Union (Withdrawal) Act 2018' [2018] PL 11.

665 Judgement of 19 November 1991, *Francovich and Bonifaci v Italy*, C-6/90 and C-9/90, EU: C:1991428.

666 3.

667 According to Section 6(7) EUWA 2018, "retained case law" means retained domestic case law and retained EU case law; "retained domestic case law" "means any principles laid down by, and any decisions of, a court or tribunal in the United Kingdom, as they have effect immediately before IP completion day and so far as they— relate to anything to which Section 2, 3 or 4 applies, and are not excluded by Section 5 or Schedule 1", "retained EU case law" means any principles laid down by, and any decisions of, the European Court, as they have effect in EU law immediately before IP completion day and so far as they – relate to anything to which Section 2, 3 or 4 applies, and are not excluded by Section 5 or Schedule 1, "retained EU law" means anything which, on or after IP completion day, continues to be, or forms part of, domestic law by virtue of Section 2, 3 or 4 or Subsection (3) or (6) above (as that body of law is added to or otherwise modified by or under this Act or by other domestic law from time to time); "retained general principles of EU law" "means the general principles of EU law, as they have effect in EU law immediately before IP completion day and so far as they— relate to anything to which Section 2, 3 or 4 applies, and are not excluded by Section 5 or Schedule 1".

668 EUWA 2018, s 6(1).

669 EUWA 2018, s 6(2). In the draft, clause 6(2) provided: "A court or a tribunal need not have regard to anything done on or after IP completion day by the European Court, another EU entity

Supreme Court or the High Court are not bound to retained EU case law,[670] lower courts must treat EU case law as having equivalent status to Supreme Court decisions, and must interpret retained law "in accordance with retained case law and any retained general principles of EU law".[671] The same applies to retained EU law modified on or after IP completion day, provided this is "consistent with the intention of the modifications".[672] Nevertheless, when deciding whether to depart from retained EU case law, the Supreme Court or the High Court must apply the same test as it would apply in determining whether to pass from its case law.[673]

3 Articles 7, 8 and 47 CFR in the post-Brexit UK

The UK Government assured that the removal of the Charter in accordance with Section 5(4) EUWA 2018 would not negatively affect the level of protection of fundamental rights.[674] In the following, it is examined if and how EUWA 2018 affected the status quo of rights guaranteed by Articles 7, 8 and 47 CFR in the UK.

a Status as General Principles

In order to play any role in the *post*-Brexit UK, the rights guaranteed in Articles 7, 8 and 47 CFR must apply irrespective of the Charter.[675] This would be the case if these rights already had the status as general principles of EU law prior to the entry into force of the Charter.[676] According to Article 6(3) TEU "[f]undamental rights, as guaranteed by the European Convention for the Protection of Human Rights and Fundamental Freedoms and as they result from the constitutional traditions common to the Member States, shall constitute general principles of the

---

or the EU but may do so if it considers it appropriate to do so." This vagueness and lack of clarity was largely criticised by senior judges and the Constitution Committee (House of Lord, Select Committee on the Constitution, Nineth Report of Session 2017–19, 'European Union (Withdrawal) Bill', HL Paper 69 paras 134 et seq. and 137 <https://publications.parliament.uk/pa/ld201719/ldselect/ldconst/69/69.pdf>).

670 EUWA 2018, s 6(4).

671 EUWA 2018, s 6(3).

672 EUWA 2018, s 6(6).

673 EUWA 2018, s 6(5).

674 Department for Exiting the European Union, 'Legislating for the United Kingdom's Withdrawal from the European Union' (n 659) 2.25.

675 EUWA 2018, s 5(5).

676 cf EUWA 2018, sch 1 para 3(1).

Union's law." Those fundamental rights were eventually incorporated into the Charter.[677]

The rights constituted in Articles 7 and 8 CFR initially derived from Article 8 ECHR.[678] Furthermore, both rights result from member states' constitutions: While the right to respect for privacy was reflected in most member states' constitutions before the entry of force of the Charter,[679] this was not the case for the right to the protection of personal data. Article 8 CFR was an "innovative" provision.[680] However, there were already six member states' constitutions that explicitly protected personal data in 2000.[681] Other member states' constitutions guaranteed the right to protect personal data as a partial guarantee of the right to protect private life[682] or as an expression of the right to the protection of communication[683]. In the German constitution, the right to the protection of personal data is covered by the general right of personality, in its manifestation of a person's right to informational self-determination.[684]

Furthermore, the right to an effective remedy, constituted in Article 47(1) CFR, derives from Article 13 ECHR, while the right to a fair hearing, established in Article 47(2) CFR, corresponds to Article 6(1) ECHR.[685] Regarding the right to legal aid, constituted in Article 47(3) CFR, the explanations refer to the ECtHR's judgement in its case *Airey v Ireland*, in which the Strasbourg Court held that Article 6(1) ECHR may require the state to provide legal aid where necessary for adequate access to a court.[686] A third of the EU member states guarantees the right to an effective remedy (Article 47(1) CFR).[687] The right to an independent

---

677 Judgement of 1 March 2011, *Association Belge des Consommateurs Test-Achats and Others*, C-236/09, EU:C:2011:100, para 16.

678 Kingreen (n 83) para 2.

679 A respective list can be found in Norbert Bernsdorff, 'Art. 7 GRCh' in Jürgen Meyer and Sven Höscheidt (eds) (n 58) para 2.

680 Bernsdorff (n 58) para 12.

681 Austria (s 1), Finland (s 10(1), second sentence), Netherlands (art 10), Spain (art 18(4)), Sweden (s 22(2)) and Portugal (art 35). The constitutions of Croatia (art 37), Hungary (art IV(2) and (3)), Slovakia (artt 19(3) and 22), Slovenia (art 38) and Poland (art 51) (as "new member states") also explicitly provide the right to the protection of personal data.

682 Belgium (art 22) and Greece (art 9(1), second sentence)

683 Denmark (s 72, second sentence), Estonia (s 43) and Italy (art 15).

684 Grundgesetz (German Basic Law), artt 1(1) and 2(1); BVerfG, 15 December 1983 – 1 BvR 209/83, 269/83, 362/83, 420/83, 440/83, 484/93 = BVerfGE 65, 1 (*Volkszählung*).

685 Explanations relating to the Charter of Fundamental Rights, OJ C 303/29.

686 Explanations relating to the Charter of Fundamental Rights, OJ C 303/30.

687 Germany (art 19(4)), Estonia (s 15), Finland (s 21), Lithuania (art 30), Portugal (art 20(5)), Romania (art 21(1)), Slovakia (art 46(1)), Slovenia (art 23), Spain (art 24(1)), Czech Republic (art 36(1)).

tribunal[688] and a public hearing[689] (Article 47(2) CFR) is represented in almost all of the member states' constitutions; the principle of fairness[690] and the right to a hearing within a reasonable time[691] (Article 47(2) CFR) is only found in comparably few member states' constitutions. The latter also applies to the constitutional guarantee of legal aid.[692] Consequently, the rights protected in Articles 7, 8 and 47 CFR are general principles of the EU's law and would, within the meaning of Section 5(5) EUWA 2018, exist irrespective of the Charter.[693]

According to Schedule 1 Paragraph 2 EUWA 2018, general principles of EU law can only be part of domestic law *post*-Brexit, provided they were thus recognised by the CJEU "in a case decided before IP completion day (whether or not it is an essential part of the decision)". The CJEU had already recognised the fundamental importance of protecting personal data as a general principle before the coming into force of the Charter in its early judgement *Stauder v Ulm*.[694] This recognition continued in the CJEU's subsequent judgements before the Charter.[695] The right to a private and family life was also recognised as a general principle of EU law before the Charter in *National Panasonic*.[696] The CJEU recognised the right to effective legal protection in Article 47 CFR as a general principle of EU law, among other things in its *Gavieiro Gavieiro and Iglesias Torres*

---

688 Belgium (art 151 s 1), Bulgaria (art 117(2)), Germany (art 97(1) and art 101), Estonia (s 146), Finland (s 3), France (art 64), Greece (art 87(1)), Ireland (art 35(2)), Italy (art 104), Lithuania (artt 31 and 109), Malta (art 39(1)), Austria (art 87), Poland (artt 45(1), 173 and 178(1)), Portugal (art 203), Romania (art 123(2)), Slovakia (art 46(1)), Slovenia (art 23 and 125), Spain (art 117(1)), Czech Republic (artt 81 and 82(1)), Hungary (artt 50(3) and 57(1)).

689 Belgium (artt 148 and 149), Bulgaria (art 121(3)), Denmark (s 65), Estonia (s 24), Finland (s 21), Greece (art 93(2)), Ireland (art 34(1)), Lithuania (artt 31 and 117), Luxembourg (artt 88 and 89), Malta (art 39(3)), Netherlands (art 121), Austria (art 90), Poland (art 45(1)), Portugal (art 206), Romania (art 126), Sweden (chapter 2 s 11), Slovakia (art 48(2)), Slovenia (art 24), Spain (artt 24(2) and 120(1) and (3)), der Czech Republic (art 96(2)), Hungary (art 57(1)), Cyprus (art 154).

690 Bulgaria (art 121(1)), Italy (art 111), Malta (art 39(1)).

691 Bulgaria (art 31(1)), Malta (art 39(1)), Portugal (art 20(4)), Sweden (chapter 2, s 9), Slovakia (art 48(2)), Spain (art 24(2)).

692 Malta (art 39(6)(c)), Portugal (art 20(1)), Spain (art 119), der Czech Republic (art 40(3)), Cyprus (art 30(3)(d)).

693 See also Andrew Murray 'Data Transfers between the EU and UK Post Brexit?' (2017) 7 IDPL 149, 154 who takes a different view on the status of the right to the protection of personal data as a general principle.

694 Judgement of 12 November 1969, *Stauder v City of Ulm*, C-29/69, EU:C:1969:57, para 7.

695 Instead of many: Judgement of 7 November 1985, *Adams v Commission*, C-145/83, EU:C:1985:448, para 34; Judgement of 14 September 2000, *Fisher*, C-369/98, EU:C:2000:443, paras 32 et seq.

696 Judgement of 26 June 1980, *National Panasonic v Commission*, C-136/79, EU:C:1980:169.

judgement.[697] However, in its decisions since 2009, the CJEU explicitly refers to the Charter rights and not to fundamental rights as general principles.[698] Consequently, it could be assumed that the general principles are "frozen" since the introduction of the Charter in 2009 and that only the Charter rights evolved further with the CJEU case law.[699] On the contrary, the Explanatory Note to Section 5(5) EUWA 2018 inclines a broad interpretation[700] so that it can be concluded that the respective general principles evolved further with the corresponding Charter rights.

In summary, the rights guaranteed in Articles 7, 8 and 47 CFR are recognised as general principles and may be part of domestic law in accordance with Schedule 1 Paragraph 2 EUWA 2018.

b Reduced Level of Protection

However, the EUWA 2018's reduction of Charter rights' status as fundamental rights to general principles also leads to significant differences regarding the level and scope of protection of the rights guaranteed in Articles 7, 8 and 47 CFR.

First, it is very likely that discrepancies between interpretations in the UK and the EU regarding the general principles or other retained EU law (such as the GDPR) occur: On the one side, British courts and tribunals may still regard the case law under the Charter in order to contour the general principles of law *post*-Brexit so far as relevant. Furthermore, any question as to the meaning of retained EU law must, so far as that law is unmodified, be determined in UK courts following the relevant pre-exit general principle of EU law and applicable case law.[701] Where it is possible to do so, retained EU law needs to be read consistently with general principles of EU law. On the other side, the CJEU case law after the IP completion day has no binding effect on British courts or tribunals. Hence, people in the UK lose potential additional protection that may arise from the future interpretation of the Charter rights.[702] According to *Aysem Diker Vanberg* and *Maelya Maunick*, these discrepancies might confuse and adversely af-

---

697 Judgement of 22 December 2010, *Gavieiro Gavieiro and Iglesias Torres*, C-444/09 and C-456/09, EU:C:2010:819, para 75.
698 Barnard (n 622) 363.
699 Explanatory Note to the EUWA 2018, paras 106 et seq.
700 Explanatory Note to the EUWA 2018, para 106; Barnard (n 622) 363.
701 EUWA 2018, s 6(3).
702 House of Lords, Committee Stage, 'Supplementary Note on the Impact of the Loss of the EU Charter of Fundamental Rights' (2018) 6.

fect the UK securing a (future) adequacy decision.[703] However, other third countries – to which the EU Commission adopted an adequacy decision – are in no way bound by the case law of the CJEU and its interpretation of Article 8 CFR or other fundamental rights. Also, Section 6(2) EUWA 2018 explicitly accords the UK courts discretion to take *post*-exit CJEU rulings into account. This provision gives UK courts legitimacy to draw on CJEU case law and could "help to shield them from criticism from those who might disapprove of such linkage".[704] At this stage no relevant *post*-Brexit case law in this context exist. The EU Commission is obligated to monitor any developments in this matter under Article 45(4) GDPR.

Second, the principle of supremacy and justiciability will continue to apply only to a limited extent: Where directly enforceable rights exist (direct EU legislation or domestic legislation implementing EU obligations), it will still be possible to bring a claim to a court. Courts will still disapprove legislation due to incompatibility with that right, provided it was passed or made before IP completion day.[705] However, this excludes general principles: including the fundamental rights of the Charter. These general principles cannot be used as a cause of action, nor can they be the ground for annulment or disapplication of any enactment, the rule of law or other conduct *post*-Brexit.[706] In other words, the Charter rights are unenforceable in the UK.[707] Instead, general principles are retained only for interpretative purposes.[708] The rationale behind the limited effect of EU general principles in the UK[709] is to collude with parliamentary sovereignty.[710] However, according to *Paul Craig*, this only explains the principle of supremacy in UK primary legislation but not the preclusion of recourse to the general principle of law in judicial review actions.[711] In this way, the protection of fundamental rights, including personal data protection, is highly weakened. It remains to be seen what interpretative weight British courts accord-

---

[703] Aysem Diker Vanberg and Maelya Maunick, 'Data Protection in the UK Post-Brexit: The Only Certainty Is Uncertainty' (2018) 32 Int. Rev.Law Comput. 190, 194.

[704] Paul Craig, 'Constitutional Principle, the Rule of Law and Political Reality: The European Union (Withdrawal) Act 2018' (2019) 82 Mod. L. Rev. 319, 335 et seq.

[705] EUWA 2018, s 4.

[706] EUWA 2018, sch 1 para 3.

[707] House of Lords, Committee Stage (n 702) 5.

[708] Department for Exiting the European Union, 'Charter of Fundamental Rights of the EU – Rights by Rights Analysis' (2017) 5 <https://assets.publishing.service.gov.uk/government/up loads/system/uploads/attachment_data/file/664891/05122017_Charter_Analysis_FINAL_VER SION.pdf>.

[709] This limited effect is constituted in Schedule 1 Paragraph 3(b) EUWA 2018.

[710] Craig (n 704) 333.

[711] ibid.

ing to Section 6(3) EUWA 2018 accord to general principles of law.[712] The UK Government took the view that there are other domestic routes of challenges, including a claim that commences as a judicial review, a claim on the grounds of an incompatibility[713] with the corresponding right protected under HRA 1998[714] or a claim under common law.[715;] In this way, executive action and secondary legislation could be struck down by the court due to a successful judicial review or under the HRA 1998.[716] Whether this is the case is discussed below.[717]

Third, Schedule 1 Paragraph 4 EUWA 2018 constitutes that there is no right in domestic law on or after IP completion day to damages for breach of any rights, presumably fundamental rights, in accordance with the rule in *Francovich and Bonifaci v Italy* [718]: Any misapplication or misinterpretation of EU law, even pre-Brexit that could cause a damages claim will not be available. The loss of the *Francovich* principle "weakens both an avenue for remedy and also a powerful preventive mechanism".[719] However, the *Francovich* principle is not of high practical relevance. Claimants must overcome serious impediments: Not only must they convince a court that there has been a breach of their Charter rights by a member states authority acting within the scope of EU law but also that this has caused them to suffer damage. They must also convince the court that the breach of EU law was "sufficiently serious"[720], which in practice is somewhat dif-

---

712 Craig (n 704) 333.
713 Yet, in the UK law order, the declaration of incompatibility does not affect the validity, operation or enforcement of the law (cf under II.2.).
714 The question whether the HRA 1998 provides the same level of protection of fundamental rights as the Charter is assessed below under II.
715 In *R (UNISON) v Lord Chancellor* [2017] UKSC 51 [64] the Supreme Court held that "the right to access to justice [...] has long been deeply embedded in [the UK's] constitutional law". The common law also recognizes the right to procedural fairness, due process and access to justice. The latter have their root in the Magna Carta. See for common law in more detail under III.
716 Department for Exiting the European Union, 'Charter of Fundamental Rights of the EU – Rights by Rights Analysis' (n 708) 23 et seq.
717 A.II. and A.III.
718 *Francovich and Bonifaci v Italy* (n 665) in which the CJEU established that member states could be liable to pay compensation who suffered a loss by reason of the member state's failure to transpose an EU directive into national law.
719 Grogan (n 660) 690.
720 Sufficiently serious breach was not explicitly mentioned in the *Francovich* decision but the later Judgement of 5 March 1996, *Brasserie du Pêcheur v Bundesrepublik Deutschland and The Queen / Secretary of State for Transport, ex parte Factortame and Others*, C-46/93 and C-48/93, ECLI:EU:C:1996:79.

ficult.[721] Consequently, the negative impact of this loss of the *Francovich* principle, within *post*-Brexit UK, is decidedly insignificant in practice.

4 Conclusion to I

The rights guaranteed in the Charter will only play an insignificant role in the UK as general principles of EU law. General principles only serve interpretative purposes, especially shown by the limitation of justiciability, which constitutes that those general principles are not enforceable in front of UK courts. The UK Government promised that the Brexit process would not have a negative impact on fundamental rights. This position downplayed the relevance of the Charter in the framework of rights protection in the UK and has argued that existing provisions in the common law and the HRA 1998 will provide sufficient, if not equivalent, safeguards.[722] Whether the HRA 1998 provides an equivalent level of protection is assessed now.

II ECHR and Human Rights Act 1998

The UK has established a dualist system due to the HRA 1998 which brings the ECHR rights "out of the Strasbourg context by creating "Convention rights" enforceable in domestic law".[723] With the loss of the fundamental rights of the Charter, the focus lies even more on the ECHR and the HRA 1998 in the UK. The HRA 1998 incorporates most of the ECHR into domestic law.[724] The Department for Exiting the EU analysis stated that eighteen Charter rights "correspond, entirely or largely, to articles" of the ECHR and are "as a result, protected both internationally and, through the Human Rights Act 1998 and devolution statutes".[725] The following will elaborate whether the ECHR and the HRA 1998 provide equal and adequate protection to the one guaranteed within the Charter. The focus will be on the protection of personal data and the judicial rights.

---

721 In detail Tobias Lock, 'Is Private Enforcement of EU Law through State Liability a Myth?: An Assessment 20 Years after Francovich' (2012) 49 CML Rev 1675.
722 Grogan (n 660) 683.
723 Richard S Kay, 'The European Convention on Human Rights and the Control of Private Law' [2005] European Human Rights Law Review 466, 478.
724 More information below under II.2.
725 Department for Exiting the European Union, 'Charter of Fundamental Rights of the EU – Rights by Rights Analysis' (n 708).

1 UK and ECHR

The UK's withdrawal from the EU did not affect the UK's participation in the ECHR, which is an international law instrument of the Council of Europe.[726] Although there is no formal obligation and the EU is not (yet) member to the ECHR, the EU Commission has regularly assessed compliance with the ECHR as part of commitment to Article 2 TEU values, expecting member states to be part of the Council of Europe.[727] However, since Brexit, there is no implicit requirement for the UK to be part of the ECHR. It could be said that the UK's future as a member of the ECHR is fragile. In 2014, the Conservative Government stated the intention to withdraw from the ECHR.[728] The (non-binding) Political Declaration in 2019 included the UK's continued commitment to respect the framework of the ECHR.[729] In early 2020, *Boris Johnson* refused to commit to keep the UK in the ECHR.[730]

In the press release concerning the launch of the adequacy decision draft, the EU Commission stated that the UK has committed to remain a party of the ECHR (and the Convention 108). It emphasises that "continued adherence to such international convention is of particular importance for the stability and durability of the proposed adequacy findings".[731] However, the TCA does not explicitly require the UK's membership in the ECHR. Nevertheless, the EU and UK reaffirmed their respect for the Universal Declaration of Human Rights and the international human rights treaties they are parties to, including the ECHR to which the UK is a party.[732] The EU has the right to suspend or terminate the

---

726 This was also confirmed by the former UK Government in Department for Exiting the European Union, 'Legislating for the United Kingdom's Withdrawal from the European Union' (n 659) 2.22.

727 For example: EU Commission, 'EU Enlargement Strategy' Communication to the European Parliament, the Council, the European Economic and Social Committee and the Committee of the Regions COM(2015) 611 final.

728 Chris Grayling, 'Protection Human Rights in the UK: The Conservatives' Proposals for Changing Britain's Human Rights Law' (Conservative Party 2014) <https://www.theguardian.com/politics/interactive/2014/oct/03/conservatives-human-rights-act-full-document>.

729 EU, 'Political Declaration Setting out the Framework for the Future Relationship between the European Union and the United Kingdom' (2019) 2019/C 384 I/02 para 7 presented to Parliament pursuant to Section 1 of the European Union (Withdrawal) Act (No 2) 2019 and Section 13 of the European Union (Withdrawal) Act 2019.

730 Jon Stone, 'Boris Johnson Refuses to Commit to Keeping UK in Human Rights Convention' *Independent* (Brussels, 5 March 2020) <https://www.independent.co.uk/news/uk/politics/boris-johnson-brexit-human-rights-convention-echr-michel-barnier-a9378141.html>.

731 EU Commission, 'Data Protection: European Commission Launches Process on Personal Data Flows to UK' (n 619); see also UK Adequacy Decision (n 14) recital 277.

732 TCA, art COMPROV.4.

TCA if there has been a "serious and substantial failure" by the UK to fulfil the obligation to uphold the values and principles of democracy, the rule of law, and respect for human rights, which underpin their domestic and international policies.[733] However, this does not necessarily mean that denouncing the ECHR will automatically lead to a suspension or termination of the TCA.

2 Human Rights Act 1998

The HRA 1998 became effective on 9 November 1998. Its main provisions came into force on 2 October 2000. Strictly speaking, the HRA 1998 has not incorporated the ECHR into domestic law but instead gives "further effect" to the ECHR rights in national law in the UK.[734] Consequently, the ECHR has only limited effect in UK domestic law due to its lack of serious enforcement mechanism (unlike the EU law with Article 258 TFEU) and the lack of possibilities of private enforcement through a doctrine of direct effect. Also, the ECtHR's decisions are not enforceable in the UK legal order. The HRA 1998 provides the possibility to take a case in which human rights have been breached to a court. While the ECHR binds UK public bodies, UK courts are still not required to follow the Strasbourg Court. Nevertheless, the ECtHR's judgements are persuasive in arguments before UK courts. Section 2(1) HRA 1998 states that "[a] court [...] determining a question which has arisen in connection with a Convention right must take into account any judgement, decision, declaration or advisory opinion of the ECtHR whenever made or given, [...] so far as in the opinion of the court [...], it is relevant to the proceedings in which that question has arisen". Legislation must be read and given effect in a way that is compatible with the Convention rights.[735] Under the HRA 1998, higher courts have the power to declare an act of parliament to be incompatible with Convention rights.[736] However, such a declaration of incompatibility does not have any legal effect on the respective act, which continues in force unless amended or repealed by Parliament. The Parliament is ultimately sovereign. The declaration of incompatibility would not affect the validity, operation or enforcement of the law.[737] If claimants fail in domestic courts, they can proceed in Strasbourg once domestic remedies have been fully exhausted. Section 6(1) states that "[i]t is unlawful for a public authority

---

733 TCA, art INST.35 in conjunction with art COMPROV.12.
734 Introduction text of the HRA 1998.
735 HRA 1998, s 3.
736 HRA 1998, s 4.
737 In Germany, the Federal Constitutional Court (*Bundesverfassungsgericht*) can strike down incompatible legislation.

to act in a way which is incompatible with a Convention right"; the term public authority includes courts or tribunals[738]. Sections 7 and 8 HRA 1998 deal with proceedings and remedies concerning actions against such public authority.

3 British Bill of Rights

In 2014, the Conservative Party set out a proposal to repeal the HRA 1998 and replace it with a new British Bill of Rights. [739] In 2015, the Conservative Party promised to "scrap the Human Rights Act 1998 and introduce a British Bill of Rights.[740] The intention was later confirmed by former Prime Minister *Theresa May.* The motive was to break the link between the British courts and the ECtHR.[741] The Supreme Court should be made "the ultimate arbiter of human rights matters in the UK".[742] The House of Lord's concluded that a British Bill of Rights "would severely strain the UK's relations and cooperation with [...] EU states".[743] In December 2020, the UK Government announced that it would review, among other things, the relationship between the domestic courts and the ECtHR, including the duty to "take into account" ECtHR case law (Section 2 HRA 1998), the impact of the human rights legislation on the relationship between the judiciary, the executive and Parliament and how the HRA 1998 applies outside the UK and whether there is a "case for change".[744] In the Queen's Speech 2022, it was once again confirmed that the UK Government will introduce a Bill of Rights.[745] At this point, it is still uncertain to which extent a British Bill of Rights may depart from the level of protection provided for under the ECHR and the HRA 1998.[746] However, it is planned that the Bill clarifies that there is

---

738 HRA 1998, s 6(3).
739 Grayling (n 728).
740 The Conservative Party, 'Strong Leadership, a Clear Economic Plan, a Brighter, More Secure Future: The Conservative Party Manifesto 2015' 60 <https://www.conservatives.com/manifesto>.
741 ibid.
742 The Conservative Party (740) 60.
743 House of Lords, European Union Committee, Twelfth Report of Session 2015 – 16, 'The UK, the EU and a British Bill of Rights' HL Paper 136 para 36 <https://publications.parliament.uk/pa/ld201516/ldselect/ldeucom/139/139.pdf>.
744 Ministry of Justice, 'Government Launches Independent Review of Human Rights Act' (2020) Press Release of 7 December 2020 <https://www.gov.uk/government/news/government-launches-independent-review-of-the-human-rights-act>.
745 The Queen's Speech 2022, 118 et seqq. <https://assets.publishing.service.gov.uk/government/uploads/system/uploads/attachment_data/file/1074113/Lobby_Pack_10_May_2022.pdf>.
746 House of Lords, European Union Committee, Twelfth Report of Session 2015 – 16 (n 743) para 124.

no requirement to follow the Strasbourg case law and that UK Courts cannot interpret rights in a more expansive manner than the Strasbourg Court.[747]

4 Article 8 ECHR

Article 8 ECHR could provide an equivalent level of personal data protection to Articles 7 and 8 CFR in the UK. According to the ECtHR and its extensive interpretation of private life, personal data is protected by Article 8 ECHR as part of an individual's private life.[748] The ECtHR's interpretation of the protection of personal data is assessed, focusing mainly on (potential) discrepancies to the Articles 7 and 8 CFR.

a Human Rights Act 1998

Article 8 ECHR was given full effect by the HRA 1998. However, one might say that since the right to the protection of personal data is not explicitly included in Article 8 ECHR, it has not been given further effect in the national law by the HRA 1998.[749] According to Section 2 HRA 1998, the ECtHR's case law is not binding for British courts or other public authorities. However, it appears that the UK largely complies with the ECHR and follows the ECtHR's case law.[750] The British courts are obliged to treat the case law of the ECtHR as a mandatory relevant consideration in determining a question in connection with Convention rights, they also have discretion in this context.[751] However, according to *Philip Sales,* this discretion is not intended to be an individual discretion for each court to exercise according to its judgement. It is instead a judicial or legal evaluative discretion under the guidance of the Supreme Court.[752] *Lord Neuberger* stated in a dictum the following: "Where [...] there is a clear and constant line of decisions whose effect is not inconsistent with some fundamental substantive or procedural aspect of our law, and whose reasoning does not appear to overlook or misunderstand some argument or point of principle, we consider that it

---

747 The Queen's Speech 2022 (n 745) 118.
748 This was already shown in Chapter 2, A.III.1.
749 For instance: *AB, R (on the application of) v Secretary of State for the Home Department* [2013] EWHC 3453 (Admin) [16].
750 See in detail Alice Donald, Jane Gordon and Philip Leach, Human Rights and Social Justice Research Institute, London Metropolitan University 'The UK and the European Court of Human Rights', (Equality and Human Rights Commission Research report 83, 2012) <https://www.equalityhumanrights.com/sites/default/files/83._european_court_of_human_rights.pdf>.
751 Philip Sales, 'Strasbourg Jurisprudence and the Human Rights Act: A Response to Lord Irvine' [2012] PL 253, 257.
752 ibid.

would be wrong for this [Supreme] court not to follow that line."[753] Personal data protection is subject to a direct and constant line of decisions in Strasbourg.[754] Hence, it appears rather unlikely that British courts would deny that the right to the protection of personal data has been given effect by the HRA 1998. Nevertheless, the extension of the protection of personal data given by the British courts is unclear at this point. *Philip Sales* expects the Supreme Court to adopt a relatively conservative approach since, unlike public authorities and governmental bodies, individuals can apply directly to the ECtHR after having exhausted domestic remedies.[755] Consequently, it cannot yet be clearly said if the HRA 1998 gave the right to protect personal data full effect.

In its adequacy decision favouring the UK, the EU Commission declared that the right to data protection as part of the right to respect for private and family life is also further affected by the HRA 1998.[756] The EU Commission has by no means questioned the protection of personal data under the HRA 1998. Nor did the EU Commission give a justification for its view. Furthermore, the EU Commission states that "any individual who claims [their] rights to privacy and data protection have been violated by public authorities can obtain redress before the UK courts under Section 7(1) [HRA 1998]".[757] A court may then grant relief or remedy. It can also declare a provision to be incompatible with Convention rights. However, as stated above, such a declaration of incompatibility only has a limited impact on the act in question.[758]

The Parliament can repeal the HRA 1998[759], although not by implied repeal.[760] The EUWA 2018 explicitly excluded the HRA 1998 from amendment, repeal or revocation by powers delegated under the EUWA 2018.[761] Some might argue that any law subject to parliamentary repeal cannot adequately replace

---

753 *Manchester City Council v Pinnock* [2010] UKSC 45 [48].

754 For example, the following cases: *S and Marper v United Kingdom* (n 117); *Uzun v Germany*, no 35623/05, ECHR 2010; *L.H. v Latvia*, no 52019/07, 29 April 2014.

755 Sales (n 751) 263.

756 UK Adequacy Decision (n 14) recital 10.

757 ibid recitals 109 et seq.

758 See under II.2.

759 As far as Scotland is concerned, the HRA 1998 is protected from modification by the Scottish Parliament, cf Scotland Act 1998, sch 4.

760 *Thoburn v Sunderland City Council* [2002] EWHC 195 (Admin), [2003] QB 151; *R (HS2 Action Alliance Ltd) v Secretary of State for Transport* [2014] USKC 3, [2014] 1 WLR 324; *Kennedy v Charity Commissioner* [2014] UKSC 20, [2015] AC 455.

761 EUWA 2018, s 8(7)(f).

a fundamental right to data protection.[762] From this point of view, equivalent protection of a natural person's data to the one within the EU would only be provided if the UK Government were to adopt a fundamental right to data protection in the proposed British Bill of Rights.[763] In this context, a concept of fundamental right would be understood as a right not subject to a simple parliamentary repeal. Hence, the question appears whether a fundamental right to data protection is mandatory to provide an adequate level of data protection to the one within the EU. The GDPR does not explicitly require the third country to provide a right to data protection in the form of a fundamental right. The third country must provide "respect for human rights and fundamental freedoms". However, this does not imply the need for a formal level of fundamental data protection. The requirement of a fundamental right to data protection would go too far. Many countries might not even have an established concept of fundamental rights, let alone a fundamental right to protect personal data or respect for privacy. For example, in Japan, which obtained an adequacy decision under the GDPR[764], the legislative regime does not contain a fundamental right to protect personal data, which is not subject to a simple repeal by the Parliament. The EU Commission still adopted an adequacy decision. Furthermore, the CJEU did not require a fundamental domestic right to protect personal data – neither in its *Schrems* and *Facebook Ireland* judgements[765] nor *Avis 1/15*[766].

b Scope of Application

The Strasbourg Court does not explicitly limit the right to data protection to only private information strictly.[767] However, this does not mean that Article 8 ECHR

---

762 Murray (n 693) 151. However, *Murray* raised these concerns not in regard to the HRA 1998, but in regard to the DPA 2018 and section 2 DPA (see below under B.II.). *Murray* states: 'A domestic UK Data Protection Act cannot adequately replace the fundamental right to data protection found in the EU Charter. Such an Act, which is always subject to Parliamentary repeal, will only replicate the framework of data protection as found in the subordinate EU Legislation (the GDPR). Only if the UK Government were to adopt a right to data protection in some form in the proposed British Bill of Rights would there be true equivalence for Article 8 in domestic law'.
763 ibid.
764 Adequacy Decision Japan (n 27).
765 *Schrems* (n 71); *Facebook Ireland and Schrems* (n 64). The USA also do not have a constitutional right to the protection to informational privacy. For more information on the existing data protection regulations in the USA see Bastian Baumann, *Datenschutzkonflikte zwischen der EU und den USA* (2016).
766 *Accord PNR EU-Canada* (n 80).
767 *Amann v Switzerland* [GC], no 27798/95, para 65, ECHR 2000-II (Chapter 2, A.III.1.)

does not extend to all types of personal data.[768] Article 8 ECHR applies mostly to information closely related to the private or family life of the natural persons concerned.[769] The fact that personal data are already in the public domain or can be accessed by the public does not necessarily remove such data from the protection of Article 8 ECHR.[770] However, public data may almost only fall within the "private life" in the case of the systematic collection or storage of (public available) personal information.[771] This also became clear, when the Strasbourg Court took the view that sparse information concerning the applicant, which had been gathered coincidentally and was of no relevance for the investigation in question, had in no way constituted systematic or permanent gathering of data and thus did not interfere with the right to respect for their private life.[772] A significant element, although not necessarily decisive, is whether an individual is reasonably entitled to expect protection of their private life.[773]

For example, the Strasbourg Court noted that "the normal use of security cameras *per se* whether in the public street or on premises, such as shopping centres or police stations where they serve a legitimate and foreseeable purpose, do not raise issues under Article 8(1) ECHR".[774] Furthermore, results of the personal data processing must attain a certain level of seriousness and in a manner causing prejudice to personal enjoyment of the right to respect for private life.[775]

c Horizontal Application

According to *Andrew Murray*, the is one key difference between the right to protect personal data guaranteed in Article 8 CFR and the one guaranteed in Article 8 ECHR would be their horizontal application. *Murray* states that the horizontal application of Article 8 CFR would be afforded clearly by Article 8(2) CFR. However, this view is not supported by the clear wording of the first sentence

---

768 cf Lynskey (n 35) 122 et seqq.

769 Luzius Wildhaber, Article 8 EMRK in Luzius Wildhaber, 'Article 8 EMRK' in Katharina Pabel and Stefanie Schmahl (eds), *Internationaler Kommentar zur Europäischen Menschenrechtskonvention* (27th edn, 2020) para 336.

770 *Satakunnan Markkinapörssi Oy and Satamedia Oy v Finland* (n 114) para 134.

771 cf *Rotaru v Romania* (n 113); *Powell v the United Kingdom* (dec.), no 45305/99, paras 58 et seq., ECHR 2000-V; *Perry v the United Kingdom*, no 63737/00, para 38, ECHR 2003-IX (extracts).

772 *Mehmedovic v Switzerland* (dec.), no 41953/98, para 18, ECHR 2001-VII.

773 *Perry v the United Kingdom* (n 771) para 37 (in this case, information has been made made public in a manner or to an extent which exceeds what the subjects could reasonably have expected); *Bărbulescu v Romania* [GC], no 61496/08, para 80, 5 September 2017.

774 *Perry v the United Kingdom* (n 771) para 40.

775 *M.L. and W.W. v. Germany*, nos 60798/10 and 65599/10, para 88, 28 June 2018.

of Article 51(1) CFR, according to which only the EU and the member states, when implementing EU law, are obliged by the Charter rights. Private individuals are not (directly) covered by this obligation. Nevertheless, the fundamental right is of great importance among private individuals. Provisions that violate Article 8 CFR are inapplicable; provisions are to be interpreted and applied in the light of the fundamental right. The binding nature of private individuals also extends to the activities of associated companies in other EU countries. This leads to an indirect horizontal effect of Article 8 CFR.[776] It could be viewed as if the CJEU tended towards a direct third-party effect for the right to be forgotten in its *Google Spain* judgement, when it qualified the processing of personal data by private search engine operators as an interference with the fundamental rights of the data subjects.[777] However, in the case the Court only derived the obligations of the search engine operator from an interpretation of the Data Protection Directive in conformity with fundamental rights.[778] The distinction between the direct fundamental rights obligation of the public bodies mentioned in the first sentence of Article 51(1) CFR and the indirect fundamental rights obligation of private actors must be clearly maintained.[779]

According to the ECtHR, Convention rights can determine relations between private parties through the doctrine of "positive obligations", which requires states to take concrete steps to secure fundamental rights.[780] In this way, the ECHR guarantees protection of the right to privacy not only against the state, but also by the state against acts of another private individual.[781] Although the HRA 1998 does not explicitly mention any form of horizontal effect under the Convention and does not refer to the common law, there might be indications that Convention rights in common law have applied indirectly horizontal. The HRA 1998 requires all legislation, whether public or private nature[782], to be interpreted in a way that is compatible with Convention rights.[783] According to Section 6(1) HRA 1998, "[i]t is unlawful for a public authority to act in a way

---

776 See instead of many Hans Jarass, 'Art. 8' in *Charta der Grundrechte der EU* (4th edn, C.H.Beck 2021), para 3 with further references.

777 Jens-Peter Schneider, 'B. Völker- und unionsverfassungsrechtliche Grundlagen' in Heinrich Amadeus Wolff and Stefan Brink (eds) (n 149) para 39.

778 *Google Spain and Google* (n 95) paras 79 et seq., 82, 85, 88.

779 See in detail: Marsch (n 43) 255.

780 For example: *X and Y v Netherlands*, 26 March 1985, para 23, Series A no 91.

781 Andrew Clapham, 'The "Drittwirkung" of the European Convention', *R. St J. Macdonald, F. Matscher and H. Petzold (eds) The European System for the Protection of Human Rights (Dordrecht, Nijhoff)* (Springer Netherlands 1996) 190.

782 ibid 825.

783 HRA 1998, s 8.

which is incompatible with a Convention right" in domestic law. This provision and Section 7 and 8 HRA 1998, which deal with proceeding and remedies only against public authorities, confirm the exclusion of a direct horizontal effect of Convention rights.[784] Courts and tribunals must comply with Convention rights when developing the common law in disputes between private parties.[785] This rule indicates an indirect horizontal effect of Convention rights in common law litigation between private parties.[786] The theory of an indirect horizontal effect has been approved in *Campbell v MGM Limited*.[787] It was argued that "the value embodied in Article 8 [...] [is] as much applicable in disputes between individuals or between an individual and a non-governmental body [...] as they are in disputes between an individual and a public authority".[788] There are several models of indirect horizontal effects established in the relevant literature, e.g. "full indirect horizontal effect"[789], "strong indirect horizontal effect"[790], "weak indirect horizontal effect" [791], or a "constraint constitutional model"[792]. However, the British courts have not yet reached a consensus on the nature and the extent of the court's duty to give horizontal effect to the Convention rights in the domestic common law.[793]

d Limited Range of Rights included in Article 8 ECHR

A potential discrepancy between Article 8 CFR and Article 8 ECHR could also provide the right to data access and rectification[794] and the right to have reference to a supervisory authority[795]. Whereas Article 8 CFR explicitly provides these rights, Article 8 ECHR does not. The ECtHR confirmed a right to access personal information under certain circumstances: The Strasbourg Court found that

---

784 Gavin Phillipson and Alexander Williams, 'Horizontal Effect and the Constitutional Constraint' (2011) 74 Mod. L. Rev. 878, 880; Gavin Phillipson, 'The Human Rights Act, "Horizontal Effect" and the Common Law: A Bang or a Whimper?' (1999) 62 Mod. L. Rev. 824, 826.

785 HRA 1998, s 6(3)(a).

786 Phillipson and Williams (n 784) 880.

787 *Campbell v MGM Limited* [2004] UKHL 22, [2004] 2 AC 457.

788 ibid [17].

789 HRW Wade, 'Horizons of Horizontality' (2000) 116 LQR 217; Jonathan Morgan, 'Privacy, Confidence and Horizontal Effect. "Hello" Trouble' (2003) 62 CLJ 444; Deryck Beyleveld and Shaun D. Pattinson, 'Horizontal Applicability and Horizontal Effect' (2002) 118 LQR 623.

790 Murray Hunt, 'The "Horizontal Effect" of the Human Rights Act' [1998] PL 423.

791 Phillipson (n 784).

792 Phillipson and Williams (n 784).

793 ibid 878.

794 Chapter 2, A.I.4.

795 Chapter 2, A.I.5.

obstacles to access personal information held by security services might constitute violations of Article 8 ECHR.[796] However, the ECtHR has recognised that, in
particular, "in cases concerning the operations of [intelligence service] agencies,
there may be legitimate grounds to limit access to certain documents".[797] The
ECtHR also ruled that "the law must provide an effective and accessible procedure, enabling applicants to [access any vital] information concerning
them".[798] The other rights, provided for in Article 8(2) CFR, have not yet been
subject to a process before the ECtHR. Also, the ECtHR has not yet recognised
a right to object to certain processing nor a right not to be made subject to a decision with significant effects on the data subject based on automated processing.[799] However, in UK domestic law, these rights are still found in the UK
GDPR and the Data Protection Act 2018, further discussed under B.

e ECtHR's Case Law on Surveillance Measures

One may also find discrepancies between the ECtHR's and the CJEU's case concerning data gathering for national security reasons. In several judgements, both
courts have decided on matters concerning data retention, data acquisition, and
data interception.[800] While the CJEU's case law on these matters is discussed in
detail below under C.II., the ECtHR's case law is briefly reviewed in the following.

Overall, the Strasbourg Court acknowledged signals intelligence and bulk interception as an essential instrument for the protection of national security.[801]
The ECtHR gives national legislators more room for manoeuvre to establish surveillance measures than the CJEU.[802] This approach was confirmed in the most

---

796 *Haralambie v Romania*, no 21737/03, para 96, 27 October 2009; *Joanna Szulc v Poland*,
no 43932/08, para 87, 13 November 2012.
797 *Turek v Slovakia*, no 57986/00, para 115, ECHR 2006-II (extracts).
798 *Yonchev v Bulgaria* no 12504/09, paras 49 et seqq., 7 December 2017.
799 Lynskey (n 35) 128.
800 For instance: *Digital Rights Ireland and Seitlinger and Others* (n 73); *Tele2 Sverige* (n 81);
Judgement of 6 October 2020, *Privacy International*, C-623/17, EU:C:2020:790; Judgement of 6 October 2020, *La Quadrature du Net and Others*, C- 511/18, C-512/8 and C-520/18, EU:C:2020:791;
ECtHR in *Weber and Saravia v Germany* (dec.), no 54934/00, ECHR 2006-XI; *Kennedy v the United
Kingdom*, no 26839/05, 18 May 2010; *Roman Zakharov v Russia* [GC], no 47143/06, ECHR 2015; *Big
Brother Watch and Others v the United Kingdom* [GC], nos 58170/13, 62322/14 and 24960/15, 21 May
2021.
801 For instance: *Centrum för rättvisa v Sweden*, no 35252/08, para 179, 19 June 2018; *Big Brother
Watch and Others v the United Kingdom* (n 800) paras 323 et seq.
802 Irena Ilic, 'Post-Brexit Limitations to Government Surveillance: Does the UK Get a Free
Hand?' (2020) 25 Communications Law 31, 33.

recent case *Big Brother Watch and Others v the United Kingdom* in May 2021, in which the Grand Chamber accepted bulk interception regimes by intelligence agencies.[803] The CJEU, on the other hand, has a more rigorous approach and is far stricter on general and indiscriminate data collection and retention itself. The CJEU finds general and indiscriminate data retention unlawful and targeted data retention only lawful under strict requirements.[804] The CJEU once again confirmed this case law in 2020.[805] These different approaches are the most significant divergence of the ECtHR's case law from the CJEU's case law.

Nonetheless, despite accepting bulk interception of communications and recognising that states have an extensive "margin of appreciation"[806] in deciding which interception regime is required to protect national security interest, the ECtHR "recalls that there is considerable potential for the bulk interception to be abused in a manner adversely affecting the rights of individuals to respect for private life".[807] The Strasbourg Court found that whatever measure surveillance system is adopted, there must be "adequate and effective guarantees against abuse".[808] According to the ECtHR, secret access to citizens' data is tolerable only as strictly necessary for safeguarding democratic institutions.[809] "The interference must be supported by relevant and sufficient reasons and proportionate to the legitimate aim or aims pursued".[810] This view shows convergence with the CJEU's case law, where the principle of necessity and proportionality also play a significant role. In light of this, the Grand Chamber established a new set of eight criteria for bulk interception[811], which the domestic legal framework must clearly define: "1. the grounds on which bulk interception may be authorised; 2. the circumstances in which an individual's communications may be

---

803 *Big Brother Watch and Others v the United Kingdom* (n 800) para 423.
804 This is discussed in detail below under C.II.
805 *Privacy International* (n 800).
806 *Big Brother Watch and Others v the United Kingdom* (n 800) para 347.
807 ibid para 425.
808 *Weber and Saravia v Germany* (n 800) para 106.
809 *Klass and Others v Germany* (n 128) para 42; *Szabó and Vissy v Hungary*, no 37138/14, paras 72 et seq., 12 January 2016.
810 *Segerstedt-Wiberg and Others v Sweden*, no 62332/00, para 88, ECHR 2006-VII.
811 For targeted data interception and retention, the ECtHR has defined a set of six minimum requirements that should be set out in law in order to avoid abuses of power: "(i) the nature of offences which may give rise to an interception order; (ii) a definition of the categories of people liable to have their communications intercepted; (iii) a limit on the duration of interception; (iv) the procedure to be followed for examining, using and storing the data obtained; (v) the precautions to be taken when communicating the data to other parties; and (vi) the circumstances in which intercepted data may or must be erased or destroyed" (for example in *Weber and Saravia v Germany* (n 800) para 95).

intercepted; 3. the procedure to be followed for granting authorisation; 4. the procedures to be followed for selecting, examining and using intercept material; 5. the precautions to be taken when communicating the material to other parties; 6. the limits on the duration of interception, the storage of intercept material and the circumstances in which such material must be erased and destroyed; 7. the procedures and modalities for supervision by an independent authority of compliance with the above safeguards and its powers to address non-compliance; 8. the procedures for independent *ex post facto* review of such compliance and the powers vested in the competent body in addressing instances of non-compliance."[812]

It is noteworthy that the CJEU and the ECtHR also have made plenty of references to each other's judgements: In *Roman Zakharov v Russia*, the ECtHR cited the CJEU's *Digital Rights Ireland and Seitlinger and Others* ruling[813], and in *Tele 2 Sverige*, the CJEU referred to the ECtHR's rulings in *Roman Zakharov v Russia* and *Szabó and Vissy v Hungary* [814].[815] In light of this, the CJEU and the ECtHR show a decent level of convergence in surveillance matters. Also, the CJEU found that "account must be taken of the corresponding rights of the ECHR [including the relevant jurisprudence of the ECtHR] for the purpose of interpreting the Charter, as a minimum threshold of protection".[816]

f Conclusion to 4

Although, Article 8 CFR provides a wider protection of personal data, Article 8 ECHR may provide an adequate level of personal data protection. Nevertheless, the extension of the protection of personal data given by the British courts under the HRA 1998 is unclear at this point. Also, the horizontal effect of Article 8 ECHR under the HRA 1998 and in common law is uncertain.

---

812 *Big Brother Watch and Others v the United Kingdom* (n 800) para 361.
813 *Roman Zakharov v Russia* (n 800) para 147.
814 *Tele2 Sverige* (n 81) paras 119 et seq.
815 Serena Crespi, 'The Applicability of Schrems Principles to the Member States: National Security and Data Protection within the EU Context' (2018) 43 Eur. Law Rev 669, 686.
816 *La Quadrature du Net and Others* (n 800) para 124.

5 Articles 6 and 13 ECHR

Article 6 ECHR provides the right to a fair trial.[817] Article 13 ECHR stipulates the right to an effective remedy.[818] With the loss of Article 47 CFR, these provisions will play a more significant role in *post*-Brexit. However, the loss of Article 47 CFR could lead to a decrease of effective remedies for rights infringement: Article 47 CFR provides more substantial protection of the right to a fair trial than Article 6 ECHR since the latter is limited to cases concerning a person's "determination of [their] civil rights and obligations or of any criminal charge against him". The protection under Article 47(1) CFR goes beyond Article 6 ECHR's scope and includes administrative proceedings, e. g. immigration processes[819], such as deportation hearings or tax[820]. In the CJEU's case *ZZ*, a dual French and Algerian national was refused admission to the UK by the Home Office on the grounds of Article 27 of the Citizens' Rights Directive[821].[822] The Directive allows Member States to restrict the free movement of EU citizens "on grounds of public policy, public security or public health".[823] The claimant's appeal of this decision lied with the Special Immigration Appeals Commission (SIAC), which decides where the Secretary of State has issued a notification to that effect based on the grounds of national security. The procedure before the SIAC consists of an open and a closed procedure; from the latter, the applicant and his or her lawyers are excluded. The case was based mainly on closed materials. However, the applicant was not informed of the grounds to exclude him from the UK. The CJEU ruled that a national authority must prove that state security would be compromised if full disclosure of the reasons were affected.[824] Furthermore, the national

---

817 See for more information: European Court of Human Rights, 'Guide on Article 6 of the European Convention on Human Rights' (2021) <https://www.echr.coe.int/documents/guide_art_6_criminal_eng.pdf>.

818 See for more information: European Court of Human Rights, 'Guide on Article 13 of the European Convention on Human Rights' (2021) <https://www.echr.coe.int/Documents/Guide_Art_13_ENG.pdf>.

819 Judgement of 4 June 2013, *ZZ*, C-300/11, EU:C:2013:363.

820 *Totel Limited v The Commissioner for HM Revenue and Customs* [2014] UKUT 0485 (TCC) [91].

821 Directive 2004/38/EC of the European Parliament and of the Council on the right of citizens of the Union and their family members to move and reside freely within the territory of the Member States amending Regulation (EEC) No 1612/68 and repealing Directives 64/221/EEC, 68/360/EEC, 72/194/EEC, 73/148/EEC, 75/34/EEC, 75/35/EEC, 90/364/EEC, 90/365/EEC and 93/96/EEC [2004] OJ L 158/77; transposed into UK law as the Immigration (European Economic Area) Regulations 2006 (SI 2006/1003).

822 *ZZ* (n 819).

823 cf Regulation 19(1) of Immigration (European Economic Area) Regulations 2006 (SI 2006/1003).

824 *ZZ* (n 819) para 61.

procedure must ensure that to the greatest possible extent, the adversarial principle is complied with;[825] the person concerned must still be informed of the essence of the grounds that constitute the basis of the decision.[826] The standard
adopted by the CJEU in (administrative) immigration cases comes very close to
that of the ECtHR in criminal cases.[827] Article 6 ECHR would not have applied
in the ZZ case due to its limited scope of application.

Another example of the discrepancies between the remedies available under
the HRA 1998 and the Charter is the case of *Benkharbouche and Janah,* which
concerned Article 47 CFR.[828] The Court of Appeal dealt with whether the right
to a fair trial can be invoked to restrict the scope of the State Immunity Act
1978. The two claimants were employees working as members of the domestic
staff of two foreign embassies in the UK. Both employees complained about
the failure to pay minimum wage and arrears of pay and breaches of the Working
Time Regulations 1998 (based on EU-derived law[829]), racial discrimination, and
harassment. Article 47 CFR could be revoked. The State Immunity Act confers
general immunity from jurisdiction in other states. Consequently, both claims
could not be successful as their employers were immune from jurisdiction.[830]
The Court of Appeal concluded that the relevant provisions of the State Immunity Act did indeed breach Article 6 ECHR and Article 47 CFR. Although the Court
of Appeal confirmed that the right to fair proceedings, including a right of access
to a court in general, may be limited, it found that the limitations established
through the State Immunity Act were too extensive and, thus, disproportionate.[831] Under the HRA 1998, the court was limited to making a declaration of incompatibility. However, the Charter violation allowed the Court to disapply the
provisions of the State Immunity Act and hence, provide an effective remedy
for the claimants.[832] In the absence of Article 47 CFR, such cases may result in
a different outcome, especially with the adoption of Schedule 1 Paragraph 3(1)

---

825 ZZ (n 819) para 65.
826 ibid para 68.
827 Tobias Lock, 'Human Rights Law in the UK after Brexit' (2017) Nov Supp (Brexit Special
Extra Issue 2017) PL 117, 5.
828 *Benkharbouche v Secretary of State for Foreign and Commonwealth Affairs and Secretary of
State for Foreign and Commonwealth Affairs and Libya v Janah* [2017] UKSC 62, [2019] AC 777.
829 Council Directive 93/104/EC concerning certain aspects of the organisation of working time
[1993] OJ L 307/18, and provisions concerning working time in Council Directive 94/33/EC on the
protection of young people at work [1994] OJ L 216/12.
830 *Benkharbouche v Secretary of State for Foreign and Commonwealth Affairs and Secretary of
State for Foreign and Commonwealth Affairs and Libya v Janah* (n 828) [4].
831 ibid [34].
832 ibid [78].

EUWA 2018.[833] The case *Benkharbouche and Janah* was cited in the right-by-right analysis by the UK Department to Exit the EU to underline the view that remedies for rights will not be impacted by the Brexit process,[834] although review shows that this will be the case.

Although Article 13 ECHR only ensures a possibility to appeal to a national authority, the right to an effective remedy protected in Article 13 ECHR is mainly consistent with the right protected in Article 47(1) CFR. However, fatally, Article 13 ECHR has not been incorporated into domestic law by the HRA 1998. The scope of the right to an effective remedy may diminish after IP completion day in domestic law. This also shows that the remedies under EU law are stronger than those available under the HRA 1998.

6 Conclusion to II

In summary, it can be said that Article 8 ECtHR provides an equivalent level of protection of personal data to the one guaranteed by Article 8 CFR. This can also be said regarding Article 13 ECHR and Article 47(1) CFR but not about Article 6 ECHR and Article 47(2) CFR as the application scope of the latter is much broader. However, it is not clear whether the protection of personal data under Article 8 ECHR was given further effect under the HRA 1998 in domestic law. Article 13 ECHR was not given any effect under the HRA 1998.

Overall, it can be said that the ECHR is consistent with the Charter. The risk of any long-term discrepancies between the Charter *post*-Brexit and the CJEU judgements and the respective ECHR rights and their interpretation by the ECtHR is relatively low. The ECtHR tends to refer to developments under the Charter when dynamically interpreting ECHR rights.[835] The ECtHR treats the Charter as an updated version of the Convention;[836] references to the Charter by the ECtHR are used to demonstrate contemporary European consensus.[837] In judgements by the ECtHR with the UK as a respondent, a reference to the Charter or other EU law (such as the GDPR) will not be sufficient to substantiate consensus. International instruments, such as the Convention 108,[838] which had

---

833 The principle of supremacy in the *post*-Brexit UK was reviewed under I.2.b.
834 Department for Exiting the European Union, 'Charter of Fundamental Rights of the EU – Rights by Rights Analysis' (n 708) para 24.
835 See in detail Tobias Lock, 'The Influence of EU Law on Strasbourg Doctrines' (2016) 41 ERE 804.
836 ibid 806.
837 ibid 820.
838 See under IV.

been signed up to by the UK, can be considered sources of consensus regarding data protection and Article 8 ECHR.

However, the loss of the principle of supremacy will impact fundamental rights in the UK: The supra-national character of the Charter makes it much more entrenched in domestic law. UK courts are not bound by the ECtHR's decisions; they must only take these into account in so far as they are, in their opinion, relevant to the matter before the court.[839] Also, UK courts cannot strike down a law incompatible with the ECHR and HRA 1998. The Supreme Court and the High Court may only declare it incompatible, but ultimately the Parliament must amend or repeal it. Consequently, even under HRA 1998, the ECHR rights have only limited effect in the UK legal order. However, at this point, the UK appears to largely comply with the ECHR and to follow the ECtHR's judgements.

It is uncertain if and how long the UK will commit to the ECHR, given the ambitions of the Conservative Party to leave the ECtHR's jurisdiction. If the UK would leave the ECHR, this will have a significant negative impact on the future adequacy decisions in favour of the UK since one of the main reasons why the EU Commission found that the UK provides an adequate level of data protection is that the UK has remained a member of the EU privacy "family" by committing to remain a party to the ECHR and the Convention 108.[840]

III Constitutional Rights in Common Law

In recent years, there has been an ongoing controversy on the potential of common law constitutional rights.[841] Since the activation of the HRA 1998, there has been a "tendency to overlook the common law".[842] With the future of the HRA 1998 being somewhat indeterminate[843], the Supreme Court has begun to place

---

839 HRA 1998, s 2.

840 EU Commission, 'Data Protection: European Commission Launches Process on Personal Data Flows to UK' (n 619).

841 For example, Mark Elliot, 'Beyond the European Convention: Human Rights and the Common Law' (2015) 68 Current Legal Problems 85; Philip Sales, 'Rights and Fundamental Rights in English Law' (2016) 75 CLJ 86; Christina Lienen, 'Common Law Constitutional Rights: Public Law at a Crossroads?' [2018] PL 649; Mark Elliot and Kirsty Hughes (eds), *Common Law Constitutional Rights* (1st edn, Bloomsbury 2020).

842 *Kennedy v Charity Commission* [2014] UKSC 20, [2015] AC 455 [133].

843 The Conservative Party proposed in the repeal of the HRA 1998 and a British Bill of Rights (see under II.3.).

renewed emphasis on the common law.[844] The question that arises is whether the common law can substitute the existing rights protection system rooted in the HRA 1998 and ECHR.[845] Many voices in the relevant literature say that common law constitutional rights can guarantee fundamental rights a level of protection that comes close to that of the HRA 1998.[846] In particular, this might be the case where the right in question reflects or is closely related to fundamental constitutional principles, such as the right to access to courts.[847] Although common law might have the potential to offer a comparable level of protection that can be afforded under the HRA 1998, the level of protection offered depends on the specific right in question.[848] Core common law rights may be immune to legislative invalidation, while others may have a lesser form of protection.[849] Presently, the former kind of rights is almost non-existent. At this point, it is very difficult to determine the development and evolution of common law constitutional rights since the introduction of the HRA 1998.[850] In terms of resilience, the capacity to remain exercisable in given circumstances in the face of incompatible legislation, the position of common law rights is uncertain.[851] Although the HRA 1998 does not prioritise Convention rights over incompatible primary legislation, the Convention rights are binding to the UK as a contractual state.[852]

On the other hand, common law rights may be vulnerable to legislative change or displacement and inferior to parliamentary acts.[853] In any case, compared to the HRA 1998, the existential resilience of common law rights is consid-

---

844 cf *R (Guardian News and Media Ltd) v City of Westminster Magistrates' Court* [2012] EWCA Civ 420 (concerning the right to open justice); *R (Osborn) v Parole Board* [2013] UKSC 61, [2014] AC 1115 (concerning the right to procedural fairness); *Kennedy v Charity Commission* (n 842) (concerning the right to open justice); *A v British Broadcasting Corp* [2014] UKSC 25, [2015] AC 588 (concerning the right to open justice); *R (UNISON) v Lord Chancellor* (n 715) (concerning the right of access to justice).

845 Elliot, 'Beyond the European Convention: Human Rights and the Common Law' (n 841) 86.

846 For a detailed discussion see Mark Elliot, 'The Fundamentality of Rights at Common Law' in Mark Elliot and Kirsty Hughes (eds) (n 841) 19.

847 The common law expressly recognizes a fundamental right of access to justice and to the courts, see for instance *R v Secretary of State for the Home Department ex parte Leech* [1994] QB 198 [210 A].

848 In detail Elliot, 'Beyond the European Convention: Human Rights and the Common Law' (n 841) 20.

849 ibid 20.

850 ibid 95.

851 For a detailed discussion see Elliot, 'Beyond the European Convention: Human Rights and the Common Law' (n 841).

852 ibid 20.

853 ibid.

ered more significant.[854] The HRA 1998 can quickly be repealed by the Parliament. While this could also be the case with common law constitutional rights, the legislative attempt to do so would be a project which would be difficult to enforce in "both technical and political terms".[855]

It becomes apparent that a great deal of uncertainty regarding the concept of common law constitutional rights exists. The main reason for this lies in the nature of the UK constitution and whether parliamentary sovereignty is still the core principle or is based on and determined by the common law.[856] Furthermore, the current lack of coherence in common law fundamental rights jurisprudence increases the legal uncertainty.[857] In order to safeguard the rule of law, there is a need for clarity and consistency regarding constitutional rights at common law and foundational principles that shape the content of such rights.[858]

IV Other International Commitments

Article 45(2)(c) GDPR encourages the EU Commission to consider all the international commitments the third country has entered – not only the ECHR. Recital 105 GDPR explicitly requires the EU Commission to consider if the third country has acceded the Convention 108 and its Additional Protocol. The UK is a member of the Convention 108 that was already reviewed.[859] The EU Commission emphasises that the adherence to such instruments is crucial to assessing the proposed adequacy findings.[860] In 2018, the UK had signed the Convention 108+[861] and is currently working on its ratification.

The Department for Exiting the EU stated that fundamental rights could also be covered in international treaties, such as the UN's Universal Declaration of Human Rights of 1948[862] (after this: UDHR).[863] However, this view overlooks that international treaties do not confer enforceable rights upon individuals

---

854 Elliot, 'Beyond the European Convention: Human Rights and the Common Law' (n 841) 21.
855 ibid 22.
856 Lienen (n 842) 650 et seq.
857 ibid 665.
858 ibid 666 et seq.
859 See for more information on the Convention 108 and 108+ in Chapter 2, A.III.2.
860 UK Adequacy Decision (n 14) recital 120.
861 Convention 108+.
862 The UDHR is available at the following link <https://www.un.org/en/universal-declaration-human-rights/> accessed 9 June 2022.
863 Department for Exiting the European Union, 'Charter of Fundamental Rights of the EU – Rights by Rights Analysis' (n 708) para 12.

where they have not been incorporated into domestic laws.[864] The UDHR is not incorporated and not legally binding and cannot be relied upon in proceedings. In the context of the loss of the Charter, these international legal instruments do not hold the same status and level of protection of personal data as the EU Charter.[865] However, this does not indicate that these international commitments do not have some influence on national laws. The influence of such international commitments on national laws was also shown back in 1984, when the Convention 108 caused the UK Government to adopt the Data Protection Act 1984 (after this: DPA 1984) due to its fear of being excluded from data transfers from other European countries.[866] In any case, Article 45(2)(c) GDPR does not necessarily require the international commitments to contain enforceable rights.

V Conclusion to A

It can be concluded that the loss of the Charter does have a negative impact on the framework of fundamental rights protected in the UK. Charter rights will only play a role as "general principles" in the *post*-Brexit UK to serve the purpose of interpretation but are not enforceable itself. Effective remedies against rights infringements are weakened. The ECHR that still applies has only limited effects in domestic law (through the HRA 1998). However, the ECHR essentially provides an equivalent level of protection of fundamental rights to the one guaranteed under the Charter and is broadly consistent with the Charter. The Charter right's scope of application is broader or developed further by the CJEU; the ECtHR tends to follow the CJEU.[867] One of the main reasons why the EU Commission found that the UK provides an adequate level of data protection compared to the one within the EU is that the UK has remained a member of the EU privacy "family" by committing to remain a party to the ECHR and the Convention 108.[868] If the UK were to leave the ECHR, this could have a significant negative impact on the adequacy decisions in favour of the UK as the respect for human rights and fundamental freedoms of a third country is essential for the adequacy as-

---

864 Grogan (n 660) 693 et seq.
865 ibid 694.
866 Paul M Schwartz, 'The Data Privacy Law of Brexit: Theories of Preference Change', *Theoretical Inquiries in Law* 135 <https://ssrn.com/abstract=3895999>.
867 Although this cannot be expected in regard with Article 6 ECHR as the clear wording limits the scope of application to civil and criminal proceedings.
868 EU Commission, 'Data Protection: European Commission Launches Process on Personal Data Flows to UK' (n 619).

sessment. Also, the recurring ambition to replace the HRA 1998 with a new British Bill of Rights could negatively affect the protection of fundamental rights in the UK, depending on the content of such Bill of Rights.[869]

B Data Protection Act 2018

In the following, the national data protection framework in the UK is further reviewed. The focus lies on the DPA 2018, which is the "third-generation" of data protection law-making in the UK. The UK's first legislation to exclusively concern personal data protection was the DPA 1984. The introduction of the DPA 1984 followed the Council of Europe's adoption of Convention 108. Convention 108 encouraged the blocking of data transfers to countries with no data protection in place. Only against the background of Convention 108's economic consequences of trade barriers, the UK Government decided, due to market considerations, to establish a data protection law, in line with the Convention 108's principles.[870] Since the adoption of the DPA 1984, the UK follows the European data protection "path".[871] The Data Protection Act 1998 (after this: DPA 1998), which transposed the Data Protection Directive into UK law and replaced the DPA 1984, came into force on 1 March 2000. Following the introduction of the GDPR, the DPA 2018 has repealed and replaced the DPA 1998 on 23 May 2018.

Several purposes were pursued with the introduction of the DPA 2018. One of the DPA 2018's primary functions was to legislate the "opening clauses" in the GDPR[872] and other areas of data protection, which are open to legislation by the member states. The latter would be the case with processing unstructured manual files by public authorities, which is not included in the GDPR's scope of application.[873] The DPA 2018 extended the data protection law into areas of data processing that the GDPR would not otherwise reach: for example, law enforce-

---

869 However, the "Strasbourg Effect" could prevent the UK to leave the ECHR or replace the HRA 1998 with a proposed British Bill of Rights. See for more information on the "Strasbourg Effect" in Lee A Bygrave, 'The "Strasbourg Effect" on Data Protection in Light of the "Brussels Effect": Logic, Mechanics and Prospects (n 133).

870 cf Schiedermair (n 44) para 79 with further references; Schwartz, 'The Data Privacy Law of Brexit: Theories of Preference Change' (n 866) 124 et seqq. who called the DPA 1984 a result of a "pre-Brussels Effect" (based on *Anu Bradford*'s concept of the "Brussel Effect") or a result of a "Strasbourg Effect".

871 Schwartz, 'The Data Privacy Law of Brexit: Theories of Preference Change' (n 866) 124.

872 The GDPR's opening clauses provide different categories of option of action for the national legislator: concretisation (art 88(1)), addition (art 37(4)) and modification (art 17(3)(b)).

873 Chapter 2, A.IV.1.a.bb.

ment or intelligence activity (Part 3 and 4 of the DPA 2018). A third primary purpose of the DPA 2018 was to guarantee that the UK can exchange personal data freely with the EU after the transitional period.[874]

Under the EUWA 2018, the GDPR was incorporated into the law of the UK as a so-called "retained EU law".[875] The GDPR as "retained EU law" was modified by the Data Protection, Privacy and Electronic Communications (Amendments etc.) (EU Exit) Regulations 2019[876] (after this: DPPEC Regulations). Under this statutory instrument, the GDPR, which is now called the EU GDPR in the UK, and the applied GDPR (Chapter 3 of Part 2 of the DPA 2018) merged to form the "UK GDPR". The UK GDPR closely mirrors the corresponding rules in the EU GDPR.[877] In this way, the data protection standards under the GDPR and the DPA 2018 are maintained after the IP completion day[878] , and a regime for general processing activities was introduced. The DPPEC Regulations, in a technical way, amended the UK GDPR[879] and the DPA 2018[880] to ensure that the UK legal framework for data protection functions correctly after the end of the transition period. For this purpose, several references in the GDPR that no longer make sense in a purely domestic context (for example, references to member states, EU law and the EU Commission) were removed from the UK GDPR. Many functions conferred on the EU Commission by the GDPR were transferred to the Secretary of State, and the Information Commissioner (after this: IC). Thus, the Secretary of State has the power to make "adequacy regulations"[881] and issue SCCs[882]; the IC continues to approve BRCs[883]. In the UK, the IC is the data protection supervisory authority responsible for monitoring compliance with the DPA

---

874 Karen Mc Cullagh, 'UK: GDPR Adaptions and Preparations for Withdrawal from the EU', *National Adaptions of the GDPR* (2019) 116.

875 cf EUWA 2018, s 3. This provision was already discussed under A.I.2.a.

876 Data Protection, Privacy and Electronic Communications (Amendments etc) (EU Exit) Regulations 2019, SI 2019/419, available at the following link <https://www.legislation.gov.uk/uksi/2019/419/contents/made> accessed 9 June 2022.

877 UK Adequacy Decision (n 14) recital 16.

878 Data Protection Privacy and Electronic Communications (Amendments etc) (EU Exit) Regulations 2020, SI 2020/1586 replaces "exit day" with "IP completion day", available at the following link <https://www.legislation.gov.uk/uksi/2020/1586/contents/made> accessed 9 June 2022.

879 DPPEC Regulations, s 3 in conjunction with sch 1.

880 DPPEC Regulations, s 4 in conjunction with sch 2.

881 DPPEC Regulations, sch 1 para 38 and DPA 2018, ss 17A and 17B.

882 DPPEC Regulations, sch 1 para 39 and DPA 2018, s 17C.

883 DPPEC Regulations, sch 1 para 40.

2018 and the UK GDPR by controllers and processors.[884] The IC is a separate legal entity constituted in a single person and supported by the Information Commissioner's Office (after this: ICO).

To summarise, the domestic framework for protecting personal data in the UK now consists of (1) the UK GDPR – as incorporated by the EUWA 2018 and amended by the DPPEC Regulations –, and (2) the DPA 2018[885], as amended by the DPPEC Regulations.[886] It is primarily based on the EU data protection framework.[887] Consequently, the EU Commission and the EDPB found a "strong alignment" between the GDPR framework and the UK legal framework on many core provisions.[888] The EU Commission concluded that the implementation of the GDPR into domestic law and the DPA 2018 build a comprehensive domestic data protection regime that ensures that the UK provides protection "essentially equivalent" to the one within the EU.[889]

In the following an overview of the DPA 2018 is provided (under I.). Then, the controversial Section 2 of the DPA 2018 will be reviewed (under II.). The focus lies on several provisions that constitutes exemptions of data subject's rights and key data processing principles in the context of national security, intelligence agencies' practices, and immigration (under III). Finally, the role of the IC (and the ICO) and its tasks and powers under the DPA 2018 will be looked at (under IV.)

I Overview

The DPA 2018 consists of seven parts: Part 1 gives an overview of the DPA 2018 and defines the key terms. Part 2 contains definitions and general remarks (first

---

884 For more information see under https://ico.org.uk. *John Edwards* is the current IC and took over the post on 3 January 2022 from *Elizabeth Denham* (https://ico.org.uk/about-the-ico/who-we-are/information-commissioner/). The role and functioning of the IC will also be discussed under II.

885 Because the DPA 2018 constantly refers to the UK GDPR, it must be read side by side with the UK GDPR.

886 UK Adequacy Decision (n 14) recital 15.

887 EDPB, 'Opinion 14/2021 Regarding the European Commission Draft Implementing Decision Pursuant to Regulation (EU) 2016/679 on the Adequate Protection of Personal Data in the United Kingdom' (n 615) recital 38.

888 ibid recitals 8 and 57 et seqq.

889 UK Adequacy Decision (n 14) recital 273.

chapter), addresses areas left for member state implementation under the GDPR (second chapter) and applies a broadly similar regime to certain types of processing not covered by the GDPR (including the processing of unstructured manual files by public authorities, law enforcement and intelligence services (Article 2(2) (a)[890]) (so-called "applied GDPR"). Part 3 transposes the LED, which concerns the police and criminal justice sector into UK law. Part 4 provides intelligence services with a specific data protection regime for the processing of personal data.[891] Part 5 clarifies the role of the IC and its functions, and part 6 consolidates the enforcement of the data protection legislation, including powers to issue enforcement notices and penalties. Part 7 contains additional provisions, e. g. information about offences, the tribunal and territorial applications.

II Section 2 DPA 2018

The implementation of the GDPR without the implementation of the Charter received some backlash. It was criticised that in this way only the "shadow" of the right to data protection as found in Article 8 CFR would be retained.[892] The UK GDPR would only provide a framework for recognising and enforcing the fundamental right to the protection of personal data found in Article 8 CFR.[893] This line of argumentation is based on Article 1(2) GDPR, stating that GDPR has the objective to protect "fundamental rights and freedoms of natural persons and, in particular, their right to the protection of personal data".

Section 2 of the DPA 2018 states, "(1) The GDPR, the applied GDPR and this Act protect individuals with regard to the processing of personal data, in particular by – (a) requiring personal data to be processed lawfully and fairly, on the basis of the data subject's consent or another specified basis, (b) conferring rights on the data subject to obtain information about the processing of personal data and to require inaccurate personal data to be rectified, and (c) conferring functions on the Commissioner, giving the holder of that office responsible for monitoring and enforcing their provisions. (2) When carrying out functions under the GDPR, the applied GDPR and this Act, the Commissioner must have regard to the importance of securing an appropriate level of protection for per-

---

890 However, the GDPR applies for activities involving personal data that were initially collected by private entities (such as telecommunications providers) and then used by intelligence services (below under C.).

891 Part 4 of the DPA 2016 is discussed below under III.2.

892 Murray (n 693) 151.

893 ibid.

sonal data, taking account of the interests of data subjects, controllers and others and matters of general public interest." This wording closely mirrors the wording of Article 8 CFR. However, according to the respective Explanatory Notes, Section 2 is only declaratory and does not constitute a new right. The UK Government takes the point of view that the right to personal data protection is already protected within the UK regime under the HRA 1998. The EU Commission agrees with this point of view.[894] However, as pointed out, uncertainties exist regarding whether and to what extent the right to the protection of personal data has been given effect under the HRA 1998.[895]

Regardless of the question on whether Article 8 ECHR has been given further effect *via* the HRA 1998 and irrespective of the criticism concerning the absence of the Charter in UK domestic law, it can generally be said that the UK GDPR and the DPA 2018 provide a distinct domestic data protection law with substance. The UK GDPR and the DPA provide data subjects with several data protection rights irrespective of the lack of implementation of Article 8 CFR. The declaration that only the "shadow" of the Article 8 CFR is retained is not correct. Article 1(1) GDPR states that the GDPR "lays down rules relating to the protection of natural persons with regard to the processing of personal data and rules relating to the free movement of personal data." Such rules can be established in national law regardless of the implementation of Article 8 CFR.

III Controversial Restrictions and Exemptions

The DPA 2018 was introduced to complement the GDPR and is therefore largely compliant with the European data protection law. Hence, the focus in the following lies on those particular restrictions and exemptions to individual's data protection rights that raised some concerns in the context of assessing adequacy.

In EU law, "any limitation on [exercising] the rights and freedoms recognised by the Charter must be provided for by law and respect the essence of those rights and freedoms" (first sentence of Article 52(1) CFR). Also, such limitations are subject to the principle of proportionality. Hence, they "must be necessary and genuinely meet objectives of general interest recognised by the [EU] or the need to protect the rights and freedoms of others" (second sentence of Article 52(1) CFR).[896]

---

894 UK Adequacy Decision (n 14) recital 10.
895 A.II.4.a.
896 The requirements of Article 52(1) CFR were already laid out in Chapter 2, A.I.2.

The UK authorities have explained to the EU Commission that the restrictions and exemptions in DPA 2018 are guided by the principle of specificity – taking a granular approach, splitting more comprehensive restrictions into multiple, more specific provisions – and the principle of conditionality – each provision has appropriate safeguards in the form of limitations or conditions to prevent abuse.[897] Whether these are sufficient to establish an adequate level of protection is evaluated in the following.

1 National Security and Defence Exemption

Article 45(2)(a) GDPR explicitly stipulates that the EU Commission shall, in particular, take into account the third country's relevant legislation concerning national security and defence as well as the implementation of such legislation.[898] The DPA 2018 sets out exemptions that apply to specific data protection provisions if it is required to safeguard "national security" or for "defence purposes".[899] Where "national security" or "defence purposes" are relied upon, exemptions apply to all subject data rights and data protection principles (except the principle of lawfulness), to the obligation to notify a data breach, to the rules on international transfers, to some of the duties and powers of the IC and enforcement provisions[900].[901] The DPA 2018 also allows the Ministers of State to sign a national security certificate to law enforcement authorities[902] and intelligence agencies.[903] It is noteworthy that the national security exemption is not dependent on those certificates; in most cases, the controller will determine whether the national security exemption is applicable.[904] The certificate is "conclusive evidence" where restricting the data subject's rights is necessary for national security.[905] In terms of transparency, certain information must be published by the IC, including the name of the minister who issued the certificate, the date of the

897 Department for Digital, Culture, Media & Sport, 'Explanatory Framework for Adequacy Discussions' (2020) Section E: Restrictions <https://assets.publishing.service.gov.uk/government/uploads/system/uploads/attachment_data/file/872232/E_-_Narrative_on_Restrictions.pdf>.

898 cf *Facebook Ireland and Schrems* (n 64).

899 cf DPA 2018, ss 26 et seqq., 110 et seqq. (corresponding provisions for intelligence services).

900 Except for the provision on the general conditions for imposing administrative fines set out in Article 83 of the UK GDPR and the provisions on penalties in Article 84 of the UK GDPR.

901 cf DPA 2018, ss 26(2) and 110(2).

902 DPA 2018, s 30.

903 DPA 2018, ss 27, 79 and 111.

904 UK Home Office, 'The Data Protection Act 2018 National Security Certificates' (2020) para 3 <https://assets.publishing.service.gov.uk/government/uploads/system/uploads/attachment_data/file/910279/Data_Protection_Act_2018_-_National_Security_Certificates_Guidance.pdf>.

905 cf DPA, ss 27(1) and 111(1).

issue and, where compatible with the interests of national security and the public interest or where it might not jeopardise the safety of any person, the text of the certificate. The UK Government has issued guidance to assist data controllers when considering whether to apply for such a certificate.[906]

a Controversy

The implementation of these exemptions raised some concerns: The Parliament's Joint Committee of Human Rights (after this: JCHR) criticised the breadth of these exemptions[907] and questioned why principles, such as the purpose limitation principle, should not apply in matters regarding national security interests.[908] Furthermore, the lack of definitions of "national security" and "defence purpose" received criticism.[909]

The judicial review regarding the national security certificate is practically limited: A data subject may appeal to the Upper Tribunal[910] against issuing such a national security certificate. Yet, an individual "directly affected" by a certificate would not be notified of this fact. In case of a data access request, the data subjects concerned would only be told that they have been given all the information required under the DPA 2018 but not that their data is being withheld on the grounds of a national security certificate. Consequently, it is practically uncertain, how the right to judicial review could be exercised by the data subject affected without any way of knowing whether a national security certificate has been applied to their data.[911] Also problematic could be that a tribunal may only quash a certificate for the lack of reasonable grounds for issuing the certificate.

b EU Commission's Assessment

The EU Commission found that the national security and defence purpose exemptions include sufficient and appropriate safeguards for the rights and free-

---

906 UK Home Office, 'The Data Protection Act 2018 National Security Certificates' (n 904).
907 House of Commons and House of Lords, Joint Committee of Human Rights, 'Note from Deputy Counsel, The Human Rights Implications of the Data Protection Bill' (2017) para 75 <https://www.parliament.uk/globalassets/documents/joint-committees/human-rights/corre spondence/2017 19/Note_Deputy_Counsel_DPBill.pdf>.
908 ibid.
909 ibid para 73.
910 The Upper Tribunal is the court competent to hear appeals against decisions made by lower administrative tribunals and has specific competence for direct appeals against decisions of certain government bodies.
911 House of Commons and House of Lords, Joint Committee of Human Rights (n 907) para 78.

doms of data subjects.[912] According to the EU Commission, the exemption must be considered and invoked by the controller on a case-by-case basis and compliant with human rights standards. Any interference with privacy rights should be necessary and proportionate in a democratic society.[913] Also, UK authorities stated that "a controller must consider the actual consequences to national security or defence if they had to comply with particular data protection provisions, and if they could reasonably comply with the usual rule without affecting national security or defence".[914] The EU Commission welcomed the ICO's guidance on national security and defence,[915] which stressed that the exemption in question would not be "blanket" and that, to invoke it, "it is not enough that the data is processed for national security purposes".[916] Instead, the controller relying on the exemption would have to "show that there is a real possibility of an adverse effect on national security" and, when necessary, the controller is expected to "provide [the ICO] with evidence about why [it] used this exemption". The EU Commission further emphasised that the guidance contains a checklist and a series of practical examples.[917]

However, the relevant provisions lack any indication that the exemption must be applied on a case-by-case basis as restrictively as possible and lack a clear and precise scope. The EU Commission ignores the fact that the ICO's guidance is not legally binding under domestic law. Therefore, according to CJEU's case law, the guidance cannot sufficiently define and limit the scope and application of the exemption or impose minimum safeguards.[918] Furthermore, the obligation to notify in case of a personal data breach to the IC and the data subject is extensively exempted, even at a point in time where it would no longer jeopardise the mission. Hence, it is very likely that the CJEU will disagree with the EU Commission's view on this matter. Overall, it is not ensured that the exemption is

---

912 UK Adequacy Decision (n 14) recital 63.

913 ibid recital 64 referring to *Guriev v Community Safety Development* (United Kingdom) Ltd [2016] EWHC 643 (QB) [45] (which concerned section 29 DPA 2018); *Lin v Commissioner of the Police for the Metropolis* [2015] EWHC 2484 (QB) [80].

914 Department for Digital, Culture, Media & Sport, 'Explanatory Framework for Adequacy Discussions' (2020) Section H: National Security Data Protection and Investigatory Powers Framework 15 et seq. <https://assets.publishing.service.gov.uk/government/uploads/system/uploads/attachment_data/file/872239/H_-_National_Security.pdf>.

915 UK Adequacy Decision (n 14) recital 65.

916 ICO, 'Guide to the General Data Protection Regulation (GDPR) – National Security and Defence' (*ico.*) <https://ico.org.uk/for-organisations/guide-to-data-protection/guide-to-the-general-data-protection-regulation-gdpr/national-security-and-defence/>.

917 UK Adequacy Decision (n 14) recital 65.

918 cf *Privacy International* (n 800) para 68.

only used objectively, necessarily and proportionately to protect national security. No effective substantive oversight by the IC or the courts is involved. The EU Commission finds that a Memorandum of Understanding[919] between ICO and UK's Intelligence Community (UKIC) ensures that "upon the ICO receiving a complaint from a data subject, the ICO will want to satisfy themselves that the issue has been handled correctly, and, where applicable that the application of any exemption has been used appropriately."[920] However, this Memorandum of Understanding indicates that the ICO is limited to express views but cannot instruct the relevant agency to act differently.[921] The ICO must follow if the authority decides on a "Neither Confirm Nor Deny" response to the data subject.[922]

Concerning the judicial review over the national security certificate, the EU Commission took the view that the tribunal "can consider a wide range of issues" and "may determine that the certificate does not apply to specific personal data [subject to the appeal]".[923] Whether a more comprehensive judicial review applies is unclear.[924]

2 Exemptions for Intelligence Agencies

The DPA 2018 contains some additional exemptions, specifically for intelligence agencies: Unlike other (law enforcement) authorities, intelligence services have the unrestricted permission to process personal data in the controller's legitimate interest or the third party to whom the data is disclosed.[925] This provision received criticism stating that the term "legitimate interest" in such context would be "too broad" and "opaque".[926] Furthermore, where intelligence agencies

---

919 ICO and the UK Intelligence Community, 'Memorandum of Understanding' (2020) <https://ico.org.uk/media/about-the-ico/mou/2617438/uk-intelligence-community-ico-mou.pdf>.
920 UK Adequacy Decision (n 14) recital 125 and footnote 170.
921 Douwe Korff, 'The Inadequacy of the EU Commission Draft GDPR Adequacy Decision on the UK' (2021) 28 <https://www.ianbrown.tech/wp-content/uploads/2021/03/KORFF-The-In adequacy-of-the-EU-Commn-Draft-GDPR-Adequacy-Decision-on-the-UK-Executive-Summary-210303final.pdf>.
922 ibid.
923 UK Adequacy Decision (n 14) recital 131 referring to the UK Home Office, 'The Data Protection Act 2018 National Security Certificates' (n 904) para 25.
924 cf DPA 2018, s 27(4).
925 DPA 2018, sch 9(6).
926 Privacy International, 'UK Data Protection Act 2018 – 339 Pages Still Falls Short on Human Rights Protection' (13 June 2018) <https://privacyinternational.org/news-analysis/2074/uk-data-protection-act-2018-339-pages-still-falls-short-human-rights-protection>; House of Commons and House of Lords, Joint Committee of Human Rights (n 907) paras 82 et seqq.

process data for national security they are entirely exempt from the oversight of the IC.[927]

In its adequacy assessment, the EU Commission was convinced that these exceptions only apply, if necessary, proportionate, and on a case-by-case basis.[928] In practice, intelligence agencies, as controllers, would have to assess whether to submit to the oversight by the IC on a case-by-case basis. The EU Commission again refers to the abovementioned Memorandum of Understanding, which established a framework for cooperation on several issues. However, the Memorandum lacks an explanation on how the communication between ICO and intelligence agencies works in practice where oversight powers of the IC are exempted. It is uncertain whether the IC can verify the lawful application of the exemption at any point. The Memorandum addresses data breach notifications and the handling of data subjects' complaints. When receiving a complaint, the ICO assesses that the application of any national security exemption has been used appropriately.[929] However, in practice, for data subjects to make such complaints, they would first have to learn about the application of national security exemption. While law enforcement agencies are required to inform data subjects of a breach where the breach is "likely to result in a high risk to the rights and freedoms of individuals"[930], intelligence agencies are only required to report "serious" personal data breaches[931] to the IC. Data breaches considered less than serious go unreported.

The EU Commission concluded that the exemption established for intelligence agencies processing personal data have sufficient safeguards "to ensure [that] they remain within the boundaries of what is necessary and proportionate to protect national security".[932] Nevertheless, it can indeed be argued that there is a "lack of sufficient independent oversight" of intelligence services activities.[933] Also, the lack of obligation to report every data breach leads to the limitation of remedies for the data subject.

Schedule 11 DPA 2018 defines rights, principles and obligations from which intelligence services are exempted when processing data for other purposes, such as the prevention or detection of crime or economic well-being of the

---

927 DPA 2018, s 110.

928 UK Adequacy Decision (n 14) recital 248.

929 DPA 2018, s 165.

930 DPA 2018, s 68.

931 According to section 108 DPA 2018, a "serious" breach would be a breach that seriously interferes with the rights and freedoms of a data subject.

932 UK Adequacy Decision (n 14) recital 133.

933 House of Commons and House of Lords, Joint Committee of Human Rights (n 907) para 87.

UK. Nearly all of the data protection principles and all of the data protection rights may be disapplied.[934] Intelligence agencies are even exempted from the obligation to report serious personal data breaches in the cases of Schedule 11 DPA 2018.[935] However, the EU Commission found that these exemptions can only be evoked as applying the data protection provisions would be "likely to prejudice" the specific interest in question.[936] "Likely to prejudice" has been interpreted by the UK courts as "a very significant and weighty chance on prejudice to the identified public interest".[937] Hence, the exemptions must always be justified by referring to the relevant prejudice likely to occur in the individual case.[938] It remains unclear why the exemptions are so broad in scope and preclude the purpose and storage limitation principles.[939] Also, the EDPB expressed severe doubts on whether all exemptions are necessary and proportional and relevant for the work of intelligence services.[940]

3 Immigration Exemption

Also openly criticised is the immigration exemption constituted in the Schedule 2 Part 1 paragraph 4 DPA 2018. According to this exemptions data subject's rights do not apply where personal data is processed for "the maintenance of effective immigration control or the investigation or detection of activities that would undermine the maintenance of effective immigration control, to the extent that the application of those provisions would be likely to prejudice any of [such] matters".[941] The exemption omits the right to be informed, the right to access data, the right to erasure, the right to restrict processing and the right to object to processing. Furthermore, all corresponding data protection key principles are removed. Merely the right to rectification, the notification obligation regarding rectification or erasure of personal data or restriction of processing, the right to data portability, and the principle of purpose limitation continue to apply.

---

934 DPA 2018, s 110.
935 Yet, here applies the "likely to prejudice" test.
936 UK Adequacy Decision (n 14) recital 132.
937 *R (Lord) v Secretary of State for the Home Department* [2003] EWHC 2073 (Admin) [100]; *Guriev v Community Safety Development (United Kingdom) Ltd* (n 913).
938 UK Adequacy Decision (n 14) recital 132.
939 House of Commons and House of Lords, Joint Committee of Human Rights (n 907) para 86.
940 EDPB, 'Opinion 14/2021 Regarding the European Commission Draft Implementing Decision Pursuant to Regulation (EU) 2016/679 on the Adequate Protection of Personal Data in the United Kingdom' (n 615) recital 145.
941 DPA 2018, sch 2 pt 1 para 4.

A narrower set of exemptions applies where a new controller obtains the personal data from the original controller to discharge statutory functions.[942]

The immigration exemption was introduced to avoid that suspected overstayers could be "tipped off" about potential immigration investigation or enforcement actions, and to profile individuals' data to identify travel patterns that may indicate that someone is abusing their rights. According to the UK Government, the prevention or identification of such scenarios would not be possible if someone could stop processing by restricting it or objecting to it.[943] The same applies to the profiling of individual's data to identify patterns that may indicate that a marriage based on which someone is seeking to establish a right to remain in the UK is a sham.[944] The right to erasure was restricted as otherwise, an individual's immigration history could be wiped and prevent the Home Office from considering an individual's case on a proper basis.[945]

In 2018, the immigration exemption was applied in around 60 % of the responses to subject access requests relating to the border and immigration system in the first year of operation of the DPA 2018.[946] In 2020, the immigration exemption was applied in around 70 % of the cases.[947] While the Home Office stated that the exemption only prevents disclosure of small elements and not the whole set of information in most cases,[948] these figures show that the practical relevance of the exemption is significantly high.

---

942 DPA 2018, sch 2 pt 1 para 4(3) and (4).
943 *R (Open Rights Group) v the Secretary of State for the Home Department* [2019] EWHC 2562, [2020] 1 WLR 811 [20] referring to *Alison Samedi* (senior civil servant responsible for data protection policy within the Border Immigration and Citizenship System (BICS) Policy and International Group of the Home Office) in witness statement paras 62 et seqq.
944 ibid.
945 ibid.
946 ibid [22] referring to *Alison Samedi* in witness statement para 7.
947 Open Rights Group, 'Submission to the European Commission, the European Data Protection Board and the European Parliament on the UK Immigration Exemption' (2021) <https://www.openrightsgroup.org/app/uploads/2021/03/Submission-to-European-Commission-on-the-operation-of-the-UKs-immigration-exemption-in-the-Data-Protection-Act-2018-Open-Rights-Group-2-March-2021.pdf>.
948 *R (Open Rights Group) v the Secretary of State for the Home Department* (n 943) [22] referring to *Alison Samedi* in witness statement para 8.

a Controversy

While the Minister for State called this exemption a "necessary and proportionate measure to protect the integrity of the [UK's] immigration system"[949], it has overall encountered much criticism. The ICO condemned that with the exemption, "individuals [would] not be able to access their personal data to identify any factual inaccuracies and it will mean that the system lacks transparency and is fundamentally unfair".[950] According to the ICO, most of the complaints to the IC about the Home Office relate to requests for access to personal data to UK Visas and immigration (often by solicitors acting on behalf of asylum seekers).[951] The ICO also criticised the term "maintenance of effective immigration control" for being too broad and required that the term be more focused on specific statutory immigration functions.[952] The ICO acknowledged the need for sole access restrictions in scenarios of "suspected overstayers".[953] Beyond such access restrictions, the JCHR questioned "why immigration control requires exemptions from fundamental principles such as lawfulness, fairness and accuracy to maintain its effectiveness", even in cases of a "suspected overstayer" or of someone providing false information in an application for leave to remain.[954] The exemption would be disproportionate to extend such restrictions to immigration control as a whole,[955] It is not clear, why in cases of lawful immigration, the restriction of essential data subject rights should be permitted or why key principles of Article 5 GDPR should be left disregarded. *Amnesty International* criticised the fact that the data controller – in most cases the Home Office – would be responsible for determining whether the data protection safeguards would be "likely to prejudice" effective immigration control so that the body against whom the safeguards apply would determine whether or not to exempt itself from these safeguards.[956] *Liberty* claimed that interferences lack foreseea-

---

949 Baroness Williams of Trafford in House of Lords, 'Data Protection Bill' Vol 785 column 1913 <https://hansard.parliament.uk/lords/2017-11-13/debates/EC101CF2-FA1C-4397-9A29-7F07333B396B/DataProtectionBill(HL)>.
950 ICO, 'Data Protection Bill, House of Lords Report Stage – Information Commissioner's Briefing – Annex II' (2017) para 20 <https://ico.org.uk/media/about-the-ico/documents/2172865/dp-bill-lords-ico-briefing-report-stage-annex-ii-20171207.pdf>.
951 ibid.
952 ibid para 19.
953 ibid para 21.
954 House of Commons and House of Lords, Joint Committee of Human Rights (n 907) para 50.
955 ibid.
956 ibid para 51 referring to the Written Evidence by *Amnesty International* (DPB001), November 2017, para 21.

bility and sufficient safeguards.[957] Consequently, a risk of disproportionate interference with privacy and data protection rights appears.[958]

Furthermore, the application of the immigration exemption often involves special category data within the meaning of Article 9(1) GDPR, such as data "revealing race or ethnic origin", requires higher protection from both a EU and an UK perspective.[959] Hence, in order to comply with the principle of proportionality, the immigration exemption must in particular "lay down clear and precise rules governing the scope of application of the measure in question and imposing minimum safeguards so that the persons whose data has been transferred have sufficient guarantees to protect their personal data against the risk of abuse effectively."[960] The EDPB's Guidelines on Article 23 GDPR[961] state that "any legislative measure adopted based on Article 23(1) GDPR must, in particular, comply with the specific requirements set out in Article 23(2) [...]. As a rule, all the requirements detailed below should be included in the legislative measure imposing restrictions".[962] Yet, the immigration exemption does not itself specify "the safeguards to prevent abuse or the unlawful access or transfer", "the controller or categories of controllers", "the risks to the rights and freedoms of data subjects and "the right of data subjects to be informed about the restriction, unless that may be prejudicial to the purpose of the restriction".[963] The "wraparound"[964] term "maintenance of an effective immigration control" is unclear, extensive and lacks foreseeability. It is uncertain what measures (e. g. detention, deportation, extradition, revoking driver's licences or checking bank data) are covered by the term.[965] The exemption is open to all controllers.[966] The exemption also applies in case personal data are not collected for immigra-

---

957 *R (Open Rights Group) v the Secretary of State for the Home Department* (n 943) [25].
958 ibid [25].
959 ibid [58]. Currently, the Article 9(1) UK GDPR still mirrors the Article 9(1) GDPR.
960 *Digital Rights Ireland and Seitlinger and Others* (n 73) paras 54 et seq.; *Tele2 Sverige* (n 81) paras 109 and 117; *Accord PNR EU-Canada* (80) para 141; *Facebook Ireland and Schrems* (n 64) para 176; Chapter 2, A.I.2.b.
961 Article 23 GDPR was briefly outlined in Chapter 2, A.IV.5.
962 EDPB, 'Guidelines 10/2020 on Restrictions under Article 23 GDPR. Version 1.0.' (2020) recitals 45 et seq.
963 EDPB, 'Opinion 14/2021 Regarding the European Commission Draft Implementing Decision Pursuant to Regulation (EU) 2016/679 on the Adequate Protection of Personal Data in the United Kingdom' (n 615) recital 69.
964 Open Rights Group (n 947) 22.
965 Matthew White, 'Immigration Exemption and the European Convention on Human Rights' (2019) 5 EDPL 26, 32.
966 Open Rights Group (n 947) 22.

tion control by a controller ("controller 1") but are made available by the latter to another controller ("controller 2") (e. g. the Home Office).[967] Besides, it is uncertain who may be subject to the immigration exemption. Also, the duration of measures under the immigration exemption is not limited.[968] Furthermore, there are no circumstances for the destruction of the personal data laid down.[969] The "prejudice test" does not set out the safeguards to prevent abuse or unlawful access or transfer.[970]

The UK Government speaks of "relatively limited circumstances".[971] The exemption is invoked in most cases where non-UK nationals try to exercise their data protection right to access their data. According to *Open Rights Group,* in approximately 70 % of all cases between January 2020 and December 2020 the Home Office denies access and therefore undermined the possibility and the right to effectively challenge any Home Office decision based on the inaccessible data.[972] Notably, this also concerns EU citizens.

To counter these uncertainties, the ICO published guidance for data controllers on using the immigration exemption.[973] Although the issued guidance might clarify and reduce legal uncertainty regarding the scope of application of the immigration exemption, it does not provide binding rules[974] complementing the exemption.[975] The EDPB emphasised that due to the importance of restricted rights

---

967 DPA 2018, sch 2 pt 1 para 4(3)(b) and (4).

968 See also White, 'Immigration Exemption and the European Convention on Human Rights' (n 965) 33.

969 ibid.

970 EDPB, 'Opinion 14/2021 Regarding the European Commission Draft Implementing Decision Pursuant to Regulation (EU) 2016/679 on the Adequate Protection of Personal Data in the United Kingdom' (n 615) recital 71.

971 Department for Digital, Culture, Media & Sport, 'Explanatory Framework for Adequacy Discussions' (2020) Section E3: Schedule 2 Restrictions 3 <https://assets.publishing.service.gov.uk/government/uploads/system/uploads/attachment_data/file/872235/E3_-_Schedule_2_Restrictions.pdf>.

972 Open Rights Group (n 947).

973 ICO, 'Guide to the General Data Protection Regulation (GDPR) Immigration Exemption' (*ico.*) <https://ico.org.uk/for-organisations/guide-to-data-protection/guide-to-the-general-data-protection-regulation-gdpr/exemptions/immigration-exemption/>.

974 *R (Open Rights Group) v the Secretary of State for the Home Department* (n 943) [57]: "Mr. Knight informs me that the Commissioner is finalising guidance on the Exemption, but it will have "statutory" status only in the sense of being issued by virtue of the Commissioner's powers under Article 57(1) of the GDPR. It will have no legal status under DPA 2018."

975 See also EDPB, 'Opinion 14/2021 Regarding the European Commission Draft Implementing Decision Pursuant to Regulation (EU) 2016/679 on the Adequate Protection of Personal Data in the United Kingdom' (n 615) recital 70.

and the extension of the exemption, the issue of "quality of law" is crucial.[976] Also, the data subject would still lack effective remedy: The right of data access is of great importance for the data subject as the "gateway" of exercising the other rights provided for the data subject.[977] The data controllers do not explain to data subjects that they have relied upon an exemption nor give a broad summary of the reasons so that the data subject will be unable to challenge it effectively.[978] Suppose a third party obtains personal data and Schedule 2 Paragraph 4 DPA 2018 exempts the right to be informed of this. In that case, an individual may neither challenge the application of the exemption nor the transfer itself. Following a request from *Open Rights Group*, the ICO revealed that since 25 May 2018, only three complaints were received about the Home Office's use of the immigration exemption.[979] Furthermore, although the Home Office committed to "informing individuals that the exemption was being exercised",[980] the Home Office "hold no publicly available records of the number of appeals against the exemption".[981] This reality suggests a failure to notify individuals about restrictions in place.

In its judgement in *YS and Others*, the CJEU clarified the scope of access request in the context of immigration control.[982] According to the CJEU, for the right to access personal data to be complied with, it is sufficient that the applicants have a "complete summary of those data in an intelligible form". The summary must allow that the applicants become "aware of those data and to check that they are accurate and processed in compliance with that directive so that [applicants] may, where relevant, exercise the rights conferred on [them by the Directive 95/46 (now GDPR)]".[983] Should the Home Office make erroneous deci-

---

976 EDPB, 'Opinion 14/2021 Regarding the European Commission Draft Implementing Decision Pursuant to Regulation (EU) 2016/679 on the Adequate Protection of Personal Data in the United Kingdom' (n 615) recital 70.

977 *R (Open Rights Group) v the Secretary of State for the Home Department* (n 943) [58].

978 ibid [59].

979 Open Rights Group (n 947) 11.

980 See *R (Open Rights Group) v the Secretary of State for the Home Department* (2019) (n 943) [48] referring to *Alison Samedi*'s statement third witness statement at para 5: "I recognise that the standard letter does not explicitly refer to the use of an exemption. Consequently, the Home Office will amend this standard response in the future so that if an exemption is relied upon, this is explicitly stated".

981 Open Rights Group (n 947) 11 and 23 et seq.

982 *YS and Others* (n 339).

983 ibid para 59.

sions[984] based on the immigration exemption, individuals cannot challenge it due to their restricted right to be informed, right to object, right of access and right to restrict processing. The immigration exemption is not compliant with the CJEU's judgement regarding the scope of the right to access. Compliance cannot also not be restored with Article 12(4) GDPR, acccording to which, the data controller must inform the data subject of the reasons for not taking action upon the data access request. Although the individual may then exercise his or her right to complain about applying an exemption to the IC, the data subject is not given any further information and can merely suspect that inaccurate data is held about them. The data subject is provided with a relatively poor basis to exercise a claim.

b Open Rights Group

In *Open Rights Group & Anor, R (on Application of) v Secretary of State for the Home Department & Anor* the *Open Rights Group*[985] and *the3million*[986] (the claimants) challenged the lawfulness of the immigration exemption before the High Court of Justice, claiming the exemption to incompatible with the Article 23 GDPR and Articles 7 and 8 CFR. The High Court entirely dismissed the claim. The High Court found the immigration exemption to be compliant with Article 23 GDPR. On 26 May 2021, the Court of Appeal reversed the High Court of Justice's decision and found the exemption incompatible with Article 23(2) UK GDPR.[987] According to the Court of Appeal, Article 23(2) requirements must be met by a measure that is "tailored to the derogation, legally enforceable, and contains provisions that are specific to the listed topics – to the extent these are relevant to the derogation in question – precise, and produce a reasonably foreseeable

---

984 An inspection by the Independent Chief Inspector of Borders and Immigration of data provided by the Home Office to banks found that 10% of the 169 cases inspected had incorrectly been included on the list of "disqualified persons", see Alan Travis, 'Home Office Wrongly Denying People Bank Accounts in 10% of Cases' *The Guardian* (22 September 2017) <https://www.theguardian.com/uk-news/2017/sep/22/home-office-errors-already-leading-to-people-being-denied-bank-accounts>.

985 *Open Rights Group* is a UK-based digital campaigning organisation working to protect the rights to privacy and free speech online. For more information see at the following link <https://www.openrightsgroup.org> accessed 9 June 2022.

986 *The 3million* is an organisation of EU citizens in the UK that campaigns for EU citizens who have made their home in the UK to be able to continue their life here after Brexit. For more information see at the following link <https://www.the3million.org.uk> accessed 9 June 2022.

987 *Open Rights Group v Secretary of State for the Home Department and Secretary of State for Digital, Culture, Media and Sport* [2021] EWCA Civ 800.

outcome."[988] Identifying safeguards in general principles of human rights, within the GDPR itself, or in administrative law, is insufficient. [989] The Court of Appeal found that the immigration exemption "itself contains nothing, specific or otherwise, about any of the matters listed in Article 23(2) GPDR. Even assuming, without deciding, that it is permissible for the "specific provisions" required by Article 23(2) GPDR to be contained in some separate legislative measure, there is no such measure."[990] The judge emphasised that "[t]he ICO's present guidance is doubtless of some value, but it is somewhat vague and, critically, it does not have the force of law. Its provisions might be a relevant consideration for a public law decision-maker [...] but I am not at all persuaded that this would be enough to comply with Article 23(2) GPDR. It is not to be forgotten that the Immigration Exemption applies to many private bodies and individuals. In any event, the term "legislative measure", whatever its precise scope, must refer to something other than a non-binding code promulgated by a regulator that counts as a relevant consideration for administrative decision-making."[991]

c EU Commission's Assessment

In EU Commission's adequacy decision draft, the EU Commission agreed with the High Court of Justice. It stated that "[a]lthough formulated rather broadly, the immigration restriction as interpreted by the case law and the ICO's guidance is subject to several strict conditions – very similar to the ones set in EU law for restrictions to data protection rights an obligation – that frame its application. In particular, it must be applied on a case-by-case basis, only to the extent necessary to achieve a legitimate aim and in a proportionate manner."[992] Yet, the EU Commission failed to assess whether, in practice, the immigration exemption is applied "on a case-by-case basis, only to the extent necessary to achieve a legitimate aim and in a proportionate manner".[993] Consequently, the EDPB has requested the EU Commission to further demonstrate and provide supportive evidence to the necessity and proportionality of the broad scope of the

---

988 *Open Rights Group v Secretary of State for the Home Department and Secretary of State for Digital, Culture, Media and Sport* (n 987) para 49.

989 ibid para 48.

990 ibid para 53.

991 ibid para 53.

992 EU Commission, 'Draft of Commission Implementing Decision Pursuant Regulation (EU) 2016/679 of the European Parliament and of the Council on the Adequate Protection of Personal Data by the United Kingdom' (2021) recital 65.

993 Korff, 'The Inadequacy of the EU Commission Draft GDPR Adequacy Decision on the UK' (n 921) 12.

exemption.[994] However, following the abovementioned Court of Appeal's decision, the EU Commission excluded "personal data transferred for United Kingdom immigration control purposes or which otherwise fall within the scope of the exemption from certain data subject rights for purposes of the maintenance of effective immigration control".[995] The EU Commission announced that "[o]nce the incompatibility with UK law is remedied, the immigration exemption should be reassessed, as well as the need to maintain the limitation of the scope of this Decision." [996]

However, the immigration exemption also includes personal data that are transferred from the EU to the UK, not for immigration purposes, but that may at some point be used for "immigration purposes" ("otherwise subject" to the immigration exemption).[997] Consequently, the "[p]roper application of [the EU Commission's] exemption would mean that no personal data can be freely transferred from the EU to the UK if the exemption may be applied to those data. That would cover almost any personal data sent to any UK public sector entity (including local councils and hospitals)."[998] As this seems rather unlikely and practically impossible, *Douwe Korff* predicts that "this carve-out will be ignored – and is intended to be ignored."[999] Also, an additional contractual provision that the data should not be used or disclosed by the UK data importer for immigration purposes would be insufficient (as seen in *Facebook Ireland and Schrems*[1000]), since it cannot override the UK's law.[1001]

---

994 EDPB, 'Opinion 14/2021 Regarding the European Commission Draft Implementing Decision Pursuant to Regulation (EU) 2016/679 on the Adequate Protection of Personal Data in the United Kingdom' (n 615) recitals 73 et seq.

995 UK Adequacy Decision (n 14) recital 6.

996 ibid.

997 Douwe Korff, 'European Commission Responds to Parliament's Resolution on UK Adequacy' (*Data protection and digital competition by Ian Brown and Douwe Korff*, 30 September 2021) <https://www.ianbrown.tech/2021/09/30/european-commission-responds-to-parliaments-resolution-on-uk-adequacy/>.

998 Douwe Korff, 'Initial Comments on the EU Commission's Final GDPR Adequacy Decision on the UK' (17 June 2021) <https://www.ianbrown.tech/2021/06/17/initial-comments-on-the-eu-commissions-final-gdpr-adequacy-decision-on-the-uk/>.

999 ibid.

1000 *Facebook Ireland and Schrems* (n 64) para 132.

1001 Korff, 'European Commission Responds to Parliament's Resolution on UK Adequacy' (n 997).

4 Conclusion to III

In its adequacy decision on the UK, the EU Commission concluded that the implementation of the GDPR into domestic law and the DPA 2018 build a comprehensive domestic data protection regime that ensures that the UK provides protection "essentially equivalent" to the one within the EU.[1002] However, the exemptions reviewed above might cause a future adequacy decision to be declared invalid by the CJEU. It can be argued with profound reasons that the national security and public defense exemption, limiting the data subjects' rights, lack a clear and precise scope of application. Furthermore, the obligation to notify the IC or the data subject in the case of a (serious) personal data breach does not even apply in cases where such notification would no longer jeopardise the national security mission. Also, the judicial remedy options against national security certificates appear to be only limited in practice. The IC's oversight powers over intelligence agencies are restricted. The exclusion of "personal data transferred [...] which otherwise fall within the scope of the exemption from certain data subject rights for purposes of the maintenance of effective immigration control"[1003] from the adequacy decision's scope of application cannot endure. As shown above, EU citizens, whose personal data is transferred to the EU, may still be affected by the DPA 2018's immigration exemption, which is not "limited to what is strictly necessary" and only provides very limited judicial review options.

IV Information Commissioner

When assessing adequacy, the EU Commission must also consider "the existence and effective functioning" of an independent supervisory authority.[1004] An independent supervisory authority with powers to monitor and enforce compliance with the data protection rules should be in place to ensure an adequate level of data protection is guaranteed practically.[1005] The data protection system must provide support and help to the individual data subjects to exercise their rights and appropriate redress mechanisms.[1006] The authority must act "in complete independence and impartiality in performing its duties and exercising its

---

1002 UK Adequacy Decision (n 14) recital 273.
1003 ibid recital 6.
1004 GDPR, art 45(2)(b).
1005 UK Adequacy Decision (n 14) recital 85.
1006 Art. 29 Data Protection Working Party, 'Adequacy Referential' (n 404) C.4.

powers". [1007] In the following, it is reviewed whether the IC meets these requirements.

1 Independence

Article 52 UK GDPR deals with the independence of the IC, making no substantive changes to Article 52(1) to (3) GDPR. The IC is appointed by Her Majesty on a
recommendation from the Government under fair and open competition and can
be removed from office by Her Majesty following an Address by both Houses of
Parliament. [1008] The latter requires that a minister submits a report to Parliament
stating that the IC is guilty of serious misconduct or no longer fulfils the conditions required for the performance of their duties.[1009] This could be seen as an
equivalent "state supervision", which could lead to a form of "prior compliance"[1010] by the IC about the decision-making practice, since the mere threat
of influence on the IC's decisions is sufficient to impair their independent exercise of their functions.[1011] In light of this, the EU Parliament criticised that the
recommendations by the Constitutional Affairs Committee in 2004[1012] and the
Public Affairs Committee of the UK Parliament in 2014[1013] recommended securing the ICO's independence by making them an officer of parliament who
would report to the Parliament rather than continuing to be appointed by the

---

1007 EU Commission, 'Draft of Commission Implementing Decision Pursuant Regulation (EU)
2016/679 of the European Parliament and of the Council on the Adequate Protection of Personal
Data by the United Kingdom' (n 992) recital 85.
1008 DPA 2018, sch 12.
1009 DPA 2018, sch 12 para 3(b).
1010 *Commission v Austria* (n 88) para 51.
1011 Jens Brauneck, 'Vereinfachter Datenfluss zwischen der EU und dem Vereinigten Königreich – Rechtmäßigkeit des DS-GVO-Angemessenheitsbeschlusses?' [2021] Recht Digital 425,
16 referring to *Commission v Austria* (n 88) paras 63 et seq.
1012 House of Commons, Seventh Report of Session 2005–06, Select Committee on Constitutional Affairs, <https://publications.parliament.uk/pa/cm200506/cmselect/cmconst/991/99102.
html>, para 108: "We see considerable merit in the Information Commissioner becoming directly
responsible to, and funded by, Parliament, and recommend that such a change be considered
when an opportunity arises to amend the legislation".
1013 House of Commons, Public Administration Committee, First Report of Session 2014–15,
'Who's Accountable? Relationships between Government and Arm's-Length Bodies' HC Paper
110 <https://publications.parliament.uk/pa/cm201415/cmselect/cmpubadm/110/110.pdf>, para
64: "The Information Commissioner and HM Inspectorate of Prisons should be more fully independent of Government and should report to Parliament. The Information Commissioner, Commissioner for Public Appointments and the Chair of the Committee on Standards in Public Life
should become Officers of Parliament, as the Parliamentary and Health Service Ombudsman
and the Controller and Auditor General already are."

Minister for Digital Media and Sports.[1014] Unlike, Article 52 GDPR, Article 52 UK GDPR does not set out obligations that ensure that the respective supervisory authority is provided with the necessary resources for the effective performance of its tasks and exercise of its powers. Nevertheless, the EDPB also recognised that the DPA 2018 contains provisions[1015] that aim to secure appropriate funding of the ICO.[1016] The EDPB has "invite[d] the European Commission to observe any developments about the allocation of resources to the ICO, which would be detrimental to the proper fulfilment of the ICO's tasks."[1017]

The Department for Digital, Culture Media and Sport (after this: DCMS) is the IC's sponsoring department within the UK Government, but the IC is an independent public body (constituted in a single person).[1018] The ICO is primarily funded by controllers paying the data protection fee[1019] (around 85% to 90% of the ICO's annual budget).[1020] This funding is supplemented by a grant-in-aid from the government[1021] to fund the ICO's regulation of other laws (such as the Freedom of Information Act (FOIA), the Network and Information System Regulations (NIS), the Electronic Identification and Trust Services (eIDAS) and the IPA 2016). *Jens Brauneck* critically argued since no other sponsor or financier is named, the term "finance" would be more accurate named under the more innocuous term "sponsor".[1022] *Brauneck* questioned the IC's economic independence.[1023] Schedule 12 Section 9 DPA 2018 confirms that the Secretary of States may make payments to the IC from parliamentary funds. Also, under Section 137 DPA 2018, the Secretary of State alone can determine fees of a specified amount to be paid to the IC.

1014 EU Parliament, 'Resolution on the Adequate Protection of Personal Data by the United Kingdom' (n 616) para 8.

1015 DPA 2018, ss 137 et seq., 182 and sch 12 para 9.

1016 EDPB, 'Opinion 14/2021 Regarding the European Commission Draft Implementing Decision Pursuant to Regulation (EU) 2016/679 on the Adequate Protection of Personal Data in the United Kingdom' (n 615) recital 110.

1017 ibid recital 111.

1018 ICO, 'Relationship with the Department for Digital, Culture Media and Sport' (*ico.*) <https://ico.org.uk/about-the-ico/who-we-are/relationship-with-the-dcms/>.

1019 Set by the Secretary of State's Data Protection (Charges and Information) Regulations 2018 (cf DPA 2018, s 137); DPA 2018, recital 16.

1020 ICO, 'How We Are Funded' (*ico.*) <https://ico.org.uk/about-the-ico/who-we-are/how-we-are-funded/>-

1021 Grant aid is mainly used to finance the operating costs of the Information Commissioner as regards non-data protection related tasks.

1022 Brauneck, 'Vereinfachter Datenfluss zwischen der EU und dem Vereinigten Königreich – Rechtmäßigkeit des DS-GVO-Angemessenheitsbeschlusses?' (n 1011) 15.

1023 ibid.

2 General Functions

The IC carries numerous functions and is granted various powers.[1024] The IC is required to execute the functions established in Article 57 UK GDPR, which closely mirrors the corresponding rule in the GDPR[1025], and, for example, includes monitoring and enforcing the application of the GDPR to promote public awareness of data protection issues and to handle complaints by data subjects. Furthermore, the IC must advise parliament, the government, and other bodies on legislative measures relating to processing personal data and power to issue to parliament, the government, other institutions, and public opinions on personal data protection.[1026] When carrying out functions, the IC must regard the importance of securing an appropriate level of protection for personal data, taking account of the interests of data subjects, controllers and others and matters of general public interest.[1027]

3 Investigatory and Enforcement Powers

Moreover, the IC is granted the powers in Article 58 UK GDPR, which closely mirrors the corresponding article in the GDPR[1028].[1029] The powers include conducting investigations in data protection audits and obtaining access to personal data and information from controllers and processors necessary to perform its functions. The DPA 2018 sets out supplement provisions on how the powers can be exercised. The IC advises and assists individuals as well as investigates any complaints made by individuals and other bodies. The IC's central enforcement powers are: (1) The issuing of information notices requiring controllers or processors to provide specified information and obtaining court orders where a person fails to comply;[1030] (2) issuing undertakings to a particular course of action to improve its compliance; (3) serving enforcement notices where there have been failures to comply with data protection law;[1031] (4) conducting consensual audits to assess whether a controller or processor is complying with good prac-

---

1024 DPA 2018, s 115.
1025 Article 57 was already outlined in Chapter 2, A.V.6.
1026 DPA 2018, s 115(3).
1027 DPA 2018, s 2(2).
1028 Article 58 GDPR was already outlined in Chapter 2, A.V.6.
1029 EDPB, 'Opinion 14/2021 Regarding the European Commission Draft Implementing Decision Pursuant to Regulation (EU) 2016/679 on the Adequate Protection of Personal Data in the United Kingdom' (n 615) recital 112.
1030 DPA 2018, ss 142–145. The newly introduced Section 142 obligates data controllers to respond to urgent information requests within 24 hours.
1031 DPA 2018, ss 149–153.

tice in the processing of personal data;[1032] (5) serving assessment notices to allow assessment of whether a controller or processor is complying with data protection law;[1033] (6) issuing monetary penalty notices, requiring payment of specified amounts for serious breaches of the DPA;[1034] and (6) prosecuting those who commit criminal offences under the DPA 2018[1035]. The EDPB emphasised the importance of effective sanctions to ensure respect for rules.[1036] It welcomed that the ICO provides comprehensive information and guidelines on its website but "invites the European Commission to continuously observe the level of support the ICO provides specifically to individuals, whose personal data have been transferred to the UK under the adequacy decision".[1037]

However, some have questioned the effective functioning of the ICO, notably in relation to its action against real time bidding and the ad tech sector (and also in relation to the possibility of complaining about the ICO).[1038] The ICO is said to have a reputation for being rather lenient with companies in the event of data protection breaches.[1039] A few members of parliament "slammed" the IC for failing to protect people's rights during the Covid-19 pandemic.[1040] *Lorna Woods* brings up the ICO's limited success in enforcing the DPA in the law enforcement sector, including the concerns that have been raised about the way the police deployed Microsoft Office Word[1041], as well as the police use of rape victim's data

---

1032 DPA 2018, s 129.

1033 DPA 2018, s 146.

1034 DPA 2018, s 146. The maximum fine that the ICO can impose has been increased to EUR 20 million or 4% of the worldwide annual turnover (DPA 2018, s 157(7)).

1035 DPA 2018, s 197. It is an offence if a data controller destroys, falsifies or conceals information (DPA 2018, s 148).

1036 EDPB, 'Opinion 14/2021 Regarding the European Commission Draft Implementing Decision Pursuant to Regulation (EU) 2016/679 on the Adequate Protection of Personal Data in the United Kingdom' (n 615) recital 112.

1037 ibid recital 116.

1038 For example, Irish Council of Civil Liberties, 'The Commission's Obligation to Refuse an "Adequacy Decision" to the United Kingdom Due to Inadequacy of Enforcement of Personal Data Protection in That Jurisdiction' (2020).

1039 Ander Lozano Zurita, 'Datenschutz nach dem Brexit: Auf was Sie jetzt achten sollten' (*DataGuard*, 12 November 2020) <https://www.dataguard.de/magazin/brexit-und-ds-gvo-was-än dert-sich-mit-dem-eu-austritt-des-vereinigten-königreiches-beim-datenschutz>.

1040 Apsana Begum and others, 'Letter to Elizabeth Denham, UK Information Commissioner' (21 August 2020) <https://www.openrightsgroup.org/app/uploads/2020/08/Letter-for-MPs-Final-sigs-1.pdf>.

1041 Sebastian Klovig Skelton, 'UK Police Unlawfully Processing over a Million People's Data on Microsoft 365' *ComputerWeekly.com* (17 December 2020) <https://www.computerweekly.com/

stored on mobile phones[1042].[1043] *Douwe Korff* called the ICO's enforcement practice "soft". From the numbers looked at by the EU Commission[1044], he identified that the ICO found infringement in approximately 10.000 cases and only issued serious enforcement in twenty-four cases (twenty-two penalty notices and two enforcement notices).[1045] *Douwe Korff*'s calculation suggests that in the UK, even in cases where the IC found that law has been broken, it fails to enforce data protection law in most cases properly. Consequently, one could raise doubts about a serious enforcement practice by the ICO.[1046]

4 Redress

To ensure adequate protection and, mainly, the enforcement of individual rights, the data subject should be given an effective administrative and judicial redress, including compensation for damages.[1047] First of all, data subjects have the right to complain to the IC if they suspect an infringement of the GDPR or DPA 2018 related to personal data relating to them.[1048] Secondly, data subjects have a right to a remedy against the IC. The data subject has a right to effective judicial rem-

---

news/252493673/UK-police-unlawfully-processing-over-a-million-peoples-data-on-Microsoft-365>.

1042 End Violence Against Women, 'New ICO Report Says Consent from Rape Victims "Too Difficult" as Basis for Phone Downloads' <https://www.endviolenceagainstwomen.org.uk/new-ico-report-says-consent-from-rape-victims-too-difficult-as-basis-for-phone-downloads/>.

1043 Lorna Woods, 'Data Protection, the UK and the EU: The Draft Adequacy Decisions' (*EU Law Analysis*, 24 February 2021) <http://eulawanalysis.blogspot.com/2021/02/data-protection-uk-and-eu-draft.html>.

1044 UK Adequacy Decision (n 14) footnotes 98 and 101.

1045 Korff, 'The Inadequacy of the EU Commission Draft GDPR Adequacy Decision on the UK' (n 921) paras 22 et seqq.

1046 Irrelevant for the assessment according to Article 45(2)(b) GDPR is the fact that seemingly, the ICO's enforcement practice does not appear to differ from many data protection authorities within the EU. In May 2021, the EU Parliament noted with concern limited enforcement practices among the member states' data protection supervisory authorities (EU Parliament, 'Resolution of 25 March 2021 on the Commission Evaluation Report on the Implementation of the General Data Protection Regulation Two Years after Its Application' (2021) (2020/2717(RSP)) paras 12 et seqq.) According to the EU Parliament, only a very small share of submitted complaints have been followed up and the amount of fines varies significantly across member states; also, the case investigation periods would take too long. Most member states' data protection authorities would claim that they are underfunded and do not have sufficient means and resources for a strong enforcement practice (which means that these member states are in breach of Art. 52(4) GDPR).

1047 UK Adequacy Decision (n 14) recital 104.

1048 UK GDPR, art 77 (no material modifications to Article 77 GDPR) and DPA 2018, s 165.

edy (before a First Tier Tribunal) against a legally binding decision of the IC concerning them[1049] and in cases where the IC fails to handle a complaint made by the data subject appropriately[1050]. Thirdly, individuals can obtain judicial redress against controllers and processors directly before the courts.[1051] Individuals who have suffered (material or non-material) damages because of an infringement of the UK GDPR have the right to receive compensation from the responsible controller or processor.[1052]

5 Post-Brexit

The IC's involvement and influence in the regulatory cooperation mechanism between the member states' supervisory authorities have stopped after the transition period. The IC will no longer be part of the one-stop-shop dispute resolution system[1053] or the GDPR's consistency mechanism. Also, the IC will not be permitted to act as the lead authority for BCRs applications.[1054] Consequently, organisations and companies that previously had a "main establishment" in the UK will likely be subject to regulation by the IC in the UK and all relevant supervisory authorities in which it is established – unless it designates a leading establishment in an EU member state. If the UK secures an adequacy decision, the IC might be granted "observer status" at the meeting of the EDPB but no voting rights.[1055] The TCA also does not enable the IC to take part in the EDPB.[1056] In 2018, the UK Government stated that it sought more than an adequacy decision and established an appropriate ongoing role for the ICO.

Further, the UK Government declared its desire to participate in the GDPR's one-stop-shop mechanism.[1057] Currently, no non-member states have a status as

---

1049 UK GDPR, art 78.

1050 UK GDPR, art 78(2) and DPA 2018, s 166.

1051 UK GDPR, art 79 and DPA 2018, s 167.

1052 UK GDPR, art 82 and DPA 2018, s 168.

1053 A single supervisory authority can act as a company's "lead authority", based on the location of its sole or "main establishment" (for instance, the place where the main processing activities take place). The lead authority will act as a "one stop shop" to supervise all the processing activities of that business that have an impact throughout the EU. Yet, the appointment of a lead supervisory authority would not exclude other supervisory authorities from asserting jurisdiction over matters that concern them.

1054 See for more information in Chapter 4, B.I.3.

1055 Cullagh (n 874) 119.

1056 cf TCA, art COMPROV.10(3).

1057 Department for Exiting the European Union, 'The Future Relationship between the United Kingdom and the European Union' (2018) 11 <https://assets.publishing.service.gov.uk/govern

contributors. The EDPB and the ICO both support a "constructive and fruitful relation" with each other "to benefit of the protection of personal data".[1058] The EDPB stated that "[w]henever necessary and in compliance with [...] the Withdrawal Agreement, the EDPB will invite [the IC] to continue this exchange to anticipate as good as we can the potential impact of the Brexit on ongoing one-stop-shop cases."[1059] Closer cooperation between the ICO and EU Data Protection Authorities might be possible in the future – either under Article 50 GDPR or under a bespoke supplementing agreement[1060].

6 Conclusion to IV

The IC has comprehensive powers and responsibilities as member states' supervisory authorities. However, it has only restricted powers concerning the processing of personal data by intelligence services.[1061] Furthermore, some concerns were raised regarding the IC's economical and personal independence.[1062] Although, the IC is given extensive enforcement mechanisms, the IC's enforcement practice could be considered to be rather "soft", since no enforcement measures have been issued in a vast majority of cases where the IC found an infringement.

V Conclusion to B

Despite the EU Commission's conclusion that the DPA 2018 guarantees a comprehensive and "essentially equivalent" data protection regime, the review above showed severe doubts. The DPA 2018' exemptions in the context of national security (for intelligence agencies) and immigration could cause a future adequacy decision to be declared invalid by the CJEU. The national security and public defense exemption limits the data subjects' rights and lacks a clear and precise scope of application. In addition, the judicial remedy options are also limited

---

ment/uploads/system/uploads/attachment_data/file/786626/The_Future_Relationship_be tween_the_United_Kingdom_and_the_European_Union_120319.pdf>.
1058 EDPB, 'Response to Ms Elizabeth Denham (ICO) Regarding Invitation to Attend Cooperation Subgroup Meeting and Open Transnational Cases' (2020) <https://edpb.europa.eu/our-work-tools/our-documents/letters/edpb-response-ms-elizabeth-denham-ico-regarding-in vitation_de>.
1059 ibid.
1060 cf TCA, art COMPROV.2.
1061 This was already assessed under III.2.
1062 Brauneck, 'Vereinfachter Datenfluss zwischen der EU und dem Vereinigten Königreich – Rechtmäßigkeit des DS-GVO-Angemessenheitsbeschlusses?' (n 1011) 15 et seq.

due to the absence of an obligation to notify the concerned data subject at all. Against the national security certificate, there is only limited judicial remedy options available to the data subjects concerned. Furthermore, the IC's oversight powers are restricted in the context of intelligence agencies' activities.

The above also showed that the exclusion of transfers of personal data for the maintenance of effective immigration control from the adequacy decision's scope of application cannot endure. EU citizens may still be affected by the DPA 2018's immigration exemption, which is not "limited to what is strictly necessary" and only provides very limited judicial review options.

C Investigatory Powers Act 2016

Remarkably after *Facebook Ireland and Schrems*, the issue of access to personal data, transferred from the EU to a third country, by public authorities, particularly by intelligence agencies, in the recipient third country, is essential in light of assessing adequacy.[1063] In the EU, the competence regarding the protection of national security lies with the member states according to Article 4(2) TEU and Article 2(2) GDPR. In *Facebook Ireland and Schrems,* the CJEU was asked whether this reservation would imply that the legal order of the EU does not include a standard of protection with which the safeguards in place in a third country, concerning the processing of (transferred) data by the public authorities for national security protection purposes, could be compared in the context of the adequacy assessment.[1064] The CJEU denied this and declared that the level of protection of fundamental rights must always be determined based on the provisions of the GDPR, read in the light of the Charter. The validity of provisions of EU law should never "be construed in the light of national law" or the ECHR[1065].[1066] In this context, the Court further referred to recital 10 GDPR,

---

1063 Korff, 'The Inadequacy of the EU Commission Draft GDPR Adequacy Decision on the UK' (n 921) 26.

1064 Reference for a preliminary ruling from the High Court (Ireland) made on 9 May 2018 – Question 2; Opinion of Advocate General *Saugmandsgaard Øe* in *Facebook Ireland and Schrems,* EU:C:2019:1145, para 203; see also for an overview of the discussion Jonas Botta, 'Eine Frage des Niveaus: Angemessenheit Drittstaatlicher Datenschutzregime im Lichte Der Schlussanträge in "Schrems II" Der Prüfungsmaßstab der Gleichwertigkeit und Seine Reichweite im Bereich der Nationalen Sicherheit' [2020] CR 82, paras 25 et seqq.

1065 Opinion of Advocate General *Saugmandsgaard Øe* in *Facebook Ireland and Schrems* (n 1064) paras 203 et seqq.

1066 *Facebook Ireland and Schrems* (n 64) paras 98 et seqq.; approved by Paal and Kumkar (n 575) 735 who argue that the examination of the equivalence of the level of protection of a

which demands to ensure a "[c]onsistent and homogeneous application" of rules protecting fundamental rights and freedoms of data subjects concerning the processing of personal data throughout the EU.[1067] Despite this, even though at the time of the transfers or after that, those data are likely to be processed by the authorities of that third country for purposes of public security, defence and state security, such transfers would fall either way in the scope of the GDPR. Article 4(2) TEU and Article 2(2)(a), (b) and (d) GDPR would not apply to such transfers since they only refer to state activities or state authorities' activities and do not relate to transfers between private data controllers and processors.[1068] Furthermore, Article 45(2)(a) GDPR explicitly includes the adequacy assessment of legislation (and its effective implementation) "concerning public security, defence, national security and criminal law and the access of public authorities to personal data".

The EU Commission assessed the UK's legal framework for the collection and subsequent use of personal data transferred to business operators in the UK by public authorities for the purposes of criminal law enforcement and national security.[1069] This assessment included part 3 and 4 of the DPA 2018[1070] and the IPA 2016[1071]. The IPA 2016 became effective on 1 January 2017, replacing the Data Retention and Investigatory Powers Act 2014 (after this: DRIPA)[1072]. The DRIPA came into force as an "emergency legislation" following the CJEU's judgement in April 2014 in the *Digital Rights Ireland and Seitlinger and Others* case, in which the CJEU declared the former Data Retention Directive[1073] invalid.[1074] Two

---

third country's legal system must be separated from the question of the distribution of competences between the Union and the member states. Some commentators criticise that the CJEU requires a third country to provide a level of protection that is not required within the EU since data subjects cannot invoke the GDPR or the Charter against EU member states' intelligence services (see in more detail in Chapter 5, B.II.2.).

1067 *Facebook Ireland and Schrems* (n 64) para 101.

1068 ibid paras 80 et seqq. referring to the Irish High Court's first question; Advocate General *Saugmandsgaard Øe* came to the same conclusion as he also stated that Article 4(2) TEU only applied to State activities, but not to cases where economic operators are – by law – required to grant public authorities access to data or transfer data to public authorities (see Opinion of Advocate General *Saugmandsgaard Øe* in *Facebook Ireland and Schrems* (n 1064) para 211).

1069 UK Adequacy Decision (n 14) recital 112.

1070 B.III.1 and 2.

1071 The IPA 2016 was famously nicknamed "Snooper's Carter".

1072 The DRIPA was subject to a sunset clause to be repealed on 31 December 2016.

1073 Directive 2006/24/EC of the European Parliament and of the Council on the retention of data generated or processed in connection with the provision of publicly available electronic communications services or of public communications networks and amending Directive

years later, the DRIPA was subject to the CJEU's decision in the joined cases *Tele2 Sverige AB v Post-och telestyrelsen* and *Secretary of State for Home Department v Tom Watson, Peter Brice and Geoffrey Lewis* (after this: *Tele2 Sverige*) and was also declared partly invalid.[1075]

In the following, an overview of the IPA 2016 is provided (under I.), followed by a review of the CJEU's leading judgements concerning the retention and acquisition of communications data and other bulk powers (under II.). The EDPB also published "Essential Guarantees for surveillance measures", which interpret the relevant judgements by the CJEU (under III.). Afterwards, the IPA 2016 is assessed with regard to its compatibility with the Charter, interpreted by the CJEU, and its adequate level of protection for personal data transferred from the EU (under IV.). The EU Commission found no issues concerning adequacy in the IPA 2016.

I Overview

The IPA 2016 generally prohibits the use techniques that allow access to communication content or communications data or equipment interference without lawful authority.[1076] Yet, it also covers a variety of law enforcement and investigatory techniques employed by law enforcement bodies and intelligence agencies that may be used under specific circumstances. The IPA 2016 includes different types of investigatory powers, such as the interception of communications[1077], acquisition and retention of communications data[1078] and equipment interference, and

---

2002/58/EC [2006] OJ L 105/54 (Data Retention Directive). The DRIPA replaced the Data Retention (EC Directive) Regulations 2009 (SI 2009/859).

1074 *Digital Rights Ireland and Seitlinger and Others* (n 73) (II.1.).

1075 *Tele2 Sverige* (n 81) (II.2.).

1076 UK Adequacy Decision (n 14) recital 177.

1077 "Communication" within the meaning of the IPA 2016 covers person-to-person, person-to-machine, machine-to-person and machine-to-machine communication (IPA 2016, s 261(2)).

1078 "Communications data" (or metadata) includes certain types of entity data and events data but is distinguished from the "content" of a communication (IPA 2016, s 261(5) and (6)). Communications data is the information about electronic communication concerning when, how, where and in what form electronic communication is transmitted or stored. Such information can reveal which individuals, groups or devices or computers had connected or communicated with each other, where they were when such communication took place, for how long and how often they communicated and which servicers (and websites) they have connected to. Unlike the interception of data, the acquisition and retention of communications data are not aimed at obtaining the content of the communication.

various types of other powers, either exercised on a specific target[1079] or in bulk[1080]. Targeted powers are available to intelligence agencies and certain law enforcement authorities however bulk powers are only available to the intelligence agencies.

Part 1 of the IPA 2016 imposes specific duties, contains protections for privacy, and restricts various general powers to obtain communications data (in the IPA known as "secondary data") and the circumstances under which equipment interference and specific requests of communications interception may occur. Part 2 legislates lawful interception of communications. Part 3 concerns the authorisations for the acquisition of communications data. Part 4 deals with the retention of communications data ("secondary data"). On 27 April 2018, following the CJEU's decision in *Tele2 Sverige*, the British High Court ruled in *Liberty v Secretary of State for the Home Department* that part 3 and 4 of the IPA 2016 were incompatible with the Charter.[1081] Part 4 was amended by the Data Retention and Acquisition Regulations 2018/1123 (after this: DRAR).[1082] Part 5 provides warrants for equipment interference, commonly known as "hacking" of devices, systems or networks. Part 6 deals with bulk interception and bulk acquisition warrants. Part 6 will be one of the main focuses in the following paragraphs due to the increased role of bulk powers in the public debate and the recent CJEU judgements in *Privacy International*[1083] and *La Quadrature du Net and Others*[1084], which concerned the bulk acquisition. Part 7 deals with bulk personal dataset warrants. Part 8 stipulates oversight arrangements for regimes in the IPA 2016. Part 9 contains further general provisions, including amendments to the Intelligence Services Act 1994 and provisions about combined warrants and authorisation.

1079 IPA 2016, ss 15 et seqq. (targeted interception of communication), ss 60 A et seqq. (targeted acquisition and retention of communications data), s 99 (targeted equipment interference).
1080 IPA 2016, ss 136 et seqq. (bulk interception), ss 158 et seqq. (bulk acquisition of communications data), ss 176 et seqq. (bulk quipment interference), ss 199 et seqq. (bulk personal dataset).
1081 *R (Liberty) v Secretary of State for the Home Department* [2018] EWHC 975 (Admin) [2019] QB 481.
1082 *Liberty v Secretary of State for the Home Department and Others* [2019] EWHC 2057 (Admin).
1083 *Privacy International* (n 800). *Privacy International* is a UK-based charity that active in privacy matters, for more information see under https://privacyinternational.org.
1084 *La Quadrature du Net and Others* (n 800). *La Quadrature du Net* is a French NGO that promotes digital rights and freedom of citizens, for more information see under https://www.la quadrature.net/en/.

II CJEU's Judgements regarding Data Retention and Bulk Powers

The following focuses on the leading judgements of the CJEU concerning the retention of communications data and bulk powers (under 1.–5.).[1085] Finally, the most important aspects of these rulings are summarised (under 6.).

1 Digital Rights Ireland and Seitlinger and Others

The judgement in *Digital Rights Ireland and Seitlinger and Others* became a "landmark case" in many ways.[1086] It concerned the validity of two laws in Ireland[1087] and Austria[1088], which transposed the Data Retention Directive that allowed for the generalised retention of metadata and its access by public authorities. The Data Retentive Directive created an extensive derogation scheme to the pre-existing EU data protection framework. Member states were to adopt measures obligating electronic communications providers to retain all traffic and location data from electronic communication, for a period of no less than sixth months and up to two years.[1089] Furthermore, it set up data retention schemes so the data could be accessed later by law enforcement agencies, intelligence services and may be used for the detection investigation and prosecution of serious crime. The Court concluded that the Data Retentive Directive exceeded the limit imposed by compliance with the principle of proportionality in light of Articles 7, 8 and 52(1) CFR.[1090]

Overall, it would fail to "lay down clear and precise rules governing the scope and application of the measure in question and imposing minimum safeguards so that the persons whose data have been retained have sufficient guar-

---

1085 *Accord PNR EU-Canada* (n 80) concerning the EU-Canada Agreement on the transfer of PNR data will not be further reviewed in this context. It concerned the retention and use of PNR data as well as the disclosure to such data to government authorities.

1086 Marie-Pierre Granger and Kristina Irion, 'The Court of Justice and the Data Retention Directive in Digital Rights Ireland: Telling off the EU Legislature and Teaching a Lesson in Privacy and Data Protection' (2014) 39 Eur. Law Rev 835, 840, the authors provide a detailed analysis of the judgement.

1087 Criminal Justice (Terrorist Offences) Act 2005, pt 7.

1088 Paragraph 102a of the Telekommunikationsgesetz 2003 ("law on telecommunication"), which was inserted into Austrian Law and amended for the purpose of transposing the Data Retention Directive into Austrian national law.

1089 Data Retention Directive, art. 6.

1090 *Digital Rights Ireland and Seitlinger and Others* (n 73) para 68 referring to Case C-614/10 *Commission v Austria* (n 88) para 69.

antees to effectively protect their personal data against the risk of abuse and against any unlawful access and use of that data"[1091] for the following reasons:

The Data Retentive Directive would cover "all persons and all means of electronic communication as well as all traffic data without any differentiation, limitation or exception being made in the light of the objective of fighting against serious crime."[1092] It would "not require any relationship between the data whose retention is provided for and a threat to public security".[1093] The Data Retentive Directive would also lack "substantive and procedural conditions" relating to the data access and the subsequent use of the data by the national authorities when it "must be strictly restricted to the purpose of preventing and detecting precisely defined serious offences or of conducting criminal prosecutions relating thereto".[1094] Moreover, "the access by the competent national authorities to the data retained [was] not made dependent on a prior review carried out by a court or by an independent administrative body".[1095] Last but not least, the Data Retentive Directive would require that the data be retained for an extended period of at least six months and a maximum of 24 months without any differentiation based on security purposes and without objective justification.[1096] The CJEU found severe problems with the provisions relating to security and the protection of data retained by providers of publicly available electronic communications services or public communications networks as the Directive did not "lay down rules which are specific and adapted to (i) the vast quantity of data [retained], (ii) the sensitive nature of that data and (iii) the risk of unlawful access to that data".[1097] The CJEU also stated that the Data Retentive Directive failed to "require the data in question to be retained within the European Union, with the result that it cannot be held that the control, explicitly required by Article 8(3) Charter, by an independent authority of compliance with the requirements of protecting and security [...] is fully ensured."[1098] The Data Retentive Directive was declared invalid.

1091 *Digital Rights Ireland and Seitlinger and Others* (n 73) para 54.
1092 ibid para 57.
1093 ibid para 59.
1094 ibid para 61.
1095 ibid para 62.
1096 ibid paras 63 et seq.
1097 ibid 66.
1098 ibid para 68 referring to *Commission v Austria* (n 88) para 37.

2 Tele2 Sverige

In reaction to the *Digital Rights Ireland and Seitlinger and Others* judgement, the UK enacted the DRIPA as a short-term solution in 2014 till the end of 2016. The DRIPA addressed some of the CJEU's concerns, e. g. providing a maximum retention period of one year[1099] and oversight by an independent reviewer.[1100] However, it was challenged before the CJEU in *Tele2 Sverige* and also declared invalid by the Court. After *Digital Rights Ireland and Seitlinger and Others*, there were still uncertainties about whether EU law prohibited all measures of generalised data retention.[1101] Additionally, the CJEU was asked whether the safeguards and requirements laid down in *Digital Rights Ireland and Seitlinger and Others* were classified as mandatory or merely indicative requirements.[1102]

Most importantly, the CJEU held that all generalised retention of metadata is unlawful and should therefore be prohibited. Only measures of targeted retention could be lawful under the established requirements, which are mandatory.[1103] Combating serious crime would be the only justification for accessing retained data. Public bodies could only access retained data where they have reasons to suspect that an individual is planning, has or might have committed or is implicated in the planning of the serious crime.[1104] However, access might be lawful, where terrorist activities threaten vital national security, defence or public security interests and where there is objective evidence to suggest that accessing personal data of persons not suspected of having committed a serious crime might make an effective contribution to combating such activities.[1105] To enable persons to exercise their right to legal remedy where their rights have been infringed, the authority to whom access to the retained data has been granted must notify the persons affected. The notification must be made as soon as it is no longer liable to jeopardise the investigation undertaken by those authorities.[1106] The member states must also ensure that retained data is maintained in the EU.[1107]

1099 DRIPA, s 1(5).
1100 DRIPA, s 7(1)-(8).
1101 Will R Mbioh, 'Post-Och Telestyrelsen and Watson and the Investigatory Powers Act 2016' (2017) 3 EDPL 273, 275.
1102 Question 2 of Case C-293/12 and Question 1 of Case C-594/12.
1103 *Tele2 Sverige* (n 81) para 108.
1104 ibid para 119 with reference by analogy to ECtHR, *Roman Zakharov v Russia* (n 800) para 26.
1105 ibid para 120.
1106 ibid para 121.
1107 ibid para 122.

3 Ministerio Fiscal

In the case of *Ministerio Fiscal,* the Spanish police requested to order electronic communications services providers to disclose telephone numbers that had been activated on a stolen mobile device and the names and addresses of the subscriber for the SIM cards used for this activation. The request was denied because the robbery and theft of the mobile phone could not be classified as a serious offence. The CJEU emphasised that the objective pursued by the access must always be proportionate to the seriousness of the interference with the fundamental rights: "As regards to the objective of preventing, investigating, detecting and prosecuting criminal offences, in accordance with the principle of proportionality, only action to combat serious crime and measures to prevent serious threats to public security are capable of justifying serious interference with the fundamental rights enshrined in Articles 7 and 8 Charter, such as the interference entailed by the retention of traffic and location data. Accordingly, only non-serious interference with those fundamental rights, such as solely obtaining the subscriber identity, may be justified by the objective of preventing, investigating, detecting and prosecuting criminal offences in general."[1108] In the case of *Tele2 Sverige* the access to retained data as a whole was concerned, which was be classified as a very serious interference with the fundamental rights. Contrary, the access to obtain the subscriber identity is classified as a non-serious interference and therefore could be justified by the objective of fighting criminal offences generally.[1109]

4 Privacy International and La Quadrature de Net and Others

The existence of practices for acquiring and using bulk communications data by security and intelligence agencies, such as the GCHQ, MI5 and MI6, was revealed by *Edward Snowden* in 2013.[1110] The practices were based on Section 94 of the Telecommunications Act 1984, which has now been replaced by the bulk acquis-

---

1108 Judgement of 2 October 2018, *Ministerio Fiscal,* C-207/16, EU:C:2018:788, paras 56 et seq.
1109 ibid para 63.
1110 James Ball, Julian Borger and Glenn Greenwald, 'Revealed: How US and UK Spy Agencies Defeat Internet Privacy and Security' *The Guardian* (6 September 2013) <http://www.the guardian.com/world/2013/sep/05/nsa-gchq-encryption-codes-security>; Jeff Larson, 'Revealed: The NSA's Secret Campaign to Crack, Undermine Internet Security' (5 September 2013) <https://www.propublica.org/article/the-nsas-secret-campaign-to-crack-undermine-internet-en cryption>; Carol Cadwalladr, 'Edward Snowden: State Surveillance in Britain Has No Limits' *The Guardian* (12 October 2014) <https://www.theguardian.com/world/2014/oct/12/snowden-state-surveillance-britain-no-limits>.

ition warrant under the IPA 2016[1111]. The NGO *Privacy International* brought an action before the Investigatory Powers Tribunal (after this: IPT) challenging the lawfulness of those practices.[1112] The IPT referred this matter to the CJEU, which decided on it in October 2020. On the same day, the CJEU decided on the joined cases *La Quadrature du Net and Others* and *Ordre des barreaux francophones et germanophone and Others* (after this: *La Quadrature du Net and Others*) in very similar matters. The latter cases concerned the 2015 French Decree on specialised intelligence services[1113] and the 2016 Belgian Law on collecting and retaining communications data[1114]. *Digital Rights Ireland and Seitlinger and Others* and *Tele2 Sverige* mainly concerned the (targeted) data retention for the purpose of criminal investigations. In contrast, *Privacy International and La Quadrature de Net and Others* concerned the bulk acquisition by security and intelligence agencies for national security purposes.

In the *Privacy International* case, the CJEU confirmed that national legislation requiring electronic communications services providers to disclose traffic data and location data through general and indiscriminate transmission cannot be justified within a democratic society as required by Article 15(1) of the e-Privacy Directive (read in the light of Article 4(2) TEU) and Articles 7, 8, 11 and 52(1) CFR); it would exceed the limits of what is strictly necessary.[1115] The CJEU referred to the requirements established in its judgements in *Digital Rights Ireland and Seitlinger and Others* and confirmed their application to bulk acquisition. Obligations requiring general and indiscriminate data retention remain impermissible.

In *La Quadrature du Net and Others*, the Court found that the e-Privacy Directive "precludes legislative measures requiring providers of electronic communications services to carry out the general and indiscriminate retention of traffic data and location data as a preventive measure.[1116] Those obligations to forward and retain such data in a general and indiscriminate way would constitute particularly serious interferences with the fundamental rights guaranteed by the Charter, where there is no link between the conduct of the persons whose data is affected and the objective pursued by the legislation at issue."[1117]

1111 IPA 2016, ss 158 et seqq. These provisions are reviewed under IV.1.a.bb.
1112 *Privacy International v Secretary of State for Foreign and Commonwealth Affairs and Others*, UKIPTrib 15_110-CH, [2016] HRLR 21.
1113 Code de la sécurité intérieure (Internal Security Code).
1114 Belgian Law of 29 May 2016.
1115 *Privacy International* (n 800) para 81.
1116 *La Quadrature du Net and Others* (n 800).
1117 ibid para 145.

However, the CJEU established several exceptions: Legislative measures which permit the competent authorities to order the general and indiscriminate retention of traffic and location data of all users of electronic communications systems for a limited period are not precluded as long as there are "sufficiently solid grounds" for a situation presenting a "genuine and present or foreseeable" "serious threat" to national security.[1118] The instruction for the preventive retention of data of all users must be limited in time to what is strictly necessary. However, they may "be renewed, the duration of each instruction cannot exceed a foreseeable period".[1119] For the same situations, the CJEU decided that obligations requiring general and indiscriminate automated analysis of traffic and location data retained by a service provider are permissible.[1120] The decision imposing these obligations must be subject to effective review either by a court or a binding decision of an independent administrative body to verify whether this situation justifies such measures and that the necessary conditions and safeguards are observed.[1121] The CJEU further emphasised that regarding automated analysis systems, it should be ensured that pre-established models, criteria and databases are non-discriminatory, not based on sensitive personal data in isolation and subject to regular re-examination.[1122] Also, any positive result should be subject to an individual manual re-examination before being acted upon.[1123] Legislative measures requiring general and indiscriminate retention of source IP addresses would be permissible only "to safeguard national security, combating serious crime and preventing serious threats to public security".[1124] IP addresses would enable the tracking of a web user's complete clickstream and, therefore, their entire online activity; that data allows for a detailed profile of the user to be produced.[1125] Legislative measures requiring general and indiscriminate retention of civil identity data would be permissible for safeguarding national security, combating crime and safeguarding public security in general.[1126] Targeted real-time access to retained traffic located data would not be precluded for persons who previously were identified as having links to a terroristic threat.[1127]

1118 *La Quadrature du Net and Others* (n 800) para 137.
1119 ibid para 138.
1120 ibid paras 172 et seqq.
1121 ibid para 139.
1122 ibid paras 180 et seqq.
1123 ibid.
1124 ibid paras 152 et seqq.
1125 ibid para 153.
1126 ibid paras 157 et seqq.
1127 ibid paras 183 et seqq.

Such access must also be subject to prior review by a court or a binding decision of an independent administrative body or, in urgent cases, within a short time afterwards to ensure that the real-time collection is authorised only within the limits of what is strictly necessary.[1128]

Nevertheless, the CJEU emphasised that all those measures, employing clear and precise rules, ensure "that the retention of data at issue is subject to compliance with the applicable substantive and procedural conditions and that the persons concerned have effective safeguards against the risks of abuse".[1129]

5 Prokuratuur

In March 2021, in the case *Prokuratuur,* the CJEU ruled once again on member states' data retention rules.[1130] The appealing court asked whether the Estonian national data retention regimes are permissible in accordance with Article 15(1) of the e-privacy Directive, read in the light of Arts. 7, 8, 11, and 52(1) CFR, although they are not confined to the prevention, detection, and prosecution of serious crimes, but contain limitations concerning the period of duration of access and the quantity and nature of the data available. The CJEU stated that the findings of the abovementioned previous decisions would apply "regardless of the length of the period in respect of which access to those data is sought and the quantity or nature of the data available in respect of such a period, when, as in the main proceedings, that set of data is liable to allow precise conclusions to be drawn concerning the private life of the person or persons concerned. Even access to a limited quantity of traffic or location data or access to data in respect of a short period may be liable to provide precise information on the private life of a user of a means of electronic communication."[1131]

6 Summary

The CJEU judgements can be summarised as follows: All generalised and indiscriminate retention of communications data is unlawful. Bulk acquisition is only permissible (for a limited period of time) in a few cases specified in *La Quadrature du Net and Others,* for example in situations presenting a "genuine and present or foreseeable serious threat to national security" under specific safeguards. Targeted data retention measures must provide the safeguards to comply with Articles 7, 8 and 52(1) CFR. They must be strictly restricted to the purpose of pre-

---

1128 *La Quadrature du Net and Others* (n 800) para 189.
1129 ibid para 132.
1130 Judgement of 2 March 2021, *Prokuratuur,* C-746/18, EU:C:2021:152.
1131 ibid paras 39 et seq.

venting and detecting precisely defined serious crimes or of conducting criminal prosecutions relating to that and to the purpose of preventing serious threats to public security (through terrorist activities).[1132] In the context of the principle of proportionality, non-serious interferences (such as obtaining subscriber identity[1133] but not source IP addresses[1134]) can be justified by the objective of fighting criminal offences in general. The following requirements are mandatory under EU law:

1. All data retention measures must be based on public law, that allows individuals to reasonably foresee when their personal data might be retained or accessed (clear and precise rules).[1135]
2. All such rules must be legally binding. [1136]
3. Except in the case of urgencies, access by the competent national authorities to the data retained is dependent on a prior review carried out by a court or by an independent administrative body.[1137]
4. The data is to be retained for no longer than required, with precise rules of retention.[1138]
5. Effective protection of the data retained against the risk of abuse and any unlawful access and use of that data must be ensured by sufficient safeguards.[1139]
6. Providers must ensure a high level of protection and security of data retention by means of technical and organisational measures.[1140]
7. Provisions must be made available to individuals for seeking a remedy or the judicial review of public measures for their compatibility with EU fundamental rights.[1141]
8. Individuals must be notified when their personal data has been accessed in cases when doing so does not jeopardise law enforcement or national security investigations.
9. The retained data must be maintained within the EU.[1142]

1132 *Digital Rights Ireland and Seitlinger and Others* (n 73) para 61; *Tele2 Sverige* (n 81) para 119.
1133 *Ministerio Fiscal* (n 1108) para 63.
1134 *La Quadrature du Net and Others* (n 800) paras 152 et seqq.
1135 *Tele2 Sverige* (n 81) para 119.
1136 ibid para 117.
1137 *Digital Rights Ireland and Seitlinger and Others* (n 73) para 62; *Tele2 Sverige* (n 81) para 120.
1138 *Digital Rights Ireland and Seitlinger and Others* (n 73) paras 63 et seq.
1139 ibid para 66.
1140 *Tele2 Sverige* (n 81) para 122.
1141 ibid para 121.
1142 *Digital Rights Ireland and Seitlinger and Others* (n 73) para 68 referring to *Commission v Austria* (n 88) para 37.

Most recently, the CJEU once again confirmed its case law in *Commissioner of An Garda Síochána and others*.[1143] The consideration of these judgements is necessary when assessing the UK's level of adequate protection.[1144]

III European Essential Guarantees for Surveillance Measures

Following the *Schrems* decision, the Article 29 Working Party identified four essential guarantees that "need to be respected for access to data, whether for national security purposes or law enforcement purposes, by all third countries [...] to be considered adequate".[1145] First, data processing "should be based on clear, precise and accessible rules (legal basis)". Second, "necessity and proportionality with regards to legitimate objectives pursued need to be demonstrated". Third, the data processing must be "subject to independent oversight". Last, but not least effective "remedies need to be available to the individuals".

The EDPB further developed the essential guarantees for surveillance measures in 2020 by reflecting the new clarifications provided by the CJEU, particularly in its *Facebook Ireland and Schrems* judgement and the *Privacy International* and *La Quadrature du Net and Others* judgements.[1146] According to the EDPB, they should not be assessed independently but "on an overall basis".[1147] Also, the third country legislation does not have to be identical to the EU legal framework.[1148]

1143 Judgement of 5 April 2022, *Commissioner of An Garda Síochána and others*, EU:C:2022:258, C-140/20. The CJEU is expected to soon decide on the compatibility of the German data retention regulations as designed in the Law on Telecommunications (*SpaceNet and Telekom Deutschland*, C-793/19 and C-794/19) as well as whether there is an independent obligation for the (French) national legislature to require electronic communications operators to retain connection data on a temporary but general basis in order to enable the administrative authority to comply with EU Directive 2003/6 and Regulation 596/2014 (*VD and SR*, C-339/20 and C-397/20).

1144 cf *Schrems* (n 71) paras 91 et seqq.; *Facebook Ireland and Schrems* (n 64) para 171.

1145 Art. 29 Data Protection Working Party 'Adequacy Referential' (n 404) referring to Working Document 01/2016 on the justification of interferences with the fundamental rights to privacy and data protection through surveillance measures when transferring personal data (European Essential Guarantees), adopted on 13 April 2016.

1146 EDPB, 'Recommendations 02/2020 on the European Essential Guarantees for Surveillance Measures' (2020).

1147 ibid para 48.

1148 ibid para 49.

IV Assessment of the IPA 2016

The following provides an assessment on whether the provisions of the IPA 2016 ensure an adequate level of protection for personal data transferred under the GDPR from the EU to the UK.[1149]

1 Principle of Necessity and Principle of Proportionality

Any limitation on exercising the rights and freedoms recognised by the Charter must respect the essence of those rights and freedoms.[1150] Limitations may be made to those rights and freedoms only if they are "necessary and genuinely meet objectives of general interest recognised by the Union or the need to protect the rights and freedoms of others" (principle of proportionality).[1151] Legislation in the UK that does not indicate any limitation on the powers it confers to implement surveillance programmes for foreign intelligence cannot ensure adequate protection.[1152] In *Schrems*, the CJEU clarified that legislation "authorising, on a generalised basis, storage of all the personal data of all the persons whose data has been transferred from the European Union [...] without differentiation, limitation or exception being made in the light of the objective pursued and without an objective criterion being laid down by which to determine the limits of the access of the public authorities to the data and its subsequent use, for purposes which are specific, strictly restricted and capable of justifying the interference which both access to the data and its use entail" do not comply with the principle of necessity.[1153] Laws permitting public authorities access on a generalised basis to the content of electronic communications interfere with the essence of the fundamental right[1154] guaranteed by Article 7 CFR.[1155]

1149 See for a detailed commentary on the IPA 2016: Simon McKay, Blackstone's Guide to The Investigatory Powers Act 2016, (1st edn Oxford University Press 2017).
1150 CFR, art 52(1), first sentence (already discussed in Chapter 2, A.I.2.a.).
1151 CFR, art 52(1), second sentence (already discussed in Chapter 2, A.I.2.b.).
1152 *Facebook Ireland and Schrems* (n 64) para 180.
1153 *Schrems* (n 71) para 93.
1154 The guarantee to the essence of the fundamental rights was already discussed in Chapter 2, A.I.2.a.
1155 *Schrems* (n 71) para 94.

a Bulk Warrants

Part 6 of the IPA 2016 governs bulk interception warrants,[1156] bulk equipment warrants[1157] and bulk acquisition warrants[1158]. Bulk interception could be classified as "direct access" to personal data by public authorities and bulk acquisition warrants as "indirect access".[1159]

aa Bulk Interception and Bulk Equipment Interference

Bulk interception warrants concern the interception of overseas-related communications from the British Islands to outside or from outside to the British Islands[1160], as occurred under the surveillance program TEMPORA[1161], and the subsequent selection for examination of the intercepted material or obtaining secondary data[1162] from such communications[1163].[1164] Bulk equipment warrants

---

1156 IPA 2016, chapter 1, ss 136 et seqq.

1157 IPA 2016, chapter 3, ss 176 et seqq.

1158 IPA 2016, chapter 2, ss 158 et seqq.

1159 Douwe Korff, 'Amid the Spying by EU Member States' Intelligence Agencies, Is EU Law Silent?' (*Data protection and digital competition by Ian Brown and Douwe Korff*, 27 August 2021) <https://www.ianbrown.tech/2021/08/27/amid-the-spying-by-eu-member-states-intelligence-a gencies-is-eu-law-silent/>. According to *Douwe Korff* any direct access of data by the intelligence agencies on the basis of law that does not does not meet the CJEU requirements and EDPB's Essential Guarantees constitutes "unauthorises" and "unlawful" access. Under the GDPR, any controller and processor must protect any personal data they process from such unauthorised access. According to *Korff*, controllers and processors, subject to the GDPR, should treat the risk of such access by EU member states' intelligence agencies the same way as the risk of access by third countries' intelligence agencies. Also, EU data protection supervisory authorities would have the power to order controllers and processors, subject to the GDPR, to not carry out processing operations if the data involved are at "high risked" of an unlawful access of EU member states' intelligence agencies or to adopt supplementary measures as safeguards.

1160 The British Islands constitute the United Kingdom, the Channel Islands and the Isle of Man, Interpretation Act 1978, sch 1, available at the following link <https://www.legislation. gov.uk/ukpga/1978/30/schedule/1> accessed 9 June 2022.

1161 For more information on TEMPORA see Open Rights Group, 'Report on GCHQ and UK Mass Surveillance, Part One Chapter One: Passive Collection' (2015) section 1.3 <https://www. openrightsgroup.org/app/uploads/2020/03/01-Part_One_Chapter_One-Passive_Collection.pdf>.

1162 Secondary data means systems data or identifying data associated with or attached to the communications being transmitted. System data and identifying data are defined in Section 263(4) and in Section 263(2) IPA 2016. Systems data is comprised in, included as a part of, attached to or logically associated with the communications being intercepted. Identifying data is comprised in, included as part of, attached to or logically associated with the communication, which is capable of being logically separated from the remainder of the communi-

authorise the addressee to secure interference with any equipment to obtain overseas-related communications, equipment data, or other information.[1165] Since the concerns as regards to bulk interception warrants also largely apply to bulk equipment warrants, the focus in the following will be on the former practices.[1166]

The dimension of the use of bulk interception powers by the UK (and the US) was exposed and brought to the public's attention by *Edward Snowden* in 2013. [1167] *Snowden* revealed that under TEMPORA, the system used by GCHQ to buffer most internet communications extracted from bearers[1168], bulk data from over 200 cables landing in the UK were intercepted for one and a half years.[1169] TEMPORA functions very similar to the US-PRISM program, the legal basis of which was subject to the *Facebook Ireland and Schrems* judgement.

For a better understanding of the bulk interception process, it can be further divided into the following stages: "(a) the interception and initial retention of communications and related communications data (that is, the traffic data belonging to the intercepted communications); (b) the application of specific selectors to the retained communications/related communications data; (c) the examination of selected communications/related communications data by analysts; and (d) the subsequent retention of data and use of the "final product", including the sharing of data with third parties."[1170] Bulk interception powers are used "to investigate communications of individuals already known to pose a threat or generate new intelligence leads" to identify previously un-

---

cation and which, once separated, does not reveal anything of what might reasonably be considered to be the meaning (if any) of the communication (IPA 2016, ss 16 and 137).

1163 The term "communications" is defined in IPA 2016, s 261(2) and includes "anything comprising speech, music, sounds, visual images or data of any description, and signals serving either for the impartation of anything between persons, between a person and a thing or between things or for the actuation or control of any apparatus".

1164 IPA 2016, ss 136 et seq.

1165 IPA 2016, s 176.

1166 For more information on bulk equipment warrants and the predecessor provisions in Intelligence Services Act 1994 see Paul F Scott, 'General Warrants, Thematic Warrants, Bulk Warrants: Property Interference for National Security Purposes' (2017) 68 NI Legal Quarterly 99.

1167 Ball, Borger and Greenwald (n 1100); Larson (n 1100); Cadwalladr (n 1100).

1168 A bearer can be a fibre within a cable or an optical channel within a fibre.

1169 Ewen MacAskill and others, 'GCHQ Taps Fibre-Optic Cables for Secret Access to World's Communications' *The Guardian* (21 June 2013) <https://www.theguardian.com/uk/2013/jun/21/gchq-cables-secret-world-communications-nsa>.

1170 *Big Brother Watch and Others v the United Kingdom* (n 800) para 325.

known threats to national security (e.g. terrorist plots, cyber-attacks).[1171] Intercepted materials are filtered and analysed to determine communications of intelligence value.[1172] These bulk interception powers may also concern the interception of communications data from EU citizens. Hence, bulk interception warrants have an essential role in the adequacy assessment. The CJEU has so far dealt with bulk interception and collection in its *Facebook Ireland and Schrems* judgement. In *Big Brother Watch v United Kingdom*, the ECtHR held that bulk interception powers under the RIPA 2000 were not *per se* incompatible with Article 8 ECHR.[1173] However, this shows one of the main differences between the ECtHR and the CJEU regarding surveillance measures. While the ECtHR finds that bulk interception is a crucial instrument for the protection of national security – owing to the multitude of threats states face in modern society –,[1174] the CJEU finds general and indiscriminate data retention to be unlawful in general.[1175]

1171 House of Commons, Intelligence and Security Committee, 'Privacy and Security: A Modern and Transparent Legal Framework' HC Paper 1705 para 25 <https://www.pdpjournals.com/docs/88433.pdf>.

1172 ibid para 28.

1173 *Big Brother Watch and Others v the United Kingdom* (n 800). However, the Strasbourg Court found that, such a regime had to be subject to "end-to-end safeguards", "meaning that, at the domestic level, an assessment should be made at each stage of the process of the necessity and proportionality of the measures being taken"; "that bulk interception should be subject to independent authorisation at the outset, when the object and scope of the operation" were being defined; and "that the operation should be subject to supervision and independent *ex post facto* review" (para 350). Having regard to the bulk interception regime operated in the UK, the Court identified the following deficiencies: bulk interception had been authorised by the Secretary of State, and not by a body independent of the executive (para 377); categories of search terms defining the kinds of communications that would become liable for examination had not been included in the application for a warrant (paras 381 et seq.); and search terms linked to an individual (that is to say specific identifiers such as an email address) had not been subject to prior internal authorisation (para 383).

1174 *Centrum för rättvisa v Sweden* (n 801) para 179; *Big Brother Watch and Others v the United Kingdom*, nos 58170/13, 62322/14 and 24960/15, para 314, 13 September 2018; *Big Brother Watch and Others v the United Kingdom* (n 800) paras 323 and 424.

1175 In detail under C.II.

(1) Under the IPA 2016

The IPA 2016 empowers the Secretary of State[1176] to issue authorisations to intercept and analyse communications data without a specific suspicion to identify persons who may pose a threat. The Secretary of State is obligated to conclude that the warrant is necessary "in the interests of national security", "for the purpose of preventing or detecting serious crime" or "in the interests of the economic well-being of the United Kingdom so far as those interests are also relevant to the interests of national security" (necessity test).[1177] Furthermore, the Secretary of State must examine whether "the conduct authorised by the warrant is proportionate to what is sought to be achieved" (proportionality test).[1178] The heads of the intelligence agencies manage a comprehensive list of valid operational purposes that were once specified in a warrant.[1179] This list must be approved by the Secretary of State but is not public. The Secretary of State must find that the intelligence agencies' operational purposes for obtaining and examining the data are necessary.[1180] The operational purposes must be specified in a greater level of detail than the statutory purposes.[1181] However, those statutory purposes are very broadly phrased. UK Government gave as an example for such an operational purpose, the "attack planning by ISIL in Syria against the UK".[1182]

A Judicial Commissioner must also approve the decision to issue the warrant.[1183] In doing so, the Judicial Commissioner must regard "(a) whether what is sought to be achieved by the warrant, authorisation or notice could reasonably be achieved by other less intrusive means, (b) whether the level of protection to be applied in relation to any obtaining of information by virtue of the warrant, authorisation or notice is higher because of the particular sensitivity of that information, (c) the public interest in the integrity and security of telecommunication systems and postal services, and (d) any other aspects of the public interest

---

1176 The Secretary of State is an appointee of the Prime Minister and head of the Department responsible for security and terrorism; more information at the following link <https://www.gov.uk/government/ministers/secretary-of-state-for-the-home-department> accessed 9 June 2022.
1177 IPA 2016, s 138(1)(b) and (2) (s 158(1)(a) and (2) for bulk acquisition).
1178 IPA 2016, s 138(1)(c) (s 158(1)(b) for bulk acquisition).
1179 IPA 2016, s 142 (s 162 for bulk acquisition).
1180 IPA 2016, s 138(1)(d) (s 158(1)(c) for bulk acquisition).
1181 IPA 2016, s 142(7) (s 161(7) for bulk acquisition).
1182 UK Government, 'Factsheet Bulk Interception' (2015) <https://assets.publishing.service.gov.uk/government/uploads/system/uploads/attachment_data/file/473751/Factsheet-Bulk_Interception.pdf>.
1183 IPA 2016, s 138(1)(g) (s 158(1)(e) for bulk acquisition). The role of the Judicial Commissioner is discussed below under 2.a.

in the protection of privacy".[1184] In addition, any other considerations relevant to whether the proposed notice is necessary and proportionate for any of the statutory purposes, as well as the requirements of the HRA 1998 and public law, must be taken into account.[1185]

(a) Untargeted, General and Indiscriminate Bulk Interception

Bulk interceptions under the IPA 2018 can very well be classified as untargeted, indiscriminate and general data collections.[1186] The algorithmic detection of bearers to intercept entails "three main problems", such as "base-rate-fallacy"[1187], "built-in biases"[1188] and the "black-box phenomenon"[1189].[1190] The only "targeting" measure that appears in the process of bulk interception is the selection of the bearer.[1191] When GCHQ taps into a selected bearer, it screens all the data that flow through that bearer indiscriminately.[1192] "Once bearers are selected or accessed, then a copy of everything flowing through it is collected including communications and associated communications data [(in the IPA 2016 known as "secondary data")]."[1193] The Parliament's Intelligence and Security Committee (after this: ISC) emphasised that some filtering of the communications content occurs at the selected bearer, resulting in either the continued re-

---

1184 IPA 2016, s 2(2).

1185 IPA 2016, s 2(4).

1186 Douwe Korff and Ian Brown, 'The Inadequacy of UK Data Protection Law in General and in View of UK Surveillance Laws, Part Two: UK Surveillance' (2020) 10 <https://www.ianbrown.tech/wp-content/uploads/2020/11/Korff-Brown-Submission-to-EU-re-UK-adequacy-Part-Two-DK-IB201130.pdf>.

1187 B Schneider, 'Data Mining for Terrorists' (*Schneier on Security*, 9 March 2006) <https://www.schneier.com/blog/archives/2006/03/data_mining_for.html> emphasising that it is mathematically unavoidable to have a large number of false positives or false negatives when searching for rare instances in large data sets.

1188 David Barnard-Wills, 'Book Review of Oscar H. Gandy, Jr. 2009. Coming to Terms with Chance: Engaging Rational Discrimination and Cumulative Disadvantage' (2011) 8 Marketing, Consumption and Surveillance 379, 379.

1189 "Black Box" phenomenon means the opaque processing of personal data.

1190 EU Parliament, 'EU-UK Private Sector Data Flows after Brexit. Settling on Adequacy' (2021) 15 <https://www.europarl.europa.eu/RegData/etudes/IDAN/2021/690536/EPRS_IDA(2021)690536_EN.pdf>.

1191 Korff and Brown, 'The Inadequacy of UK Data Protection Law in General and in View of UK Surveillance Laws, Part Two: UK Surveillance' (n 1186) 41.

1192 ibid 10.

1193 Center for Democracy and Technology, 'Not a Secret: Bulk Interception Practices of Intelligence Agencies' (2019) 22 <https://cdt.org/wp-content/uploads/2019/09/2019-09-13-Not-A-Secret-Bulk-Interception-Practices-of-Intelligence-Agencies-FINAL.pdf>.

tention or discarding of information.[1194] However, such filtering of communications – applying specific selectors to the retained communications/related communications data – only occurs after the interception.[1195] The ISC also confirmed that GCHQ collects all secondary data associated with these communications before extracting the data most likely to be of intelligence value.[1196] The GCHQ's primary source of communications data is a by-product of the bulk interception activities. Moreover, a warrant may provide for the obtaining of only secondary data.[1197] These communications data are retained.

The bulk, indiscriminate extraction of (at least secondary) data constitutes a breach of the fundamental right to privacy and data protection.[1198] In the adequacy decision favouring the UK, the EU Commission gave the impression that the extraction and retention of secondary data are not as intrusive and that only relevant material for the national security purpose is retained and examined.[1199] However, the CJEU already confirmed that communications data are highly revealing and are "no less sensitive than the actual content of communications" as they can be used to create profiles of individuals.[1200] The ECtHR was also "not persuaded that the acquisition of related communications data is necessarily less intrusive than the acquisition of content".[1201] This case law especially applies for identifying data which falls under the definition of secondary data (in Sections 16 and 137 IPA 2016), such as the location of a meeting in a calendar appointment, the photograph information, including the date and location it was taken, and the contact "mailto" addresses within a webpage.[1202] Hence,

---

1194 House of Commons, Intelligence and Security Committee (n 1171) paras 61 et seqq.

1195 Eric King, 'Witness Statement of Eric King on Behalf of Privacy International in Privacy International v the Secretary of State for Foreign and Commonwealth Affairs & Government Communication Headquarters (Case No IPT/13/92/CH)' para 45 <https://privacyinternational. org/sites/default/files/2018-03/2014.06.08%20Eric%20King%20witness%20statement.pdf>; Center for Democracy and Technology (n 1193) 12 referring to the UK Government's own observation to the ECtHR.

1196 House of Commons, Intelligence and Security Committee (n 1171) footnote 56.

1197 Korff, 'The Inadequacy of the EU Commission Draft GDPR Adequacy Decision on the UK' (n 921) 34.

1198 See also EDPB, 'Opinion 14/2021 Regarding the European Commission Draft Implementing Decision Pursuant to Regulation (EU) 2016/679 on the Adequate Protection of Personal Data in the United Kingdom' (n 615) recital 176 et seq.

1199 UK Adequacy Decision (n 14) recital 239.

1200 *Privacy International* (n 800) para 71.

1201 *Big Brother Watch and Others v the United Kingdom* (n 800) (concerning RIPA 2000).

1202 Examples were given by the UK Home Office, in 'Code of Practice (Draft) on Interception of Communications' (2017) para 2.20 <https://assets.publishing.service.gov.uk/government/up

the indiscriminatory bulk extraction of secondary data compromises the very essence of the fundamental rights to privacy and data protection.[1203]

(b) Principle of Necessity and Proportionality

The objective pursued with the access must always be in proportion to the seriousness of the interference with the fundamental rights. In *La Quadrature du Net and Others*, the CJEU found that legislative measures of member states which permit the competent authorities to order the general and indiscriminate retention of "traffic and location data of all users of electronic communications systems for a limited period of time" are not precluded as long as there are "sufficiently solid grounds" for a situation presenting a genuine and present or foreseeable serious threat to national security.[1204] The broader purpose of "interest of national security" would not be a proportionate purpose for the general and indiscriminate retention. Also, the definition of serious crime in Section 263(1) IPA 2016 does not comply with the CJEU's case law.[1205] Serious crime is defined by Section 263(1) IPA 2016 as an "offence, or one of the offences, which is or would be constituted by the conduct concerned is an offence for which a person who has reached the age of 18 [...] and has no previous convictions could reasonably be expected to be sentenced to imprisonment for a term of 3 years or more," or where "the conduct involves the use of violence, results in substantial financial gain or is conducted by a large number of persons in pursuit of a common purpose". The CJEU requires a relatively high threshold of serious crime and has specified offences related to fighting terrorism or organised crime as serious crimes.[1206] In *La Quadrature du Net and Others*, the CJEU found that to combat crime (in general), the general and indiscriminate retention of only data relating to the civil identity of users of electronic communications systems would be permitted.[1207]

The bulk powers exceed the limit of what is strictly necessary: The IPA 2016 does not itself define the scope and application of its powers concerning direct

---

loads/system/uploads/attachment_data/file/668941/Draft_code_-_Interception_of_Communica tions.pdf>.

1203 Korff and Brown, 'The Inadequacy of UK Data Protection Law in General and in View of UK Surveillance Laws, Part Two: UK Surveillance' (n 1186) 41.

1204 *La Quadrature du Net and Others* (n 800) paras 135 et seqq.

1205 See below under b. for the threshold of serious crime in the context of data retention and targeted acquisition.

1206 Opinion of Advocate General *Saugmandsgaard Øe* of 19 July 2016, *Tele2 Sverige*, C-203/15 and C-698/15, EU:C:2016:572, paras 102 and 108.

1207 *La Quadrature du Net and Others* (n 800) para 157.

access to the system to communications beyond the broad term "interest of national security".[1208] The specific scope and limit of any specific bulk interception are set out in the "operational purposes", which are not available to the public.[1209] Under these circumstances, the IPA 2016 does not meet the requirements set out by the CJEU. The Secretary of State should only validate operational purpose when the intelligence agency answers to objective criteria, including the identifiability of the persons concerned, the quantity of data aggregated and the purpose specification.[1210] Furthermore, the specifics about the operational purposes should be also presented to a Judicial Commissioner[1211], who should also assess the operational purposes themselves, not only to the Secretary of State.[1212] The EDPB criticised the difficulty of determining the scope of these operational purposes, especially in cases where data collection is circumscribed to a geographical area, which could be a few streets but also the EEA as a whole.[1213]

Furthermore, the IPA 2016 permits that data collected in bulk is retained for a long period. Section 150(5) and (6) IPA 2016 provides only for the destruction of the copies of the data collected and only if their retention is not necessary or likely to become necessary, in the interests of national security or any other grounds according to Section 138(2) IPA 2016 or other purposes in accordance with Section 150(3) and (6) IPA 2016.[1214] In addition, the IPA 2016 itself does not preclude the targeting of improper targets.[1215] It does not "define the categories of people on whom data can be collected under the bulk power warrants".[1216] Data subjects "who have no personal link or some link in time or place to the offences or threats in question" should be excluded from collecting personal data by the legislation itself.[1217] The lack of a link between the individ-

---

1208 Korff and Brown, 'The Inadequacy of UK Data Protection Law in General and in View of UK Surveillance Laws, Part Two: UK Surveillance' (n 1186) 40.
1209 ibid.
1210 Rubin S Warrant, 'Digital Rights Ireland Deja Vu? Why the Bulk Acquisition Warrant Provisions of the Investigatory Powers Act 2016 Are Incompatible with the Charter of Fundamental Rights of the European Union' (2017) 50 Geo. Wash. Int'l L. Rev. 209, 234.
1211 More information on Judicial Commissioners is outline below 2.a.
1212 Warrant (n 1210) 234.
1213 EDPB, 'Opinion 14/2021 Regarding the European Commission Draft Implementing Decision Pursuant to Regulation (EU) 2016/679 on the Adequate Protection of Personal Data in the United Kingdom' (n 615) recital 170.
1214 ibid recital 171.
1215 bid 41.
1216 Korff 'The Inadequacy of the EU Commission Draft GDPR Adequacy Decision on the UK' (n 921) 33.
1217 *Big Brother Watch and Others v the United Kingdom* (n 1174) paras 307 and 423; *Big Brother Watch and Others v the United Kingdom* (n 800) para 382 (both concerning RIPA 2000).

uals who may be concerned by the data collection and the purposes pursued by the legislation was also criticised by the EDPB.[1218] The group of individuals targeted by bulk interception programs lacks foreseeability. The ECtHR specified that in the context of the interception of communications, "foreseeability cannot mean that an individual should be able to foresee when the authorities are likely to intercept his communications so that he can adapt his conduct accordingly".[1219] However, the ECtHR stated that in bulk interception situations, the risks of arbitrariness are evident: "The domestic law must be sufficiently clear to give citizens an adequate indication as to the circumstances in which and the conditions on which public authorities are empowered to resort to any such measures".[1220] This requirement is not provided by the IPA 2016. Neither the circumstances nor the conditions under which bulk interception occurs are sufficiently clarified because the operational purposes are kept from the public.[1221] The IPA 2016 does not specify any procedural safeguards, oversights, or review mechanism in the process of the selection of "bearers from which to intercept communications, selectors to sort through the intercepted data to decide what to retain" and any initial search criteria.[1222] It is unclear how closely the Judicial Commissioner reviews and oversees selections of bearers and other processes involved with a bulk interception as part of bulk warrant approval.[1223]

Consequently, the IPA 2016's bulk power provisions do not comply with the principle of proportionality.

(2) EU Commission's Assessment
The EU Commission considered that concerns regarding the "surveillance" practices by UK authorities raised by the *Snowden* revelations, have been sufficiently

---

1218 EDPB, 'Opinion 14/2021 Regarding the European Commission Draft Implementing Decision Pursuant to Regulation (EU) 2016/679 on the Adequate Protection of Personal Data in the United Kingdom' (n 615) recital 151.

1219 *Roman Zakharov v Russia* (n 800) para 233.

1220 ibid; *Big Brother Watch and Others v the United Kingdom* (n 800) para 333.

1221 The ECtHR also criticized the RIPA 2000 for the lack of foreseeability of the circumstances in which (related) communications could be examined, *Big Brother Watch and Others v the United Kingdom* (n 800) paras 391 and 416.

1222 *Big Brother Watch and Others v the United Kingdom* (n 1174) para 347; *Big Brother Watch and Others v the United Kingdom* (n 800) paras 377 et seqq. (concerning RIPA 2000).

1223 Korff and Brown, 'The Inadequacy of UK Data Protection Law in General and in View of UK Surveillance Laws, Part Two: UK Surveillance' (n 1186) 43; EDPB, 'Opinion 14/2021 Regarding the European Commission Draft Implementing Decision Pursuant to Regulation (EU) 2016/679 on the Adequate Protection of Personal Data in the United Kingdom' (n 615) recital 173; EU Parliament, 'EU-UK Private Sector Data Flows after Brexit. Settling on Adequacy' (n 1190) 17.

dispelled by the reform of IPA 2000, concluding in the IPA 2016.[1224] The EU Commission found the necessity and proportionality test, conducted by the Secretary of State (and the Judicial Commissioner) to be a sufficient safeguard.[1225] The Home Office's Code of Practice on Interception would specify that the assessment must involve "balancing the seriousness of the intrusion onto the privacy against the need for the activity in investigative, operational and capability terms. The conduct authorised should offer a realistic prospect of bringing the expected benefit and should not be disproportionate or arbitrary."[1226] Further on, the EU Commission found that the list of operational purposes would limit the scope of selection of interception material for the audit phase.[1227] According to the ISC, these safeguards and power restrictions would prevent the GCQH from conducting "indiscriminate blanket interception[s] of all communications".[1228] However, the EU Commission's assessment failed to analyse the UK's intelligence agencies' actual bulk interception practices.[1229] It downplayed the significance of the interception and subsequent retention of secondary data, which can be highly revealing. Also, the EU Commission's assessment lacks an analysis of whether the UK legal surveillance practices met the requirements of the relevant EU case law[1230],[1231].

In light of the CJEU's *Facebook Ireland and Schrems* judgement, the IPA 2016's provisions regarding the bulk interception powers do not provide a level of protection of personal data, which is "essentially equivalent" to the one guaranteed within the EU. The EDPB highlighted three "points of attention":[1232] First, the EU Commission should have assessed preciseness, clarity, and exhaustiveness of the IPA 2016 and broad definitions in the relation of proportionality of the interception measures.[1233] The EDPB stressed that about the

---

1224 UK Adequacy Decision (n 14) footnote 473.
1225 ibid recitals 218 et seqq.
1226 UK Home Office, 'Code of Practice (Draft) on Interception of Communications' (n 1202) para 4.10.
1227 UK Adequacy Decision (n 14) recital 222.
1228 House of Commons, Intelligence and Security Committee (n 1171) para 58.
1229 Korff, 'The Inadequacy of the EU Commission Draft GDPR Adequacy Decision on the UK' (n 921) 11 and 26.
1230 The CJEU's requirements were outline under II.6.
1231 EU Parliament, 'EU-UK Private Sector Data Flows after Brexit. Settling on Adequacy' (n 1190) 23.
1232 EDPB, 'Opinion 14/2021 Regarding the European Commission Draft Implementing Decision Pursuant to Regulation (EU) 2016/679 on the Adequate Protection of Personal Data in the United Kingdom' (n 615) recitals 148 et seqq.
1233 ibid recital 156.

nature of the law, the CJEU implied that the core elements must be provided in legislation providing for actionable and enforceable rights before a court. Consequently, internal codes containing non-actionable rights would not be sufficient.[1234] Second, the EDPB called the EU Commission out to clarify its understanding of the scope of the IPA 2016, including its sense of the term "users of telecommunications services" and whether data from telecommunication operators' establishments in the EEA are concerned.[1235] Third, the EU Commission should have assessed and demonstrated appropriate safeguards (*ex post* oversight, redress possibilities) within the UK legal framework that would be provided in cases in which the "double-lock" procedure does not apply.[1236] However, the EU Commission failed to do so.

bb Bulk Acquisition

Bulk acquisition warrants allow telecommunications operators to disclose retained communications data to intelligence agencies.[1237] Intelligence agencies are also permitted to acquire bulk personal datasets containing personal information about many people.[1238]

The EU Commission found that the bulk acquisition of communications data would not usually concern the personal data of EU data subjects transferred under an adequacy decision to the UK.[1239] According to the EU Commission, this would follow from the definition of communications data in Section 261(5) IPA 2016 and the definition of telecommunications operators in Section 261(10) IPA 2016: "communications data is held or obtained by a telecommunications operator"; "telecommunications operator is a person who offers or provides a telecommunication service to persons in the UK or who controls or provides a telecommunications system which is (wholly or partly) controlled from the UK". The EU Commission argued these definitions would show "that obligations under the IPA 2016 cannot be imposed on telecommunications operators whose equipment is not in or controlled from the UK and who do not offer or provide services to persons in the UK".[1240] "If EU subscribers (whether located in the EU

1234 EDPB, 'Opinion 14/2021 Regarding the European Commission Draft Implementing Decision Pursuant to Regulation (EU) 2016/679 on the Adequate Protection of Personal Data in the United Kingdom' (n 615) recital 154 and 157.
1235 ibid recital 159.
1236 ibid recital 160.
1237 IPA 2016, s 158.
1238 IPA 2016, pt 7.
1239 UK Adequacy Decision (n 14) recital 231.
1240 ibid footnote 399.

or the UK) made use of the services in the UK, any communications in relation to the provisions of this service would be collected directly by the service provider in the UK rather than be subject to a transfer from the EU". [1241]

The EDPB criticised the lack of clarity that only establishments located within the UK could receive requests from the competent supervisory authority. It would not comply with the abovementioned broad definition of telecommunications operators (in Section 261(10) IPA 2016). [1242] It found that personal data of EU data subjects could certainly be concerned in the case of data collection or generation by an establishment of a UK telecommunications operator located within the EEA, transferred to an establishment of the same operator in the UK based on the adequacy decision and then collected within the UK by a public authority.[1243]

The explanation of the EU Commission gives the impression that the routing of data through third countries and collecting data by third-country entities directly from data subjects in the EU should be exempted from Article 44 et seqq. GDPR. The consequence would be that non-EU companies could be bound by the GDPR, according to Article 3(2) GDPR, but without an EU data exporter, they could not be bound by its specific regime of Article 44 et seqq. GDPR. The EU Commission seems to follow the same approach as the ICO, which distinguishes between so-called "non-restricted transfers" (data importer is subject to the GDPR according to the marketplace principle) and "restricted transfers" (Article 44 et seqq. GDPR apply).[1244] A transfer is only restricted if made "to a receiver to which the GDPR does not apply".

This view conflicts with the opinion of the EDPB following the *Facebook Ireland and Schrems* judgement, which stresses that "remote access by an entity from a third country to data located in the EEA is also considered a transfer".[1245] A data transfer can be classified as a cross-border transfer of data that "are moved from one country to another – or are made accessible from another coun-

---

1241 UK Adequacy Decision (n 14) foontnote 399.

1242 EDPB, 'Opinion 14/2021 Regarding the European Commission Draft Implementing Decision Pursuant to Regulation (EU) 2016/679 on the Adequate Protection of Personal Data in the United Kingdom' (n 615) recital 158.

1243 ibid.

1244 'Guide to the General Data Protection Regulation (GDPR) – International Transfers after the UK Exit from the EU Implementation Period' (*ico.*) <https://ico.org.uk/for-organisations/guide-to-data-protection/guide-to-the-general-data-protection-regulation-gdpr/international-transfers-after-uk-exit/>.

1245 EDPB, 'Recommendations 01/2020 on Measures That Supplement Transfer Tools to Ensure Compliance with the EU Level of Protection of Personal Data – Version 1.0' (2020) paras 13 and 90 et seq.

try than the one in which they are held – [...] irrespective of whether the data are collected directly by an entity in one country from data subjects in another country".[1246] Such data may also be exposed to access by authorities in third countries." International electronic communications data flow through various systems controlled by a different entities with "complex inter-operability and inter-billing arrangements in place".[1247] Regarding modern electronic communications, it is relatively far away from reality to assume that UK communications service providers only collect data from their UK subscribers through their own infrastructure in the UK.[1248] Also, the GDPR provisions apply to all providers outside the EU offering their goods or services to individuals in the EU (Article 3(2)(a) GDPR).[1249] Consequently, the UK telecommunications operators providing services to EU citizens must regard the GDPR and are required to put appropriate safeguards (Article 44 et seqq. GDPR) in place when directly collecting personal data on EU persons. Furthermore, the EU Commission's view would contradict the objective of the GDPR to ensure an equivalent and high level of data protection (recital 10 GDPR).[1250] Article 44 et seqq. also aim to guarantee such a level beyond the EU. It can therefore be assumed that the CJEU would also apply Article 44 GDPR to those controllers in third countries who directly collect the personal data of EU citizens – provided that the GDPR applies geographically. Article 3(2) GDPR does not release these controllers from the obligations of Chapter V GDPR but is rather constitutive for them. The EU Commission's view also ignored the fact that the definition of telecommunications operator is very broad. According to the Communications Data Code of Practice "[t]he definition of a telecommunications operator also includes application and website providers but only insofar as they provide a telecommunications service. For example an online market place may be a telecommunications operator as it provides a connection to an application/website. It may also be a telecommunications operator if and in so far as it provides a messaging service. This means that numerous businesses will be considered telecommunications operators in respect of

---

1246 Korff, 'The Inadequacy of the EU Commission Draft GDPR Adequacy Decision on the UK' (n 921) 16.
1247 ibid.
1248 ibid 16 et seq.
1249 For more information on the "marketplace principle" see in Chapter 2, A.IV.1.c.bb.
1250 Jonas Botta, 'Zwischen Rechtsvereinheitlichung und Verantwortungsdiffusion: Die Prüfung grenzüberschreitender Datenübermittlungen nach "Schrems II"' [2020] CR 505, 512.

some of their operations, even where the majority of their work is unrelated to telecommunications services or telecommunication systems".[1251]

In any case, the IPA 2016's bulk acquisition powers provisions do not comply with the principle of proportionality and the principle of necessity: The remarks above regarding bulk interception warrants[1252] also apply to the bulk acquisition provisions of the IPA 2016. In the IPC's Annual Report in 2019, it was pointed out that an internal GCHQ compliance review of warrants in March 2019 showed that 50% of the justifications for bulk acquisition warrants did not meet the required standard.[1253] Although the GCHC compliance team has taken measures to improve GCHQ's compliance in this area and the IPC does not "expect to slip in this standard at future inspections",[1254] the EU Commission must further review and monitor such implementation and the concrete application of the IPA 2016.[1255]

b (Targeted) Data Acquisition and Retention

Parts 3 and 4 of the IPA 2016 concern the targeted acquisition of communications data and data retention, which are both powers that are available to certain law enforcement agencies[1256] and intelligence agencies. The Secretary of State holds the power to require telecommunications operators to retain the communications data for a maximum period of 12 months.[1257] The targeted nature of acquisition does not relate to the number of operators but to the name or description of the "target", a "description of the nature" and "the activities for which the equipment is used". [1258] Also noteworthy is that notices can be addressed to a "description of operators" and therefore, "a notice may be broader than the proce-

---

1251 UK Home Office, 'Communications Data Code of Practice' (2018), para 2.4 <https://assets. publishing.service.gov.uk/government/uploads/system/uploads/attachment_data/file/757850/ Communications_Data_Code_of_Practice.pdf>.
1252 aa.(1)(b).
1253 IPCO, 'Annual Report of the Investigatory Powers Commissioner 2019' 10.48 <https://www. ipco.org.uk/docs/IPC%20Annual%20Report%202019_Web%20Accessible%20version_final.pdf>
1254 ibid.
1255 EDPB, 'Opinion 14/2021 Regarding the European Commission Draft Implementing Decision Pursuant to Regulation (EU) 2016/679 on the Adequate Protection of Personal Data in the United Kingdom' (n 615) recital 181.
1256 These law enforcement authorities are listed in Schedule 4 DPA 2018.
1257 IPA 2016, s 87.
1258 EDPB, 'Opinion 14/2021 Regarding the European Commission Draft Implementing Decision Pursuant to Regulation (EU) 2016/679 on the Adequate Protection of Personal Data in the United Kingdom' (n 615) recital 164.

dure for targeted retention may seem to imply".[1259] In the view of the EU Commission's the data retention powers established in the IPA 2016 typically do not concern personal data of individuals located within the EU, which are transferred under an adequacy decision.[1260] In this regard, the remarks above regarding the bulk acquisitions apply.

In *Liberty v Secretary of State for the Home Department,* the High Court concluded that Part 4 of the IPA 2016 does not permit general and indiscriminate retention of communications data.[1261] It requires a range of factors to be considered and imposes controls to ensure that the Secretary of State's decision satisfies the test of necessity and proportionality.[1262] The necessity and proportionality test is more distinct than the one stipulated in part 6: Section 88 IPA 2016 requires the Secretary of State to consider further "the telecommunication services to which the retention notice relates, the appropriateness of limiting the data to be retained by reference to location or descriptions of persons to whom telecommunications services are provided." However, in any case, the statutory purposes are not in line with the principle of proportionality. The statutory purposes for which data may be retained are interests for applicable crime purposes, the economic well-being of the UK as far as those interests are also relevant for the interest of national security, in the interests of public safety, for preventing death or injury or any damage to a person's physical or mental health, or of mitigating any injury or damage to a person's physical or mental health and assisting investigations into alleged miscarriages of justice.[1263] These statutory purposes are not in line with the principle of proportionality: Access and the subsequent use of the data by public bodies "must be strictly restricted to the purpose of preventing and detecting precisely defined serious crimes or of conducting criminal prosecutions relating thereto" as well as to the purpose to prevent serious threats to public security (through terrorist activities).[1264] Contrary to the UK Government's view, this would exclude the damages to someone's mental health. In the context of the principle of proportionality, only non-serious interferences (such as ob-

---

1259 EDPB, 'Opinion 14/2021 Regarding the European Commission Draft Implementing Decision Pursuant to Regulation (EU) 2016/679 on the Adequate Protection of Personal Data in the United Kingdom' (n 615) recital 164.
1260 UK Adequacy Decision (n 14) recital 199.
1261 *R (Liberty) v Secretary of State for the Home Department* (n 1081) [127].
1262 ibid.
1263 IPA 2016, s 87(1)(a).
1264 *Digital Rights Ireland and Seitlinger and Others* (n 73) para 61; *Tele2 Sverige* (n 81) para 119.

taining subscriber identity[1265] but not source IP addresses[1266]) can be justified by the objective of fighting criminal offences in general.

Also, the threshold for "serious crime" set out in the IPA 2016 in the context of targeted acquisition and data retention is too low.[1267] According to Section 86(2 A) (targeted acquisition) and Section 87(10B) (data retention), "serious crime" means "crime where the offence, or one of the offences, which is or would be constituted by the conduct concerned is – (a) an offence for which an individual who has reached the age of 18 (or, in relation to Scotland or Northern Ireland, 21) is capable of being sentenced to imprisonment for a term of 12 months or more (disregarding any enactment prohibiting or restricting the imprisonment of individuals who have no previous convictions), or (b) an offence – (i) by a person who is not an individual, or (ii) which involves, as an integral part of it, the sending of a communication or a breach of a person's privacy."[1268] This definition of serious crime does not abide by the ruling of the CJEU in *Tele2 Sverige*.[1269] The CJEU suggests a higher threshold of serious crime, and specified offences related to fighting terrorism or organised crime are serious.[1270] The EU Commission underlies the misconception that the DRAR has followed the *Tele2 Sverige* judgement and has established a higher threshold to "serious crime" than Section 263(1) IPA.[1271] Section 263 IPA 2016 covers offences for which an individual who "has no previous conviction could reasonably be expected to be sentenced to imprisonment for a term of 3 years and more". Consequently, a maximum sentence of three years or more is established by IPA 2016. However, the DRAR defines serious crime as an offence for which someone can be sentenced to 12 months, which means a maximum of 12 months or more. In this way, the threshold to serious crime is significantly lowered by the DRAR.[1272] Any offence committed by a body corporate and any offence that involves, as an integral part of the offence, the sending of a communication or a breach of privacy" is included under the term "serious crime". Hence, there is a high

---

1265 *Ministerio Fiscal* (n 1108) para 63.
1266 *La Quadrature du Net and Others* (n 800) paras 152 et seqq.
1267 a.aa.(2).
1268 IPA 2016, s 263(1).
1269 Lord Paddrick in House of Lords, 'Data Retention and Acquisition Regulations 2018' Vol 793 column 1292 <https://hansard.parliament.uk/Lords/2018-10-30/debates/F2B04417-1038-4179-8EFC-BBEC51692D35/DataRetentionAndAcquisitionRegulations2018>.
1270 cf Opinion of Advocate General *Saugmandsgaard Øe* in *Tele2 Sverige* (n 1206) paras 102 and 108.
1271 UK Adequacy Decision (n 14) recital 202.
1272 Lord Paddrick (n 1269) column 1292.

risk that minor offences will also be included.[1273] The definition of serious crime is not in line with the principle of proportionality.

2 Independent oversight mechanism

In the context of (targeted) data retention and bulk acquisition warrants in member states, the CJEU ruled that access by the competent national authorities to the personal data shall be dependent on a prior review carried out by a court or by an independent administrative body whose decision is binding.[1274] The evaluation aims to verify that a situation justifying the measure exists and "the conditions and safeguards that must be laid down are observed".[1275] In the context of adequacy, the CJEU took the independent oversight over the implementation of surveillances measures into account in the *Facebook Ireland and Schrems* judgement.[1276]

a Investigatory Powers Commissioner and Judicial Commissioners

The oversight over investigatory powers is exercised by the Investigatory Powers Commissioner (after this: IPC) that is appointed by the Prime Minister.[1277] The IPC is the chief Judicial Commissioner and is assisted by other Judicial Commissioners (collectively known as the Judicial Commissioners).[1278] A Judicial Commissioner is only qualified if they hold or have held a high judicial office[1279] and was jointly recommended by a combination of five political and judicial officials.[1280] The term of office is three years with the option of reappointment.[1281] The Judicial Commissioners can be removed from office either by the Prime Min-

---

1273 Lord Paddrick (n 1269) column 1293.

1274 *La Quadrature du Net and Others* (n 800) paras 168 and 189.

1275 ibid.

1276 *Facebook Ireland and Schrems* (n 64) paras 179 and 183. The CJEU took into account an oversight mechanism, which did not cover individual surveillance measures but surveillance programs (para 179).

1277 IPA 2016, s 227.

1278 IPA 2016, s 227(7) and (8).

1279 A "high judicial office" means office as a judge of any of the following courts: the Supreme Court, the Court of Appeal in England and Wales, the High Court in England and Wales, the Court of Session, the Court of Appeal in Northern Ireland, the High Court in Northern Ireland, or as a Lord of Appeal in Ordinary (Constitutional Reform Act 2005, pt 3 s 60(2)).

1280 IPA 2016, s 227(2) and (4).

1281 IPA 2016, s 227(2).

ister in specific circumstances according to Section 228(5) IPA 2016 or if each House of Parliament has passed a respective resolution.[1282]

In the recent *Liberty v Secretary of State for the Home Department* case, the High Court found the Judicial Commissioner to be independent.[1283] So did the EU Commission.[1284] The CJEU has set high standards in this respect. It must be strictly avoided that the Judicial Commissioner as the supervisory authority is subject to any kind of (direct or indirect) external influence.[1285] The independence of the Judicial Commissioners could be questioned since the IPC, and the Judicial Commissioners are appointed by the Prime Minister, who is part of the executive.[1286] The number of appointed Judicial Commissioners depends on the Prime Minister's assessment, which means that in this way, the Prime Minister could control the Judicial Commissioners' effectiveness.[1287] Nevertheless, the Judicial Commissioners' appointment and reappointment have high thresholds that provide sufficient safeguards to prevent any dependency from the executive. The increased requirements that a Judicial Commissioner must meet to be qualified for the position and the high thresholds set out in Section 228(5) for the Commissioners' dismissal is likely to guarantee the Judicial Commissioners' independence.

To obtain warrants for the targeted interception, equipment interference, bulk personal datasets, bulk acquisition of communications data, and retention notices for communications data, law enforcement bodies or intelligence agencies must make a reasoned request which is reviewed and authorised by the Secretary of State. The Secretary of State's decision to approve the warrants is then reviewed and must be approved by a Judicial Commissioner ("double-lock" procedure).[1288] This "double-lock" mechanism is a crucial difference to the prede-

---

1282 IPA 2016, s 228(5).

1283 *Liberty v Secretary of State for the Home Department and Anor* (n 1082) [224].

1284 UK Adequacy Decision (n 14) recital 250.

1285 cf *Commission v Germany* (n 89).

1286 Matthew White, 'The Threat to the UK's Independent and Impartial Surveillance Oversight Comes Not Just from the Outside, but from Within' [2019] EHRLR 512 analysed the IPA 2016' oversight mechanism against the ECtHR' case law. The author argued that the cumulative effects of appointments, tenure, dismissal, directions/instructions, staffing/resources, and the possibility function alteration posed a serious threat to the independence of the oversight system. The author further criticised that the oversight mechanism lacks institutional separation between the IPC and the Judicial Commissioners.

1287 Friederike Gräfin von Brühl and Thomas Nietsch, 'Internationale Datentransfer im Lichte des "Brexit"' (2017) Tagungsband Herbstakademie Recht 4.0. – Innovationen aus den rechtswissenschaftlichen Laboren 171, 182.

1288 IPA 2016, s 229. If a Judicial Commissioner refuses to approve a warrant, the Secretary of State can appeal to the IPC, whose decision is final.

cessor provision of DRIPA and was called to be "one of the most significant new safeguards introduced by the IPA 2016".[1289] The EDPB also welcomed the introduction of Judicial Commissioners as a significant improvement.[1290] However, some critics are concerned that the "double-lock" system does not provide a sufficient safeguard on the exercise of power by the Secretary of State as the Judicial Commissioner is not supplied with the same level of authority as the latter.[1291] Some would prefer a "single-lock" mechanism that only the Judicial Commissioner would decide on the issue.[1292] This mechanism was not implemented due to concerns regarding the lack of ability for the Parliament to hold the Judicial Commissioners accountable.[1293] Others prefer an "equal-lock" mechanism so that Judicial Commissioners can make substantive decisions rather than simply review the decisions made by the Secretary of State.[1294]

The IPC and Judicial Commissioners are obligated to carry out the oversight only in a way that would not jeopardise the success of an intelligence or security operation, or compromise the safety of those involved or unduly impede the operational effectiveness of intelligence services.[1295] In May 2019, concerns from the IPC that the MI5 had failed to comply with warrant safeguards relating to interception were made public.[1296] It shows that unlawful activities continue to happen despite the new oversight mechanism.[1297] Furthermore, the Judicial Commis-

---

1289 UN Special Rapporteur, 'End of Mission Statement on the Right to Privacy at the Conclusion of His Mission to the United Kingdom of Great Britain and Northern Ireland' (2018) <https://www.ohchr.org/EN/NewsEvents/Pages/DisplayNews.aspx?NewsID=23296&LangID=E>.

1290 EDPB, 'Opinion 14/2021 Regarding the European Commission Draft Implementing Decision Pursuant to Regulation (EU) 2016/679 on the Adequate Protection of Personal Data in the United Kingdom' (n 615) recital 202.

1291 Phoebe Hirst, 'Mass Surveillance in the Age of Terror Bulk Powers in the Investigatory Powers Act 2016' [2019] EHRLR 403, 414 et seq.

1292 ibid 413.

1293 House of Lords, 'Debate on the Investigatory Powers Bill' Vol 774 <https://hansard.par liament.uk/Lords/2018-10-30/debates/F2B04417-1038-4179-8EFC-BBEC51692D35/Data RetentionAndAcquisitionRegulations2018>.

1294 *Joanna Cherry* MP stated that "judicial review is not the same as judicial authorisation [since] judicial review creates the illusion of judicial control over surveillance, and it does not achieve enough movement away from the status quo" (House of Commons, Official Report Session 2015–2016, Vol 607 column 843) <https://www.parliament.uk/globalassets/documents/ publications-records/house-of-commons-publications/hcbv607.pdf>).

1295 IPA 2016, s 229(7). This does not apply for the IPC in the context of Section 60 A, where the IPC grants authorisation for most of the communications data request.

1296 Sajid Javid, 'Written Statement, Investigatory Powers Act 2016: Safeguard Relating to Retention and Disclosure of Material' (2019) HCWS1552.

1297 Hirst (n 1291) 417.

sioners' review is marginal and the review standards applied are minimal as there are only three grounds of judicial review: "illegality, procedural unfairness and irrationality".[1298] *Douwe Korff* analysised that in the *Begum* case[1299], the UK Supreme Court's took the approach that Judicial Commissioners are obliged to be respectful and deferential to the Secretary of State who issues bulk power warrants and only opposes it if there is clear evidence that the warrant is not necessary nor proportionate.[1300] This practice is also shown in the annual report of the IPC for 2019 for bulk powers, as all of the bulk warrants in question were approved by Judicial Commissioners.[1301] Also, the EDPB pointed out that affected individuals cannot directly address the IPC but must lodge a complaint with the ICO. However, the ICO has limited competence in national security[1302], which leads to uncertainties on whether it is legally ensured that the IPCO addresses such complaints.[1303]

b Internal Authorisations

The EDPB criticised that "in specific limited cases lawful interception without a warrant is possible and only prior authorisation by the competent IC authorities themselves is required [...] including for interceptions in accordance with overseas requests [pursuant to Section 52 IPA 2016]".[1304] When data is required for the "interest of national security" or "economic well-being of the UK", as long as it is "relevant" for national security, or where a member makes an application of an intelligence agency for "applicable crime purposes",[1305] the acquisition may also be authorised by a designated senior officer (Section 61 IPA). The des-

---

1298 Korff, 'The Inadequacy of the EU Commission Draft GDPR Adequacy Decision on the UK' (n 921) 10 et seq. referring to the Raphael Hogarth, 'Judicial Review' (*Institute for Government*, 9 March 2020) <https://www.instituteforgovernment.org.uk/explainers/judicial-review>.
1299 *R (Begum) v Special Immigration Appeals Commission and Secretary of State for the Home Department* [2021] UKSC 7.
1300 Korff, 'The Inadequacy of the EU Commission Draft GDPR Adequacy Decision on the UK' (n 921) 33.
1301 IPCO (n 1253) 140.
1302 As already established in B.III.1 and 2.
1303 EDPB, 'Opinion 14/2021 Regarding the European Commission Draft Implementing Decision Pursuant to Regulation (EU) 2016/679 on the Adequate Protection of Personal Data in the United Kingdom' (n 615) recital 211.
1304 ibid recital 160.
1305 IPA 2016, s 61(7)(b). "Applicable crime purpose" means, according to Section 61(7)(A) IPA 2016 "where the communications data is wholly or partly events data, the purpose of preventing or detecting serious crime; in any other case, the purpose of preventing or detecting crime or of preventing disorder".

ignated senior officer varies depending on the relevant public authority.[1306] While the EU Commission refers to the Home Office's Code of Practice on Communication Data[1307] that emphasises that the designated officer "must be independent from the investigation or operation concerned and have working knowledge of human rights principles and legislation",[1308] the authorisation is still classified as an internal authorisation. In *Tele 2 Sverige*, the CJEU recognised internal authorisation to be solely acceptable in cases of validly established urgency.[1309] Hence, provisions that allow interception of communications[1310], obtaining communications data[1311], equipment interferences[1312], bulk equipment interferences[1313] and bulk personal dataset[1314], without prior authorisation by a Judicial Commissioner in urgent cases, would be compliant with the CJEU's case law.[1315] In all other cases, the access of competent national authorities to retained data should be subject to a prior review carried out either by a court or by an independent administrative body. However, Section 61 A IPA 2016, introduced by the DRAR, goes further and permits internal authorisation for cases where requests for communications data made for national security purposes or the purpose of the economic well-being of the UK, as far as those interests are also relevant for the national security and will be maintained.[1316] In its assessment, the EU Commission did not consider this CJEU case law on the internal authorisation.[1317] An *ex-post* oversight by the IPC through an audit, inspection and investigation would not be sufficient according to the CJEU's case law. The EDPB had called the EU Commission out to clarify further the conditions

---

1306 IPA 2016, s 70(3).

1307 UK Home Office, 'Code of Practice (Draft) on Interception of Communications' (n 1202) paras 4.12 et seqq.

1308 UK Adequacy Decision (n 14) recital 203.

1309 *Tele2 Sverige* (n 81) para 120.

1310 IPA 2016, s 23.

1311 IPA 2016, s 16 A.

1312 IPA 2016, s 109.

1313 IPA 2016, s 180.

1314 IPA 2016, s 209.

1315 The Judicial Commissioner must be informed that a warrant has been issued and must approve it within three working days (cf IPA 2016, s 109(2) and (3). In cases, where the Judicial Commissioner refuses to approve the warrant, it ceases to have affect and may not be renewed (cf IPA 2016, s 109(4)).

1316 IPA 2016, new s 61(7)(a) and (c).

1317 UK Adequacy Decision (n 14) recital 203.

under which urgency can be invoked.[1318] However, the EU Commission failed to do so.[1319]

c EU Commission's Assessment

The EU Commission found that the IPA 2016 set out an effective independent oversight mechanism.[1320] However, the EU Commission failed to assess the procedural arrangements in practice and mistakes that the Judicial Commissioners only can conduct a marginal and limited judicial review in practice. The CJEU could very well conclude that the review of the Judicial Commissioners is ineffective in practice. If the CJEU were to review the oversight mechanism in the future, Section 61 IPA 2016 could also be an obstacle for confirming the validation of the EU Commission's adequacy decision.

1318 EDPB, 'Opinion 14/2021 Regarding the European Commission Draft Implementing Decision Pursuant to Regulation (EU) 2016/679 on the Adequate Protection of Personal Data in the United Kingdom' (n 615) recital 166.

1319 UK Home Office, 'Code of Practice (Draft) on Interception of Communications' (n 1202) para 5.31"[c]ircumstances in which an urgent authorisation may be appropriate include but are not limited to: an immediate threat of loss or serious harm to human life – this may include those situations where, for example, there is serious concern for the welfare of a vulnerable person including children at imminent risk of being abused or otherwise harmed; an urgent operational requirement where, within no more than 48 hours of the urgent authorisation being granted, the acquisition of communications data will directly assist the prevention or detection of the commission of a serious crime or the making of arrests or the seizure of illicit material, or where that operational opportunity will be lost; or a credible and immediate threat to national security or a time-critical and unique opportunity to secure, or prevent the loss of, information of vital importance to national security where that threat might be realised, or that opportunity lost. A situation where there has been a loss of life or serious harm to an individual, or where a person is otherwise unable to identify themselves, and the acquisition of communications data will assist with locating the next of kin of the affected individual where there are no other methods to locate the next of kin."; UK Home Office, 'Code of Practice on Equipment Interference – Pursuant to Schedule 7 to the Investigatory Powers Act 2016' (2018) para 5.67 <https://assets.pub lishing.service.gov.uk/government/uploads/system/uploads/attachment_data/file/715479/Equi Equip_Interference_Code_of_Practice.pdf> para 5.67: "Urgency is determined by whether it would be reasonably practicable to seek the Judicial Commissioner's approval to issue the warrant in the time available to meet an operational or investigative need. Urgent warrants should fall into one or both of the following categories: (i) imminent threat to life or serious harm – for example, if an individual has been kidnapped and it is assessed that their life is in imminent danger; or (ii) an intelligence-gathering or investigative opportunity with limited time to act – for example, a consignment of Class A drugs is about to enter the UK and law enforcement agencies want to have coverage of the perpetrators of serious crime in order to effect arrests."

1320 UK Adequacy Decision (n 14) recitals 250 et seqq.

3 Effective Remedies

On the grounds of Article 47(1) CFR, individuals must have an effective remedy to satisfy their rights when they consider that they are not or have not been respected. "[L]egislation not providing for any possibility for an individual to pursue legal remedies in order to have access to personal data relating to him, or to obtain the rectification or erasure of such data, does not respect the essence of the fundamental right to effective judicial protection, as enshrined in Article 47 of the Charter."[1321] Article 47(1) CFR refers to a "tribunal". According to the CJEU, "data subjects must have the possibility of bringing legal action before an independent and impartial court [or body which offers guarantees essentially equivalent to those required by Article 47 CFR,][1322] in order to have access to their personal data, or to obtain the rectification or erasure of such data".[1323] The court or body must be independent, especially from the executive, with all necessary guarantees, including its conditions of dismissal or revocation of appointment and powers.[1324] The body shall have the power to adopt decisions binding on the intelligence services in accordance with legal safeguards on which data subjects can rely.[1325]

a Investigatory Powers Tribunal

The IPT is the judicial body for any complaint by a person aggrieved by conduct under the IPA 2016, RIPA 2000 or any conduct of the intelligence services.[1326] It is a specialist tribunal whose members must have specified judicial experience. The quality of the membership in terms of judicial expertise and independence is very high;[1327] members must hold or have held high judicial office or be a qualified lawyer of a least ten years.[1328] The IPT is independent of the executive.[1329] Her Majesty appoints members for a period of five years.[1330] They also may be removed from office by Her Majesty on an address presented to her by

---

1321 *Schrems* (n 71) para 95.
1322 *Facebook Ireland and Schrems* (n 64) para 197.
1323 ibid para 194.
1324 ibid para 195.
1325 ibid para 196.
1326 RIPA 2000, s 65.
1327 *R (Privacy International) v Investigatory Powers Tribunal* [2019] UKSC 22, [2020] AC 491.
1328 RIPA 2000, s 65(1).
1329 UK Adequacy Decision (n 14) recital 264.
1330 RIPA 2000, s 65.

both Houses of Parliament.[1331] The tribunal is a judicial body of similar standing and authority to the High Court.[1332]

The IPT has jurisdiction regarding claims brought against public authorities regarding all the powers provided for in the IPA 2016.[1333] Two forms of challenges are allowed: a claim under Section 7 of the HRA 1998 for any breach of Convention rights (Section 65(2)(a) RIPA 2000) or a complaint against a public authority (Section 65(2)(b) RIPA 2000) "by a person who is aggrieved by any conduct [by and or on behalf of any intelligence services, for or in connection with the interception of communications in the course of their transmission by means of a postal service or telecommunications system, or of a kind which may be required or permitted by communication retention authorisation or notice or a bulk acquisition warrant] which he believes (a) to have taken place in relation to him, to any of his property, to any communications sent by or to him, or intended for him, or to use of any postal services, telecommunications service or telecommunication systems; and (b) to have taken place in challengeable circumstances or to have been carried out by or on behalf of any of the intelligence services".[1334] The latter complaint is permitted by any person who believes that they have been subject to any use of investigatory powers.[1335] Individuals may claim to be victims of violation committed by the mere existence of secret measures or legislation permitting secret measures if they can show that they are potentially at risk of being subject to such measures due to their personal situation.[1336] The IPT called this a "low hurdle" for a claimant;[1337] the ECtHR agreed.[1338] The IPC cannot refer a case to the IPT for investigation. Individuals are provided with a domestic route of appeal from a decision or determination of the IPT on a legal issue to the Court of Appeal in England or Wales:[1339] The decision on whether to grant permission to appeal will be taken by the IPT in the first instance. If the IPT refuses to grant permission to appeal, this decision may be reviewed by the appeal court.[1340] The Supreme Court has decided that the IPT is amenable to judicial review.[1341]

1331 RIPA 2000, sch 3 para 1(5).

1332 *R (A) v Director of Establishments of the Security Service* [2009] UKSC 12, [2010] 2 AC 1.

1333 IPA 2016, s 243 (amending RIPA 2000, ss 65 and 67).

1334 RIPA 2000, s 65(4).

1335 RIPA 2000, s 65(2)(b), (4) and (5).

1336 *Human Rights Watch Inc and Others v Secretary of State for Foreign and Commonwealth Affairs and Others* [2016] UKIPTrib 15 165-CH [46].

1337 ibid. The EU Commission agreed with this view (UK Adequacy Decision (n 14) recital 266).

1338 *Roman Zakharov v Russia* (n 800) para 171.

1339 IPA 2016, s 242(1) and RIPA 2000, new s 67 A.

1340 In England and Wales this would be the Court of Appeal.

The "IPT will generally proceed on the assumption that the facts asserted by the applicant are true and then, acting upon that assumption, decide whether they would constitute lawful or unlawful conduct".[1342] The IPT takes "both the generic compliance of the relevant interception regime" (based on "assuming there to have been an interception as alleged") into consideration "as well as, at a subsequent stage, the specific question of whether the individual applicant's rights have [...] been breached".[1343] Those involved in the authorisation and execution of a warrant are required to disclose to the IPT all documents it may need, including "below the waterline" documents that could not be made public for national security reasons,[1344] irrespective of whether those documents support or undermine their defence. The IPT has the discretion to hold (oral) hearings in public, where possible.[1345] In closed proceedings, it may appoint a counsel to the tribunal to make submissions on behalf of claimants who cannot be represented.[1346] The IPT has the power to award compensation and make any other order it deems fit, including quashing or cancelling any warrant and requiring the destruction of any records.[1347] However, the possibility to grant the data subject the right to rectify data or provide access to data, which the CJEU required in *Facebook Ireland and Schrems*[1348], is not explicitly mentioned. However, the term "any order it sees fit" indicates a discretionary power of the tribunal.

b ECtHR's Assessment
In the case *Kennedy v United Kingdom* the ECtHR found that the IPT was compliant with Articles 6 and 13 ECHR, offering a fair trial and effective judicial reme-

---

1341 *R (Privacy International) v Investigatory Powers Tribunal* (n 1327).
1342 *Big Brother Watch and Others v the United Kingdom* (n 1174) para 250.
1343 *Big Brother Watch and Others v the United Kingdom* (n 1174) para 250. *Big Brother Watch and Others v the United Kingdom* (n 800) para 413. The ECtHR has altered its view in *Kennedy v the United Kingdom* (n 800). Here, the ECtHR warned that the powers of the IPT insufficiently provided for a legal complaint regarding the general operation of legislative surveillance rather than a specific complaint of interception in an individual case as the IPT "is not able to disclose information to an extent, or in a manner, contrary to the public interest or prejudicial to national security or the prevention or detection of serious crime" (*Kennedy v the United Kingdom* (n 800) para 110).
1344 RIPA 2000, s 68(6) and (7).
1345 The Investigatory Powers Tribunal Rules 2018, No 10 (former No 9).
1346 *Liberty and Others v the Security Service, SIS, GCHQ* [2015] UKIPTrib 13_77-H_2.
1347 RIPA 2000, s 67(7).
1348 *Schrems* (n 71) para 95.

dy.[1349] The IPT negotiates in a mixture of open *inter partes* proceedings based on "assumed facts", avoiding risks to the national security, and closed hearings in private to apply the legal conclusion from the open hearings to the facts.[1350] The ECtHR found that the restrictions in IPT proceedings qualify as necessary and proportionate, weighing the interest of national security and the need to keep secret methods in criminal investigations against the general right to adversarial proceedings. The Strasbourg Court emphasised "the extensive jurisdiction of the IPT to examine any complaint or unlawful interception. [...] [A]ny person who suspects that his communications have been or are being intercepted may apply to the IPT. The jurisdiction of the IPT does not [...] depend on notification to the interception subject that there has been an interception of his communications".[1351] In *Big Brother Watch*, it was further emphasising that "in fact, depending on the circumstances it may even offer better guarantees of a proper procedure than a system based on the notification. Regardless of whether the material was acquired through targeted or bulk interception, the existence of a national security exception could deprive a notification requirement of any real practical effect."[1352] "[W]hile the evidence submitted by the Government may not yet demonstrate the existence of a "binding obligation" requiring it to remedy any incompatibility identified by the IPT, in light of the IPT's "special significance" in secret surveillance cases which arises from its "extensive powers [...] to investigate complaints before it and to access confidential information" (see *Kennedy*, para 110) the Court would nevertheless accept that the practise of giving effect to its findings on the incompatibility of domestic law with the

---

1349 *Kennedy v the United Kingdom* (n 800) para 190 (concerning the RIPA 2000); see also *Big Brother Watch and Others v the United Kingdom* (n 1174) para 265; *Big Brother Watch and Others v the United Kingdom* (n 800) para 413.

1350 IPT, 'Closed and Open Procedures' <https://www.ipt-uk.com/content.asp?id=13>.

1351 *Kennedy v the United Kingdom* (n 800) para 167. In *Roman Zakharov v Russia* (n 800) para 171, the ECtHR stated that where the domestic system does not afford an effective remedy to a person who suspects that they were subjected to secret surveillance, widespread suspicion and concern among the general public that secret surveillance powers are being abused cannot be said to be unjustified. In such circumstances the individual does not need to demonstrate the existence of any risk that secret surveillance measures were in fact applied to them but rather may claim to be a victim of a violation occasioned by the mere existence of secret measures or of legislation permitting secret measures. "By contrast, if the national system provides for effective remedies, a widespread suspicion of abuse is more difficult to justify. In such cases, the individual may claim to be a victim of a violation occasioned by the mere existence of secret measures or of legislation permitting secret measures only if he [or she] is able to show that, due to [their] personal situation, he [or she] is potentially at risk of being subjected to such measures."

1352 *Big Brother Watch and Others v the United Kingdom* (n 800) para 348.

Convention is sufficiently certain for it to be satisfied as to the effectiveness of the remedy."[1353] According to the Strasbourg Court "the relevant question is not whether the IPT can issue a Declaration of Incompatibility, but whether the practice of giving effect to its findings is sufficiently certain";[1354] "where the IPT has found a surveillance regime to be incompatible with the Convention, the Government have ensured that any defects are rectified and dealt with."[1355] According to the ECtHR, "the IPT has shown itself to be a remedy, available in theory and practice, which is capable of offering redress to applicants complaining of both specific incidences of surveillance and the general Convention compliance of surveillance regimes."[1356] Whether the CJEU would agree with the ECtHR and confirm that the IPT provides an effective remedy to the individual is yet to be seen, but the ECtHR judgement is likely to be indicative.

c IPT's Jurisdiction

However, the IPT may fail to provide an effective remedy for individuals located in the EU. In 2016, the IPT ruled that the UK "owes no obligation under Article 8 [ECHR] to persons both of whom are situated outside its territory in respect of electronic communications between them which pass through [the UK]".[1357] These individuals are not within the jurisdiction of the UK in the sense of Article 1 ECHR[1358] and accordingly do not have any of the rights under that Convention.[1359] The IPT mainly referred to and formed an analogy to the ECtHR's judgement in *Banković and Others v Belgium and Others*.[1360] It cannot fully apply the ECHR for EU citizens if there were located outside of the UK. Nevertheless, EU citizens outside the UK may still lodge a complaint pursuant to Section 65(2)(b) IPA 2016.

1353 *Big Brother Watch and Others v the United Kingdom* (n 800) para 262.
1354 ibid para 264.
1355 ibid para 258.
1356 ibid para 265.
1357 *Human Rights Watch Inc and Others v Secretary of State for Foreign and Commonwealth Affairs and Others* (n 1336) [60].
1358 "The high contracting parties shall secure to everyone within their jurisdiction the rights and freedoms defined in Section 1 of this convention."
1359 *Human Rights Watch Inc and Others v Secretary of State for Foreign and Commonwealth Affairs and Others* (n 1336) [60] et seq.
1360 *Banković and Others v Belgium and Others* (dec.) [GC], no 52207/99 ECHR 2001-XII.

d Notification

The IPA 2016 does not provide individuals with the right to be notified when their electronic communication has been accessed.[1361] The "fact that data are retained and subsequently used without the subscriber or registered user being informed is likely to generate in the minds of the persons concerned the feeling that their private lives are the subject of constant surveillance."[1362] Section 231 IPA 2016 obligates the IPC to inform an individual of any error in relation to the retention and accessing of their data in only two scenarios: if the error is considered a serious error and if it is in the public interest to inform the person of the error. However, the IPA 2016 does not hold a breach of fundamental rights to be serious *per se*. This is contrary to the CJEU's judgement in *Schrems* which has confirmed that interference with a fundamental right (in these cases the right to data protection), regardless of the harm they caused, provide individuals with legal standing to seek a remedy or judicial protection as such.[1363] Section 231(4) IPA 2016 further limits the right to a notification to the extent to which disclosing the error would be prejudicial to the economic well-being of the UK.

The CJEU recognised in its judgements regarding surveillance measures in member states that the notification of persons whose data has been collected must occur "only to the extent and as soon as the notification no longer jeopardises the mission for which the authorities are responsible".[1364] This view was also confirmed in the context of (PNR) data transfer, in the CJEU's *Opinion 1/15*.[1365] Yet, in its *Schrems* judgements, the CJEU did not find that the notification obligation is a mandatory requirement to respect the essence of Article 47 CFR. Also, according to ECHR, the individual concerned does not need to be notified to make a complaint before the IPT since there is no evidential burden to overcome to apply with it.[1366]

e EU Commission's Assessment

The EU Commission concluded that the IPT provides an effective remedy for individuals under the IPA 2016.[1367] The EDPB agreed that the functioning of the IPT

1361 Mbioh (n 1101) 280.

1362 *Digital Rights Ireland and Seitlinger and Others* (n 73) para 37.

1363 *Schrems* (n 71) paras 87 and 89.

1364 *Tele2 Sverige* (n 81) para 121; *La Quadrature du Net and Others* (n 800) para 191. See also similarly ECtHR in *Kennedy v the United Kingdom (n 800) para 60 and in Roman Zakharov v Russia* (n 800) para 234.

1365 *Accord PNR EU-Canada* (n 80) para 220

1366 As already outline under b.

1367 UK Adequacy Decision (n 14) recitals 263 et seqq.

is compliant with Article 47 CFR.[1368] The CJEU will likely decide in line with the EU Commission and the ECtHR. The establishment of the IPT also fulfils the criteria regarding judicial protection established by the Court in *Schrems* and *Facebook Ireland and Schrems*[1369].

V Conclusion to C

The above analysis shows that, overall, the IPA 2016 does not comply with the Charter and the CJEU's established requirements in *Digital Rights Ireland and Seitlinger and Others*, *Tele2 Sverige* and others. In its adequacy decision, it appears that the EU Commission instead reproduced and summarised the "UK's self-valedictory self-description" [1370] of its surveillance regime but did not provide a proper analysis of the surveillance regime's compliance with EU law. The IPA 2016 in its current form significantly increases the likelihood of the CJEU invalidating an adequacy decision in favour of the UK. The strict standard applied by the CJEU when assessing an adequate level of protection ("essentially equivalent") became particularly clear in the recent *Facebook Ireland and Schrems* ruling. Although the EU Commission did not find any issues with the IPA 2016, the IPA 2016 is very likely to become relevant in proceedings before the CJEU:

1. The bulk interception powers and bulk acquisition powers set out in the IPA 2016 are untargeted, general, and indiscriminate powers. The EU Commission's assessment failed to assess the UK's intelligence agencies' actual bulk interception practices.[1371] It downplayed the significance of the interception and subsequent retention of secondary data, which can be highly revealing.

2. The bulk powers and the powers for the retention of communications data do not comply with the principle of proportionality: This is, among other things, due to the broad definition of "serious crime". In *La Quadrature du Net and Others*, the bulk acquisition might only be permitted in exceptional cases for a limited period as long as there are "sufficiently solid

---

1368 EDPB, 'Opinion 14/2021 Regarding the European Commission Draft Implementing Decision Pursuant to Regulation (EU) 2016/679 on the Adequate Protection of Personal Data in the United Kingdom' (n 615) recital 213.
1369 Chapter 2, B.I.3.a.
1370 Korff, 'Initial Comments on the EU Commission's Final GDPR Adequacy Decision on the UK' (n 998) referring to the EU Commission's UK Adequacy Decision (n 14) recital 275.
1371 ibid 11 and 26.

grounds" for a "situation presenting a genuine and present or foreseeable serious threat to national security". The "interest of national security" includes a broader range.

3. Furthermore, the bulk powers exceed the limit of what is strictly necessary: The IPA 2016 does not itself define the scope and application of its powers in relation to direct access to the system to communications beyond the broad term "interest of national security". Neither the circumstances nor the conditions under which bulk interception occurs are sufficiently clarified, as the operational purposes are kept from the public. Furthermore, the IPA 2016 does not preclude the targeting of improper targets.

4. The EU Commission did not further assess the procedural practice and mistakes that the Judicial Commissioners only have powers to conduct a marginal and limited judicial review in practice. Further on, it is unclear if and how closely the Judicial Commissioner reviews and oversees selections of bearers and other processes involved with a bulk interception as part of bulk warrant approval.[1372] The CJEU could very well conclude that the review of the Judicial Commissioners is ineffective in practice.

5. In cases of retention of communications data and bulk warrants for the purpose of national security interests, an internal authorisation is not sufficient. Only in exceptional urgent cases, an internal authorisation should be permitted.

6. According to the ECtHR, an effective remedy is in place: "[T]he IPT has shown itself to be a remedy, available in theory and practice, which is capable of offering redress to applicants complaining of both specific incidences of surveillance and the general Convention compliance of surveillance regimes."[1373] The CJEU will likely agree.

7. Further on, the onward transfer to other third countries could be problematic, which is discussed below under D.

D Onward Transfer of Personal Data to Third Countries

As already indicated, a further obstacle to adopting an adequacy decision by the EU Commission should have been transferring personal data from the UK to other third countries. The EU Commission did not review the Secretary of State's

---

1372 Korff and Brown, 'The Inadequacy of UK Data Protection Law in General and in View of UK Surveillance Laws, Part Two: UK Surveillance' (n 1186) 43.
1373 *Big Brother Watch and Others v the United Kingdom* (n 1174) para 265.

practices within the UK when defining adequacy. Article 44 GDPR explicitly mentions that the conditions laid down for the data transfer also apply for the onward transfer from the third country to other third countries.[1374] When assessing the level of protection provided in the UK, the EU Commission must consider rules for the onward transfer of personal data in other third countries.[1375] The CJEU ruling in *Facebook Ireland and Schrems* highlights the severe sensitivities attached to any transfer of EU personal data to the US.[1376] In the following, the data transfer from the UK to third countries in general will be examined (under I.). This is followed by a review of the UK's specific onward transfer practices in the context of law enforcement (under II.) and in the intelligence agencies' areas of practice (under III.).

I Data Transfer from the UK to Third Countries

For most parts, the UK has mirrored Chapter V of the GDPR in the UK GDPR. According to the EU Commission, the regime in Articles 44–49 UK GDPR for transfer of personal data from the UK to other third countries "mirrors the one set out in Chapter V of the GDPR.[1377] The Secretary of State can make adequacy regulations, stipulating that a third country (or a territory or a sector within a third country) ensures adequate personal data protection. The Secretary of State considers the same elements that the EU Commission is required to assess under Article 45(2) GDPR, interpreted together with the retained EU case law. When assessing a third country's adequate level of protection, the relevant standard would be whether the third country ensures a level of protection "essentially equivalent" to that guaranteed within the UK. The UK Government has published manual guidance with a manual template for the Secretary of State for Digital, Culture, Media and Sport on collecting relevant information to inform decision-making as to whether a third country provides adequate levels of data protection according to UK law.[1378]

1374 cf *Accord PNR EU-Canada* (n 80) para 214.

1375 GDPR, art 45(2)(a).

1376 House of Commons, Home Affairs Committee, 'UK-EU Security Cooperation after Brexit' (2018) <https://publications.parliament.uk/pa/cm201719/cmselect/cmhaff/635/63508.htm#_id TextAnchor047>, para 121.

1377 UK Adequacy Decisions (n 14) recital 74.

1378 Secretary of State for Digital, Culture, Media, and Sport, 'Data Adequacy Assessment Manual' <https://assets.publishing.service.gov.uk/government/uploads/system/uploads/at tachment_data/file/1013033/Manual_Guidance.pdf>.

Notably, UK authorities and courts may depart from "retained case law" and evolve a different view of what "essential equivalence" under the UK GDPR means.[1379] The EU Commission did not review the Secretary of State's practices within the UK when defining adequacy.[1380] The EU's adequacy decisions and the SCCs also apply in the UK.[1381] Transfers to an EEA state, Gibraltar or third countries, which were subject to an adequacy decision at the end of the transition period, are treated as if they are based on adequacy regulations.[1382] In this regard, it should be kept in mind that the EU Commission is required under Article 45(3) GDPR to review the adequacy decisions at least every four years. Hence, some adequacy decisions could very well be repealed, amended, or suspended by the EU Commission.

Consequently, the EDPB requests that the EU Commission monitors a country deemed to no longer provide for an adequate level of protection, which is still considered as such by the UK.[1383] Furthermore, the UK might recognise third countries as adequate that might not yet benefit from an adequacy decision issued by the EU Commission. Hence, the EDPB wants the EU Commission to closely monitor the adequacy assessment process and criteria by UK authorities, especially third countries not recognised as adequate under the GDPR.[1384] In both cases described above, the EU Commission must take appropriate measures to remedy the situations, e.g. adding specific requirements or suspending the adequacy decision.[1385] The EU Commission stated that it is planning to do so and simultaneously emphasised cooperation between the ICO and the EDPB to avoid conflicts due to "problematic divergence".[1386] However, it seems noteworthy that the EU Commission "overlooked" the fact that – unlike the EU – the UK held the territory of Gibraltar to have an adequate level of protection.[1387]

1379 Korff, 'The Inadequacy of the EU Commission Draft GDPR Adequacy Decision on the UK' (n 921) 17 et seq.

1380 Brauneck, 'Vereinfachter Datenfluss zwischen der EU und dem Vereinigten Königreich – Rechtmäßigkeit des DS-GVO-Angemessenheitsbeschlusses?' (n 1011) 20.

1381 DPA 2018, sch 21 para 4.

1382 DPA 2018, sch 21 paras 4 and 5.

1383 EDPB, 'Opinion 14/2021 Regarding the European Commission Draft Implementing Decision Pursuant to Regulation (EU) 2016/679 on the Adequate Protection of Personal Data in the United Kingdom' (n 615) recital 83.

1384 ibid recital 81.

1385 ibid recitals 81 and 83.

1386 UK Adequacy Decision (n 14) recital 82.

1387 Korff, 'Initial Comments on the EU Commission's Final GDPR Adequacy Decision on the UK' (n 998).

In the absence of regulations, a cross-border transfer can occur where the controller or processor has provided appropriate safeguards (Article 46 UK GPDR). Nevertheless, following the *Facebook Ireland and Schrems* judgement, data exporters must ensure that data subjects are afforded a level of protection "essentially equivalent" to that guaranteed within the EU.[1388] Data exporters are responsible "to verify, on a case-by-case basis" if the law or practice in the respective third country impacts the effectiveness of the appropriate safeguards transfer tool.[1389] The EDPB calls out the EU Commission to accordingly reassure that data exporters take such appropriate measures where necessary to ensure the effective respect of the safeguard contained in the chosen transfer tool.[1390] In the absence of an adequacy decision or appropriate safeguards, a transfer can occur based on derogations (Article 49 UK GDPR). Correspondingly, the EU Commission must monitor the UK's interpretation on the use of derogations and that it remains aligned to the EU's interpretation; otherwise, the adequacy decision must be amended accordingly.[1391]

The EDPB has expressed concerns that the UK has not included Article 48 GDPR in the UK GDPR.[1392] Article 48 GDPR requires that a transfer or disclosure of personal data may only be recognised or enforceable in any manner if based on an international agreement in force between requesting the third country and the UK. The EDPB considers the safeguards in Article 48 GDPR to be very important as to requests for access to data in the UK made by USA or other third countries' authorities, which are discussed below.[1393] The EDPB recalls that "request from a foreign authority does not in itself constitute a legal ground for transfer". [1394] The order can only be recognised "if based on an international agreement such as a mutual legal assistance treaty, in force between the requesting third country and the Union or a Member State".[1395] The EU Commission stated that "the same effect is guaranteed by other legal provisions and principles". "[I]n order to enforce a foreign judgement, courts in the UK need to be able to

---

1388 Discussed in detail in Chapter 4, A.I.3.
1389 *Facebook Ireland and Schrems* (n 64) para 134.
1390 EDPB, 'Opinion 14/2021 Regarding the European Commission Draft Implementing Decision Pursuant to Regulation (EU) 2016/679 on the Adequate Protection of Personal Data in the United Kingdom' (n 615) recital 87.
1391 ibid recital 98.
1392 UK Adequacy Decision (n 14) footnote 71.
1393 II.3 and III.3.
1394 EDPB, 'Opinion 14/2021 Regarding the European Commission Draft Implementing Decision Pursuant to Regulation (EU) 2016/679 on the Adequate Protection of Personal Data in the United Kingdom' (n 615) recital 103.
1395 ibid.

point to common law or to a statute that allows its enforceability. However, neither common law[1396] nor statutes provide for the enforcement of foreign judgements requiring the transfer of data without an international agreement in place. Therefore, requests for data are unenforceable under UK law, absent such an international agreement. Furthermore, any transfer of personal data to third countries – including upon request from a foreign court or administrative authority – remains subject to the restrictions set out in Chapter V of the UK GDPR which are identical to the corresponding provisions of Regulation (EU) 2016/679, and therefore require to rely on one of the grounds for transfer available under Chapter V in accordance with the specific conditions to which it is subject under that Chapter."[1397]

II Onward Transfer for Law Enforcement Purposes

In the following, the legal framework for onward transfers of personal data from the UK to other third countries for the purposes of law enforcement is reviewed.

1 Data Protection Act 2018

When a competent authority intends to share personal data processed under part 3 of the DPA 2018 with law enforcement authorities of a third country, the transfer may only take place based where the transfer is necessary for law enforcement purposes and, either is based on adequacy regulations or, in the absence of such rules, appropriate safeguards are ensured.[1398] Furthermore, where the personal data was initially transmitted or otherwise made available to the controller or another competent authority by an EU member state, the onward transfer must be authorised by that member state or competent authority in accordance with the law of the member state.[1399] Appropriate safeguards are in place, where established by a legal instrument, which binds the recipient, or where the controller concludes that appropriate safeguards exist to protect the data, after having assessed all circumstances surrounding the transfer of that type of personal data to the third country in question.[1400] If a transfer is not based on an adequacy regulation or appropriate safeguards, it can occur in "spe-

---

1396 *Adams and Others v Cape Industries Plc.*, [1990] 2 W.L.R. 657.
1397 UK Adequacy Decision (n 14) footnote 71.
1398 DPA 2018, s 73(1).
1399 DPA 2018, s 73(1)(b).
1400 DPA 2018, s 75.

cial circumstances". Special circumstances are assumed where a transfer is necessary (a) to protect the vital interests of the data subject or another person, (b) to safeguard the legitimate interest of the data subject, (c) for the prevention of an immediate and serious threat to the public security of a member state or third country, (d) in individual cases for any of the law enforcement purposes; or (e) in individual cases for a legal purpose.[1401] Authorisation to the onward transfer by the competent authority, which transferred the personal data to the UK, is not mandatory in cases where the transfer is necessary for the prevention of an immediate and serious threat either to the public security of a member state or a third country or to the essential interests of a member state, and the authorisation cannot be obtained in good time.[1402]

2 Investigatory Powers Act 2016

Under the IPA 2016, "overseas disclosures", where material acquired by law enforcement authorities under a warrant authorising the use of interception or equipment interference is handed over to a third country, are allowed if the Secretary of State considers that specific appropriate arrangements are in place.[1403] Such appropriate safeguards must limit the number of persons to whom the data is disclosed, the extent to which any material is copied, and the number of copies made. Furthermore, the issuing authority may consider arrangements to ensure that any part of that material is destroyed when there are no longer relevant grounds for retaining it.[1404]

3 UK-US Agreement on Access to Electronic Data for the Purpose of Countering Serious Crime

On 3 October 2019, the UK and USA signed the bilateral "Agreement on Access to Electronic Data for the Purpose of Countering Serious Crime" (after this: UK-US Agreement).[1405] The Agreement is established under the UK Crime (Overseas Production Orders) Act 2019 and the US Clarifying Lawful Overseas Use of Data (CLOUD) Act 2018.[1406] The Agreement has still not entered into force. It allows

---

1401 DPA 2018, s 76.
1402 DPA 2018, s 73(5).
1403 IPA 2016, ss 54 and 130.
1404 IPA 2016, ss 54 and 130.
1405 See for a detailed review of the UK-US Agreement in
1406 In September 2019, the USA and EU released a joint statement that they had commenced negotiating a data access agreement, US Department of Justice – Office of Public Affairs, 'Joint US-EU Statement on Electronic Evidence Sharing Negotiations' (2019) Press Release of 26 Sep-

law enforcement authorities in either the UK or the US ("Issuing Parties") to request access to electronic evidence held by communications service providers or by state authorities in the respective other country ("Receiving Parties") to prevent and prosecute serious crime.[1407] Under this Agreement, data transferred from the EU to service providers in the UK could be subject to orders to produce electronic evidence issued by competent US law enforcement authorities and made applicable in the UK.[1408] In light of the *Schrems* and the *Facebook Ireland and Schrems* judgement, the assessment of the UK-US Agreement should have been essential to the EU Commission's evaluation of adequacy.[1409]

a Data Transfer

Before the UK-US Agreement, the respective law enforcement agencies could only request information held by a company abroad or a third country's authority through so-called Mutual Legal Assistance Treaties (MLAT). These requests are submitted to the country's government in which the respective company is based, which then reviews the request, obtains, and serves an order, collects the data and returns it to the requesting law enforcement agencies. These MLAT stipulate a multi-stage process, which can take months or even years. Under the new UK-US Agreement, an overseas production order by the respective UK or US law enforcement agencies must be served within three months and produced within seven days. The USA can request electronic data related to a serious crime[1410] investigation from UK-based communications service providers or UK governmental entities or authorities if the targeted person is located in the USA or a third country (including the EU27) but not if the target is located in the UK.[1411] The UK can request electronic data related to a serious crime[1412] inves-

---

tember 2019 <https://www.justice.gov/opa/pr/joint-us-eu-statement-electronic-evidence-sharing-negotiations>.

1407 Secretary of State for Foreign and Commonwealth Affairs by Command of Her Majesty, 'Agreement between the Government of the United Kingdom of Great Britain and Northern Ireland and the Government of the United States of America on Access to Electronic Data for the Purpose of Countering Serious Crime' (2019) USA No 6.

1408 cf EU Commission, 'Draft of Commission Implementing Decision Pursuant Regulation (EU) 2016/679 of the European Parliament and of the Council on the Adequate Protection of Personal Data by the United Kingdom' (n 992) recital 151.

1409 UK Adequacy Decision (n 14) recital 153.

1410 "Serious crime" is defined as "an offense that is punishable by a maximum term of imprisonment of at least three years" (UK-US Agreement, art 1(14)).

1411 The oversea production orders are subject to the conditions and safeguards appearing in Articles 7 and 8 of the UK-US Agreement and to the requirements on the respective domestic laws.

tigation from a US-based communications service or US governmental entities or authorities provider if the targeted person is located in the UK and is not a US person[1413] and if the target is located in a third country (including the EU27) and is not a US-person (Article 4 of the UK-US Agreement). Suppose the targeted person is in a third country. In that case, these countries should be notified[1414] unless the targeted person is a US-person or a UK citizen, and the USA or the UK considers notification could impede investigations or pose other problems.[1415] The UK-US Agreement does not distinguish whether the data are stored in the UK, the USA, or any other country.

Consequently, personal data relating to EU citizens and personal data protected by the GDPR are subject to the UK-US Agreement. The Agreement also does not compel a communications service provider or a state authority in the other party's jurisdiction to comply with a request.[1416] Any actions taken in the event of non-compliance are governed by the legislation of the country making the request. However, obligations are placed on the two countries to remove the barriers in domestic law within the communication service providers' jurisdiction, which would otherwise prevent disclosure of this data recognized by this Agreement.[1417] The Agreement does not allow law enforcement agencies to access data, which they would not otherwise have had a right to access under the existing domestic legislation.

b Safeguards

The UK-US Agreement (and the respective domestic laws) include several safeguards, which limit the scope of the regime: The UK-US Agreement provides targeting restriction, which include a prohibition on overseas production orders that may be used to violate freedom of speech or disadvantage for specific

---

1412 The first part of the Cloud Act is not limited to "serious crime" but concerns all type of crimes.

1413 "US Person" means: (i) a citizen or national of the United States; (ii) a person lawfully admitted for permanent residence; (iii) an unincorporated association a substantial number of members of which fall into Subsections (i) or (ii); or (iv) a corporation that is incorporated in the United States (Article 1(16)).

1414 UK-US Agreement, art 5(1).

1415 UK-US Agreement, art 5(1).

1416 Foreign & Commonwealth Office, 'Explanatory Memorandum to the Agreement between the Government of the United Kingdom of Great Britain and Northern Ireland and the Government of the United States of America on Access to Electronic Data for the Purpose of Countering Serious Crime' (2019) para 7 <https://www.gov.uk/government/publications/ukusa-agreement-on-access-to-electronic-data-for-the-purpose-of-countering-serious-crime-cs-usa-no62019>.

1417 ibid para 8.

groups (based on their race, sex, sexual orientation, religion, ethnic origin or political opinions)[1418] and the prohibition on the onward transfer to another third country or issuing an overseas production order on behalf of the third country.[1419] Furthermore, the overseas production orders must be targeted, must identify their objective[1420] and must be subject to review or oversight under the domestic law by a judicial body or independent authority.[1421] UK law enforcement agencies ask a domestic court to issue a production order directly against the communications service provider (email providers, mobile phone networks, social media companies and cloud storage services) or state authority located in the US. The UK enforcement authorities must satisfy the judge that the entity has possession or control of the electronic data and that the data is likely to be of "substantial value" to the investigation; the accessing or production of the data must be in the public interest.[1422] Suppose the UK court grants authorisation, in that case, UK law enforcement agencies will serve the production order of electronic data directly on the receiving communications service provider or the state authority in the other country. A designated authority will review such production order and ensure its compliance with the Agreement. Also, the remedy of judicial review against the Secretary of State's decision to transmit the production order is available. The application for an overseas production order shall be made with a notice to the receiving communications service provider or receiving authority.[1423] Furthermore, the UK Crime Act 2019 provides for an application to be made to vary or revoke an overseas production order.[1424] The application for a variation must specify the relevant designated international cooperation arrangement by reference to which it is made and must specify or describe the data in respect of which the varied order is sought. Excepted electronic data may not be specified. The US Cloud Act also provides the receiving parties with the option to modify or quash the overseas production warrant.[1425]

1418 UK-US Agreement, art 4(2).

1419 UK-US Agreement, art 5(4).

1420 UK-US Agreement, art 4(5).

1421 UK-US Agreement, art 5(2).

1422 UK Crime Act 2019, s 4.

1423 UK-US Agreement, art 5(8).

1424 UK Crime Act 2019, s 7.

1425 US Cloud Act, s 3(2). US Courts should conduct a limited comity analysis when deciding whether to quash a warrant, *inter alia* taking into account the investigative interest of the US authority, the interests of foreign states, and the likelihood and severity of penalties abroad (UK Cloud Act, s 3).

The UK-US Agreement further provides the option of objecting with the designated authority in the issuing state – the Secretary of State in the UK – in a reasonable time after receiving the order.[1426] The Secretary of State must respond to the objections and, if not resolved, must raise the complaints with the designated authority in the receiving state. While the two designated authorities can confer "in an effort to resolve" the objections, it is not clear whether the recipient of the production order will be involved in the decision-making process. The overseas production order must not conflict with domestic data privacy laws, which means that the recipient must also comply with the UK GDPR.[1427]

c EU Commission's Assessment

The EU Commission did not consider the UK-US Agreement to be an obstacle to an adequacy decision. It found that data of EU citizens, which is obtained under the agreement, "benefit from equivalent protections to the specific safeguards provided by the so-called "EU-US Umbrella Agreement".[1428] The EU-US Umbrella Agreement[1429] is an agreement concluded by the EU and the USA in December 2016 and entered into force on 1 February 2017. The EU-US Umbrella Agreement sets out safeguards and rights applicable to data transfers in law enforcement cooperation.

According to the EU Commission, the safeguards and rights established in the EU-US Umbrella Agreement are incorporated into the UK-US Agreement "by reference on a *mutatis mutandis* basis to notably take into account the specific nature of the transfers (i.e. transfers from private operators to a law enforcement, rather than transfers between law enforcement authorities). The UK-US Agreement would specifically provide for equivalent protections to those provided by the EU-US Umbrella Agreement, applied to "all personal information produced in the execution of Orders subject to the Agreement to produce equivalent protections".[1430] The EU Commission states that "[d]ata transferred under the UK-US Agreement should therefore benefit from protections provided by an EU law instrument, with the necessary adaptions to reflect the nature of the transfer at issue."[1431] Furthermore, the EU Commission emphasised that "the UK author-

---

1426 UK-US Agreement, art 11.
1427 UK-US Agreement, art 3(1).
1428 UK Adequacy Decision (n 14) recital 154.
1429 Agreement between the United States of America and the European Union on the protection of personal information relating to the prevention, investigation, detection and prosecuting of criminal offences, OJ L 336.
1430 UK Adequacy Decision (n 14) recital 154 referring to Article 9(1) of the UK-US Agreement.
1431 ibid recital 155.

ities have confirmed that they will only let the Agreement enter into force once they are satisfied that its implementation complies with the data protection standards for any data requested with respect to compliance with the data protection standards for any data requested under this Agreement."[1432] "[A]ny future clarification regarding the way the US will comply with its obligations under the Agreement should be communicated by the UK to the European Union, as soon as it becomes available, to ensure proper monitoring of [the adequacy] decision".[1433]

Once the UK-US Agreement enters into force, personal data transferred from the EU to the UK under the adequacy decision would be subject to the UK-US Agreement's provision laying down conditions for indirect access by US authorities, impacting the UK Data Protection Framework, including the provisions on onward transfers.[1434] The EU Commission's arguments above are not reassuring. The EDPB criticised that the EU Commission only refers to explanations given by UK authorities without quoting or providing any concrete written assurance or commitment, nor pointing out specific legal provisions under UK law that would affect such explanations.[1435] There are no fundamental safeguards to ensure that the UK Government informs the EU Commission of "any future clarification regarding the way the US will comply with its obligations under the Agreement".[1436] It is left to the UK to decide what to communicate with the EU Commission regarding the UK-US Agreement and its practical implementation.[1437] There is no efficient guarantee that the safeguards of the EU-US Umbrella Agreement will be fully applied under the UK-US Agreement. [1438] Article 9(1) of the UK-US Agreement only stipulates that they are applied "*mutatis mutanda*" and with "adaptions to reflect the nature of the transfers at issues." The EDPB has legitimate concerns whether this "would meet the criteria of clear, precise

---

1432 UK Adequacy Decision (n 14).

1433 ibid recital 155.

1434 EDPB, 'Opinion 14/2021 Regarding the European Commission Draft Implementing Decision Pursuant to Regulation (EU) 2016/679 on the Adequate Protection of Personal Data in the United Kingdom' (n 615) recital 88.

1435 ibid referring to the EU Commission, 'Draft of Commission Implementing Decision Pursuant Regulation (EU) 2016/679 of the European Parliament and of the Council on the Adequate Protection of Personal Data by the United Kingdom' (n 992) recital 153.

1436 Korff, 'The Inadequacy of the EU Commission Draft GDPR Adequacy Decision on the UK' (n 921) 20.

1437 ibid.

1438 ibid.

and accessible rules when it comes to access to personal data".[1439] It has requested that the EU Commission clarifies how and based on which legal instrument
equivalent protections to the specific safeguards provided by the EU-US Umbrella Agreement would be given effect and be binding under UK law.

Furthermore, many find the safeguards established in the EU-US Umbrella
Agreement insufficient, particularly the availability of judicial redress for EU citizens[1440].[1441] In 2020, the EDPB, yet again, called for a further improvement to the
level of safeguards established.[1442]

d EDPB's Analysis

In its preliminary analysis, the EDPB had "doubts as to whether the safeguards
in the US-UK Agreement for access to personal data in the UK would apply in
case of disclosure obligations applicable to providers of electronic communication service or remote computing service under the jurisdiction of the United
States, regardless of whether the data requested is located within or outside of
the United States." [1443] Section 3(1) of the US Cloud Act states that "[a] provider
of electronic communication service or remote computing service shall comply
with the obligations of this chapter to preserve, backup, or disclose the contents
of a wire or electronic communication and any record or other information about
a customer or subscriber within such provider's possession, custody, or control,
regardless of whether such communication, record or other information is located within or outside of the United States." The EU Commission failed to clarify
the interplay between the UK-US Agreement and the US domestic law and did not
define and assess the specific safeguards of the UK-US Agreement.[1444] Instead it
merely acknowledged that "the details of the concrete implementation of the

---

1439 EDPB, 'Opinion 14/2021 Regarding the European Commission Draft Implementing Decision Pursuant to Regulation (EU) 2016/679 on the Adequate Protection of Personal Data in
the United Kingdom' (n 615) recital 91.
1440 The right to take legal action of EU citizens is limited by the US as far as internal security
interests are concerned. Further the right to take legal action is only intended for EU-citizens but
not for third country citizens who live in the EU.
1441 Korff, 'The Inadequacy of the EU Commission Draft GDPR Adequacy Decision on the UK'
(n 921) 20.
1442 EDPB, 'Letter to the European Parliament' (2020) <https://edpb.europa.eu/sites/edpb/
files/files/file1/edpb_letter_out_2020-0054-uk-usagreement.pdf.>.
1443 ibid; see also EDPB, 'Opinion 14/2021 Regarding the European Commission Draft Implementing Decision Pursuant to Regulation (EU) 2016/679 on the Adequate Protection of Personal
Data in the United Kingdom' (n 615) recital 93.
1444 EU Parliament, 'EU-UK Private Sector Data Flows after Brexit. Settling on Adequacy'
(n 1190) 24.

data protection safeguards are still subject to discussions between the UK and the US"[1445].[1446] The EDPB found it unclear whether the safeguards enshrined in the UK-US Agreement (including the one provided by the EU-US Umbrella Agreement) would apply to all the requests to access made by US authorities under the US Cloud Act.[1447] The US Cloud Act remains in full effect after UK-US Agreement.[1448] The first part of the US Cloud Act is not limited to "serious crime" but concerns all types of crime. US law enforcement agents could then request stored communications data relating to all kinds of criminal investigations.

Furthermore, the US Cloud Act does not require notification of third affected countries. The EDPB criticised that it is not evident whether, in the event of a conflict between the US-UK Agreement and the Cloud Act, especially with data protection, the US-UK Agreement will prevail. This shows that the dual system, consisting of the US-UK Agreement and the respective domestic law, lacks legal certainty as provisions of domestic law could overturn safeguards and provisions of the US-UK Agreement.[1449]

The EDPB further criticised that the agreement between the UK and the USA did not "include a mandatory prior judicial authorisation as an essential guarantee for access to metadata and content data".[1450] The US-UK Agreement only refers to the judicial review under the application of domestic law.[1451] Although the UK Crime Act 2019 requires prior judicial review by the UK law enforcement authority,[1452] and the US Cloud Act states that a court or a competent authority

---

1445 UK Adequacy Decision (n 14) recital 155.

1446 Brauneck, 'Vereinfachter Datenfluss zwischen der EU und dem Vereinigten Königreich – Rechtmäßigkeit des DS-GVO-Angemessenheitsbeschlusses?' (n 1011) 20; EU Parliament, 'EU-UK Private Sector Data Flows after Brexit. Settling on Adequacy' (n 1190) 24.

1447 EDPB, 'Letter to the European Parliament' (n 1442); see also EDPB, 'Opinion 14/2021 Regarding the European Commission Draft Implementing Decision Pursuant to Regulation (EU) 2016/679 on the Adequate Protection of Personal Data in the United Kingdom' (n 615) recital 93.

1448 US-UK Agreement, art 6(3).

1449 Theodore Christakis, '21 Thoughts and Questions about the UK-US Cloud Act Agreement (And an Explanation of How It Works – with Charts)' (*European Law Blog*, 17 October 2019) para 3 <https://europeanlawblog.eu/2019/10/17/21-thoughts-and-questions-about-the-uk-us-cloud-ACT-agreement-and-an-explanation-of-how-it-works-with-charts/>.

1450 EDPB, 'Opinion 14/2021 Regarding the European Commission Draft Implementing Decision Pursuant to Regulation (EU) 2016/679 on the Adequate Protection of Personal Data in the United Kingdom' (n 615) recital 90.

1451 cf UK-US Agreement, art 3.

1452 UK Crime Act 2019, s 4(2)-(7).

must issue the warrant,[1453] the US-UK Agreement is criticised for not being sufficiently clear on this matter. The UK-US Agreement also lacks an obligation to
notify the targeted persons.[1454]

The EU Commission did not consider the EDPB's criticism concerning the
data sharing under the UK-US Agreement. EDPB's concerns have partly been
dealt with in the TCA. Article LAW.EUROJUST.72 TCA addresses the onward transfer of data shared for law enforcement purposes. Law enforcement authorities
are prohibited from making onward transfers without obtaining the consent of
whichever authority provided the information and without appropriate safeguards regarding personal data protection. However, this would only apply to
the data provided to the UK law enforcement authority by Eurojust[1455], and
whose disclosure is requested by US law enforcement authorities. It does not
cover the constellation in which the communications service providers based
in the UK disclose personal data, which were previously transferred from the
EU to the UK, to US law enforcement authorities. The criticism regarding the
US-UK Agreement's lack of legal certainty on safeguards and judicial authorisation, as well as the lack of obligation to notify a targeted person, remains. These
issues might be an obstacle to the affirmation by the CJEU that the US-UK Agreement provides an adequate level of protection. The EDPB also emphasised that
the EU Commission must assess the impact and potential risks of provisions on
personal data contained in international agreements recently signed (such as
CEPA[1456]) or signed by the UK in the future.[1457]

1453 US Cloud Act, s 2703(a). The US law enforcement authority must offer specific and artic-
ulable facts showing that there are reasonable grounds to believe that the contents of a wire or
electronic communication, or the records or other information sought, are relevant and material
to an ongoing criminal investigation (US Cloud Act, s 2703(d)).
1454 Christakis, '21 Thoughts and Questions about the UK-US Cloud Act Agreement (And an Explanation of How It Works – with Charts)' (n 1449) para 9.
1455 Eurojust is an EU agency dealing with the judicial co-operation in criminal matters among
agencies of the member states. See for more information about Eurojust at the following link
<https://www.eurojust.europa.eu> accessed 9 June 2022.
1456 Agreement for a Comprehensive Economic Partnership between UK and Japan, CS Japan
No 1/2020, 23 November 2020.
1457 EDPB, 'Opinion 14/2021 Regarding the European Commission Draft Implementing Decision Pursuant to Regulation (EU) 2016/679 on the Adequate Protection of Personal Data in
the United Kingdom' (n 615) recital 94.

III Onward Transfer by Intelligence Agencies

In the following, the legal framework for onward transfer of personal data from the UK to other third countries by intelligence agencies is reviewed.

1 Data Protection Act 2018

Section 109 DPA 2018 allows intelligence agencies to make cross-border transfers, where necessary and proportionate, in accordance with their statutory functions or provisions of the Security Services Act 1989[1458] or Intelligence Services Act 1994[1459] (for the Security Service the prevention or detection of serious crime or any criminal proceedings, for the Intelligence Service the interests of national security, the prevention or detection of serious crime, or any criminal proceedings, and for the GCHQ any criminal proceedings).[1460] The safeguards for these disclosures only comprise the requirement that the recipient of the data respects data security, the extent of disclosure limited to what is necessary, data retention and the restriction of access to data to a limited number of persons.[1461]

1458 Security Services Act 1989, available at the following link <https://www.legislation.gov.uk/ukpga/1989/5/contents> accessed 9 June 2022. Section 2(2) of the Security Service Act 1989 provides that "The Director-General shall be responsible for the efficiency of the Service and it shall be his duty to ensure— (a) that there are arrangements for securing that no information is obtained by the Service except so far as necessary for the proper discharge of its functions or disclosed by it except so far as necessary for that purpose or for the purpose of the prevention or detection of] serious crime or for the purpose of any criminal proceedings]; and (b) that the Service does not take any action to further the interests of any political party; and (c) that there are arrangements, agreed with Director General of the National Crime Agency, for co-ordinating the activities of the Service in pursuance of Section 1(4) of this Act with the activities of police forces, the National Crime Agency and other law enforcement agencies.

1459 Intelligence Services Act 1994, available at the following link <https://www.legislation.gov.uk/ukpga/1994/13/contents> accessed 9 June 2022. Section 2(2) of the Intelligence Service Act 1994 provides that "The Chief of the Intelligence Service shall be responsible for the efficiency of that Service and it shall be his duty to ensure— (a) that there are arrangements for securing that no information is obtained by the Intelligence Service except so far as necessary for the proper discharge of its functions and that no information is disclosed by it except so far as necessary— (i) for that purpose; (ii) in the interests of national security; (iii) for the purpose of the prevention or detection of serious crime; or (iv) for the purpose of any criminal proceedings; and (b) that the Intelligence Service does not take any action to further the interests of any United Kingdom political party".

1460 DPA 2018, s 109.

1461 EDPB, 'Opinion 14/2021 Regarding the European Commission Draft Implementing Decision Pursuant to Regulation (EU) 2016/679 on the Adequate Protection of Personal Data in the United Kingdom' (n 615) recital 190.

Although Section 109(2) DPA 2018 applies in cases in which the national security exemption is invoked,[1462] Section 110 DPA 2018, still leads to situations of overseas disclosures where safeguards as well as individuals' rights, oversight and redress would not be entirely provided or respected in the designated third country if considered necessary to safeguard national security.[1463]

2 Investigatory Powers Act 2016

Overseas disclosures are allowed where intelligence agencies consider the transfer to be necessary and proportionate for national security purposes or in relation to serious crime, "provided that the recipient agency treats the data securely".[1464] The IPA 2016 sets out safeguards regarding "overseas disclosures" – transfers to a third country of material collected through targeted interception[1465], targeted equipment interference[1466], bulk interception[1467], bulk acquisition of communications data[1468] and bulk equipment interference[1469]. It must be ensured that arrangements are in force for securing that the third country receiving the data limits the number of persons who see the material, and the extent of disclosure and the number of copies made of any material to the minimum necessary for the authorised purposes set out in the IPA 2016.[1470] Hence, every copy made of any of that material collected under the warrant must be stored securely and destroyed when there are no longer any relevant grounds for retaining it (including every copy made of it).[1471] These arrangements apply to such extent as the Secretary of State considers appropriate, in relation to any of the material, which is handed over, or any copy which is given to the authorities in question and that restrictions are in force, which would prevent, to

---

1462 Section 110 DPA 2018 does not list Section 109 DPA 2018 as one of the provisions that can be disapplied exceptionally; UK Adequacy Decision (n 14) recital 196.

1463 EDPB, 'Opinion 14/2021 Regarding the European Commission Draft Implementing Decision Pursuant to Regulation (EU) 2016/679 on the Adequate Protection of Personal Data in the United Kingdom' (n 615) recital 190.

1464 See in Korff, 'The Inadequacy of the EU Commission Draft GDPR Adequacy Decision on the UK' (n 921) 38.

1465 IPA 2016, s 54.

1466 IPA 2016, s 130.

1467 IPA 2016, s 151.

1468 IPA 2016, s 171(9).

1469 IPA 2016, s 192.

1470 IPA 2016, ss 54(2) and 53(2), 130(2) and 129(2), 151(2) and 150(2), 171(9) and 171(2), 192(2) and 191(2).

1471 IPA 2016, ss 54(2) and 53(5), 130(2) and 129(5), 151(2) and 150(5), 171(9) and 171(5), 192(2) and 191(5).

such extent as the Secretary of State considers appropriate, the doing of anything in, for the purposes of or in connection with any proceedings outside the UK, which would result in a prohibited disclosure.[1472] In 2019, the Investigatory Powers Commissioner's Office (after this: IPCO) published a report after reviewing existing GCHQ procedures concerning sharing intelligence and bulk datasets. In the report, it stated that "[o]ne significant challenge the review faced was the commencement [...] of the parts of the IPA 2016 relating to the various bulk powers. [...] This includes the requirement under the IPA 2016 that, before approving the sharing of material obtained as a consequence of conduct under a bulk warrant, the Secretary of State must be satisfied (to such an extent (if any) as the Secretary of State considers appropriate) that the overseas authority with whom material is being shared has in place safeguards in relation to retention, disclosure and examination."[1473] This statement confirms that the data-sharing system essentially is a discretionary matter in the hands of the Secretary of State.[1474] Furthermore, safeguards are instead set out regarding data security but not with judicial oversight.[1475]

3 Five Eyes Alliance

One of the main concerns regarding the onward transfer of personal data from the UK is the *Five Eyes* alliance. It is considered to be the oldest and most prominent intelligence alliance worldwide.[1476] It consists of the following five intelligence services: US' National Security Agency (NSA), UK's GCHQ, Canada's Communications Security Establishment (CSEC), Australia's Defence Signals Directorate (DSD) and New Zealand's Government Communications Security Bureau (GCSB). In 1999, a global surveillance alliance was revealed as the head of Australia's DSD openly acknowledged Australia's involvement in the alliance;[1477] the alliance was later confirmed in 2010. The USA and the UK cooperated on sig-

---

1472 IPA 2016, ss 54(2),130(2), 151(2), 171(9) and 192(2).
1473 IPCO (n 1253) para 10.42.
1474 Korff, 'The Inadequacy of the EU Commission Draft GDPR Adequacy Decision on the UK' (n 921) 39.
1475 ibid.
1476 Corey Pfluke, 'A History of the Five Eyes Alliance: Possibility for Reform and Additions' (2019) 38 Comparative Strategy 302, 305.
1477 Duncan Campbell, 'Australia First to Admit We're Part of a Global Surveillance System' *Heise Online* (28 May 1999) <https://www.heise.de/tp/features/Australia-first-to-admit-we-re-part-of-global-surveillance-system-3440779.html>.

nal intelligence operations during World War II, e. g. decrypting *Enigma*[1478]. After World War II, the USA and the UK continued to share their intelligence service and signed the British-US Communication Agreement (BRUSA) in March 1946, which was renamed UKUSA.[1479] The agreement included all intelligence gathered, produced, or disseminated dealing with foreign communications and the techniques and methods.[1480] Canada joined the agreement in 1948, and Australia and New Zealand followed in 1956.[1481] In February 2021, the NSA stated that the UKUSA alliance would allow "to share information between the two agencies as much as possible, with minimal restriction" and that "this ground-breaking document created the policies and procedures for UK and US intelligence professionals for sharing communication, translation, analysis, and code-breaking information".[1482] The *Five Eyes* countries share all intelligence gathered within their group with each other.[1483] The countries involved work on a high level of cooperation and practice burden-sharing.[1484] The level of cooperation under the UKUSA agreement is so far-reaching that "the national product is often indistinguishable."[1485] The *Five Eyes* countries participate in cooperative global operations and develop and analyse technologies together.[1486] Their most famous surveillance program is called *ECHELON* – a highly automated, tiered system and surveillance network to analyse data obtained by intercepting communications traffic from around the world. In some cases, the *Five Eyes* alliance also shares intelligence with third-party nations, e. g. when intelligence is relevant

---

1478 Enigma is a cipher machine developed and used in the early to mid-20th century to protect commercial, diplomatic and military communications by and from Nazi Germany.
1479 Margarete Warner, 'An Exclusive Club: The 5 Countries That Don't Spy On Each Other' [2013] PBS News Hour <https://www.pbs.org/newshour/world/an-exclusive-club-the-five-coun tries-that-dont-spy-on-each-other>; see in detail Pfluke (n 1476) 303 et seq.
1480 ibid 303.
1481 Pfluke (n 1476) 302.
1482 National Security Agency/Central Security Service, 'GCHQ and NSA Celebrate 75 Years of UKUSA Agreement' (2021) Press Release of 4 March 2021 <https://www.nsa.gov/Press-Room/News-Highlights/Article/Article/2524368/gchq-and-nsa-celebrate-75-years-of-ukusa-agreement/>.
1483 Pfluke (n 1476) 305.
1484 ibid.
1485 Erich King, 'Witness Statement of Eric King on Behalf of Privacy International in Privacy International v the Secretary of State for Foreign and Commonwealth Affairs & Government Communication Headquarters (Case No. IPT/13/92/CH)' <https://privacyinternational.org/sites/default/files/2018-03/2014.06.08%20Eric%20King%20witness%20statement.pdf> para 80 who is referring to Richard J. Aldrich, *Transatlantic Intelligence and security co-operation* (2006).
1486 Pfluke (n 1476) 305.

to a country's safety.[1487] The *Five Eyes* countries agreed to share sensitive intelligence on ISIS with France after the Paris terror attacks in November 2015.[1488]

The *Edward Snowden* leaks in 2013 initiated an open debate on how and to what extent the *Five Eyes* alliance infringes on privacy rights. The controversial issue in the context of the UK adequacy decision is the possible transfer of personal data from the EU through the UK to the United States under the *Five Eyes* alliance. Data on individuals in the EU, subject to the GCHQ's bulk powers, will also be available to the NSA. The CJEU recently declared the personal data protection level within the USA "inadequate" and the *Privacy Shield* invalid.[1489] The relevant provisions do not correlate to the minimum safeguards resulting from the principle of proportionality.[1490] In the US, non-US citizens have no right to an effective remedy as neither PPD-28 nor E.O. 12333 grants data subject rights that are actionable against US authorities in US courts.[1491] Yet, in the 2016 Report of the Interception of Communications Commissioner, it was found that "GCHQ provided comprehensive details of the sharing arrangements whereby Five Eyes partners can access elements of the product of GCHQ's interception warrants on their own systems. [The] inspectors also met representatives of the Five Eyes community and received a demonstration of how other Five Eyes members can request access to GCHQ's data. Access to GCHQ systems is tightly controlled and has to be justified in accordance with the laws of the host country and handling instructions of Section 15/16 safeguards. Before getting any access to GCHQ data, Five Eyes analysts must complete the same legalities training as GCHQ staff."[1492]

In 2001, Australia was considered for an adequacy decision by the EU Commission. The Article 29 Working Party found that several areas in the Australia Privacy Act would not meet the adequacy standard.[1493] The Australian Government subsequently did not revise Australia's data protection laws in order to

---

1487 Pfluke (n 1476) according to who, other intelligence-sharing networks (e. g. NATO and Interpol) only share their intelligence on a 'need-to-know basis' or based on a barter system.

1488 Jason Hanna, 'What Is the Five Eyes Intelligence Pact' [2017] CNN <https://edition.cnn.com/2017/05/25/world/uk-us-five-eyes-intelligence-explainer/index.html>.

1489 *Facebook Ireland and Schrems* (n 64). See in more detail above in Chapter 2, B.I.3.a.bb.

1490 ibid para 183.

1491 ibid para 192.

1492 Sir Stanley Burnton, 'Report of the Interception of Communications Commissioner Annual Report' (2016) 46 <https://assets.publishing.service.gov.uk/government/uploads/system/uploads/attachment_data/file/670219/IOCCO_annual_report_2016_2.PDF>.

1493 Art. 29 Data Protection Working Party, 'Opinion 3/2001 on the Level of Protection of the Australian Privacy Amendment (Private Sector) Act 2000' (2001) WP 40 final.

meet the required standard.[1494] The Australian Privacy Act does not apply to small businesses[1495] and employee data, and lacks several data subject's rights.[1496] Also, the Australian Privacy Commissioner can only investigate an interference with privacy, if Australian citizens and the permanent residents are concerned.[1497] As a result, EU citizens that are no permanent residents in Australia but whose data was transferred from the EU to Australia may not exercise access and correction rights in relation to their data.[1498]

4 EU Commission's Assessment

The EU Commission did not include the *Five Eyes* Alliance in its adequacy assessment.[1499] Instead, the EU Commission had only considered Part 4 DPA and the IPA 2016 concerning "requests" to exchange intelligence with foreign partners but not such a broader form of intelligence sharing. The EDPB also pointed out that the secret nature of the *Five Eyes* Alliance makes it very challenging in terms of clarity and foreseeability of the law in relation to the further use and overseas disclosure of information collected by UK authorities for national security purposes. Nevertheless, the Grand Chamber of the ECtHR found in its judgement in *Big Brother Watch* that there has been no violation of Article 8 ECHR for UK intelligence agencies' requests for intercepted material from foreign intelligence agencies as "[t]he British-US Communication Intelligence Agreement of 5 March 1946 specifically permits the exchange of material".[1500] The Grand Chamber stated that "sufficient safeguards had been in place to protect against abuse and to ensure that UK authorities had not used requests for intercept material from foreign intelligence partners as a means of circumventing their duties

---

1494 Nicholas Blackmore, 'Feeling Inadequate? Why Adequacy Decisions Are Rare (and May Get Rarer) in Asia-Pacific' (26 March 2019) <https://kennedyslaw.com/thought-leadership/article/feeling-inadequate-why-adequacy-decisions-are-rare-and-may-get-rarer-in-asia-pacific/>.
1495 Australian Privacy Act, sch 1.
1496 For a comparison of the GDPR and the Australian Privacy Act see Office of the Australian Information Commissioner, 'Australian Entities and the EU General Data Protection Regulation (GDPR)' (2018) <https://www.oaic.gov.au/privacy/guidance-and-advice/australian-entities-and-the-eu-general-data-protection-regulation>.
1497 Australian Privacy Amendment Act 2000, s 41(4) and National Privacy Principle 6 and 7.
1498 Art. 29 Data Protection Working Party, 'Opinion 3/2001 on the Level of Protection of the Australian Privacy Amendment (Private Sector) Act 2000' (n 1493) 5.
1499 EDPB, 'Opinion 14/2021 Regarding the European Commission Draft Implementing Decision Pursuant to Regulation (EU) 2016/679 on the Adequate Protection of Personal Data in the United Kingdom' (n 615) recital 192.
1500 *Big Brother Watch and Others v the United Kingdom* (n 800) para 500.

under domestic law and the Convention".[1501] However, the EDPB highlighted that the most recent public version of the UKUSA Agreement dates back to 1956[1502], which appears somewhat outdated regarding the significant development of communication technology and signal intelligence since then. [1503] More recent versions are publicly inaccessible. The EDPB also pointed out media reports that undersea cables that land in the UK are intercepted by the GCHQ and disclosed to the NSA.[1504] Also, it is unclear whether Section 109 DPA 2018 and the provisions of the IPA 2016 continue to apply in the context of the *Five Eyes* alliance.

The UK Parliament stated that the UK benefits significantly from the *Five Eyes* alliance and recommends working proactively with EU institutions to ensure that the UK's onward data transfer regime allows both an EU adequacy decision and the continuance of the existing *Five Eyes* relationship.[1505] It also "urge[d] the EU to recognise the value of these parallel security relationships, and to work flexibly to come to an agreed solution."[1506] However, it is evident by the *Facebook Ireland and Schrems* outcome that the CJEU has set a high bar for any data transfer between the EU and the US, and this will also apply for the onward transfer to the USA by the UK. The EU and its member states are interested in being granted access to intelligence databases by the UK.[1507] Many EU countries are Tier-B countries, with whom the *Five Eyes* alliance has a "focused cooperation".[1508] The UK could restrict the access to its own intelligence databases, which "given the pre-eminence of UK intelligence gathering

---

1501 *Big Brother Watch and Others v the United Kingdom* (n 800) para 513.

1502 Available at the following link <https://www.nsa.gov/Portals/70/documents/news-fea tures/declassified-documents/ukusa/new_ukusa_agree_10may55.pdf> accessed 9 June 2022.

1503 EDPB, 'Opinion 14/2021 Regarding the European Commission Draft Implementing Decision Pursuant to Regulation (EU) 2016/679 on the Adequate Protection of Personal Data in the United Kingdom' (n 615) recital 195.

1504 ibid.

1505 House of Commons, Home Affairs Committee, 'UK-EU Security Cooperation after Brexit' (2018) para 123 <https://publications.parliament.uk/pa/cm201719/cmselect/cmhaff/635/63508. htm#_idTextAnchor047>.

1506 ibid.

1507 National Crime Agency, 'Suspicious Activity Reports (SARs) Annual Report 2015' <https:// www.nationalcrimeagency.gov.uk/who-we-are/publications/2-sars-annual-report-2015/file> indicated that the UK Financial Intelligence Unity (UKFIU) received 1,566 requests for financial intelligence from its international partners between October 2014 and September 2015 – and almost 800 requests came from EU member states.

1508 Privacy International, 'Five Eyes' <https://privacyinternational.org/learn/five-eyes>.

on terrorism, crime and perceived international threats, is not insignificant".[1509] It might also be one of the political reasons the EU Commission did not find the UK's involvement in the *Five Eyes* alliance an obstacle to an adequacy decision. However, in *Facebook Ireland and Schrems*, the CJEU also overrode EU interests in sustaining the trading relationship with the US, the interests of the USA in protecting national security and differences between the EU and US data protection systems. From the EU's perspective, the USA had even more "leverage" than the UK has now, considering that many EU citizens are much more dependent on US-based platforms (e. g. *Google* and *YouTube*) in their daily lives.[1510] A disrupted data flow between the EU and the UK would have a more significant impact on UK citizens than *vice versa*.[1511] Consequently, this interest of the EU and member states in the context of access to intelligence information will likely not positively impact a CJEU's decision to assess the UK's adequacy level in the future.[1512]

IV Conclusion to D

While the EU Commission found that the UK's transfer practices in the context of law enforcement and national security would not be an obstacle to adopting an adequacy decision in favour of the UK, the remarks above show that it is very likely that the CJEU will decide otherwise. There is a high risk that the CJEU would invalidate such an adequacy decision. To be able to provide an adequate level of data protection in the context of onward transfer of personal data from the EU, the UK would have to re-evaluate their onward transfer practices, in particular to the US, in the context of law enforcement and intelligence agencies cooperation and implement appropriate safeguards, which comply with the CJEU's requirement in *Facebook Ireland and Schrems*. However, it does not seem to be a realistic chance that the UK will do so soon. Especially not with the adoption of an adequacy decision, which will apply for until June 2025.

1509 Clowance Wheeler-Ozanne, 'Deal or No-Deal: Does It Matter? Data Protection Predictions for Post-Brexit Britain' (2020) 24 Edinburgh Law Review 275, 278.
1510 ibid 278.
1511 In detail in Chapter 5, A.IV.
1512 Wheeler-Ozanne (n 1509) 278.

E Conclusion to Chapter 3

The EU Commission decided that the UK provides an adequate level of protection within the meaning of Article 45 GDPR read in light of the Charter.[1513]

However, in this chapter, several issues within the UK legislative system were pointed out that stipulate a high chance that the CJEU will declare the adequacy decision invalid.

The loss of the Charter *post*-Brexit does have a negative impact on the framework of fundamental rights protected in the UK (under A.). Charter rights only play a role as "general principles" in the *post*-Brexit UK to serve the purpose of interpretation but are not enforceable itself. Consequently, effective remedies against rights infringements are weakened. However, the UK is still a member of the ECHR and Convention 108. Although the ECHR has only limited effects in domestic law (through the HRA 1998), it provides an equivalent level of protection of fundamental rights to the one guaranteed under the Charter and is broadly consistent with the Charter. This membership was one of the main reasons the EU Commission found that the UK provides an adequate level of data protection compared to the EU.[1514] Over the last few years, the Conservative Party, which currently forms the UK's government, openly opposed the UK's membership in the ECHR and sought to weaken the role of the ECtHR at a national level.[1515] If the UK were to leave the ECHR, this could have a significant negative impact on the adequacy decision in favour of the UK. It could lead to an absence of respect for human rights and fundamental freedoms in the UK if no equivalent Bill of Rights would be introduced. The TCA provides the possibility for the EU to suspend or terminate the TCA if there has been a "serious and substantial failure" by the UK to fulfil the obligation "to uphold the values and principles of democracy, the rule of law, and respect for human rights, which underpin their domestic and international policies".[1516] This "serious and substantial failure" could occur if the UK were to leave the ECHR. Hence, this can be seen as leverage over the UK to stay a member of the ECHR and the Convention 108. However, even if the UK were to leave the ECHR, this does not necessarily lead to impossibility to uphold the rule of law. A new British Bill of Rights replacing the HRA 1998 could, depending on the respective content, affect the level of protection of

---

1513 See above in the introduction to Chapter 3.
1514 UK Adequacy Decision (n 14) recital 276.
1515 cf 'EU Enlargement Strategy' Communication to the European Parliament, the Council, the European Economic and Social Committee and the Committee of the Regions COM(2015) 611 final (n 727).
1516 TCA, art INST.35 in conjunction with art COMPROV.12.

fundamental rights in the UK. In light of this, the EU Commission must monitor, on an ongoing basis, relevant developments in the UK.

The DPA 2018 came into force under the GDPR, when the UK was still a member state to the EU. However, the review (under B.) showed that there is a chance that some of the exemption provisions in the DPA 2018 might cause a future adequacy decision to be declared invalid by the CJEU. There is no effective substantive oversight by the ICO or the courts over the use of the national security exemptions. The judicial remedy options against national security certificates are limited in practice. Further, it must be monitored whether *Douwe Korff*'s fear that the EU Commission's exclusions of "personal data transferred [from the EU to the UK] for United Kingdom immigration control purposes which otherwise falls within the scope of the [immigration] exemption" will be ignored in practice will prove to be true.[1517] Hence, The UK could soon administer a new data protection regime that is no longer subject to EU law.[1518] The EU Commission took this into account, stating that under this circumstance, the monitoring, on an ongoing basis, of relevant development in the UK is crucial.[1519] However, although political statements indicate that the UK's future data protection law might diverge from the GDPR, other factors, such as the digital services and IT sector's dependency on digital data from the EU and the "Brussels Effect", could suggest otherwise.[1520]

A controversial issue concerning the data transfer from the EU to the UK is the IPA 2016 (under C.).[1521] It does not comply with the Charter and the CJEU's established requirements of *Digital Rights Ireland and Seitlinger and Others, Tele2 Sverige* and other relevant judgements. Although the EU Commission did not find any issues with the IPA 2016, the UK's intelligence agencies' bulk interception and acquisition practices significantly increase the likelihood that the CJEU invalidates an adequacy decision in favour of the UK: The bulk interception powers and bulk acquisition powers set out in the IPA 2016 are untargeted, general and indiscriminate powers. The EU Commission's assessment failed to include the UK's intelligence agencies' actual bulk interception practices and the significance of the interception and subsequent retention of secondary data, which can be highly revealing. The bulk powers and the powers to the retention

---

1517 Korff, 'Initial Comments on the EU Commission's Final GDPR Adequacy Decision on the UK' (n 998).
1518 Further plans were announced in August 2021, in detail in Chapter 5, A.
1519 Adequacy Decision UK (n 14) recital 281.
1520 In detail in Chapter 5, A.IV.
1521 Korff, 'The Inadequacy of the EU Commission Draft GDPR Adequacy Decision on the UK' (n 921).

of communications data do not comply with the principle of proportionality and the principle of necessity.[1522] The IPA 2016 does not itself define the scope and application of its powers in relation to direct access to the system to communications beyond the broad term "interest of national security". Furthermore, the EU Commission failed to assess the procedural arrangements in practice and mistakes that the Judicial Commissioners only have powers to conduct a marginal and limited judicial review in practice.[1523]

Furthermore, the CJEU will likely invalidate the adequacy decision in favour of the UK due to the onward sharing practices (under D.), particularly by UK intelligence agencies, to the USA (through the *Five Eyes* alliance).

The Partnership Council[1524], which supervises the operation of the TCA on a political level, may make (non-binding) recommendations and advise the parties regarding the transfer of personal data in areas covered by the Agreement.[1525] In this way, difficulties can be dealt with before they cause disruption. If the CJEU invalidates the adequacy decision, the Partnership Council may also provide (strategic) solutions. The EU Commission could have considered different approaches for the adequacy decision. The UK adequacy decision could have been reduced as partial adequacy finding, whereby the UK would only be found to provide an adequate level of protection with respect to personal data transferred for commercial purposes.[1526] However, since the application scope of the provisions of the IPA 2016 are broad, it cannot be guaranteed that such personal data would not fall under the IPA 2016's scope. Also the broad practice of onward transfer to the US could not be prevented by a partial adequacy decision. Therefore, such a solution would not have been effective in addressing the inadequate protection of EU personal data in the UK system. Another consideration for the EU Commission could have been the implementation of a data transfer framework following the examples of *Safe Harbour*, *Privacy Shield* and the new *Trans-Atlantic Privacy Data Transfer Framework*. Under such a framework, organisations would self-certify to comply with the GDPR and provide an adequate level of protection for personal data transferred from the EU to the UK. Different than under the US law, EU citizens already have a right to appeal before the IPT (Section 65(2)(b) IPA 2016). However, such a framework could not modify the broad national provisions of the IPA 2016, which do not comply

---

1522 C.IV.1.
1523 C.IV.2.
1524 TCA, Titel III pt 1.
1525 TCA, art INST.1(h).
1526 Bradford, *The Brussels Effect: How the European Union Rules the World* (n 147) 280.

with the principle of proportionality.[1527] These provisions would still apply to personal data from the EU. Another consideration could have been that the UK, following Japan's example, implements additional safeguards, which would (solely) apply to data transferred from the EU to the UK and would compensate for certain differences between the EU and UK data protection systems.[1528] The EU Commission could have demanded to limit the scope of the IPA 2016 and onward transfers to the US of personal data from the EU. This would have been in fact be the most effective solution. However, it is not very likely that the UK would agree to implement safeguards that, in practice, effectively exclude the personal data transferred from the EU from the extensive investigatory powers at issue as well as from the onward transfers to third countries that do not provide an adequate level of protection (especially through the *Five Eyes* alliance to the US).

1527 With regard to the new EU-US Trans-Atlantic Data Privacy Framework it will also be relevant if and in what way the framework changes the extensive access of US intelligence agencies to personal data from the EU under the FISA and the E.O., which the CJEU considered to not comply with the proportionality principle (cf *Facebook Ireland and Schrems* (n 64) para 184). See for further concerns Douwe Korff and Ian Brown, 'Some brief initial comments on the announcement of an "agreement principle" on a new Trans-Atlantic Data Privacy Framework & on the EDPB's statement on the agreement in principle' (11 April 2022) <https://www.ian brown.tech/wp-content/uploads/2022/04/Early-comments-on-TADPF.pdf>.

1528 Japan implemented several measures before the adoption of the adequacy decision. These included an expansion of Japan's definition of sensitive data, facilitating the exercise of individual rights, and providing a higher level of protection for European data transferred from Japan to another third country. Japan also agreed to establish a complaint handling and resolution system under the supervision of the Japanese data protection authority to ensure that possible complaints from EU citizens related to access to their data by Japanese law enforcement and security authorities are effectively investigated and resolved, cf Annex 1 to the Japan Adequacy Decision ("Supplementary Rules"). See in detail for the 'Japanese Way', Flora Y. Wang, 'Cooperative Data Privacy: The Japanese Model of Data Privacy and the EU-Japan GDPR Adequacy Agreement' 33 Harvard Law and Technology Review (2020) 661.

Chapter 4 Alternative Data Transfer Tools

Since 28 June 2021, the UK benefits from an adequacy decision by the EU Commission. However, businesses should keep in mind that the adequacy decision includes a "sunset clause", setting the adequacy decision to automatically expire on 27 June 2025, four years after it entered into force.[1529] Additionally, the UK Government declared that it would in the future develop "separate and independent policies" in the area of data protection.[1530] The EU Commission is obligated to monitor all such relevant developments on a permanent and ongoing basis and eventually "repeal, amend or suspend the decision" in case of third country's lack of compliance with EU requirements.[1531] As concluded in the previous chapter, there is a high chance that the CJEU renders the adequacy decision in favour of the UK invalid as the Court has done before with *Safe Harbor* and the *Privacy Shield*. Hence, the "sword of Damocles" of invalidation is already hanging over the newly adopted adequacy decision.[1532] When an adequacy decision is rendered invalid by the CJEU, there is no transitional period for businesses to change data export provisions.[1533] In such a case, data exporters must immediately switch to alternative transfer tools, such as appropriate safeguards established in Article 46 GDPR, or use the derogation-provisions in Article 49 GDPR as a legal transfer basis.[1534] Consequently, businesses that export personal data from the EU to the UK must anticipate all changes to the adequacy decision before the expiration date and act and modify their transfer practices accordingly.[1535]

This Chapter focuses on all relevant alternative transfer tools for data exporters, which should be considered in the event that one of the aforementioned

---

1529 UK Adequacy Decision (n 14) art 4.

1530 Boris Johnson, 'UK/EU Relations' Written Statement on 3 February 2021 in the House of Commons UIN HCWS86 <https://questions-statements.parliament.uk/written-statements/detail/2020-02-03/HCWS86>. However, according to Schwartz, 'The Data Privacy Law of Brexit: Theories of Preference Change' (n 866) the chances of the UK developing a completely independent and separate data protection law are low due to the so-called "Brussels Effect". This effect will be discussed in detail in Chapter 5 under A.I.

1531 GDPR, art 45(3).

1532 Botta, 'Zwischen Rechtsvereinheitlichung und Verantwortungsdiffusion: Die Prüfung grenzüberschreitender Datenübermittlungen nach "Schrems II"' (n 1250) 509.

1533 EDPB, 'Frequently Asked Questions on the Judgement of the Court of Justice of the European Union in Case C-311/18 – Data Protection Commissioner v Facebook Ireland Ltd and Maximillian Schrems' (n 587).

1534 Such alternative transfer tools were already briefly reviewed in Chapter 2, B. II. and B.III.

1535 Wagner (n 4) 320.

https://doi.org/10.1515/9783110988253-006

cases occurs. Article 46 GDPR provides different appropriate safeguards, based on which personal data can be transferred despite the absence of an adequacy decision. First, the SCCs, the most popular appropriate safeguard (under A.), will be looked at. Following the *Facebook Ireland and Schrems* judgement, SCCs have undergone major developments. Nevertheless, there might be great potential to the other appropriate safeguards (under B.). Many of those have not yet been enough explored, such as codes of conduct and certification mechanisms. Also, the potential of Article 49 GDPR, constituting several derogations for specific situations, in which personal data may be transferred despite the absence of an adequacy decision or appropriate safeguards, are examined (under C.). The focus in the following mainly lies in providing practical guidelines for businesses as data exporters and analysing whether these tools are a suitable alternative for data transfer from the EU to the UK. Additionally, an overview of any further obligations, established under the GDPR, for data exporters transferring personal data outside the EU, is provided (under D.). If data exporters (and data importers in third countries, which are subject to the GDPR) fail to comply with the obligations under the GDPR when transferring personal data outside the EU, heavy sanctions might await them (under E.). Finally, the latest developments in the UK concerning alternative transfer tools are reviewed (under F.).

A Standard Contractual Clauses

SCCs are the most adopted alternative transfer tool. The *IAPP* found that 88 % of survey respondents whose organisations move personal data outside the EU rely on SCCs.[1536] In practice, SCCs are often already in place as a precautionary measure, even where businesses could rely on an adequacy decision since the EU Commission may amend or suspend these adequacy decisions.[1537] Once the SCCs are adopted (or approved) by the EU Commission, their use does not require an additional notification or any further authorisation by an authority. Therefore, SCCs have the advantage of quick implementation and fewer uncertainties regarding administrative procedures for the contracting parties.[1538] Also, the use of SCCs offers a high degree of legal certainty.[1539] However, the con-

---

1536 IAPP, 'IAPP-EY Annual Governance Report 2019' <https://iapp.org/store/books/a191P000003Qv5xQAC/>.
1537 EU Parliament, 'EU-UK Private Sector Data Flows after Brexit. Settling on Adequacy' (n 1190).
1538 Pauly, 'Art. 46 DS-GVO' (n 519) para 20.
1539 ibid.

tracting parties must take action if the EU Commission's decision is amended, replaced or repealed by EU Commission or the decision is declared invalid by the CJEU.[1540]

The implementation and use of SCCs were already briefly reviewed.[1541] In the following, the most recent developments will be discussed. The obligations of parties and data protection supervisory authorities as well as data subject rights under the SCCs were subject to the CJEU's review in the *Facebook Ireland and Schrems* judgement (under I.). Following the *Facebook Ireland and Schrems* judgement, the EU Commission adopted a new and modernised set of SCCs on 4 June 2021 (under II.). This modernisation aimed to extend the parties obligations under SCCs, especially regarding data access by public authorities in the respective third country, but also to strengthen the data subjects' rights. The EDPB published some Recommendations on supplementary measures for the practical use of the appropriate safeguards (under III.). Yet, there are still some practical and legal uncertainties concerning the use of SCCs (under IV.). Finally, a few examples of the practical implementation of the new SCCs will be briefly outlined (under VI.).

I CJEU: Facebook Ireland and Schrems

In *Facebook Ireland and Schrems*, the CJEU decided on the validity of the EU Commission's Decision 2010/87/EU[1542], which implemented SCCs concerning the data transfer between an EU-based controller to a controller outside the EU.[1543] Background to the dispute in the main proceedings was that the personal data of *Facebook* users in the EU are transferred, wholly or partly, from *Facebook Ireland*, the subsidiary of *Facebook Inc.*, to servers located in the US, where the data are being processed. The data transfer between *Facebook Ireland* and *Facebook Inc.* is based on a data transfer processing agreement that relied on the abovementioned Decision 2010/87/EU. *Maximilian Schrems* then requested from the Irish Data Protection Commissioner to suspend the transfer of data in application of Decision 2010/87/EU, claiming that, since US entities may be re-

---

1540 Pauly, 'Art. 46 DS-GVO' (n 519) para 20.
1541 Chapter 2, B.II.3.
1542 Commission Decision 2010/87/EU on standard contractual clauses for the transfer of personal data to processors established in third countries under Directive 95/46 of the European Parliament and of the Council, as amended by Commission Implementing Decision [2010] OJ L 39/5.
1543 *Facebook Ireland and Schrems* (n 64).

quired to grant access to personal data to US security services, data subjects concerned have no remedy to invoke their rights guaranteed in Articles 7 and 8 CFR in the US. The Data Protection Commissioner brought the proceedings before the Irish High Court and demanded to refer questions to the CJEU; the High Court then requested a preliminary ruling.[1544]

1 SCCs' Validity

The CJEU was requested to decide on the issue of whether the EU Commission's Decision 2010/87/EU is valid in the light of Articles 7, 8 and 47 CFR and the fact that SCCs are not binding on third country's national authorities, which may require the data importer to make personal data available to security services.[1545] The Court found that the mere fact that SCCs do not legally bind third country authorities could not affect the validity of the EU Commission SCCs decision.[1546] In the Court's view, the validity would depend on whether the SCCs, consistently with Article 46(1) and (2)(c) GDPR, interpreted in the light of the Charter, incorporate "effective mechanisms that make it possible, in practice, to ensure compliance with the level of protection required by EU law, and that transfer of personal data under the clauses of such a decision are suspended or prohibited in the event of the breach of such clauses or it being impossible to honour them."[1547] The CJEU clarified that the mere implementation of one of the instruments under Article 46(2) GDPR is not necessarily sufficient for a data transfer "subject to appropriate safeguards". Instead, Article 46(2) GDPR only clarifies that appropriate safeguards "may" exist in one of the listed transfer tools, but it is not necessarily given.[1548] According to this reading, Article 46(2) GDPR provides a selection concerning the "how" to transfer personal data outside the EU but says nothing about "whether" appropriate safeguards can be achieved at all with the chosen transfer tool in a specific transfer.[1549]

1544 Reference for a preliminary ruling from the High Court (Ireland) made on 9 May 2018 in *Facebook Ireland and Schrems*, OJ C 249/15.

1545 ibid Questions 7 and 11.

1546 *Facebook Ireland and Schrems* (n 64) para 136.

1547 ibid para 127.

1548 ibid para 128.

1549 Philippe Heinzke, 'Schrems II: Neue Anforderungen an den Transfer personenbezogener Daten in Drittländer' [2020] GRUR-Prax 436, 437.

2 Required Level of Protection

The CJEU confirmed that the use of SCCs requires the guarantee to a level of protection "essentially equivalent" to that within the EU.[1550] The Court pointed out that Article 46 GDPR is systematically placed in Chapter V of the GDPR and, therefore, must be read in the light of Article 44 GDPR.[1551] Article 44, Article 46(1) and Article 46(2)(c) GDPR, interpreted in the light of the Charter, require that the level of protection of natural persons guaranteed by the GDPR is not undermined. [1552] Furthermore, the CJEU referred to recital 108 GDPR, which emphasises the responsibility of the controller or processor "to compensate for the lack of data protection in a third country" where an adequate level of data protection is absent. Consequently, such appropriate safeguards must be capable of ensuring that data subjects are afforded a level of protection "essentially equivalent" to the one guaranteed in the EU.[1553] Whether the level of protection is sufficient must be assessed in the light of the Charter and view of Article 46 GDPR in each case by the data exporter. Article 46(1) GDPR states that the data subjects must be afforded appropriate safeguards, enforceable rights and effective legal remedies.[1554] In this context, not only the contractual relationship between both parties to the planned transfer but also possible access by authorities in the third country to the personal data to be transferred and the legal system of the destination country must be taken into account.[1555]

3 Data Exporters' Obligations

According to the CJEU, SCCs, interpreted in the light of Article 44 GDPR and the Charter, put the data exporter under various obligations to ensure compliance with the data protection requirements within the EU. As SCCs provide contractual guarantees independently of the level guaranteed in each third country, it is the obligation of the controller or the processor established in the EU to guarantee appropriate safeguards.[1556] In cases where SCCs cannot provide guarantees

---

1550 *Facebook Ireland and Schrems* (n 64) para 96.

1551 ibid paras 92 et seq., also referring to Opinion of Advocate General *Saugmandsgaard Øe* in *Facebook Ireland and Schrems* (n 1064) para 117.

1552 ibid para 132.

1553 ibid paras 95 et seq., also referring to Opinion of Advocate General *Saugmandsgaard Øe* in *Facebook Ireland and Schrems* (n 1064) para 115.

1554 *Facebook Ireland and Schrems* (n 64) para 103.

1555 ibid para 104.

1556 ibid para 133; the Court underlines this by referring to recitals 108 and 114 of the GDPR, stating that the controller or the processor "should take measures to compensate for the lack of data protection in a third country by way of appropriate safeguards for the data subject" (GDPR,

beyond a contractual obligation, the controllers or processors may be required to adopt additional safeguards to ensure compliance with that level of protection.[1557] Consequently, before any data transfer, the data exporter must "verify, on a case-by-case basis, whether the law of the third country of destination ensures adequate protection of personal data transferred" based on SCCs and, where necessary, must install additional safeguards (transfer impact assessment).[1558] The transfer of personal data based on SCCs must be suspended or prohibited in the case of a breach of the obligation under the SCCs and where it is (practically) impossible to be compliant. The contractual mechanism provided for in Article 46(2)(c) GDPR is based on the responsibility of the data exporter established in the EU and, where the controllers fail to act, the competent national supervisory authority.[1559]

4 National Supervisory Authorities' Obligations and Enforcement of SCCs

The CJEU confirmed that without a valid adequacy decision, the competent supervisory authority must suspend or prohibit a transfer of data to a third country based on SCCs, if, in the supervisory authority's opinion and the light of all circumstances of the transfer, the SCCs are not or cannot be complied within the third country in question and the level of protection guaranteed by the GDPR and the Charter cannot be ensured by other means, e.g. by the controller's suspension of the data transfer.[1560] This obligation would derive from Article 8(3) CFR, Article 51(1) GDPR and Article 57(1)(a) GDPR, according to which the national supervisory authorities are responsible for monitoring compliance with

---

recital 108) and "those safeguards should ensure compliance with data protection requirements and the rights of the data subjects appropriate to processing within the Union, including the availability of enforceable data subject rights and of legal remedies" (GDPR, recital 114).

1557 *Facebook Ireland and Schrems* (n 64) para 133 and recital 109 GDPR: "The possibility for the controller or processor to use standard data-protection clauses adopted by the Commission or by a supervisory authority should prevent controllers or processors neither from including the standard data-protection clauses in a wider contract, such as a contract between the processor and another processor, nor from adding other clauses or additional safeguards provided that they do not contradict, directly or indirectly, the standard contractual clauses adopted by the Commission or by a supervisory authority or prejudice the fundamental rights or freedoms of the data subjects. Controllers and processors should be encouraged to provide additional safeguards via contractual commitments that supplement standard protection clauses."

1558 ibid para 135.

1559 ibid para 126; Opinion of Advocate General *Saugmandsgaard Øe* in *Facebook Ireland and Schrems* (n 1064) para 126.

1560 *Facebook Ireland and Schrems* (n 64) para 121; Opinion of Advocate General *Saugmandsgaard Øe* in *Facebook Ireland and Schrems* (n 1064) para 148.

the EU rules concerning personal data protection. Such monitoring is particularly important where personal data is transferred to a third country. There is an increased risk of a data subject's ability to exercise data protection rights, primarily to protect themselves from unlawful use or revelation of the data.[1561] In the Court's opinion, the supervisory authority must determine whether the action is appropriate and necessary and is required to execute its responsibility for ensuring that the GDPR is fully enforced with all due diligence.[1562]

Moreover, the CJEU emphasises that the SCCs "[do] not prevent a national supervisory authority from exercising its powers to oversee data flows, including the power to suspend or ban a transfer of personal data when it determines that the transfer is carried out in violation of EU or national data protection law, such as, for instance, when the data importer does not respect the standard contractual clauses."[1563] The risk that various member states may be adopting diverging decisions – since, according to Article 55(1) GDPR and Article 57(1)(a) GDPR the task of enforcing that regulation lies with each supervisory authority on the territory of its member state – is decreased by Article 64(2) GDPR. The latter provision provides the possibility for a supervisory authority to refer the matter to the EDPB for an opinion, which may adopt a binding decision (Article 65 GDPR), remarkably where a supervisory authority does not follow the opinion issued.[1564]

5 Implementation in Practice

The consequences of *Facebook Ireland and Schrems* were considerable. Data exporters needed to go through the immense task of reviewing all data exports to third countries based on SCCs.[1565] In each case, data exporters needed to check whether the guarantees contained in these clauses are sufficient to establish an adequate level of protection against the background of the legal situation in the

---

[1561] *Facebook Ireland and Schrems* (n 64) para 108 referring to recital 106 GDPR.

[1562] ibid para 112. According to the CJEU this comes from the synopsis of various provisions: Furthermore, Article 57(1)(f) GDPR requires each supervisory authority to handle complaints on its territory with all due diligence, Article 78(1) and (2) GDPR establishes the right of each person to an effective judicial review where an supervisory authority fails to deal with his or her complaint, and Article 58(1) GDPR confers extensive investigative powers on each supervisory authority to handle complaints lodged; Article 58(2) GDPR lists various corrective powers which the authority may adopt if it takes the view that a data subject whose personal data have been transferred to a third country is not afforded an adequate level of protection in that third country.

[1563] ibid para 114.

[1564] ibid para 147.

[1565] Barbara Sandfuchs, 'The Future of Data Transfers to Third Countries in Light of the CJEU's Judgement C- 311/18 – Schrems II' [2021] GRUR Int. 245, 246.

recipient country. This assessment required an in-depth examination of the legal circumstances. It must be examined which (security) laws the respective third-country company to which or with the help of which personal data is transferred is subject to, which access possibilities of third-country public authorities result from this and which rights the data subjects are entitled to. The use of SCCs alone without additional technical or organisational measures was no longer enough to legitimise the transfer to the third countries where public authorities have access to personal data and where data subjects' rights and safeguards are limited. In practice, the *Facebook Ireland and Schrems* judgement appeared to be ignored – especially by US providers.[1566] US providers still preserved the right to transfer data to the US without referring to additional (technical) measures.[1567] Hence, it appears that the practice is not necessarily in conformity with data protection law. It follows mainly from the leniency of the data protection supervisory authorities and/or their financial and personnel resources.[1568] Also, US companies have significant market power in the digital sector. For example, the cloud market is currently dominated by US operators (*Amazon, Microsoft*, and *Google*), followed by (a wide margin of) Chinese providers.[1569] The failure to comply with the data protection requirements for third-country transfers can result in severe fines of up to four per cent of the worldwide (group) turnover of the previous year.[1570] However, no substantial fines have been made yet in praxis following the *Facebook Ireland and Schrems* ruling. This *status quo* may change since the EU Commission adopted its new SCCs decision (under II.) and the EDPB published its "Recommendations 01/2020 on measures that supplement transfer tools to ensure compliance with the EU level of protection of personal

---

1566 cf Thorsten Sörup and Danyal Parvez, 'Nutzung von Microsoft Office 365 im Unternehmen. Datenschutz- und betriebsverfassungsrechtliche Fragestellungen und Gestaltungshinweise' [2021] ZD 291, 293.

1567 State Commissioner for Data Protection and Freedom of Information in Mecklenburg-Western Pomerania, 'Pressemitteilung des Landesbeauftragten für Datenschutz und Informationsfreiheit Mecklenburg-Vorpommern' (2021) Press Release of 17 March 2021 <https://www.datenschutz-mv.de/presse/?id=168438&processor=processor.sa.pressemitteilung>.; Rolf Schwartmann and Lucia Burkhardt, '"Schrems II" als Sackgasse für die Datenwirtschaft? Verfahrensrechtliche Grenzen datenschutzrechtlicher Sanktionen' [2021] ZD 235, 236 et seq.

1568 Botta, 'Zwischen Rechtsvereinheitlichung und Verantwortungsdiffusion: Die Prüfung grenzüberschreitender Datenübermittlungen nach "Schrems II"' (n 1250) 512.

1569 Mathias Brandt, 'USA sind Cloud-Macht Nr. 1' (*Statista*, 12 January 2021) <https://de.statista.com/infografik/22251/geschaetzter-public-cloud-umsatz-in-den-top-5-maerkten/>.

1570 GDPR, art 83(5)(c). The sanction mechanisms under the GDPR are briefly outlined below under E.

data" (after this: EDPB Recommendations on supplementary measures) (under III.)

II New SCCs

On 4 June 2021, following the *Facebook Ireland and Schrems* judgement, the EU Commission published an implementing decision on SCCs, and a new set of SCCs (Annex) (after this: new SCCs).[1571] The motivation behind were "important developments [...] in the digital economy, with the widespread use of new and more complex processing operations, often involving multiple data importers and exporters, long and complex processing chains as well as evolving business relationships."[1572] According to the EU Commission these developments had called "for a modernisation of the standard contractual clauses to better reflect those realities, by covering additional processing and transfer situations and to use a more flexible approach, for example concerning the number of parties able to join the contract."[1573] "In order to provide appropriate safeguards, the standard modernisation contractual clauses should ensure that the personal data transferred on that basis are afforded a level of protection essentially equivalent to that which is guaranteed within the Union."[1574] Depending on the designation of the parties as controllers or processors, the modular clauses for transfers include data protection safeguards;[1575] provisions regarding the appointment of sub-processors in controller-to-processor transfers and processor-to-processor transfers;[1576] data subject rights and the parties' obligations in the event of a data subject rights request;[1577] and provisions concerning the parties' liability under the SCCs[1578]. Annex I to the SCCs comprises a description of the transfers, including the categories of data subjects whose personal data is transferred, the categories of personal data transferred, the purpose(s) of the transfer and further processing, the maximum data retention periods, and, for further details on transfers to (sub)processors, as well as a list of parties to the contract. Notably, the new SCCs explicitly consider the involvement of three or more parties and the

---

1571 SCCs Decision 2021 (n 549).
1572 ibid recital 6.
1573 ibid.
1574 ibid recital 11.
1575 ibid Annex clause 8.
1576 ibid Annex clause 9.
1577 ibid Annex clauses 10 and 11.
1578 ibid clause 12.

accession of other parties throughout the contract's life cycle.[1579] Annex III to the SCCs lists the sub-processors used by the processor. Concerning onward transfers to additional recipients in third countries, transfers are allowed only if the recipient accedes to the SCCs, the protection of the personal data transferred is ensured by other means, or data subjects provide an informed and explicit consent.[1580]

The EDPB and the EDPS have adopted joint opinions on the new sets of SCCs. Overall, they concluded that the draft SCCs present a reinforced level of protection for data subjects. Significantly, the provisions that intended to address some of the main issues identified in the *Facebook Ireland and Schrems* judgement were welcomed by the EDPB and EDPS. However, the EDPB and EPDS requested several amendments to the draft SCCs in order to ensure more clarity and legal certainty for day-to-day operations of data exporters.[1581] Hence, the EDPB also published a new version of its Recommendations on supplementary measures for data exporters (under III.). Parties to the SCCs should be aware to ensure sufficient accuracy in determining which party takes which role in a specific transfer or a set of transfers.[1582] The best practice would be that a new and separate Annex would be used for each transfer or set of transfers, which should only be signed by those involved in effectively carrying out the specific processing.[1583] Roles and responsibilities in a transfer should be simplified through the relevant *Annex* to set out the relevant processing activities in detail and clarify the third-party accession mechanism.[1584] Parties to the SCCs should be aware that combining different modules within a single set may eventually lead to the parties' blurring of roles and responsibilities.[1585]

1 Processor-to-Processor and Processor-to-Controller Transfer

The new SCCs constitute a modular approach and no longer only cover data transfers in controller-to-controller (now Module One) and controller-to-process-

---

1579 SCCs Decision 2021 (n 549) recital 10.

1580 For a detailed discussion of practical problems concerning former SCCs and data processors see Paul Voigt, 'Praxisprobleme im Zusammenhang mit den EU-Standardvertragsklauseln zur Auftragsverarbeitung – mehr als "nur" Schrems II ...' [2020] CR 513.

1581 EDPB and EDPS, 'Joint Opinion 2/2021 on the European Commission's Implementing Decision on Standard Contractual Clauses for the Transfer of Personal Data to Third Countries for the Matters Referred to in Article 46(2)(c) of Regulation (EU) 2016/679' (2020) recitals 14, 112, 123 and 127.

1582 ibid recital 128.

1583 ibid.

1584 ibid recitals 45 et seq.

1585 ibid recital 31.

or (now Module Two) relationships but also transfers in processor-to-processor (now Module Three) and processor-to-controller relationships (now Module Four). Controllers and processors should "select the module applicable to their situation", making it possible to adapt their obligations under the SCCs to their roles and responsibilities concerning the data processing.[1586] The lack of SCCs for processor-to-processor transfers used to be a problem in practice: The old SCCs were only constituted suitable guarantees if the controller was located in the EU and the processor in the third country. However, in practice, only a sub-processor is usually located in the third country, while the processor is situated in the EU.[1587]

2 Parties' Obligations

The SCCs must provide specific safeguards to address any effects of third country's laws on the data importer's compliance with the clauses and how to deal with binding requests by public authorities for disclosure of the personal data transferred.[1588] First, the data transfer should only take place if the laws in the receiving country do not prevent the data importer from complying with its contractual obligations.[1589] Hence, the new SCCs require the data importer and the data exporter to conduct a risk-based assessment considering the specific circumstances of the transfer, the laws and practices of the third country of destination and the safeguards put in place.[1590] When agreeing to the new SCCs, the parties must warrant that "they have no reason to believe that the laws applicable to the data importer are not in line with these requirements."[1591] The assessment must be documented and re-evaluated by the parties if changes in the relevant legislation are observed.[1592] The assessment must also be provided to supervisory authorities at their request. The EDPB and EDPS doubted whether there could be room for a risk-based assessment that includes subjective factors, such as the parties' prior experience with governmental data access requests.[1593] Notably, the Joint Opinion stressed that the public authorities' absence of requests for disclosure should not be relevant factors for the local law assess-

---

1586 SCCs Decision 2021 (n 549) recital 10.
1587 Google Cloud, 'Google Cloud's Approach to the New EU Standard Contractual Clauses' (2021) 8 <https://services.google.com/fh/files/misc/gc_new_eu_scc.pdf>.
1588 SCCs Decision 2021 (n 549) recital 18.
1589 ibid recital 19 and Annex clause 14.
1590 ibid Annex clause 14(b).
1591 ibid recital 19.
1592 ibid Annex clause 14(d).
1593 EDPB and EDPS (n 1581) recitals 86 et seqq.

ment.[1594] However, the EDPB changed its point of view in the new version of its Recommendations on supplementary measures.[1595] Furthermore, the EDPB and EDPS have criticised the absence of a master version for documenting the data importer and data exporter's risk-based assessment.[1596] Also, the Joint Opinion pointed out that the EU Commission did not consider cases in which the level of data protection in the third country is adequate, but, in practice, the authorities have not followed the law.[1597] This would follow from Article 45(2) GDPR, according to which not only the legislation in the respective third country but also the effective implementation practice is relevant for the adequacy assessment. The EDPB included such cases in its Recommendations on supplementary measures.[1598]

Second, the data importer must immediately notify the data exporter if there is reason to believe that the data importer can no longer comply with the SCCs.[1599] The data exporter is then obligated to identify appropriate measures – technical or organisational measures to ensure security and confidentiality – and, if necessary, consult the competent supervisory authority.[1600] Annex II to the new SCCs includes a description of such technical and organisational measures that must be implemented to ensure an appropriate level of security for the data transferred.[1601] Also, the EDPB has specified examples for such technical and organisational measures in its Recommendations on supplementary measures.[1602] The data importer should additionally notify "the data subject if it receives a legally binding request by a public authority under the law of the country of destination for disclosure of personal data or becomes aware of any direct access by public authorities to personal data" transferred under the SCCs by the law of the receiving third country.[1603] The data importer must provide the data exporter with relevant information on the requests received but also regularly

---

1594 EDPB and EDPS (n 1581) recital 87.
1595 Under IV.3.b.
1596 EDPB and EDPS (n 1581) recital 89.
1597 ibid recital 81.
1598 EDPB, 'Recommendations 01/2020 on Measures That Supplement Transfer Tools to Ensure Compliance with the EU Level of Protection of Personal Data – Version 2.0' (2021) paras 43 et seqq.
1599 SCCs Decision 2021 (n 549) recital 21.
1600 ibid.
1601 The EDBP and the EDPS recommended that Annex 2 includes more specified measures to the respective transfer to avoid generic remarks related to various transfers, see in EDPB and EDPS (n 1581) recital 131.
1602 Under III.2.a. and c.
1603 SCCs Decision 2021 (n 549) recital 22 and Annex clause 15.1 (a)(i).

with any aggregate information. The data importer must document any request for disclosure received and the response provided and make that information available to the data exporter and the competent supervisory authority upon request.[1604] Moreover, the data importer is obligated to challenge governmental access requests to the extent legally possible.[1605]

Third, the data exporter must suspend the transfer if the competent supervisory authority cannot ensure or instruct the appropriate safeguards.[1606] In severe cases, the data exporter has "the right to terminate the contract where the data importer is in breach of, or unable to comply with" the new SCCs.[1607]

3 Extended Data Subjects' Rights

The data subject's rights have also been extended and strengthened under the new SCCs. The data subjects are granted direct rights against the data importers.[1608] To what extent these rights will be granted depends on each transfer scenario. In case of a data transfer between controllers (Module One), the data subject may enforce the full range of GDPR rights. Furthermore, data subjects must be provided with a copy of the SCCs upon request and informed of any change of purpose and identity of any third party to whom the personal data is disclosed. The SCCs require the data importer to inform data subjects of a contact point and promptly deal with any complaints or requests.[1609]

Also, redress mechanisms must be available to data subjects:[1610] Data subjects must be able to invoke, and where necessary enforce, the SCCs as third-party beneficiaries.[1611] Excluded from this are clauses targeted to solely regulate the relationship between the data exporter and data importer.[1612] Data subjects must be provided with the possibility to complain to the competent supervisory authority or refer to the competent courts in the EU in a dispute with the data importer.[1613] The data importer must submit to the jurisdiction of such authorities and courts and must commit to comply with any binding decision under

---

1604 SCCs Decision 2021 (n 549) recital 22 and Annex clause 15.1 (a)(i).
1605 ibid and Annex clause 15.1 (b).
1606 ibid Annex clause 14(f).
1607 ibid recital 17 and Annex clause 16(b).
1608 SCCs Decision 2021 (n 549) Annex clause 16(c).
1609 ibid recital 12 and clause 8.5(e) (Module One), clause 8.6(c) (Module Two and Module Three), clause 11(a) (Module Four).
1610 ibid Annex clause 11.
1611 ibid recital 12 and Annex clause 3.
1612 ibid recital 12.
1613 ibid.

the applicable member state law.[1614] Additionally, "the data importer should have the option to offer data subjects the possibility to seek redress before an independent dispute resolution body at no cost."[1615]

4 Liability

The new SCCs also introduced a stricter liability regime, comparable to the liability rules under the GDPR. Where the clauses are breached, data subjects are entitled to damage compensation (material and non-material). The data exporter and data importer may be jointly and severally liable vis-à-vis data subjects.[1616] In cases of transfers from the controller to processor (Module Two) and from processor to (sub-)processor (Module Three), the data exporter will even be subjected to strict liability for breaches of the data importers.[1617] Furthermore, each party is liable to the other party for any damage it causes the other party by a breach of the clauses.[1618]

5 Extraterritoriality and Retransfers

Data exporters outside the EU may also use the new SCCs. The processor-to-controller clauses (Module Four) cover retransfers, for instance data transfers from a processor in the EU (to which the processor rules of the GDPR apply directly) to a controller outside the EU (which is not subject to the GDPR). According to the EU Commission, the SCCs decision would not cover transfers to non-EU data importers already subject to the GDPR under Article 3(2) GDPR.[1619]

1614 SCCs Decision 2021 (n 549) recital 13 and Annex clause 11(e) (does not apply for Module Four).

1615 ibid recital 13.

1616 ibid Annex clause 12(b) and (c) (Module One and Module Four) and clause 12(b) and (e) (Module Two and Three).

1617 SCCs Decision 2021 (n 549) Annex clause 12(c) and (d). This was called for by the Joint Opinion of the EDPB and the EDPS (n 1581): Regarding controller-to-processor (Module Two) and processor-to-processor (Module Three), the possibility of seeking redress from the data exporter for any damages caused by the data importer should not only be allowed under the condition of action against the data importer (GDPR, recitals 121 et seq.).

1618 ibid Annex clause 12(a).

1619 EDPB and EDPS (n 1581) recital 27. This restricted scope of application raised some concerns and will be further discussed below under IV.2.a.

III EDPB's Recommendation for Supplementary Measures

On 10 November 2020, the EDPB published its Recommendations on supplementary measures for transfer tools to ensure compliance with EU data protection level ("Version 1.0"). It followed the CJEU's ruling in *Facebook Ireland and Schrems*. The purpose was "[t]o help exporters [...] with the complex task of assessing third countries and identifying appropriate supplementary measures where needed".[1620] On 18 June 2021, following the adoption of the new SCCs, the EDPB published an updated "Version 2.0".[1621]

These Recommendations on supplementary measures provide an extensive guideline for businesses using or plan on using (any) appropriate safeguards as an alternative transfer tool. *Andrea Jelinek*, EDPB Chair, stated that concerning "ad-hoc supplementary measures in order to ensure that data subjects are afforded a level of protection essentially equivalent to that guaranteed within the EU, the new SCCs will have to be used along with the EDPB Recommendations on supplementary measures".[1622] Data exporters are strongly advised to follow the specific guidelines set out in the EDPB Recommendations on supplementary measures.[1623] According to the EDPB, the "roadmap" to apply the principle of accountability to data transfers in practice consists of six steps. Data exporters should carefully consider these if they deliberate a data transfer outside the EU.

1 Six-Steps Evaluation

First, data exporters need to know their transfers.[1624] They should record and map their transfers to establish which transfers require further action.[1625]. Further, the exporters should validate that the transferred data is relevant and limited to what is necessary concerning the purposes they are transferred to and

---

1620 EDPB, 'Recommendations 01/2020 on Measures That Supplement Transfer Tools to Ensure Compliance with the EU Level of Protection of Personal Data – Version 1.0' (n 1245) 2.
1621 EDPB, 'Recommendations 01/2020 on Measures That Supplement Transfer Tools to Ensure Compliance with the EU Level of Protection of Personal Data – Version 2.0' (n 1598).
1622 European Data Protection Board and European Data Protection Supervisor, 'EDPB & EDPS Adopt Joint Opinion on New Sets of SCCs' (2021) Press Release of 15 January 2021 <https://edpb.europa.eu/news/news/2021/edpb-edps-adopt-joint-opinions-new-sets-sccs_en>.
1623 Sandfuchs (n 1565) 247.
1624 EDPB, 'Recommendations 01/2020 on Measures That Supplement Transfer Tools to Ensure Compliance with the EU Level of Protection of Personal Data – Version 2.0' (n 1598) paras 8 et seqq.
1625 These transfers include onward transfers, remote access, and cloud solutions.

processed for in the third country.[1626] A second step is to verify the transfer tool the transfer relies upon amongst enlisted in Chapter V of the GDPR.[1627] A third step is assessing the third-country law and practice and any risk of impingement "on the effectiveness of the appropriate safeguards of the transfer tools the data exporter" relies on for a specific transfer ("transfer impact assessment").[1628] The tool is only effective if the transferred personal data is provided a level of protection in the third country that is "essentially equivalent" to that guaranteed in the EU. Subsequently, the data exporter will need to determine how the domestic legal order of the third country applies to each transfer and its specific characteristics. First and foremost, the data exporters need to assess in detail if any applicable third country laws affect the obligations contained in the chosen transfer tool.[1629] In this regard, the EDPB refers to its "European Essential Guarantees" Recommendations[1630].[1631] Practices in the third country must be considered alongside the relevant local legislation.[1632] The EDPB also provides data exporters with possible sources of information and emphasises that the parties may also consider "documented practical experience of the importer with the relevant prior instances of requests for access received from public authorities in the third country."[1633] However, these prior experiences may only be used "if the legal framework of the third country does not prohibit the importer [...] from providing information [on disclosure requests] by public authorities [...] or [...] in the absence of such requests".[1634] Also, the EDPB clarifies that the "absence of prior instances of such requests" cannot be considered "a decisive factor on the effectiveness" of the chosen transfer tool.[1635] If the assessment under the third step has revealed that the transfer tool is ineffective, then, in a fourth step, the data controller must "identify and adopt supplementary measures".[1636] The EPDB stresses that the supplementary measures must be identified on a

---

1626 EDPB, 'Recommendations 01/2020 on Measures That Supplement Transfer Tools to Ensure Compliance with the EU Level of Protection of Personal Data – Version 2.0' (n 1598) para 11.
1627 ibid paras 14 et seqq.
1628 ibid paras 28 et seqq.
1629 ibid paras 32 et seqq.
1630 See in Chapter 3, C.III.
1631 EDPB, 'Recommendations 01/2020 on Measures That Supplement Transfer Tools to Ensure Compliance with the EU Level of Protection of Personal Data – Version 2.0' (n 1598) para 41.
1632 ibid paras 43 et seqq.
1633 ibid para 47.
1634 EDPB, 'Recommendations 01/2020 on Measures That Supplement Transfer Tools to Ensure Compliance with the EU Level of Protection of Personal Data – Version 2.0' (n 1598) para 47.
1635 ibid.
1636 ibid paras 50 et seqq.

case-by-case basis.[1637] Contractual or organisational measures alone will not prevent access to personal data by public authorities of the third country.[1638] The EDPB provides a "(non-exhaustive) list" of the following factors, which could help the data exporter with identifying effective supplementary measures: the "format of the data to be transferred"; the "nature of the data"; the "length and complexity of the data processing workflow, the number of actors involved [...] and the relationship between them" as well as the possibility of onward transfers.[1639] Annex 2 to the EDPB Recommendations on supplementary measures provides examples of technical, contractual and supplementary measures (under 2.).[1640] A fifth step consists of any formal procedural actions that the adoption of the supplementary measures may require.[1641] A sixth step is to "re-evaluate" the protection of the personal data transferred to the third country at "appropriate intervals" and monitor any changes and development that may affect it.[1642] The data exporter "should put sufficiently sound mechanisms in place to ensure that it promptly suspends or ends transfers where the importer has breached or is unable to honour the commitments it has taken in the transfer tool; or the supplementary measures are then no longer effective in that third country".[1643]

2 Supplementary Measures

In the case that the transfer impact assessment (third step) reveals that the chosen Article 46 GDPR transfer tool does not ensure adequate protection, supplementary measures are required (fourth step).[1644]

1637 EDPB, 'Recommendations 01/2020 on Measures That Supplement Transfer Tools to Ensure Compliance with the EU Level of Protection of Personal Data – Version 2.0' (n 1598) para 51.
1638 ibid para 53.
1639 ibid para 54.
1640 The Annex 2 is divided into technical measures (sub-divided into scenarios for which effective measures could be found and scenarios in which no effective measures could be found), additional contractual measures and organizational measures. For each section/additional measure a (non-exhaustive) list of examples is provided for businesses.
1641 EDPB, 'Recommendations 01/2020 on Measures That Supplement Transfer Tools to Ensure Compliance with the EU Level of Protection of Personal Data – Version 2.0' (n 1598) paras 59 et seqq.
1642 ibid paras 67 et seq.
1643 ibid para 68.
1644 Center for Information Policy Leadership (CIPL), 'A Path Forward for International Data Transfers under the GDPR after the CJEU Schrems II Decision' (2020) <https://www.in formationpolicycentre.com/uploads/5/7/1/0/57104281/cipl_white_paper_gdpr_transfers_post_ schrems_ii__24_september_2020__2_.pdf> providing a toolkit of possible supplementary mea-

a Technical Measures

Technical safeguards[1645] appear to be the most effective supplementary measure since data exporters should primarily take measures that *de facto* completely prevent access by third-country authorities incompatible with the EU guarantees of the rule of law.[1646]

Organisations should include a comprehensive security infrastructure, including state of the art technical security measures such as firewalls, antivirus and intrusion prevention, regular auditing, testing and controls, access controls and audit logging, physical security infrastructure, application security and device management and law enforcement ID verification.[1647]

Technical tools might be anonymisation and pseudonymisation of personal data. Anonymisation of the data eliminates the reference to persons, which is why the GDPR would no longer apply to the transmission of such data. Pseudonymisation is the process of disguising identities.[1648] Personal data is processed "in such a manner that the personal data can no longer be attributed to a specific data subject without the use of additional information, provided that such additional information is kept separately and is subject to technical and organisational measures to ensure that the personal data are not attributed to an identified or identifiable natural person".[1649] Unlike anonymous information, pseudonymised data remain personal data in the meaning of the GDPR but reduce the risks of natural persons being identified by an unauthorised person. Thus, it is a way of designing data processing in a less invasive way.[1650] Pseudonymisation of personal data can ensure adequate protection provided that the data importer does not have access to additional information through which the pseudonyms can be attributed to the respective data subject.[1651]

---

sures organisation can put in place to protect transferred data. However, the following focuses on the official EDPB Recommendation.

1645 Such additional technical safeguards would be necessary regardless of Articles 25 and 32 GDPR, which require the implementation of technical measures independently from any export of personal data.

1646 Barbara Scheben and Konstantin von Busekist, 'Dürfen personenbezogene Daten die EU noch verlassen?' [2021] WPg 329, 333.

1647 Center for Information Policy Leadership (CIPL) (n 1644) 12.

1648 Art. 29 Data Protection Working Party, 'Opinion 4/2007 on the Concept of Personal Data' (2007) WP 136 18.

1649 GDPR, art 4(5).

1650 Rücker (n 154) para 102.

1651 EDPB, 'Recommendations 01/2020 on Measures That Supplement Transfer Tools to Ensure Compliance with the EU Level of Protection of Personal Data – Version 2.0' (n 1598) para 85. Data exporter should be aware that IP addresses, cookie IDs, advertising IDs, unique user IDs or other

Technical measures may include strong data encryption before transmission. Data encryption is expressly recognised as an appropriate technical measure to ensure a level of security appropriate to the risk (Article 32 GDPR). Encryption is already widely used by organisations in the context of their data processing activities.[1652] The main goal of encryption is to limit access to the content of personal data to authorised parties.[1653] However, encryption is not a one-size-fits-all solution but instead is deployed on a case-by-case analysis depending on the type of threats, level of risks, type of data and processing as well as state of the art.[1654] When deploying encryption, businesses should be aware that key management is essential for encrypting and decryption of personal data.[1655] The appropriate management approach requires an organisation to consider potential security risks, operational risks, necessary costs and functional limitations.[1656] However, the encryption must be in line with the EDPB's requirement, including conformity to the state of art and retaining the decryption keys solely in the EU or a country with an adequate level of protection according to Article 45 GDPR, where the data importer has no access.[1657]

Another effective technical safeguard could be the split or multi-party processing where data is split to different data importers located in different jurisdictions to prevent that no processor receives enough data to reconstruct the personal data. No data exchange must take place between these different data

---

identifiers are used to (re)identify users, are not pseudonymisation measures within the meaning of the GDPR. Unlike in cases where data are pseudonymised in order to disguise or delete the identifying data so that the data subjects can no longer be addressed, IDs or identifiers are used to make the individual distinguishable and addressable, cf Konferenz der unabhängigen Datenschutzaufsichtsbehörden des Bundes und der Länder (Datenschutzkonferenz), 'Orientierungshilfe der Aufsichtsbehörden für Anbieter von Telemedien' (March 2019) 15 <https://www.da tenschutzkonferenz-online.de/media/oh/20190405_oh_tmg.pdf>.

1652 CIPL (n 1644) 13.

1653 ibid.

1654 ibid 14.

1655 ibid.

1656 ibid.

1657 EDPB, 'Recommendations 01/2020 on Measures That Supplement Transfer Tools to Ensure Compliance with the EU Level of Protection of Personal Data – Version 2.0' (n 1598) para 84. The Recommendations also include additional guidance on how to assess the strength of encryption algorithms (footnotes 80 and 81) and how cryptographic algorithms may be utilised to pseudonymise personal data (footnote 83). For example, a data importer subject to FISA 702 is obligated to provide access to or surrender imported data in its possession or custody or under its control. This obligation may expressly extend to the cryptographic keys without which the data cannot be read (para 81).

importers.[1658] *CIPL* suggest that similarly, access to data stored in the EU could be limited to EU employees of EU entities, whereas access from outside the EU would be reviewed, approved, and supervised by an EU employee.[1659]

Although technical measures might be the most effective safeguard to prevent access by public authorities in a third country, they may not be a sufficient tool in the cases of transfer to processors which require access to personal data in the clear[1660] or in cases involving remote access to clear data for business purposes[1661].

b Contractual Measures

Contractual measures may accompany technical safeguards. Contractual measures cannot bind local third-country authorities that are not a party to the contract or prevent the application of the third-country legislation in those cases in which the legislation obliges importers to comply with the disclosure orders they receive from public authorities.[1662] Hence such measures should be combined with other technical and organisational measures to provide the level of data protection required.[1663] The EDPB specified some examples, such as providing for the contractual obligation to use specific technical measures,[1664] transparency obligations (e. g. disclosing whether the importer has created back doors to facilitate government access),[1665] obligations to take specific actions,[1666] and empowering data subjects to exercise their rights[1667]. The obligation to take specific actions includes the data exporters' demand from data importers to commit to reviewing potential governmental orders requesting access and, where there are grounds to do so, legally challenge the orders.[1668] Particular attention must be paid to the specific wording of such additional contractual safeguards not to violate the prohibition of amendments to the SCCs.[1669] However, no viola-

---

1658 EDPB, 'Recommendations 01/2020 on Measures That Supplement Transfer Tools to Ensure Compliance with the EU Level of Protection of Personal Data – Version 2.0' (n 1598) para 92.
1659 CIPL (n 1644) 13.
1660 EDPB, 'Recommendations 01/2020 on Measures That Supplement Transfer Tools to Ensure Compliance with the EU Level of Protection of Personal Data – Version 2.0' (n 1598) para 94.
1661 ibid para 96.
1662 ibid para 101.
1663 ibid para 99.
1664 ibid paras 103 et seq.
1665 ibid paras 105 et seqq.
1666 ibid paras 118 et seqq.
1667 ibid paras 122 et seqq.
1668 SCCs Decision 2021 (n 549) Annex clause 15.2(a).
1669 Scheben and Busekist (n 1646) 333.

tion would occur where the amendments do not contradict the SCCs and are exclusively beneficial for the data subjects concerned.[1670]

c Organisational Measures

Lastly, additional organisational measures may be implemented. These would include internal policies and organisational standards, which data exporters could apply to themselves and impose on data importers in third countries. However, while organisational measures play an essential role in ensuring consistency in the entire processing cycle, internal oversight of processing activities, and reacting to potential governmental data access requests quickly, they mainly support the technical and contractual measures.[1671] The examples of organisational measures provided by the EDPB include transparency and accountability measures and data minimisation measures. Another organisational measure could be the decision to partially relocate some of the EU's data or move the data to adequate countries, when technically possible and when compliant with costs and risks assessments.[1672]

3 No Effective Supplementary Measures

The EDPB considers technical measures, meaning encryption or pseudonymisation, to be the most promising safeguard measure when transferring personal data outside the EU based on Article 46 GDPR. It appears to be "highly suspicious" of the use of solely non-technical measures.[1673] Although the list of "examples of technical measures" in Annex 2 is non-exhaustive[1674], it gives the impression that the EDPB only accepts transfers if the data are made unreadable through encryption.[1675]

1670 Scheben and Busekist (n 1646) 333 referring to recital 109 GDPR.
1671 EDPB, 'Recommendations 01/2020 on Measures That Supplement Transfer Tools to Ensure Compliance with the EU Level of Protection of Personal Data – Version 2.0' (n 1598) paras 128 et seq.
1672 CIPL (n 1644) 12.
1673 Theodore Christakis, '"Schrems III"? First Thoughts on the EDPB Post-Schrems II Recommendations on International Data Transfers (Part 2)' (*European Law Blog*, 16 November 2020) <https://europeanlawblog.eu/2020/11/16/schrems-iii-first-thoughts-on-the-edpb-post-schrems-ii-recommendations-on-international-data-transfers-part-2/>.
1674 EDPB, 'Recommendations 01/2020 on Measures That Supplement Transfer Tools to Ensure Compliance with the EU Level of Protection of Personal Data – Version 2.0' (n 1598) para 77.
1675 Christakis, '"Schrems III"? First Thoughts on the EDPB Post-Schrems II Recommendations on International Data Transfers (Part 2)' (n 1673).

The request for strong encryption faces criticism. Encryption might not always be a suitable solution since it blocks data usability and prevents data processing by data importers.[1676] Also it appears to be practically almost impossible to adopt technical safeguards that resist the highly advanced technologies, used by GCHQ and the NSA to try and access encrypted data streams of internet communication services (bulk interception powers)[1677], which was revealed by *Edward Snowden* in 2013[1678].[1679] Encryption would merely make access by technically advanced public authorities more difficult, which according to *Douwe Korff* might lead to a more focused approach on data relevant to operational purposes on the intelligence agencies' side.[1680] Moreover, *CIPL* has pointed out that in some EU member states, organisations might face political pressure not to encrypt data to be available to government security, intelligence, and law enforcement agencies.[1681] On 24 November 2020, the EU Council's Committee of Permanent Representatives published a non-binding resolution on encryption,[1682] promoting the idea that state authorities' access to encrypted data should be possible. This points out a dilemma, the data exporter might face when encryption personal data.

The two examples of scenarios in which effective technical measures are not identified and data transfer would have to be suspended could be accounted for the vast majority of "real world transfers".[1683] According to the EDPB, technical measures would be insufficient safeguards in transfers to cloud services providers or other processors that require access to data in the clear and remote access

---

1676 Christakis, '"Schrems III"? First Thoughts on the EDPB Post-Schrems II Recommendations on International Data Transfers (Part 2)' (n 1673).
1677 See Chapter 3, C.IV.1.a.aa.
1678 Ball, Borger and Greenwald (n 1100); Larson (n 1100); Cadwalladr (n 1100).
1679 Korff, 'Amid the Spying by EU Member States' Intelligence Agencies, Is EU Law Silent?' (n 1159) 13.
1680 ibid.
1681 EDPB, 'Recommendations 01/2020 on Measures That Supplement Transfer Tools to Ensure Compliance with the EU Level of Protection of Personal Data – Version 2.0' (n 1598) para 85.
1682 Council of Europe, 'Council Resolution on Encryption – Security through Encryption and Security despite Encryption' (2020) 12863/20 <https://www.statewatch.org/media/1510/eu-council-encryption-declaration-13084-20-rev1.pdf>.
1683 Omer Tene, 'Quick Reaction to EDPB Schrems II Guidance' (*LinkedIn*, 12 November 2020) <https://www.linkedin.com/pulse/quick-reaction-edpb-schrems-ii-guidance-omer-tene/?utm_source=POLITICO.EU&utm_campaign=a48677014b-EMAIL_CAMPAIGN_2020_11_13_02_43&utm_medium=email&utm_term=0_10959edeb5-a48677014b-190373637>.

to data for business purposes.[1684] In these cases, personal data, which has been exported, must be returned or destroyed by the data importer. If a data exporter wishes to continue transfers to third country data importers without adequate protection, the competent supervisory authority must be informed, which will, in turn, suspend or prohibit the transfer. In this context, the data exporter should prepare itself to plausibly explain why it cannot reasonably be expected to switch to alternative offers without transfer problems.[1685] Data exporters could consider and examine the possibility of switching to service providers in the EU or countries that have been afforded an adequacy decision.[1686] A complete switch to providers in the EU or adequate third countries is challenging to realise, especially in cloud-based services, as the European digital sovereignty is not yet far enough advanced in this respect.[1687] However, UK cloud providers do not have a dominant market position. For example, the estimated turnover of public cloud providers (including software as a service, service infrastructure and service platform) in 2021 in the UK was around EUR 13.3 million – yet, closely followed by the turnover in Germany in 2021 (EUR 12.2 million). Consequently, the switch from UK service providers to service providers in the EEA or other adequate third countries appears to be realisable. Nevertheless, it is doubtful whether data protection concerns can be dispelled by relocating data processing to servers in the EU, if companies are legally obliged to hand over data stored by subsidiaries in the EU[1688] With regard to UK companies that are situated in the EU, the EU Commission considers this would not be the case.[1689] However, this is not convincing since the IPA broadly defines telecommunications operators in section 261(10) IPA 2016. Consequently, data collection or generation by an establishment of a UK telecommunications operator located within the EEA, or data transferred to an establishment of the same operator in the UK based on

---

1684 EDPB, 'Recommendations 01/2020 on Measures That Supplement Transfer Tools to Ensure Compliance with the EU Level of Protection of Personal Data – Version 2.0' (n 1598) paras 94 et seqq.

1685 Scheben and Busekist (n 1646) 335.

1686 Sandfuchs (n 1565) 248; Maximilian Mense, 'EU-US-Privacy-Shield – Der kleinste gemeinsame Nenner angemessenen Datenschutzes? Angemessenheit des Datenschutzniveaus und aktuelle Entwicklungen' [2019] ZD 351, 355.

1687 cf Brandt (n 1569).

1688 Kühling and Heberlein (n 577) 11.

1689 UK Adequacy Decision (n 14) footnote 399.

the adequacy decision and then collected within the UK by a public authority can also concern data subjects located within the EU.[1690]

Data exporters could alternatively consider the concept of a "data trustee".[1691] An EU company can be interposed as an intermediary with data servers in the EU (or in a third country with an adequate level of protection) that would process on behalf of but without any access of the third country company.[1692] The agreement between the data trustee and the third country company ensures that the third country company or its subsidiaries have no legal claim to access costumer data nor do they have technical access. The contract between the data trustee and the customer provides that the data trustee may only grant access to third parties, which includes the third county company and its subsidiaries, if permitted by the customer, national provisions or the contract (for example for maintenance purposes). The EDPB has not yet published an opinion on the concept of a data trustee. However, the implementation of a data trustee appears to be very effective to prevent unlawful access to personal data. The possibility of access by courts, authorities or private parties to data located abroad depends on whether the data controller claimed is personally subject to the third country jurisdiction ("personal jurisdiction") or whether the data is accessible to its physical or *de facto* control. The data trustee model would address both issues by physically relocating the data extraterritorially. Legally and factually, the access to the stored data from data controllers (processors and licensors) would be removed, subject to the third country jurisdiction, and transferred to a territorially external data trustee.[1693] This concept also seems to be fitting for small and medium-sized companies.

1690 EDPB, 'Opinion 14/2021 Regarding the European Commission Draft Implementing Decision Pursuant to Regulation (EU) 2016/679 on the Adequate Protection of Personal Data in the United Kingdom' (n 615) recital 158. See in detail in Chapter 3 under C.IV.1.a.bb.

1691 This concept was used by the *Microsoft Group* as a response to the case *Microsoft Corp. v United States*, 829 F.3d 197 (2d Cir. 2016).

1692 In detail Paul M Schwartz and Karl-Nikolaus Peifer, 'Datentreuhändermodelle – Sicherheit vor Herausgabeverlangen US-Amerikanischer Behörden und Gerichte?' [2017] CR 165; Botta, 'Zwischen Rechtsvereinheitlichung und Verantwortungsdiffusion: Die Prüfung grenzüberschreitender Datenübermittlungen nach "Schrems II"' (n 1250) 510.

1693 Schwartz and Peifer (n 1692) 174.

IV Practical and Legal Uncertainties

Although the *Facebook Ireland and Schrems* judgement and the EDPB Recommendations on supplementary measures clarified the use of appropriate safeguards as transfer tools, there are still some legal uncertainties and unresolved issues. As the Court laid down specific requirements outlined for the SCCs, such as the verification and the careful assessment that the third country's legislation is adequate compared to the EU level of protection, many data exporters needed time to re-evaluate their data transfers under SCCs and, where necessary, need to implement additional safeguards.[1694] The above has shown that data exporters face demanding, costly and sometimes impossible challenges to ensure sufficient additional safeguards for data exports based on SCCs.[1695] This will be very hard on small and medium-sized businesses (under 1.). Also, competent supervisory authorities will have an increased workload with, at this time, only insufficient resources (under 2.). Legal certainty is not enhanced by the fact that the EDPB and the EU Commission take different approaches to the concept of "transfer" (under 3.).

1 Small and Medium-Sized Businesses

The new SCCs are significantly more comprehensive than the previous sets and contain far more specific regulations. In future, it will no longer be sufficient only to sign the SCCs. Instead, it is up to the data exporter to assess the level of protection for the transferred data that prevails in the recipient country. Thus, data exporters are expected to carry out a comparative study of foreign law (transfer impact assessment). However, such a task is difficult to accomplish even with experts from all countries involved.[1696] The data exporter must determine on a case-by-case basis that the SCCs establish an adequate level of data protection, particularly considering the third country's law. If this is not the case, the SCCs would have to be supplemented with additional safeguard measures. Although the EDPB provided some examples of additional safeguard measures that could be effective in practice, establishing additional safeguard measures for a data transfer under SCCs would constantly be under the risk of supervisory intervention.[1697] While large companies will have the resources

---

1694 Chuches and Zalnieriute (n 586).
1695 Sandfuchs (n 1565) 248.
1696 Heinzke (n 1549) 438.
1697 Alexander Golland, 'Datenschutzrechtliche Anforderungen an internationale Datentransfers' [2020] NJW 2593, 2596.

and legal departments to identify data protection compliance issues and to ensure compliance with SCCs, for small and medium-sized businesses, the case-by-case assessment of the adequacy of third countries legal framework, as well as the identification of effective additional safeguard measures, will be a significant challenge difficult to meet.[1698] Most apparent, many small and medium-sized businesses do not have the necessary financial and organisational means to deploy strong encryption.

2 Insufficient Resources

As already mentioned before[1699], member states' data protection authorities claim that they are underfunded[1700] and do not have sufficient means and resources for a strong enforcement practice.[1701] There appear to be only limited enforcement practices among the member states' data protection supervisory authorities.[1702] According to the EU Parliament, only a very small share of submitted complaints have been followed up and the amount of fines varies significantly across member states[1703]; also, the case investigation periods would take too long.[1704] With the adoption of the new SCCs, the workload of the national supervisory authority will increase, as they, now explicitly, must monitor actions more (closely) and act on data subjects' complaints where data transfers under SCCs do not afford protection equivalent to the EU law. Supervisory authorities must adopt correcting measures where data controllers fail to act or suspend or prohibit the data transfer under the SCCs. Also, the multitude of private and official actors responsible for reviewing third-country data transfers includes the severe risk of a diffusion of responsibility.[1705] It is up to the EDPB, as an instrument of inter-authority cooperation, to ensure consistent country assessments. The national data protection authorities (and the EU Commission and the committee chair) may submit questions on third-country data protection lev-

---

1698 See also Paal and Kumkar (n 575) 737.
1699 Chapter 3, B.IV.3.
1700 With underfunded data protection authorities, these member states are in breach of Article 52(4) GDPR, cf EU Parliament, 'Resolution of 25 March 2021 on the Commission Evaluation Report on the Implementation of the General Data Protection Regulation Two Years after Its Application' (n 1046).
1701 ibid para 15.
1702 ibid paras 12 et seqq.
1703 cf *CMS*, 'GDPR Enforcement Tracker' <https://www.enforcementtracker.com>.
1704 ibid paras 13 et seq.
1705 Botta, 'Zwischen Rechtsvereinheitlichung und Verantwortungsdiffusion: Die Prüfung grenzüberschreitender Datenübermittlungen nach "Schrems II"' (n 1250) 513.

els to the EDPB as these are "matter[s] of general application" (Article 64(2) GDPR). The CJEU considers this system efficient to deal with different national supervisory authorities' divergent legal opinions and decisions.[1706] The EDPB may adopt a binding decision under Article 65(1)(c) GDPR, especially where a supervisory authority does not follow the opinion issued.[1707]

3 EDPB vs EU Commission?

The EU Commission and the EDPB seem to disagree and take different approaches on the concept of "transfer", which leads to legal uncertainties (under a.). The issue of whether subjective factors should be included in the transfer impact assessment has been resolved (under b.).

a Concept of Transfer

The EU Commission seems to again take the view point that the term "transfer" only includes cases where the data importer is not subject to the extraterritorial scope of the GDPR.[1708] This approach was also taken in the adequacy decision favouring the UK.[1709] In the context of appropriate safeguards, these would not cover data imports that take place outside the EU but are still subject to the GDPR under Article 3(2) GDPR. Such transfers would not fall under Article 46 GDPR.

In favour of the narrow interpretation, one could argue that effective fundamental legal protection also falls within the scope of the GDPR.[1710] Where the data importer is already subject to GDPR principles, there would be no need for additional appropriate safeguards. Furthermore, it can be argued that Article 3(2) GDPR and recitals 22 to 25 show that data processing is not crucial but rather a mandatory application of the GDPR.[1711] The EU Commission pursues the same approach with the new SCC as the ICO in the UK, which distinguishes

---

1706 *Facebook Ireland and Schrems* (n 64) para 147.

1707 ibid.

1708 cf Draft of Commission Implementing Decision (EU) on standard contractual clauses for the transfer of personal data to third countries pursuant to Regulation (EU) 2016/679 of the European Parliament and of the Council (2020) <https://ec.europa.eu/info/law/better-regulation/have-your-say/initiatives/12741-Data-protection-standard-contractual-clauses-for-transferring-personal-data-to-non-EU-countries-implementing-act-_en> (Draft SCCs Decision 2021), art 1(1).

1709 As already reviewed in Chapter 3, C.IV.1.a.bb.

1710 Axel Spies, 'EU-Standardvertragsklauseln bei internationaler Datenübermittlung' [2021] ZD-Aktuell 05011 referring to recitals 141 and 148 (with regard to Article 47 CFR) and to recital 1 (with regard to Article 8 CFR).

1711 ibid.

between so-called "non-restricted transfers" (data importer is subject to the GDPR under Article 3(2) GDPR) and "restricted transfers" (Article 44 et seqq. of the GDPR apply).

While some arguments could speak for this narrow interpretation, it has overall received much criticism. The EDPB and the EDPS requested that the EU Commission clarifies that Article 1(1) of the SCC Draft Decision is "only intended to address the issue of the scope of the Draft Decision and the draft SCCs themselves, and not the scope of the notion of transfers."[1712] According to the EDPB and EDPS, the wording of Article 44 GDPR does not exempt companies that comply with and fall under the extraterritorial scope of the GDPR.[1713] Instead, the provisions of Chapter V should always apply if the recipient of the transfer is located in a third country. Also, the third country status is not affected by the extraterritorial applicability of the GDPR because only the individual recipient but not the entire country in which it is located could be subject to the GDPR under the marketplace principle.[1714] Moreover, it is doubtful whether the extraterritorial applicability of the GDPR, according to Article 3(2) GDPR alone is sufficient to ensure an adequate level of data protection.[1715] In the *Schrems* and *Facebook Ireland and Schrems* rulings, the CJEU emphasised that the adequacy of the level of data protection can only be assessed based on careful and overall consideration of the legal and factual circumstances in the third country regarding the protection of personal data.[1716] The extraterritorial applicability of the GDPR alone does not say anything about whether the transferred data in the third country are sufficiently protected from access by authorities or courts of the third country or whether the data subjects have sufficiently effective and enforceable legal remedies at their disposal.[1717] The normative environment in the receiving state must be fully taken into account, irrespective of which rules apply to the processing of the data by the receiving body for its purposes.[1718] This hurdle cannot be overcome by the data subjects' rights and remedies granted under the GDPR as their enforcement by European supervisory au-

---

1712 EDPB and EDPS (n 1581) recital 28.
1713 Spies (n 1710); Meike Kamp, 'Art. 44 DS-GVO' in Heinrich Amadeus Wolff and Stefan Brink (eds) (n 149) para 36.
1714 Christian Schröder, 'Art. 44 DS-GVO' in Jürgen Kühling and Benedikt Buchner (eds) (n 174) para 16b.
1715 Peter Schantz, 'Art. 44 DSGVO' in Spiros Simitis, Gerrit Hornung and Indra Spiecker (eds) (n 29) para 14.
1716 *Schrems* (n 71) para 75.
1717 Schröder, 'Art. 44 DS-GVO' (n 1714) para 16b; Schantz, 'Art. 44 DSGVO' (n 1715) para 14.
1718 *Schrems* (n 71) para 75.

thorities in third countries is often limited and encounters considerable practical difficulties.[1719] For the applicability of Chapter V to be based solely on whether or not the GDPR applies in the third country is likely to fall short.[1720] The first sentence of Article 44 GDPR explicitly includes the constellation that personal data "are intended for processing after transfer". However, the mention of such constellations would only make sense where personal data have not been processed before the transfer but are to be processed for the first time in the third country.[1721] Data are only processed for the first time if they are collected directly from the data subject, and no other controller or processor is interposed.

Furthermore, with a narrow interpretation of the term "transfer", it would be advantageous for a company to process data only in a third country without interposing an establishment in the EU. This would contradict the GDPR's aim to encourage businesses to establish within the EU and benefit from one-stop-shop privilege.[1722] Also, Article 46(2)(b) GDPR, which concerns BCRs as alternative appropriate safeguards, would be redundant if the data importer already has access to EU data because it is subject to the GDPR.[1723]

The CJEU has not yet decided on the interplay between Article 44 GDPR and Article 3(2) GDPR. The Court did not even mention the territorial scope of the GDPR in *Facebook Ireland and Schrems* and only comprehensively examined its material scope of application.[1724] However, as shown above, a narrow understanding of the concept "transfer" would contradict the general regulatory objective of the GDPR, which is to ensure an equivalent level of protection and a high level of data protection even beyond the EU.[1725] It can therefore be assumed that the CJEU would also apply Article 44 et seqq. GDPR apply to those controllers that fall under Article 3(2) GDPR. This assumption should be kept in mind by data exporters. Contrary to the EU Commission's view, Article 3(2) GDPR does not release data controllers from the obligations of Chapter V of the Regulation but is rather constitutive for them.[1726]

1719 Andreas Börding, 'Ein neues Datenschutzschild für Europa' [2016] CR 431, 433 et seq.
1720 Schröder, 'Art. 44 DS-GVO' (n 1714) para 16b.
1721 Schantz, 'Art. 44 DSGVO' (n 1715) para 15.
1722 ibid.
1723 Spies (n 1710).
1724 *Facebook Ireland and Schrems* (n 64) paras 82 et seqq.
1725 cf GDPR, recital 10.
1726 Botta, 'Zwischen Rechtsvereinheitlichung und Verantwortungsdiffusion: Die Prüfung grenzüberschreitender Datenübermittlungen nach "Schrems II"' (n 1250) 512.

b Subjective Factors in Local Law Assessment

When assessing whether the local laws affect the compliance with the SCCs, the EU Commission requested the data exporter and data importer to consider "any relevant practical experience with prior instances, or the absence of requests for disclosure from public authorities received by the data importer for the type of data transferred".[1727]

The EDPB and the EDPS stressed that the third country's local law and practice assessment should only be based on objective factors, such as the legal framework, regardless of the likelihood of access to personal data.[1728] It should include aspects such as the purposes of the data transfer or processing, the "[t]ypes of entities involved in the processing"; "[s]ector in which the transfer occurs"; "[c]ategories of personal data" concerned; "[w]hether data [is] stored in the third country" or within the EU; the "[f]ormat of the data", the possibility of any onward transfers of the personal data to another third country.[1729] The EDPB and the EDPS criticised that SCCs drafting can be misunderstood to permit data to be exported if the data importer has not yet received any order to disclose data to a public authority, even if it is subject to local laws permitting such orders.[1730] The EDPB and EDPS referred to the CJEU's judgement in *Facebook Ireland and Schrems*, in which the Court did not consider any subjective factors, such as the likelihood of access by public authorities.[1731] In practice, the assessment of subjective factors would be complicated and hardly verifiable.[1732]

However, in the updated second of the Recommendations on supplementary measures, the EDPB changed its view and now finds that the data exporter may also consider "documented practical experience" of the data importer with "relevant prior instances of requests for access received from the public authorities in the third country".[1733] Nevertheless, the EDPB suggested higher requirements than the EU Commission has established: only documented prior practical experiences should be considered and only together with other (objective) information. Most importantly, the data importer's experience "should be corroborated

---

1727 Draft SCCs Decision 2021 (n 1708), Annex Section II clause 2(b)(i).
1728 EDPB and EDPS (n 1581) recital 86.
1729 EDPB, 'Recommendations 01/2020 on Measures That Supplement Transfer Tools to Ensure Compliance with the EU Level of Protection of Personal Data – Version 1.0' (n 1245) paras 33 et seq.
1730 EDPB and EDPS (n 1581) recital 87.
1731 ibid para 87.
1732 ibid.
1733 EDPB, 'Recommendations 01/2020 on Measures That Supplement Transfer Tools to Ensure Compliance with the EU Level of Protection of Personal Data – Version 2.0' (n 1598) para 47.

and not contradicted by relevant, objective, reliable, verifiable and publicly available or otherwise accessible information on the practical application of the relevant law (e. g. the existence or absence of requests for access received by other actors operating within the same sector and/or related to similar transferred personal data and/or the application of the law in practice, such as case law and reports by independent oversight bodies)."[1734] In the final version of the SCCS, the EU Commission also slightly altered its approach and now complies with the EDPB's view: Only "relevant and documented experience with prior instances", which should mainly include "internal records or other documentation, drawn up on a continuous basis in accordance with due diligence and certified at senior management level", provided it is "supported by other relevant, objective criteria", may be taken into account.[1735] Also, it should be considered whether the practical experience is corroborated and not contradicted by other reliable (objective) sources of information.[1736]

In this context, a recent decision of the Austrian national supervisory authority (*DSB*) is noteworthy.[1737] The authority stressed that Article 44 GDPR did not have a risked-based approach for transfer of personal data outside the EU. The success of a complaint of a violation of Article 44 GDPR would not depend on whether there is a certain "minimum risk" of national authorities accessing the data.[1738] In other provisions, where the GDPR-regulator wanted a risk-based approach ("the higher the processing risk, the more measures are to be implemented"), such approach is explicitly standardised.[1739] It could not be concluded that recital 20 of the SCCs Decision includes is a risk-based approach. *DBS* even stated that the SCCs Decision of the EU Commission could not in any case subject the requirements of Art. 44 GDPR to a completely new content due to the primacy of the text of the regulation. This decision shows that data exporters must be aware that risk-based argumentations, e. g. that the personal data being transferred would not be sensitive data or that the national authori-

---

1734 EDPB, 'Recommendations 01/2020 on Measures That Supplement Transfer Tools to Ensure Compliance with the EU Level of Protection of Personal Data – Version 2.0' (n 1598) para 47
1735 SCCs Decision 2021 (n 549) footnote 12.
1736 ibid.
1737 DBS, Decision of 22 April 2022 <https://noyb.eu/sites/default/files/2022-01/E-DSB%20-%20Google%20Analytics_EN_bk.pdf> 44 et seqq.
1738 The DSB argued with the wording of Article 44 GDPR, according to which a violation already exists if personal data are transferred to a third country without an adequate level of protection.
1739 GDPR, art. 24(1) and (2), 25(1), 30(5), 32(1) and (2), 34(1), 35(1) and (3), 37(1)(b) and (c).

ties of the third country would not be interested in the transferred data, will most likely not convince national supervisory authorities.

V Practical Approaches to Implementation of new SCCs

Businesses have been taking different approaches in implementing the new SCCs in their data transfer practices. The following focuses on a few companies' approaches to implementing the new SCCs.[1740]

1 Google

Google Cloud Service uses Module Three (processor-to-processor) to transfer personal data outside the EU.[1741] *"Google Europe"*, a *Google* company, located in Dublin, acts as the contractual partner for customers, located in the EEA. Transfers of personal data between the customer and *Google Europe* usually take place between countries with an adequate level of data protection and do not require SCC protection. However, depending on the products, personal data may also be accessed from outside the EEA, e.g. by the US company *Google LCC*. For such "onward transfers" to countries without an adequate level of data protection, *Google Europe* uses Module Three of the new SCC with the corresponding data recipients. This module covers the situation between a processor as a data exporter (*Google Europe*) and its sub-processor as a data importer (*Google LLC*). *Google Cloud Services* explained its approach to the implementation of the new SCCs in more detail in a white paper.[1742] It has overall differentiated between three scenarios: customers who are located in the EEA, UK or Switzerland, customers who are located in adequate countries outside the EEA, UK or Switzerland with *Google* service providers in adequate countries and, customers who are located in adequate or non-adequate countries with *Google* service providers in non-adequate countries.[1743]

1740 cf Lena Götzinger and Hannes Meyle, 'Wie Google, Microsoft und Salesforce die neuen SCC umsetzen und was dies für Verantwortliche im EWR und in der Schweiz bedeutet' (*daten:recht – das Datenschutz-Team von Walder Wyss*, 18 October 2021) <https://datenrecht. ch/wie-google-microsoft-und-salesforce-die-neuen-scc-umsetzen-und-was-dies-fuer-verantwor tliche-im-ewr-und-in-der-schweiz-bedeutet/>.
1741 Google Cloud Platform, Workspace & Cloud Identity: EU Standard Contractual Clauses (Module 3: Processor-to-Processor, Google Exporter), available at https://cloud.google.com/ terms/sccs/eu-p2p-google-exporter.
1742 Google Cloud (n 1587).
1743 ibid.

2 Microsoft

Microsoft implements the new SCCs similarly to *Google Cloud Services*. For customers of *Microsoft* products and services from the EEA, the contract partner is usually *Microsoft Ireland Operations Limited*, located in Dublin. In some circumstances, Microsoft uses the US-based *Microsoft Corporation* as a sub-processor. *Microsoft Ireland Operations Limited* uses Module Three for data transfer to *Microsoft Corporation*.[1744] Additionally, *Microsoft* offers its customers different encryption standards for the purpose of supplementary safeguards, which not even *Microsoft* would be able to decrypt.[1745]

3 Salesforce

Salesforce customers from the EEA generally conclude their contracts with *Salesforce Ireland*, an Irish subsidiary. Where data are transferred to or accesses are made from the US American *salesforce.com, Inc. (Salesforce Inc.)*, the new SCCs are implemented. *Salesforce* takes a different approach than *Google* and *Microsoft:* The SCC are agreed directly between the customer and *Salesforce Inc.* For customers that are data controllers, *Salesforce* offers Module 2.[1746]

4 Facebook

Facebook also uses Module Three for data transfers from *Facebook Ireland* to *Facebook, Inc.*[1747]

1744 Microsoft, 'Microsoft Products and Services Data Protection Addendum (DPA)' (2021) <https://www.microsoft.com/licensing/docs/view/Microsoft-Products-and-Services-Data-Protection-Addendum-DPA>.
1745 For more information on Microsoft see Fatih Ataoglu, 'Faktencheck Datenschutz: Wie wir unsere Kundendaten nach dem Schrems-II-Urteil schützen' (*Microsoft*, 14 October 2021) <https://news.microsoft.com/de-de/datenschutz-wie-wir-unsere-kundendaten-nach-dem-schrems-ii-urteil-schuetzen/>; Stratos Komotoglou, 'Das 1x1 der IT-Sicherheit: Lückenloser Schutz in der Cloud mit Confidential Computing' (*Microsoft*, 12 July 2021) <https://news.microsoft.com/de-de/das-1x1-der-it-sicherheit-lueckenloser-schutz-in-der-cloud-mit-confidential-computing/>.
1746 Salesforce, 'Data Processing Addendum' (2021) <https://www.salesforce.com/content/dam/web/en_us/www/documents/legal/Agreements/data-processing-addendum.pdf>.
1747 facebook, 'Facebook European Data Transfer Addendum Effective on 27 September 2021' <https://www.facebook.com/legal/EU_data_transfer_addendum/update>.

5 Amazon

Amazon Web Services have also updated their Data Processing Addendum and included the new SCCs.[1748] Module Two applies, provided that the customer acts as a data controller; Module Three applies, should the customer be a data processor. In the latter scenario, *Amazon Web Services* adds the following passus: "Taking into account the nature of the processing, Customer agrees that it is unlikely that AWS will know the identity of Customer's controllers because AWS has no direct relationship with Customer's controllers and therefore, Customer will fulfil AWS's obligations to Customer's controllers under the Processor-to-Processor Clauses".[1749]

VI Conclusion to A

Suppose the UK adequacy decision would be declared invalid by the CJEU or repealed or suspended by the EU Commission. In that case, SCCs could provide an effective alternative transfer tool. The EU Commission's new set of SCCs fully implements the CJEU's *Facebook Ireland and Schrems* decision. It grants the data exporters a transitional period of one year.[1750] As from entry into force of the new SCCs on 27 June 2021, controllers and processors could enter into the old SCCs for three months. [1751] Those entities that have implemented the old SCCs can continue to rely on the old SCCs for an additional transitional period of 15 months until 27 December 2022, provided that the processing operations that are the subject matter of the contract remain unchanged, apart from necessary supplementary measures to ensure that the transfer is subject to appropriate safeguards.[1752] However, during the transitional period, data exporters must still observe the requirements established in *Facebook Ireland and Schrems* by the CJEU.

EU-based controllers and processors must check their data flows. They are advised to closely follow the EDPB Recommendations on supplementary measures and complete the six-step evaluation[1753] and, where necessary, implement

---

1748 Amazon Web Services, 'AWS GDPR Data Processing Addendum' <https://d1.awsstatic.com/legal/aws-gdpr/AWS_GDPR_DPA.pdf>.
1749 ibid.
1750 SCCs Decision 2021 (n 549) recital 24.
1751 ibid.
1752 ibid.
1753 III.1.

supplementary measures[1754]. It is necessary to carefully select the contractual partner and check about any obligations to disclose personal data to authorities to which it might be subject under UK law. The EU-based controllers and processors must closely study the UK's surveillance law and practices, adopt supplementary measures (robust encryption on a mandatory basis, fully anonymised or strongly pseudonymised data), and may even consult their national data protection supervisory authority in relation to any doubts as to whether the data that are to be transferred can be effectively protected against the access by UK public authorities. Failure to carry out these tasks, and failure to protect the data against unlawful access by UK public authorities would constitute a personal data breach for which the EU-based data exporter will be liable.[1755] In many practical relevant cases, there might not be any effective supplementary measure available.[1756] In these cases, data exporters should consider the option of establishing a "data trustee", although this model is currently still rather uncommon.

B Other Appropriate Safeguards

Article 46 GDPR also includes other appropriate safeguards as transfer tools. Although SCCs are the most popular appropriate safeguards in practice, the other safeguards could also have significant potential. This potential will be analysed in the following. In particular, BCRs could be an attractive alternative transfer tool for larger companies (under I.). CoC (under II.) or the certification mechanism (under III.) have not yet been sufficiently exploited as appropriate safeguards but might also hold great potential for international data transfer.

I Binding Corporate Rules

Many multinational organisations such as *Airbus*, *American Express*, and *eBay* use BCRs for transferring personal data outside the EEA but within their group of entities and subsidiaries.[1757] Article 4(20) GDPR defines BCRs as "personal data protection policies which are adhered to by a controller or processor estab-

---

1754 III.2.
1755 This is outlined below under E.
1756 III.3.
1757 See list of companies for which the EU BCR cooperation procedure is closed (updated on 24 May 2018), available at the following link <http://ec.europa.eu/newsroom/article29/docu ment.cfm?doc_id=50116> accessed 9 June 2022.

lished on the territory of a Member State for transfers or a set of transfers of personal data to a controller or processor in one or more third countries within a group of undertakings, or group of enterprises engaged in a joint economic activity". Article 47(1) GDPR generally requires BCRs to be "(a) [...] legally binding and apply to and are enforced by every member concerned of the group of undertakings, or group of enterprises engaged in a joint economic activity, including their employees; (b) expressly confer enforceable rights on data subjects with regard to the processing of their personal data; and (c) fulfil the requirements laid down in paragraph 2". Article 47(2) GDPR contains a comprehensive catalogue of what content the BCRs shall specify at least.[1758] This includes (a) the structure and the contact of the group, (b) the circumstances of the data transfers (categories of personal data, type of processing, purposes, types of data subjects affected and the third countries in question), (c) the legally binding nature internally and externally, (d) the application of the data protection principles, (e) the data subjects' rights and the means to exercise those rights, (f) the acceptance by the controller or processor in the EEA for any breaches by a member which is not established in the EEA, (g) the information notice on BCRs to the data subjects, (h) the task of any data protection officer or the person or entity in charge of monitoring compliance with BCRs, (i) the complaint procedures, (j) the mechanisms for ensuring the verification of compliance with the BCRs, (k) the mechanisms for reporting and recording changes to the rules and reporting those changes to the supervisory authority, (l) the cooperation mechanism with the supervisory authority to ensure compliance, (m) the mechanism for reporting conflicting third-country legislation, (n) the appropriate data protection training to personnel having access to personal data.

Concerning their legally binding nature (Article 47(2)(c) GDPR), BCRs must be (internally) binding for members of the organisation, including each employee, e. g. "by way of specific obligations contained in a contract and by linking observance of the rules with disciplinary procedures"[1759] or "setting up special education programmes"[1760], as well as for subcontractors handling the

---

1758 See for a detailed figure that indicates the differences between the substantive requirements for BCR set out by the Art. 29 Data Protection Working Party under the DPD and those included in Article 47 GDPR in Kuner, 'Art. 47 GDPR' (n 525) 817 et seqq.
1759 Art. 29 Data Protection Working Party, 'Working Document Establishing a Model Checklist Application for Approval of Binding Corporate Rules' (2005) WP 108, 5.9.
1760 'Working Document: Transfers of Personal Data to Third Countries: Applying Article 26 (2) of the EU Data Protection Directive to Binding Corporate Rules for International Data Transfers' (2003) WP 74, 3.3.1.

data[1761]. Externally, data subjects concerned must be granted "third party beneficiaries" – either by legal effects or by contractual agreements between the group members – and must be able to enforce compliance with the rules, both via the competent data protection authorities and the competent courts.[1762] Data subjects must at least be able to enforce elements of the BCRs, such as data protection principles[1763], transparency and easy access to the BCRs[1764], the right of access, rectification, erasure, restriction and objection to processing, right not to be subject to decisions based solely on automated processing, including profiling[1765], national legislation preventing respect of BCR[1766], the right to complain through the internal complaint mechanism of the companies[1767], cooperation duties with supervisory authorities[1768], liability and jurisdiction provisions[1769] – in particular, the right to lodge a complaint with the competent supervisory authority and before the competent court. Further, according to the Art. 29 Working Party, the BCRs should "expressly" contain the data subject's "right to judicial remedies and right to obtain redress and, where appropriate, compensation in case of any breach of one of the enforceable elements of the BCRs as enumerated above".[1770]

1 Advantages and Disadvantages of BCRs as Appropriate Safeguards

The process of implementing BCRs and getting their approval is complex and time-consuming for businesses.[1771] So far, only a few international companies

---

1761 Art. 29 Data Protection Working Party, 'Working Document Establishing a Model Checklist Application for Approval of Binding Corporate Rules' (n 1759), 5.10.

1762 See in more detail Art. 29 Data Protection Working Party, 'Working Document: Transfers of Personal Data to Third Countries: Applying Article 26 (2) of the EU Data Protection Directive to Binding Corporate Rules for International Data Transfers' (n 1760), 3.3.2; Art. 29 Data Protection Working Party, 'Working Document Establishing a Model Checklist Application for Approval of Binding Corporate Rules' (n 1759) No 5.12 et seq.

1763 GDPR, art 47(2)(d).

1764 GDPR, art 47(2)(g).

1765 GDPR, art 47(2)(e).

1766 GDPR, art 47(2)(m).

1767 GDPR, art 47(2)(i).

1768 GDPR, art 47(2)(k) and (l).

1769 GDPR, art 47(2)(e) and (f).

1770 Art. 29 Data Protection Working Party, 'Working Document Setting up a Table with the Elements and Principles to Be Found in Binding Corporate Rules' (2018) WP 256 rev.01, 1.3.

1771 Emanuel von Towfigh and Jacob Ulrich, 'Art. 47 DSGVO' in Gernot Sydow (ed) (n 163) para 34.

have adopted BCRs.[1772] Setting up BCRs is "more costly and burdensome for organisations than setting up SCCs".[1773] Due to this cost-intense approval process, primarily large companies have adopted or are expected to adopt BCRs.[1774] On the other side, large companies prefer to set up BCRs, where large-scale investments are cost-effective to demonstrate accountability, to deal with changes in the corporate structures, or where complex webs of data processing require flexibility.[1775] The catalogue of requirements for BCRs is broad and detailed. Up to this date, the practical relevance of the BCRs model is manageable since not all intercontinental corporations are willing to align their global data processing with EU standards.[1776] Companies are free to limit the BCRs to data from the EU or the EEA.[1777] However, such differentiation in the processing of personal data may be undesirable from a corporate policy point of view, so that it is preferable to refrain from applying a set of rules with a global regulatory approach from the outset.[1778] On the other side, due to the marketplace principle, many companies are already subject to the GDPR. The GDPR's extraterritoriality makes it hard for businesses to circumvent the GDPR.[1779] Different data protection and privacy rules mean additional costs for businesses. With the GDPR-compliance businesses can conduct business everywhere.[1780] Also, the GDPR has the standing of strongly enhancing the privacy and data protection rights of citizens.[1781]

The GDPR has reduced the administrative efforts to implement BCRs since the authorisation, by the competent supervisory authority, is not required for each data transfer between the undertakings bound by the BCRs.[1782] Once the BCRs are approved, they provide a solution which the significant advantage of

---

1772 See for a list of approved BCRs under EDPB, 'Approved Binding Corporate Rules' <https://edpb.europa.eu/our-work-tools/accountability-tools/bcr_en>; see for an overview of approved BCRs before the GDPR EDPB, 'Pre-GDPR BCRs Overview List' <https://edpb.europa.eu/our-work-tools/our-documents/other/pre-gdpr-bcrs-overview-list-0_en>.
1773 McCann, Patel and Ruiz (n 19) 7.
1774 Towfigh and Ulrich 'Art. 47 DSGVO' (n 1771) para 34.
1775 EU Parliament 'EU-UK Private Sector Data Flows after Brexit. Settling on Adequacy' (n 1190) 7; Schröder, 'Art. 47 DS-GVO' (n 528) para 4 takes a different view, stating that the broad and detailed catalogue in Article 47 GDPR is at the expense of flexibility.
1776 Ambrock (n 577) 1496; Alexander Filip, 'Binding Corporate Rules (BCR) aus der Sicht einer Datenschutzaufsichtsbehörde -Praxiserfahrungen mit der europaweiten Anerkennung von BCR' [2013] ZD 51, 56.
1777 Filip (n 1776) 56.
1778 Schröder, 'Art. 47 DS-GVO' (n 528) para 4.
1779 See in Chapter 5 under B.I.2.
1780 Bradford, *The Brussels Effect: How the European Union Rules the World* (n 147) 143.
1781 This will be also outlined below in Chapter 5 under B.I. (GDPR as "gold standard").
1782 Kugler (n 524) 873.

being tailored to the specifics of data transfer within a particular group of undertakings or enterprises engaged in a joint economic activity.[1783] Also, once approved, BCRs provide a very high degree of legal certainty.[1784]

2 CJEU: Facebook Ireland and Schrems

In its *Facebook Ireland and Schrems* ruling, the CJEU did not explicitly state whether the requirements, which the CJEU established regarding the use of SCCs as a transfer tool, must also be observed for all other transfer mechanisms under Article 46(2) GDPR – including BCRs.[1785] The effectiveness of BCRs as a transfer tool is comparable to the effectiveness of SCCs according to the CJEU's requirements.[1786] BCRs only internally bind a multinational company but no third country state authorities. It cannot be assumed that any self-regulatory commitment can guarantee a higher level of protection.[1787] According to the EDPB, "[t]he reasoning put forward by the *Facebook Ireland and Schrems* judgement also applies to other transfer instruments pursuant to Article 46(2) GDPR since all of these instruments are contractual, so the guarantees foreseen and the commitments taken by the parties therein cannot bind third country public authorities."[1788] The principles established by the CJEU concerning the SCCs should also be observed when using the BCRs or any other transfer tools under Article 46(2) GDPR.[1789] The abovementioned Recommendations on supplementary measures by the EDPB also apply.[1790]

1783 See for a detailed analysis of the (potential of) BCRs in Loekke Moerel, *Binding Corporate Rules: Corporate Self-Regulation of Global Data Transfers* (1st edn, 2012). See also Olivier Proust and Emmanuelle Bartoli, 'Binding Corporate Rules: A Global Solution for International Data Transfers' (2012) 2 IDPL 35 who view BCRs as the future of global data flows.
1784 Tim Wybitul, Lukas Ströbel and Marian Ruess, 'Übermittlung personenbezogener Daten in Drittländer. Überblick und Checkliste für die Prüfung nach der DS-GVO' [2017] ZD 503, 506.
1785 EDPB, 'Frequently Asked Questions on the Judgement of the Court of Justice of the European Union in Case C-311/18 – Data Protection Commissioner v Facebook Ireland Ltd and Maximillian Schrems' (n 587).
1786 Golland (n 1697) 2594.
1787 Paal and Kumkar (n 575) 438.
1788 EDPB, 'Recommendations 01/2020 on Measures That Supplement Transfer Tools to Ensure Compliance with the EU Level of Protection of Personal Data – Version 2.0' (n 1598) recital 62.
1789 Heinzke (n 1549) 438; Paal and Kumkar (n 575) 438.
1790 See under A.III.

3 Companies with the ICO as Lead Supervisory Authority

In the past, the ICO authorised around 25% of all BCRs.[1791] Also, it assured businesses that "no BCR authorisations will be cancelled because of Brexit".[1792] The ICO aims to continue to work with other EU supervisory authorities, regardless of how the ICO finds itself in a *post*-Brexit world. The ICO expressed its intention to continue as "leading expertise in BCR [and remaining] ...continually available to the international controller and processor community".[1793] However, as the ICO has lost its status as an EU supervisory authority, UK companies will no longer benefit from the One-Stop-Shop mechanism.[1794] Other EEA but non-EU members such as Norway, Iceland, or Switzerland have also not been given any special dispensation. Hence, this is neither to be expected to be the case for the ICO. Companies with the BCRs initially authorised by the ICO that continue to transfer data from the EU to the UK need to find a new lead authority. Such companies must now consider whether another supervisory authority has jurisdiction over their data processing in the EU, resulting from establishments under Article 3(1) GDPR or activities under Article 3(2) GDPR. Additionally, UK companies need to be aware that Article 27 GDPR requires them to appoint a representative in the EU that supervisory authorities and data subjects can address all issues that are related to processing activities.

Recently, the EDPB adopted an information note on BCRs for companies with the ICO as BCRs lead supervisory authority that continue to transfer data from the EU to the UK based on BCRs.[1795] These BCRs holders must identify a new BCRs lead supervisory authority in the EEA. Such identification should take place according to the criteria laid down in Working Paper 263 rev.01, according to which an applicant group should justify the proposal of the BCRs lead supervisory authority based on relevant criteria such as: "the location(s) of the Group's [EEA] headquarters; the location of the company within the Group with delegated data protection responsibilities; the location of the company which is best placed (in terms of management function, administrative bur-

---

1791 cf List of companies for which the EU BCRs cooperation procedure is closed (n 1757).

1792 James Dipple-Johnstone, 'Blog: Changes to Binding Corporate Rules Applications to the ICO' (*ico.*, 20 November 2017) <https://ico.org.uk/about-the-ico/news-and-events/news-and-blogs/2017/11/blog-changes-to-binding-corporate-rules-applications-to-the-ico/>.

1793 ibid.

1794 ICO, 'EU Regulatory Oversight' (*ico.*) <https://ico.org.uk/for-organisations/dp-at-the-end-of-the-transition-period/data-protection-and-the-eu-in-detail/the-uk-gdpr/eu-regulatory-over sight/>.

1795 EDPB, 'Information Note on BCRs for Companies Which Have ICO as BCR Lead Supervisory Authority' (2020) <https://edpb.europa.eu/sites/default/files/files/file1/edpb_information noteforgroupswithicoasbcrleadsa_20200722_en.pdf>.

den, etc.) to deal with the application and to enforce the binding corporate rules in the Group; the place where most decisions in terms of the purposes and the means of the processing (e. g. transfer) are taken; and the member state within the EU from which most or all transfers outside the EEA will take place."[1796] The business can then make a formal application to the supervisory authority in the EEA, which will consider on a case-by-case basis, based on criteria set out in WP 263 and cooperation with other supervisory authorities, whether it is the appropriate BCRs lead supervisory authority.[1797] It is noteworthy that businesses selecting a new lead supervisory authority should consider that some supervisory authorities are taking a stricter interpretation of the abovementioned criteria to avoid an "impression of forum shopping".[1798] The EDPB stressed that the change of BCRs lead supervisory authority should have taken effect at the latest at the end of the Brexit transition period (30 June 2021).[1799] For BCRs already approved under the GDPR, the new BCRs lead supervisory authority in the EEA should have issued a new approval decision before the end of the transition period.[1800] However, the public list of approved BCRs under the GDPR indicates that this only applies to one BCRs that was approved by the ICO.[1801] For BCRs for which ICO acted as the lead authority under Directive 95/46, no issued approval by the new BCRs lead supervisory authority is necessary.[1802] Because the Article 29 Working Party published working papers that set out referential tables and approach uniformity for the approval criteria among the supervisory authority,[1803] the documents submitted for approval should be substantially in the same format as those that were initially submitted to the ICO so that the new approval should be rather something of a formality.[1804] The ICO provided

---

1796 Art. 29 Data Protection Working Party, 'Working Document Setting Forth a Co-Operation Procedure for the Approval of "Binding Corporate Rules" for Controllers and Processors under the GDPR' (2018) WP 263 rev.01 1.2.

1797 EDPB, 'Information Note on BCRs for Companies Which Have ICO as BCR Lead Supervisory Authority' (n 1795).

1798 Sian Rudgard, 'BCR and Brexit – A Practical Way Forward' (6 October 2020) <https://www.engage.hoganlovells.com/knowledgeservices/news/bcr-and-brexit-a-practical-way-forward>.

1799 EDPB, 'Information Note on BCRs for Companies Which Have ICO as BCR Lead Supervisory Authority' (n 1795).

1800 ibid.

1801 BCRs of *Equinix Inc.*, see EDPB, 'Approved Binding Corporate Rules' (n 1772).

1802 EDPB, 'Information Note on BCRs for Companies Which Have ICO as BCR Lead Supervisory Authority' (n 1795).

1803 Art. 29 Data Protection Working Party, 'Working Document Setting up a Table with the Elements and Principles to Be Found in Binding Corporate Rules' (n 1770).

1804 Rudgard (n 1798).

an Annex with a checklist of elements to be amended.[1805] Working Paper 256[1806] and Working Paper 257[1807] specify the requirements. Some amendments may cover liability provisions (e. g. a designated entity in the country of the new lead supervisory authority responsible for claims under the BCR);[1808] others may require changes in the administrative process (e. g. cooperation duty[1809]). If those BCRs holders have not yet changed their BCRs accordingly, they can no longer rely on their BCRs as valid transfer mechanisms of data outside the EEA.[1810]

Companies should keep in mind that the takeover of a BCRs by a new lead supervisory authority does not imply verifying any necessary update. Instead, the new lead supervisory authority can request that any relevant changes be made and adopt any consequent decision.[1811] The EDPB stresses that all the supervisory authorities "reserve their right to exercise their powers including, the power to investigate BCRs, including of the BCRs implementation itself, or to give a special attention to certain aspects of such BCRs in the context of a broader investigation of the company, and, where appropriate, an approval."[1812] Hence, there is a chance that some residual uncertainty as to whether any updates will be subject to further comment or scrutiny remains.[1813]

A business organisation that operates across the EU and in the UK should combine EU and UK requirements into one BCRs policy since, at the moment, the substantive obligations are identical (Article 46(2)(b) and 47 UK GDPR).[1814] Whether this will be the case in the future remains to be seen.

1805 Annex to the ICO, 'Data Protection Bill, House of Lords Report Stage – Information Commissioner's Briefing – Annex II' (n 950).
1806 Art. 29 Data Protection Working Party, 'Working Document Setting up a Table with the Elements and Principles to Be Found in Binding Corporate Rules' (n 1770).
1807 ibid.
1808 Annex to the EDPD, 'Information Note on BCRs for Companies Which Have ICO as BCR Lead Supervisory Authority' (n 1795) 1.5.
1809 Annex to ibid 3.
1810 EDPB, 'Information Note on BCRs for Companies Which Have ICO as BCR Lead Supervisory Authority' (n 1795).
1811 ibid.
1812 ibid.
1813 Rudgard (n 1798).
1814 ibid.

4 Conclusion to I

In cases where SCCs cannot effectively guarantee essential equivalent protection of personal data, BCRs are usually also out of the question.[1815] In practice, it seems impossible to protect data access by UK public authorities with bulk interception powers transferred to the UK under BCRs any more than under SCCs. The concerns about using the SCCs as an appropriate transfer tool largely apply to the use of BCRs. Such data exporters must conduct a transfer impact assessment and check whether an adequate level of protection exists in the recipient country and, if this is not the case, take further measures to mitigate the risk.[1816] Yet, a business with approved BCRs could be more advantageous in addressing concerns raised in *Facebook Ireland and Schrems* because Article 47(1) and (2) GDPR contain many obligations that relate to those concerned.[1817] However, a process must be implemented, followed by requests from third country state authorities and commitments to be transparent about local law requirements that prevent the BCRs company from fulfilling its BCRs obligations under local law. One advantage the structure of BCRs has is the "in-built flexibility to respond to changes". If the EDPB issues guidance on potential additional requirements for the use of BCRs, businesses with approved BCRs could incorporate them into their BCRs policies.[1818]

II Codes of Conduct

Approved CoC[1819] might also be considered as alternative transfer tools to the SCCs or BCRs. This transfer tool is still at a very early stage; practical examples are still emerging. Approved CoC can be used to transfer personal data between entities that have subscribed to the same code.

1 Use of CoC

In July 2021, the EDPB has published Guidelines on CoC as a tool for transfers.[1820] The data importer in the third country must adhere to the CoC and its enforcement in a binding manner, mainly through contractual arrangements. CoC in-

---

1815 Golland (n 1697) 2594.
1816 Heinzke (n 1549) 438.
1817 Rudgard (n 1798).
1818 ibid.
1819 Chapter 2, B.II.4.
1820 EDPB, 'Guidelines 04/2021 on Codes of Conduct as Tools for Transfers' (n 554).

tended for transfers adhered by a data importer in a third country can be relied on by data exporters, subject to the GDPR, without the need for such data exporters to adhere to the CoC themselves. Yet, provided a commitment to comply with certain obligations processing the transferred data must be included in a binding instrument.[1821] Such "binding and enforceable commitments" aim to address this discrepancy between the CoC member in the EU and outside the EU contractually and ensure that they also guarantee the level of data protection provided in the GDPR.[1822] Notably, the "binding and enforceable commitments" should address the following: the data subject's right to enforce CoC-rules as a third party beneficiaries; the issue of liability in case of breaches to the rules under the CoC members outside of the EU; the possibility for a data subject to bring a claim in case of violation of the CoC rules before a EU supervisory authority or court; the possibility for a data subject to bring any claim arising out or from the respect by the importer to the CoC against the data exporter before the supervisory authority or court of the data exporter's establishment or of the data subject's habitual residence;[1823] the possibility of representation of the data subject by a not-for-profit organisation (Article 80(1) GDPR); the possibility that the data exporter can enforce the CoC rules against a CoC member as third-party beneficiary; the obligation to notify the data exporter and the data exporter's supervisory authority of any detected violation of the CoC outside the EU.[1824]

In order to classify as an appropriate safeguard in the meaning of Article 46 GDPR, essential principles, rights and obligations arising under the GDPR for controllers/processors and guarantees that are specific to the context of transfers, such as concerning the issue of onward transfers and conflict of laws in the third country, must be addressed in the CoC.[1825] The EDPB's Guidelines provide a checklist with "minimum guarantees" to be included in a CoC intended transfer, taking into account the CJEU *Facebook Ireland and Schrems* ruling. Such "minimum guarantees" include the following: a description of transfers to be covered and data protection principles to be complied with; accountability measures; appropriate governance through DPO; a suitable training program on

---

1821 EDPB, 'Guidelines 04/2021 on Codes of Conduct as Tools for Transfers' (n 554) para /.
1822 ibid para 29.
1823 This liability should be without prejudice to the mechanisms to be implemented under the code with the monitoring body that can also act against controllers/processors in accordance with the code by imposing corrective measures.
1824 In detail EDPB, 'Guidelines 04/2021 on Codes of Conduct as Tools for Transfers' (n 554) para 34.
1825 ibid para 12.

the obligations; data protection audit or other internal mechanisms for monitoring compliance with the CoC (independently from the oversight to be performed by the monitoring body as for any CoC)[1826]; transparency measures; data subject rights of information, access, rectification, erasure, restriction, notification, objection, not to be subject to decisions based solely on automated processing; data subjects' third-party-beneficiary rights; appropriate complaint handling process maintained by the monitoring body; warranty that at the time of adhering to the CoC the data importer has no reason to believe that the laws applicable prevent it from fulfilling its obligations under the code, and to implement where necessary together with the data exporter supplementary measures[1827]; mechanisms for dealing with changes to the CoC and consequences of withdrawal from the CoC; commitment to cooperate with EU supervisory authorities; commitment to accept the jurisdiction of EU supervisory authority and EU courts; criteria of selection of the monitoring body[1828].[1829]

2 CoC as Promising Transfer Tool

CoC represent an opportunity to establish a set of rules which contribute to the proper application of the GDPR in a practical, transparent, and cost-effective manner.[1830] They can take into account specific characteristics of data processing in certain sectors.[1831] For example, codes could be drawn up by bodies representing a sector and separate sectors with common processing activities sharing the same processing characteristics and needs (e. g. human resources code).[1832] Also, CoC can be a very beneficial transfer tool for small and medium-sized enterprises, taking into account their particular needs and allowing them to achieve GDPR compliance in a more cost-effective manner.[1833] Solutions can be devel-

---

1826 The aim of the data protection audit program is to ensure and demonstrate compliance with the code. The aim of the audits performed by the monitoring body is to assess whether the applicant is eligible to participate to the code and whether sanctions are necessary in case of infringements.

1827 A.II.2. and A.III.2.

1828 It must be demonstrated that the monitoring body has the requisite level of expertise to carry out its role in an effective manner for such a code intended for transfers.

1829 EDPB, 'Guidelines 04/2021 on Codes of Conduct as Tools for Transfers' (n 554) para 35.

1830 EDPB, 'Guidelines 1/2019 on Codes of Conduct and Monitoring Bodies under Regulation 2016/679 – Version 2.0' (n 551) 11.

1831 ibid.

1832 ibid para 6.

1833 ibid 11; critically EU Parliament 'EU-UK Private Sector Data Flows after Brexit. Settling on Adequacy' (n 1190) 9 stating that not all associations will have the means to develop such codes

oped, combining an innovation-friendly approach, state of the art practices and a robust data protection implementation, and are likely to face wide market adoption.[1834] The EDPB finds that they are also beneficial to develop and foster the data subject's trust and confidence in processing data outside the EEA.[1835] There are currently no CoC for third-country transfers. However, it becomes clear that CoC could have great potential as a transfer tool.[1836] Compared to other transfer mechanisms under Article 46 GDPR CoC could be a more "adapted tool".[1837] They can be used as a transfer tool for multiple transfers to a third country specific to a sector or processing activities.[1838] Also, due to sector-specific development CoC will likely be accompanied by implementation guidelines.[1839] In comparison to SCCs, CoC has the advantage that multiple transfers can be addressed with a single tool compared to (fully) contractual solutions.[1840] Furthermore, entities using CoC – unlike BCRs – do not need to be within the same group to frame their transfers.[1841] Also, their deployment may relax the burden of proof for compliance (e.g. Article 4(3), 28(5) or 32(3) GDPR) and serve as an attenuating circumstance in the face of fines (Article 83(2)(j) GDPR).[1842]

3 Conclusion to II

As the above and the remarks in Chapter 2[1843] showed, CoC are not just another self-regulatory approach, such as the *Privacy Shield*.[1844] Once the competent data protection supervisory authority approves them, it is insufficient for controllers

---

and not all actors (for instance, small and medium- sized enterprises (so-called SMEs)) possess the negotiating power to see their interests reflected in relevant codes.

1834 Cornelius Witt, Frank Ingenrieth and Jörn Wittmann, 'Could Codes of Conduct Be the Answer to "Schrems II"?' (*IAPP*, 29 September 2020) <https://iapp.org/news/a/could-codes-of-conduct-be-the-answer-to-schrems-ii/>.

1835 EDPB, 'Guidelines 1/2019 on Codes of Conduct and Monitoring Bodies under Regulation 2016/679 – Version 2.0' (n 551) para 17.

1836 Witt, Ingenrieth and Wittmann (n 1834).

1837 EDPB, 'Guidelines 04/2021 on Codes of Conduct as Tools for Transfers' (n 554) para 6.

1838 ibid.

1839 EU Parliament 'EU-UK Private Sector Data Flows after Brexit. Settling on Adequacy' (n 1190) 9.

1840 EDPB, 'Guidelines 04/2021 on Codes of Conduct as Tools for Transfers' (n 554) para 7.

1841 ibid para 6.

1842 EU Parliament 'EU-UK Private Sector Data Flows after Brexit. Settling on Adequacy' (n 1190) 8.

1843 Chapter 2, B.II.4.

1844 Witt, Ingenrieth and Wittmann (n 1834).

and processors to self-declare compliance.[1845] Instead, compliance will be enforced by an independent monitoring body.[1846] Some find CoC far ahead of SCCs or the *Privacy Shield* in terms of effective and trusted implementation of the GDPR.[1847] Yet, the aforementioned concerns about the access to data by public authorities through bulk interception also applies to data transfer under CoC.[1848]

III Certification

The GDPR first introduced the possibility of a certification mechanism set out in Article 42 GDPR.[1849] The certification mechanism currently lacks procedures and criteria and is practically not available to businesses.[1850] Businesses that plan on exporting personal data based on Article 46(2)(f) GDPR will need to implement such certification procedure pursuant to Article 42 GDPR successfully. Similarly, to the use of CoC, the data importer must make "binding and enforceable commitments" to apply the certification as an appropriate safeguard. Applicants must operate and process data compliant to the GDPR to get a certification. Also in place must be supplementary measures that compensate for any voids of privacy in the respective third countries.[1851] The accredited[1852] certification body[1853] then states GDPR conformity and potentially grant the use of a logo or symbol signifying the successful completion of the certification procedure (e. g. seal or mark).[1854] The certification could cover all or at least many transfer cases and, therefore, could be a promising transfer tool, especially for larger

---

1845 Lisa-Marie Lange and Alexander Filip, 'Art. 46 DS-GVO' in Heinrich Amadeus Wolff and Stefan Brink (eds) (n 149) para 50 peaking of self-regulatory instruments but under sovereign control.
1846 Chapter 2, B.II.4.
1847 Witt, Ingenrieth and Wittmann (n 1834).
1848 cf Paal and Kumkar (n 575) 738 concerning data transfer to the US.
1849 Chapter 2, B.II.5.
1850 cf EDPB, 'Register of Certification Mechanisms, Seals and Marks' <https://edpb.europa.eu/our-work-tools/accountability-tools/certification-mechanisms-seals-and-marks_de>.
1851 cf A.III.2.
1852 EDPB, 'Guidelines 4/2018 on the Accreditation of Certification Bodies under Article 43 of the General Data Protection Regulation (2016/679) – Version 3.0' (n 566).
1853 GDPR, art 43.
1854 EDPB, 'Guidelines 1/2018 on Certification and Identifying Certification Criteria in Accordance with Articles 42 and 43 of the Regulation – Version 3.0' (2019) 8.

companies in the UK that regularly process data from the EU.[1855] Also, such certification criteria and bodies support businesses in implementing the GDPR and inspire consumer trust and confidence in business-to-business relationships.[1856] Also, accredited certification can help with regulatory authorities demanding proof of compliance.[1857] It can further reduce imposed fines.[1858] Considering these aspects, businesses should closely monitor developments in this area.[1859] Some found that the delays of certification mechanisms available to data controllers and processors were "worrying" and would noticeably impact small and medium-sized businesses.[1860] The longer the data controllers and processors cannot rely on certificates from service providers, the more the transaction costs and compliance efforts increase.[1861] The EDPB has announced that it will publish new guidance on certification as a transfer tool to third counties in accordance with Article 42(2) GDPR.[1862] Yet, the aforementioned concerns about the access to data by public authorities through bulk interception also applies to data transfer under certification.[1863]

IV Conclusion to B

Most importantly, when using appropriate safeguards as transfer tools, businesses must always take into account the *Facebook Ireland and Schrems* decision (A.I.) and the EDPB Recommendations on supplementary measures (A.III.). CoC, certification and BCRs (for transfer within an organisation) could provide a more promising transfer tool for data transfers outside the EU to the UK. However, the latter appears to be unfitting for smaller or medium-sized businesses. Despite great potential, CoC and the certification mechanism are lacking practical relevance up to this point. They have not yet been sufficiently exploited as

---

1855 Johanna Hofmann and Benjamin Stach, 'Soft Brexit – Die Ruhe vor dem Sturm? Was müssen Unternehmen ab 2021 beachten?' [2021] ZD 3, 7.

1856 Alisha Gühr, Irene Karper and Sönke Maseberg, 'Der lange Weg zur Akkreditierung nach Art. 42 DSGVO' (2020) 44 DuD 649, 650.

1857 ibid.

1858 GDPR, art 83(2)(j).

1859 Hofmann and Stach (n 1855) 7.

1860 Alexander Duisberg, 'Zertifizierung und der Mittelstand – Quo Vadis?' [2018] ZD 53, 53.

1861 ibid.

1862 EDPB, 'Guidelines 1/2018 on Certification and Identifying Certification Criteria in Accordance with Articles 42 and 43 of the Regulation – Version 3.0' (n 1854) 28.

1863 cf Paal and Kumkar (n 575) 738 concerning data transfer to the US.

appropriate safeguards. Therefore, companies should monitor further developments in this area.

C Derogation for Specific Situations

In *Facebook Ireland and Schrems*, the CJEU emphasised that the derogations, established in Article 49 GDPR[1864], prevent a "legal vacuum" since it "details the conditions under which transfers of personal data to third countries may take place in the absence of an adequacy decision under Article 45(3) of the GDPR or appropriate safeguards under Article 46 of the GDPR".[1865] The Article 29 Working Party and the EDPB published practical guidance for data controllers to transfer personal data under Article 49 GDPR derogations.[1866] Businesses should take these Guidelines into account when considering a transfer of personal data based on Article 49 GDPR. The following is looking at the different derogations, taking into account the EDPB's Guidelines, especially focusing on the data subject's consent (II. and III.). Prior to this, the status of these scenarios as "derogations" and the standing of Article 49 GDPR within the system of GDPR's Chapter V will be reviewed (I.).

I Status as Derogations

The Article 29 Working Party and (later) the EDPB have advocated a layered approach within the system of Chapter V[1867]: Data exporters should first endeavour to frame the transfer with one of the mechanisms established in Article 45 and 46 GDPR and only in their absence use the derogations provided in Article 49(1)

1864 Chapter 2, B.III.
1865 *Facebook Ireland and Schrems* (n 64) para 202.
1866 Art. 29 Data Protection Working Party, 'Working Document on a Common Interpretation of Article 26(1) of Directive 95/46/EC of 24 October 1995' (n 570); EDPB, 'Guidelines 2/2018 on Derogations of Article 49 under Regulation 2016/679' (n 570).
1867 In favor of a 'layered approach' are Ambrock and Karg (n 77) 156; Emanuel von Towfigh and Jacob Ulrich, 'Art. 49 DSGVO' in Gernot Sydow (ed) (n 163) para 16; for different approach see Kai von Lewinski, 'Privacy Shield – Notdeich nach dem Pearl Harbor für die transatlantischen Datentransfers' [2016] EuR 405, 156, who might consider the adequacy decisions, the appropriate safeguards and the derogations as alternatives (however, does not further evaluate).

GDPR.[1868] Derogations under Article 49 GDPR would be exemptions from the general principle that personal data may only be transferred to third countries if an adequate level of protection is provided for in the third country or if appropriate safeguards have been adduced and the data subjects enjoy enforceable and effective rights to continue to benefit from their fundamental rights and safeguards.[1869] According to this approach, personal data transfers, which are based on Article 49 GDPR, would be subject to a "mandatory double subsidiarity".[1870] The EDPB emphasises that in order to prevent the exception from becoming the rule, Article 49 GDPR should be interpreted restrictively.[1871] To support its argument, EDPB refers to the wording of the title of Article 49 GDPR "Derogations for specific situations".[1872] Also, recital 114 GDPR states that in the absence of an adequacy decision, "the controller or processor should make use of solutions that provide data subjects with enforceable and effective rights as regards to the processing of their data in the Union once those data have been transferred so that that they will continue to benefit from fundamental rights and safeguards." This may favour the implementation of appropriate safeguards over applying the derogation.

Lit. (b), (c), (d), (e) and (f) can only apply in situations where the data transfer is "necessary" for the specific purpose of the derogation to be used. Recital 111 GDPR makes a further restriction for the derogations established in lit. (b), (c) and (e) to only apply in cases of "occasional" data transfer. The term "occasional" indicates that such transfer may happen more than once, but not regularly.[1873] The EDPB emphasises that a data transfer that occurs regularly within a

---

1868 Art. 29 Data Protection Working Party, 'Working Document on a Common Interpretation of Article 26(1) of Directive 95/46/EC of 24 October 1995' (n 570) 9; EDPB, 'Guidelines 2/2018 on Derogations of Article 49 under Regulation 2016/679' (n 570) 3 et seq.

1869 EDPB, 'Guidelines 2/2018 on Derogations of Article 49 under Regulation 2016/679' (n 570) 3.

1870 Botta, 'Zwischen Rechtsvereinheitlichung und Verantwortungsdiffusion: Die Prüfung grenzüberschreitender Datenübermittlungen nach "Schrems II"' (n 1250) 511.

1871 EDPB, 'Guidelines 2/2018 on Derogations of Article 49 under Regulation 2016/679' (n 570) 3 referring to the CJEU case law: 'the protection of the fundamental right to respect for private life at EU level requires that derogations from and limitations on the protection of personal data should apply only in so far as is strictly necessary' (*Satakunnan Markkinapörssi and Satamedia* [GC], no 931/13, para 56, 27 June 2017; *Volker and Markus Schecke and Eifert* (n 56) para 77; *Digital Rights Ireland and Seitlinger and Others* (n 73) para 52; *Schrems* (n 64) para 92; *Tele2 Sverige* (n 81) para 96); also Art. 29 Data Protection Working Party, 'Working Document on a Common Interpretation of Article 26(1) of Directive 95/46/EC of 24 October 1995' (n 570) 7.

1872 EDPB, 'Guidelines 2/2018 on Derogations of Article 49 under Regulation 2016/679' (n 570) 3 et seq.

1873 ibid 4.

stable transfer relationship would have to be deemed systematic and repeated and would not be considered "occasional".[1874] Although the derogations that are established in lit. (a), (d), (f) and (g) are not limited to such "occasional" transfers, the Article 29 Working Party and the EDPB go further and recommended that all derogations are applied restrictively.[1875] Whether this approach is convincing and practicable, in particular for lit. (a) will be discussed below.[1876] The EDPB supports its alleged argument with the fourth sentence of recital 115 to the GDPR, which states that "[t]ransfers should only be allowed where the conditions of this Regulation for a transfer to third countries are met". Yet, this remark would also include Article 49 GDPR. Hence, the EDPB's argumentation is circular.

In practice, these derogations are needed frequently as some of the derogations have everyday recurring transfers as their subject matter – hotel bookings, flight reservation, bank transfers or orders for goods.[1877] In a global world, contracts concluded with companies in third countries or services provided in the direct interest of the data subjects and data transfers for the exercise, assertion or defence of legal claims, especially before US courts, are frequent.[1878] Public bodies are also increasingly working on an international level.[1879] Against this background, *Christian Schröder* emphasises that it will be an important but difficult task for both data controllers and supervisory authorities not to let the derogations "get out of hand" in practice and at the same time to allow the necessary flexibility in individual cases.[1880]

Other authors refer to WP 114 and find that the derogations under Article 49(1) GDPR are fundamentally unsuitable for processing operations carried out *en masse*, repeatedly, or routinely.[1881] It is argued that transfers, which

---

1874 EDPB, 'Guidelines 2/2018 on Derogations of Article 49 under Regulation 2016/679' (n 570).

1875 ibid; Art. 29 Data Protection Working Party, 'Working Document on Transfers of Personal Data to Third Countries: Applying Articles 25 and 26 of the EU Data Protection Directive' (1998) WP 12 24.

1876 See in detail Ambrock and Karg (n 77) 154.

1877 Daniel A Pauly, 'Art. 49 DS-GVO' in Boris P Paal and Daniel A Pauly (eds) (n 157) para 2; Paal and Kumkar (n 575) 738; Lisa-Marie Lange and Alexander Filip, 'Art. 49 DS-GVO' (n 557) para 2.

1878 Christian Schröder, 'Art. 49 DS-GVO' in Jürgen Kühling and Benedikt Buchner (eds) (n 174) para 2.

1879 ibid.

1880 ibid.

1881 Thomas Zerdick, 'Art. 49 DS-GVO' in Eugen Ehmann and Martin Selmayr (eds) (n 538) para 4 referring to Art. 29 Working Party 'Working Document on a Common Interpretation of Article 26(1) of Directive 95/46/EC of 24 October 1995' (n 570) 11.

are based on Article 49 GDPR, may only be carried out if the risks for the data subject are minor (e. g. in the case of international money transfers). However, WP 114, to which these remarks refer, also states that the derogations in Article 49 GDPR "for the most part concern cases where risks to the data subject are relatively small or where other interests (public interests or those of the data subject himself) override the data subject's right to privacy."[1882] From this, it can be concluded that the regulatory legislator has already weighed up the interests in advance and has deliberately decided that only in some instances of derogations the restrictive term "occasional" or "necessity test" must be applied, but otherwise, derogations apply without further restriction. Furthermore, repeatedly and routinely situations could also fall under the term "specific situations". Hence, the restrictive interpretation of the exceptions is by no means mandatory (apart from the derogations that only apply for "occasional transfers").

The CJEU might have confirmed this point of view in *Facebook Ireland and Schrems*, stating that Article 49 GDPR prevents a "legal vacuum" since it "details the conditions under which transfers of personal data to third countries may take place in the absence of an adequacy decision under Article 45(3) of the GDPR or appropriate safeguards under Article 46 of the GDPR."[1883] The CJEU made the statement despite being aware of the frequent data flows between the EU and the US. A "legal vacuum" is not prevented by interpreting Article 49(1) GDPR restrictively. However, despite *Facebook Ireland and Schrems*, the EDPB continues to maintain its view.[1884] Also, *Jonas Botta* rightfully argued that the CJEU did not give an extensive interpretation of the Article 49 GDPR but only referred to its existence.[1885] The Court did not examine how and whether the provisions of Article 49 GDPR are practically enforceable in the data transfer between the EU and the US.[1886]

1882 Art. 29 Data Protection Working Party, 'Working Document on a Common Interpretation of Article 26(1) of Directive 95/46/EC of 24 October 1995' (n 570) 7.

1883 *Facebook Ireland and Schrems* (n 64) para 202.

1884 EDPB, 'Frequently Asked Questions on the Judgement of the Court of Justice of the European Union in Case C-311/18 – Data Protection Commissioner v Facebook Ireland Ltd and Maximillian Schrems' (n 587) 4.

1885 Botta, 'Zwischen Rechtsvereinheitlichung und Verantwortungsdiffusion: Die Prüfung grenzüberschreitender Datenübermittlungen nach "Schrems II"' (n 1250) 511.

1886 ibid.

II Consent of the Data Subject

The general requirements for transferring personal data based on the data subject's consent were already reviewed.[1887] In the case of personal data transfer in the UK, a declaration of consent must include a summary of the essential findings of the collection and processing practices of the UK intelligence services.[1888] Also, the general requirements of "informed" consent as a lawful basis under Article 6(1)(a) GDPR apply, which would include that the data subject is adequately informed about "the data controller's identity, the purpose of the transfer, the type of data, the existence of the right to withdraw consent, the identity, or the categories of recipients".[1889] Noteworthy, the data subject must be informed of the absence of an adequacy decision and appropriate safeguards and further of the possible risks of such transfer for the data subject resulting from the lack of an adequacy decision and appropriate safeguards.[1890]

Overall, the data transfer based on the data subject's consent could be rather challenging to realise in practice. Many data transferring companies, such as cloud providers, have no direct relationship with the data subjects and are already factually unable to obtain consent.[1891] From a company's point of view, the transfer based on the data subject's consent also has the disadvantage that the data subject can withdraw consent at any time, making it a more unsuitable transfer tool for long-term and comprehensive data transfers.[1892] However, on the other side, this derogation gives businesses the great advantage of adapting the scope of the consent or contract to their specific situation.[1893] Difficulties may arise from the requirement of freely given consent.[1894]

1887 Chapter 2, B.III.1.

1888 cf Ambrock (n 577) 1496 referring to the US.

1889 EDPB, 'Guidelines 2/2018 on Derogations of Article 49 under Regulation 2016/679' (n 570) 7.

1890 In the relevant literature, there is disagreement about whether the controller must additionally fulfil Article 13 and 14 GDPR for the consent to be informed cf n 308.

1891 Lothar Determann and Michaela Weigl, 'EU-US-Datenschutzschild und Alternativen für internationale Datentransfers' [2016] EuZW 811, 814; Paal and Kumkar (n 575) 737.

1892 Jörg Hladjk, 'Art. 47 DSGVO' in Martin Eßer, Philipp Kramer and Kai von Lewinski (eds) (n 176) para 2; Determann and Weigl (n 1891) 813; Nadine Geppert, 'Überprüfung der Modelle zur Datenübermittlung in Drittländer. Die Zukunft von EU-US-Privacy-Shield, BCRs und Standardvertragsklauseln' [2018] ZD 62, 65; Flemming Moos and Jens Schefzig, '"Safe Harbor" hat Schiffbruch erlitten. Auswirkungen des EuGH-Urteils C-362/14 in Sachen Schrems ./. Data Protection Commissioner' [2015] CR 625, 632; von Lewinski, 'Privacy Shield – Notdeich nach dem Pearl Harbor für die transatlantischen Datentransfers' (n 1867) 407; Paal and Kumkar (n 575) 737.

1893 Determann and Weigl (n 1891) 813.

1894 See above in Chapter 1 under A.IV.3.a with further references.

It is questionable whether the EDPB's restrictive interpretation of Article 49 GDPR should also apply to the data subject's consent.[1895] The fact that recital 111 GDPR does not explicitly limit this derogation to "occasional" transfers shows that the legislator understood that the data subject's will is manifested by the consent and the autonomy of the data subject should be given effect, even if a large number of transfers take place. Some authors see the data subject's consent as an expression and exercise of the individual's right to informational self-determination[1896].[1897] Consistent with this view, exercising the right to infor mational self-determination, data subjects could further be permitted to disclose their data in a self-determined manner if, for example, the data subject concerned decides for themselves that the positive consequences thereby outweigh the negative ones. Following this line, *Jens Ambrock* argued that the data subject are permitted to consciously expose their data to complete "surveillance" when consenting to a data transfer to third countries without adequate data protection.[1898] The extent to which the data subject releases information would be up to the data subject concerned, compatible with the right to self-determination.[1899] However, *Ambrock* changed his point of view and noticed together with *Moritz Karg* that in exceptional cases, some intrusive measures could not even be legalised by the data subject's consent.[1900] An individual cannot choose

---

1895 See in detail Voigt (n 286) 288 who concludes that consent within the framework of Article 8 CFR must be qualified – at least in conjunction with Article 7 CFR – as the active exercise of self-determination in the area of data protection law and thus as the exercise of fundamental rights.

1896 Kai von Lewinski classifies today's European data protection law under the concept of informational heteronomy. Consent should give the data subject the possibility to (co-)determine the processing of their personal data by a third party. The data subject is given a leeway through informational heteronomy, in which informational self-determination can then take place, cf Kai von Lewinski, 'Einführung' in Martin Eßer, Philipp Kramer and Kai von Lewinski (eds) (n 176) para 29; see also von Lewinski *Die Matrix des Datenschutzes – Besichtigung und Ordnung eines Begriffsfeldes* (n 115) 48.

1897 Many authors view that in addition to protection against interferences in the protected private sphere – Article 7 CFR also includes elements of self-determination, cf Hubertus Gersdorf, 'Art. 7 GrCh' in Boris P Paal and Hubertus Gersdorf (eds), *BeckOK Informations- und Medienrecht* (33rd edn, 2021), para 23; Thorsten Kingreen, 'Art. 7 EU-GRCharta' in Christian Callies and Matthias Ruffert (eds) (n 83). According to *Norbert Bernsdorff* the right to information self-determination is also protected by Article 8 CFR, cf Bernsdorff (n 58) para 14. *Marlene Voigt* views that the right to the information self-determination is protected by Article 8 CFR in conjunction with Article 7 CFR, cf Voigt (n 286) 287 et seq.

1898 Ambrock (n 577) 1496.

1899 ibid.

1900 Ambrock and Karg (n 77) 158.

to contract away their rights privately since the EU data protection framework offers a "minimum and non-negotiable level of privacy protection for all individuals".[1901] This line of argumanetation is convincing. Even if one would not classify the consent as a exercise of a fundamental right to the informational self-determination but as a waiver of the exercise of fundamental rights, one would come to the similar conclusion that the will of the data subject concerned must largely be taken into account through his or her consent. [1902] A legal basis that justifies interference with the "essence" of a fundamental right would itself disregard the "respect to essence" and would have to be declared "null and void" as a violation of Article 52(1) CFR.[1903] The CJEU has not yet fully defined the "essence" of Article 8 CFR.[1904] The violation of the essence of Article 8 CFR appears to depend on whether the recipient third country's regulation contains a minimum level of restrictions and limitation of data processing.[1905] The essence to the right guaranteed by Article 7 CFR would be violated by "a rule that allows the authorities to access the content of electronic communications generally"[1906] Legislation not providing legal remedies for an individual to have access to their data or to obtain the rectification or erasure of it violated the essence of the right to effective judicial protection in Article 47 CFR.[1907] Consequently, any data transfer disrespecting the "essence" of Articles 7, 8 and 47 CFR cannot be justified by the data subject's consent. The principle of respect to the essence is directed at member states and European bodies in the legislative process as well as data protection supervisory authorities in the implementation process of legal norms. The EU regulator was only allowed to enact Article 49(1)(a) GDPR in such a way that a data subject's consent would only justify the transfer to a third country

---

1901 Art. 29 Data Protection Working Party, 'Opinion 1/98 on Platform for Privacy Preferences (P3P) and the Open Profiling Standard (OPS)' (1998) WP 11 2. For example, further exploitation, such as in the sense of an exclusive licence or the construction of a genuine 'data property' is excluded.

1902 cf Kai von Lewinski in von Lewinski, Rüpke, Eckhardt, *Datenschutzrecht* (n 286) 182 et seq, (with further references); Kranenborg (n 92) paras 08.25 et seqq. This view is supported by the history of origins in the Convention on Fundamental Rights, in which a right to self-determination was deliberate excluded from the wording as well as the common constitutional tradition of the member states, which shows that the right to informational self-determination is a "German Concept".

1903 See in detail on the guarantee of essence as an absolute limitation in data protection law Bock and Engeler (n 97) 599.

1904 Chapter 2, A.I.2.b.

1905 *Accord PNR EU-Canada* (n 80) paras 151 et seq.

1906 *Schrems* (n 71) para 94.

1907 ibid para 187.

without an adequate level of data protection if it does not legitimise any data processing that constitutes an interference with the essence of the fundamental right. Otherwise, the data subjects' freedom of will and choice is restricted, preventing them from disposing of their fundamental positions themselves.[1908] Data exporters should consider these considerations when using the data subject's consent as a legal basis for the transfer of personal data to the UK since data protection authorities are required to intervene in cases where the essence of fundamental rights is violated. Special attention should be paid to investigatory powers established under the IPA 2016.[1909]

III Other Derogations

In the following, other derogations that are constituted in Article 49(1) GDPR will be looked at. It must be kept in mind that Article 13(1)(f) and 14(1)(f) GDPR apply when using one of the following derogations.

1 Necessary for the Performance of a Contract or the Implementation of Precontractual Measures

Article 49(1)(b) and (c) GDPR are limited to "occasional transfers".[1910] Lit. (b) may serve as a legal basis for transferring personal data concerning individual clients by travel agents to hotels to organise the client's stay at the hotel.[1911] The EDPB stresses that the derogation cannot be used "when a corporate group has, for business purposes, centralised its payment and human resources management functions for all its staff in a third country as there is no direct and objective link between the performance of the employment contract and such transfer."[1912] The term "necessity" "requires a close and substantial connection between the data subject [...] and the purposes of the contract.[1913] The data transfer must be without alternatives, to the purpose of the performance of this con-

---

1908 Bock and Engeler (n 97).
1909 See in detail in Chapter 3, C.IV.
1910 GDPR, recital 111.
1911 EDPB, 'Guidelines 2/2018 on Derogations of Article 49 under Regulation 2016/679' (n 570) 8; Art. 29 Data Protection Working Party, 'Working Document on a Common Interpretation of Article 26(1) of Directive 95/46/EC of 24 October 1995' (n 570) 13.
1912 EDPB, 'Guidelines 2/2018 on Derogations of Article 49 under Regulation 2016/679' (n 570) 8.
1913 Art. 29 Data Protection Working Party, 'Working Document on a Common Interpretation of Article 26(1) of Directive 95/46/EC of 24 October 1995' (n 570) 15.

tract or these precontractual measures.[1914] It would be the case of a transfer by travel agents concerning personal data of their individual clients to hotels or other commercial partners for the client's stay abroad.[1915] An example for an occasional transfer would be "if personal data of a sales manager, who in the context of his/her employment contract travels to different clients in third countries, are to be sent to those clients in order to arrange the meetings" or "if a bank in the EU transfers personal data to a bank in a third country in order to execute a client's request for making a payment, as long as this transfer does not occur in the framework of a stable cooperation relationship between the two banks".[1916] In lit. (c) scenarios, the data subject is not a party to the agreement, but the contract must be concluded in the data subject's interest between the controller and a third party. The Article 29 Working Party found that lit. (c) is an insufficient legal basis for international data transfers concerning the data controller's employees to providers established outside the EU, to which the data controllers outsource their payroll management.[1917]

2 Necessary for Important Reasons of Public Interest

Article 49(1)(d) GDPR is mainly used by public authorities but can also be relied upon by private entities.[1918] It is not limited to "occasional" transfers.[1919] Consequently, the respective transfer purposes are considered important enough that transfers based on it "can take place on a large scale and in a systematic manner".[1920] Yet, the EDPB "strongly encourages" data exporters to base transfers that "are made in the usual course of business or practice" on appropriate safeguards instead of Article 49(1)(d) GDPR.[1921] According to recital 112 GDPR, "important reasons of public interest" might be given in "cases of international data exchanges between competition authorities, tax or customs administra-

---

1914 Art. 29 Data Protection Working Party, 'Working Document on a Common Interpretation of Article 26(1) of Directive 95/46/EC of 24 October 1995' (n 570) 13.
1915 EDPB, 'Guidelines 2/2018 on Derogations of Article 49 under Regulation 2016/679' (n 570) 9.
1916 Art. 29 Data Protection Working Party, 'Working Document on a Common Interpretation of Article 26(1) of Directive 95/46/EC of 24 October 1995' (n 570).
1917 Art. 29 Data Protection Working Party, 'Working Document on a Common Interpretation of Article 26(1) of Directive 95/46/EC of 24 October 1995' (n 570) 14.
1918 GDPR, recital 112.
1919 GDPR, recital 111.
1920 EDPB, 'Guidelines 2/2018 on Derogations of Article 49 under Regulation 2016/679' (n 570) 11.
1921 ibid.

tions, between financial supervisory authorities, between services competent for social security matters, or for public health or in order to reduce and/or eliminate doping in sport." When using Article 49(1)(d) GDPR as transfer legal basis it is not sufficient to transfer personal data for public interest specific only to a third country because this could lead to third-country authorities easily circumventing the requirement for adequate protection in this country by unilaterally establishing public interests.[1922] Instead, the public interest, "in the spirit of reciprocity for international cooperation" [1923], must be recognised in the EU or member state's law to which the controller is subject.[1924] An international agreement or convention to which the EU or the member states are parties and recognises a specific objective and provides for international cooperation can be an indicator.[1925] Notably, there may be restrictions in the information obligations pursuant to Article 14(1) GDPR if the provision of "such information proves impossible or would involve a disproportionate effort, in particular for processing for archiving purposes in the public interest, scientific or historical research purposes or statistical purposes".[1926]

3 Necessary for Establishment, Exercise or Defence of Legal Claims

This derogation is limited to "occasional" transfers.[1927] The term "legal claims" is interpreted broadly, including legal claims in a judicial, administrative, or "any out-of-court procedure".[1928] The legal claim must already exist; in the context of this derogation, it is not sufficient that there is a possibility that a claim might be brought up one day.[1929] The derogation covers data transfers "for the purpose of defending oneself or for obtaining a reduction or waiver of a fine legally foreseen" and "for the purpose of formal pre-trial discovery procedures in civil litigation".[1930] The EDPB emphasises that "[a]s a transfer needs to be made in a pro-

---

1922 Kugler (n 524) para 928.
1923 EDPB, 'Guidelines 2/2018 on Derogations of Article 49 under Regulation 2016/679' (n 570) 10.
1924 GDPR, art 49(4).
1925 EDPB, 'Guidelines 2/2018 on Derogations of Article 49 under Regulation 2016/679' (n 570) 10.
1926 GDPR, art 14(5)(b).
1927 GDPR, recital 111.
1928 GDPR, recital 111.
1929 EDPB, 'Guidelines 2/2018 on Derogations of Article 49 under Regulation 2016/679' (n 570) 12; Art. 29 Data Protection Working Party, 'Working Document on a Common Interpretation of Article 26(1) of Directive 95/46/EC of 24 October 1995' (n 570) 15.
1930 EDPB, 'Guidelines 2/2018 on Derogations of Article 49 under Regulation 2016/679' (n 570) 11.

cedure, a close link is necessary between a data transfer and a specific procedure regarding the situation in question. The abstract applicability of a certain type of procedure would not be sufficient."[1931] "T[he] "necessity test" requires a close and substantial connection between the data in question and the specific establishment, exercise or defense of the legal position".[1932] The data exporter must generally be aware of the principle of data minimisation[1933] and should also consider, in a preliminary step, whether anonymised data would be sufficient and, if not, in a second step, whether pseudonymised data could be an option.[1934]

4 Necessary in order to Protect the Vital Interests of the Data Subject or Another Person, where the Data Subject is Physically or Legally Incapable of Giving Consent

This derogation is not limited to "occasional" transfers.[1935] Consequently, transfer based on it may also be repeated and systematic transfers. The derogation applies where the data subject is incapable of making a valid decision and providing consent (due to physical, mental or legal incapability) and requires urgent medical care, and only his or her doctor established in the EU can provide these data.[1936] The GDPR respects the will of individuals to value their data sovereignty even higher than their own lives.[1937] However, it is not sufficient to transfer personal medical data to persons responsible for the treatment and established outside the EU if their purpose is to carry out general medical research that will not yield results until sometime in the future.[1938] Instead, the transfer must be necessary for an essential diagnosis.[1939]

1931 EDPB, 'Guidelines 2/2018 on Derogations of Article 49 under Regulation 2016/679' (n 570) 11.
1932 ibid.
1933 For more information on the principle of data minimisation see in Chapter 2 under A.IV.2.c
1934 EDPB, 'Guidelines 2/2018 on Derogations of Article 49 under Regulation 2016/679' (n 570) 12.
1935 cf GDPR, recital 111.
1936 EDPB, 'Guidelines 2/2018 on Derogations of Article 49 under Regulation 2016/679' (n 570) 13; Art. 29 Data Protection Working Party, 'Working Document on a Common Interpretation of Article 26(1) of Directive 95/46/EC of 24 October 1995' (n 570) 15.
1937 Ambrock and Karg (n 77) 159.
1938 EDPB, 'Guidelines 2/2018 on Derogations of Article 49 under Regulation 2016/679' (n 570) 13; Art. 29 Data Protection Working Party, 'Working Document on a Common Interpretation of Article 26(1) of Directive 95/46/EC of 24 October 1995' (n 570) 16.
1939 ibid.

5 Transfer Made from a Public Register

In the context of this derogation, the EDPB defines a register as an electronic or written "record containing regular entries of items or details" or as "an official list or record of names or items", which be by law intended to provide information to the public.[1940] Registers that are the responsibility of private bodies do not fall under this derogation.[1941] Registers open to consultation by either the public or any person with a legitimate interest could be "registers of companies, registers of associations, registers of criminal convictions, (land) title registers or public vehicle registers".[1942] Data exporters should be aware that, "[w]here a transfer is made from a register to be consulted by persons having a legitimate interest, the transfer can only be made at the request of those persons or if they are recipients, taking into account the data subjects' interests and fundamental rights".[1943]

6 Compelling Legitimate Interests of the Data Controller

The derogations under the second sentence of Article 49(1) GDPR could be interpreted as a "last resort" legal basis.[1944] The EDPB views that this derogation should be interpreted very strictly due to this derogation's subsidiary nature.[1945] In line with the principle of accountability,[1946] the data exporter must demonstrate that it was impossible to frame the data transfer by appropriate safeguards or apply one of the above derogations.[1947] The EDPB notices that this might be the case with international data transfers by small and medium-sized companies, for which the establishment of appropriate safeguards according to Article 46 GDPR as transfer tools could be a disproportionate burden due to a lack of financial and organisational means, or in scenarios where cooperation with the data importer is practically impossible.[1948]

1940 EDPB, 'Guidelines 2/2018 on Derogations of Article 49 under Regulation 2016/679' (n 570) 13.
1941 ibid.
1942 ibid.
1943 EDPB, 'Guidelines 2/2018 on Derogations of Article 49 under Regulation 2016/679' (n 570) 14.
1944 ibid.
1945 ibid 15.
1946 Chapter 2, A.IV.2.g.
1947 EDPB, 'Guidelines 2/2018 on Derogations of Article 49 under Regulation 2016/679' (n 570) 14.
1948 ibid 15.

Since the derogations in Article 49(1) GDPR already define situations where legitimate interests override the interest of a data subject's protection, it is challenging to define interests which, on the one hand, are not yet covered by Article 49(1) GPDR and, on the other hand, are sufficiently "compelling".[1949] There is no clear definition of the term "compelling legitimate interest". It likely includes such interests that the European regulators could not adjust in a future-oriented provision, open to development.[1950] The EDPB finds that a high threshold applies, requiring the compelling legitimate interest to be essential for the data controller. It provides the example of a data controller that is "compelled to transfer the personal data in order to protect its organisation or systems from serious immediate harm or from a severe penalty which would seriously affect its business." Recital 113 does provide some guideline: In the case of scientific or historical research purposes or statistical purposes, the legitimate expectations of society for an increase of knowledge should be considered.[1951]

When assessing the necessity of the transfer, a balancing test must be performed. All possible adverse effects, including any possible damage, to the data subject's interest, rights and freedoms must be "carefully forecasted and assessed, by taking into consideration their likelihood and severity".[1952] To determine "suitable safeguards" for the data subject's rights and freedoms, the data exporter must consider the "nature of the data, the purpose and duration of the processing" and "the situation in the country of origin, the third country and, if any, the country of final destination of the transfer".[1953] Also, the data exporter must be aware that it is mandatory by law to apply additional safeguards to minimise identified risks resulting from the personal data transfer. Such additional measures could be technical (pseudonymisation or encryption) and organisational.[1954] The controller is also required to inform the transfer's supervisory authority in advance and inform the data subject of the transfer and on the compelling legitimate interests pursued.[1955]

1949 Ambrock and Karg (n 77) 160.
1950 ibid.
1951 GDPR, recital 113.
1952 EDPB, 'Guidelines 2/2018 on Derogations of Article 49 under Regulation 2016/679' (n 570) 15.
1953 ibid.
1954 See in detail under A.III.2.a. and c.
1955 GDPR, art. 49(1), second and third sentence.

IV Conclusion to C

The above shows that some of the derogations established in Article 49 GDPR apply to various scenarios that occur on an everyday basis in a globally connected world, such as hotel bookings, flight reservation, bank transfers or orders for goods.[1956] In a global world, contracts concluded with companies in third countries or services provided in the direct interest of the data subjects and data transfers for the exercise, assertion or defence of legal claims, especially before US courts, are frequent.[1957] Nevertheless, businesses that transfer personal data based on the derogations under Article 49 GDPR should be aware that neither the respective third country provides an adequate level of protection nor does the data exporters provide adequate protection or appropriate safeguards to the personal data transferred.[1958] Since it is not required to have any kind of prior authorisation from a supervisory authority, transfers based on derogations lead to increased risks for the rights and freedoms of the data subjects concerned.[1959] The examination of the specific transfer – if necessary, with the involvement of the data protection authority – requires a comprehensive legal analysis that can hardly be carried out by a single company and is accompanied by considerable legal uncertainty.[1960] Businesses should keep in mind that, currently, in the prevailing view – supported by the EDPB – the derogations must be interpreted restrictively. However, the necessary flexibility in individual cases must be allowed.[1961] Derogations that only apply for "occasional transfers" may also be used as a legal basis for the repeated and systematic transfer. This includes transfer based on the data subject's consent, provided that the consent is explicit and informed. Yet, in practice, many data exporters have no direct relationship with the data subjects and are already factually unable to obtain consent.[1962] Also, transfer based on the data subject's consent has the dis-

---

1956 Pauly, 'Art. 49 DS-GVO' (n 1877) para 2; Paal and Kumkar (n 575) 73; Lange and Filip, 'Art. 49 DS-GVO' (n 1877) para 2.
1957 Schröder, 'Art. 49 DS-GVO' (n 1878) para 2.
1958 EDPB, 'Guidelines 2/2018 on Derogations of Article 49 under Regulation 2016/679' (n 570) 4.
1959 EDPB, 'Guidelines 2/2018 on Derogations of Article 49 under Regulation 2016/679' (n 570) 4.
1960 Moos and Schefzig (n 1892) 632.
1961 Schröder, 'Art. 49 DS-GVO' (n 1878) para 2.
1962 Determann and Weigl (n 1891) 814; Paal and Kumkar (n 575) 737.

advantage that the data subject can withdraw consent at any time, making it a more unsuitable transfer tool for long-term and comprehensive data transfers.[1963]

In *Facebook Ireland and Schrems*, the CJEU did not further evaluate whether and how the derogations under Article 49 GDPR are effective in practice. It remains to be seen, whether in the future the CJEU is given cause to take a more comprehensive position on the interpretation of the derogations within Chapter V GDPR. In January 2021, CJEU judge-rapporteur *Thomas von Danwitz* mentioned, without anticipating much, that Article 49 GDPR derogations could be considered an option for intra-group transfers and that should be more attentively explored.[1964]

Data exporters should also be aware that EU or member state legislation might expressly limit transfers of specific categories of personal data to a third country in the future (Article 49(5) GDPR).

D Further Obligations

Besides the general data controllers' and processors' general obligations under the GDPR, which were already reviewed in Chapter 2[1965] the data exporter must be aware of additional obligations if personal data is transferred from the EU to the UK. First, the information provided to the data subjects must be updated. According to Article 13(1)(f) GDPR and Article 14(1)(f) GDPR separate information must be provided about the intention to transfer data to a third country. Second, data subjects have the right to obtain information on "the recipients or categories of recipient to whom the personal data have been or will be disclosed, in particular recipients in third countries or international organisations" (Article 15(1)(c), (2) GDPR). Third, the procedures in which personal data is transferred to third countries must be included in the data controller's "record of processing activities" (Article 30(1)(d) and (e) GDPR). For data processors, this also applies according to Article 30(2)(c) GDPR. Naturally, compliance with the

---

1963 Hladjk (n 1892) para 2; Determann and Weigl (n 1891) 813; Geppert (n 1892) 65; Moos and Schefzig (n 1892) 632; von Lewinski, Privacy Shield – Notdeich nach dem Pearl Harbor für die transatlantischen Datentransfers' (n 1867) 407; Paal and Kumkar (n 575) 737.
1964 Thomas von Danwitz, 'Internationaler Datentransfer in der Rechtsprechung des EuGH' (European Data Protection Day 2021 – Transborder Transfers. Challenges of international data transfer from the perspective of the Convention 108+ and GDPR. 40 Years of Convention 108, 28 January 2021) <https://cdn.pottkinder.de/streaming/stream2.html>.
1965 Chapter 2, A.IV.2. and 4.

general legal requirements for the transmission of personal data is required.[1966] UK companies, which fall under the application scope of the GDPR, must appoint an EU representative under Article 27 GDPR.[1967]

E Sanctions

In non-compliance with the GDPR, undertakings[1968] may be sanctioned and face financial exposure (Article 83 GDPR). The GDPR introduced the possibility for national supervisory authorities to impose effective and dissuasive fines. Most recently, the Irish Data Protection Commissioner imposed a EUR 250 million fine on *WhatsApp*.[1969] The Luxembourg National Commission issued the highest fine for Data Protection (CNDP) to *Amazon.com* Inc (EUR 746 million).[1970] The French National Commission on Informatics and Liberty (CNIL) fined *Google* a EUR 50 million fine;[1971] the Hamburg Commissioner for Data Protection and Freedom of Information (BfDI) fined *Hennes & Mauritz* with a EUR 35,3 million fine[1972]. The imposition of a fine is one of the several means available to super-

---

1966 Chapter 2 under A.IV.3.

1967 cf in more detail Paul Voigt and Niklas Drexler, 'Pflichten für Verantwortliche und Auftragsverarbeiter nach Art. 27 DS-GVO und UK-GDPR' [2021] ZD 409. EU companies, which fall under the application scope of the UK GDPR must also appoint an UK representative under Article 27 UK GDPR.

1968 "Where administrative fines are imposed on an undertaking, an undertaking should be understood to be an undertaking in accordance with Articles 101 and 102 Treaty on the Functioning of the European Union ("TFEU") for those purposes" (recital 150 GDPR). The CJEU case law definition is: "the concept of an undertaking encompasses every entity engaged in an economic activity regardless of the legal status of the entity and the way in which it is financed" (Judgement of 23 April 1991, *Höfner and Elsner v Macroton*, C-41/90, EU:C:1991:161, para 21). An undertaking "must be understood as designating and economic unit even if in law that economic unit consists of several persons, natural or legal" (cf Judgement of 14 December 2006, *Confederación Española de Empresarios de Estaciones de Servicio*, C-217/05, EU:C:2006:784, para 40).

1969 GDPR Hub, 'DPC (Ireland) – WhatsApp Ireland Limited – IN-18 – 12 – 2' <https://gdprhub.eu/index.php?title=DPC_(Ireland)_-_WhatsApp_Ireland_Limited_-_IN-18-12-2&mtc=today>.

1970 Data Privacy Manager, '20 Biggest GDPR Fines so Far [2019, 2020 & 2021]' (2021) <https://dataprivacymanager.net/5-biggest-gdpr-fines-so-far-2020/>. This blog article provides an overview of the highest fines so far issued by member states' supervisory authorities. *Amazon.com* plans to appeal this decision.

1971 CNIL, 'The CNIL's Restricted Committee Imposes a Financial Penalty of 50 Million Euros against GOOGLE LLC' (21 January 2019) <https://www.cnil.fr/en/cnils-restricted-committee-imposes-financial-penalty-50-million-euros-against-google-llc>.

1972 Martin Schramm, '35,3 Millionen Euro Bußgeld wegen Datenschutzverstößen im Servicecenter von H&M' (*Der Hamburgische Beauftragte für Datenschutz und Informationsfreiheit*, 1 Oc-

visory authorities to enforce compliance with the GDPR.[1973] Such "administrative" fines are administered by the data protection supervisory authority in each EU member state.[1974] A data controller involved in the processing of personal data which infringes the GDPR is liable for the damage caused by it. Hence, the involvement of third parties, such as email or cloud storage services, does not absolve the data controller from ensuring that personal data is processed accordingly to the GDPR.[1975] A data processor is liable if it has not complied with the GDPR obligations specifically directed to processors or where it has acted outside or contrary to lawful instructions of the controller.[1976] Data controllers or processors are only exempted from liability if they prove that they were not "in any way responsible for the event giving rise to the damage".[1977]

According to Article 83 GDPR, fines must be "effective, proportionate and dissuasive".[1978] The supervisory authority will determine whether an infringement has occurred and the severity of the penalty. The criteria established in Article 83(2)(a)-(k) GDPR support in determining whether a fine will be assessed and in what amount: the nature, gravity and duration of the infringement as well as the number of data subjects affected; whether the infringement was intentional or the result of negligence; whether the organisation took any actions to mitigate the damage suffered by the affected data subjects; the amount of technical and organisational preparation the organisation had previously implemented to comply with the GDPR; the history of any relevant previous infringements; whether the organisation cooperated with the supervisory authority to discover and remedy the infringement; what type of personal data the infringement effect; whether the organisation proactively reported the infringement to the supervisory authority; whether the organisation allowed approved codes of conduct or was previously certified; as well as any other aggravating and mitigating factors.

In the case of "minor" infringements, a supervisory authority should issue a reprimand instead of a fine.[1979] However, infringements on Article 44 et seqq.

---

tober 2020) <https://datenschutz-hamburg.de/pressemitteilungen/2020/10/2020-10-01-h-m-ver fahren>.

1973 Art. 58 GDPR; recital 150 GDPR: "Imposing an administrative fine or giving a warning does not affect the application of other powers of the supervisory authorities or of other penalties under this Regulation".

1974 For an overview of fines and penalties which data protection authorities within the EU have imposed under the GDPR see *CMS*, 'GDPR Enforcement Tracker' (n 1703).

1975 GDPR, art 82(2).

1976 GDPR, art 82(2).

1977 GDPR, art 82(3).

1978 GDPR, art 83(1).

1979 GDPR, recital 148.

GDPR, when transferring personal data to a recipient country, are classified as "serious infringements", which "go against the very principles of the right to privacy and the right to be forgotten that are at the heart of the GDPR".[1980] These infringements could result in a fine of up to EUR 20 million, or 4 % of the group's worldwide annual revenue from the preceding financial year – whichever amount is higher.[1981] For example, on 11 March 2021, the Spanish Data Protection Authority (AEPD) issued a EUR 8.15 million fine to *Vodafone Spain* because, among other things, they approved an international data transfer that did not meet the requirements of the GDPR.[1982]

In a case in which an organisation has multiple GDPR infringements, it will only be sanctioned for the gravest infringement, provided all the infringements are part of the same or linked processing operation.[1983] Additionally, member states must foresee other penalties (e. g. penalties under criminal law).[1984] However, "the imposition of criminal penalties for infringements of such national rules should not lead to a breach of the principle of *ne bis in idem*[1985], as interpreted by the Court of Justice".[1986]

F Current Developments in the UK

The ICO provides guidance for UK businesses that receive data from or have offices in the EU and EEA.[1987] The guidance gives a very brief and basic overview of the changes in data protection since the UK left the EU. The ICO also published an "interactive tool" for UK businesses that receive personal data into the UK from the EEA to keep data flowing from the EEA to the UK.[1988] This tool aims to help businesses to determine whether SCCs are necessary to maintain the

---

1980 GDPR EU, 'What are the GDPR Fines?'<https://gdpr.eu/fines/.

1981 GDPR, art 83(5).

1982 Data Privacy Manager (n 1970).

1983 GDPR, art 83(3).

1984 GDPR, art 84.

1985 The principle of *ne bis in idem* is a fundamental right enshrined in Article 50 CFR and Article 4 of Protocol No VII to the ECHR. It means that the same infringement should not be punished twice.

1986 GDPR, recital 149.

1987 ICO, 'Overview – Data Protection and the EU' (*ico.*) <https://ico.org.uk/for-organisations/dp-at-the-end-of-the-transition-period/overview-data-protection-and-the-eu/>.

1988 ICO, 'Keep Data Flowing from the EEA to the UK – Interactive Tool' (*ico.*) <https://ico.org.uk/for-organisations/dp-at-the-end-of-the-transition-period/keep-data-flowing-from-the-eea-to-the-uk-interactive-tool/>.

data flow, to select the right SCCs and to understand and complete them. It supports businesses to clarify whether and to what extent they use EU based service providers to process their data. Notably, many UK businesses fall under the GDPR's extraterritorial scope of application. Under Article 3(2) GDPR, the scope of European data protection law is extended to all business activities of companies not established in the EU that involve any processing of personal data connected to the internal market. In these scenarios, UK companies must comply with the GDPR. In practice, it is advisable to comply with the provisions of the GDPR – even if the DPA 2018 provides any deviations from it.[1989]

Since the new EU SCCs are not binding to UK businesses that are not subject to the GDPR. Currently, the old EU SCCs continue to be valid in the UK. Yet, the ICO has consulted on an alternative transfer tool to govern transfers of personal data from the UK to third countries.[1990] On 2 February 2022, the IDTA[1991], the international data transfer addendum to the EU SCCs (Addendum)[1992] and a document setting out transitional provisions were laid before the UK Parliament and came into force on 21 March 2022.[1993] The IDTA and the Addendum replace the old EU SCCs – following the *Facebook Ireland v Schrems* judgement – for personal data transfers outside the UK that are not covered by an adequacy decision. However, in substance it only differs a little from the new EU SCCs. For example, the IDTA also includes sub-processor to processor transfers.[1994] Also, the ICO considers introducing an alternative dispute resolution mechanism (arbitration mechanism).[1995] Unlike than the modular approach of the new EU SCCs, the draft IDTA adopt a tabular structure. This tabular format includes clauses that apply to all data transfers. These tables must be filled out by the transferring parties for each transfer (Part 1), extra protection clauses (Part 2), to be filled out if the transfer risk assessment identifies that the transfer mechanism requires additional safeguards, commercial clauses (Part 3), which are optional and mandato-

---

1989 Hofmann and Stach (n 1855) 5. This is advisable vis-à-vis EU customers in general.

1990 ICO, 'Guide to the General Data Protection Regulation (GDPR) – Standard Contractual Clauses (SCCs) after the Transition Period Ends' (*ico.*) <https://ico.org.uk/for-organisations/guide-to-data-protection/guide-to-the-general-data-protection-regulation-gdpr/international-transfers-after-uk-exit/sccs-after-transition-period/>.

1991 ICO, 'International Data Transfer Agreement, Version A1.0' (*ico.*) <https://ico.org.uk/media/for-organisations/documents/4019538/international-data-transfer-agreement.pdf>.

1992 ICO, 'International Data Transfer Addendum to the EU Commission Standard Contractual Clauses' (*ico.*) <https://ico.org.uk/media/for-organisations/documents/4019539/international-data-transfer-addendum.pdf>.

1993 These documents are issued under Section 119 A DPA 2018.

1994 ibid 7.

1995 ibid 43.

ry clauses (Part 4) to be adopted in their entirety. However, at this point, it is still unclear whether the IDTA will be adopted and if it develops relevance in practice. Since the ICO has also published an Addendum to the new EU SCCs to allow organisations to adapt the EU SCCs to work in the context of UK transfers,[1996] most businesses might use the Addendum since it covers them for exports from the EU and the UK.[1997]

Furthermore, in August 2021, the ICO published a draft of the transfer risk assessment (so-called TRA) that sets out measures to evaluate the risks associated with transfers to third countries (possibly under the new IDTA) to determine whether the relevant transfer mechanism can be relied on.[1998] The TRA is very similar to the EDPB's Guidance on supplementary measures. It includes three steps: The first step includes an assessment of the transfer and whether the TRA tool is suitable for this specific transfer, considering the nature of the importer, the onward transfers, the purposes, transfer method and regularity.[1999] In a second step, the data exporter must assess whether the IDTA is likely to be enforceable in the destination country.[2000] If the data exporter has doubts, it must perform a supplementary risk assessment considering any potential harm to data subjects and ways to reduce any risks. The ICO provides comprehensive guidance for this supplementary assessment.[2001] In a third step, the data exporter must assess whether there is appropriate protection for the data from third-party access.[2002] The ICO also provides guidelines on safeguarding data subject's rights and on assessing the likelihood of third-party access.[2003] The ICO encourages the data exporter to make the transfer even though there would be a minimal risk or even more than minimal risk with a low risk of

---

1996 ICO, 'Draft Standard Data Protection Clauses to be issued by the Commissioner under Section 119 A(1) Data Protection Act 2018 – UK Addendum to the EU Commission Standard Contractual Clauses' (August 2021) <https://ico.org.uk/media/about-the-ico/consultations/2620398/draft-ico-addendum-to-com-scc-20210805.pdf>.

1997 The Addendum makes it clear that in the event of any conflict between the Addendum and UK data protection law, UK data protection law will prevail (recital 6); in a conflict between the Addendum and the EU SCCs (to which the Addendum is appended), the Addendum will prevail unless the inconsistent or conflicting terms of the EU SCCs afford greater protection for data subjects (recital 10).

1998 ICO, 'Draft International Transfer Risk Assessment and Tool' (August 2021) <https://ico.org.uk/media/about-the-ico/consultations/2620397/intl-transfer-risk-assessment-tool-20210804.pdf>.

1999 ibid 11 et seqq.

2000 ibid 16 et seqq.

2001 ibid 19 et seqq.

2002 ibid 29 et seqq.

2003 ibid 32 et seqq.

harm to data subjects.[2004] The TRA must be reviewed no less than annularly[2005], which would be contrary to the EU SCCs that oblige parties to take into account any change to law or practice that might affect the transfer[2006].

G Conclusion to Chapter 4

The assessment above is essential for EU-based businesses transferring data to the UK for the case that the adequacy decision favouring the UK is invalidated by the CJEU or repealed or suspended by the EU Commission. Appropriate safeguards require far more supervisory and safeguard measures than data transfers based on an adequacy decision. Since the CJEU's ruling in *Facebook Ireland and Schrems* (under A.I.), the data exporter and, subsidiarily, the competent supervisory authority must fulfil strict oversight – mainly to supervise the legal situation in the recipient country regarding the fundamental rights of the data subject concerned, and where necessary to suspend the data transfer (under A.II.). When transferring personal data based on SCCs or other appropriate safeguards, businesses are strongly advised to consider and follow the EDPB's Recommendations on supplementary measures (under A.III.). Businesses must do a data transfer impact assessment, concerning the need for the implementation of supplementary measures, and should start this process on time as it will only be possible to do so until 27 December 2022. Data controllers and processors must trace data flows and check which sub-processors have access to the personal data. Businesses should then particularly ask the following questions:[2007] Is the respective data importer or its (sub)processor in the third country subject to laws that could thwart its assumed data protection obligations? What does the competent data supervisory authority say? Which technical and organisational measures can be implemented to ensure an adequate level of data protection? Are all relevant company units and data importers in third countries informed about the possible inadmissibility of transfers and the adjustments that may become necessary? Who is responsible for analysing the further development of the legal situation? What are the consequences of suspending data transfers in specific business processes or departments or switching to alternative providers in the EU or safe third countries? In light of the principle of accountability (Article 5(2)

2004 ICO, 'Draft International Transfer Risk Assessment and Tool' (n 1998) 29.
2005 ICO, 'Draft International Data Transfer Agreement' (August 2021) <https://ico.org.uk/media/about-the-ico/consultations/2620396/intl-data-transfer-agreement-202100804.pdf> 16.
2006 A.II.2.
2007 cf Scheben and Busekist (n 1646) 335 concerning data transfer from the EU to the US.

GDPR), the assessment carried out and any measures taken should also be comprehensively documented.

According to Article 49 GDPR, if no appropriate safeguards are used as a transfer tool, businesses should carefully evaluate an exceptional circumstance (under C.I.). Article 49 GDPR might even take on greater importance in the context of data transfer to third countries. The importance of derogations is already shown in practice. However, businesses should keep in mind that the Article 29 Working Party and EDPB still strongly advocate a restrictive interpretation of Article 49 GDPR.

Chapter 5 Future Developments

In Chapter 2 and Chapter 3, the status quo data protection regime in the EU and *post*-Brexit UK has been reviewed and analysed. This Chapter focuses on possible developments in data protection in the UK (under A.) and in the EU (under B), which could be relevant for future data flows between the EU and the UK. In particular, the UK's new data plans (under A.I.), the new internal data transfer strategy (under A.II.), the planned adequacy partnerships (under A.III.), as well as the chances of a possible future divergence from the EU legal system, will be looked at (under A.IV.).

Furthermore, the EU's global data strategy will be looked at (under B.II). The focus here lies on the GDPR's standing as the "gold standard" (under B.II.1.). Also relevant for the analysis is the criticism the EU adequacy processes has received (under B.II.2.). Finally, the relationship between the CJEU and the EU Commission will be reviewed in the context of global data transfer and "adequacy" (under B.II.3.). This Chapter aims to provide a "look into the future" and provides a better understanding of what might happen in cross-border data protection, particularly in the EU-UK relation.

A The UK's Future Data Protection Regime

Věra Jourová, Vice-President for Values and Transparency, said in the context of the adoption of the adequacy decision by the EU Commission in favour of the UK: "The UK has left the EU but today its legal regime of protecting personal data is as it was. Because of this, we are adopting these adequacy decisions today. At the same time, we have listened very carefully to the concerns expressed by the Parliament, the Members States and the European Data Protection Board, in particular on the possibility of future divergence from our standards in the UK's privacy framework. We are talking here about a fundamental right of EU citizens that we have a duty to protect. This is why we have significant safeguards and if anything changes on the UK side, we will intervene".[2008]

From this, it can be deduced that any deviation from the European data protection system entails the EU Commission's risk of reviewing the adequacy decision and even of repealing or suspending it. *Post*-Brexit, the UK administers, ap-

---

2008 EU Commission, 'Commission Adopts Adequacy Decisions for the UK' (2021) Press Release of 28 June 2021 <https://ec.europa.eu/commission/presscorner/detail/ro/ip_21_3183>.

https://doi.org/10.1515/9783110988253-007

plies, and enforces its own data protection regime, notably involving amendments or changes to the data protection framework assessed in the EU Commission's adequacy decision.[2009] In light of this, the UK Government's planned *post-*Brexit (global) data regime will be examined in the following. Furthermore, any indications and chances of future divergence from EU data protection law are reviewed.

I UK Government's post-Brexit Data Plans

In early 2020, the UK Government, under Prime Minister *Boris Johnson*, confirmed that it would develop "separate and independent policies" in data protection.[2010] This position on adopting a divergence from EU data protection was a significant change from former Prime Minister *Theresa May*'s view, who committed to ensuring that the GDPR would be in domestic UK law long-term.[2011]

The current UK Government highlights that "[h]aving left the European Union, the UK will champion the benefits that data can deliver. [It] will promote domestic best practice and work with international partners to ensure data is not inappropriately constrained by national borders and fragmented regulatory regimes so that it can be used to its full potential."[2012] In this paper, the UK Government also emphasised the intention to "remove unnecessary barriers to international data flow".[2013] This view was once again confirmed in a UK Government commissioned "Report of the Taskforce on Innovation, Growth and Regulatory Reform" that was released in May 2021, stating "[the EU] GDPR is prescriptive, and inflexible and particularly onerous for smaller companies and charities to operate. It is challenging for organisations to implement the necessary processes to manage the sheer amounts of collected and stored data and need to be tracked from creation to deletion. Compliance obligations should be more proportionate, with fewer obligations and lower compliance burdens on charities,

---

2009 EDPB, 'Opinion 14/2021 Regarding the European Commission Draft Implementing Decision Pursuant to Regulation (EU) 2016/679 on the Adequate Protection of Personal Data in the United Kingdom' (n 615) recital 50.

2010 Johnson, 'UK/EU Relations' (n 1530).

2011 Theresa May, 'In Full: Theresa May's Speech on Future UK-EU Relations' (2 March 2018) <https://www.bbc.com/news/uk-politics-43256183>.

2012 Department for Digital, Culture, Media & Sport, 'National Data Strategy' (2020) Policy Paper <https://www.gov.uk/government/publications/uk-national-data-strategy/national-data-strategy>.

2013 ibid.

SMEs and voluntary organisations."[2014] "The government plans to promote the free flow of personal data globally and across borders, including through ambitious new trade deals and new data adequacy agreements with some of the fastest-growing economies, while ensuring people's data continues to be protected to a high standard. All future decisions will be based on what maximises innovation and keeps up with evolving tech. As such, the government's approach will seek to minimise burdens on organisations seeking to use data to tackle some of the most pressing global issues, including climate change and the prevention of disease."[2015] The UK could "amend its data protection statute in a unilateral fashion".[2016]

The DCMS launched a consultation "on changes to break down barriers to innovative and responsible uses of data so it can boost growth, especially for start-ups and small firms, speed up scientific discoveries and improve public services".[2017] For example, the UK Government proposed to revise the "legitimate interests" lawful basis for processing (Article 6(1)(f) UK GDPR), so that, rather than the controller needing in each cases to balance its interests against the rights of the subject, there would be a set of defined categories where the interest in favour of processing is presumed.[2018] Also, rules relating to AI-driven processing should be modified in order to incentivise further innovation in this field.[2019] Another modification might be the replacement of administrative accountability duties through an introduction of a "risk-based privacy management programme" that "reflects the volume and sensitivity of the personal information it handles, and the type(s) of data processing it carries out".[2020] Other sugges-

---

2014 Rt Hon Sir Iain Duncan Smith, Rt Hon Theresa Villiers and George Freeman, 'Taskforce on Innovation, Growth and Regulatory Reform' (2021).

2015 Department for Digital, Culture, Media & Sport, 'EU Adopts "Adequacy" Decisions Allowing Data to Continue Flowing Freely to the UK. UK Businesses and Other Organisations Will Benefit from Unrestricted Personal Data Transfers' (n 21).

2016 Schwartz, 'The Data Privacy Law of Brexit: Theories of Preference Change' (n 866) 145.

2017 *Oliver Dowden* in Department for Digital, Culture, Media & Sport, 'UK Unveils Post-Brexit Global Data Plans to Boost Growth, Increase Trade and Improve Healthcare' (2021) Press Release of 26 August 2021 <https://www.gov.uk/government/news/uk-unveils-post-brexit-global-data-plans-to-boost-growth-increase-trade-and-improve-healthcare>. For an overview of the consultation paper see Marc Stauch, 'UK: Government Publishes Proposal for Reforming UK Data Protection Law' [2021] ZD-Aktuell, 05532 and Julius Nickoleit and Johannes Müller, 'Regierungspapier: Datenschutz-Reforminitiative in UK' [2021] ZD-Aktuell, 05522.

2018 DCMS, 'Data: A New Direction' (10 September 2021) para 60 <https://assets.publishing. service.gov.uk/government/uploads/system/uploads/attachment_data/file/1022315/Data_Re form_Consultation_Document__Accessible_.pdf>.

2019 ibid paras 63 et seqq.

2020 ibid paras 151 et seqq.

tions include changing the threshold for reporting privacy breaches to the ICO,[2021] and making the subject access request mechanism in Article 15 UK GDPR subject to a general fee[2022]. Furthermore, the government paper includes some reforms of the ICO, such as introducing further review powers over the ICO to the Secretary of State[2023].[2024] The former *IC Elizabeth Denham* warned that "[f]or the future ICO to be able to hold government account, it is vital its governance model preserves its independence and is workable within the context of the framework set by Parliament and with effective accountability. The current proposal for the Secretary of State to approve ICO guidance and to appoint the CEO does not sufficiently safeguard this independence."[2025] In the Queen's Speech 2022, the Government confirmed the Data Reform Plans.[2026] Yet, it remains to be seen if and what kind of amendments the UK will implement in its data protection legislative system in the future and whether such amendments will endanger the UK's adequacy decision.

II UK's New Internal Data Transfer Regime

Nevertheless, on 26 August 2021, the Department for Digital, Culture, Media and Sport (after this: DCMS) unveiled a more specific UK's *post*-Brexit new data transfer regime.[2027] The UK seeks to "move quickly and creatively to develop global partnerships which will make it easier for UK organisations to exchange data with important markets and fast-growing economies".[2028] Data power should be used to "drive growth and create jobs while keeping high data protection standards".[2029] The future UK's data regime aims to become "even more ambitious, pro-growth and innovation-friendly, while still being underpinned by secure and trustworthy privacy standards".[2030] According to Digital Secretary *Oliver*

2021 DCMS, 'Data: A New Direction' para 180.
2022 ibid para 188.
2023 ibid para 373.
2024 ibid paras 307 et seqq.
2025 Elizabeth Denham, 'Foreword to ICO response to DCMS consultation "Data: a new direction"' (ico.) (7 October 2021) <https://ico.org.uk/about-the-ico/news-and-events/news-and-blogs/2021/10/response-to-dcms-consultation-foreword/>.
2026 The Queen's Speech 2022 (n 745) 57 et seq.
2027 Department for Digital, Culture, Media & Sport, 'UK Unveils Post-Brexit Global Data Plans to Boost Growth, Increase Trade and Improve Healthcare' (n 2017).
2028 ibid.
2029 ibid.
2030 ibid.

Dowden, which now holds power to adopt the UK's adequacy decisions, the UK aims to develop a "world-leading data policy".[2031] The DCMS highlighted the need for international data sharing for clinical trials or medical research. As popular examples for the benefits of unhindered international data flows, the availability of the NHSX' national database of chest X-Rays and images to researchers that investigate Covid-19 or clinical trials like the Oxford *AstraZeneca* vaccine development[2032] are used. The UK Government also published guidance on international data transfer.[2033] Furthermore, a new International Data Transfers Expert Council has launched in May 2021.[2034] This Council will consist of fifteen leading individuals, which will provide independent and expert advice, which "will enable the government to deliver on its mission to champion[2035] the international flow of data".[2036]

One of the new developments is the planned introduction of a new exemption for data transfers, known as the reverse transfer exemption.[2037] In this scenario data, which are originating from a country not subject to an adequacy decision and are transferred to a processor in the UK, can be freely transferred back to the country of origin. According to EU law this would a restricted transfer and the SCC's currently do not permit such a reverse transfer.

2031 *Oliver Dowden* in ibid.

2032 Department for Digital, Culture, Media & Sport, 'International Data Transfers: Building Trust, Delivering Growth and Firing up Innovation, 26 August 2021' (2021) Guidance UK adequacy (i) <https://www.gov.uk/government/publications/uk-approach-to-international-data-transfers/international-data-transfers-building-trust-delivering-growth-and-firing-up-innovation>.

2033 ibid.

2034 Department for Digital, Culture, Media & Sport, 'The Government's New International Data Transfers Expert Council' (2021) News Story <https://www.gov.uk/government/news/the-governments-new-international-data-transfers-expert-council>.

2035 Department for Digital, Culture, Media & Sport, 'National Data Strategy' (n 2012).

2036 Department for Digital, Culture, Media & Sport, 'The Government's New International Data Transfers Expert Council' (n 2034).

2037 Department for Digital, Culture, Media & Sport, 'Data: A New Direction' (10 September 2021) para 260 <https://assets.publishing.service.gov.uk/government/uploads/system/uploads/attachment_data/file/1022315/Data_Reform_Consultation_Document__Accessible_.pdf>.

III Planned Adequacy Decisions

The UK has listed the US and Australia, Columbia, Dubai, the Republic of Korea, and Singapore as its "top priorities" for negotiations on adequacy.[2038] The UK announced new "multi-billion-pound global data partnerships with the US, Australia and Republic of Korea".[2039] The announcement also states that "longer-term priorities" would be adequacy partnerships with Brazil, India, Indonesia, and Kenya. According to the UK Government, there are already 80 billion pounds of data-enabled service exports from the UK to these destinations.[2040] Regarding whether to commence an adequacy assessment in respect of a country, policy factors will be taken into account. Such factors include the trade and diplomatic relationship between the UK and the third country.[2041] It remains to be seen how the UK will establish these "adequacy partnerships" and how this will affect the EU Commission's adequacy decision towards the UK.

1 UK–US

Significantly, the indicated adequacy arrangement between the UK and the US will be relevant from the EU perspective. A UK adequacy decision on the US would be a threat to the EU Commission's adequacy decision on the UK. Since 92% of the UK's service exports to the US are data-enabled, amounting to 67 billion pounds, the US is the UK's most important national trading partner in data-enabled exports.[2042] The UK Government emphasised its disappointment in the CJEU *Facebook Ireland and Schrems* ruling in October 2020, invalidating the *Privacy Shield*. It plans to remove trading and data flow barriers to the US. The UK might find that the US provides adequate protection around national security. The legal standard for measuring "adequacy" or "essential equivalence" could change in the UK.[2043] In *Facebook Ireland and Schrems*, the CJEU applied the

---

2038 Department for Digital, Culture, Media & Sport, 'Map UK Data Partnerships' <https://assets.publishing.service.gov.uk/government/uploads/system/uploads/attachment_data/file/1013047/UK_Data_Partnerships___Map_V2_.jpg>.
2039 Department for Digital, Culture, Media & Sport, 'UK Unveils Post-Brexit Global Data Plans to Boost Growth, Increase Trade and Improve Healthcare' (n 2017).
2040 ibid.
2041 Department for Digital, Culture, Media & Sport, 'International Data Transfers: Building Trust, Delivering Growth and Firing up Innovation, 26 August 2021' (n 2032).
2042 Department for Digital, Culture, Media & Sport, 'UK Unveils Post-Brexit Global Data Plans to Boost Growth, Increase Trade and Improve Healthcare' (n 2017).
2043 Peter Swire, 'UK's Post-Brexit Strategy on Cross-Border Data Flows' (*Lawfare*, 1 September 2021) <https://www.lawfareblog.com/uks-post-brexit-strategy-cross-border-data-flows>.

Charter. *Post*-Brexit, a UK and US adequacy arrangement review would instead be subject to the UK courts and the applicable law to assess adequacy would be UK law. The current and future data flow relations between the UK and the US were already discussed in Chapter 4 under D. However, the chances of a wider trade deal between the UK and the US were recently "played down" by US President *Joe Biden.*

2 UK–Australia

Australia is one of the UK's largest trading partners, especially in digital and tech sectors.[2044] The UK has already signed an "agreement in principle" with Australia on 16 June 2021.[2045] This document sets out what the UK and Australia have agreed to be included in the free trade agreement once finalised. The agreement would include "ambitious commitments that will increase opportunities for digital trade across all sectors of the economy, while also ensuring world-leading standards for personal data protection and for legitimate public policy services".[2046] Particularly, "unjustifiable data localisation requirements [should be prohibited] to create a more certain and secure online environment and support growth in digital trade between Australia and the United Kingdom."[2047] The UK believes Australia to have a "strong data protection regime, which is designed to foster transparent and robust personal data handling practices and business accountability".[2048] The EU Commission does not find Australia providing an "adequate" level of protection.[2049] Consequently, any UK adequacy decision favour-

---

[2044] The UK digital industry has exported 841 million pounds worth of services to Australia in 2019, cf Department for International Trade, 'UK-Australia Free Trade Agreement: Benefits for the UK <https://assets.publishing.service.gov.uk/government/uploads/system/uploads/attachment_data/file/1041548/uk-australia-free-trade-agreement-fta-benefits-for-the-uk.pdf>.

[2045] Department for International Trade, 'UK-Australia FTA Negotiations: Agreement in Principle' (2021) <https://www.gov.uk/government/publications/uk-australia-free-trade-agreement-negotiations-agreement-in-principle/uk-australia-fta-negotiations-agreement-in-principle#services>.

[2046] ibid Digital Trade 3.2.

[2047] ibid.

[2048] Department for Digital, Culture, Media & Sport, 'UK Unveils Post-Brexit Global Data Plans to Boost Growth, Increase Trade and Improve Healthcare' (n 2017).

[2049] This was already briefly reviewed in Chapter 3, D.III.3. A comprehensive overview of the data protection laws in the South Pacific is provided by the Research Centre for Law and Digitalisation, 'Data Protection Laws in the South Pacific' (last revised 28 October 2021) < https://www.jura.uni-passau.de/fileadmin/dokumente/fakultaeten/jura/lehrstuehle/hennemann/Mapping_Global_Data_Law/L_08_-_Data_Protection_Laws_in_South_Pacific_01.pdf>.

ing Australia could also become a problem in the context of the onwards transfer of personal data from the EU.

3 UK–South Korea

There should be no concerns on the intended adequacy "partnership" with South Korea on the part of the EU since the EU has, most recently, adopted an adequacy decision on the protection of personal data by South Korea under the Personal Information Protection Act.[2050]

4 UK–Columbia

Columbia was the UK's third-largest trading partner in South America[2051] in 2019.[2052] The UK emphasises that it has a "comprehensive data protection framework".[2053] In fact, the chances of Columbia obtaining an adequacy decision by the EU Commission could be considered high.[2054] Columbia does ensure a high standard of the protection of personal data, including key principles and data subject's rights (such as access, rectification, update and deletion), obligations of data controllers and processors, a fundamental right to a judicial remedy, protection for sensitive data, the principle of proportionality and necessity concerning access to data by public authorities, etc.[2055] One obstacle for obtaining an adequacy decision could be the Columbian Data Protection Authority's

---

2050 South Korea Adequacy Decision (n 28). A comprehensive overview of the data protection laws in Asia is provided by the Research Centre for Law and Digitalisation, 'Data Protection Laws in Asia' (last revised on 1 February 2022) < https://www.jura.uni-passau.de/fileadmin/do kumente/fakultaeten/jura/lehrstuehle/hennemann/Mapping_Global_Data_Law/L03_-_Asia. pdf>.

2051 A comprehensive overview of the data protection laws in South America is provided by the Research Centre for Law and Digitalisation, 'Data Protection Laws in South America' (last revised on 16 September 2021) <https://www.jura.uni-passau.de/fileadmin/dokumente/fa kultaeten/jura/lehrstuehle/hennemann/Mapping_Global_Data_Law/L_05_-_Data_Protection_ Laws_in_South_America.pdf>.

2052 Department for Digital, Culture, Media & Sport, 'UK Unveils Post-Brexit Global Data Plans to Boost Growth, Increase Trade and Improve Healthcare' (n 2017).

2053 Columbia has two data protection laws: Law 1266 of 200 and Law 1581 of 2021. See for more information on the Columbian data protection laws at One Trust DataGuidance, February 2021, https://www.dataguidance.com/notes/colombia-data-protection-overview.

2054 cf Luis Alberto Montezuma, 'Obtaining Adequacy Standing for Colombia' (*IAPP*, 2 August 2018) <https://iapp.org/news/a/obtaining-adequacy-standing-for-colombia/>.

2055 Department for Digital, Culture, Media & Sport, 'UK Unveils Post-Brexit Global Data Plans to Boost Growth, Increase Trade and Improve Healthcare' (n 2017).

decision to declare certain third countries adequacy, including Australia, Costa Rica, US, Mexico, Peru and Serbia.[2056]

5 UK–Singapore

Singapore is the UK's biggest trading partner in South-East Asia.[2057] According to the DCMS, Singapore has a "strong private sector data protection regime"[2058].[2059] Singapore has never attempted to obtain an adequacy decision by the EU Commission.[2060]

6 UK–Dubai International Finance Centre

The Dubai International Finance Centre has "strong links with UK financial services".[2061] In fact, it has adopted a new data protection law, which came into effect in July 2020. The new data protection mirrors many aspects of the GDPR.[2062] Yet, it remains to be seen how the chances for an adequacy finding by an EU Commission stand.[2063]

IV Future Divergence from the EU's Data Protection System

The UK chose to follow EU data protection during and, up to this date, *post*-Brexit.[2064] However, the UK Government's remarks and the recent announcement of

---

2056 Montezuma (n 2054).

2057 Department for Digital, Culture, Media & Sport, 'UK Unveils Post-Brexit Global Data Plans to Boost Growth, Increase Trade and Improve Healthcare' (n 2017).

2058 See for more information on the Singapore Personal Data Protection Act 2012 (No 26 of 2012) (PDPA) at OneTrust DataGuidance, April 2021, https://www.dataguidance.com/notes/singapore-data-protection-overview.

2059 Department for Digital, Culture, Media & Sport, 'UK Unveils Post-Brexit Global Data Plans to Boost Growth, Increase Trade and Improve Healthcare' (n 2017).

2060 cf Blackmore (n 1494).

2061 Department for Digital, Culture, Media & Sport, 'UK Unveils Post-Brexit Global Data Plans to Boost Growth, Increase Trade and Improve Healthcare' (n 2017).

2062 Hunton Andrews Kurth, 'New Dubai International Financial Centre Data Protection Law Comes Into Effect' (July 2020) <https://www.huntonprivacyblog.com/wp-content/uploads/sites/28/2020/07/new-dubai-ifc-data-protection-law-1.pdf>.

2063 Satvik Kapoor, 'The Data Protection Law of the Dubai International Finance Centre and the GDPR' (*LinkedIn*, 10 December 2020) <https://www.linkedin.com/pulse/data-protection-law-dubai-international-finance-centre-satvik-kapoor> provides an overview of relevant divergences.

2064 Schwartz, 'The Data Privacy Law of Brexit: Theories of Preference Change' (n 866) 133.

the new data plans indicate that the days of the UK following the EU's data protection approach are about to expire. The prevailing narrative seems to be that leaving the EU is an opportunity for a new, more global data regime and breaking down data flow barriers to other third countries. "We have taken back control of laws and our destiny. We have taken back control of every jot and title of our regulation. In a way that is complete and unfettered", Prime Minister *Boris Johnson* claimed.[2065] However, such a promise of restoring the UK's regulatory sovereignty *post*-Brexit is misleading.[2066] The "Leave" campaign[2067] and the Brexit debate did not focus on data privacy matters or other legislative matters but rather on "immigration policy, UK funding of the EU, fishery issues, and a wish for legislative independence".[2068]

However, the following might suggest that the chances of the UK's deviation from the EU's privacy legislation may, on the contrary, be limited.[2069] Suppose the UK deviates too far from providing a system of data protection law for data transfers from the EU, one that is consistent with European constitutional requirements. In that case, the EU Commission or the CJEU will likely find the UK system to no longer be "adequate".[2070]

The disruption of data flows from the EU to the UK would have a massive impact on the UK's economy. The EU is a large commercial market – in fact, the largest single market worldwide.[2071] As already mentioned, the UK's economy, especially the IT sector and the digital service industry, is mainly dependent on data transfer from the EU. Three-quarters of the UK's cross-border data flows are with EU countries.[2072] Digital companies comprise 10% of the UK's GDP.[2073]

2065 David Hughes, 'Boris Johnson's Speech in Full: Every Word of Brexit Deal Announcement as He Hails UK "Taking Back Control"' (*i news*, 24 December 2020) <https://inews.co.uk/news/politics/boris-johnson-speech-full-brexit-deal-announcement-trade-agreement-text-video-808170>.
2066 Bradford, *The Brussels Effect: How the European Union Rules the World* (n 147) 278.
2067 For more information on the "Leave" campaign see at the following link <http://www.voteleavetakecontrol.org/why_vote_leave.html> accessed 9 June 2022.
2068 Schwartz, 'The Data Privacy Law of Brexit: Theories of Preference Change' (n 866) 135.
2069 ibid in detail clarifies and analyses different models of preference change.
2070 ibid 143.
2071 EU, 'Trade' <https://europa.eu/european-union/topics/trade_en>.
2072 House of Lords, European Union Committee, Third Report of Session 2017–19, 'Brexit: The EU Data Protection Package', HL Paper 7 para 5 <https://publications.parliament.uk/pa/ld201719/ldselect/ldeucom/7/708.htm>.
2073 The Boston Consulting Group, 'The Internet Now Contributes 10 Percent of GDP to the UK Economy, Surpassing the Manufacturing and Retail Sectors' (2015) <https://www.globenewswire.com/news-release/2015/05/01/924211/0/en/The-Internet-Now-Contributes-10-Percent-of-GDP-to-the-UK-Economy-Surpassing-the-Manufacturing-and-Retail-Sectors.html?culture=en-us>.

The UK economy has the highest percentage of GDP attributed to the digital economy in Europe.[2074] Services contribute 44% to the UK's global exports, and trades in services is highly dependent on digital technologies and data flows. [2075] Consequently, adequacy status is essential for the UK.[2076] From a UK's perspective, conformity with EU data protection could be seen as a "necessary price for participation in the digital economy".[2077] This perspective is not necessarily a new finding for the UK since it enacted its first data protection law, the DPA 1984, due to market forces and the fear of being excluded from data transfers from other European countries caused by Convention 108[2078].[2079] Nowadays, the UK's economy has become even more dependent on digital data coming from the EU. The so-called "Brussels Effect" might be the most influential factor in retaining EU data protection law under Brexit.[2080]

The concept of the "Brussels Effect" was first introduced by *Anu Bradford* in 2012.[2081] It attributes an extraterritorial influence to the EU legislation.[2082] The "Brussels Effect" results from a large internal market (market power)[2083], a relative regulatory capacity[2084] and the political will to create strict rules (stringent standards)[2085]. It appears on consumer markets (inelastic markets)[2086] and markets with a non-divisible service or product[2087]. *Bradford* further differentiates between the *de jure*[2088] and *de facto*[2089] "Brussels Effect".[2090]

2074 The Boston Consulting Group (n 2073).

2075 House of Lords, European Union Committee, Third Report of Session 2017–19 (n 2072) para 5.

2076 ibid para 50.

2077 Schwartz, 'The Data Privacy Law of Brexit: Theories of Preference Change' (n 866) 135.

2078 The Convention 108 was already reviewed in Chapter 2, A.III.2.b.

2079 Schwartz, 'The Data Privacy Law of Brexit: Theories of Preference Change' (n 866) 135.

2080 ibid 140.

2081 Anu Bradford, 'The Brussels Effect' (2012) 107 Nw. U. L. Rev. According to the author the "Brussels Effect" occurs in antitrust law, privacy regulations, health protection (regulation of chemicals), environmental protection and food safety; See also most recently Bradford, *The Brussels Effect: How the European Union Rules the World* (n 147).

2082 ibid. Prior to the Brussels Effect, Jack L. Goldsmith and Tim Wu spoke of a 'California effect' applied on a global scale in Jack Goldsmith and Tim Wu, *Who Controls the Internet?: Illusions of a Borderless World* (Oxford University Press 2006).

2083 Bradford, 'The Brussels Effect' (n 2081) 11 et seq.

2084 ibid 12 et seqq.

2085 ibid 14 et seqq.

2086 ibid 16 et seq.

2087 ibid 17 et seqq.

2088 In detail Bradford, *The Brussels Effect: How the European Union Rules the World* (n 147) 147 et seqq.

According to *Anu Bradford*, European data protection and privacy is a prime example of the Brussels Effect.[2091] This is mainly due to the ban of data transfer from the EU to third countries that fail to ensure "an adequate level of protection" of data privacy rights.[2092] With *Schrems* and *Facebook Ireland and Schrems*, the CJEU has "effectively dictated the rest of the world's data protection legislation", at least for the countries that depend on the adequacy decisions for their data transfer.[2093] This is not changed by the fact that the UK was the second-largest economy in the EU by GDP[2094] and the third-largest population[2095] and that, consequently, since Brexit, the EU's market size is diminished by 15 %, reducing the remaining EU market size compared to other third countries. Brexit will not "dampen" the Brussels effect.[2096] The *de jure* Brussels has already occurred in the significant retention of EU legislation in UK domestic law and adopting a UK GDPR.[2097] As the above numbers show, the UK is still highly dependent on "inclusion" in the EU's digital data economy.[2098] Consequently, the UK Government should retain close regulatory alignment to ensure "adequacy". Otherwise, many UK companies could no longer do business in the EU, at least not without high compliance costs[2099].

In light of the Brussels Effect, the Conservative Party's ambition to develop an entirely new data protection system, which completely deviates from the EU data protection system, appears unlikely.[2100] The option for the EU to withdraw this adequacy decision in case of non-compliance on the part of the UK is a "Damocles sword" for domestic data protection legislative developments.[2101]

2089 In detail ibid 142 et seqq.

2090 Bradford, 'The Brussels Effect' (n 2081) 8 and 28.

2091 ibid 22 et seqq.

2092 ibid 24. Moritz Hennemann calls the instrument of adequacy decisions the GDPR's 'pull effect', cf Moritz 'Das Schweizer Datenschutzrecht im Wettbewerb der Rechtsordnungen' (n 411) 372.

2093 Bradford, *The Brussels Effect: How the European Union Rules the World* (n 147) 149.

2094 Eurostat, 'GDPR and Main Components (Output, Expenditure and Income)' (2020) <https://ec.europa.eu/eurostat/databrowser/view/namq_10_gdp/default/table?lang=en>.

2095 Eurostat, 'EU Population up to over 513 Million on 1 January 2019' (2019) News Release of 10 July 2019 <https://ec.europa.eu/eurostat/documents/2995521/9967985/3-10072019-BP-EN.pdf/e152399b-cb9e-4a42-a155-c5de6dfe25d1>.

2096 Bradford, *The Brussels Effect: How the European Union Rules the World* (n 147) 278.

2097 Schwartz, 'The Data Privacy Law of Brexit: Theories of Preference Change' (n 866) 141.

2098 ibid 142.

2099 cf McCann, Patel and Ruiz (n 19).

2100 Schwartz, 'The Data Privacy Law of Brexit: Theories of Preference Change' (n 866) 145.

2101 ibid.

Besides the Brussels Effect, *Paul M. Schwartz* investigated further reasons the GDPR might have been applied in the UK and factors speaking against a future divergence from the EU data protection system. The UK might have accepted the EU's data protection law and such acceptance could be manifested in the public opinion or in the preferences of the legal system.[2102] A second reason might be that the UK's data protection preferences were always aligned with the EU. The UK has influenced the European data protection system along with the other member states. Hence, the GDPR also reflects "values" and "decades of input from the UK".[2103] A third reason might be that the UK changed its values to align with those of the EU through a process of "persuasion or acculturation".[2104] A fourth reason could be the easy accessibility of a legal transplant of the GDPR.[2105]

The UK's decision to preserve the GDPR can be identified as "passive"[2106] and a decision not to reject EU data protection law[2107]. It was a decision to maintain stability and avoid the high costs associated with changing the data protection law.[2108] *Tal Zarsky* identifies a "Hotel California" Effect: Even though the UK wants to "check out" of the GDPR[2109], it is finding that it "can never leave" because a high bureaucracy effort would be involved.[2110]

V EU Commission

In its adequacy decision, the EU Commission widely ignored the intentions of the UK to diverge from EU law.[2111] It was pointed out by *Douwe Korff* that this ap-

---

2102 Schwartz, 'The Data Privacy Law of Brexit: Theories of Preference Change' (n 866) 115 et seq. referring to *Robert Cooter's* theory, focused on individual preferences (see Robert Cooter, Models of Morality in Law and Economics: Self-Control and Self-Improvement for the "Bad Man" of Holmes, 78 B.U. L. Rev. 903 [1998]).
2103 ibid 147.
2104 ibid 117.
2105 ibid 118 et seq. referring to Alan Watson, Legal Transplants 94 (2d ed. 1993).
2106 Tal Zarsky, 'The Hotel California Effect: The Future of E.U. Data Protection Influence in the U.K. (Reviewing Paul M. Schwartz, The Data Privacy Law of Brexit: Theories of Preference Change, 22(2) Theoretical Inquires in Law 111 (2021))' (*Jotwell*, 23 November 2021) <https://cyber.jotwell.com>.
2107 Schwartz, 'The Data Privacy Law of Brexit: Theories of Preference Change' (n 866) 137.
2108 ibid 137.
2109 Such intentions were made clear by the UK Government (I.-III.).
2110 Zarsky (n 2106).
2111 See UK Adequacy Decision (n 14) recitals 3, 7, 20, 23, 34, 39 and 41.

proach was contrary to the one with the EU Commission's adequacy decision on Israel in 2011[2112], in which adequacy was declared largely based on the testimony that it could be expected that existing deficiencies would be restored soon.[2113]

After the DCMS announcement in August 2021, it was reported that an EU official said that Brussels was "monitoring the UK's decision very closely," adding that "in case of justified urgency that threatened its citizens, it would immediately revoke its data-sharing arrangement with the UK."[2114] However, the EU Commission has never revoked any adequacy decision issued so far."[2115] Some state that unless the UK's new data protection regime would take "radical" steps contrary to the EU decision, it is very unlikely that the EU Commission will "act even on very significant divergence".[2116] Yet, exceptionally, any developments in the UK-US data transfer relationship will be essential from an EU perspective. Since *Facebook Ireland and Schrems*, onward transfer of personal data to the US appears to be a delicate topic for the EU. The EU Commission would have to take steps if the US would become an "adequate" third country under the UK GDPR "to avoid the UK becoming blatantly a personal data laundering haven".[2117]

VI Conclusion to A

Post-Brexit, the UK tries to set out a new global data strategy, opening up data flows to several key trading partners through adequacy partnerships. However, it becomes clear that, contrary to what the government is presenting to the outside and its citizens ("We have taken back control of laws and our destiny"), the UK's options are limited. This is mainly due to a strong "Brussels Effect" in privacy and data protection. The UK's economy, especially the IT sector and the digital service industry, is primarily dependent on data transfer from the EU. If the UK deviates too far from providing a system of data protection law for data trans-

---

2112 Commission Decision 2011/61/EU pursuant to Directive 95/46/EC of the European Parliament and of the Council on the adequate protection of personal data by the State of Israel with regard to automated processing of personal data [2011] OJ L 27/39.
2113 Korff, 'European Commission Responds to Parliament's Resolution on UK Adequacy' (n 997).
2114 Alexander Mühlauer, 'Goodbye, verhasste Cookie-Banner' *Süddeutsche Zeitung* (London, 26 August 2021) <https://www.sueddeutsche.de/wirtschaft/brexit-dsgvo-1.5393086>.
2115 Korff, 'European Commission Responds to Parliament's Resolution on UK Adequacy' (n 997).
2116 ibid.
2117 ibid.

fers from the EU, the EU Commission or the CJEU will likely find the UK system to no longer be "adequate".[2118] The disruption of data flows from the EU to the UK would have a massive impact on the UK's economy. Consequently, the UK Government should retain close regulatory alignment to ensure "adequacy". Otherwise, many UK companies will be faced with high compliance costs[2119].

Should the level of protection for personal data in the UK decrease in the context of onward transfers due to new adequacy decisions with a lower standard of "adequacy", the data transfers to the UK could only be possible under the strict conditions of Article 46 of the GDPR.[2120] The DCMS's planned global data strategy indicates such a potential decrease. However, the "Brussels Effect" is so strong that the UK's acceptance of the loss of its adequacy status is not very likely. The UK is aware of it. The future will show whether the UK "succeeds" in its planned global data strategy and, at the same time, keeping its adequacy decision. If the UK's announced global data strategy would be implemented, it would create fundamental challenges for the UK's adequacy status.[2121] Such developments could indicate that the UK did not leave to "cave to the economic pressures of commercial entities".[2122]

B Global Data Strategy in the EU

The following focuses on the current global data strategy in the EU and any (necessary) developments in this field. The EU has been marketing the GDPR as the "gold standard" in terms of data protection regimes (under I.). The GDPR not only served as a model regime ("export of the GDPR") or initiated an implementation or modernisation of data protection law. It also has a global reach due to the "Brussels Effect", which has been strengthened by the GDPR's data transfer system and marketplace principle. Despite its current worldwide standing, the GDPR has faced many criticisms. Especially, the process of obtaining an adequacy decision by the EU Commission has been criticised (under II.). Finally, the relationship between the CJEU and the EU Commission, in the context of global data transfer and adequacy will be looked at (under III.).

2118 Schwartz, 'The Data Privacy Law of Brexit: Theories of Preference Change' (n 866) 143.
2119 cf McCann, Patel and Ruiz (n 19).
2120 cf Adrian Fischer, 'UK: Großbritannien bald kein sicheres Drittland i.S.d. Art. 45 DS-GVO mehr?' [2021] ZD-Aktuell 05346; Chapter 4, A. and B.
2121 Zarsky (n 2106) calling such challenges 'possibly workable'.
2122 ibid.

I The GDPR as "Gold Standard"

The EU praises[2123] its data protection regime as the "gold standard" of data protection regimes.[2124] In its two-year anniversary review of the GDPR, the EU Commission called the GDPR an "overall success".[2125] According to the EU Commission, "citizens are more empowered and aware of their rights".[2126] Also, all businesses in the internal market are bound by a harmonised framework and the same rules. The GDPR would constitute "an essential and flexible tool to ensure the development of new technologies in accordance with fundamental rights."[2127]

The EU has essentially influenced how the world thinks about data protection.[2128] *Jack L. Goldsmith* and *Tim Wu* called the EU the "effective sovereign of global privacy law".[2129] The EU has recognised the importance of cross-border transfer and has promoted international standards for personal data protection.[2130] It sought to shape the global standard on data privacy ("if we do not shape standards now, others do"), stating that alternative global standards may be less desirable in requiring data localisation or leveraging data protection for censorship and state surveillance.[2131] Also, European citizens view privacy as (very) important.[2132] Political scandals, such as the 2013 *Edward Snowden* revelation regarding unauthorised NSA surveillance programs, or in 2018, the *Cam-*

2123 *Thomas Hoeren* holds a different view and calls the GDPR the 'greatest catastrophe of the 21st century', see in Stefan Krempl, 'Rechtsexperte: Datenschutz-Grundverordnung als "größte Katastrophe des 21. Jahrhunderts"' (*heise online*, 27 April 2016).
2124 Jan Philipp Albrecht, 'How the GDPR Will Change the World' 2 EDPL 287, 288.
2125 EU Commission, 'Two Years of the GDPR: Questions and Answers' (2020) Press Release of 24 June 2020 <https://ec.europa.eu/commission/presscorner/detail/en/qanda_20_1166>.
2126 ibid.
2127 ibid.
2128 Paul M Schwartz, 'Global Data Privacy: The EU Way' (2019) 94 N.Y.U. L. Rev. 771, 773.
2129 Goldsmith and Wu (n 2082) 176.
2130 EU Commission, 'A Comprehensive Approach on Personal Data Protection in the European Union' (2010) Communication to the European Parliament, the Council, the Economic and Social Committee and the Committee on the Region (COM) 2010 609 final 19.
2131 Bradford, *The Brussels Effect: How the European Union Rules the World* (n 147) 137 referring to an interview with *Bruno Gencarelli*, Head of the International Data Flosw and Protection Unit, European Commission, Directorate General Justice and Consumers, in Brussels, Belgium, 17 July 2018.
2132 EU Commission, 'Flash Barometer 443 (EPrivacy)' (2016) Report <https://europa.eu/eurobarometer/surveys/detail/2124>.

bridge Analytica scandal[2133], enhanced the EU's standing in the privacy discourse and strengthened its positions to advocate stronger data protection laws.[2134] Some emphasise that the EU should never compromise fundamental standards in a global world. *Graham Greenleaf* states that "[r]espect for [the US and China's] domestic prerogatives should not be confused with any need to reduce fundamental aspects of global data privacy standards."[2135] He even goes so far as saying that "[t]here are no alternative global standards worth considering".[2136]

1 The GDPR's Global Export and Reach

For many countries, the GDPR served as a model regime or initiated an implementation or modernisation of data protection law.[2137] The "export" of the GDPR seemed to be successful over the years.[2138] Various countries have essentially "copied" the GDPR, while others have made use of only specific components of the GDPR.[2139]

The US, besides California[2140] and more recently Virginia[2141], and Colorado[2142], with a sector-specific regulation approach[2143], has been an exception

---

2133 *Cambridge Analytica*, a British consulting firm, acquired private data obtained from Facebook users. Such unauthorised data were used in political campaigns.

2134 Bradford, *The Brussels Effect: How the European Union Rules the World* (n 147) 141.

2135 Graham Greenleaf, 'The Influence of European Data Privacy Standards Outside Europe: Implications for Globalisation of Convention 108' (2012) 2 IDPL 68.

2136 ibid.

2137 Graham Greenleaf, 'Global Data Privacy Laws 2019: 132 National Laws & Many Bills' (2019) 157 PL&B Reports 14, 14.

2138 cf Greenleaf (n 2135) who identified the influence of 'European standards' (especially Convention 108) in 33 laws outside Europe in 2012.

2139 cf Hennemann, Wettbewerb der Datenschutzrechtsordnungen? – Zur Rezeption der Datenschutz-Grundverordnung –' (n 209) 871.

2140 California Consumer Privacy Act of 2018 (CCPA), Assembly Bill No 375; see for a more detailed comparison of the CCPA and the GDPR in Schwartz, 'Global Data Privacy: The EU Way' (n 2128).

2141 The Virginia Consumer Data Protection Act came into law on 2 March 2021, see for an overview Sarah Rippy, 'Virginia passes the Consumer Data Protection Act' (*IAPP*, 3 March 2021) <https://iapp.org/news/a/virginia-passes-the-consumer-data-protection-act/>.

2142 The state of Colorado officially enacted the Colorado Privacy Act on 8 July 2021, see for an overview Sarah Rippy, 'Colorado Privacy Act becomes law' (*IAPP*, 8 July 2021) < https://iapp.org/news/a/colorado-privacy-act-becomes-law/>.

2143 The US takes a sectoral approach to data protection: there is no overarching data protection law, but (only) sectoral protection provisions for certain constellations in which the individual is considered particularly in need of protection (for example in the health sector, the Insurance Portability and Accountability Act 1996).

with resisting the EU's lead in privacy protection.[2144] China has emulated some elements of the EU's data protection laws, at least on paper, since it recently enacted its Personal Information Protection Law (PIPL).[2145] It incorporates several GDPR concepts, such as purpose limitation (Article 6 PIPL) and the individual's consent as a legal basis for data processing (Article 13(1) PIPL). By creating regulations similar to those in the EU, Chinese technology exporters, can better adapt to its regulations. However, China's practice of deploying data as a tool of social control[2146] and state surveillance practice shows that any "Brussels Effect" "on the paper" does not necessarily mean that EU laws and principles are effectively employed in practice.[2147] Also, PIPL was mainly introduced due to the state's concern about uncontrolled mass data collection by private companies, which takes place beyond state control.[2148]

India is one of the jurisdictions that are in the process of adopting a GDPR "inspired" law.[2149] Yet, this draft bill significantly departs from the GDPR insofar as it contains a generalised data localisation requirement, under which data controllers must ensure the storage of at least one serving copy of critical personal data in India.[2150] Japan adapted its data protection law to the GDPR in 2017 in

---

2144 Bradford, *The Brussels Effect: How the European Union Rules the World* (n 147) 154.

2145 An English translation can be found at the following link <http://www.lawinfochina.com/display.aspx?id=36358&lib=law&SearchKeyword=&SearchCKeyword=%B8%F6%C8%CB%D0%C5%CF%A2%B1%A3%BB%A4%B7%A8> accessed 9 June 2022.

2146 China has implemented a social credit system that rated citizens for their trustworthiness on issues such as paying taxes or committing a crime. An untrustworthy rating has significant negative consequences for the individual, cf Lily Kuo, 'China Bans 23 m From Buying Travel Tickets as Part of "Social Credit" System' *The Guardian* (1 March 2019) <https://www.theguardian.com/world/2019/mar/01/china-bans-23m-discredited-citizens-from-buying-travel-tickets-social-credit-system>; reports have surfaced that China uses a large-scale deployment of the facial recognition technique for law enforcement purposes, cf Paul Mozur, 'Inside China's Dystopian Dreams: A.I., Shame and Lots of Cameras' *The New York Times* (15 October 2018) <https://www.nytimes.com/2018/07/08/business/china-surveillance-technology.html>.

2147 Bradford, *The Brussels Effect: How the European Union Rules the World* (n 147) 154.

2148 Dennis-Kenji Kipker, 'Das neue chinesische Datenschutzgesetz PIPL ist da!' (*beck.de*, 22 August 2021) <https://community.beck.de/2021/08/22/das-neue-chinesische-datenschutzgesetz-pipl-ist-da>.

2149 Vijay Govindarajan, Anup Srivastava and Luminita Enache, 'How India Plans to Protect Consumer Data' *HBR* (18 December 2019) <https://hbr.org/2019/12/how-india-plans-to-protect-consumer-data>.

2150 Ministry of Law and Justice, 'The Personal Data Protection Bill 2019', available at the following link <https://prsindia.org/billtrack/the-personal-data-protection-bill-2019> accessed 9 June 2022; cf Naomi Shiffman and Jochai Ben-Avi, 'Data Localization: Bad for Users, Business, and Security' (*Mozilla*, 22 June 2018) <https://blog.mozilla.org/netpolicy/2018/06/22/data-localization-india/>.

order to obtain an adequacy decision.[2151] Also, many Latin American countries, such as Columbia, Costa Rica, Mexico, Peru, and Brazil,[2152] have transplanted concepts inspired by the EU data protection regime.[2153] The Ibero-American Data Protection Network (RIDP) aims to establish common principles for protecting personal data.[2154] On 1 July 2021, the South African Protection of Personal Information Act 2013 (POPIA) [2155], primarily based on the Directive 95/46 but with stricter provisions, entered into force.[2156] The Nigeria Data Protection Regulation 2019 is based on the GDPR.[2157]

The EU is said to have power in the "market for regulatory ideas" (regulatory market power)[2158].[2159] The EU's "market power" on the "market of regulatory ideas" – also in terms of data protection regulation[2160] – can be attributed above all to the existing economic relevance of the internal market, in which companies, in particular, want to participate.

[2151] cf Act on the Protection of Personal Data (APPI) (Act No 57 of 2003), available at the following link <https://www.cas.go.jp/jp/seisaku/hourei/data/APPI.pdf> acccessed 20 December 2021; Schwartz, 'Global Data Privacy: The EU Way' (n 2128) 786 et seqq. provides a summary of the process of the adoption of the adequacy decision on Japan. For more detail see Wang (n 1528).

[2152] The Brazilian Data Protection Law (LGPD) was adopted in 2018 in strong alignment with the GDPR.

[2153] Ana Brian Nougrères, 'Data Protection and Enforcement in Latin America and in Uruguay' in David Wright and Paul de Hert (eds), *Enforcing Privacy: Regulatory, Legal and Technological Approaches* (Springer 2016) 153.

[2154] More information on the RIDP available at the following link <https://www.redipd.org/en> accessed 20 December 2020.

[2155] Available at the following link <https://www.gov.za/sites/default/files/gcis_document/201409/3706726-11act4of2013protectionofpersonalinforcorrect.pdf> accessed 20 December 2020.

[2156] See for more information on data protection regimes in Africa in Hennemann, Boshe and von Meding (n 445).

[2157] Nigerian Data Protection Regulation 2019, available at the following link <https://ndpr.nitda.gov.ng/Content/Doc/NigeriaDataProtectionRegulation.pdf> accessed 9 June 2022.

[2158] See for a general assessment of the competition of legal systems on the market of regulatory ideas in Lothar Michael, 'Wettbewerb von Rechtsordnungen' (2009) 124 DVBl 1062; Eva-Maria Kieninger, 'Competition between Legal Systems' in Jürgen Basedow, Klaus J Hopt and Reinhard Zimmermann (eds), *The Max Planck Encyclopedia of European Private Law* (Oxford University Press 2012); Jens Kersten, '§ 233 Wettbewerb der Rechtsordnungen?' in Josef Isensee and Paul Kirchhof (eds), *Handbuch des Staatsrechts*, vol 11 (3rd edn, 2013); Hennemann, Wettbewerb der Datenschutzrechtsordnungen? – Zur Rezeption der Datenschutz-Grundverordnung –' (n 209) 867 et seqq.

[2159] Bradford, 'The Brussels Effect' (n 2081) 22 et seqq.; Hennemann, Wettbewerb der Datenschutzrechtsordnungen? – Zur Rezeption der Datenschutz-Grundverordnung –' (n 209) 15.

[2160] ibid.

2 Brussels Effect

The regulatory instruments "marketplace principle" (Article 3 GDPR) and Chapter V of the GDPR contribute to the extraterritorial influence of the GDPR.[2161] *Orla Lynskey* uses the term "supremacy by default" in this context.[2162] The "Brussels Effect" caused by the EU Commission's instrument of adequacy decisions was already evaluated above in the context of the UK.[2163] Due to the marketplace principle[2164], the GDPR covers almost every offer of goods via the internet and every digital service. This leads to global obligations and commitments under EU data protection standards.[2165] The GDPR's extraterritoriality makes it hard for businesses to circumvent the GDPR.[2166] This *de facto* Brussels Effect[2167] occurs where global companies conduct business under unilateral EU rules.[2168] Many (US) companies have already harmonised practices under the GDPR (such as *Google*[2169] or *Facebook*[2170]) since the EU is an important market for many data-driven businesses.[2171] The EU represents the third-largest economy in the world[2172] and the second-largest consumer market in the world[2173]. Because of

---

2161 More detail in ibid.

2162 Lynskey (n 35) 43. The author uses the term 'supremacy by design' in the context of Article 3(2) GDPR.

2163 A.IV.

2164 Chapter 2, A.IV.1.c.bb.

2165 Hennemann Wettbewerb der Datenschutzrechtsordnungen? – Zur Rezeption der Datenschutz-Grundverordnung –' (n 209) 881.

2166 Bradford, *The Brussels Effect: How the European Union Rules the World* (n 147) 142.

2167 In detail ibid 142 et seqq. *Moritz Hennemann* also identifies this phenomenon as the GDPR's legislative 'push effect' (n 415) 373.

2168 Schwartz, 'The Data Privacy Law of Brexit: Theories of Preference Change' (n 866) 140.

2169 *Google* has a search market share over 90% in most EU member states, exceeding its market share in the US, cf Robinson Meyer, 'Europeans Use Google Way, Way More Than Americans Do' *The Atlantic* (15 April 2015) <https://www.theatlantic.com/technology/archive/2015/04/europeans-use-google-way-way-more-than-americans-do/390612/>.

2170 *Facebook* has 250 million users in Europe, contributing 25% of Facebook's global revenue, Shona Ghosh, 'Facebook in Europe Is about to Get Massively Disrupted by New Laws Meant to Bring It to Heel' *Business Insider* (11 April 2018) <https://www.businessinsider.com/gdpr-privacy-law-eu-massive-timely-facebook-2018-4>.

2171 cf Schwartz, 'The Data Privacy Law of Brexit: Theories of Preference Change' (n 866) 147.

2172 Eurostat, 'The 2017 Results of the International Comparison Program: China, US and EU Are the Largest Economies in the World' (2020) News Release of 19 May 2020 <https://ec.europa.eu/eurostat/documents/portlet_file_entry/2995521/2-19052020-BP-EN.pdf/bb14f7f9-fc26-8aa1-60d4-7c2b509dda8eThe 2017 results of the International Comparison Program China, US and EU are the largest economies in the world>.

2173 The World Bank, 'Households and NPISHs Final Consumption Expenditure (Current US$)' (2020) <https://data.worldbank.org/indicator/NE.CON.PRVT.CD?year_high_desc=true>.

this "enormous market power",[2174] it would be "out of the question" for global companies to "pull out of the European market altogether".[2175] Consequently, most of the prominent (digital) companies commonly "obey the European rules".[2176] Many global companies even completely adhere to EU privacy standards rather than customise for different markets due to technical non-divisibility of products or services and compliance costs (for example, *Facebook*[2177], *Google*, *Netflix*[2178]).[2179] Different data protection and privacy rules mean additional costs for businesses. When opting for a single global policy, companies typically choose the GDPR as the most stringent regulation to retain the ability to conduct business everywhere.[2180] Also, companies follow the GDPR worldwide for "reputational and brand-related" reasons.[2181]

3 Risk of Foreclosure of the "Market of Regulatory Ideas"

However, the global reach of the GDPR faced lots of criticism. Businesses criticised that the proliferation of more restrictive EU regulations is costly and hinders innovation.[2182] Notably, the costs of complying with EU regulations are often even prohibitively high for small and medium-sized enterprises since they do not have the capacity to develop their products and services to meet EU standards. In contrast, large organisations, such as *Facebook* or *Google*, have the resources to meet the high data protection standards.[2183] The GDPR does not provide any notable exceptions for smaller companies and non-profit

---

2174 Goldsmith and Wu (n 2082) 176.

2175 ibid 175.

2176 In 2006, this already reflected a common practice for large companies, cf ibid 176.

2177 Natasha Lomas, 'Facebook Urged to Make GDPR Its "Baseline Standard" Globally' (*Tech-Crunch*, 9 April 2018) <https://techcrunch.com/2018/04/09/facebook-urged-to-make-gdpr-its-baseline-standard-globally/?guccounter=1&guce_referrer=aHR0cHM6Ly93d3-cuZ29vZ2xlLmNvbS88&guce_referrer_sig=AQAAAKidzFclSICBMnwHYOqS82N-ZhpELnUb4bY-jICHCAdHpuR0vh_I1KZzmSZTYFoZax0sKl3HxzOWnWxqWIRUZgsY3FlhAOFBDns7v3ty6tSvuQ-vuwjiztDnyqqAScooKgB0unVd9s6PFU2yLRzxH8 V8pZgumJ_2S6Ig15zBYdKBbj>.

2178 For example, *Netflix* does not differentiate between EU and US customers with regard to the right of access (within the meaning of Art. 15 of the GDPR) and other transparency requirements, cf Heinrich-Böll-Stiftung, 'Privacy in the EU and US: Consumer Experiences across Three Global Platforms' (2019) 7.

2179 Bradford, *The Brussels Effect: How the European Union Rules the World* (n 147) 142 et seq.

2180 ibid 143.

2181 ibid 144.

2182 Gregory Shaffer, 'Globalization and Social Protection: The Impact of EU and International Rules in the Ratcheting Up of U.S. Privacy Standards' (2000) 25 Yale J. Int'l L. 75.

2183 Bradford, *The Brussels Effect: How the European Union Rules the World* (n 147) 238.

organisations.[2184] Also, many governments and companies abroad find that the EU data protection rules are disguised protectionism.[2185] Furthermore, many criticise the Brussels effect as "EU's regulatory imperialism".[2186] According to *Kai von Lewinski*, the extraterritoriality of the GDPR's scope of application, admittedly overall, shows an "imperial tendency" of European data protection law.[2187] *Niko Härting* speaks of a "claim to global validity".[2188] Article 3(2) GDPR may well be perceived as intrusive outside of the EU and have adverse effects on the EU's external relations.[2189]

In his opinion in *Facebook Ireland and Schrems*, Advocate General *Saugmandsgaard Øe* emphasised that: "the law of the third State of destination may reflect its own scale of values according to which the respective weight of the various interests involved may diverge from that attributed to them in the EU legal order. [...] The 'essential equivalence' test should [...] be applied in such a way as to preserve a certain flexibility in order to take the various legal and cultural traditions into account."[2190] In line with this, *Moritz Hennemann* points out that a regulatory approach often expresses specific (legal) cultural experiences.[2191] (Legal) traditions would shape the specific application or form the basis for an acceptance of certain norms. Especially, the cultural differences between the individual-oriented West and the more community-oriented cultures in Asia and Africa are immense.[2192] *Kai von Lewinski* rightly points out that the European data protection model cannot be established here without exposing one-

---

2184 Ernst, 'Art. 2 DS-GVO' (n 157) paras 14 et seq. and 19.

2185 cf William Alan Reinsch, 'Must Third Countries Choose Between EU or U.S. Digital Trade Protection Preferences?' (*CSIS, The Future of Digital Trade Policy and the Role of the U.S. and UK*, 11 July 2018) <https://www.csis.org/blogs/future-digital-trade-policy-and-role-us-and-uk/must-third-countries-choose-between-eu-or-us>; Philip Stephens, 'Europe Rewrites the Rules for Silicon Valley' *Financial Times* (3 November 2016); Yet, Anu Bradford presented several examples that disprove the EU as a "biased regulator" targeting US companies to afford protectionism for EU companies, cf Bradford, *The Brussels Effect: How the European Union Rules the World* (n 147) 242 et seqq.

2186 See for an overview Bradford, *The Brussels Effect: How the European Union Rules the World* (n 147) 247 et seqq.

2187 von Lewinski, 'Art. 3 DSGVO' (n 219) para 24.

2188 Niko Härting, 'Starke Behörden, schwaches Recht – der neue EU-Datenschutzentwurf' [2012] Der Betriebsberater 459.

2189 von Lewinski, 'Art. 3 DSGVO' (n 219) para 24.

2190 Opinion of Advocate General *Saugmandsgaard Øe* in *Facebook Ireland and Schrems* (n 1064) para 249.

2191 Moritz Hennemann, 'Exportbeschränkungen für den Datenschutz?' *Frankfurter Allgemeine Tageszeitung Einspruch*, 1 October 2020.

2192 von Lewinski, 'Einführung' (n 1896) para 15.

self to the accusation or appearance of "cultural imperialism".[2193] Beyond that, the "import" of law into another legal system likely has a different "effect" than in the legal system of origin.[2194] For example, if there is a different understanding of autonomy, individual protection and the common good, the "imported" law might potentially not unfold in an intended way and instead constitute a "foreign body" in the domestic legal construct.[2195] The balance between different data protection and privacy cultures and orders that is affected due to Article 3 GDPR could be a global problem.[2196] *Moritz Hennemann* emphasises that Article 45 of the GDPR constitutes a "mandate" for comparing different data protection and privacy laws or data protection concepts[2197].[2198] Narrowing the regulatory concept of the GDPR alone will eventually lead to a foreclosure effect on the "market for regulatory ideas"[2199].[2200] At this point, Chapter V of the GDPR has a "network effect" on the legal framework favoured by third countries.[2201] Whereas competition between jurisdictions generates diversity and innovation[2202], complete or extensive harmonisation leads to a loss of innovation.[2203] "Alternative regulatory approaches – potentially even more innovative and appropriate – are to be evaluated carefully by means of a functional and/or contextual comparative approach".[2204]

2193 von Lewinski, 'Einführung' (n 1896) para 15.

2194 Kersten (n 2158) para 6.

2195 ibid.

2196 von Lewinski, 'Art. 3 DSGVO' (n 219) para 24.

2197 As constituted by von Lewinski *Die Matrix des Datenschutzes – Besichtigung und Ordnung eines Begriffsfeldes* (n 115) 64 et seqq.

2198 Hennemann, Wettbewerb der Datenschutzrechtsordnungen? – Zur Rezeption der Datenschutz-Grundverordnung –' (n 209) 890.

2199 See in general on the role of comparative law in the context of competition between legal systems: Gralf-Peter Calliess, 'Die Rolle der Rechtsvergleichung im Kontext des Wettbewerbs der Rechtsordnungen' in Reinhard Zimmermann (ed), *Zukunftsperspektiven der Rechtsvergleichung* (Mohr Siebeck 2016).

2200 Hennemann, Wettbewerb der Datenschutzrechtsordnungen? – Zur Rezeption der Datenschutz-Grundverordnung –' (n 209) 891. The author also outlines three central (substantive) course settings of a data protection law comparison in the context of Article 45 GDPR (893).

2201 Lynskey (n 35) 43.

2202 Calliess (n 2199) 179.

2203 Hennemann, Wettbewerb der Datenschutzrechtsordnungen? – Zur Rezeption der Datenschutz-Grundverordnung –' (n 209) 895 with further references.

2204 ibid.

II Criticism Concerning the EU's Adequacy Process

The EU views adequacy decisions as a "key pillar of maintaining" the "gold standard".[2205] Yet, overall, the process has been facing much criticism.

1 Strict Standard and No Flexibility in Judicial Review over "Adequacy"

The CJEU applies a strict standard in exercising judicial review over the "adequacy" of third countries' data protection regimes. In *Schrems*, the CJEU first introduced the definition of "adequate" as "essentially equivalent".[2206] According to *Paul M. Schwartz*, the CJEU even "constitutionalise" the "adequacy" standard by grounding its opinion in Articles 7 and 8 of the Charter.[2207] The CJEU's approach was criticised.[2208] According to *Christian Schröder*, the term "adequacy" would suggest that the level of protection in the third country does not have to be identical to the European level of data protection, nor does it have to be equivalent.[2209] The EU Commission as a political authority would require some discretion in assessing the adequacy of the level of protection in third countries, which would be in line with economic policy and entrepreneurial freedoms.[2210] *Christian Schröder* argued that the CJEU's interpretation hinders the EU Commission in finding flexible and pragmatically solutions in the case of fundamentally different approaches about the protection of personal data in third countries, which would neither undermine the protection rights of the data subjects nor require third countries to almost wholly approximate their legal system to European protection.[2211] Before *Schrems*, it was partly argued that the level of protection was adequate if the data processing provided a level of protection that "substantially complies with the core set of protection principles of the Directive".[2212] *Christian Schröder* views that this would have allowed for a certain undercutting of the level of protection as a whole or concerning individual protection instruments, but would have better taken into account the fact that the EU is dependent on

---

2205 Vincent Manancourt, 'Why Brussels Went Easy on Britain in Its Data Deal' *Politico* (30 June 2021) <https://www.politico.eu/article/why-brussels-went-easy-on-britain-in-data-adequacy-deal/>.

2206 *Schrems* (n 71) para 60.

2207 Schwartz, 'Global Data Privacy: The EU Way' (n 2128) 881.

2208 Kühling and Heberlein (n 577) 9; Schröder, 'Art. 45 DSGVO' (n 455) paras 11 et seqq. with further references.

2209 Schröder, 'Art. 45 DSGVO' (n 455) para 11.

2210 ibid.

2211 ibid.

2212 cf Bastian Baumann, *Datenschutzkonflikte zwischen der EU und den USA* (2016) 99.

trade with third countries and that these third countries rarely want to ensure comprehensively equivalent protection of personal data or adapt their legal system accordingly.[2213] Now, the CJEU's definition of "adequacy" is further given effect in recital 104 GDPR.

Advocate General *Saugmandsgaard Øe* also criticised the lack of pragmatism and flexibility. He referred to the former Data Protection Supervisor *Peter Hustinx*, who stated that the provisions in Article 45 et seqq. GDPR "are based on a reasonable degree of pragmatism in order to allow interaction with other parts of the world."[2214] In his analysis, the Advocate General sought to find a balance between the "reasonable degree of pragmatism", on the one hand, on the other hand, the "need to assert the fundamental values recognised in the legal orders of the Union and its Member States".[2215] In this context, Advocate General *Saugmandsgaard Øe* promoted that since the EU provides a very "high standard by comparison with the level of protection in force in the rest of the word", "[t]he 'essential equivalence' test should [...] be applied in such a way as to preserve a certain flexibility so as to take the various legal and cultural traditions into account. That test implies, however, if it is not to be deprived of its substance, that certain minimum safeguards and general requirements for the protection of fundamental rights that follow from the Charter and the ECHR have an equivalent in the legal order of the third country of destination."[2216] Consequently, the recipient third country's legislation could establish a scale of values according to which the respective weight of the various interests may diverge from the weight recognised by the EU legislation.[2217] Although this open and more liberal approach is welcomed in the relevant literature,[2218] the Court stuck to its *Schrems* ruling without further remarks. However, the *Privacy Shield* was invalidated because the essence of Article 7 and Article 47 CFR was not respected. Respect to the essence of fundamental rights is the absolute minimum that must be ensured. In its *Schrems* and *Facebook Ireland and Schrems* judgements, CJEU merely

---

2213 Schröder, 'Art. 45 DSGVO' (n 455) para 11.

2214 Peter Hustinx, 'EU Data Protection Law: The Review of Directive 95/46/EC and the Proposed General Data Protection Regulation' (Juli 2013) S. 43 <https://edps.europa.eu/sites/edp/files/publication/14-09-15_article_eui_en.pdf>.

2215 Opinion of Advocate General *Saugmandsgaard Øe* in *Facebook Ireland and Schrems* (n 1064) para 7.

2216 ibid para 249.

2217 ibid.

2218 Hennemann, Wettbewerb der Datenschutzrechtsordnungen? – Zur Rezeption der Datenschutz-Grundverordnung –' (n 209) 889; Schröder, 'Art. 45 DS-GVO' (n 455) para 11.

highlighted several aspects[2219], such as "effective independent data protection supervision"[2220], "legal remedies in order to have access to personal data relating to [the data subject], or to obtain the rectification or erasure of such data"[2221], "derogations and limitations in relation to the protection of personal data to apply only in so far as is strictly necessary"[2222].[2223] Consequently, the *Schrems* and *Facebook Ireland and Schrems* judgments cannot be interpreted as fully rejecting the Advocate General's approach.[2224] From a fundamental rights perspective, the CJEU's approach is consistent because it effectively prevents the EU's level of data protection from being circumvented by a transfer to a third country.[2225]

The CJEU's ruling points out a dilemma: Particularly with the US, a reasonable compromise between the conflicting must be found. Some propose that the successor to the *Privacy Shield* should exclude the activities of US intelligence agencies.[2226] However, the planned *Trans-Atlantic Data Privacy Framework* appears to continue to include the activites of US intelligence agencies. According to a published factsheet, the following will be put in place: a new set of rules and binding safeguards to limit access to data by US intelligence authorities to what is necessary and proportionate to protect national security, procedures to ensure effective oversight of new privacy and civil liberties standards, a new two-tier redress system to investigate and resolve complaints of EU citizens on access of data by US Intelligence authorities, which includes a Data Protection Review Court, strong obligations for companies processing data transferred from the EU, which will continue to include the requirement to self-certify their adherence to the principles through the US Department of Commerce, as well as specific monitoring and review mechanisms.[2227] With the implementation of a redress system for EU citizens, one of the main issue the CJEU had with the

---

2219 Wagner (n 4) 323; Hennemann, Wettbewerb der Datenschutzrechtsordnungen? – Zur Rezeption der Datenschutz-Grundverordnung –' (n 209) 889.

2220 *Schrems* (n 71) para 81 ("effective detection and supervision mechanism"); *Facebook Ireland and Schrems* (n 64) para 188.

2221 *Schrems* (n 71) para 95; *Facebook Ireland and Schrems* (n 64) para 187.

2222 ibid para 92.

2223 Hennemann, Wettbewerb der Datenschutzrechtsordnungen? – Zur Rezeption der Datenschutz-Grundverordnung –' (n 209) 889.

2224 cf Wagner (n 4) 323.

2225 GDPR, art 44, second sentence.

2226 Mathias Lejeune, 'Datentransfer personenbezogener Daten in die USA vor dem aus?! – Kritische Anmerkungen zur EuGH Entscheidung C-311/18 vom 16.7.2020' [2020] CR 522, 528.

2227 EU Commission, Factsheet Trans-Atlantic Data Privacy Framework (March 2022), <https://ec.europa.eu/commission/presscorner/detail/en/FS_22_2100>.

US system could be resolved. However, it remains to be seen how the new framework addresses the US's provisions' lack of proportionality in terms of access to personal data from the EU by intelligence agencies.[2228]

If the UK adequacy decision is declared invalid, the EU might disrupt data flow to one of the leading countries in artificial intelligence, leading to the EU falling further behind in the digital economy. Nevertheless, beyond that, suggesting that the UK is not adequate would "set the bar for adequacy impossibly high" since the UK has already shown its adherence to the GDPR as a former member state, and a national replication of the GDPR remains in place *post*-Brexit ("UK GDPR").[2229]

2 Differential Treatment of Member States and Third Countries in respect to National Security Legislation and Practices

Under the Article 4(2) TEU national security is the sole responsibility of each member state; the CJEU has no competence to review electronic surveillance conducted by a member state in the field of national security. National security activities also fall outside the scope of the GDPR (Article 2(2)(d) GDPR). In light of this, some commentators argue, it would be difficult to explain to third countries that activities of intelligence services within the EU are to be regarded as a necessary component of the respective national security and should not be subject to the requirements of the GDPR. However, the related activities of the intelligence services of a third country must nevertheless be measured against the requirements of the GDPR.[2230] It would be "ironic" that European citizens can invoke neither the GDPR nor the Charter rights against European intelligence services.[2231] The CJEU differentiates: Transfers to a private data importer do fall under the scope of the GDPR, even though at the time of the transfer or after that, those data are likely to be processed by the authorities of that third country for public security, defence and state security; Article 4(2) TEU and Article 2(2) (a), (b) and (d) GDPR do not apply in such cases as they only refer to activities of the state or state authorities and do not relate to fields in which individuals

---

2228 See for some initial comments: Korff and Brown, 'Some brief initial comments on the announcement of an "agreement principle" on a new Trans-Atlantic Data Privacy Framework & on the EDPB's statement on the agreement in principle' (n 1527).

2229 Eleonor Duhs, 'EU-UK Data Flows, Adequacy and Regulatory Changes from 1st January 2021' (*LinkedIn*, 28 December 2020) <https://www.linkedin.com/pulse/eu-uk-data-flows-ad equacy-regulatory-changes-from-1st-eleonor-duhs>.

2230 Lejeune (n 2226) 523.

2231 Niko Härting, 'Danke, Max Schrems!' (*beck-aktuell*, 24 August 2020) <https://rsw.beck.de/ aktuell/daily/magazin/detail/danke-max-schrems!>.

are active.[2232] *Douwe Korff*[2233] calls these scenarios "indirect access".[2234] It occurs in mandatory retaining and disclosing personal data to intelligence agencies, required of agencies in this processing, subject to EU data protection.[2235] Notably, where the CJEU has seized the competence of judicial review over the EU and its member states' national security legislation (cases of "indirect access"), in *Digital Rights Ireland and Seitlinger and Others*, *Tele2 Sverige*, *La Quadrature du Net and Others* and *Privacy International*,[2236] the CJEU's assessment was consistent with the one in *Schrems* and *Facebook Ireland and Schrems*.[2237] Consequently, the CJEU holds high standards for data retention and bulk acquisition in member states, leading to a rapprochement of the standards applicable to member states and third countries. In the cases of "direct access" to data by intelligence agencies (for example, through "hacking" in provider's system),[2238] member states must meet the ECHR and national constitutional law.[2239] The CJEU has no jurisdiction to assess whether EU member states' direct access ("direct implemented measures") meet EU law.[2240] Whether the member states comply with the ECHR can only be assessed by the ECtHR or national courts. However, most EU member states failed to comply with the EU law standards for "indirect access", as the CJEU judgements have shown. Currently, the German data retention law is subject to the CJEU's review.[2241] There has also been criticism of whether EU coun-

---

2232 *Facebook Ireland and Schrems* (n 64) paras 80–89 referring to the Irish High Court's first question; Advocate General *Saugmandsgaard Øe* came to the same conclusion as he also stated that Article 4(2) TEU only applied to State activities, but not to cases where economic operators are – by law – required to grant public authorities access to data or transfer data to public authorities (Opinion of Advocate General *Saugmandsgaard Øe* in *Facebook Ireland and Schrems* (n 1064) para 211).
2233 Korff, 'Amid the Spying by EU Member States' Intelligence Agencies, Is EU Law Silent?' (n 1159).
2234 ibid 3.
2235 ibid.
2236 Chapter 3, C.II.
2237 cf Kristina Irion, 'Schrems II and Surveillance: Third Countries' National Security Powers in the Purview of EU Law' (*European Law Blog*, 24 July 2020) <https://europeanlawblog.eu/2020/07/24/schrems-ii-and-surveillance-third-countries-national-security-powers-in-the-purview-of-eu-law/>.
2238 Korff, 'Amid the Spying by EU Member States' Intelligence Agencies, Is EU Law Silent?' (n 1159) 4.
2239 *La Quadrature du Net and Others* (n 800) para 103.
2240 The CJEU confirmed this again in ibid.
2241 The Advocate General *Sánchez-Bordona* already delivered his opinion, stating the German data retention law does not comply with EU Law since it permanently permits data retention, cf

tries live up to their own standards, including assertions of considerable incon-sistency and non-enforcement by EU members[2242].[2243] Some argue that it was "hypocritical" for the CJEU in the *Facebook Ireland and Schrems* judgment to concern itself with the standard of data protection for intelligence surveillance outside the EU when the standards that apply in the EU seem lacking in many respects.[2244] Several EU member states, including Germany, France, the Nether-lands and Sweden, are implicated in electronic surveillance.[2245] If the CJEU de-clares the adequacy decision favouring the UK invalid, the EU will also be faced with criticisms due to recent developments in France.[2246] The French Gov-ernment asked the Council of State, the highest administrative authority, to not follow the CJEU judgement in *La Quadrature du Net and Others* concerning data retention rules in France.[2247] Following the *La Quadrature du Net and Others* judgement, the French Government has argued with "constitutional identity" and that matters related to security remain national competence (Article 4(2) TEU)[2248]. However, the French Council of State has rejected the latter argument

---

Opinion of Advocate General *Campos Sánchez-Bordona* of 18 November 2021, *Space Net AG*, C-793/19 and C-794/19, EU:C:2021:939.

2242 Chapter 3, B.IV.3.

2243 See for instance, Greenleaf, 'The Influence of European Data Privacy Standards Outside Europe: Implications for Globalisation of Convention 108' (n 2135) 78.

2244 Christopher Kuner, 'Reality and Illusion in EU Data Transfer Regulation Post Schrems' (2017) 18 German Law Journal 881, 898 with further references; European Union Agency For Fun-damental Right, 'Surveillance by Intelligence Services: Fundamental Rights Safeguards and Remedies in the European Union – Volume II: Summary' <https://fra.europa.eu/sites/default/files/fra_uploads/fra-2017-surveillance-intelligence-services-vol-2-summary_en.pdf> provides an overview.

2245 cf Didier Bigo and others, 'Mass Surveillance of Personal Data by EU Member States and Its Compatibility with EU Law' (2013) No 62 <https://www.ceps.eu/wp-content/uploads/2013/11/No%2062%20Surveillance%20of%20Personal%20Data%20by%20EU%20MSs.pdf>.

2246 Manancourt, 'Why Brussels Went Easy on Britain in Its Data Deal' (n 2205).

2247 Vincent Manancourt, 'EU to US on Surveillance: Do as I Say, Not as I Do. A French-Led Push to Keep Personal Data Is Undermining the EU's Position on Surveillance' *Politico* (17 March 2021) <https://www.politico.eu/article/eu-to-us-surveillance-data-flows/>.

2248 The CJEU once again confirmed in *La Quadrature du Net* (*La Quadrature du Net and Others* (n 800) para 99) that according to the Court's settled case law, although "it is for the Member States to define their essential security interests and to adopt appropriate measures to ensure their internal and external security, the mere fact that a national measure has been taken for the purpose of protecting national security cannot render EU law inapplicable and exempt the Member States from their obligation to comply with that law" (*Commission v Austria* (n 88) paras 75 et seq.; *ZZ* (n 819) para 38; Judgement of 2 April 2020, *Commission v Poland (Tem-porary mechanism for the relocation of applicants for international protection)*, C-715/17, C-718/17 and C-719/17; EU:C:2020:257, paras 143 and 170).

and ordered the French Government to repeal the rules obliging telecommunication operators to keep communications data for a year. However, while the CJEU ruled that large-scale data retention is permissible for national security, it does not prevent and detect serious crime.[2249] For the latter, only narrow, targeted data retention "according to the categories of persons concerned or using a geographical criterion" is permissible.[2250] The French Council of State disagreed and stated that "those strictures are not technically feasible nor operationally efficient" and stated that communications data, such as localisation, is indispensable for successful investigations.[2251] Also noteworthy in this context, intelligence agencies of several member states, such as Germany[2252], Sweden[2253], France[2254] and the Netherlands[2255], cooperate with the NSA similarly to the UK.[2256] In the long run, *Douwe Korff* and *Ian Brown* plead for a "minilateral" framework for the leading advanced economy democracies (in particular, the EU and EEA states as well as the *Five Eyes* countries).[2257] The EU Commission is currently consulting on possible approaches and solutions for harmonising the data retention within the EU in light of the CJEU's case law.[2258]

2249 *La Quadrature du Net and Others* (n 800) paras 136 and 141.

2250 ibid para 147.

2251 cf Laura Kayali, 'French Administrative Court Walks Data Retention Tightrope' *Politico* (21 April 2021) <https://www.politico.eu/article/french-administrative-authority-partially-revokes-data-retention-scheme/>.

2252 Research by ZDF, 'Washington Post' and SRF shows how the BND and CIA secretly spied on states and concealed human rights violations, Elmar Theveßen, Peter F Müller and Ulrich Stoll, '"Operation 'Rubikon'"' – #Cryptoleaks: Wie BND und CIA alle täuschten' (*zdf.de*, 11 February 2020) <https://www.zdf.de/nachrichten/politik/cryptoleaks-bnd-cia-operation-rubikon-100.html>; Bigo and others (n 2245) 49 et seq.

2253 Bigo and others (n 2245) 47.

2254 ibid 49.

2255 ibid 59.

2256 Korff and Brown, 'The Inadequacy of UK Data Protection Law in General and in View of UK Surveillance Laws, Part Two: UK Surveillance' (n 1186) 10.

2257 Ian Brown and Douwe Korff, 'Study Requested by the European Parliament's LIBE Committee: Exchanges of Personal Data After the Schrems II Judgement' (Policy Department for Citizens' Rights and Constitutional Affairs) <https://www.europarl.europa.eu/RegData/etudes/STUD/2021/694678/IPOL_STU(2021)694678_EN.pdf>.

2258 See recently leaked EU Commission, 'Non-Paper on the Way Forward on Data Retention – Presentation by the Commission to the Delegations and Exchange of Views' (2021) <https://cdn.netzpolitik.org/wp-upload/2021/07/wk07294.en211.pdf.>. The EU Commission is considering three policy approaches: no EU initiative, non-binding guidance or EU legislative initiative. For the latter, the EU Commission is considering five regulatory initiatives, including the generalised retention of traffic and location data for national security purposes, the targeted data retention of traffic and location data for serious crime and serious threats to public security and

In its adequacy assessment, the CJEU analysed the access by public authorities to protect national security in third countries without first examining whether there is any deterioration in the level of data protection in the third country compared to that in the EU.[2259] Some requests that in the area of conflict between data protection and national security, the EU Commission must first examine the data protection regimes of the member states in a comparative law analysis before reviewing a third-country legal system to determine the scope of the existing comparative standard.[2260] Advocate General *Saugmandsgaard Øe* argued that due to Article 4(2) TEU, EU law, could not be the relevant comparator for provisions concerning public authorities' processing of personal data for national security purposes. The restrictions on the data subject's fundamental rights by the legislation of the recipient third country may only be compared to those restrictions, the member states may impose in accordance with EU law and, only in so far as similar rules of a member state fall within the scope of EU law.[2261] Consequently, in the view of the Advocate General, the relevant comparator for an adequacy assessment in the abovementioned case is the level of protection within the EU, under the law of the member states, including their commitments under the ECHR – as they constitute a common denominator in the member states.[2262] However, Advocate General *Saugmandsgaard Øe* stressed that this should only apply where rules govern only state activities and do not apply to any activity carried out by individuals.[2263] The CJEU disagreed, stating that the level of protection of fundamental rights must always be determined based on the provisions of the GDPR, read in the light of the fundamental rights enshrined in the Charter, and not based on the ECHR – as the EU has not yet acceded to the ECHR and it, therefore, does not constitute a legal instrument which has been formally incorporated into EU law – despite Article 6(3) TEU and

---

national security, the expedited retention (quick-freeze) of traffic and location data for serious crime and the safeguarding of national security, the generalised retention of IP addresses assigned to the source of an Internet connection for serious crime and serious threats to public security, the generalised retention of civil identity data to fight crime and public security threats in general.

2259 Schröder, 'Art. 45 DS-GVO' (n 455) para 13.

2260 Botta, 'Eine Frage des Niveaus: Angemessenheit Drittstaatlicher Datenschutzregime im Lichte Der Schlussanträge in "Schrems II" Der Prüfungsmaßstab der Gleichwertigkeit und Seine Reichweite im Bereich der Nationalen Sicherheit' (n 1064) 85.

2261 Opinion of Advocate General *Saugmandsgaard Øe* in *Facebook Ireland and Schrems* (n 1064) para 205.

2262 ibid para 207.

2263 ibid para 211.

Article 52(3) of the Charter.[2264] The validity of provisions of EU law should never be construed in the light of national law.[2265]

Christopher Kuner, as well as *Boris P. Paal* and *Katharina Kumkar*, accurately point out the fact that the allocation of legislative competence in EU law is not the same as the scope of application of the Charter.[2266] Strictly speaking, the data protection standards of member state intelligence agencies are irrelevant for judging the standard of protection offered by third countries.[2267] In the case of a data transfer, the focus is solely on whether, according to the legal situation there, any encroachment on fundamental rights would have to be feared in the recipient country based on the transfer authorisation.[2268] The fact that equal access by member state security authorities may lie outside the scope of application of EU law and the CJEU's review competence is irrelevant in this respect.[2269] A violation of fundamental rights by a third country, based on permitted transfer by the EU Commission[2270], cannot be excused because member state standards may be lacking.[2271] However, in a moral and political sense, the legitimacy of EU fundamental rights protection is undermined if the EU is viewed as holding third countries to standards that it is not willing to abide by itself. [2272] The question is whether the EU can demand a higher level of protection of third countries than EU member states, for which no adequacy test is provided.[2273] In order to strengthen the legitimacy of EU data protection law, it should be avoided that the high standard of protection under EU law is undermined "through the back door", as it were, by access powers in the member states.[2274]

2264 *Facebook Ireland and Schrems* (n 64) paras 98 et seqq.

2265 ibid.

2266 Kuner, 'Reality and Illusion in EU Data Transfer Regulation Post Schrems' (n 2244) 896 with further references; Paal and Kumkar (n 575) 735.

2267 Kuner, 'Reality and Illusion in EU Data Transfer Regulation Post Schrems' (n 2244) 899.

2268 Paal and Kumkar (n 575) 735.

2269 Kuner 'Reality and Illusion in EU Data Transfer Regulation Post Schrems' (n 2244); Paal and Kumkar (n 575) 735.

2270 Peter Schantz, 'Art. 45 DSGVO' in Spiros Simitis, Gerrit Hornung and Indra Spiecker (eds) (n 29) para 15.

2271 Kuner 'Reality and Illusion in EU Data Transfer Regulation Post Schrems' (n 2244); Paal and Kumkar (n 575) 735.

2272 ibid 735.

2273 Jens Brauneck, 'Privacy Shield – zu Recht für ungültig erklärt? Zugleich Besprechung von EuGH, Urt. v. 16.7.2020 in der Rs. C-311/18 – Schrems II' (n 467) 936.

2274 Kuner 'Reality and Illusion in EU Data Transfer Regulation Post Schrems' (n 2244); Paal and Kumkar (n 575) 735.

3 Slow, Non-Transparent, Inconsistent and Inflexible Adequacy Process

There are more and more complaints about the adequacy decision process in Brussels since it takes a very long period (on an average of 28 months)[2275] for the EU Commission to adopt an adequacy decision.[2276] Typically, a third country approaches the EU Commission and requests open discussions about an adequacy decision. When determining with which third countries a dialogue on adequacy should be pursued, the EU Commission has considered the following criteria to be taken into account: the extent of commercial relations with the third country in question, the extent of personal data flows from the EU, "the pioneering role the third country plays in the field of privacy and data protection that could serve as a model for other countries in its region, and the overall political relationship with the third country" (such as common values).[2277] The negotiations may take several years as economic and political factors usually play an essential role and must be considered. In the 26 years since Directive 95/46 came into effect in 1995, only 13 countries have obtained an adequacy decision.[2278] Since the introduction of the GDPR, only Japan, the UK and South Korea have obtained adequacy decisions so far.[2279] The adequacy decision for South Korea was only adopted in December 2021, although there have been adequacy talks with the EU Commission since late 2017.[2280] Also, some criticise the adequacy process for its lack of transparency.[2281] The EU Commission has con-

---

2275 cf Pieter Lamens and Evelyn Caesar, 'GDPR & Brexit: Is There a Need for an Adequacy Decision? What Are the Consequences of Brexit in Relation to Data Transfers?' (*Deloitte*) <https://www2.deloitte.com/nl/nl/pages/risk/articles/cyber-security-privacy-gdpr-and-brexit-is-there-a-need-for-an-adequacy-decision.html>.

2276 Manancourt, 'Why Brussels Went Easy on Britain in Its Data Deal' (n 2205); Greenleaf, 'The Influence of European Data Privacy Standards Outside Europe: Implications for Globalisation of Convention 108' (n 2135) 78.

2277 EU Commission, 'Adequacy Decisions – How the EU Determines If a Non-EU Country Has an Adequate Level of Data Protection' <https://ec.europa.eu/info/law/law-topic/data-protection/international-dimension-data-protection/adequacy-decisions_en>.

2278 Without *Safe Harbor* and the *Privacy Shield*, which both were invalidated by the CJEU.

2279 EU Commission, Adequacy Decisons, available at the following link <https://ec.europa.eu/info/law/law-topic/data-protection/international-dimension-data-protection/adequacy-decisions_en> accessed 9 June 2022. For a comprehensive overview of the EU Commission's adequacy decisions see Research Centre for Law and Digitalisation, 'Adequacy Decisions by the European Commission' (n 414).

2280 EU Commission, 'Communication from the Commission to the European Parliament and Council. Exchanging and Protecting Personal Data in a Globalised World' (n 142) 8.

2281 Manancourt, 'Why Brussels Went Easy on Britain in Its Data Deal' (n 2205); Greenleaf, 'The Influence of European Data Privacy Standards Outside Europe: Implications for Globalisation of Convention 108' (n 2135) 78.

sidered "applications" from third countries but found them not to be adequate; the reasons for these negative conclusions were not publicised.[2282] Morocco applied for an adequacy decision in 2009, with this request still pending.[2283]

The *Information Technology and Innovation Foundation* (ITIF)[2284] criticised that the EU would apply its privacy principles and the limits of the adequacy-based data transfer approach inconsistently.[2285] *ITIF* pointed out that the fact that the adequacy decisions, which were adopted under Directive 94/46, have continued effect under the GDPR would show inconsistency on the part of the EU Commission. The EU Commission has not reviewed its adequacy decisions with countries that would likely not meet the EU's new standards under the GDPR, such as Israel.[2286] According to commentators, the Israeli Privacy Protection Act (PPA) fails to meet the GDPR standards (and former Directive 95/46 standards) concerning the substance, procedure, enforcement and, access by Israeli security and intelligence agencies.[2287] *The New York Times* recently pointed out Israel's initiative to source data without users' explicit consent, allowing the police to use the anti-terrorism location tracking system to track the mobile phones of Covid-19 positive individuals.[2288] Also, while the US adequacy deci-

---

2282 Greenleaf, 'The Influence of European Data Privacy Standards Outside Europe: Implications for Globalisation of Convention 108' (n 2135) 78.

2283 cf Hind Chenaoui, 'Moroccan Data Protection Law: Moving to Align with EU Data Protection?' (*IAPP*, 11 September 2018) <https://iapp.org/news/a/moroccan-data-protection-law-moving-to-align-with-eu-data-protection/>.

2284 The ITIF is a nonprofit, nonpartisan research and educational institute focusing on the intersection of technology innovation and public policy, for more information see at the following link <https://itif.org/about> accessed 20 December 2020.

2285 Information Technology & Innovation Foundation, 'Response to the Consultation of the EU Commission on Transfers of Personal Data to Third Countries and Cooperation between Data Protection Authorities' (2020) 3 <https://www2.itif.org/2020-gdpr-two-year-review.pdf>.

2286 ibid 4 et seq.

2287 Detailed Douwe Korff, 'Opinion on the Future of Personal Data Transfers from the EU/EEA to Israel & the Occupied Territories' (*Data protection and digital competition by Ian Brown and Douwe Korff*, 4 February 2021) 23 et seqq. <https://www.ianbrown.tech/wp-content/uploads/2021/07/KORFF-Opinion-EU-Israel-data-transfers-final.pdf>. Currently, Israel is in the process of updating its Privacy Protection Act, see for more details in Douwe Korff, 'Israel's Privacy Protection Act amendments and EU adequacy decision (*Data protection and digital competition by Ian Brown and Douwe Korff*, 23 February 2022) < https://www.ianbrown.tech/2022/02/23/israels-privacy-protection-act-amendments-and-eu-adequacy/> who questions the adequate level of protection provided even with the planned changes.

2288 David M Halbfinger, Isabel Kershner and Ronen Bergman, 'To Track Coronavirus, Israel Moves to Tap Secret Trove of Cellphone Data' *The New York Times* (16 March 2020) <https://www.nytimes.com/2020/03/16/world/middleeast/israel-coronavirus-cellphone-tracking.html>.

sions were several times reviewed and re-affirmed by the EU Commission[2289] (later validated by the CJEU), the adequacy decision for Israel has not been similarly scrutinised.[2290] Eleven adequacy decisions were up for review in 2020; however, up to this date, none of these has been repelled or amended.[2291]

In practice, businesses have so far benefitted only little from adequacy decisions as a transfer tool.[2292] Only a few businesses transfer personal data solely to countries covered by adequacy decisions. The EU Commission did not use its two-year anniversary review of GDPR to speed up adequacy processes or make it and other legal tools more effective in allowing easier international transfers of EU personal data to more countries.[2293] Although the EU Commission stated that, the extent of commercial relations with the third country in question would be essential to start adequacy talks[2294], notably, only a few "top trading partner" of the EU have been granted an adequacy decision or even only a partial adequacy decision: US (invalidated by *Schrems* and *Facebook Ireland and Schrems*), Canada (only for commercial activities), Switzerland, Japan, and the UK.[2295] So far, the EU Commission named Chile, Brazil, Kenya, India, Tunisia, Indonesia, Taiwan, and California as potential adequacy countries.[2296] As mentioned above, South Korea "waited" since 2017 for an adequacy decision. The re-

---

2289 The EU-US *Privacy Shield* was reviewed three times by the EU Commission since its adoption in 2016.

2290 Information Technology & Innovation Foundation (n 2285) 6.

2291 According to the EU Commission, in 2020, the Commission services have already engaged in an intense dialogue with each of the 11 concerned third countries and territories to assess how their data protection systems have evolved since the adoption of the adequacy decision and whether they meet the standard set by the GDPR. The EU Commission stated that it will report separately on the evaluation of the existing adequacy decisions after the CJEU decided in *Facebook Ireland and Schrems* (n 64), cf EU Commission, 'Data Protection as a Pillar of Citizens' Empowerment and the EU's Approach to the Digital Transition – Two Years of Application of the General Data Protection Regulation' Communication to the European Parliament and the Council COM/2020/264 final 11.

2292 Information Technology & Innovation Foundation (n 2285) 5.

2293 ibid.

2294 EU Commission, 'Communication from the Commission on the Legal Nature of the Charter of Fundamental Rights of the European Union' (n 53) 8.

2295 The EU's top trading parties in 2020 were (ordered by highest trade volume): China, USA, United Kingdom, Switzerland, Russia, Turkey, Japan, Norway, South Korea, India, Canada, Brazil, Mexico, Taiwan, Vietnam, Singapore, Saudi Arabia, Ukraine, Australia and Malaysia, cf EU Commission, Directorate General for Trade, 'Client and Supplier Countries of the EU27 in Merchandise Trade (Value %) (2020, Excluding Intra-EU Trade)' <https://trade.ec.europa.eu/do clib/docs/2006/september/tradoc_122530.pdf>.

2296 EU Commission, 'Two Years of the GDPR: Questions and Answers' (n 2125).

cently completed EU-Singapore Free Trade Investment Protection Agreement[2297] does not include any agreements on digital trade and data flows, although Singapore is one of the EU's largest trading partners in Southeast Asia.[2298] As already mentioned, Singapore has not yet formally applied to an adequacy decision; however, it might be the right time for the EU Commission to become more proactive about adequacy processes.[2299]

According to the *ITIF*, "the limited number of adequacy decisions is also because the cost and complexity for a country to live up to GDPR are high—and getting higher with the EU's own evolving interpretation, application, and enforcement."[2300] An adequacy decision may not permanently alleviate the administrative impact of GDPR on data transfer given what equivalence means for these countries and their firms in having to harmonize their data protection frameworks and practices to GDPR.[2301] The UK might offer a new alternative to third countries that the EU has not yet granted adequacy. *Joe Jones*, Head of UK International Transfer Regime, stated UK plans on doing "adequacy differently" from the EU and getting more deals done quicker. Furthermore, *Jones* stated that the UK needs "to embrace the fact that different countries will take slightly different approaches to data protection and privacy".[2302] However, it seems unlikely that the UK adequacy decision or trade agreement could replace or be an adequate alternative to an adequacy decision by the EU Commission. This is especially true against the background of the Brussels Effect, which, according to the above, has not been weakened by Brexit.[2303]

Moreover, *Paul. M. Schwartz* finds that the EU Commission does have a "considerable negotiating flexibility".[2304] The process of the adequacy finding of Japan and the US had shown "openness to varied and customized approaches".[2305]

2297 For more information on the EU-Singapore Free Trade Agreement Investment Protection Agreement see at the following link <https://ec.europa.eu/trade/policy/in-focus/eu-singapore-agreement/> accessed 9 June 2022.
2298 cf Information Technology & Innovation Foundation (n 2285) 4.
2299 cf Greenleaf, 'The Influence of European Data Privacy Standards Outside Europe: Implications for Globalisation of Convention 108' (n 2135) 78.
2300 Information Technology & Innovation Foundation (n 2285) 4.
2301 ibid.
2302 Jedidiah Bracy, 'Government Leaders Discuss State of Play for UK Adequacy, Data Transfers' (*IAPP*, 27 January 2021) <https://iapp.org/news/a/government-leaders-discuss-state-of-play-for-u-k-adequacy-data-transfers/> quoting Joe Jones from a LinkedIn Live Panel Discussion, organised by *IAPP*.
2303 cf Bradford, *The Brussels Effect: How the European Union Rules the World* (n 147) 278.
2304 Schwartz, 'Global Data Privacy: The EU Way' (n 2128) 774 and 804.
2305 ibid 803 et seqq.

While Japan engaged in a formal process of seeking an adequacy decision, the EU Commission and the US developed two voluntary private sector compliance programs.[2306] In its two-year anniversary review of the GDPR, the EU Commission promoted new ways of international cooperation: "Over the last two years, the Commission has stepped up bilateral, regional, and multilateral dialogue, fostering a global culture of respect for privacy and convergence between different privacy systems to benefit citizens and businesses alike. The Commission is committed to continuing this work as part of its broader external action, for example, in the context of the Africa-EU Partnership[2307] and in its support for international initiatives, such as "Data Free Flow with Trust", which was initiated by Japan[2308].[2309] In 2020, the EU Commission emphasized that it actively seeks engagement with key partners to reach an "adequacy decision", allowing free data flow and embracing trade relations.[2310] Putting aside the abovementioned inconsistencies that only a few top trade partner countries have been granted an adequacy decision so far, the adequacy decision for Japan, the UK and South Korea could also be seen as a "kick-off" for many future adequacy decisions to follow. The EU Commission stated that exploratory talks are ongoing with other countries in Asia and Latin America but did not further specify the countries.[2311] It remains to be seen whether the abovementioned problems can be reduced or even resolved in future adequacy processes.

III CJEU vs EU Commission?

For the EU Commission, an adequacy decision appears to be an economic and political decision. However, the CJEU's approach to assessing adequacy severely

---

2306 Schwartz, 'Global Data Privacy: The EU Way' (n 2128).

2307 For more information on the partnership between the African Union and the EU see at the following link <https://africa-eu-partnership.org/en> accessed 9 June 2022.

2308 World Economic Forum, 'Data Free Flow with Trust (DFFT): Paths towards Free and Trusted Data Flows' (2020) White Paper <https://www3.weforum.org/docs/WEF_Paths_Towards_Free_and_Trusted_Data%20_Flows_2020.pdf>. The White Paper "maps a multi-dimensional architecture for international cooperation on data flows between governments, as well as involving business, with recommendations to increase level of governance trust and build openness through trade rules and other tools".

2309 EU Commission, 'Data Protection as a Pillar of Citizens' Empowerment and the EU's Approach to the Digital Transition – Two Years of Application of the General Data Protection Regulation' (n 2291) 12.

2310 ibid 10.

2311 ibid.

restricts the discretion of the EU Commission.[2312] In particular, it does not allow the EU Commission to determine the adequacy of a third country for overriding political reasons.[2313] These approaches can be demonstrated using the example of the *Privacy Shield* and *Facebook Ireland and Schrems*. In both *Schrems* decisions, the bounds of the EU's exceptionalism regarding data protection were extended. The CJEU overrode the EU Commission's accommodation of EU interests in sustaining the EU's most important trading relationship, sovereign interests of the US and other governments in protecting security, and differences between American and European legal systems[2314].[2315] The outcome in *Facebook Ireland and Schrems* not only set a high bar for a new data transfer arrangement between the EU and the US but also for all future adequacy decisions, including the UK. However, as analysed in in Chapter 3, the EU Commission did not comply with EU law and the CJEU's approach to an adequacy assessment but has instead tried to weaken the standard of review of Article 45 GDPR to become more flexible in its data protection diplomacy. Now the adequacy decision favouring the UK runs the risk of failing again before the CJEU. The CJEU has anchored the standard of review in the Charter itself, which is why a departure from the equivalence requirement would be contrary to primary law in the Court's view.[2316] The UK adequacy decision shows the EU Commission's fear to lose its position as a global standard-setter on data protection" by being "too hard on third-party countries".[2317] *Politico* found e-mails in which the EU Commission expresses its concerns to regulators that if their own "critical opinions" are adopted "without being significantly rebalanced".[2318] This would "show that [the EU] model is not credible as a global solution and that adequacy is basically 'mission impos-

---

2312 *Schrems* (n 71) para 78.

2313 Schantz, 'Art. 45 DSGVO' (n 2270) para 6.

2314 For more information on the differences between the EU and the US data protection systems see Manuel Klar and Jürgen Kühling, 'Privatheit und Datenschutz in der EU und den USA – Kollision zweier Welten?' (2016) 141 Archiv des öffentlichen Rechts 165.

2315 Cameron F Kerry, 'The Oracle at Luxembourg: The EU Court of Justice Judges the World on Surveillance and Privacy' (2021) <https://www.brookings.edu/research/the-oracle-at-luxembourg-the-eu-court-of-justice-judges-the-world-on-surveillance-and-privacy/>.

2316 Botta, 'Zwischen Rechtsvereinheitlichung und Verantwortungsdiffusion: Die Prüfung grenzüberschreitender Datenübermittlungen nach "Schrems II"' (n 1250) 509; Botta speaks here of a 'disempowerment of the Commission' by the CJEU: Due to its strict requirements for adequacy decisions, the CJEU has *de facto* deprived the EU Commission of its primary regulatory instrument for non-European data flows, which also deprived it of its primacy in the system of Article 44 et seqq. GDPR system.

2317 Manancourt, 'Why Brussels Went Easy on Britain in Its Data Deal' (n 2205).

2318 ibid.

sible' if even a former Member State that has decided to keep the same data protection rules essentially is not considered adequate".[2319] This shows the ambivalence of the system. On the one hand, the EU praises its data protection regime as a "gold[en] standard"[2320] and sees adequacy decisions as a "key pillar of maintaining that standard"[2321]. On the other hand, the EU Commission issues adequacy decisions – for political and economic reasons (*Safe Harbor* and *Privacy Shield*, most recently the adequacy decision in favour of the UK). In the case of the UK, the CJEU will most likely follow its line from the past and correct the EU Commission's approach by declaring the adequacy decision – in its current form – invalid.[2322]

To be able to provide an adequate level of data protection in the context of onward transfer of personal data from the EU, the UK would have to re-evaluate their onward transfer practices, in particular to the US, in the context of law enforcement and intelligence agencies cooperation and implement appropriate safeguards which comply with the CJEU's requirement in *Facebook Ireland and Schrems*. The EU Commission emphasised the monitoring of any developments in the UK, especially any details the details of the UK-US Agreement that still need to be clarified.[2323] However, notably, the EU Commission has never repealed, suspended or amended any adequacy decision even when it would be evident that a third country's law and practices do not (anymore) provide for adequate protection.[2324] The EU Commission's approach was shown in the case of the EU-US *Privacy Shield*. In October 2019, the EU Commission published its annual review and found that the Privacy Shield provided adequate protection for data transfers from the EU to the US. This practice shows that the adequacy decision obtained by the UK is not an exception due to the UK's status as a former member state. The EU Commission turned a blind eye to the activities of the UK intelligence agencies affecting EU citizens.

The CJEU's *Facebook Ireland and Schrems* judgement can be seen as a "corrective" to the very powerful position of the EU Commission when adopting adequacy decisions.[2325] The CJEU pointed out that the competent national supervi-

---

2319 Manancourt, 'Why Brussels Went Easy on Britain in Its Data Deal' (n 2205).
2320 Albrecht (n 2124) 288.
2321 Manancourt, 'Why Brussels Went Easy on Britain in Its Data Deal' (n 2205).
2322 Korff, 'Initial Comments on the EU Commission's Final GDPR Adequacy Decision on the UK' (n 998).
2323 UK Adequacy Decision (n 14) recital 155.
2324 Korff, 'The Inadequacy of the EU Commission Draft GDPR Adequacy Decision on the UK' (n 921) 7.
2325 Schantz, 'Art. 45 DSGVO' (n 2270) para 34.

sory authority must, even if there is an adequacy decision, be able to examine in complete independence, as regards the protection of the data subject's rights and freedoms with regard to the processing of their personal data, "whether the transfer of those data complies with the requirements [of the GDPR]" and, if necessary, "bring an action before the national courts" so that they may, in case of doubt, seek a preliminary ruling.[2326] Data subjects must be able to take action against the supervisory authority pursuant to Article 78 GDPR (right to an effective judicial remedy) if the authority dismisses their complaint referring to the adequacy decision since this complaint could then be referred to the CJEU by national courts pursuant to Article 267 TFEU.[2327] The CJEU's approach could be understood as an expression of distrust towards the EU Commission's previous practices.[2328] Furthermore, the CJEU appears to recall that an adequacy decision is a unilateral measure[2329] by the EU Commission and not the result of negotiations, such as the recent negotiations with the US on the *Privacy Shield*, in the context of which the EU Commission could make concessions.[2330] The judgment is emblematic of the formal strength of the EU's fundamental rights approach to personal data protection and limits in the age of digital interdependency.[2331]

C Conclusion to Chapter 5

Currently, the EU promotes the GDPR as the "gold standard". It is undeniable that the GDPR has a wide global reach and has often served as a model regime or initiated an implementation or modernisation of data protection law.[2332] The *de facto* Brussels Effect in data protection is enhanced by the GDPR's "adequacy" mechanism and extraterritorial scope of application (marketplace principle). However, this global "export" of the GDPR brings a risk of foreclosure of the "market of regulatory ideas", which may hinder innovation.

The EU has faced lots of criticisms regarding its data transfer regime and practice. Some have criticised that the CJEU's interpretation of "adequacy" hinders the EU Commission in finding flexible and pragmatic solutions in the cases

---

2326 *Facebook Ireland and Schrems* (n 64) para 120.
2327 ibid para 110.
2328 Schantz, 'Art. 45 DSGVO' (n 2270) para 34.
2329 See for a different view Schwartz, 'Global Data Privacy: The EU Way' (n 2128).
2330 Schantz 'Art. 45 DSGVO' (n 2270) para 6.
2331 Irion (n 2237).
2332 Greenleaf, 'Global Data Privacy Laws 2019: 132 National Laws & Many Bills' (n 2137) 14.

of fundamentally different ideas about the protection of personal data in third countries.[2333] The EU should revise its restriction approach to data transfers and set out a new, more flexible strategy. Data transfer should be based "on a reasonable degree of pragmatism in order to allow interaction with other parts of the world."[2334] "[T]he 'essential equivalence' test should [...] be applied in such a way as to preserve a certain flexibility to take the various legal and cultural traditions into account. That test implies, however, if it is not to be deprived of its substance, that certain minimum safeguards and general requirements for the protection of fundamental rights that follow from the Charter and the ECHR have an equivalent in the legal order of the third country of destination."[2335] However, as clarified above, the *Facebook Ireland and Schrems* judgement cannot necessarily be interpreted as rejecting a flexible approach.

Yet, it becomes clear from the above that there is much room for improvement regarding the EU's data transfer regime. In practice, businesses have so far benefitted only little from adequacy decisions as a transfer tool.[2336] Only a few EU key trading partners have been granted an adequacy decision so far. The adequacy process is too slow and lacks transparency. Hopefully, the adequacy decision for Japan and South Korea could also be seen as a "kick-off" for more future adequacy decisions in Asia and Latin America to follow. In 2020, the Commission emphasised that it would actively seek engagement with key trading partners and also promoted broader external actions (African-EU Partnership) and other international initiatives concerning global data flow ("Data Flow with Trust").

Nevertheless, the EU Commission must be more aware of its inconsistent adequacy practice regarding adequacy decisions for countries like Israel and, recently, the UK, as already evaluated in Chapter 3. On the one hand, the EU praises its data protection regime – as already mentioned above – as a "gold standard"[2337] and sees adequacy decisions as a "key pillar of maintaining that standard"[2338]. On the other hand, the EU Commission issues adequacy decisions – notably for political and economic reasons. The CJEU does not grant the EU Commission any room for discretion in determining the adequacy decision of

---

2333 Schröder, 'Art. 45 DS-GVO' (n 455) para 11.
2334 Hustinx (n 2214) 43.
2335 Opinion of Advocate General *Saugmandsgaard Øe* in *Facebook Ireland and Schrems* (n 1064) para 249.
2336 Information Technology & Innovation Foundation (n 2285) 5.
2337 Albrecht (n 2124) 288.
2338 Manancourt, 'Why Brussels Went Easy on Britain in Its Data Deal' (n 2205).

a third country;[2339] it thus clarifies that the recognition of the adequacy of the level of data protection of a third country may not be based solely on political motives. About the adequacy decision towards the UK, the CJEU will most likely follow its line from the past and correct the EU Commission's approach by declaring the UK adequacy decision – in its current form – invalid.[2340] This would show again that the EU is not the perfect fit as a global solution.[2341]

2339 *Schrems* (n 71) para 78.
2340 Korff, 'Initial Comments on the EU Commission's Final GDPR Adequacy Decision on the UK' (n 998).
2341 Manancourt, 'Why Brussels Went Easy on Britain in Its Data Deal' (n 2205).

Chapter 6 Conclusion

In general, the EU views its high data protection standard as the "gold standard"[2342]. The basis for this view is that the right to the protection of personal data in the EU is fundamentally guaranteed and protected through Article 7[2343] and Article 8[2344] CFR as well as the GDPR[2345] and the LED. The fundamental right character of privacy is reflected in the design and interpretation of the GDPR's provisions.[2346] The GDPR further has an extraterritorial reach due to the introduction of the marketplace principle.[2347] Above that, the Charter and the GDPR provide various key data protection principles[2348], which form a fundamental basis for data protection law in the EU and go hand in hand with the various rights[2349] and enforcement mechanisms guaranteed to the data subjects concerned. Undermining the protection standard guaranteed within the EU when transferring personal data to a third party is not permitted. Where a third country fails to ensure "an adequate level of protection of personal data", data transfers are generally not allowed, except under the specifics of Article 46 and Article 49 GDPR.[2350] The CJEU defines "adequate" as "essentially equivalent".[2351]

The EU Commission decided that the UK provides an adequate level of protection within the meaning of Article 45 GDPR read in light of the Charter and adopted an adequacy decision on the UK on 28 June 2021.[2352]

However, contrary to the EU Commission's point of view, this study revealed that several issues point out a lack of adequacy within the UK legislative and implementation system.[2353] Being a member of the ECHR and the remaining member of the EU privacy "family"[2354] appears not to be sufficient in the UK's case.

2342 Albrecht (n 2124).
2343 Chapter 2, A.II.
2344 Chapter 2, A.I.
2345 Chapter 2, A.IV.
2346 ibid 38 et seq.
2347 Chapter 2, A.IV.1.c.bb.
2348 Chapter 2, A.IV.2.
2349 Chapter 2, A.V.4.
2350 Chapter 2, B.I.3.
2351 *Schrems* (n 71); *Facebook Ireland and Schrems* (n 64).
2352 UK Adequacy Decision (n 14) recital 276 (Chapter 3, Introduction).
2353 Chapter 3.
2354 EU Commission, 'Data Protection: European Commission Launches Process on Personal Data Flows to UK' (n 619).

https://doi.org/10.1515/9783110988253-008

First, the DPA 2018 has several exemption provisions that might cause a future adequacy decision to be declared invalid by the CJEU.[2355] There is no effective substantive oversight provided by the ICO or the courts over the use of the national security exemptions.[2356] The judicial remedy options against national security certificates are limited in practice.[2357] Also, it is practically impossible to exclude all personal data that would fall within the scope of the DPA 2018's immigration exemption from the adequacy decision.[2358]

Second, the IPA 2016 does not comply with the Charter and the CJEU's established requirements[2359].[2360] The UK's intelligence agencies' bulk interception and acquisition practices based on the IPA 2016 significantly increase the likelihood that the CJEU invalidates an adequacy decision in favour of the UK. While the EU Commission did not find any issues with the IPA 2016, the bulk interception powers and bulk acquisition powers set out in the IPA 2016 are untargeted, general and indiscriminate powers.[2361] The EU Commission did not thoroughly assess the UK's intelligence agencies' actual bulk interception practices.[2362] Also, it did not raise any concerns regarding the the interception and subsequent retention of secondary data, which can be highly revealing. The bulk powers and the powers to the retention of communications data do not comply with the principle of proportionality and the principle of necessity. [2363] The EU Commission also did not assess the implemented procedural arrangements in practice and left out of consideration that the Judicial Commissioner only have powers to conduct a marginal and limited judicial review in practice.[2364]

Third, the UK's onward transfer practices, especially to the US – in the context of law enforcement (under the UK-US Agreement[2365]) and national security (within the *Five Eyes* alliance[2366]) – should have been an obstacle to the adequacy decision.[2367] One reason why such practice was not an obstacle to the adequa-

---

2355 Chapter 3, B.III.
2356 Chapter 3, B.III.1 and 2.
2357 Chapter 3, B.III.1 and 2.
2358 Chapter 3, B.III.3.
2359 These judgements are reviewed in Chapter 3 under C.II.
2360 Chapter 3, C.IV.
2361 Chapter 3, C.IV.1.aa.(1).(a). and (2).
2362 Chapter 3, C.IV.1.a.aa.(2).
2363 Chapter 3, C.IV.1.a.aa.(1).(b).
2364 Chapter 3, C.IV.2.a.
2365 Chapter 3, D.II.3.
2366 Chapter 3, D.III.3.
2367 Chapter 3, D.II.4 and III.4.

cy decision can probably be seen in the assumption that the EU has an interest in such intelligent data.

To be able to provide an adequate level of data protection, the UK would have to re-evaluate its data retention and bulk warrant practices as well as its onward transfer practices, in particular to the US, and implement appropriate safeguards, which comply with the CJEU's requirement in *Facebook Ireland and Schrems*[2368]. However, it does not seem to be a realistic chance that the UK will do so in the near future – especially not since the EU Commission adopted the adequacy decision, which applies until 28 June 2025.

Should the CJEU have the opportunity to decide on the UK's level of adequacy, it will likely declare the adequacy decision invalid. It would be unjustifiable to not declare the adequacy decision in its current form invalid against the background of the inadequacy identified in this study. However, in the event of the declaration of invalidity, the "dilemma" of the EU's data protection "philosophy" in a globally connected world would become even more apparent.[2369] Criticisms regarding the EU's data transfer regime and practice would increase.[2370] The EU Commission should modernise its approach to data transfer outside the EU and set out a new and more flexible strategy, which could simplify finding more pragmatic solutions in cases where the data protection approach in a third country differs fundamentally from the one within the EU. The EU should revise its restriction approach to data transfers and set out a new, more flexible strategy. This appeal is also supported by the fact that, in practice, businesses have so far benefitted only little from adequacy decisions as a transfer tool.[2371] Due to the lengthy and rather intransparent adequacy process, only a few EU key trading partners have been granted an adequacy decision so far.[2372]

Post-Brexit, it appears that the UK is in the process of modernising its current data protection law. The EU Commission took this into account, stating that under this circumstance, the monitoring, on an ongoing basis, of relevant development in the UK is crucial.[2373] In the process of developing a new data protection strategy, the UK's Government will most likely take into account that if the UK deviates too far from providing a system of data protection law for data transfers from the EU, the EU Commission or the CJEU will likely find the

---

2368 *Facebook Ireland and Schrems* (n 64).
2369 cf Manancourt, 'Why Brussels Went Easy on Britain in Its Data Deal' (n 2205).
2370 Chapter 5, B.II.
2371 Information Technology & Innovation Foundation (n 2285).
2372 Chapter 5, B.II.3.
2373 UK Adequacy Decision (n 14) recital 281.

UK system to no longer be "adequate". The disruption of data flows from the EU to the UK would have a massive impact on the UK's economy.

Overall, it can be said that despite the adoption of the adequacy decision by the EU Commission on 28 June 2021, the future of data flows from the EU to the UK remains uncertain. Since the EU Commission has not yet revoked any issued adequacy decision, it will likely not revoke the one for the UK. At most, the EU Commission could take steps if the UK declares the US – that has no adequate level of data protection pursuant to the CJEU's rulings[2374] – as an "adequate" third country under the UK GDPR "to avoid the UK becoming blatantly a personal data laundering haven".[2375] It does not contribute to a legal certainty that the EU Commission has largely disregarded the CJEU's case law. If the CJEU were to declare the UK adequacy decision invalid, there would be no transitional period. Hence, EU-based businesses as data exporters should anticipate changes to the adequacy decisions and be ready to switch to other transfer tools.[2376]

In case the CJEU declares the adequacy decision invalid, data exporters may use other transfer tools under strict conditions[2377] or exceptionally transfer data in specific situations laid down by the GDPR[2378]. Appropriate safeguards are an alternative transfer tool but require far more supervisory and control measures than data transfers based on an adequacy decision. Since the CJEU's *Schrems II* ruling, the data exporter and, subsidiarily, the competent supervisory authority must fulfil strict oversight – mainly to supervise the legal situation in the recipient country regarding the fundamental rights of the data subject concerned, and where necessary to suspend the data transfer.[2379] Businesses must do a data transfer impact assessment and determine the possible need for the implementation of supplementary safeguard measures.[2380] It is necessary for data exporters to carefully select the contractual partner and check about any obligations to disclose personal data to authorities to which it might be subject under UK law. The EU-based controllers and processors must closely study the UK's surveillance law and practices, and, where necessary, adopt supplementary measures. Failure to carry out these tasks, and failure to protect the data against unlawful access by UK public authorities would constitute a personal data breach for

---

2374 *Schrems* (n 71); *Facebook Ireland and Schrems* (n 64).

2375 Korff, 'European Commission Responds to Parliament's Resolution on UK Adequacy' (n 997).

2376 cf Wagner (n 4) 320.

2377 Chapter 2, B.II. and Chapter 4, A and B.

2378 Chapter 2, B.III and Chapter 4, C.

2379 Chapter 4, A.I.2 and 3.

2380 Chapter 4, A.III.1 and 2.

which the EU-based data exporter will be liable.[2381] Alternatives in form of CoC, certifications and BCRs (for transfer within an organisation) could provide a more promising transfer tool for data transfers outside the EU to the UK.[2382] However, the latter appears to be unfitting for smaller or medium-sized businesses and CoC and the certification mechanism are lacking practical relevance up to this point since they have not yet been sufficiently exploited as appropriate safeguards. Also, Article 49 GDPR could also take on greater importance in the context of data transfer to third countries.[2383] Derogations established in Article 49 GDPR apply to various scenarios that occur on an everyday basis in a globally connected world.[2384] In these cases, neither the respective third country nor data exporters provide adequate protection or appropriate safeguards to the personal data transferred. Furthermore, there is an increased risks for the rights and freedoms of the data subjects concerned since data transfers based on the derogations in Article 49 GDPR do not require any kind of prior authorisation from a supervisory authority. The Article 29 Working Party and EDPB still strongly advocate a restrictive interpretation of Article 49 GDPR. The examination of the specific transfer requires a comprehensive legal analysis and is often accompanied by considerable legal uncertainty.[2385]

In view of the above, it finally must be said that it would have been pleasant if the EU Commission had shown more consistency and used the adequacy decision for the UK as an opportunity to disclose the problems of the European data transfer regime. It could have deliberately tried to make the adequacy regime more flexible and, where adequacy is not simply ensured given, openly excluded these parts or, at least, requested the implementation of explicit supplementary measures and safeguards for personal data from the EU. Instead, the EU Commission has tried to somehow "bend" the adequacy of the UK "into shape". In doing so, it showed inconsistency and turned a blind eye to obvious inadequacy. Instead, the EU Commission reproduced and summarised the "UK's self-valedictory self-description". This also damages the credibility of the EU's data protection regime, which already has been subject to criticism in the past – and will be closely monitored in the future.

2381 Chapter 4, E.
2382 Chapter 4, B.
2383 Chapter 4, C.
2384 cf Pauly, 'Art. 49 DS-GVO' (n 1877) para 2; Paal and Kumkar (n 575) 738; Lange and Filip, 'Art. 49 DS-GVO' (n 1877) para 2.
2385 cf Moos and Schefzig (n 1892) 632.

Table of Cases

I UK Cases

https://doi.org/10.1515/9783110988253-009

Thoburn v Sunderland City Council [2002] EWHC 195 (Admin), [2003] QB 51
Totel Limited v The Commissioner for HM Revenue and Customs [2014] UKUT 0485 (TCC)

II CJEU Cases

Albako Margarinefabrik Maria von der Linde GmbH & Co. KG v Bundesanstalt für
    landwirtschaftliche Marktordnung, C-249/85, EU:C:1987:245 (21 May 1987)
Amministrazione delle finanze dello Stato v Simmenthal SpA, C-106–77, EU:C:1978:49
    (9 March 1978)
Andrea Francovich and Danila Bonifaci and others v Italian Republic, C-6/90 and C-9/90, EU:
    C:1991:428 (19 November 1991)
Asociación Nacional de Establecimientos Financieros de Crédito (ASNEF) and Federación de
    Comercio Electrónico y Marketing Directo (FECEMD) v Administración del Estado, C-468/
    10 and C-469/10, EU:C:2011:777 (24 November 2011)
Association Belge des Consommateurs Test-Achats ASBL and Others v Conseil des ministres,
    C-236/09, EU:C:2011:100 (1 March 2011)
Avis 2/13, EU:C:2014:2454 (Opinion) (18 December 2014)
Avis 1/15 – Accord PNR EU-Canada, EU:C:2017:592 (Opinion) (26 July 2017)
Bernard Conolly v European Commission, C-274/99, EU:C:2001:127 (6 March 2001)
Brasserie du Pêcheur SA v Bundesrepublik Deutschland and The Queen v Secretary of State
    for Transport, ex parte Factortame Ltd and Others, C-46/93 and C-48/93, EU:C:1996:79
    (5 March 1996)
Bundesrepublik Deutschland v SpaceNet AG and Telekom Deutschland GmbH, C-793/19 and
    C-794/19, Opinion of Advocate General Campos Sánchez-Bordona, EU:C:2021:939 (18
    November 2021)
Bundesverband der Verbraucherzentralen und Verbraucherverbände – Verbraucherzentrale
    Bundesverband e.V. v Planet49 GmbH, C-673/17, EU:C:2019:801 (1 October 2019)
Camera di Commercio, Industria, Artigianato e Agricoltura di Lecce v Salvatore Manni, C-398/
    15, EU:C:2017:197 (9 March 2017)
College van burgemeester en wethouders van Rotterdam v M. E. E. Rijkeboer, C-553/07, EU:
    C:2009:293 (7 May 2009)
Confederación Española de Empresarios de Estaciones de Servicio v Compañía Española de
    Petróleos SA.,
    C-217/05, EU:C:2006:784 (14 December 2006)
Data Protection Commissioner v Facebook Ireland Limited and Maximilian Schrems, C-311/18,
    EU:C:2020:559 (16 July 2020)
Data Protection Commissioner v Facebook Ireland Limited and Maximilian Schrems, C-311/18,
    EU:C:2020:559 (16 July 2020), Opinion of Advocate General Saugmandsgaard Øe, EU:
    C:2019:1145 (19 December 2019)
Digital Rights Ireland Ltd v Minister for Communications, Marine and Natural Resources and
    Others and Kärntner Landesregierung and Others, C-293/12, EU:C:2014:238 (8 April
    2014)
Elliniki Radiophonia Tiléorassi AE and Panellinia Omospondia Syllogon Prossopikou v
    Dimotiki Etairia Pliroforissis and Sotirios Kouvelas and Nicolaos Avdellas and Others, C-
    260/89, EU:C:1991:254 (18 June 1991)

Erich Stauder v City of Ulm, Sozialamt, C-29/69, EU:C:1969:57 (12 November 1969)
European Parliament v Council of the European Union and Commission of the European
    Communities, C- 317/04 and C-318/04, EU:C:2006:346 (30 May 2006)
European Commission v Federal Republic of Germany, C-518/07, EU:C:2010:125 (9 March
    2010)
European Commission v Republic of Austria, C-614/10, EU:C:2012:631 (16 October 2012)
European Commission v Republic of Poland (Temporary mechanism for the relocation of
    applicants for international protection), C-715/17, C-718/17 and C-719/17; EU:C:2020:257
    (2 April 2020)
Flaminio Costa v E.N.E.L., C-6 – 64, EU:C:1964:66 (15 July 1964)
Google LLC, successor in law to Google Inc. v Commission nationale de l'informatique et des
    libertés (CNIL),
    C-507/17, EU:C:2019:772 (24 September 2019)
Google Spain SL and Google Inc. v Agencia Española de Protección de Datos (AEPD) and
    Mario Costeja González, C-131/12, EU:C:2014:317 (13 May 2014)
Institut professionnel des agents immobiliers (IPI) v Geoffrey Englebert and Others, C-473/12,
    EU:C:2013:715 (7 November 2013)
Internationale Handelsgesellschaft mbH v Einfuhr- und Vorratsstelle für Getreide und
    Futtermittel, C-11/70, EU:C:1970:114 (17 December 1970)
Klaus Höfner and Fritz Elser v Macrotron GmbH, C-41/90, EU:C:1991:161 (23 April 1991)
La Quadrature du Net and Others v Premier ministre and Others, C-511/18, C-512/8 and C-
    520/18, EU:C:2020:791 (6 October 2020)
Marleasing SA v La Comercial Internacional de Alimentación SA, C-106 – 89, EU:C:1990:395
    (13 November 1990)
Maximilian Schrems v Data Protection Commissioner, C-362/14, EU:C:2015:66 (6˙October
    2015)
Mediaset SpA v Ministero dello Sviluppo economico, C-69/13, EU:C:2014:71 (13 February
    2014)
Ministerio Fiscal, C-207/16, EU:C:2018:788 (2 October 2018)
N.S. v Secretary of State for the Home Department and M.E. and Others v Refugee
    Applications Commissioner and Minister for Justice, Equality and Law Reform, C-411/10
    and C-493/10, EU:C:2011:865 (21 December 2011)
N.S. v Secretary of State for the Home Department and M.E. and Others v Refugee
    Applications Commissioner and Minister for Justice, Equality and Law Reform, Opinion of
    Advocate General Trstenjak, EU:C:2011:611 (22 September 2011)
N.V. Algemene Transport- en Expeditie Onderneming van Gend & Loos v Netherlands Inland
    Revenue Administration, C-26/62, EU:C:1963:1 (5 February 1963)
National Panasonic (UK) Limited v Commission of the European Communities, C-136/79, EU:
    C:1980:169 (26 June 1980)
Patrick Breyer v Bundesrepublik Deutschland, C-582/14, EU:C:2016:779 (19 October 2016)
Peter Nowak v Data Protection Commissioner, C-434/16, EU:C:2017:994 (20 December 2017)
Peter Pammer v Reederei Karl Schlüter GmbH & Co. KG and Hotel Alpenhof GesmbH v Oliver
    Heller, C-585/08 and C-144/09, EU:C:2010:740 (7 December 2010)
Privacy International v Secretary of State for Foreign and Commonwealth Affairs and Others,
    C-623/17, EU:C:2020:790 (6 October 2020)
Prokuratuur, C-746/18, EU:C:2021:152 (2 March 2021)

III ECtHR Cases

Gardel v France, no 16428/05, ECHR 2009
Gaskin v United Kingdom, 7 July 1989, Series A no 160
Haralambie v Romania, no 21737/03, 27 October 2009
I v Finland, no 20511/03, 17 July 2008
Joanna Szulc v Poland, no 43932/08, 13 November 2012
Kennedy v the United Kingdom, no 26839/05, 18 May 2010
Klass and Others v Germany, 6 September 1978, Series A no 28
L.H. v Latvia, no 52019/07, 29 April 2014
M.L. and W.W. v. Germany, nos 60798/10 and 65599/10, 28 June 2018
M.N. and others v San Marino, no 28005/12, 7 July 2015
Mehmedovic v Switzerland (dec.), no 41953/98, ECHR 2001-VII
Österreichischer Rundfunk v Austria, no 35841/02, 7 December 2006
Perry v the United Kingdom, no 63737/00, ECHR 2003-IX (extracts)
Powell the United Kingdom (dec.), no 45305/99, ECHR 2000-V
Roman Zakharov v Russia [GC], no 47143/06, ECHR 2015
Rotaru v Romania [GC], no 28341/95, ECHR 2000-V
S and Marper v United Kingdom [GC], nos 30562/04 and 30566/04, ECHR 2008
Satakunnan Markkinapörssi Oy and Satamedia Oy v Finland [GC], no 931/13, 27 June 2017
Segerstedt-Wiberg and Others v Sweden, no 62332/00, ECHR 2006-VII
Szabó and Vissy v Hungary, no 37138/14, 12 January 2016
Turek v Slovakia, no 57986/00, ECHR 2006-II (extracts)
Uzun v Germany, no 35623/05, ECHR 2010
Vgt Verein gegen Tierfabriken v Switzerland, no 24699/94, ECHR 2001-VI
Von Hannover v Germany, no 59320/00, ECHR 2004-VI
Weber and Saravia v Germany (dec.), no 54934/00, ECHR 2006-XI
X and Y v Netherlands, 26 March 1985, Series A no 91
Yonchev v Bulgaria no 12504/09, 7 December 2017
Z v Finland, 25 February 1997, Reports of Judgements and Decisions 1997-I

III Other Jurisdictions

BGH, 12 July 2018 – III ZR 183/17 = BGHZ 219, 243
BVerfG, 14 October 2014 – 2 BvR 1481/104 = BVerfGE 111, 307 (Görgülü)
BVerfG, 15 December 1983 – 1 BvR 209/83, 269/83, 362/83, 420/83, 440/83, 484/93
    = BVerfGE 65, 1 (Volkszählung)
BVerfG, 15 January 1958 – 1 BvR 400/51 = BVerfGE 7, 198 (Lüth)
Second Circuit (USA), Microsoft Corp. v United States 829, F.3d 197 (2016)
Datenschutzbehörde (DSB) (Austrian Data Protection Authority), Decision of 22 April 2022
    <https://noyb.eu/sites/default/files/2022-01/E-DSB%20-%20Google%20Analytics_EN_bk.
    pdf> accessed 9 June 2022

Table of Legislation

I UK Legislation

Agreement between the Government of the United Kingdom of Great Britain and Northern
Ireland and the Government of the United States of America on Access to Electronic
Data for the Purpose of Countering Serious Crime' (2019) USA No 6.
Agreement for a Comprehensive Economic Partnership between UK and Japan, CS Japan
No 1/2020, 23 November 2020
Data Protection Act 2018
Data Protection Privacy and Electronic Communications (Amendments etc) (EU Exit)
Regulations 2020, SI 2020/1586
Data Retention (EC Directive) Regulations 2009 (SI 2009/859)
Data Retention and Investigatory Powers Act 2018
European Union (Withdrawal Agreement) Act 2020
European Union (Withdrawal) Act (No 2) 2019
European Union (Withdrawal) Act 2018
Intelligence Services Act 1994
Investigatory Powers Act 2000
Regulation 19(1) of Immigration (European Economic Area) Regulations 2006 (SI 2006/1003)
Regulation of Investigatory Powers Act 2000
Scotland Act 1998
Security Services Act 1989
Telecommunications Act 1984
The British Islands constitute the United Kingdom, the Channel Islands and the Isle of Man,
Interpretation Act 1978
UK Crime (Overseas Production Orders) Act 2019
UK General Data Protection Regulation

II EU Legislation

Agreement between the United States of America and the European Union on the protection
of personal information relating to the prevention, investigation, detection and
prosecuting of criminal offences, OJ L 336
Commission Decision 2000/520/EC pursuant to Directive 95/46/EC of the European
Parliament and of the Council on the adequacy of the protection provided by the safe
harbor privacy principles and related frequently asked questions issued by the US
Department of Commerce [2000] OJ L 215/7
Commission Decision 2001/497/EC on standard contractual clauses for the transfer of
personal data to third countries, under Directive 95/46 [2001] OJ L 181/19
Commission Decision 2002/2/EC pursuant to Directive 95/46/EC of the EU Parliament and of
the Council on the adequate protection of personal data provided by the Canadian
Personal Information Protection and Electronic Documents Act [2001] OJ L 2/13

https://doi.org/10.1515/9783110988253-010

Commission Decision 2004/915/EC amending Decision 2001/497/EC as regards the
introduction of an alternative set of standard contractual clauses for the transfer of
personal data to third countries [2004] OJ L 385/74

Commission Decision 2006/253/EC on the adequate protection of personal data contained in
the Passenger Name Record of air passengers transferred to the Canada Border Services
Agency [2005] OJ L 91/49

Commission Decision (EU) 2010/87 on standard contractual clauses for the transfer of
personal data to processors established in third countries under Directive 95/46 of the
EU Parliament and of the Council [2010] OJ L 39/5

Commission Decision 2011/61/EU pursuant to Directive 95/46/EC of the European Parliament
and of the Council on the adequate protection of personal data by the State of Israel
with regard to automated processing of personal data [2011] OJ L 27/39

Commission Implementing Decision (EU) 2016/1250 pursuant to Directive 95/46/EC of the
European Parliament and of the Council on the adequacy of the protection provided by
the EU-U.S. Privacy Shield [2016] OJ L 207/1

Commission Implementing Decision (EU) 2016/2295 amending Decisions 2000/518/EC, 2002/
2/EC, 2003/490 EC, 2003/821/EC, 2004/411/EC, 2008/393/EC, 2010/146/EU, 2010/625/
EU, 2011/61/EU and Implementing Decisions 2012/848/EU, 2013/65/EU on the adequate
protection of personal data by certain countries, pursuant to Article 25(6) of Directive
95/46/EC of the European Parliament and of the Council [2016] OJ L 344/83

Commission Implementing Decision (EU) 2019/419 pursuant to Regulation (EU) 2016/679 of
the EU Parliament and of the Council on the adequate protection of personal data by
Japan under the Act on the Protection of Personal Information [2019] OJ L 76/1

Commission Implementing Decision (EU) 2021/1772 pursuant to Regulation (EU) 2016/679 of
the European Parliament and of the Council on the adequate protection of personal data
by the United Kingdom [2021] OJ L 360/1

Commission Implementing Decision (EU) 2021/1773 pursuant to Directive (EU) 2016/680 of
the European Parliament and of the Council on the adequate protection of personal data
by the United Kingdom [2021] OJ L 360/69

Commission Implementing Decision (EU) 2021/914 on standard contractual clauses for the
transfer of personal data to third countries pursuant to Regulation (EU) 2016/679 of the
European Parliament and of the Council [2021] OJ L 199/13

Commission Implementing Decision pursuant to Regulation (EU) 2016/679 of the European
Parliament and of the Council on the adequate protection of personal data by the
Republic of Korea under the Personal Information Protection Act, C(2021) 4800 final

Council Directive 93/104/EC concerning certain aspects of the organisation of working time
[1993] OJ L 307/18

Council Directive 94/33/EC on the protection of young people at work [1994] OJ L 216/12

Directive 95/46/EC of the European Parliament and of the Council of 24 October 1995 on the
protection of individuals with regard to the processing of personal data and on the free
movement of such data [1995] OJ L 281/31

Directive 2004/38/EC of the European Parliament and of the Council on the right of citizens
of the Union and their family members to move and reside freely within the territory of
the Member States amending Regulation (EEC) No 1612/68 and repealing Directives 64/
221/EEC, 68/360/EEC, 72/194/EEC, 73/148/EEC, 75/34/EEC, 75/35/EEC, 90/364/EEC,
90/365/EEC and 93/96/EEC [2004] OJ L 158/77

Directive 2006/24/EC of the European Parliament and of the Council on the retention of data generated or processed in connection with the provision of publicly available electronic communications services or of public communications networks and amending Directive 2002/58/EC [2006] OJ L 105/54

Directive (EU) 2016/680 of the EU Parliament and of the Council on the protection of natural persons with regard to the processing of personal data by competent authorities for the purposes of the prevention, investigation, detection or prosecution of criminal offences or the execution of criminal penalties, and on the free movement of such data, and repealing Council Framework Decision 2008/977/JHA [2016] *OJ L 119/8*

Regulation (EU) 2016/679 of the European Parliament and of the Council on the protection of natural persons with regard to the processing of personal data and on the free movement of such data, and repealing Directive 95/46/EC (General Data Protection Regulation) [2016] OJ L 119/1

Trade and Cooperation Agreement between the EU and the Euratom, of the one part, and the UK, of the other part, 31 December 2020, OJ L 444/14 (TCA)

III Council of Europe

Additional Protocol to the Convention for the Protection of Individuals with regard to Automatic Processing of Personal Data, regarding supervisory authorities and transborder data flows, No 181, 8 November 2001

Convention for the Protection of Individuals with Regard to Automatic Processing of Personal Data, No 108, 28 January 1981

European Convention on Human Rights

Protocol amending the Convention for the Protection of Individuals with regard to Automatic Processing of Personal Data, No 233, 18 May 2018

IV Other Legislation

African Union Convention on Cyber Security and Personal Data African Union Convention on Cyber Security and Personal Data

Australian Privacy Act

Austrian Telekommunikationsgesetz 2003 ("Telecommunications Act")

Belgian Law of 29 May 2016

Brazilian Data Protection Law (LGPD)

California Consumer Privacy Act of 2018 (CCPA)

Chinese Personal Information Protection Law (PIPL)

Criminal Justice (Terrorist Offences) Act 2005

French Code de la sécurité intérieure (Internal Security Code)

German Grundgesetz ("Basic Law")

Japanese Act on the Protection of Personal Data (APPI) (Act No 57 of 2003)

Nigeria Data Protection Regulation 2019

US Clarifying Lawful Overseas Use of Data (CLOUD) Act 2018

US Foreign Intelligence Surveillance Act

US Executive Order (E.O.) 12333
US Presidential Policy Directive 28
South African Protection of Personal Information Act 2013 (POPIA)

Bibliography

Albrecht JP, 'How the GDPR Will Change the World' (2016) 2 EDPL 287

Aldrich, RJ, Transatlantic Intelligence and security co-operation (2006)

Alsenoy B van, Data Protection Law in the EU: Roles, Responsibilities and Liability (Cambridge University Press 2019)

Amazon Web Services, 'AWS GDPR Data Processing Addendum' <https://d1.awsstatic.com/legal/aws-gdpr/AWS_GDPR_DPA.pdf> accessed 9 June 2022

Ambrock J, 'Nach Safe Harbor: Schiffbruch des Transatlantischen Datenverkehrs?' [2015] NZA 1493

Ambrock J and Karg M, 'Ausnahmetatbestände der DS-GVO als Rettungsanker des internationalen Datenverkehrs? Analyse der Neuerungen zur Angemessenheit des Datenschutzniveaus' [2017] ZD 154

Art. 29 Data Protection Working Party, 'Opinion 1/98 on Platform for Privacy Preferences (P3P) and the Open Profiling Standard (OPS)' (1998) WP 11

Art. 29 Data Protection Working Party, 'Working Document on Transfers of Personal Data to Third Countries: Applying Articles 25 and 26 of the EU Data Protection Directive' (1998) WP 12

Art. 29 Data Protection Working Party, 'Opinion 3/2001 on the Level of Protection of the Australian Privacy Amendment (Private Sector) Act 2000' (2001) WP 40 final

Art. 29 Data Protection Working Party, 'Working Document: Transfers of Personal Data to Third Countries: Applying Article 26 (2) of the EU Data Protection Directive to Binding Corporate Rules for International Data Transfers' (2003) WP 74

Art. 29 Data Protection Working Party, 'Working Document on Data Protection Issues Related to RFID Technology' (2005) WP 105

Art. 29 Data Protection Working Party, 'Working Document Establishing a Model Checklist Application for Approval of Binding Corporate Rules' (2005) WP 108

Art. 29 Data Protection Working Party, 'Working Document on a Common Interpretation of Article 26(1) of Directive 95/46/EC of 24 October 1995' (2005) WP 114

Art. 29 Data Protection Working Party, 'Opinion 4/2007 on the Concept of Personal Data' (2007) WP 136

Art. 29 Data Protection Working Party, 'Working Document on Frequently Asked Questions (FAQs) Related to Binding Corporate Rules' (2008) WP 155

Art. 29 Data Protection Working Party, 'Opinion 1/2010 on the Concepts of "Controller" and "Processor"' (2010) WP 169

Art. 29 Data Protection Working Party, 'Opinion 8/2010 on Applicable Law' (2010) WP 179

Art. 29 Data Protection Working Party, 'Opinion 15/2011 on the Definition of Consent' (2011) WP 187

Art. 29 Data Protection Working Party, 'Opinion 03/2013 on Purpose Limitation' (2013) WP 203

Art. 29 Data Protection Working Party, 'Opinion 06/2014 on the Notion of Legitimate Interests of the Data Controller under Article 7 of Directive 95/46/EC' (2014) WP 217

Art. 29 Data Protection Working Party, 'Guidelines on the Implementation of the Court of Justice of the European Union Judgement on "Google Spain and Inc v Agencia Espanola de Protección de Datos (AEPD) and Mario Costeja González"' (2014) WP 225

https://doi.org/10.1515/9783110988253-011

Art. 29 Data Protection Working Party, 'Guidelines on Automated Individual Decision-Making and Profiling for the Purposes of Regulation 2016/679' (2017) WP 251 rev.01

Art. 29 Data Protection Working Party, 'Adequacy Referential' (2018) WP 254 rev.01

Art. 29 Data Protection Working Party, 'Working Document Setting up a Table with the Elements and Principles to Be Found in Binding Corporate Rules' (2018) WP 256 rev.01

Art. 29 Data Protection Working Party, 'Working Document Setting up a Table with the Elements and Principles to Be Found in Processor Binding Corporate Rules' (2018) WP 257 rev.01

Art. 29 Data Protection Working Party, 'Working Document Setting Forth a Co-Operation Procedure for the Approval of "Binding Corporate Rules" for Controllers and Processors under the GDPR' (2018) WP 263 rev.01

Ataoglu F, 'Faktencheck Datenschutz: Wie wir unsere Kundendaten nach dem Schrems-II-Urteil schützen' (*Microsoft*, 14 October 2021) <https://news.microsoft.com/de-de/daten schutz-wie-wir-unsere-kundendaten-nach-dem-schrems-ii-urteil-schuetzen/> accessed 9 June 2022

Ausloos J, *The Right to Erasure: Safeguard for Informational Self-Determination in a Digital Society?* (Oxford University Press 2018)

Ball J, Borger J and Greenwald G, 'Revealed: How US and UK Spy Agencies Defeat Internet Privacy and Security' *The Guardian* (6 September 2013) <http://www.theguardian.com/world/2013/sep/05/nsa-gchq-encryption-codes-security> accessed 9 June 2022

Barnard C, 'So Long, Farewell, Auf Wiedersehen, Adieu: Brexit and the Charter of Fundamental Rights' (2019) 82 Mod. L. Rev. 350

Barnard-Wills D, 'Book Review of Oscar H. Gandy, Jr. 2009. Coming to Terms with Chance: Engaging Rational Discrimination and Cumulative Disadvantage' (2011) 8 Marketing, Consumption and Surveillance 379

Baumann B, *Datenschutzkonflikte zwischen der EU und den USA* (2016)

Begum A and others, 'Letter to Elizabeth Denham, UK Information Commissioner' (21 August 2020) <https://www.openrightsgroup.org/app/uploads/2020/08/Letter-for-MPs-Final-sigs-1.pdf> accessed 9 June 2022

Belling V, 'Supranational Fundamental Rights or Primacy of Sovereignty? Legal Effects of the So-Called Opt-Out from the EU Charter of Fundamental Rights' (2012) 18 ELJ 251

Berg M, 'Die Bestimmbarkeit als Grundproblem des Datenschutzrechts – Überblick über den Theorienstreit und Lösungsvorschlag' [2015] ZD 365

Bernsdorff N, 'Art. 7 GRCh' in Jürgen Meyer and Sven Höscheidt (eds), *Nomos Kommentar: Charta der Grundrechte der Europäischen Union* (5th edn, 2019)

Bernsdorff N, 'Art. 8 GRCh' in Jürgen Meyer and Sven Höscheidt (eds), *Nomos Kommentar: Charta der Grundrechte der Europäischen Union* (5th edn, Nomos 2019)

Beyleveld D and Pattinson SD, 'Horizontal Applicability and Horizontal Effect' (2002) 118 LQR 623

Bigo D and others, 'Mass Surveillance of Personal Data by EU Member States and Its Compatibility with EU Law' (2013) No. 62 <https://www.ceps.eu/wp-content/uploads/2013/11/No%2062%20Surveillance%20of%20Personal%20Data%20by%20EU%20MSs.pdf> accessed 9 June 2022

Blackmore N, 'Feeling Inadequate? Why Adequacy Decisions Are Rare (and May Get Rarer) in Asia-Pacific' (26 March 2019) <https://kennedyslaw.com/thought-leadership/article/feel ing-inadequate-why-adequacy-decisions-are-rare-and-may-get-rarer-in-asia-pacific/> accessed 9 June 2022

Bock K and Engeler M, 'Die Verfassungsrechtliche Wesensgehaltsgarantie als absolute Schranke im Datenschutzrecht' (2016) 131 DVBl 593

Börding A, 'Ein neues Datenschutzschild für Europa' [2016] CR 431

Bühlmann, L and Reinle, M, 'DSG Revision: Vergleich zum geltenden Recht und zur EU-DSGVO' <https://www.mll-news.com/wp-content/uploads/2020/10/DSG-Revision_Gegenü berstellung.pdf>

Botta J, 'Eine Frage des Niveaus: Angemessenheit drittstaatlicher Datenschutzregime im Lichte der Schlussanträge in "Schrems II" – Der Prüfungsmaßstab der Gleichwertigkeit und seine Reichweite im Bereich der nationalen Sicherheit' [2020] CR 82

Botta J, 'Zwischen Rechtsvereinheitlichung und Verantwortungsdiffusion: Die Prüfung grenzüberschreitender Datenübermittlungen nach "Schrems II"' [2020] 36 CR 505

Bracy J, 'Government Leaders Discuss State of Play for UK Adequacy, Data Transfers' (IAPP, 27 January 2021) <https://iapp.org/news/a/government-leaders-discuss-state-of-play-for-u-k-adequacy-data-transfers/> accessed 9 June 2022

Bradford A, 'The Brussels Effect' (2012) 107 Nw. U. L. Rev.

Bradford A, The Brussels Effect: How the European Union Rules the World (Oxford University Press 2020)

Brandt M, 'USA sind Cloud-Macht Nr. 1' (Statista, 12 January 2021) <https://de.statista.com/in fografik/22251/geschaetzter-public-cloud-umsatz-in-den-top-5-maerkten/> accessed 9 June 2022

Brauneck J, 'Marktortprinzip der DSGVO: Weltgeltung für EU-Datenschutz?' [2019] EuZW 494

Brauneck J 'Privacy Shield – Zu Recht für ungültig erklärt? Zugleich Besprechung von EuGH, Urt. v. 16.7.2020 in der Rs. C-311/18 – Schrems II' [2020] EuZW 933

Brauneck J 'Vereinfachter Datenfluss zwischen der EU und dem Vereinigten Königreich – Rechtmäßigkeit des DS-GVO-Angemessenheitsbeschlusses?' [2021] Recht Digital 425

Brink S and Eckhardt J, 'Wann ist ein Datum ein personenbezogenes Datum? Anwendungsbereich des Datenschutzrechts' [2015] ZD 205

Brkan M, 'The Concept of Essence of Fundamental Rights in the EU Legal Order: Peeling the Onion to Its Core' (2018) 14 EuConst 332

Brown I and Korff D, 'Study Requested by the European Parliament's LIBE Committee: Exchanges of Personal Data After the Schrems II Judgement' (Policy Department for Citizens' Rights and Constitutional Affairs) <https://www.europarl.europa.eu/RegData/ etudes/STUD/2021/694678/IPOL_STU(2021)694678_EN.pdf> accessed 9 June 2022

Brühl F von and Nietsch T, 'Internationale Datentransfer im Lichte des "Brexit"' (2017) Tagungsband Herbstakademie Recht 4.0. – Innovationen aus den rechtswissenschaftlichen Laboren 171

BSA, 'BSA Welcomes EU Decision For UK Adequacy, Encourages Global Convergence on Data Flows' (2018) <https://www.bsa.org/news-events/news/bsa-welcomes-eu-decision-for-uk-adequacy-encourages-global-convergence-on-data-flows> accessed 9 June 2022

Burnton SS, 'Report of the Interception of Communications Commissioner Annual Report' (2016) <https://assets.publishing.service.gov.uk/government/uploads/system/uploads/at tachment_data/file/670219/IOCCO_annual_report_2016_2.PDF> accessed 9 June 2022

Bygrave LA, *Data Privacy Law: An International Perspective* (2014)

Bygrave LA, 'The "Strasbourg Effect" on Data Protection in Light of the "Brussels Effect":
Logic, Mechanics and Prospects' (2020) 40 CLSR <https://doi.org/10.1016/j.clsr.2020.
105460> accessed 9 June 2022

Cadwalladr C, 'Edward Snowden: State Surveillance in Britain Has No Limits' *The Guardian*
(12 October 2014) <https://www.theguardian.com/world/2014/oct/12/snowden-state-sur
veillance-britain-no-limits> accessed 9 June 2022

Calliess G P, 'Die Rolle der Rechtsvergleichung im Kontext des Wettbewerbs der
Rechtsordnungen' in Reinhard Zimmermann (ed), *Zukunftsperspektiven der
Rechtsvergleichung* (Mohr Siebeck 2016)

Campbell D, 'Australia First to Admit We're Part of a Global Surveillance System' *Heise Online*
(28 May 1999) <https://www.heise.de/tp/features/Australia-first-to-admit-we-re-part-of-
global-surveillance-system-3440779.html> accessed 9 June 2022

Center for Democracy and Technology, 'Not a Secret: Bulk Interception Practices of
Intelligence Agencies' (2019) <https://cdt.org/wp-content/uploads/2019/09/2019-09-13-
Not-A-Secret-Bulk-Interception-Practices-of-Intelligence-Agencies-FINAL.pdf> accessed
9 June 2022

Center for Information Policy Leadership (CIPL), 'A Path Forward for International Data
Transfers under the GDPR after the CJEU Schrems II Decision' (2020) <https://www.in
formationpolicycentre.com/uploads/5/7/1/0/57104281/cipl_white_paper_gdpr_transfers_
post_schrems_ii__24_september_2020__2_.pdf> accessed 9 June 2022

Chenaoui H, 'Moroccan Data Protection Law: Moving to Align with EU Data Protection?' (*IAPP*,
11 September 2018) <https://iapp.org/news/a/moroccan-data-protection-law-moving-to-
align-with-eu-data-protection/> accessed 9 June 2022

Christakis T, '21 Thoughts and Questions about the UK-US Cloud Act Agreement: (And an
Explanation of How It Works – with Charts)' (*European Law Blog*, 17 October 2019)
<https://europeanlawblog.eu/2019/10/17/21-thoughts-and-questions-about-the-uk-us-
cloud-act-agreement-and-an-explanation-of-how-it-works-with-charts/> accessed 9 June
2022

Christakis T, '"Schrems III"? First Thoughts on the EDPB Post-Schrems II Recommendations
on International Data Transfers (Part 2)' (*European Law Blog*, 16 November 2020)
<https://europeanlawblog.eu/2020/11/16/schrems-iii-first-thoughts-on-the-edpb-post-
schrems-ii-recommendations-on-international-data-transfers-part-2/> accessed 9 June
2022

Chuches G and Zalnieriute M, 'A Groundhog Day in Brussels. Schrems II and International
Data Transfer' (*Verfassungsblog*, 16 July 2020) <https://verfassungsblog.de/a-groundhog-
day-in-bruessels/> accessed 9 June 2022

Clapham A, 'The "Drittwirkung" of the European Convention', *R. St J. Macdonald, F. Matscher
and H. Petzold (eds) The European System for the Protection of Human Rights
(Dordrecht, Nijhoff)* (Springer Netherlands 1996)

Clifford D and Ausloos J, 'Data Protection and the Role of Fairness' (2018) 37 YEL 130

CMS, 'GDPR Enforcement Tracker' <https://www.enforcementtracker.com> accessed 9 June
2022

CNIL, 'The CNIL's Restricted Committee Imposes a Financial Penalty of 50 Million Euros
against GOOGLE LLC' (21 January 2019) <https://www.cnil.fr/en/cnils-restricted-commit
tee-imposes-financial-penalty-50-million-euros-against-google-llc> accessed 9 June 2022

Council of Europe, 'Welcome to Mexico, 53rd Party to Convention 108' (2018) Press Release of 28 June 2018 <https://www.coe.int/en/web/data-protection/-/welcome-to-mexico-53rd-party-to-convention-108> accessed 9 June 2022

Council of Europe 'Explanatory Report to Protocol Amending the Convention for the Protection of Individuals with Regard to Automatic Processing of Personal Data' CM(2018)2-addfinal

Council of Europe 'Council Resolution on Encryption – Security through Encryption and Security despite Encryption' (2020) 12863/20 <https://www.statewatch.org/media/1510/eu-council-encryption-declaration-13084-20-rev1.pdf> accessed 9 June 2022

Craig P, 'Constitutional Principle, the Rule of Law and Political Reality: The European Union (Withdrawal) Act 2018' (2019) 82 Mod. L. Rev. 319

Crespi S, 'The Applicability of Schrems Principles to the Member States: National Security and Data Protection within the EU Context' (2018) 43 European Law Review 669

Cullagh KM, 'UK: GDPR Adaptions and Preparations for Withdrawal from the EU', *National Adaptions of the GDPR* (2019)

Danwitz T von, 'The Rule of Law in the Recent Jurisprudence of the ECJ' (2014) 37 Fordham International Law Journal

Danwitz T von, 'Internationaler Datentransfer in der Rechtsprechung des EuGH' (European Data Protection Day 2021 – Transborder Transfers. Challenges of international data transfer from the perspective of the Convention 108+ and GDPR. 40 Years of Convention 108, 28 January 2021) <https://cdn.pottkinder.de/streaming/stream2.html> accessed 9 June 2022

Data Privacy Manager, '20 Biggest GDPR Fines so Far [2019, 2020 & 2021]' (2021) <https://dataprivacymanager.net/5-biggest-gdpr-fines-so-far-2020/> accessed 9 June 2022

Denham, E, 'Foreword to ICO response to DCMS consultation "Data: a new direction"' (*ico.*) (7 October 2021) <https://ico.org.uk/about-the-ico/news-and-events/news-and-blogs/2021/10/response-to-dcms-consultation-foreword/> accessed 9 June 2022

Department for Digital, Culture, Media & Sport, 'A New Data Protection Bill: Our Planned Reforms' (2017) Statement of Intent <https://assets.publishing.service.gov.uk/government/uploads/system/uploads/attachment_data/file/635900/2017-08-07_DP_Bill_-_Statement_of_Intent.pdf> accessed 9 June 2022

Department for Digital, Culture, Media & Sport 'Explanatory Framework for Adequacy Discussions' (2020) Section E3: Schedule 2 Restrictions <https://assets.publishing.service.gov.uk/government/uploads/system/uploads/attachment_data/file/872235/E3_-_Schedule_2_Restrictions.pdf> accessed 9 June 2022

Department for Digital, Culture, Media & Sport 'Explanatory Framework for Adequacy Discussions' (2020) Section E: Restrictions <https://assets.publishing.service.gov.uk/government/uploads/system/uploads/attachment_data/file/872232/E_-_Narrative_on_Restrictions.pdf> accessed 9 June 2022

Department for Digital, Culture, Media & Sport 'Explanatory Framework for Adequacy Discussions' (2020) Section H: National Security Data Protection and Investigatory Powers Framework <https://assets.publishing.service.gov.uk/government/uploads/system/uploads/attachment_data/file/872239/H_-_National_Security.pdf> accessed 9 June 2022

Department for Digital, Culture, Media & Sport National Data Strategy' (2020) Policy Paper <https://www.gov.uk/government/publications/uk-national-data-strategy/national-data-strategy> accessed 9 June 2022

Department for Digital, Culture, Media & Sport 'EU Adopts "Adequacy" Decisions Allowing Data to Continue Flowing Freely to the UK. UK Businesses and Other Organisations Will Benefit from Unrestricted Personal Data Transfers.' (2021) Press Release of 28 June 2021 <https://www.gov.uk/government/news/eu-adopts-adequacy-decisions-allowing-data-to-continue-flowing-freely-to-the-uk> accessed 9 June 2022

Department for Digital, Culture, Media & Sport 'International Data Transfers: Building Trust, Delivering Growth and Firing up Innovation, 26 August 2021' (2021) Guidance <https://www.gov.uk/government/publications/uk-approach-to-international-data-transfers/international-data-transfers-building-trust-delivering-growth-and-firing-up-innovation> accessed 9 June 2022

Department for Digital, Culture, Media & Sport 'Data: A New Direction' (*DCMS blog*, 16 December 2021) <https://dcmsblog.uk/2021/12/data-a-new-direction/>.

Department for Digital, Culture, Media & Sport 'The Government's New International Data Transfers Expert Council' (2021) News Story <https://www.gov.uk/government/news/the-governments-new-international-data-transfers-expert-council> accessed 9 June 2022

Department for Digital, Culture, Media & Sport 'UK Unveils Post-Brexit Global Data Plans to Boost Growth, Increase Trade and Improve Healthcare' (2021) Press Release of 26 August 2021 <https://www.gov.uk/government/news/uk-unveils-post-brexit-global-data-plans-to-boost-growth-increase-trade-and-improve-healthcare> accessed 9 June 2022

Department for Digital, Culture, Media & Sport 'Data: a New Direction' (2021) <https://assets.publishing.service.gov.uk/government/uploads/system/uploads/attachment_data/file/1022315/Data_Reform_Consultation_Document__Accessible_.pdf> accessed 9 June 2022

Department for Digital, Culture, Media & Sport 'Map UK Data Partnerships' <https://assets.publishing.service.gov.uk/government/uploads/system/uploads/attachment_data/file/1013047/UK_Data_Partnerships___Map_V2_.jpg> accessed 9 June 2022

Department for Exiting the European Union, 'Legislating for the United Kingdom's Withdrawal from the European Union' (2017) CM 9446 <https://assets.publishing.service.gov.uk/government/uploads/system/uploads/attachment_data/file/604514/Great_repeal_bill_white_paper_print.pdf> accessed 9 June 2022

Department for Exiting the European Union 'Charter of Fundamental Rights of the EU – Rights by Rights Analysis' (2017) <https://assets.publishing.service.gov.uk/government/uploads/system/uploads/attachment_data/file/664891/05122017_Charter_Analysis_FINAL_VERSION.pdf> accessed 9 June 2022

Department for Exiting the European Union 'The Exchange and Protection of Personal Data. A Future Partnership Paper' (2017)

Department for Exiting the European Union 'The Future Relationship between the United Kingdom and the European Union' (2018) <https://assets.publishing.service.gov.uk/government/uploads/system/uploads/attachment_data/file/786626/The_Future_Relationship_between_the_United_Kingdom_and_the_European_Union_120319.pdf> accessed 9 June 2022

Department for International Trade, 'UK-Australia FTA Negotiations: Agreement in Principle' (2021) <https://www.gov.uk/government/publications/uk-australia-free-trade-agreement-negotiations-agreement-in-principle/uk-australia-fta-negotiations-agreement-in-principle#services> accessed 9 June 2022

Determann L and Weigl M, 'EU-US-Datenschutzschild und Alternativen für internationale Datentransfers' [2016] EuZW 811

Dienst S, 'C. Lawful Processing of Personal Data in Companies under the General Data Protection Regulation' in Tobias Kugler and Daniel Rücker (eds), *New European General Data Protection Regulation: A Practitioner's Guide* (1st edn, Nomos 2018)

Dipple-Johnstone J, 'Blog: Changes to Binding Corporate Rules Applications to the ICO' (*ico.*, 20 November 2017) <https://ico.org.uk/about-the-ico/news-and-events/news-and-blogs/2017/11/blog-changes-to-binding-corporate-rules-applications-to-the-ico/> accessed 9 June 2022

Donald A, Gordon J and Leach P, Human Rights and Social Justice Research Institute, London Metropolitan University 'The UK and the European Court of Human Rights', (Equality and Human Rights Commission Research report 83, 2012) <https://www.equalityhumanrights.com/sites/default/files/83._european_court_of_human_rights.pdf> accessed 9 June 2022

Duhs E, 'EU-UK Data Flows, Adequacy and Regulatory Changes from 1st January 2021' (*LinkedIn*, 28 December 2020) <https://www.linkedin.com/pulse/eu-uk-data-flows-adequacy-regulatory-changes-from-1st-eleonor-duhs> accessed 9 June 2022

Duisberg A, 'Zertifizierung und der Mittelstand – Quo Vadis?' [2018] ZD 53

Dunham E, 'ICO Statement in Response to the EU Commission's Announcement on the Approval of the UK's Adequacy' (28 June 2021) <https://ico.org.uk/about-the-ico/news-and-events/news-and-blogs/2021/06/ico-statement-in-response-to-the-eu-commission-s-announcement-on-the-approval-of-the-uk-s-adequacy> accessed 9 June 2022

ECHR, 'Guide on Article 8 of the European Convention on Human Rights' (2020) <https://www.echr.coe.int/documents/guide_art_8_eng.pdf> accessed 9 June 2022

ECHR 'Guide on Article 6 of the European Convention on Human Rights' (2021) <https://www.echr.coe.int/documents/guide_art_6_criminal_eng.pdf> accessed 9 June 2022

ECHR 'Guide on Article 13 of the European Convention on Human Rights' (2021) <https://www.echr.coe.int/Documents/Guide_Art_13_ENG.pdf> accessed 9 June 2022

EDPB, 'Guidelines 2/2018 on Derogations of Article 49 under Regulation 2016/679' (2018)

EDPB 'Guidelines 1/2018 on Certification and Identifying Certification Criteria in Accordance with Articles 42 and 43 of the Regulation – Version 3.0' (2019)

EDPB 'Guidelines 1/2019 on Codes of Conduct and Monitoring Bodies under Regulation 2016/679 – Version 2.0' (2019)

EDPB 'Guidelines 4/2018 on the Accreditation of Certification Bodies under Article 43 of the General Data Protection Regulation (2016/679) – Version 3.0' (2019)

EDPB 'Guidelines 3/2018 on the Territorial Scope of the GDPR (Article 3)' (2019)

EDPB 'Letter to the European Parliament' (2020) <https://edpb.europa.eu/sites/edpb/files/files/file1/edpb_letter_out_2020-0054-uk-usagreement.pdf.> accessed 9 June 2022

EDPB 'Information Note on BCRs for Companies Which Have ICO as BCR Lead Supervisory Authority' (2020) <https://edpb.europa.eu/sites/default/files/files/file1/edpb_informationnoteforgroupswithicoasbcrleadsa_20200722_en.pdf> accessed 9 June 2022

EDPB 'Frequently Asked Questions on the Judgement of the Court of Justice of the European Union in Case C-311/18 – Data Protection Commissioner v Facebook Ireland Ltd and Maximillian Schrems' (2020) <https://edpb.europa.eu/sites/default/files/files/file1/20200724_edpb_faqoncjeuc31118_en.pdf> accessed 9 June 2022

EDPB 'Response to Ms Elizabeth Denjam (ICO) Regarding Invitation to Attend Cooperation Subgroup Meeting and Open Transnational Cases' (2020) <https://edpb.europa.eu/our-work-tools/our-documents/letters/edpb-response-ms-elizabeth-denham-ico-regarding-invitation_de> accessed 9 June 2022

EDPB 'Recommendations 01/2020 on Measures That Supplement Transfer Tools to Ensure Compliance with the EU Level of Protection of Personal Data – Version 1.0' (2020)

EDPB 'Recommendations 02/2020 on the European Essential Guarantees for Surveillance Measures' (2020)

EDPB 'Guidelines 10/2020 on Restrictions under Article 23 GDPR. Version 1.0.' (2020)

EDPB 'Opinion 14/2021 Regarding the European Commission Draft Implementing Decision Pursuant to Regulation (EU) 2016/679 on the Adequate Protection of Personal Data in the United Kingdom' (2021)

EDPB 'Recommendations 01/2020 on Measures That Supplement Transfer Tools to Ensure Compliance with the EU Level of Protection of Personal Data – Version 2.0' (2021)

EDPB 'Guidelines 04/2021 on Codes of Conduct as Tools for Transfers' (2021)

EDPB 'Approved Binding Corporate Rules' <https://edpb.europa.eu/our-work-tools/accountability-tools/bcr_en> accessed 9 June 2022

EDPB 'Pre-GDPR BCRs Overview List' <https://edpb.europa.eu/our-work-tools/our-documents/other/pre-gdpr-bcrs-overview-list-0_en> accessed 9 June 2022

EDPB 'Register of Certification Mechanisms, Seals and Marks' <https://edpb.europa.eu/our-work-tools/accountability-tools/certification-mechanisms-seals-and-marks_de> accessed 9 June 2022

EDPB and EDPS, 'Joint Opinion 2/2021 on the European Commission's Implementing Decision on Standard Contractual Clauses for the Transfer of Personal Data to Third Countries for the Matters Referred to in Article 46(2)(c) of Regulation (EU) 2016/679' (2020)

EDPB and EDPS, 'EDPB & EDPS Adopt Joint Opinion on New Sets of SCCs' (2021) Press Release of 15 January 2021 <https://edpb.europa.eu/news/news/2021/edpb-edps-adopt-joint-opinions-new-sets-sccs_en> accessed 9 June 2022

EDPS, 'Opinion 8/2016 on Coherent Enforcement of Fundamental Rights in the Age of Big Data' (2016)

Eichenhofer J, '"e-Privacy" im Europäischen Grundrechtsschutz: Das "Schrems"-Urteil des EuGH' [2016] EuR 76

Eichenhofer J, 'Privatheit im Internet als Vertrauensschutz. Eine Neukonstruktion der Europäischen Grundrechte auf Privatleben und Datenschutz' (2016) 55 Der Staat 41

Elliot M, 'Beyond the European Convention: Human Rights and the Common Law' (2015) 68 Current Legal Problems 85

Elliot M, 'The Fundamentality of Rights at Common Law' in Mark Elliot and Kirsty Hughes (eds), *Common Law Constitutional Rights* (1st edn, Bloomsbury 2020)

Elliot M and Hughes K (eds), *Common Law Constitutional Rights* (1st edn, 2020)

Elliot M and Tierney S, 'Political Pragmatism and Constitutional Principle: The European Union (Withdrawal) Act 2018' [2018] PL

End Violence Against Women, 'New ICO Report Says Consent from Rape Victims "Too Difficult" as Basis for Phone Downloads' <https://www.endviolenceagainstwomen.org.uk/new-ico-report-says-consent-from-rape-victims-too-difficult-as-basis-for-phone-downloads/> accessed 9 June 2022

English R, 'The EU Charter: Are We in or Out?' (*UK Human Rights Blog*, 1 March 2011) <https://ukhumanrightsblog.com/2011/03/01/the-eu-charter-are-we-in-or-out/> accessed 9 June 2022

Ernst S, 'Art. 2 DS-GVO' in Boris P Paal and Daniel A Pauly (eds), *Datenschutz-Grundverordnung. Bundesdatenschutzgesetz: DS-GVO BDSG* (3rd edn, C.H. Beck 2021)

Ernst S, 'Art. 3 DS-GVO' in Boris P Paal and Daniel A Pauly (eds), *Datenschutz-Grundverordnung. Bundesdatenschutzgesetz: DS-GVO BDSG* (3rd edn, C.H. Beck 2021)

EU, 'Political Declaration Setting out the Framework for the Future Relationship between the European Union and the United Kingdom' (2019) 2019/C 384 I/02

EU, 'Trade' <https://europa.eu/european-union/topics/trade_en> accessed 9 June 2022

EU Commission, 'A Comprehensive Approach on Personal Data Protection in the European Union' (2010) Communication to the European Parliament, the Council, the Economic and Social Committee and the Committee on the Region (COM) 2010 609 final

EU Commission, 'Proposal for a Regulation of the European Parliament and of the Council on the Protection of Individuals with Regard to the Processing of Personal Data and on the Free Movement of Such Data (General Data Protection Regulation)' (2012) COM(2012) 11 final

EU Commission, 'Proposal for a Council Decision on the Conclusion of the Agreement between Canada and the European Union on the Transfer and Processing of Passenger Name Record Data' (2013) COM/2013/0528 final

EU Commission, 'Communication from the Commission to the European Parliament and the Council. A New EU Framework to Strengthen the Rule of Law' (2014) COM(2014) 158 final

EU Commission, 'Communication from the Commission on the Legal Nature of the Charter of Fundamental Rights of the European Union' COM(2014) 644 final

EU Commission, 'Flash Barometer 443 (EPrivacy)' (2016) Report <https://europa.eu/euro barometer/surveys/detail/2124> accessed 9 June 2022

EU Commission, 'Communication from the Commission to the European Parliament and Council. Exchanging and Protecting Personal Data in a Globalised World' (2017) COM(2017) 7 final

EU Commission, 'Report from to the European Parliament and the Council on the Third Annual Review of the Functioning of the EU-U.S. Privacy Shield' (2019) COM(2019) 495 final

EU Commission, 'Report from the Commission to the EU Parliament and the Council on the third annual review of the functioning of the EU-U.S. Privacy Shield' (2019) COM(2019) 495 final

EU Commission, 'Two Years of the GDPR: Questions and Answers' (2020) Press Release of 24 June 2020 <https://ec.europa.eu/commission/presscorner/detail/en/qanda_20_1166> accessed 9 June 2022

EU Commission, 'Draft of Commission Implementing Decision (EU) on standard contractual clauses for the transfer of personal data to third countries pursuant to Regulation (EU) 2016/679 of the European Parliament and of the Council (2020) <https://ec.europa.eu/ info/law/better-regulation/have-your-say/initiatives/12741-Data-protection-standard-con tractual-clauses-for-transferring-personal-data-to-non-EU-countries-implementing-act-_en> accessed 9 June 2022

EU Commission, 'Intensifying Negotiations on transatlantic Data Privacy Flows: A Joint Press Statement by European Commissioner for Justice Didier Reynders and U.S. Secretary of Commerce Gina Raimondo' (2021) Press Release of 25 March 2021 <https://ec.europa. eu/commission/presscorner/detail/en/STATEMENT_21_1443> accessed 9 June 2022

EU Commission, 'Data Protection: European Commission Launches Process on Personal Data Flows to UK' (2021) Press Release of 19 February 2021 <https://ec.europa.eu/commis sion/presscorner/detail/en/ip_21_661> accessed 9 June 2022

EU Commission, 'Draft of Commission Implementing Decision Pursuant Regulation (EU) 2016/ 679 of the European Parliament and of the Council on the Adequate Protection of Personal Data by the United Kingdom' (2021) <https://ec.europa.eu/info/sites/info/files/ draft_decision_on_the_adequate_protection_of_personal_data_by_the_united_king dom_-_general_data_protection_regulation_19_feb_2020.pdf> accessed 9 June 2022

EU Commission, 'Non-Paper on the Way Forward on Data Retention – Presentation by the Commission to the Delegations and Exchange of Views' (2021) <https://cdn.netzpolitik. org/wp-upload/2021/07/wk07294.en211.pdf.> accessed 9 June 2022

EU Commission, 'Data Protection: Commission Adopts Adequacy Decisions for the UK' (2021) Press Release of 28 June 2021 <https://ec.europa.eu/commission/presscorner/detail/ro/ ip_21_3183> accessed 9 June 2022

EU Commission, 'European Commission and United States Joint Statement on Trans-Atlantic Data Privacy Framework' (2022) Press release of 19 February 2021 <https://ec.europa.eu/ commission/presscorner/detail/en/ip_22_2087>.

EU Commission, 'Adequacy Decisions – How the EU Determines If a Non-EU Country Has an Adequate Level of Data Protection' <https://ec.europa.eu/info/law/law-topic/data-pro tection/international-dimension-data-protection/adequacy-decisions_en> accessed 9 June 2022

EU Commission, 'Data Protection as a Pillar of Citizens' Empowerment and the EU's Approach to the Digital Transition – Two Years of Application of the General Data Protection Regulation' Communication to the European Parliament and the Council COM/2020/264 final

EU Commission, 'EU Enlargement Strategy' Communication to the European Parliament, the Council, the European Economic and Social Committee and the Committee of the Regions COM(2015) 611 final EU Commission, Directorate General for Trade, 'Client and Supplier Countries of the EU27 in Merchandise Trade (Value %) (2020, Excluding Intra-EU Trade)' <https://trade.ec.europa.eu/doclib/docs/2006/september/tradoc_122530.pdf> accessed 9 June 2022

EU Parliament, 'EU-UK Private Sector Data Flows after Brexit. Settling on Adequacy' (2021) <https://www.europarl.europa.eu/RegData/etudes/IDAN/2021/690536/EPRS_IDA(2021) 690536_EN.pdf> accessed 9 June 2022

EU Parliament, 'Resolution of 25 March 2021 on the Commission Evaluation Report on the Implementation of the General Data Protection Regulation Two Years after Its Application' (2021) (2020/2717(RSP))

EU Parliament, 'Resolution on the Adequate Protection of Personal Data by the United Kingdom' (2021) (2021/2594(RSP))

European Union Agency for Fundamental Right, 'Surveillance by Intelligence Services: Fundamental Rights Safeguards and Remedies in the European Union – Volume II: Summary' <https://fra.europa.eu/sites/default/files/fra_uploads/fra-2017-surveillance-in telligence-services-vol-2-summary_en.pdf> accessed 9 June 2022

European Union Agency for Fundamental Rights and others (eds), *Handbook on European Data Protection Law* (2014)

Eurostat, 'EU Population up to over 513 Million on 1 January 2019' (2019) News Release of 10 July 2019 <https://ec.europa.eu/eurostat/documents/2995521/9967985/3-10072019-BP-EN.pdf/e152399b-cb9e-4a42-a155-c5de6dfe25d1> accessed 9 June 2022

Eurostat, 'GDPR and Main Components (Output, Expenditure and Income)' (2020) <https://ec.europa.eu/eurostat/databrowser/view/namq_10_gdp/default/table?lang=en> accessed 9 June 2022

Eurostat, 'The 2017 Results of the International Comparison Program: China, US and EU Are the Largest Economies in the World' (2020) News Release of 19 May 2020 <https://ec.europa.eu/eurostat/documents/portlet_file_entry/2995521/2-19052020-BP-EN.pdf/bb14f7f9-fc26-8aa1-60d4-7c2b509dda8e> accessed 9 June 2022

facebook, 'Facebook European Data Transfer Addendum Effective on 27 September 2021' <https://www.facebook.com/legal/EU_data_transfer_addendum/update> accessed 9 June 2022

Filip A, 'Binding Corporate Rules (BCR) aus der Sicht einer Datenschutzaufsichtsbehörde – Praxiserfahrungen mit der europaweiten Anerkennung von BCR' [2013] ZD 51

Fischer A, 'UK: Großbritannien bald kein sicheres Drittland i. S. d. Art. 45 DS-GVO mehr?' [2021] ZD-Aktuell 05346

Foreign & Commonwealth Office, 'Explanatory Memorandum to the Agreement between the Government of the United Kingdom of Great Britain and Northern Ireland and the Government of the United States of America on Access to Electronic Data for the Purpose of Countering Serious Crime' (2019)

Frenzel EM, 'Art. 5 DS-GVO' in Boris P Paal and Daniel A Pauly (eds), *Datenschutz-Grundverordnung. Bundesdatenschutzgesetz: DS-GVO BDSG* (3rd edn, C.H. Beck 2021)

Frontier Economics, 'The UK Digital Sectors after Brexit' (2017)

Gady F-S, 'EU/U.S. Approaches to Data Privacy and the "Brussels Effect": A Comparative Analysis' (2014) Georget. J. Int. Aff. 12

GDPR EU, 'What are the GDPR Fines?'<https://gdpr.eu/fines/> accessed 9 June 2022

GDPR Hub, 'DPC (Ireland) – WhatsApp Ireland Limited – IN-18 – 12 – 2' <https://gdprhub.eu/index.php?title=DPC_(Ireland)_-_WhatsApp_Ireland_Limited_-_IN-18-12-2&mtc=today> accessed 9 June 2022

Geppert N, 'Überprüfung der Modelle zur Datenübermittlung in Drittländer. Die Zukunft von EU-US-Privacy-Shield, BCRs und Standardvertragsklauseln' [2018] ZD 62

Gersdorf H, 'Art. 7 GrCh' in Boris P Paal and Hubertus Gersdorf (eds), *BeckOK Informations- und Medienrecht* (35rd edn, 2022)

Ghosh S, 'Facebook in Europe Is about to Get Massively Disrupted by New Laws Meant to Bring It to Heel' *Business Insider* (11 April 2018) <https://www.businessinsider.com/gdpr-privacy-law-eu-massive-timely-facebook-2018-4> accessed 9 June 2022

Goldsmith J and Wu T, *Who Controls the Internet?: Illusions of a Borderless World* (Oxford University Press 2006)

Golland A, 'Datenschutzrechtliche Anforderungen an internationale Datentransfers' [2020] NJW 2593

Gömann M, 'The New Territorial Scope of EU Data Protection Law: Deconstruction a Revolutionary Achievement' (2017) 54 CML Rev 567

González EG and Hert P de, 'Understanding the Legal Provisions That Allow Processing and Profiling of Personal Data—an Analysis of GDPR Provisions and Principles' (2019) 19 ERA Forum 597

Google Cloud, 'Google Cloud's Approach to the New EU Standard Contractual Clauses' (2021) <https://services.google.com/fh/files/misc/gc_new_eu_scc.pdf> accessed 9 June 2022

Götzinger L and Meyle H, 'Wie Google, Microsoft und Salesforce die neuen SCC umsetzen und was dies für Verantwortliche im EWR und in der Schweiz bedeutet' (*daten:recht – das Datenschutz-Team von Walder Wyss*, 18 October 2021) <https://datenrecht.ch/wie-google-microsoft-und-salesforce-die-neuen-scc-umsetzen-und-was-dies-fuer-verantwor tliche-im-ewr-und-in-der-schweiz-bedeutet/> accessed 9 June 2022

Govindarajan V, Srivastava A and Enache L, 'How India Plans to Protect Consumer Data' *HBR* (18 December 2019) <https://hbr.org/2019/12/how-india-plans-to-protect-consumer-data> accessed 9 June 2022

Granger M-P and Irion K, 'The Court of Justice and the Data Retention Directive in Digital Rights Ireland: Telling off the EU Legislature and Teaching a Lesson in Privacy and Data Protection' (2014) 39 Eur. Law Rev 835

Graux H and others, 'Study Requested by the European Parliament's LIBE Committee: The Future EU-UK Relationship: Options in the Field of the Protection of Personal Data for General Processing Activities and for Processing for Law Enforcement Purposes' (Policy Department for Citizens' Rights and Constitutional Affairs 2018) <https://www.europarl. europa.eu/RegData/etudes/STUD/2018/604976/IPOL_STU(2018)604976_EN.pdf> accessed 9 June 2022

Grayling C, 'Protection Human Rights in the UK: The Conservatives' Proposals for Changing Britain's Human Rights Law' (Conservative Party 2014) <https://www.theguardian.com/politics/interactive/2014/oct/03/conservatives-human-rights-act-full-document> accessed 9 June 2022

Greenleaf G, 'The Influence of European Data Privacy Standards Outside Europe: Implications for Globalisation of Convention 108' (2012) 2 IDPL 68

Greenleaf G, 'Global Data Privacy Laws 2019: 132 National Laws & Many Bills' (2019) 157 PL&B Reports 14

Griffis, K, 'US-EU Privacy Shield Talks Inching Closer to A Deal' (LAW60, 28 February 2022) <https://www.law360.com/articles/1468909/us-eu-privacy-shield-talks-inching-closer-to-a-deal>

Grogan J, 'Rights and Remedies at Risk: Implications of the Brexit Process on the Future of Rights in the UK' [2019] PL 683

Gühr A, Karper I and Maseberg S, 'Der lange Weg zur Akkreditierung nach Art. 42 DSGVO' (2020) 44 DuD 649

Hachez N and Wouters J, 'Promoting the Rule of Law: A Benchmarks Approach' (Leuven Centre for Global Governance Studies 2013) Working Paper No. 105 <https://www.fp7-frame.eu/wp-content/materiale/w-papers/WP105-Hachez-Wouters.pdf> accessed 9 June 2022

Halbfinger DM, Kershner I and Bergman R, 'To Track Coronavirus, Israel Moves to Tap Secret Trove of Cellphone Data' *The New York Times* (16 March 2020) <https://www.nytimes. com/2020/03/16/world/middleeast/israel-coronavirus-cellphone-tracking.html> accessed 9 June 2022

Hanna J, 'What Is the Five Eyes Intelligence Pact' [2017] CNN <https://edition.cnn.com/2017/05/25/world/uk-us-five-eyes-intelligence-explainer/index.html> accessed 9 June 2022

Härting N, 'Starke Behörden, schwaches Recht – der neue EU-Datenschutzentwurf' [2012] Der Betriebsberater 459

Härting N, 'Danke, Max Schrems!' (*beck-aktuell*, 24 August 2020) <https://rsw.beck.de/ak tuell/daily/magazin/detail/danke-max-schrems!> accessed 9 June 2022

Heinrich-Böll-Stiftung, 'Privacy in the EU and US: Consumer Experiences across Three Global Platforms' (2019)

Heinzke P, 'Schrems II: Neue Anforderungen an den Transfer personenbezogener Daten in Drittländer' [2020] GRUR-Prax 436

Hendrick F, 'Art. 8 – Protection of Personal Data' in Filip Dorssemont and others (eds) (1st edn, 2019)

Hennemann M, 'Datenportabilität' [2017] PinG 5

Hennemann M, 'Datenrichtigkeit. Beitragsreihe "Input Control – Datenqualität und Datenvalidität als Grundlage rechtlicher Automatisierungsprozesse", Abschnitt "Allgemeines"' [2020] LRZ 77

Hennemann M, 'Wettbewerb der Datenschutzrechtsordnungen? – Zur Rezeption der Datenschutz-Grundverordnung –' (2020) 84 RabelsZ 864

Hennemann M, 'Exportbeschränkungen für den Datenschutz?' *Frankfurter Allgemeine Tageszeitung Einspruch* (1 October 2020)

Hennemann M, 'Das Schweizer Datenschutzrecht im Wettbewerb der Rechtsordnungen' in Boris P. Paal, Dörte Poelzig, Oliver Fehrenbacher (eds), *Deutsches, Europäisches und vergleichendes Wirtschaftsrecht: Festschrift für Werner F. Ebke zum 70. Geburtstag* (C.H.Beck 2021) 377

Hennemann M, Boshe P and Meding R von, 'Current Regulatory Approaches, Policy Initiatives, and the Way Forward' (2022) 3 Global Privacy Law Review 56.

Herbst T, 'Art. 5 DS-GVO' in Jürgen Kühling and Benedikt Buchner (eds), *Datenschutz-Grundverordnung, Bundesdatenschutzgesetz: DS-GVO/BDSG* (3rd edn, C.H. Beck 2020)

Hirst P, 'Mass Surveillance in the Age of Terror Bulk Powers in the Investigatory Powers Act 2016' [2019] EHRLR 403

Hladjk J, 'Art. 47 DSGVO' in Martin Eßer, Philipp Kramer and Kai von Lewinski (eds), *Auernhammer, DSGVO/BDSG - Kommentar* (7th edn, Carl Heymanns Verlag 2020)

Hofmann J and Stach B, 'Soft Brexit – die Ruhe vor dem Sturm? Was müssen Unternehmen ab 2021 beachten?' [2021] ZD 3

Hogarth R, 'Judicial Review' (*Institute for Government*, 9 March 2020) <https://www.in stituteforgovernment.org.uk/explainers/judicial-review> accessed 9 June 2022

Hornung G, 'Art. 3 DSGVO' in Spiros Simitis, Gerrit Hornung and Indra Spiecker (genannt Döhmann) (eds), *Nomos Kommentar: Datenschutzrecht: DSGVO mit BDSG* (1st edn, Nomos 2019)

Hornung G and Spiecker (genannt Döhmann) I, 'Art. 1 DSGVO' in Spiros Simitis, Gerrit Hornung and Indra Spiecker (genannt Döhmann) (eds), *Nomos Kommentar: Datenschutzrecht: DSGVO mit BDSG* (1st edn, Nomos 2019)

House of Commons, Official Report Session 2015–2016, Vol 607 <https://www.parliament.uk/ globalassets/documents/publications-records/house-of-commons-publications/hcbv607. pdf> accessed 9 June 2022

House of Commons, Select Committee on Constitutional Affairs, Seventh Report of Session 2005 – 06 <https://publications.parliament.uk/pa/cm200506/cmselect/cmconst/991/ 99102.html> accessed 9 June 2022

House of Commons, Public Administration Committee, First Report of Session 2014 – 15, 'Who's Accountable? Relationships between Government and Arm's-Length Bodies' HC Paper 110 <https://publications.parliament.uk/pa/cm201415/cmselect/cmpubadm/110/ 110.pdf> accessed 9 June 2022

House of Commons, Intelligence and Security Committee, 'Privacy and Security: A Modern and Transparent Legal Framework' (2015), HC Paper 1705 <https://www.pdpjournals.com/docs/88433.pdf> accessed 9 June 2022

House of Commons, Home Affairs Committee, 'UK-EU Security Cooperation after Brexit' (2018) <https://publications.parliament.uk/pa/cm201719/cmselect/cmhaff/635/63508.htm#_id TextAnchor047> accessed 9 June 2022

House of Commons, European Scrutiny Committee, Thirty-Fifth Report of Session 2019–21, 'Documents considered by the Committee on 3 February 2021', HC Paper 229 <https://committees.parliament.uk/publications/4604/documents/46687/default/> accessed 9 June 2022

House of Commons and House of Lords, Joint Committee of Human Rights, 'Note from Deputy Counsel: The Human Rights Implications of the Data Protection Bill' (2017) <https://www.parliament.uk/globalassets/documents/joint-committees/human-rights/correspondence/2017-19/Note_Deputy_Counsel_DPBill.pdf> accessed 9 June 2022

House of Lords, 'Data Protection Bill' Vol 785 (13 November 2017) <https://hansard.parliament.uk/lords/2017-11-13/debates/EC101CF2-FA1C-4397-9A29-7F07333B396B/DataProtectionBill(HL)> accessed 9 June 2022

House of Lords, European Union Committee, Tenth Report of Session 2007–08, 'The Treaty of Lisbon: An Impact Assessment', (2008) HL Paper 62-I <https://publications.parliament.uk/pa/ld200708/ldselect/ldeucom/62/62.pdf> accessed 9 June 2022

House of Lords, European Union Committee, Twelfth Report of Session 2015–16, 'The UK, the EU and a British Bill of Rights', (2016) HL Paper 136 <https://publications.parliament.uk/pa/ld201516/ldselect/ldeucom/139/139.pdf> accessed 9 June 2022

House of Lords, 'Debate on the Investigatory Powers Bill' Vol 774 (19 October 2016) <https://hansard.parliament.uk/lords/2016-10-19/debates/E48829E1-69FB-444C-A27B-0B914F56CFFA/InvestigatoryPowersBill> accessed 9 June 2022

House of Lords, 'Data Retention and Acquisition Regulations 2018', Vol 793 (30 October 2018) <https://hansard.parliament.uk/Lords/2018-10-30/debates/F2B04417-1038-4179-8EFC-BBEC51692D35/DataRetentionAndAcquisitionRegulations2018> accessed 9 June 2022

House of Lords, Select Committee on the Constitution, Nineth Report of Session 2017–19, 'European Union (Withdrawal) Bill', (2018) HL Paper 69 <https://publications.parliament.uk/pa/ld201719/ldselect/ldconst/69/69.pdf> accessed 9 June 2022

House of Lords, Committee Stage, 'Supplementary Note on the Impact of the Loss of the EU Charter of Fundamental Rights' (2018) <https://www.equalityhumanrights.com/sites/default/files/note_on_practical_impact_of_loss_of_the_charter.pdf> accessed 9 June 2022

House of Lords, European Union Committee, Third Report of Session 2017–19, 'Brexit: The EU Data Protection Package' HL Paper 7 <https://publications.parliament.uk/pa/ld201719/ldselect/ldeucom/7/708.htm> accessed 9 June 2022

Hughes D, 'Boris Johnson's Speech in Full: Every Word of Brexit Deal Announcement as He Hails UK "Taking Back Control"' (*i news*, 24 December 2020) <https://inews.co.uk/news/politics/boris-johnson-speech-full-brexit-deal-announcement-trade-agreement-text-video-808170> accessed 9 June 2022

Hunt M, 'The "Horizontal Effect" of the Human Rights Act' [1998] PL 423

Hunton Andrews Kurth, 'New Dubai International Financial Centre Data Protection Law Comes Into Effect' (July 2020) <https://www.huntonprivacyblog.com/wp-content/uploads/sites/28/2020/07/new-dubai-ifc-data-protection-law-1.pdf> accessed 9 June 2022

Hustinx P, 'EU Data Protection Law: The Review of Directive 95/46/EC and the Proposed General Data Protection Regulation' (July 2013) <https://edps.europa.eu/sites/edp/files/publication/14-09-15_article_eui_en.pdf> accessed 9 June 2022

IAPP, 'IAPP-EY Annual Governance Report 2019' <https://iapp.org/store/books/a191P000003Qv5xQAC/> accessed 9 June 2022

ICO, 'Briefing, Data Protection Bill, House of Lords Report Stage – Information Commissioner's Briefing – Annex II' (2017) <https://ico.org.uk/media/about-the-ico/documents/2172865/dp-bill-lords-ico-briefing-report-stage-annex-ii-20171207.pdf.> accessed 9 June 2022

ICO, 'Data Protection Bill, House of Lords Report Stage – Information Commissioner's Briefing – Annex II' (2017) <https://ico.org.uk/media/about-the-ico/documents/2172865/dp-bill-lords-ico-briefing-report-stage-annex-ii-20171207.pdf> accessed 9 June 2022

ICO, 'Draft International Transfer Risk Assessment and Tool' (August 2021), <https://ico.org.uk/media/about-the-ico/consultations/2620397/intl-transfer-risk-assessment-tool-20210804.pdf> accessed 9 June 2022

ICO, 'Draft International Data Transfer Agreement' (August 2021) <https://ico.org.uk/media/about-the-ico/consultations/2620396/intl-data-transfer-agreement-202100804.pdf> accessed 9 June 2022

ICO, Draft Standard Data Protection Clauses to be issued by the Commissioner under Section 119 A(1) Data Protection Act 2018 – UK Addendum to the EU Commission Standard Contractual Clauses' (August 2021) <https://ico.org.uk/media/about-the-ico/consultations/2620398/draft-ico-addendum-to-com-scc-20210805.pdf> accessed 9 June 2022

ICO, 'EU Regulatory Oversight' (*ico.*) <https://ico.org.uk/for-organisations/dp-at-the-end-of-the-transition-period/data-protection-and-the-eu-in-detail/the-uk-gdpr/eu-regulatory-oversight/> accessed 9 June 2022

ICO, 'Guide to the General Data Protection Regulation (GDPR) – Immigration Exemption' (*ico.*) <https://ico.org.uk/for-organisations/guide-to-data-protection/guide-to-the-general-data-protection-regulation-gdpr/exemptions/immigration-exemption/> accessed 9 June 2022

ICO, 'Guide to the General Data Protection Regulation (GDPR) – International Transfers after the UK Exit from the EU Implementation Period' (*ico.*) <https://ico.org.uk/for-organisations/guide-to-data-protection/guide-to-the-general-data-protection-regulation-gdpr/international-transfers-after-uk-exit/> accessed 9 June 2022

ICO, 'Guide to the General Data Protection Regulation (GDPR) – National Security and Defence' (*ico.*) <https://ico.org.uk/for-organisations/guide-to-data-protection/guide-to-the-general-data-protection-regulation-gdpr/national-security-and-defence/> accessed 9 June 2022

ICO, 'Guide to the General Data Protection Regulation (GDPR) – Standard Contractual Clauses (SCCs) after the Transition Period Ends' (*ico.*) <https://ico.org.uk/for-organisations/guide-to-data-protection/guide-to-the-general-data-protection-regulation-gdpr/international-transfers-after-uk-exit/sccs-after-transition-period/> accessed 9 June 2022

ICO, 'How We Are Funded' (*ico.*) <https://ico.org.uk/about-the-ico/who-we-are/how-we-are-funded/> accessed 9 June 2022

ICO, 'International Data Transfer Addendum to the EU Commission Standard Contractual Clauses, Version B1.0' (*ico.*) <https://ico.org.uk/media/for-organisations/documents/4019539/international-data-transfer-addendum.pdf> accessed 9 June 2022

ICO, 'International Data Transfer Agreement, Version A1.0' (*ico.*) <https://ico.org.uk/media/for-organisations/documents/4019538/international-data-transfer-agreement.pdf> accessed 9 June 2022

ICO, 'Keep Data Flowing from the EEA to the UK – Interactive Tool' (*ico.*) <https://ico.org.uk/for-organisations/dp-at-the-end-of-the-transition-period/keep-data-flowing-from-the-eea-to-the-uk-interactive-tool/> accessed 9 June 2022

ICO, 'Overview – Data Protection and the EU' (*ico.*) <https://ico.org.uk/for-organisations/dp-at-the-end-of-the-transition-period/overview-data-protection-and-the-eu/> accessed 9 June 2022

ICO, 'Relationship with the Department for Digital, Culture Media and Sport' (*ico.*) <https://ico.org.uk/about-the-ico/who-we-are/relationship-with-the-dcms/> accessed 9 June 2022

ICO and the UK Intelligence Community, 'Memorandum of Understanding' (2020) <https://ico.org.uk/media/about-the-ico/mou/2617438/uk-intelligence-community-ico-mou.pdf> accessed 9 June 2022

Ilic I, 'Post-Brexit Limitations to Government Surveillance: Does the UK Get a Free Hand?' (2020) 25 Communications Law 31

Information Technology & Innovation Foundation, 'Response to the Consultation of the EU Commission on Transfers of Personal Data to Third Countries and Cooperation between Data Protection Authorities' (2020) <https://www2.itif.org/2020-gdpr-two-year-review.pdf> accessed 9 June 2022

IPCO, 'Annual Report of the Investigatory Powers Commissioner 2019' <https://www.ipco.org.uk/docs/IPC%20Annual%20Report%202019_Web%20Accessible%20version_final.pdf> accessed 9 June 2022

IPT, 'Closed and Open Procedures' <https://www.ipt-uk.com/content.asp?id=13> accessed 9 June 2022

Irion K, 'Schrems II and Surveillance: Third Countries' National Security Powers in the Purview of EU Law' (*European Law Blog*, 24 July 2020) <https://europeanlawblog.eu/2020/07/24/schrems-ii-and-surveillance-third-countries-national-security-powers-in-the-purview-of-eu-law/> accessed 9 June 2022

Irish Council of Civil Liberties, 'The Commission's Obligation to Refuse an "Adequacy Decision" to the United Kingdom Due to Inadequacy of Enforcement of Personal Data Protection in That Jurisdiction' (2020)

Jarass H, 'Art. 8' in *Charta der Grundrechte der EU* (4th edn, C.H.Beck 2021)

Javid S, 'Investigatory Powers Act 2016: Safeguard Relating to Retention and Disclosure of Material' Written Statement of 9 May 2019, HCWS1552 <https://questions-statements.parliament.uk/written-statements/detail/2019-05-09/HCWS1552> accessed 9 June 2022

Johnson B, 'UK/EU Relations' Written Statement on 3 February 2021 in the House of Commons UIN HCWS86 <https://questions-statements.parliament.uk/written-statements/detail/2020-02-03/HCWS86> accessed 9 June 2022

Kamp M, 'Art. 44 DS-GVO' in Heinrich Amadeus Wolff and Stefan Brink (eds), *Beck'scher Onlinekommentar: Datenschutzrecht* (38th edn, C.H. Beck 2022)

Kapoor S, 'The Data Protection Law of the Dubai International Finance Centre and the GDPR' (*LinkedIn*, 10 December 2020) <https://www.linkedin.com/pulse/data-protection-law-dubai-international-finance-centre-satvik-kapoor> accessed 9 June 2022

Kay RS, 'The European Convention on Human Rights and the Control of Private Law' [2005] European Human Rights Law Review 466

Kayali L, 'French Administrative Court Walks Data Retention Tightrope' *Politico* (21 April 2021) <https://www.politico.eu/article/french-administrative-authority-partially-revokes-data-retention-scheme/> accessed 9 June 2022

Kerry CF, 'The Oracle at Luxembourg: The EU Court of Justice Judges the World on Surveillance and Privacy' (2021) <https://www.brookings.edu/research/the-oracle-at-luxembourg-the-eu-court-of-justice-judges-the-world-on-surveillance-and-privacy/> accessed 9 June 2022

Kersten J, '§ 233 Wettbewerb der Rechtsordnungen?' in Josef Isensee and Paul Kirchhof (eds), *Handbuch des Staatsrechts*, vol 11 (3rd edn, 2013)

Kieninger E-M, 'Competition between Legal Systems' in Jürgen Basedow, Klaus J Hopt and Reinhard Zimmermann (eds), *The Max Planck Encyclopedia of European Private Law* (Oxford University Press 2012)

King E, 'Witness Statement of Eric King on Behalf of Privacy International in Privacy International v the Secretary of State for Foreign and Commonwealth Affairs & Government Communication Headquarters (Case No. IPT/13/92/CH)' <https://privacyinternational.org/sites/default/files/2018-03/2014.06.08%20Eric%20King%20witness%20statement.pdf> accessed 9 June 2022

Kingreen T, 'Art. 7 EU-GRCharta' in Christian Callies and Matthias Ruffert (eds), *EUV/AEUV – Das Verfassungsrecht der Europäischen Union mit Europäischer Grundrechtecharta* (6th edn, C.H. Beck 2022)

Kingreen T, 'Art. 8 EU-GRCharta' in Christian Callies and Matthias Ruffert (eds), *EUV/AEUV – Das Verfassungsrecht der Europäischen Union mit Europäischer Grundrechtecharta* (6th edn, C.H. Beck 2022)

Kipker D-K, 'Das neue chinesische Datenschutzgesetz PIPL ist da!' (*beck.de*, 22 August 2021) <https://community.beck.de/2021/08/22/das-neue-chinesische-datenschutzgesetz-pipl-ist-da> accessed 9 June 2022

Klar M, 'Die extraterritoriale Wirkung des neuen europäischen Datenschutzrechts' (2017) 41 DuD 533

Klar M, 'Art. 3 DS-GVO' in Jürgen Kühling and Benedikt Buchner (eds), *Datenschutz-Grundverordnung, Bundesdatenschutzgesetz: DS-GVO/BDSG* (3rd edn, C.H. Beck 2020)

Klar M and Kühling J, 'Privatheit und Datenschutz in der EU und den USA – Kollision zweier Welten?' (2016) 141 Archiv des öffentlichen Rechts 165

Komotoglou S, 'Das 1x1 der IT-Sicherheit: Lückenloser Schutz in der Cloud mit Confidential Computing' (*Microsoft*, 12 July 2021) <https://news.microsoft.com/de-de/das-1x1-der-it-sicherheit-lueckenloser-schutz-in-der-cloud-mit-confidential-computing/> accessed 9 June 2022

Konferenz der unabhängigen Datenschutzaufsichtsbehörden des Bundes und der Länder (Conference of the independent data protection supervisory authorities in Germany), 'Orientierungshilfe der Aufsichtsbehörden für Anbieter von Telemedien' (March 2019) <https://www.datenschutzkonferenz-online.de/media/oh/20190405_oh_tmg.pdf> accessed 9 June 2022

Korff D, 'Opinion on the Future of Personal Data Transfers from the EU/EEA to Israel & the Occupied Territories' (*Data protection and digital competition by Ian Brown and Douwe Korff*, 4 February 2021) <https://www.ianbrown.tech/wp-content/uploads/2021/07/KORFF-Opinion-EU-Israel-data-transfers-final.pdf> accessed 9 June 2022

Korff D, 'The Inadequacy of the EU Commission Draft GDPR Adequacy Decision on the UK' (2021) <https://www.ianbrown.tech/wp-content/uploads/2021/03/KORFF-The-Inadequacy-of-the-EU-Commn-Draft-GDPR-Adequacy-Decision-on-the-UK-Executive-Summary-210303flnal.pdf> accessed 9 June 2022

Korff D, 'Initial Comments on the EU Commission's Final GDPR Adequacy Decision on the UK' (17 June 2021) <https://www.ianbrown.tech/2021/06/17/initial-comments-on-the-eu-commissions-final-gdpr-adequacy-decision-on-the-uk/> accessed 9 June 2022

Korff D, 'Amid the Spying by EU Member States' Intelligence Agencies, Is EU Law Silent?' (*Data protection and digital competition by Ian Brown and Douwe Korff*, 27 August 2021) <https://www.ianbrown.tech/2021/08/27/amid-the-spying-by-eu-member-states-intelligence-agencies-is-eu-law-silent/> accessed 9 June 2022

Korff D, 'European Commission Responds to Parliament's Resolution on UK Adequacy' (*Data protection and digital competition by Ian Brown and Douwe Korff*, 30 September 2021) <https://www.ianbrown.tech/2021/09/30/european-commission-responds-to-parliaments-resolution-on-uk-adequacy/> accessed 9 June 2022

Korff D, ' Israel's Privacy Protection Act amendments and EU adequacy decision (*Data protection and digital competition by Ian Brown and Douwe Korff*, 23 February 2022) < https://www.ianbrown.tech/2022/02/23/israels-privacy-protection-act-amendments-and-eu-adequacy/> accessed 9 June 2022

Korff D and Brown I, 'The Inadequacy of UK Data Protection Law in General and in View of UK Surveillance Laws, Part Two: UK Surveillance' (2020) <https://www.ianbrown.tech/wp-content/uploads/2020/11/Korff-Brown-Submission-to-EU-re-UK-adequacy-Part-Two-DK-IB201130.pdf> accessed 9 June 2022

Korff D and Brown I, 'Some brief initial comments on the announcement of an "agreement principle" on a new Trans-Atlantic Data Privacy Framework & on the EDPB's statement on the agreement in principle' (11 April 2022) <https://www.ianbrown.tech/wp-content/uploads/2022/04/Early-comments-on-TADPF.pdf accessed 9 June 2022

Kramer P, 'Art. 6 DSGVO' In Martin Eßer, Philipp Kramer and Kai von Lewinski (eds), *Auernhammer, DSGVO/BDSG - Kommentar* (7th edn, Carl Heymanns Verlag 2020)

Kranenborg H, 'Art. 8 CFR' in Steve Peers and others (eds), *The EU Charter of Fundamental Rights: A Commentary* (2nd edn, Nomos 2021)

Krempl S, 'Rechtsexperte: Datenschutz-Grundverordnung als "größte Katastrophe des 21. Jahrhunderts"' (*heise online*, 27 April 2016)

Kuenssberg L and David D, 'Joe Biden Plays down Chances of UK-US Trade Deal' (*BBC News*, 22 September 2021) <https://www.bbc.com/news/uk-politics-58646017> accessed 9 June 2022

Kugler T, 'E. Practical Examples' in Tobias Kugler and Daniel Rücker (eds), *New European General Data Protection Regulation: A Practitioner's Guide* (1st edn, Nomos 2018)

Kühling J and Heberlein J, 'EuGH "reloaded": "unsafe Harbor" USA vs. "Datenfestung" EU' [2016] NVwZ 7

Kühling J and Raab J, 'Art. 2 DS-GVO' in Jürgen Kühling and Benedikt Buchner (eds), *Datenschutz-Grundverordnung, Bundesdatenschutzgesetz: DS-GVO/BDSG* (3rd edn, C.H. Beck 2020)

Kuner C, *Transborder Data Flow and Data Privacy Law* (Oxford University Press 2013)

Kuner C, 'Reality and Illusion in EU Data Transfer Regulation Post Schrems' (2017) 18 German Law Journal 881

Kuner C, 'Art. 45 GDPR' in Christopher Kuner, Lee A Bygrave and Christopher Docksey (eds), *The EU General Data Protection Regulation (GDPR). A Commentary* (Oxford University Press 2020)

Kuo L, 'China Bans 23 m From Buying Travel Tickets as Part of "Social Credit" System' *The Guardian* (1 March 2019) <https://www.theguardian.com/world/2019/mar/01/china-bans-23m-discredited-citizens-from-buying-travel-tickets-social-credit-system> accessed 9 June 2022

Lamens P and Caesar E, 'GDPR & Brexit: Is There a Need for an Adequacy Decision? What Are the Consequences of Brexit in Relation to Data Transfers?' (*Deloitte*) <https://www2.de loitte.com/nl/nl/pages/risk/articles/cyber-security-privacy-gdpr-and-brexit-is-there-a-need-for-an-adequacy-decision.html> accessed 9 June 2022

Lange L-M and Filip A, 'Art. 46 DS-GVO' in Heinrich Amadeus Wolff and Stefan Brink (eds), *Beck'scher Onlinekommentar: Datenschutzrecht* (38th edn, C.H. Beck 2022)

Lange L-M and Filip A, 'Art. 47 DS-GVO' in Heinrich Amadeus Wolff and Stefan Brink (eds), *Beck'scher Onlinekommentar: Datenschutzrecht* (38th edn, C.H. Beck 2022)

Lange L-M and Filip A, 'Art. 49 DS-GVO' in Heinrich Amadeus Wolff and Stefan Brink (eds), *Beck'scher Onlinekommentar: Datenschutzrecht* (38th edn, C.H. Beck 2022)

Larson J, 'Revealed: The NSA's Secret Campaign to Crack, Undermine Internet Security' (5 September 2013) <https://www.propublica.org/article/the-nsas-secret-campaign-to-crack-undermine-internet-encryption> accessed 9 June 2022

Lejeune M, 'Datentransfer personenbezogener Daten in die USA vor dem aus?! – Kritische Anmerkungen zur EuGH Entscheidung C-311/18 Vom 16.7.2020' [2020] CR 522

Lewinski K von, *Die Matrix des Datenschutzes – Besichtigung und Ordnung eines Begriffsfeldes*, vol 1 (Mohr Siebeck 2014)

Lewinski K von, 'Privacy Shield – Notdeich nach dem Pearl Harbor für die transatlantischen Datentransfers' [2016] EuR 405

Lewinski K von, 'Art. 2 DSGVO' in Martin Eßer, Philipp Kramer and Kai von Lewinski (eds), *Auernhammer, DSGVO/BDSG - Kommentar* (7th edn, Carl Heymanns Verlag 2020)

Lewinski K von, 'Art. 3 DSGVO' in Martin Eßer, Philipp Kramer and Kai von Lewinski (eds), *Auernhammer, DSGVO/BDSG - Kommentar* (7th edn, Carl Heymanns Verlag 2020)

Lewinski K von, 'Einführung' in Martin Eßer, Philipp Kramer and Kai von Lewinski (eds), *Auernhammer, DSGVO/BDSG- Kommentar* (7th edn, Carl Heymanns Verlag 2020)

Lewinski K von and Rüpke G and Eckhardt J, *Datenschutzrecht* (1st edn, C.H.Beck 2018)

Lienen C, 'Common Law Constitutional Rights: Public Law at a Crossroads?' [2018] PL 649

Lock T, 'Is Private Enforcement of EU Law through State Liability a Myth?: An Assessment 20 Years after Francovich' (2012) 49 CML Rev 1675

Lock T, 'The Influence of EU Law on Strasbourg Doctrines' (2016) 41 ERE 804

Lock T, 'Human Rights Law in the UK after Brexit' (2017) Nov Supp (Brexit Special Extra Issue 2017) PL 117

Lomas N, 'Facebook Urged to Make GDPR Its "Baseline Standard" Globally' (*TechCrunch*, 9 April 2018) <https://techcrunch.com/2018/04/09/facebook-urged-to-make-gdpr-its-baseline-standard-globally/?guccounter=1&guce_referrer=aHR0cHM6Ly93d3cuZ29vZ2xlLmNvbS8&guce_referrer_sig=AQAAAKidzFclSICBMnwHYOqS82N-ZhpELnUb4bYjICHCAdHpuR0vh_I1KZzmSZTYFoZaxOsKl3HxzOWnWxqWIRUZgsY3FlhAOFBDns7v3ty6tSvuQvuwjiztDnyqqAScooKgBOunVd9s6PFU2yLRzxH8V8pZgumJ_2S6Ig15zBYdKBbj> accessed 9 June 2022

Lynskey O, *The Foundations of EU Data Protection Law* (Oxford University Press 2015)

MacAskill E and others, 'GCHQ Taps Fibre-Optic Cables for Secret Access to World's Communications' *The Guardian* (21 June 2013) <https://www.theguardian.com/uk/2013/jun/21/gchq-cables-secret-world-communications-nsa> accessed 9 June 2022

Manancourt V, 'EU to US on Surveillance: Do as I Say, Not as I Do. A French-Led Push to Keep Personal Data Is Undermining the EU's Position on Surveillance' *Politico* (17 March 2021) <https://www.politico.eu/article/eu-to-us-surveillance-data-flows/> accessed 9 June 2022

Manancourt V, 'Why Brussels Went Easy on Britain in Its Data Deal' *Politico* (30 June 2021) <https://www.politico.eu/article/why-brussels-went-easy-on-britain-in-data-adequacy-deal/> accessed 9 June 2022

Marsch N, *Das Europäische Datenschutzrecht* (Mohr Siebeck 2018)

May T, 'In Full: Theresa May's Speech on Future UK-EU Relations' (2 March 2018) <https://www.bbc.com/news/uk-politics-43256183> accessed 9 June 2022

Mbioh WR, 'Post-Och Telestyrelsen and Watson and the Investigatory Powers Act 2016' (2017) 3 EDPL 273

McCann D, Patel O and Ruiz J, 'The Cost of Data Inadequacy' *New Economics Foundation* (23 November 2020) <https://neweconomics.org/2020/11/the-cost-of-data-inadequacy> accessed 9 June 2022

McKay S, Blackstone's Guide to The Investigatory Powers Act 2016, (1st edn, Oxford University Press 2017)

Mense M, 'EU-US-Privacy-Shield – Der kleinste gemeinsame Nenner angemessenen Datenschutzes? Angemessenheit des Datenschutzniveaus und aktuelle Entwicklungen' [2019] ZD 351

Meyer R, 'Europeans Use Google Way, Way More Than Americans Do' *The Atlantic* (15 April 2015) <https://www.theatlantic.com/technology/archive/2015/04/europeans-use-google-way-way-more-than-americans-do/390612/> accessed 9 June 2022

Michael L, 'Wettbewerb von Rechtsordnungen' (2009) 124 DVBl 1062

Michl W, 'Das Verhältnis zwischen Art. 7 und Art. 8 GRCh – Zur Bestimmung der Grundlage des Datenschutzgrundrechts im EU-Recht' (2017) 41 DuD 349

Microsoft, 'Microsoft Products and Services Data Protection Addendum (DPA)' (2021) <https://www.microsoft.com/licensing/docs/view/Microsoft-Products-and-Services-Data-Protection-Addendum-DPA> accessed 9 June 2022

Ministry of Justice, 'Government Launches Independent Review of Human Rights Act' (2020) Press Release of 7 December 2020 <https://www.gov.uk/government/news/government-launches-independent-review-of-the-human-rights-act> accessed 9 June 2022

Moerel L, *Binding Corporate Rules: Corporate Self-Regulation of Global Data Transfers* (1st edn, 2012)

Montezuma LA, 'Obtaining Adequacy Standing for Colombia' (*IAPP*, 2 August 2018) <https://iapp.org/news/a/obtaining-adequacy-standing-for-colombia/> accessed 9 June 2022

Moore D, 'Art. 23 GDPR' in Christopher Kuner, Lee A Bygrave and Christopher Docksey (eds), *The EU General Data Protection Regulation (GDPR). A Commentary* (Oxford University Press 2020)

Moos F and Schefzig J, '"Safe Harbor" hat Schiffbruch erlitten. Auswirkungen des EuGH-Urteils C-362/14 in Sachen Schrems ./. Data Protection Commissioner' [2015] CR 625

Morgan J, 'Privacy, Confidence and Horizontal Effect: "Hello" Trouble' (2003) 62 CLJ 444

Mozur P, 'Inside China's Dystopian Dreams: A.I., Shame and Lots of Cameras' *The New York Times* (15 October2018) <https://www.nytimes.com/2018/07/08/business/china-surveillance-technology.html> accessed 9 June 2022

Mühlauer A, 'Goodbye, verhasste Cookie-Banner' *Süddeutsche Zeitung* (London, 26 August 2021) <https://www.sueddeutsche.de/wirtschaft/brexit-dsgvo-1.5393086> accessed 9 June 2022

Murphy CC, 'Bulletin on the EU Charter of Fundamental Rights: An Introduction: Part 2' [2016] EHRLR 273

Murray AD, 'Data Transfers between the EU and UK Post Brexit?' (2017) 7 IDPL 149

National Crime Agency, 'Suspicious Activity Reports (SARs) Annual Report 2015' <https://www.nationalcrimeagency.gov.uk/who-we-are/publications/2-sars-annual-report-2015/file> accessed 9 June 2022

National Security Agency/Central Security Service, 'GCHQ and NSA Celebrate 75 Years of UKUSA Agreement' (2021) Press Release of 4 March 2021 <https://www.nsa.gov/Press-Room/News-Highlights/Article/Article/2524368/gchq-and-nsa-celebrate-75-years-of-ukusa-agreement/> accessed 9 June 2022

Nickoleit, J and Müller, J, 'Regierungspapier: Datenschutz-Reforminitiative in UK' [2021] ZD-Aktuell 05522

Nougrères AB, 'Data Protection and Enforcement in Latin America and in Uruguay' in David Wright and Paul de Hert (eds), *Enforcing Privacy: Regulatory, Legal and Technological Approaches* (Springer 2016)

OECD, 'The OECD Privacy Framework' (2013) <https://www.oecd.org/sti/ieconomy/oecd_privacy_framework.pdf>

Office of National Statistics, 'Index of Services, UK: January 2020' (2020) <https://www.ons.gov.uk/economy/economicoutputandproductivity/output/bulletins/indexofservices/january2020> accessed 9 June 2022

Office of the Australian Information Commissioner, 'Australian Entities and the EU General Data Protection Regulation (GDPR)' (2018) <https://www.oaic.gov.au/privacy/guidance-and-advice/australian-entities-and-the-eu-general-data-protection-regulation> accessed 9 June 2022

Ojanen T, 'Making the Essence of Fundamental Rights Real: The Court of Justice of the European Union Clarifies the Structure of Fundamental Rights under the Charter. ECJ 6 October 2015, Case C-362/14, Maximilian Schrems v Data Protection Commissioner.' (2016) 12 EuConst 318

Open Rights Group, 'Report on GCHQ and UK Mass Surveillance, Part One Chapter One: Passive Collection' (2015) <https://www.openrightsgroup.org/app/uploads/2020/03/01-Part_One_Chapter_One-Passive_Collection.pdf> accessed 9 June 2022

Open Rights Group, 'Submission to the European Commission, the European Data Protection Board and the European Parliament on the UK Immigration Exemption' (2021) <https://www.openrightsgroup.org/app/uploads/2021/03/Submission-to-European-Commission-on-the-operation-of-the-UKs-immigration-exemption-in-the-Data-Protection-Act-2018-Open-Rights-Group-2-March-2021.pdf> accessed 9 June 2022

Paal BP, 'Marktmacht im Daten(schutz)Recht' (2020) 18 ZWeR 215

Paal BP, 'Art. 20 DS-GVO' in Boris P Paal and Daniel A Pauly (eds), *Datenschutz-Grundverordnung. Bundesdatenschutzgesetz: DS-GVO BDSG* (3rd edn, C.H. Beck 2021)

Paal BP and Kumkar LK, 'Datenübermittlungen nach dem Unwirksamwerden des EU-US-Privacy Shield. Bestandsaufnahme und Handlungsempfehlungen nach der EuGH-Entscheidung "Schrems II"' [2020] MMR 733

Pauly DA, 'Art. 44 DS-GVO' in Boris P Paal and Daniel A Pauly (eds), *Datenschutz-Grundverordnung. Bundesdatenschutzgesetz: DS-GVO BDSG* (3rd edn, C.H. Beck 2021)

Pauly DA, 'Art. 45 DS-GVO' in Boris P Paal and Daniel A Pauly (eds), *Datenschutz-Grundverordnung. Bundesdatenschutzgesetz: DS-GVO BDSG* (3rd edn, C.H. Beck 2021)

Pauly DA, 'Art. 46 DS-GVO' in Boris P Paal and Daniel A Pauly (eds), *Datenschutz-Grundverordnung. Bundesdatenschutzgesetz: DS-GVO BDSG* (3rd edn, C.H. Beck 2021)

Pauly DA, 'Art. 47 DS-GVO' in Boris P Paal and Daniel A Pauly (eds), *Datenschutz-Grundverordnung. Bundesdatenschutzgesetz: DS-GVO BDSG* (3rd edn, C.H. Beck 2021)

Pauly DA, 'Art. 49 DS-GVO' in Boris P Paal and Daniel A Pauly (eds), *Datenschutz-Grundverordnung. Bundesdatenschutzgesetz: DS-GVO BDSG* (3rd edn, C.H. Beck 2021)

Peers S, 'The "Opt-out" That Fell to Earth: The British and Polish Protocol Concerning the EU Charter of Fundamental Rights' (2012) 12 Human rights Law Review 375

Peers S and Prechal S, 'Art. 52 CFR' in Steve Peers and others (eds), *The EU Charter of Fundamental Rights: A Commentary* (2nd edn, Nomos 2021)

Peter Swire, 'U.K's Post-Brexit Strategy on Cross-Border Data Flows' (*Lawfare*, 1 September 2021) <https://www.lawfareblog.com/uks-post-brexit-strategy-cross-border-data-flows> accessed 9 June 2022

Pfluke C, 'A History of the Five Eyes Alliance: Possibility for Reform and Additions' (2019) 38 Comparative Strategy 302

Phillipson G, 'The Human Rights Act, "Horizontal Effect" and the Common Law: A Bang or a Whimper?' (1999) 62 Mod. L. Rev. 824

Phillipson G and Williams A, 'Horizontal Effect and the Constitutional Constraint' (2011) 74 Mod. L. Rev. 878

Prime Minister's Office and HRH The Prince of Wales, Prince Charles, The Queen's Speech 2022 (10 March 2022) <https://assets.publishing.service.gov.uk/government/uploads/system/uploads/attachment_data/file/1074113/Lobby_Pack_10_May_2022.pdf> accessed 9 June 2022

Privacy International, 'UK Data Protection Act 2018 – 339 Pages Still Falls Short on Human Rights Protection' (13 June 2018) <https://privacyinternational.org/news-analysis/2074/uk-data-protection-act-2018-339-pages-still-falls-short-human-rights-protection> accessed 9 June 2022

Privacy International, 'Five Eyes' <https://privacyinternational.org/learn/five-eyes> accessed 9 June 2022

Proust O and Bartoli E, 'Binding Corporate Rules: A Global Solution for International Data Transfers' (2012) 2 IDPL 35

Reinsch WA, 'Must Third Countries Choose Between EU or U.S. Digital Trade Protection Preferences?' (*CSIS, The Future of Digital Trade Policy and the Role of the U.S. and UK*, 11 July 2018) <https://www.csis.org/blogs/future-digital-trade-policy-and-role-us-and-uk/must-third-countries-choose-between-eu-or-us> accessed 9 June 2022

Research Centre for Law and Digitalisation, 'Adequacy Decisions by the European Commission' <https://www.jura.uni-passau.de/fileadmin/dokumente/fakultaeten/jura/lehrstuehle/hennemann/Mapping_Global_Data_Law/I01_-_Adequacy_Decisions.pdf> accessed 9 June 2022

Research Centre for Law and Digitalisation, 'Data Protection Laws in Africa' <https://www.jura.uni-passau.de/fileadmin/dokumente/fakultaeten/jura/lehrstuehle/hennemann/Mapping_Global_Data_Law/L02_-_Africa.pdf> accessed 9 June 2022

Research Centre for Law and Digitalisation, 'Data Protection Laws in Asia' <https://www.jura.uni-passau.de/fileadmin/dokumente/fakultaeten/jura/lehrstuehle/hennemann/Mapping_Global_Data_Law/L03_-_Asia.pdf> accessed 9 June 2022

Research Centre for Law and Digitalisation, 'Data Protection Laws in South America' <https://www.jura.uni-passau.de/fileadmin/dokumente/fakultaeten/jura/lehrstuehle/hennemann/Mapping_Global_Data_Law/L_05_-_Data_Protection_Laws_in_South_America.pdf> accessed 9 June 2022

Research Centre for Law and Digitalisation, Data Protection Laws in the South Pacific' <https://www.jura.uni-passau.de/fileadmin/dokumente/fakultaeten/jura/lehrstuehle/hennemann/Mapping_Global_Data_Law/L_08_-_Data_Protection_Laws_in_South_Pacific_01.pdf> accessed 9 June 2022

Research Centre for Law and Digitalisation, 'Parties to the CoE Convention 108 / 108+' <https://www.jura.uni-passau.de/fileadmin/dokumente/fakultaeten/jura/lehrstuehle/hennemann/Mapping_Global_Data_Law/I02_-_Convention_108_and_108__.pdf> accessed 9 June 2022

Rippy, S, 'Colorado Privacy Act becomes law' (*IAPP*, 8 July 2021) <https://iapp.org/news/a/virginia-passes-the-consumer-data-protection-act/> accessed 9 June 2022

Rippy, S, 'Virginia passes the Consumer Data Protection Act' (IAPP, 8 July 2021) <https://iapp.org/news/a/colorado-privacy-act-becomes-law/> accessed 9 June 2022

Roßnagel A, 'Art. 2 DSGVO' in Spiros Simitis, Gerrit Hornung and Indra Spiecker (genannt Döhmann) (eds), *Nomos Kommentar: Datenschutzrecht: DSGVO mit BDSG* (1st edn, Nomos 2019)

Roßnagel A, 'Art. 5 DSGVO' in Spiros Simitis, Gerrit Hornung and Indra Spiecker (genannt Döhmann) (eds), *Nomos Kommentar: Datenschutzrecht: DSGVO mit BDSG* (1st edn, Nomos 2019)

Rücker D, 'B. Scope of Application of the GDPR' in Tobias Kugler and Daniel Rücker (eds), *New European General Data Protection Regulation: A Practitioner's Guide* (1st edn, Nomos 2018)

Rudgard S, 'BCR and Brexit – A Practical Way Forward' (6 October 2020) <https://www.engage.hoganlovells.com/knowledgeservices/news/bcr-and-brexit-a-practical-way-forward> accessed 9 June 2022

Sales P, 'Strasbourg Jurisprudence and the Human Rights Act: A Response to Lord Irvine' [2012] PL 253

Sales P, 'Rights and Fundamental Rights in English Law' (2016) 75 CLJ 86

Salesforce, 'Data Processing Addendum' (2021) <https://www.salesforce.com/content/dam/web/en_us/www/documents/legal/Agreements/data-processing-addendum.pdf> accessed 9 June 2022

Sandfuchs B, 'The Future of Data Transfers to Third Countries in Light of the CJEU's Judgement C-311/18 – Schrems II' [2021] GRUR Int. 245

Schantz P, 'Art. 44 DSGVO' in Spiros Simitis, Gerrit Hornung and Indra Spiecker (eds), *Nomos Kommentar: Datenschutzrecht: DSGVO mit BDSG* (1st edn, Nomos 2019)

Schantz P, 'Art. 45 DSGVO' in Spiros Simitis, Gerrit Hornung and Indra Spiecker (genannt Döhmann) (eds), *Nomos Kommentar: Datenschutzrecht: DSGVO mit BDSG* (1st edn, Nomos 2019)

Schantz P, 'Art. 48 DSGVO' in Spiros Simitis, Gerrit Hornung and Indra Spiecker (genannt Döhmann) (eds), *Nomos Kommentar: Datenschutzrecht: DSGVO mit BDSG* (1st edn, Nomos 2019)

Schantz P, 'Art. 1 DS-GVO' in Heinrich Amadeus Wolff and Stefan Brink (eds), *Beck'scher Onlinekommentar: Datenschutzrecht* (38th edn, C.H. Beck 2022)

Scheben B and Busekist K von, 'Dürfen personenbezogene Daten die EU noch verlassen?' [2021] WPg 329

Schiedermair S, 'Einleitung' in Spiros Simitis, Gerrit Hornung and Indra Spiecker (eds), *Nomos Kommentar: Datenschutz: DSGVO mit BDSG* (1st edn, Nomos)

Schneider B, 'Data Mining for Terrorists' (*Schneier on Security*, 9 March 2006) <https://www.schneier.com/blog/archives/2006/03/data_mining_for.html> accessed 9 June 2022

Schneider, J-P 'B. Völker- und unionsverfassungsrechtliche Grundlagen' in Heinrich Amadeus Wolff and Stefan Brink (eds), *Beck'scher Onlinekommentar: Datenschutzrecht* (38th edn, C.H. Beck 2022)

Schramm M, '35,3 Millionen Euro Bußgeld wegen Datenschutzverstößen im Servicecenter von H&M' (*Der Hamburgische Beauftragte für Datenschutz und Informationsfreiheit*, 1 October 2020) <https://datenschutz-hamburg.de/pressemitteilungen/2020/10/2020-10-01-h-m-verfahren> accessed 9 June 2022

Schröder C, 'Art. 44 DS-GVO' in Jürgen Kühling and Benedikt Buchner (eds), *Datenschutz-Grundverordnung, Bundesdatenschutzgesetz: DS-GVO/BDSG* (3rd edn, C.H. Beck 2020)

Schröder C, 'Art. 45 DS-GVO' in Jürgen Kühling and Benedikt Buchner (eds), *Datenschutz-Grundverordnung, Bundesdatenschutzgesetz: DS-GVO/BDSG* (3rd edn, C.H. Beck 2020)

Schröder C, 'Art. 46 DS-GVO' in Jürgen Kühling and Benedikt Buchner (eds), *Datenschutz-Grundverordnung, Bundesdatenschutzgesetz: DS-GVO/BDSG* (3rd edn, C.H. Beck 2020)

Schröder C, 'Art. 47 DS-GVO' in Jürgen Kühling and Benedikt Buchner (eds), *Datenschutz-Grundverordnung, Bundesdatenschutzgesetz: DS-GVO/BDSG* (3rd edn, C.H. Beck 2020)

Schröder C, 'Art. 49 DS-GVO' in Jürgen Kühling and Benedikt Buchner (eds), *Datenschutz-Grundverordnung, Bundesdatenschutzgesetz: DS-GVO/BDSG* (3rd edn, C.H. Beck 2020)

Schumacher P, 'B. Scope of Application of the GDPR' in Tobias Kugler and Daniel Rücker (eds), *New European General Data Protection Regulation: A Practitioner's Guide* (1st edn, Nomos 2018)

Schwartmann R and Burkhardt L, '"Schrems II" als Sackgasse für die Datenwirtschaft? Verfahrensrechtliche Grenzen datenschutzrechtlicher Sanktionen' [2021] ZD 235

Schwartz PM, 'Global Data Privacy: The EU Way' (2019) 94 N.Y.U. L. Rev. 771

Schwartz PM, 'The Data Privacy Law of Brexit: Theories of Preference Change', *Theoretical Inquiries in Law* <https://ssrn.com/abstract=3895999> accessed 9 June 2022

Schwartz PM and Peifer K-N, 'Datentreuhändermodelle – Sicherheit vor Herausgabeverlangen US-Amerikanischer Behörden und Gerichte?' [2017] CR 165

Schwartz PM and Peifer K-N, 'Transatlantic Data Privacy Law' (2017) 119 Geo. L.J. 115

Scott PF, 'General Warrants, Thematic Warrants, Bulk Warrants: Property Interference for National Security Purposes' (2017) 68 NI Legal Quarterly 99

Secretary of State for Digital, Culture, Media, and Sport, 'Data Adequacy Assessment Manual' <https://assets.publishing.service.gov.uk/government/uploads/system/uploads/attach ment_data/file/1013033/Manual_Guidance.pdf> accessed 9 June 2022

Secretary of State for Foreign and Commonwealth Affairs by Command of Her Majesty, 'Agreement between the Government of the United Kingdom of Great Britain and Northern Ireland and the Government of the United States of America on Access to Electronic Data for the Purpose of Countering Serious Crime' (2019) USA No. 6 (2019)

Shaffer G, 'Globalization and Social Protection: The Impact of EU and International Rules in the Ratcheting Up of U.S. Privacy Standards' (2000) 25 Yale J. Int'l L.

Shiffman N and Ben-Avi J, 'Data Localization: Bad for Users, Business, and Security' (*Mozilla*, 22 June 2018) <https://blog.mozilla.org/netpolicy/2018/06/22/data-localization-india/> accessed 9 June 2022

Skelton SK, 'UK Police Unlawfully Processing over a Million People's Data on Microsoft 365' *ComputerWeekly.com* (17 December 2020) <https://www.computerweekly.com/news/ 252493673/UK-police-unlawfully-processing-over-a-million-peoples-data-on-Microsoft-365> accessed 9 June 2022

Smith RHSID, Villiers RHT and Freeman G, 'Taskforce on Innovation, Growth and Regulatory Reform' (2021)

Sörup T and Parvez D, 'Nutzung von Microsoft Office 365 im Unternehmen. Datenschutz- und Betriebsverfassungsrechtliche Fragestellungen und Gestaltungshinweise' [2021] ZD 291

Spies A, 'EU-Standardvertragsklauseln bei internationaler Datenübermittlung' [2021] ZD-Aktuell 05011

Stauch, M, 'UK: Government Published Proposal for Reforming UK Data Protection Law' [2021] ZD-Aktuell 05532

State Commissioner for Data Protection and Freedom of Information in Mecklenburg-Western Pomerania, 'Pressemitteilung des Landesbeauftragten für Datenschutz und Informationsfreiheit Mecklenburg-Vorpommern' (2021) Press Release of 17 March 2021 <https://www.datenschutz-mv.de/presse/?id=168438&processor=processor.sa.press emitteilung> accessed 9 June 2022

Stemmer B, 'Art. 6 DS-GVO' in Heinrich Amadeus Wolff and Stefan Brink (eds), *Beck'scher Onlinekommentar: Datenschutzrecht* (38th edn, C.H. Beck 2022)

Stephens P, 'Europe Rewrites the Rules for Silicon Valley' *Financial Times* (3 November 2016)

Stone J, 'British Bill of Rights Plan Shelved Again for Several More Years, Justice Secretary Confirms' *Independent* (23 February 2017) <https://www.independent.co.uk/news/uk/poli tics/scrap-human-rights-act-british-bill-rights-brexit-liz-truss-theresa-may-a7595336.html> accessed 9 June 2022

Stone J, 'Boris Johnson Refuses to Commit to Keeping UK in Human Rights Convention' *Independent* (Brussels, 5 March 2020) <https://www.independent.co.uk/news/uk/poli tics/boris-johnson-brexit-human-rights-convention-echr-michel-barnier-a9378141.html> accessed 9 June 2022

Sydow G, 'Einleitung' in Gernot Sydow (ed), *Nomos Kommentar: Europäische Datenschutzgrundverordnung* (2nd edn, Nomos 2018)

Tene O, 'Quick Reaction to EDPB Schrems II Guidance' (*LinkedIn*, 12 November 2020) <https://www.linkedin.com/pulse/quick-reaction-edpb-schrems-ii-guidance-omer-tene/?utm_source=POLITICO.EU&utm_campaign=a48677014b-EMAIL_CAMPAIGN_2020_11_13_02_43&utm_medium=email&utm_term=0_10959edeb5-a48677014b-190373637> accessed 9 June 2022

The Boston Consulting Group, 'The Internet Now Contributes 10 Percent of GDP to the UK Economy, Surpassing the Manufacturing and Retail Sectors' (2015) <https://www.globenewswire.com/news-release/2015/05/01/924211/0/en/The-Internet-Now-Contributes-10-Percent-of-GDP-to-the-UK-Economy-Surpassing-the-Manufacturing-and-Retail-Sectors.html?culture=en-us> accessed 9 June 2022

The Conservative Party, 'Strong Leadership, a Clear Economic Plan, a Brighter, More Secure Future: The Conservative Party Manifesto 2015' <https://www.conservatives.com/manifesto> accessed 9 June 2022

The World Bank, 'Households and NPISHs Final Consumption Expenditure (Current US$)' (2020) <https://data.worldbank.org/indicator/NE.CON.PRVT.CD?year_high_desc=true> accessed 9 June 2022

Theveßen E, Müller PF and Stoll U, '"Operation 'Rubikon'" – #Cryptoleaks: Wie BND und CIA alle täuschten' (*zdf.de*, 11 February 2020) <https://www.zdf.de/nachrichten/politik/cryptoleaks-bnd-cia-operation-rubikon-100.html> accessed 9 June 2022

Thon M, 'Transnationaler Datenschutz: Das internationale Datenprivatrecht der DS-GVO' (2020) 84 RabelsZ 25

Towfigh E von and Ulrich J, 'Art. 47 DSGVO' in Gernot Sydow (ed), *Nomos Kommentar: Europäische Datenschutzgrundverordnung* (2nd edn, Nomos 2018)

Travis A, 'Home Office Wrongly Denying People Bank Accounts in 10 % of Cases' The Guardian (22 September 2017) <https://www.theguardian.com/uk-news/2017/sep/22/home-office-errors-already-leading-to-people-being-denied-bank-accounts> accessed 9 June 2022

UK Government, 'Factsheet Bulk Interception' (2015) <https://assets.publishing.service.gov.uk/government/uploads/system/uploads/attachment_data/file/473751/Factsheet-Bulk_Interception.pdf> accessed 9 June 2022

UK Home Office, 'Code of Practice (Draft) on Interception of Communications' (2017) <https://assets.publishing.service.gov.uk/government/uploads/system/uploads/attachment_data/file/668941/Draft_code_-_Interception_of_Communications.pdf> accessed 9 June 2022

UK Home Office, 'Code of Practice on Equipment Interference – Pursuant to Schedule 7 to the Investigatory Powers Act 2016' (2018) <https://assets.publishing.service.gov.uk/government/uploads/system/uploads/attachment_data/file/715479/Equipment_Interference_Code_of_Practice.pdf> accessed 9 June 2022

UK Home Office, 'Communications Data Code of Practice' (2018) <https://assets.publishing.service.gov.uk/government/uploads/system/uploads/attachment_data/file/757850/Communications_Data_Code_of_Practice.pdf> accessed 9 June 2022

UK Home Office, 'The Data Protection Act 2018 National Security Certificates' (2020) <https://assets.publishing.service.gov.uk/government/uploads/system/uploads/attachment_data/file/910279/Data_Protection_Act_2018_-_National_Security_Certificates_Guidance.pdf> accessed 9 June 2022

UN Special Rapporteur, 'End of Mission Statement on the Right to Privacy at the Conclusion of His Mission to the United Kingdom of Great Britain and Northern Ireland' (2018) <https://www.ohchr.org/EN/NewsEvents/Pages/DisplayNews.aspx?NewsID=23296&LangID=E> accessed 9 June 2022

US Department of Justice – Office of Public Affairs, 'Joint US-EU Statement on Electronic Evidence Sharing Negotiations' (2019) Press Release of 26 September 2019 <https://www.justice.gov/opa/pr/joint-us-eu-statement-electronic-evidence-sharing-negotiations> accessed 9 June 2022

Vanberg AD and Maunick M, 'Data Protection in the UK Post-Brexit: The Only Certainty Is Uncertainty' (2018) 32 Int. Rev.Law Comput. 190

Vela JH, Plucinska J and Burchard H von der, 'EU Trade, the Martin Selmayr Way' *Politico* (18 October 2017) <https://www.politico.eu/article/eu-trade-the-martin-selmayr-way/> accessed 9 June 2022

Vermeulen G and Lievens E, *Data Protection and Privacy under Pressure – Transatlantic Tensions, EU Surveillance, and Big Data* (2017)

Voigt M, *Die Datenschutzrechtliche Einwilligung. Zum Spannungsfeld von informationeller Selbstbestimmung Und ökonomischer Verwertung personenbezogener Daten* (Nomos 2020)

Voigt P, 'Praxisprobleme im Zusammenhang mit den EU-Standardvertragsklauseln Zur Auftragsverarbeitung – mehr als "nur" Schrems II ...' [2020] CR 513

Voigt, P and Drexler, N, 'Pflichten für Verantwortliche und Auftragsverarbeiter nach Art. 27 DS-GVO und UK-GDPR' [2021] ZD 409

Wade H, 'Horizons of Horizontality' (2000) 116 LQR 217

Wagner J, 'The Transfer of Personal Data to Third Countries under the GDPR: When Does a Recipient Country Provide an Adequate Level of Protection?' (2018) 8 IDPL 318

Wang, Flora Y. 'Cooperative Data Privacy: The Japanese Model of Data Privacy and the EU-Japan GDPR Adequacy Agreement' (2020) 33 Harvard Law and Technology Review 661

Warner M, 'An Exclusive Club: The 5 Countries That Don't Spy On Each Other' [2013] PBS News Hour <https://www.pbs.org/newshour/world/an-exclusive-club-the-five-countries-that-dont-spy-on-each-other> accessed 9 June 2022

Warrant RS, 'Digital Rights Ireland Deja Vu? Why the Bulk Acquisition Warrant Provisions of the Investigatory Powers Act 2016 Are Incompatible with the Charter of Fundamental Rights of the European Union' (2017) 50 Geo. Wash. Int'l L. Rev. 209

Wheeler-Ozanne C, 'Deal or No-Deal: Does It Matter? Data Protection Predictions for Post-Brexit Britain' (2020) 24 Edinburgh Law Review 275

White M, 'Immigration Exemption and the European Convention on Human Rights' (2019) 5 EDPL 26

White M, 'The Threat to the UK's Independent and Impartial Surveillance Oversight Comes Not Just from the Outside, but from Within' [2019] EHRLR 512

Wildhaber L, 'Art. 8 EMRK' in Katharina Pabel and Stefanie Schmahl (eds), *Internationaler Kommentar zur Europäischen Menschenrechtskonvention* (27th edn, 2020)

Witt C, Ingenrieth F and Wittmann J, 'Could Codes of Conduct Be the Answer to "Schrems II"?' (*IAPP*, 29 September 2020) <https://iapp.org/news/a/could-codes-of-conduct-be-the-answer-to-schrems-ii/> accessed 9 June 2022

Wolff HA, 'Art. 8 GRC' in Matthias Pechstein, Carsten Nowak and Ulrich Häde (eds), *Frankfurter Kommentar EUV/GRC/AEUV*, vol 1 (1st edn, C.H. Beck 2017)

Wolters PTJ, 'The Control by and Rights of the Data Subject under the GDPR' (2018) 22 Journal of Internet Law 7

Woods L, 'Data Protection, the UK and the EU: The Draft Adequacy Decisions' (EU Law Analysis, 24 February 2021) <http://eulawanalysis.blogspot.com/2021/02/data-pro tection-uk-and-eu-draft.html> accessed 9 June 2022

World Economic Forum, 'Data Free Flow with Trust (DFFT): Paths towards Free and Trusted Data Flows' (2020) White Paper <https://www3.weforum.org/docs/WEF_Paths_Towards_Free_and_Trusted_Data%20_Flows_2020.pdf> accessed 9 June 2022

Wybitul T, Ströbel L and Ruess M, 'Übermittlung personenbezogener Daten in Drittländer. Überblick und Checkliste für die Prüfung nach der DS-GVO' [2017] ZD 503

Zarsky T, 'The Hotel California Effect: The Future of E.U. Data Protection Influence in the U.K. (Reviewing Paul M. Schwartz, The Data Privacy Law of Brexit: Theories of Preference Change, 22(2) Theoretical Inquires in Law 111 (2021))' (Jotwell, 23 November 2021) <https://cyber.jotwell.com> accessed 9 June 2022

Zerdick T, 'Art. 46 DS-GVO' in Eugen Ehmann and Martin Selmayr (eds), *Beck'scher Kurz-Kommentare: DSGVO* (2nd edn, C.H. Beck 2018)

Zerdick T, 'Art. 49 DS-GVO' in Eugen Ehmann and Martin Selmayr (eds), *Beck'scher Kurz-Kommentare: DSGVO* (2nd edn, C.H. Beck 2018)

Ziebarth W, 'Art. 4 DSGVO' in Gernot Sydow (ed), *Nomos Kommentar: Europäische Datenschutzgrundverordnung* (2nd edn, Nomos 2018)

Zurita AL, 'Datenschutz nach dem Brexit: Auf was Sie jetzt achten sollten' (*DataGuard*, 12 November 2020) <https://www.dataguard.de/magazin/brexit-und-ds-gvo-was-ändert-sich-mit-dem-eu-austritt-des-vereinigten-königreiches-beim-datenschutz> accessed 9 June 2022